HARMONISATION OF
FAMILY LAW IN EUROPE:
A HISTORICAL PERSPECTIVE

EUROPEAN FAMILY LAW SERIES

Published by the Organising Committee of the
Commission on European Family Law

Prof. Katharina Boele-Woelki (Utrecht)
Prof. Frédérique Ferrand (Lyon)
Dr. Cristina González Beilfuss (Barcelona)
Prof. Maarit Jänterä-Jareborg (Uppsala)
Prof. Nigel Lowe (Cardiff)
Prof. Dieter Martiny (Frankfurt/Oder)
Prof. Walter Pintens (Leuven)

HARMONISATION OF
FAMILY LAW IN EUROPE:
A HISTORICAL PERSPECTIVE

A tale of two millennia

MASHA ANTOKOLSKAIA

intersentia

Antwerpen – Oxford

Distribution for the UK:
Hart Publishing
Salter's Boat Yard
Folly Bridge
Abingdon Road
Oxford OX1 4LB
UK
Tel: + 44 1865 24 55 33
Fax: + 44 1865 79 48 82

Distribution for Switzerland and Germany:
Stämpfli Verlag AG
Wölflistrasse 1
CH-3001 Bern
Switzerland
Tel: + 41 (0)31 300 63 18
Fax: + 41 (0)31 300 66 88

Distribution for North America:
Gaunt Inc.
Gaunt Building
3011 Gulf Drive
Holmes Beach
Florida 34217-2199
USA
Tel: + 1 941 778 5211
Fax: + 1 941 778 5252

Distribution for other countries:
Intersentia Publishers
Groenstraat 31
BE-2640 Mortsel
Belgium
Tel: + 32 3 680 15 50
Fax: + 32 3 658 71 21

Harmonisation of Family Law in Europe: A Historical Perspective
Masha Antokolskaia

© 2006 Intersentia
Antwerpen – Oxford
http://www.intersentia.com

© 2006 M.V. Antokolskaia

ISBN-10: 90-5095-576-2
ISBN-13: 978-90-5095-576-8
D/2006/7849/62
NUR 822 and 828

For my mother

ACKNOWLEDGEMENTS

This research has been made possible by a fellowship from the Royal Netherlands Academy of Arts and Sciences. I am deeply indebted to the Royal Academy for supporting and financing this research. I am also deeply indebted to Katharina Boele-Woelki for granting me the opportunity to resume the thread of my academic activities in The Netherlands at the Molengraaff Instituut of Private Law of the University of Utrecht. I am very grateful to her for initiating, hosting and supporting this research, and for five years of most pleasant, fruitful and educative collaboration. A research covering such a time span and such a range of jurisdictions would be neither possible nor sensible without the invaluable help of a network of academic colleagues. I am very grateful to all those who assisted me, in particular to the colleagues who read large parts of the manuscript of this book and made helpful remarks and suggestions. Errors and conclusions are mine. Special thanks to Hans Ankum of the University of Amsterdam for commenting on the Chapter on Roman law, as well as Jan Hallebeek and Lieke Coenraad of the Vrije Universiteit Amsterdam and Chris Coppens of the University of Nijmegen for their comment on the historical chapters of this book. I owe a special dept to Katharina Boele-Woelki of the University of Utrecht, Dieter Martiny of the Europa Universität Viadrina (Frankfurt/Oder, Germany), Bente Braat of the University of Utrecht, Frédérique Ferrand of the Université Jean Moulin (Leon, France), David Bradley of the London School of Economics, Maarit Jänterä-Jareborg of the Uppsala University and Tone Sverdrup of the University of Oslo, for their remarks on the sections concerning German, French, English and Nordic law. I also owe much to the thought provoking discussions with Marie-Thérèse Meulders-Klein, University of Louvain de Neuve, Belgium, and with David Bradley. To my husband and colleague Arno Akkermans, who contributed to the coming into being of this book in many different ways, I owe more than words can say. I am also very grateful to the faculty of law of the Vrije Universiteit Amsterdam and to my colleagues there for enabling me to complete this project after I had gotten a chair there. I would like to thank Scott Curry-Sumner for revising my English and my student-assistant Naomi Spalter for helping me with the final technical touches and for her wonderful illustrations. Finally, I would like to thank my mother for her emotional support and my cat Murzik for being a most perfect anti-stress ball during the years that this research was carried out.

Masha Antokolskaia

PREFACE

The idea of this study first crossed my mind when I was asked to contribute to a report on the perspectives of the harmonisation of family law in Europe for the Netherlands Comparative Law Association.[1] I was challenged by the idea of exploring the main objection to family law harmonisation, the so-called 'cultural constraints argument'. This argument suggests that it is principally impossible to harmonise family law because the family laws of the different European countries are deeply embedded in their unique national cultures and history. The cultural constraints argument gives rise to two main questions. The first question, whether family law has converged in the past and currently converges in the present, is in principle a historical-empirical one. The other question, whether convergence and the deliberate harmonisation of family law are possible at all, also seems empirical at first sight, but an analysis of the debate on this issue will reveal that the essence of the discord is on the theoretical, rather than the empirical level.

The main purpose of this book is to suggest answers to these two questions through the analysis of convergence and divergence tendencies and the historical instances of deliberate harmonisation in the field of marriage, unmarried cohabitation, divorce, the position of extramarital children, and matrimonial property, in the majority of Europe throughout the last two millennia. In spite of the long span of time and the large geographical and institutional areas covered, this book has a rather limited scope. It does not deal with most of the issues involved in the contemporary debate surrounding the deliberate harmonisation of family law in Europe; such as whether such harmonisation is necessary or desirable, what methods should be employed to achieve it, which fields should be chosen, whether the EU has competence to harmonise family law, and so on. Save a single exception, neither does this book deal with the activities of the Commission on European Family Law (CEFL). The research for this book had already started before the CEFL was established in 2001. My inspiration for this research became all the stronger when, in 2001, I became a member of the CEFL Expert Group. This made me a 'participating observer' and allowed me to look into the 'harmonisation kitchen'. However, this study neither follows the patterns of the CEFL's work, nor comments on it. While the CEFL is primarily focussed on drafting activities – elaborating *Principles of European Family*

---

[1]   ANTOKOLSKAIA, M., DE HONDT, W., STEENHOFF, G., *Naar een Europees Familierecht* (1999).

Law – the research presented in this book is entirely devoted to historical and theoretical issues.

TABLE OF CONTENTS

PART IV. CURRENT FAMILY LAW: SWEEPING MODERNISATION.
Breakthrough of uniformity or self-reproducing diversity?

CHAPTER 12.
THE BACKGROUND OF THE REFORMS 261

CHAPTER 13.
'DEATH OF MARRIAGE' OR SEARCH FOR A NEW CONCEPT
OF MARRIAGE? 273

CHAPTER 16.

ILLEGITIMATE CHILDREN: FROM DISCRIMINATION TO EQUALITY
AN EXAMPLE OF SUCCESSFUL HARMONISATION 443

APPENDICES

LIST OF ABBREVIATIONS

†	died
1 Cor.	1st Epistle of Saint Paul to the Corinthians
A.D.	*Anno Domini*
ABGB	*Allgemeines Bürgerliches Gesetzbuch* (Austria)
ALP	*Allgemeines Landrecht für die Preussischen Staaten*
App	Appendix
Art/Arts	Article/Articles
B.C.	Before Christ
BGB	*Bürgerliches Gesetzbuch* (Germany)
Bull. civ.	*Bulletin des arrêts de la Cour de Cassation* (France*)*
BverfG	*Bundesverfassungsgericht* (Germany)
c.	*circa*
Cass. Belg.	*Cour de Cassation/Hof van Cassatie* (Belgium)
Cass. Civ. 2	*Cour de Cassation, Deuxième chambre civile* (Supreme Court, France)
Cass. Fr.	*Cour de Cassation* (Supreme Court France)
Cass. Soc.	*Cour de Cassation, chambre sociale* (Supreme Court, France)
CC	*Code Civil* (France)
CEFL	Commission on European Family Law
CFI	Court of First Instance (European Union)
Chamber	*la Chambre des Représentants de Belgique/de Belgische Kamer van volksvertegenwoordigers* (Belgium)
ch/chs	chapter/chapters
COM	European Commission documents (European Union)
D.	*Digeste*
Dir.	Directive
ECHR, ECtHR	European Court of Human Rights
ECHR	European Convention for Human Rights and Fundamental Freedoms
ECJ	European Court of Justice (European Union)
EComHR	European Commission of Human Rights
ed/eds	editor/editors
edn/edns	edition/editions

e.g.	*exempli gratia* (for example)
et al.	*et alii* (and others)
etc.	*et cetera* (and the others)
EU	European Union
EWCA Civ	Court of Appeal (Civil Division), England and Wales
FCR	*Butterworths Family Court Reports*, England and Wales
ff	folios following (following pages)
FLR	*Family Law Reports* (England and Wales)
Fr.	France/French
HR	*Hoge Raad* (Supreme Court, The Netherlands)
Ibid.	*ibidem* (from the same source)
i.e.	*id est* (that is; in other words)
Iul.	Julien
LPartG	*Lebenspartnerschaftsgesetz* (Germany)
Luke	Gospel of Saint Luke
Mark	Gospel of Saint Mark
Matt.	Gospel of Saint Matthew
L.R. 1	Law Reports (1st series) (England and Wales)
MP	Member of Parliament
NJ	*Nederlandse Jurisprudentie* (The Netherlands)
NJW	*Neue Juristischen Wochenschrift* (Germany)
no	number
No	Number (of an Act)
nr./nrs	number/numbers
O.J.	*Official Journal of European Communities*
p./pp.	Page/pages
PACS	*Pacte civil de solidarité*
para/paras	paragraph/paragraphs
PIC	*Pacte d'Intérêt Commun*
sec.	section
SOU	*Statens Offentliga Utredningar* (Sweden)
St.	Saint
sub-s/sub-ss	sub-section/sub-sections
supp/supps	supplement/supplements
trans	translated, translation
Ulp.	Ulpien
Univ.	University
v.	versus
vol/vols	volume/volumes

PART I
INTRODUCTION

CHAPTER 1
INTRODUCTION

1.1. THE HARMONISATION OF FAMILY LAW AND THE CULTURAL CONSTRAINTS ARGUMENT

Since the beginning of the 1980s, academic interest in the issue of harmonisation of private law in Europe has been evolving. From that time on, various international projects devoted to the harmonisation of private law have emerged.[1] In 2001 the *Commission on European Family Law* (further referred to as the CEFL) joined these initiatives. The objective of the CEFL is to elaborate non-binding *Principles on European Family Law*[2] that can serve as a frame of reference for national and supra-national legislatures.[3] All of the present harmonisation projects, including the CEFL, are purely academic initiatives with no political authorisation. Initially these projects developed with little interest shown from the EU institutions. However, from the beginning of the new millennium the EU attitude toward 'European private law' has shifted to significant involvement.[4] This attention from European institutions bestowed the academic initiatives with some political importance and instigated a further increase in scholarly interest.[5] As a result, European private law has grown into

---

[1]   The most important are: *The UNIDROIT Commission for the Principles for International Commercial Contracts* (further referred as *UNIDROIT Commission*) initiated in 1980; *the Commission on European Contract Law*, (further referred as *Lando Commission*), in 1982; the *European Group on Tort Law*, and the *Project on the Common Core of European Private law* (further referred as *Common Core project*), started in 1992; *The Project on the European Code of Contract*, and *The Project on Ius Commune Casebooks for the Common Law of Europe* (further referred as *Casebooks* project) were established in 1994; the international *Working Group on European Trust Law* started in 1996, and *the Study Group on a European Civil Code* (further referred as *Civil Code project*) was set up in 1998.

[2]   The first set of Principles was published in 2004: *Principles of European Family Law Regarding Divorce and Maintenance Between Former Spouses,* BOELE-WOELKI, K. et al (2004). The second set of principles regarding parental responsibility is now in the drafting process.

[3]   See: BOELE-WOELKI, K., 'Comparative Research-based Drafting of Principles of European Family Law' (2002), p. 178-185; BOELE-WOELKI, K., 'B(l)oeiend vergelijkend familierecht: de Commission on European Family Law' (2003), p. 141-159.

[4]   That change manifested itself with the 2001 *Communication From the Commission to the Council and the European Parliament on European Contract Law* (Brussels 11.07. 2001, COM (2001) 398 final–C-0471/2001, OJ C 255, 13.9.2001), followed by a number of other important initiatives of the European Parliament, the European Council and the Commission.

[5]   For a concise overview of the recent state of affairs see: HONDIUS, E., 'European Private Law –Survey 2002-2004' (2004), p. 855-899.

a new academic discipline with its own subject and methodology, an abundance of literature,[6] entire university courses and professorial chairs.

In this context family law is a relative late comer that long played the role of Cinderella. Otto Kahn-Freund reflected the negative attitude toward harmonisation of family law that used to be common by proclaiming the unification of family law 'a hopeless quest'.[7] This scepticism was rooted in the alleged fundamental unsuitability of family law for harmonisation due to strong cultural and historical constraints, resulting in the lack of shared values and objectives. The proponents of the so-called 'cultural constraints argument' maintain that differences between the family laws are embedded in unique and cherished national cultural heritages; that this cultural and historical diversity is unbridgeable and therefore family laws are not converging spontaneously and cannot be harmonised deliberately.[8] The notion of the cultural and historical embedment of family law originates from family law scholars. As early as in the 1968, Wolfram Müller-Freienfels wrote, 'Family law concepts are especially open to influence by moral, religious, political and psychological factors; family law tends to become introverted because historical, racial, social and religious considerations differ according to country and produce different family law systems'.[9] Most scholars engaged in harmonisation activities in other areas of private law rather uncritically adopted the same attitude. The political institutions of the EU were also susceptible to this perception. For instance, the European Council has quite recently stated that family law is 'very heavily influenced by the culture and tradition of national (or even religious) legal systems, which could create a number of difficulties in the context of harmonisation'.[10] Accordingly, family law has for quite some time been defined to be unsuitable for deliberate harmonisation, without substantial scrutiny of the merits of the cultural constraints argument.[11] As a result, the issue of harmonisation of family

---

[6] A recent overview of literature on general and specific harmonisation issues is given throughout the volume *Towards a European Civil Code,* A. HARTKAMP et al (eds), (2004).

[7] KAHN-FREUND, O., 'Common Law and Civil Law – Imaginary and Real Obstacles to Assimilation' (1978), p. 141.

[8] On the use of this argument see, for instance: OLIVEIRA, G., de, 'A European Family Law? Play it again, and again … Europe!' (2000), p. 272; HOHNERLEIN, M., 'Konturen eines einheitlichen europäischen Familien- und Kindschaftsrecht – die Rolle der Europäischen Menschenrechtskonvention' (2000-01), p. 252.

[9] MÜLLER-FREIENFELS, W., 'The Unification of Family Law' (1968-69), p. 175.

[10] *Council report on the need to approximate member states' legislation in civil matters* of 16 November 2001, 13017/01 justciv 129, p. 114.

[11] For instance KOOPMANS, T., 'Towards a New "Ius Commune"'(1992), p. 50; DROBNIG, U., 'Scope and General Rules of a European Civil Code' (1997), p. 493; KERAMEUS, K., 'Problems of Drafting a European Civil Code'(1997), p. 479; ALPA, G., 'European Community Resolutions and the Codification of "Private Law" (2000), p. 326; BASEDOW, J., 'Codification of Private Law in the European Union: the making of a Hybrid' (2001), p. 35-37.

law long remained on the fringes of the discussion surrounding harmonisation of private law.[12]

However, in the late 1990s the attitude towards the harmonisation of family law gradually became more positive.[13] The most tangible result of this development was the establishment of the CEFL. The CEFL has put considerable effort into turning Cinderella into a princess. Apart from making a start with the drafting of Principles, it held two conferences to promote the idea of harmonisation of family law.[14] However, in spite of the wealth of literature[15] and the blooming drafting activities of the CEFL, harmonisation of family law remains a highly controversial issue and the discussion whether it is possible at all is far from being closed.[16] The reason for this is that the cultural constraints argument has not been overcome, but rather, more or less passed over.

The persistent disagreement on the fundamental issue of whether the harmonisation of family law is possible at all led to the situation that, while the popularity of the idea of harmonisation has been notably increasing throughout the last decade, the resistance to it has not diminished. On the contrary, the advance of harmonisation activities has only sharpened the debate. The opponents of harmonisation continue to rely on the notion of the cultural and historical embedment of family law as their key argument. The perseverance of their opposition is, as such, no indication of weakness of the idea of deliberate harmonisation. It also does not mean that the CEFL has started its work prematurely without awaiting sufficient consensus. Consensus on such a controversial issue would probably never have been reached. As will be explained in the next chapter of this book, the present discourse on harmonisation is rooted in never-ending controversies surrounding the correlation of law and society, and modernist 'integrative' and post-modernist 'contrastive' comparative law

---

[12]   Rather illustrative in this respect is a remark by Ole Lando, the 'father' of the first harmonisation project, made in 2006: 'The family laws of the European Union are a fascinating subject. One would think that each of the laws reflect the national character, the dominant religion, the tradition, the family matters, which are linked to the economic and social conditions of each country. For these reasons I thought that there could never be any rapprochement of family laws and notably not in the laws of divorce. The more the laws are linked to persons and passions, I thought, the more they would differ and remain different.' LANDO, O., 'Can Europe Build Unity of Civil Law Whilst Respecting Diversity?' (2006), p. 8.

[13]   BOELE-WOELKI, K., 'Comparative Research-based Drafting of Principles of European Family Law' (2002), p. 175-177. PINTENS, W., 'Europeanisation of Family Law' (2003), p. 4 ff.

[14]   In 2002 and 2004. The conference papers are published in two volumes respectively: BOELE-WOELKI, K. (ed), *Perspectives for the Unification and Harmonisation of Family Law in Europe* (2003), and BOELE-WOELKI, K. (ed), *Common Core and Better Law in European Family Law* (2005).

[15]   For a recent overview see: MARTINY, D., 'Is Unification of Family Law Feasible or Even Desirable?' (2004), p. 328-333 and the CEFL website: http://www2.law.uu.nl/priv/cefl/ under the rubric 'publications'.

[16]   MARTINY, D., 'Is Unification of Family Law Feasible or Even Desirable?' (2004), p. 307-333.

methodology. This means that if harmonisation activities were ever to be started, they could have been started only in spite of serious opposition.

Yet, the fact that such opposition is inevitable does not mean that the proponents of harmonisation could simply disregard the opposition's arguments altogether, in the spirit of the old Persian proverb 'the dog barks but the caravan moves on'. The most extreme proponents of the cultural constraints argument submit that family laws in Europe are not converging at present and have never really converged in the past, and that their current diversity is an emanation of the irredeemable dissimilarity of national cultures. Thus, any attempt to harmonise family law is doomed to create only a virtual reality alien to, and thus alienated by, social reality. This objection is too serious to be ignored.

The notion that family law is strongly embedded in national culture has long been taken for granted without having been analysed thoroughly by either proponents or opponents of the cultural constraints argument. Even those who try to put this argument into perspective have not taken pains to investigate it in any depth. The most common counter-argument is that certain peculiarities of the family law of the country in question cannot be explained by cultural factors. For instance, Ewoud Hondius doubts that the fact that The Netherlands is the only European country that still has a total community of assets as the legal regime for matrimonial property could be explained by the particularities of Dutch national culture.[17] Others point out that certain changes in long-standing family law concepts have not brought about any cultural shocks.[18] The most elaborate criticism so far is that some culturally-imbedded rules do not coincide with the modern notion of human rights;[19] that tradition is not 'holy' and should not be protected at any rate; and that even culturally-laden family rules are not an end in themselves, but rather a means by which to promote a desired regulation of human relations.[20] In an earlier work[21] I tried to make a first step in the direction of a more fundamental qualification of the cultural constraints argument, by bringing to light the common historical roots of family law all European countries share. The analysis of other aspects of the cultural constraints argument, however, requires a much more extensive theoretical and historical study. This study is the subject of this book.

---

[17] HONDIUS, E., *Naar een Europees burgerlijk recht* (1993), p. 180.

[18] The introduction in Belgian family law of the notion of *mater semper certa est*, is used as an example thereof. PINTENS, W., VANWINCKELEN, K., *Casebook European Family Law* (2001), p. 15.

[19] DE GROOT, G.-R., 'Op weg naar een Europees personen- en familierecht?' (1995), p. 29.

[20] See for instance: PINTENS, W., VANWINCKELEN K., (*Casebook European Family Law* (2001), p. 15): '[...] law, even if imbedded in our culture, is primarily an instrument to regularize human relationships and is not a purpose in itself.'

[21] See note 1 in this chapter.

A thorough examination of the cultural constraints argument involves two dimensions, one empirical and the other theoretical. In regard to the contention that family law has never really converged in the past and is not converging in the present, the enquiry is in principle a historical-empirical one. In regard to the contention that convergence and the deliberate harmonisation of family law are not possible at all, the enquiry also seems empirical at first sight – but an analysis of the debate on this issue reveals that the essence of the discord is on the theoretical, rather than the empirical level. As was already mentioned, the present discourse on harmonisation is rooted in theoretical controversies surrounding the correlation between law and society, and comparative law methodology. In regard to the correlation of law and society, the cultural constraints argument relies on the so-called strong 'mirror' theory of law, which postulates that the correlation is very strong. In regard to comparative law methodology, the argument is related to the so-called 'relativist' epistemology, which induces the observer to search for differences rather than for similarities.[22]

The examination of the empirical-historical dimension of the cultural constraints argument involves a search for historical evidence of convergence and divergence tendencies and an evaluation of the historical instances of deliberate harmonisation of family law. The theoretical dimension of cultural constraints can only be dealt with theoretically through an analysis of the relations between (family) law and society, and different positions in regard to comparative law methodology. However, it is not my intent to try to defeat or to prove the cultural constraints argument on this theoretical level. Different theories on the relationship between law and society, in which the cultural constraints argument is rooted, have existed alongside each other for centuries and will most likely continue to exist in the centuries to come. The same is true for the relativist and universalist epistemological approaches. The history of European thought has proven the inherent impossibility of confirming or dismissing any of these theories; so the cultural constraints argument appears also neither confirmable nor dismissible on this theoretical level. For this reason, the discussion of the theoretical dimension of the cultural constraints argument in this book will essentially be no more than a theoretical introduction to the subsequent research that deals with this argument's historical-empirical dimension, which involves the lion's share of this book.

The latter research is an empirical one, dealing with the analysis and interpretation of historical facts. On this level it should be possible to empirically deny or prove the existence or absence of convergence in family law, and thereby to deny or prove the validity of the cultural constraints argument. If the historical development of family laws throughout Europe reveals a strong convergence tendency and examples of

---

[22]   See Chapter 2.

successful deliberate harmonisation, the cultural constraints argument would require fundamental qualification. Whether family laws in Europe are converging at the moment and/or have been converging in the past seems just a matter of empirical-historical research in, respectively, recent and more distant history. The same is true for historical attempts to deliberately harmonise family law. An analysis of various historical family law harmonisation attempts on national and multi-state levels in order to see whether, and to what extent, they were successful or failed to penetrate into real life, should be realisable. Therefore, one could suggest that it is enough to conduct a thorough and comprehensive historical-comparative research of family law in Europe in order to resolve the controversy surrounding the issues of the cultural constraints argument, convergence and harmonisation. The research presented herein is basically devoted to this task.

There is, however, an important complication. The theoretical dimension of the cultural constraints argument cannot be so easily dismissed. In reality, the theoretical and historical dimensions of the cultural constraints argument are closely interwoven. As will be discussed in the next chapter, the observer's position in regard to the theoretical dimension of the cultural constraints argument is often rather decisive for his evaluation of empirical historical data. This can explain why the same historical examples are sometimes employed by both proponents and opponents of the convergence hypothesis in order to support their conflicting conclusions. There appears to be a clear danger of getting entangled in a vicious circle that ends in one tending to find what one is looking for. On the ground of such reasoning, the post-modernist epistemology states the fundamental impossibility of objective comparative research because its results totally depend on the 'intellectual framework' of the observer.[23] Due to this, post-modernist thought advises against an observer's attempt to be objective and instead instructs the observer 'to confess one's culture'.[24] Fortunately, post-modernist epistemological framework relativism has been persuasively criticised and put into perspective.[25] That absolute objectivity is unattainable does not make it less imperative to strive to attain objectivity as much as possible. Still, the post-modernist warning was taken into consideration with regard to the method of this research. This method is based on the assumption that, to a certain extent, objective truth is possible to attain, but that the threat of subjectivity should be taken seriously. Also, measures to avoid selection bias should of course be taken. This has determined several choices made in the context of this study.

---

[23] See Section 2.3.1. of this chapter.

[24] GELLNER, E., *Postmodernism, Reason and Religion* (1992), p. 25. For more on this issue see Section 2.3.1. of this chapter.

[25] See for instance: PETERS, A., SCHWENKE, H., 'Comparative Law Beyond Post-Modernism' (2000), p. 811-821

1.2. TRYING TO AVOID SELECTION BIAS

As has been already mentioned, the main objective of this book is to investigate the empirical-historical dimension of the cultural constraints argument and the convergence/divergence discourse. For the validity of such research it is not only necessary to diminish, as much as possible, the effect of one's subjective inclinations on the interpretation of data. The first and most basic methodological precaution is to avoid selection bias with regard to the choice of historical periods, jurisdictions and relevant fields of family law.

1.2.1. CHOICE OF HISTORICAL PERIODS. WHY TWO MILLENNIA?

The choice of historical periods is perhaps the most crucial one. It is remarkable to see that the question of the existence of convergence in family law has been repeatedly answered in diametrically opposed ways by thorough, bona fide scholars.[26] The mere difference in perception of the observers, albeit important, cannot fully explain such a fundamental disagreement. An important factor seems to be that they all are able to invoke clear empirical evidence, as the history of family law in Europe includes both periods showing an obvious tendency of divergence, as well as periods when the convergence trend was more prominent. Thus, the mere choice of a period of investigation can be decisive for the outcome of one's research. My hypothesis is that one of the explanations for the differing appreciation of the convergence/divergence issue is an examination of time-spans that are too short. Studying this complex issue, it is easy to fall into a trap of selectiveness focusing primarily on those periods that tend to affirm one's starting point.[27] Therefore it appears that only a study of convergence and divergence tendencies throughout a broader period of history can avoid selection bias and shed true light on the convergence/divergence discourse. For these reasons, I decided that the only way to thoroughly address this problem was to take pains to go through the whole of the last two millennia of European family law history.

---

[26]   Compare, for instance: BRADLEY, D., 'Convergence in Family Law: Mirrors, Transplants and Political Economy' (1999), p. 127 – 131 with PINTENS, W., VANWINCKELEN, C., *Casebook. European Family Law* (2001), p. 16 and MARTINY, D., 'Is Unification of Family Law Feasible or Even Desirable?' (2004), p. 317-318.

[27]   Harry Willekens has rightly noticed that: 'A purely synchronic comparison or one restricted to developments within, say, "recent years" or a certain decade, will easily miss the point and will give the impression of fundamental differences, where the a comparison over a more extended period of time would rather point to mere time lag.' WILLEKENS, H., 'Explaining Two Hundred Years of Family Law in Western Europe' (1997), p. 60.

1.2.2. CHOICE OF FIELDS OF FAMILY LAW

The second problem that has to be addressed is the intentional or unintentional selection of fields of family law where convergence or divergence has been most, or least, prominent. In order to avoid this danger, very different fields of family law have been made the object of this study. Marriage and divorce are chosen; firstly, because they are the core institutions of family law, and secondly, because marriage and divorce are notoriously culturally and ideologically sensitive fields of family law, most often used as examples by the proponents of the cultural constraints argument. Extramarital cohabitation (concubinage) is also discussed because of, in the first place, its ideological and political sensitivity. In the second place, this topic is selected because it has been claimed that the present partnership legislation with regard to unmarried (same-sex) cohabitation provides one of the most convincing examples of spontaneous convergence of family laws in Europe. The regulation of the status of children born outside marriage is chosen because this area of law provides an example of an institution once politically sensitive and strongly dominated by religion and culture, whilst now forming a rare example of almost total consensus on the European level. Another reason the four aforementioned institutions were opted for is that all of them are rooted in the European *ius commune* of family law: the uniform medieval canon law of the Catholic Church. The last institution, matrimonial property law, is added by way of contrast. In the first place, this field is to a much less extent connected to religion and culture than the four previous ones. In the second place, the medieval unification of family law had little influence on matrimonial property law, nor was matrimonial property law part of the medieval *ius commune*.

1.2.3. CHOICE OF JURISDICTIONS

Jurisdictional choice could also affect findings with regard to convergence and divergence. In some European regions (for example the Nordic Region, South Europe), the development of family law continuously displays strong similarities. Others sets of countries are commonly used (for instance common law and civil law jurisdictions) as examples of perpetual diversity. In order to avoid selection bias, this study undertakes, albeit in general lines only, to cover the whole of what is now called Western and Eastern Europe, the latter represented first by Byzantium and then by Russia. Turkey becomes part of the enquiry only from the moment of Ataturk's reforms in the early 20th century, when Turkey decided to integrate itself into Europe. A further selection is made on the ground of two considerations. Three main Western European regions, which currently constitute France, England and Germany, are chosen because of their continuous importance in the history of European family law. In addition to this 'big three', a varying number of other jurisdictions is discussed in so far as they played a prominent role in the developments of family law in Europe during a certain period. For this reason, for instance, the Russian reforms of 1920s, the early 20th century Nordic co-operation and the Dutch introduction of same-sex marriage will receive some special attention. In order to broaden the scope of the geographical coverage, sometimes a global description of a certain period (for example the Protestant Reformation) is given. There will also be close-ups on some particularly illustrative events (for instance the Irish and Italian struggle surrounding the introduction of divorce in the late 20th century), or countries (for example Turkey during the reception of Western family law). As a rule, the closer to the present the events are, the more detailed their discussion becomes.

1.3. METHOD OF COMPARATIVE RESEARCH

1.3.1. LAW IN CONTEXT, LAW IN THE BOOKS AND LAW IN ACTION

I have no intention to stick my oar into the unending debate on comparative law methodology. However, a few remarks on the methods of this comparative research must be made. It almost goes without saying that comparative research cannot be reduced to the examination of legal rules only;[28] even more so for a study aimed at the delineation of convergence and divergence tendencies. On the one hand, those who allege that convergence and harmonisation are impossible claim that even if rules as such become more common, cultural constraints preclude them from producing real convergence on the deeper level of culture and mentality.[29] It is also suggested that similar rules can 'meet dissimilar – even opposing – institutional objectives',[30] and thus do not signify any convergence. On the other hand, proponents of harmonisation are accused of asserting or accepting 'all too readily, that harmonisation of rules follows and is justified by some ill-defined Europeanisation or globalisation of economic

---

[28]   For a brief recent overview see: PALMER, V., 'From Lerotholi to Lando: Some Examples of Comparative Law Methodology' (2005), p. 283.

[29]   Thus Legrand argues that even evident examples of growing proximity between legal solutions provided in civil and common law systems should be dismissed as an illusion based on a fallacious reduction of law to legal rules (LEGRAND, P., *Fragments on Law-as-Culture* (1999), p. 83-84), because, 'if one forgoes surface examination at the level of rules and concepts to conduct a deep examination in terms of legal *mentalités,* one must come to the conclusion that legal systems, despite their adjacency within the European Community, have not been converging, are not converging and will not be converging'. LEGRAND, P., 'European Legal Systems Are Not Converging' (1996), p. 61-62.

[30]   BRADLEY, D., 'Convergence in Family Law: Mirrors, Transplants and Political Economy' (1999), p. 139.

relations, values, or the like.'[31] For this reason it is crucial to examine the developments of family law within their social, political and ideological context. This requires the use of a so-called 'organic' comparative method, which 'incorporates both law and social underpinning into the same comparative act.'[32] To this purpose special attention will be given to the development of the ideas that have inspired the transformations of family law and the political debates that surrounded family law reforms.

The legal comparison in this study is not limited to mere comparison of the formal elements of law: legal concepts and legal definitions. Instead, the so-called method of 'functional equivalence'[33] is widely employed to uncover functionally equivalent solutions behind formally different legal concepts. For instance what is functionally 'divorce upon mutual consent' of the spouses is not necessary always labelled as such, but can be hidden under the headings of 'irretrievable breakdown of marriage' or 'fault'-based divorce by collusion. The use of the method of functional equivalence often involves an implicit inclination to search for similarities, rather than differences. In order to avoid such one-sidedness, a more or less opposite method – one that could be called 'functional disequivalence' – will equally be applied in this study in order to reveal functionally different phenomena behind the same legal concepts. For instance, behind one and the same label of 'irretrievable breakdown' of marriage, grounds for divorce can be hidden that are functionally completely different, such as fault, a certain period of separation or consent of the spouses.

The proponents of the cultural constraints argument claim that radical reforms and attempts to harmonise family law are often rejected by society and produce a lasting discrepancy between the law as it formally is and social reality. Therefore, another point of special attention will be uncovering the instances of, and examining the reasons for, the discrepancies between the family 'law in the books' and the 'law in action'.

1.3.2. COMBINING COMPARATIVE AND HISTORICAL RESEARCH

The mission of this book requires the combination of comparative and historical research, covering the whole of Europe over the last two millennia. Such ambition, of course, brings about serious difficulties. The problems and merits of combining

---

[31]   NOTTAGE, L., *Convergence, Divergence, and the Middle Way in Unifying or Harmonising Private Law* (2001), p. 17.

[32]   PALMER, V., 'From Lerotholi to Lando: Some Examples of Comparative Law Methodology' (2005), p. 265.

[33]   See ZWEIGERT, K., KÖTZ, H., *An Introduction to Comparative Law* (1998), p. 34 ff.

comparative and historical research have recently been the object of attention in the literature.[34] It has also more than once been suggested that profound comparative research in current European private law is only possible if it is based on the study of the Roman-canon *ius commune*. As Zimmermann has put it: '[s]ince European law consists of several legal systems, and since direct reference back to the old, genuinely European *ius commune* would entail a short-circuit, we will have to combine historical and comparative legal scholarship. [...] The legal historian will have to tell his story up to the very point where the comparative lawyer can take over – as long, of course, as neither of them is able to produce works that leave it open where legal history ends and comparative law commences'.[35] This 'as long [...] as' is of course an essential problem. Only very few scholars are able to undertake innovative historical research based on the scrutiny of primary sources, in combination with comparative research of contemporary law. Being a legal comparatist, specialised in family law, and no legal historian, I am clearly not qualified to fulfil such a task. Moreover, both the territory and the time-span covered in this book render historical research based on the analysis of basic source material as good as impossible. For this reason I was forced to resort to a combination of comparative research and historical study based on reliable secondary sources. It is of course impossible to say even one new word in legal history with the help of such acquired 'second hand' historical data, but such 'utilitarian'[36] use of legal history can perfectly serve to provide a better understanding of such general lines of development of family law as convergent/divergence trends and historical examples of harmonisation.

1.4. GENERAL OUTLINE OF THIS BOOK

Thus, this book provides a historical-comparative overview, aimed to give a concise but more or less inclusive picture of the convergence/divergence tendencies from

---

[34] See, in general: HÜBNER, H., ' Sinn und Möglichkeiten retrospektiver Rechtsvergleichung' (1987), p. 235-252. Further: KÖTZ, for instance, called legal history and comparative studies: 'twin sisters' and considers the mere question of whether they should be combined as misplaced. 'Was erwartet die Rechtsvergleichung von der Rechtsgeschichte' (1992), p. 19-22. Most vividly, the correlation between the comparative and historical method is pictured by Laurence Friedman. In his view, 'the historian is after all a comparatist by nature; her units of comparison are not two or more societies in the present but the "same" society at various points in the past.[...] The comparatist wants to measure and explain similarities and differences; the historian wants to measure and to explain continuities and change; the two themes are reducible to each other.' FRIEDMAN, L., 'Some Thoughts on Comparative Legal Culture'(1990), p. 55. For an overview of an animated discussion that has recently taken place in The Netherlands see: STEENHOFF, G., 'The Place of Legal History in the Teaching of Law and in Corporatists Formation' (1998), p. 1- 19.

[35] ZIMMERMANN, R., 'Savigny's Legacy Legal History, Comparative Law, and The Emergence of A European Legal Science' (1996), p. 602.

[36] ZIMMERMANN, R., 'Rechtsvergelijking, Rechtsgeschiedenis en *ius commune*' (1994), p. 16.

Roman times to the present, and an account of the historical attempts of deliberate harmonisation of family law in Europe. It consists of five parts. The present Part I: Introduction, deals with the theoretical dimension of the cultural-constraints argument and of the convergence/divergence and harmonisation issues. Part II: 'From Diversity to Uniformity: Medieval Canon Law – the Family Law *Ius Commune*' follows the course of the largest-ever convergence event in the history of European law – the creation of the medieval uniform canon family law. Part III: 'Modern Times – From Uniformity to the Current Diversity. Similar Developments: Difference in Timing, Resemblance in Substance' describes the development of family law from the medieval *ius commune* to the current diversity. Part IV: 'Current Family Law. Sweeping Modernisation: Breakthrough of Uniformity or Self-Reproducing Diversity?' deals with the convergence and divergence tendencies through the recent developments in family law, from the 1960s onwards. In Part V, entitled 'Conclusion' the final conclusions with regard to convergence/divergence and the cultural constraints argument are presented.

CHAPTER 2
THE CULTURAL CONSTRAINTS ARGUMENT, CONVERGENCE, AND HARMONISATION: THEORETICAL ASPECTS

2.1. INTRODUCTION

The central subject of this chapter is the cultural constraints argument, its theoretical roots and its implications for the ongoing convergence and harmonisation debate. The cultural constraints argument is not unique to family law, but it is here that this argument has the most profound and lasting influence. In this chapter the cultural constraints argument will be dealt with from the family law perspective. As was mentioned in the previous chapter, the theoretical roots of the cultural constraints argument are in the so-called strong 'mirror' theory of law and in the application of the so-called 'relativist' epistemology in the field of comparative law. The mirror theory of law postulates that the correlation between law and society is very strong. 'Relativist' epistemology induces the observer to search for differences rather than similarities and leads to 'contrastive' rather than 'integrative' comparative law. These issues will be discussed in the second and the third sections, respectively. Yet, before these two theoretical matters are addressed, some basic concepts used in this study will be introduced and clarified in the following section.

2.2. THE DANGER OF TALKING AT CROSS PURPOSES. THE CONCEPTUAL FRAMEWORK OF THIS BOOK

The ease with which such terms as 'convergence', 'harmonisation' and 'unification' are used by authors, addressing these issues, could give the impression that there is a general consensus to the meaning of these terms. Alas, this is far from true. Considerable discrepancy in the meanings attached to key concepts used in the convergence and harmonisation debate frequently leads to talking at cross purposes.

There is neither a single vested set of definitional terms,[1] nor an acknowledged classification of the forms and methods of harmonisation.[2] The purpose of the paragraphs below is to provide the mainstream definitions of some key-concepts and, where necessary, to clarify the meaning of certain terms that will be used in this book.

2.2.1. THE CONCEPTS OF CONVERGENCE, HARMONISATION, AND UNIFICATION AS USED IN THIS BOOK

Harmonisation embraces unification

Discussing the problem of harmonisation and convergence is no easy task, as neither comparative law in general, nor the newly developed discipline of European Private Law has paid much attention to developing a uniform conceptual language.[3] According to the most general definition, the **harmonisation** of law is every process that results in an increase in the degree of legal uniformity.[4] The concept of harmonisation is often used in the context of European law and normally means approximation; however, it also encompasses **unification**: making laws totally identical.[5] In the past there was an attempt to draw a fundamental distinction between the concepts of harmonisation and unification. Harmonisation was defined to imply only *'l'affinité'*, whilst unification entailed *'l'uniformité'*.[6] However, this attempt did not find much support.[7] The common opinion remains that the only difference between harmonisation and unification is in the degree of approximation.[8]

Further differentiations within the concept of harmonisation made in European law are also relevant for the debate surrounding the harmonisation of family law. European law distinguishes between total harmonisation (unification), indicating the total

---

[1] MEULDERS-KLEIN, M.-T., 'Towards a European Civil Code of Family Law? Ends and Means' (2003), p. 105.

[2] See in the same sense: CAPPELLETTI, M., SECCOMBE, M., WEILER, J., 'General Introduction' (1978), p. 36.

[3] Bernadine Trompenaars ironically suggests in her dissertation that this happened because the organisations involved were much too busy with the harmonisation activities and did not have time to think of terminology. TROMPENAARS, B., *Pluriforme unificatie en uniforme interpretatie* (1989), p. 30.

[4] Ibid, p. 29.

[5] VAN GERVEN, W., 'Harmonisation of private law: do we need it?' (2004), p. 506-507.

[6] MALINTOPPI, A., 'Les relations entre l' unification et l'harmonisation du droit et la technique de l'unification ou de l'harmonisation par la voie d'accords internationaux' (1967-1968), p. 43 ff.

[7] For an overview of this discussion see: TROMPENAARS, B., *Pluriforme unificatie en uniforme interpretatie* (1989), p. 9-10.

[8] TROMPENAARS, B., *Pluriforme unificatie en uniforme interpretatie* (1989), p. 9-10.

assimilation of laws; partial harmonisation, indicating the assimilation of laws with regard to some aspects only; and minimum harmonisation, indicating the creation of some common minimum standard only.[9]

Different forms of harmonisation and the definition of convergence

Harmonisation and unification can be imposed by a higher authority (**top-down** or centralist method) or take place on a voluntary basis (**bottom-up** or non-centralist method).[10] Harmonisation and unification can also result either from deliberate human efforts,[11] (exclusively or not exclusively) aimed at achieving more similarity between laws,[12] or as the result of a natural evolutionary process. Top-down harmonisation is always a result of deliberate efforts by a central authority. In contrast to top-down harmonisation, bottom-up harmonisation can be both deliberate, stemming from purposeful human efforts; and spontaneous, resulting from a spontaneous evolutional approximation of legal systems. The latter form of bottom-up harmonisation is also called **convergence**.[13] The word 'convergence', however, is sometimes used to describe not so much the process but rather its result. This renders the exact meaning of this term somewhat ambivalent since the result of deliberate harmonisation could also be called 'convergence'. In this book the latter meaning will be avoided as much as possible. Unless indicated otherwise, 'convergence' will mean the process of spontaneous bottom-up approximation.

Top-down harmonisation

The top-down method is characterised by three elements. Firstly, top-down harmonisation is always imposed by a higher national (for example a federal legislature, a federal court) or supranational authority (for instance the EU legislature, international courts, the Roman Catholic Church in the Middle Ages). Secondly, it always involves deliberate actions by such authority. Finally, it is accomplished through the use of binding legal instruments.[14] The history of family law in Europe shows several examples of top-down deliberate harmonisation, the most notable of which are the unification of the bulk of family law by the Roman Catholic Church in the Middle Ages, the far-reaching harmonisation of family law within the Napoleonic Empire, and the unification of family law in the framework of the formation of the national

---

9   VAN GERVEN, W., 'Harmonisation of private law: do we need it?' (2004), p. 508.
10   SMITS, J., *The Making of European Private Law* (2002), p. 6.
11   Also called 'organised' harmonisation, TROMPENAARS, B., *Pluriforme unificatie en uniforme interpretatie* (1989), p. 12.
12   Ibid, p. 9-10.
13   The words 'convergence' and 'spontaneous harmonisation' will be used as synonyms throughout the remainder of this study.
14   CAPPELLETTI, M., SECCOMBE, M., WEILER, J., 'General Introduction' (1978), p. 36.

states of Germany and Italy in the nineteenth century. In present-day Europe, the main instruments of top-down harmonisation of (family) law are EU legislation,[15] the case law of the European Court of Justice (ECJ), and the case law of the European Court of Human Rights (ECHR) based on the application of the European Convention of Human Rights and Fundamental Freedoms.[16] The method of top-down harmonisation is not popular among the scholarly groups and commissions currently involved in the harmonisation of family law in Europe. At the moment, projects committed to this method are in the clear minority. Only[17] the *Study Group on a European Civil Code* initially stated that its goal was to draft what was intended to become a binding European Civil Code, imposed by an EU Regulation.[18] However, severe critique has forced the group to moderate its ambitions. Its current strategy is defined as being aimed to pave the way for a future Code with the elaboration of *Principles of European Private Law.*[19]

Deliberate bottom-up harmonisation

The word 'bottom-up' does not mean that this form of harmonisation takes place without deliberate human efforts. It only indicates that the approximation of laws is not imposed by a higher authority. The role of the actors participating in a bottom-up harmonisation process can vary rather significantly. National states can accomplish such harmonisation through voluntary, coordinated efforts aimed at adopting similar laws. The best historical example of such bottom-up harmonisation is the 20th century Nordic co-operation. International organisations (for example the Council of Europe, UNIDROIT, UNCITRAL) can initiate bottom-up harmonisation processes by drafting

---

[15] There is a recent debate on whether the EU has competence to legislate family matters. Some authors tend to answer this question negatively, e.g. MÜLLER-GRAFF, P-C., 'Privatrecht und Europäisches Gemeinschaftsrecht' (1999), p. 246; MEULDERS-KLEIN, M.-T., 'Towards a European Civil Code of Family Law? Ends and Means' (2003), p. 113. There are, however, other voices suggesting that '[…] just as uniform rules of private international law have been proposed as necessary for the operation of the internal market, for the development of a common judicial area and as basis for developing European citizenship, it is not inconceivable that similar justification may put forward for greater harmonization of national family laws of Member States'. MCGLYNN, C., 'A Family Law for the European Union' (2000), p. 238. It is also suggested that EU competence to harmonise substantive family law can be derived from a broad interpretation of Article 64 of the EC Treaty (BOELE-WOELKI, K., 'The principles of European family law: aims and prospects' (2005), p.162). See also on this issue: DETHLOFF, N., 'Arguments for the Unification and Harmonisation of Family Law in Europe' (2003), p. 54-58 and PINTENS, W., 'Europeanisation of Family Law' (2003), p. 20-28.

[16] SMITS, J., *The Making of European Private Law* (2002), p. 6-7.

[17] Recently, the founding father of the *Commission on European Contract Law* Ole Lando has also aligned himself with top-down harmonisation. See: LANDO, O., 'Optional or Mandatory Europeanisation of Contract Law' (2000), p. 65-69.

[18] VON BAR, C., 'The Study Group on a European Civil Code' (2000), p. 326.

[19] VON BAR, C., 'Paving the Way Forward with Principles of European Private Law' (2002), p. 142-145.

an international convention, open for voluntary acceptance by the states.[20] In these cases the actors of the harmonisation process actually perform deliberate bottom-up harmonisation. The efforts of the actors of a bottom-up harmonisation process can also be aimed at promoting and facilitating spontaneous harmonisation (convergence). Several academic groups and commissions are currently pursuing such goals. The methods they employ for this purpose are rather diverse. The most notable among them are: promoting the convergence of legal systems by developing a common European legal science[21] and common European legal education,[22] as well as drafting non-binding model *Principles* of particular fields of European private law. Some of these groups have chosen a very cautious approach. Thus, the goal of the *Ius Commune Casebooks for the Common Law of Europe* is defined as trying to 'uncover the common roots of the different legal systems'[23] and to promote the creation of unification of European private law by its natural 'bottom up' growth through the 'progressive convergence of the legal systems'.[24] The project explicitly refrains from 'drafting model principles, taking the form of articles of a code'.[25] The goal of another project, *The common core of European Private law,* is described even more cautiously. The stated purposes of the project are making a map of the private law of Europe,[26] 'building a common culture', and 'shaping a truly common legal education' by virtue of the creation of 'a model "European legal school"'.[27]

Several other groups and commissions (e.g. the *UNIDROIT Commission,*[28] the *European Group on Tort Law*[29]), go a step further and set their target on the elaboration

---

[20]   Some authors regard these forms of harmonisation as centralist (top-down). See, for instance, SMITS, J., *The Making of European Private Law* (2002), p. 6-7.

[21]   See for instance: NEUMAYER, K. 'The Role of Uniform Legal Science in the Harmonisation of the Continental Legal Systems' (1962); GORDLEY, J., 'Comparative Legal Research: Its Function in the Development of Harmonized Law' (1995), p. 52-53.

[22]   See: COING, H., 'European Common Law: Historical Foundations' (1978), p. 44, KÖTZ, H., 'A common Private Law For Europe: Perspective For the Reform of European Legal Education' (1992), p. 34 ff.

[23]   VAN GERVEN, W. et al, *Torts. Scope of Protection,* (1998), p. X.

[24]   LAROUCHE, P., 'Ius Commune Casebooks for the Common Law of Europe' (2000), p. 106.

[25]   VAN GERVEN, W., 'Casebooks for the Common Law of Europe. Presentation of the Project' (1996), p. 68.

[26]   BUSSANI, M., MATTEI, U., 'The Common Core Approach to European Private Law' (1997-98), p. 340.

[27]   Ibid, p. 341.

[28]   The purposes of UNIDROIT Principles are to serve as model for the national and international legislator, to be incorporated by the parties into their contract, to be chosen by the parties as a kind of 'surrogate law' (see: BOELE-WOELKI, K., 'Principles and Private International Law. The UNIDROIT Principles of International Commercial Contract and the Principles of European Contract law. (1996), p. 659-670), and to serve 'as a mean of interpreting and supplementing of existing international instruments' BONELL, M., 'Unification of Law by Non-Legislative Means' (1992), p. 225-233.

[29]   SPIER, J., HAAZEN, O., 'The European Group on Tort Law' (1999), p. 471.

of non-binding *Principles* for particular fields of Private Law. The *Commission on European Family Law* (CEFL) also belongs to this kind of projects. The aim of the CEFL is to draft non-binding *Principles* that can serve as a frame of reference for national legislators as they contemplate the renewal of their family laws; for private parties and their counsel as they draft marriage contracts for international marriages; and for the EU legislature as it drafts secondary Community laws in the field of family law.[30] It is important to stress that the ambitions of the CEFL do not go any further than to promote the voluntary 'bottom-up' harmonisation in some fields of family law. 'Top-down' unification by means of binding instruments is not intended. This view is explicitly expressed by the chairwoman of the *Commission*, Katharina Boele-Woelki. In her programmatic article on the purposes of the CEFL, she wrote that the option of 'drafting a binding uniform family law for the whole EU […] is much too far-reaching and is neither considered to be feasible nor desirable at the present time'.[31]

The following chart provides an overview of the most notable academic projects aiming at both top-down and bottom-up harmonisation.

---

[30] Katharina Boele-Woelki clarifies that 'some of the Principles, but not all, have been drafted so that they could be implemented in a national system. Following this approach the Principles may serve two purposes: firstly, they could be considered as recommendations and, secondly, they may be used as a model for the applicable law'. BOELE-WOELKI, K., 'The principles of European family law: aims and prospects' (2005), p.167.

[31] BOELE-WOELKI, K., 'Comparative Research-based Drafting of Principles of European Family Law' (2002), p. 179.

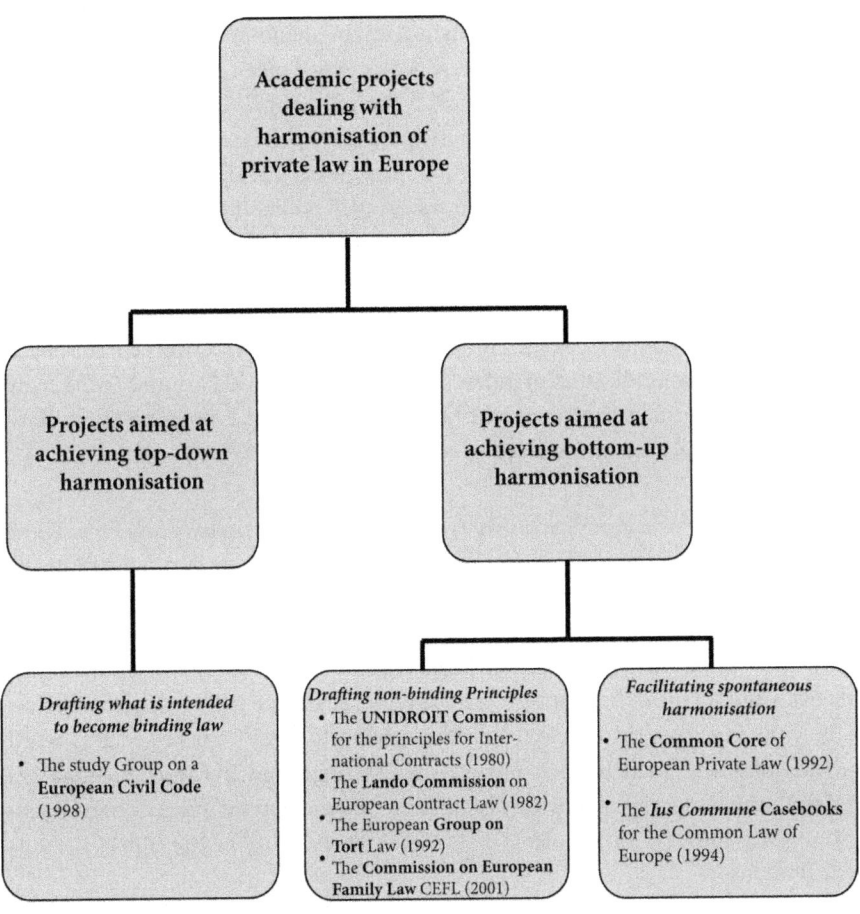

Spontaneous bottom-up harmonisation (convergence)

As was already mentioned, convergence is a form of bottom-up harmonisation that develops spontaneously in the form of approximation of legal systems due to natural evolutional processes. As we are talking about the development of legal systems, the word 'natural' does not mean that these developments take place without any participation of human actors; it rather denotes that the approximation of legal systems is beyond the immediate purpose of men.[32] Although convergence can in theory lead to a total unification of law, the history of family law in Europe presents no such examples. According to a widely shared view, the level of the achieved

---

[32] TROMPENAARS, B., *Pluriforme unificatie en uniforme interpretatie* (1989), p. 9-10.

approximation is not essential for typifying certain phenomenon as being a convergence. It is rightly stressed that 'convergence does not mean unifying everything; it simply means getting closer to each other'.[33] The following definition of convergence, given by the Italian comparatist Ugo Mattei, could be taken as a more or less common standpoint: 'in comparative law jargon, "convergence" is defined as a phenomenon of similar solutions reached by different systems from different points of departure'.[34] A minority of scholars, however, tend to perceive convergence more narrowly. For instance, David Bradley does not see evidence of convergence even in the far-reaching assimilation of Nordic family law, reached during the heydays of the Nordic co-operation.[35] This allows the suggestion that, in Bradley's view, convergence probably supposes the total eradication of differences, thus unification. This study will further operate with the mainstream notion of convergence, which denotes no more than a process of assimilation and still leaves room for differences.[36]

There is no consensus among scholars as to what actually makes laws converge. Those, who presuppose a strong correlation between law and society,[37] attribute the convergence of legal systems to economic, political, cultural and religious approximation, among others. Those, who adhere to the theory of the (relative) autonomy of law,[38] search for the sources of legal convergence within the realm of law. These theories and their implications on the convergence debate will be discussed below. One contemporary theory regarding the driving forces of convergence is worth mentioning here; namely, the controversial[39] theory of the 'free movement of legal rules',[40] which suggests that private law in Europe can be spontaneously harmonised by way of a 'competition of rules'[41] that ultimately results in the triumph of the most efficient one.[42]

---

[33]   VAN HOECKE, M., 'The Harmonisation of Private Law in Europe: Some Misunderstandings' (2000), p. 9.

[34]   MATTEI, U., *Comparative Law and Economics* (1996), p. 126.

[35]   BRADLEY, D., 'A Family Law For Europe? Sovereignty, Political Economy and Legitimation' (2003), p. 68.

[36]   ÖRÜCÜ, E., *Critical Comparative Law: Considering Paradoxes for Legal Systems in* Transition (1999), p. 22.

[37]   See Section 2.4.1. of this Chapter.

[38]   See Section 2.4.2. of this Chapter.

[39]   See critically: DROBNIG, U., *Private Law in the European Union* (1996), p. 15; HAAZEN, O., 'Comparative Law and Economics en het Europees privaatrecht als ongemengd rechtsstelsel' (1998), p. 1229-1233.

[40]   This theory was introduced in: SMITS, J., 'A European Private law as a Mixed Legal System. Towards a Ius Commune through the Free Movement of Legal Rules' (1998), p. 328-340 and further developed in his *The Making of European Private Law* (2002), p. 60-71.

[41]   SMITS, J., *The Making of European Private Law.* (2002), p. 63.

[42]   Ibid, p. 62 ff.

The paradigm of spontaneous harmonisation is when two or more legal systems mutually approach one another. The growing similarity between the common and civil law systems is a good example thereof. When one system just emulates the legal solutions of the other, as, for instance, was the case when Turkey borrowed the Swiss family law, it is sometimes suggested that this is not convergence in the strict sense of this word, but rather 'transplantation' or 'borrowing'.[43] The same suggestion is made with regard to several countries that elaborate on new laws, each building upon the same model. This phenomenon is defined as 'parallel development', following the same path, rather than convergence. Drawing on the 'Nordic model' of registered partnership in the Netherlands, Germany and Britain, Switzerland, and so on, can serve as a recent example of such parallel development. However, the effect of legal borrowing and parallel developments is very much the same as that of the paradigm of convergence. In all three cases the similarity of legal systems increases due to spontaneous, evolutionary, bottom-up processes. Therefore, the term convergence will be used in this book in order to denote all spontaneous top-down processes that lead to an increase of similarity between family laws.

The following chart can help the reader in the event of any conceptual confusion.

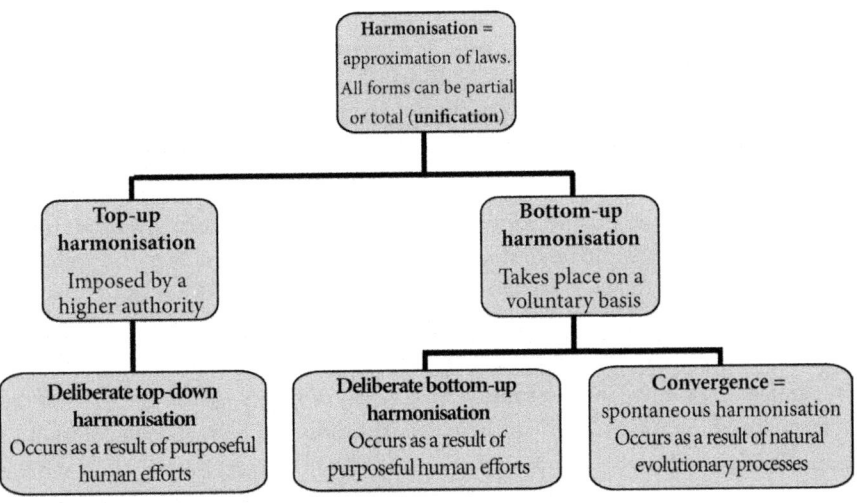

2.2.2. CONVERGENCE AND EVOLUTION

So, convergence is defined as the result of natural evolutionary processes. As was already mentioned, there is no consensus as to what actually makes laws converge.

---

[43] DAVID, R., 'The International Unification of Private Law' (1971), p. 6

Why would natural evolutionary processes make legal systems develop in each other's direction and not further apart from each other? The expectation that legal evolution leads to more similarity is strongly related to the notion that such evolution unavoidably involves the 'progress' to some higher stages of a more or less universal nature. This perception is edifyingly depicted in the following passage by John Merryman:

> 'progressive legal change is a natural process where pace and direction can be momentarily affected by human actions but will, in the longer run, be controlled by larger forces out of human control. Legal systems are more or less developed or mature, standing at different stages of evolution. When they converge it is because the less developed system is catching up with the more developed ones.'[44]

This perception goes to the heart of the issues discussed in this chapter, and indeed, in the whole of this book. The element that deserves attention here is the notion of 'progressive' legal evolution. This notion is not uncontroversial,[45] but the term 'progressive' will nonetheless be used throughout this book. John Merryman rightly points at the difficulty of discussing legal evolution in the abstract, apart from its relation to social, economic and political objectives.[46] The historical analysis in the following chapters will demonstrate that after the Protestant Reformation in the sixteenth century there was a clear development in family law towards more permissiveness. The overall history of the development of family law in Europe during the last two millennia, however, resembles a spiral rather than a linear process. During the first spin of the spiral, the permissive Classical Roman family law was replaced by the restrictive canon family law of the Middle Ages. Only few if any, would label this development 'progressive', at least from the present-day point of view. Through the second spin the medieval canon family made place for the permissive law of our times. These developments would be considered by many as 'progressive', but this appreciation is also not uncontroversial. There is no universal measure for evaluating the 'progressiveness' of family law. Obviously, the criteria for such evaluation depend largely on the ideological and political inclinations of the observer. If, for instance, one prefers to evaluate the relevant developments of family law on the basis of the buttressing of the 'traditional' family, the conclusion will be that the evolution of family law reached its zenith during the period of the Protestant Reformation and the Catholic Counterreformation. From this point of view, all subsequent developments can only be seen as regress. In contrast, if one prefers the permissiveness of family law

---

[44] MERRYMAN, J., 'On the Convergence (and Divergence) of Civil Law and the Common Law' (1978), p. 199.

[45] The legal Darwinist theories, popular in the end of the 19th century, are now 'generally discredited'. MERRYMAN, J., 'On the Convergence (and Divergence) of Civil Law and the Common Law' (1978), p. 199, note 6. For an overview of literature on this subject see: ibid.

[46] Ibid.

as the criterion, then the period of the Protestant Reformation and the Catholic Counterreformation will be seen as the nadir, and all subsequent developments as progressive evolution. Post-modernist value-relativism claims that all possible evaluation criteria are equally valuable, and none can be preferred above the other. Although modern family law literature, for the most part, does not adhere to this restriction, assessments like 'progressive', 'conservative', 'modern' or 'reactionary', which are frequently used in this book, are generally not considered to be completely politically correct. Most authors suggesting evolutionary schemes for explaining the developments of family law try to express themselves in more neutral terms and not to use this ideologically-laden terminology.

There is, however, more or less[47] a silent agreement that at least one criterion can be used for the evaluation of the 'progressiveness' of family without inducing the accusation of bias. This criterion is the level of protection of human rights.[48] Looking at the evolution of family law since the Reformation from the angle of the protection of human rights reveals that the level of such protection has been steadily growing. This allows the assessment of the whole evolution as generally **progressive**, and the whole process to be called **modernisation**.[49] If one abstracts from the various concrete human rights developed in all kinds of legal instruments, the movement towards better protection of human rights as a whole can be generally epitomised as the gradual switch from a transpersonalistic to a personalistic appreciation of the relations between society, family and family members.[50] According to the old transpersonalistic way of thinking, the individual was subservient to the family, and the family was in turn subservient to society at large. In contrast, the starting point of the modern personalistic perspective can be paraphrased by the saying: 'family is made for man, not man for the family'. In the personalistic family ideology, the concrete interests, feelings and aspirations of the individual family members are given priority above abstract general values like 'stability of the family' or 'indissolubility of marriage'. The gradual decline of the transpersonalistic approach in family ideology and family law in Europe after the Reformation in favour of a more personalistic one is a development that throughout this book will be appreciated as 'progressive'.

---

[47]   The universality of human rights is being contested by the proponents of the strict version of value relativism. See: PETERS, A., SCHWENKE, H., 'Comparative Law Beyond Post-Modernism' (2000), p. 818, and also COTTERRELL, R., 'The Concept of Legal Culture' (1997), 45-46.

[48]   See FROWEIN et al, 'The Protection of Fundamental Human Rights as a Vehicle of Integration' (1978), p. 231 ff.

[49]   For another meaning of the term 'modern' used in this book, see the introduction to Part III, note 1.

[50]   An illuminating synopsis of the philosophical background of transpersonalistic and personalistic ideologies was given by the early 20th century Russian scholar Ivan Pokrovskii in his outstanding, but alas almost forgotten, book *Osnovnie problemi grazgdanskogo prava* (1917), p. 52 ff. See also: RADBRUCH, G., *Grunzdzüge der Rechtsphilosophie* (1914), p. 97-104 and LASK, E., 'Rechtsphilosophie' (1907), p. 269-320.

This picture, however, requires some qualifications. The terms 'progress', 'modernisation' and even the criterion of the level of protection of human rights are not suitable for characterising every family law phenomenon. They fall short when describing merely technical areas, like, for instance, matrimonial property law: it is impossible to say that limited community of property is more 'progressive' than deferred community of property or the other way around. Also, 'progressiveness' and the level of protection of human rights are not always very helpful terms for describing the developments involving conflicts of interests between two individuals. Thus one cannot say that the law protecting the rights of a surrogate mother at the expense of the rights of the genetic mother of a child is more 'progressive' than the reverse version. Finally, the very notion of 'protection of human rights' is not unproblematic. Scholars like Mary Ann Glendon and Marie-Thérèse Klein point for instance at the intrinsic tension between the protection of the individual 'private' rights of a person, on the one hand, and the protection of the right to 'family life', based on the interdependency of the family members, on the other.[51] However, with these qualifications held in mind, the criterion of 'progressiveness' measured upon the level of protection of human rights is fairly workable. In line with this scheme, the designation 'progressive' or 'modern' will be used for those laws, developments and human actors that contribute to the emergence of a more personalistic family law, assuring a higher level of protection of human rights.

Contrarily, the laws, developments and persons discussed in this book will be qualified as being 'conservative' when they aim to bring these developments to a halt or turn back the clock on them. The 'conservative' stance in family law is usually related to an ideal of a traditional family of the past. An appeal to the 'traditional family' and 'traditional family values' seems to be rather universal. Restoring the 'traditional' stable and virtuous family of the past inspired reformers as diverse as the Roman Emperor Augustus (first century A.D.) and the actors of the sixteenth century Protestant Reformation. In the context of the last two centuries an appeal to the 'traditional family' involves the idealisation of a patriarchal, stable, hierarchical, male-dominated family, which is believed to have existed in the past. The historical analysis of the following chapters, however, will reveal that this ideal traditional family is more an ideological construct of the nineteenth and twentieth century conservatives, rather than a historical reality.[52]

---

[51] See MEULDERS-KLEIN, M.-T., *La personne, la famille et le droit – 1968-1998: Trois décennies de mutations en Occident* (1999), p. 467-425; 'Towards a European Civil Code of Family Law? Ends and Means' (2003), p. 108-109 and GLENDON, M.A., *Rights Talks: The Impoverishment of Political Discourse* (1991).

[52] Roderick Phillips has equally labelled 'conservatives' those who believed that the 'ideal family model had been a historical reality that could be resuscitated'. PHILLIPS, R., *Putting asunder* (1988), p. 487.

2.3. RELATIVISM, UNIVERSALISM AND PLURALISM: HARMONISATION AS PART OF THE 'UNFINISHED MODERNITY PROJECT'

2.3.1. INTEGRATIVE AND CONTRASTIVE COMPARATIVE LAW

Looking for sameness or difference?

The first of the theoretical roots of the cultural constraints argument to be discussed here is the so-called 'relativist' epistemology and the corresponding 'contrastive' method in comparative law. An important reason as to why the ongoing convergence/divergence debate in comparative law[53] seems to be endless is the fact that the subjective perspective of a comparatist influences her inclination to perceive either similarities or differences in the same events. As was already mentioned in the previous chapter, sometimes the same historical examples are employed by both proponents and opponents of the convergence thesis in support of their confliction conclusions. The reforms introducing no-fault divorce in the 1970s are a recurrent example.[54] On the one hand, the advance of no-fault divorce has been pointed to as evidence of convergence, as it has led to the eradication, or at least the attenuation, of the fault grounds. On the other hand, it has been suggested that no evidence of a convergence tendency can be derived from the no-fault movement, as, in spite of the similar general trend, the results of divorce reforms have not been the same in every country.

The opposite appreciation of the same historical events has to do with two important epistemological approaches that influence contemporary comparative legal thought: the universalistic search for similarities, on the one hand, and the relativistic emphasis on differences, on the other hand. According to Ian Ward, the debate that continues to dominate theoretical comparative law[55] is the discord between looking for 'sameness and difference'.[56]

---

[53]   See on this debate: NOTTAGE, L., *Convergence, Divergence, and the Middle Way in Unifying or Harmonising Private Law* (2001), p. 3 ff; DE WITTE, B., 'The Convergence Debate' (1996), p. 105-107.

[54]   In support of the convergence thesis see for instance: NEUMAYER, K., 'General Introduction' (1978), p. 1; PINTENS, W., VANWINCKELEN, C., *Casebook. European Family Law* (2001), p. 16; PHILLIPS, R., *Putting asunder* (1988), p. 570, against it, see for example: BRADLEY, D., 'A Family Law For Europe? Sovereignty, Political Economy and Legitimation' (2003), p. 96.

[55]   On a brief overview of this debate, see: ÖRÜCÜ, E., *The Enigma of Comparative Law* (2004), p. 179 ff.

[56]   WARD, I., 'The Limits of Comparativism: Lessons from UK-EC Integration' (1995), p. 31. A self-test suggested by Ward is in the answer to the question: 'are we identifying difference, and cherishing it, or are we trying to suppress it, by effective same-ness'. Ibid.

Historical roots of the integrative and contrastive approaches in comparative law

The two opposing trends in present-day comparative law have long historical roots. Rudolf Schlesinger has suggested a general rule, according to which periods of 'integrative' comparative law, laying emphasis on similarities, interchanges throughout the history of comparative law with periods of 'contrastive' comparative law, which tends to stress the differences.[57] This theory is widely appreciated; however, scholars are not unanimous on the exact historical boundaries of these periods. It is commonly accepted that from the sixteenth to the eighteenth century, when the old *ius commune* was still an important factor on the European legal scene, comparative law was basically dealing with the search for similarities between the local laws, and emphasising the resemblance between the legal systems.[58] Luigi Moccia describes how this attitude, based on the 'transnational spirit of jurists'[59] made place for 'a new emphasis on searching for differences',[60] when the upcoming codification movement started to weaken the *ius commune* in the end of the eighteenth century.[61] This tendency was set forth with the advent of nationalism and legal positivism in the nineteenth century.[62] In contrast, Anne Peters and Heiner Schwenke maintain that 'integrative' comparative law begins in the age of codification under the influence of the nostalgic search for 'the lost unity of the natural law,' and the 'historical optimism' of the theorists of the 'organic evolution of law'.[63] In this latter view, the nineteenth century 'contrastive' comparative law, based on the ideas of the German Historical School and legal positivism, was no successor, but rather contemporaneous with the 'integrative' comparative law.[64]

The ideas about the influence of 'contrastive' and 'integrative' comparative law in the twentieth century also differ rather significantly. According to Rudolf Schlesinger, the contrastive approach continued to prevail in comparative law until the last decades of the twentieth century.[65] In his view, it was not until the very end of the century, when the search for similarities and 'common core of legal systems' was revived under the influence of the European integration, that the integrative approach won through.[66] In contrast, some other authors suggest that 'integrative' comparative law was practised

---

[57] SCHLESINGER R., 'The Past and Future of Comparative Law' (1995), p. 477 ff.
[58] MOCCIA, L., 'Historical Overview of the Origins and Attitudes of Comparative Law' (1992), p. 616. SCHLESINGER, R., 'The Past and Future of Comparative Law' (1995), p. 478.
[59] MOCCIA, L., 'Historical Overview of the Origins and Attitudes of Comparative Law' (1992), p. 618.
[60] Ibid.
[61] SCHLESINGER, R., 'The Past and Future of Comparative Law' (1995), p. 479.
[62] MOCCIA, L., 'Historical Overview of the Origins and Attitudes of Comparative Law' (1992), p. 618.
[63] PETERS, A., SCHWENKE, H., 'Comparative Law Beyond Post-Modernism' (2000), p. 803-805.
[64] Ibid, p. 805-806.
[65] SCHLESINGER, R., 'The Past and Future of Comparative Law' (1995), p. 479.
[66] Ibid.

in Europe throughout almost the whole of the twentieth century. This opinion is supported by the fact that the first international congress of comparative law, held in Paris in 1900, was clearly dominated by the search for concepts and principles common to all 'civilised' systems of law.[67] It is also suggested that a strong politically inspired aspiration to unify the laws, which aroused after the First and the Second World Wars, shaped an entire 'ideology of convergence'.[68]

There is, however, a general consensus as to the point that at this moment the contrastive and the integrative approaches are simultaneously influencing comparative law methodology. These two opposing tendencies in comparative law reflect two opposing forces concurrently at work in contemporary Europe:[69] the tendency of creating a closer unity,[70] more interdependency and standardisation, on the one hand; and the tendency towards more sovereignty, preservation of diverse cultural identities[71] and national particularities, on the other hand.[72]

Philosophical roots of the integrative and the contrastive approach

The two long-standing trends in comparative law are in turn the reflection of two important general tendencies in European thought: universalism and relativism. Both trends can be traced far back in history, but they fully crystallised as antagonists during the Enlightenment.

The universalist tendency is typified by the two key premises of Enlightenment philosophy: universalism and anthropocentrism. The universalism of the Enlightenment expresses itself in postulating the existence of universal laws of reason and universally valid values. Anthropocentrism basically means that man is considered to be the centre of the order of things. Universalistic thought is also typified by epistemological optimism: man is supposed to be able to understand and master the causal order of the world with the help of reason. On top of that the 'Promethean spirit' of the Enlightenment involves the belief in the possibility of emancipating man and improving the human condition[73] according to the laws of reason and universally valid values.

---

[67]   See PETERS, A., SCHWENKE, H., 'Comparative Law Beyond Post-Modernism' (2000), p. 807.

[68]   NOTTAGE, L., *Convergence, Divergence, and Middle Way in Unifying or Harmonising Private Law*, (2001), p. 21.

[69]   MERRYMAN, J., 'On the Convergence (and Divergence) of Civil Law and the Common Law' (1978), p. 213-215.

[70]   COLLINS, H., 'European Private Law and the Cultural Identity of States' (1995), p. 353.

[71]   Ibid.

[72]   MERRYMAN, J., 'On the Convergence (and Divergence) of Civil Law and the Common Law' (1978), p. 213-215.

[73]   TOMESEN, L., 'Ideeënstelsels die ten grondslag liggen aan het Europese cultuurdebat' (1994), p. 6.

The universalistic way of thinking, based on the idea of universally valid values, anthropocentrism, and belief in progress, is also known as the 'Modernity'[74] modus of thinking.[75] According to Jean-François Lyotard, the appeal to universal values and the strive for emancipation gives Modernity-as-a-way-of-thinking a distinctive modus: 'a project, a target oriented will'.[76] The implementation of this project was started by the enlightened monarchs in the late eighteenth century and culminated during the French revolution. However, after the conservative Restoration of 1815, the 'Modernity project' lost its momentum and was met with severe criticism. After what could be considered to be the second major attempt to implement the 'Modernity project' – the Russian revolution of 1917 – also ended in terror and disillusionment, the credibility of the whole project dropped rather low.[77] The emancipation 'Modernity project' thus turned (according to its critics for the better and according to its proponents for the worse) into a centuries-long 'unfinished' project.[78]

The first relativist critique of the 'Modernity project' appeared almost simultaneously with the project itself, and came from the camp of the Enlightenment philosophers themselves. Jean-Jacques Rousseau, in line with his culture-pessimistic position, accused modernisation of levelling cultures and alienating man.[79] The later critics of the 'Modernity project' hold it responsible for colonialism, arrogant Europe-centrism, disregarding other cultures,[80] and, above all, for the large-scale social engineering practiced by the totalitarian regimes of the twentieth century. This critique reached its apotheosis in the allegation of Theodor Adorno that 'Modernity has ended at Auschwitz'.[81]

All the critics of the 'Modernity project' from the eighteenth century to the present have one feature in common: their argumentation is based on moral and epistemological relativism. If Modernity as a modus of thinking is typified by anthropocentrism, universalism and epistemological optimism, relativism as a modus

---

[74] The use of the term 'Modernity' in the meaning of a distinct modus of thinking contrasts with the other way of use of the same term with reference to the post-medieval period of European history. This other meaning of the term Modernity is derived from the commonly made division of European history into three major periods: Antiquity, Middle Ages and Modernity. It should be noted that the term 'Modernity' will be further used in this book in both aforementioned meanings. The meaning used in any particular case is easily discernable from the context.

[75] LYOTARD, J-F., *Het postmoderne uitgelegd aan onze kinderen* (1987), p. 31-32.

[76] Ibid, p. 61.

[77] GELLNER, E., *Postmodernism, Reason and Religion* (1992), p. 86-87.

[78] One of the best-known contemporary proponents of Modernity – Jürgen Habermas once stated that if Modernity is still an 'unfinished project,' it has to be finished. See: REIJEN, W., *De onvoltooide rede. Modern en postmodern* (1987), p. 10.

[79] TOMESEN, L., 'Ideeënstelsels die ten grondslag liggen aan het Europese cultuurdebat' (1994), p. 7.

[80] Ibid, p. 8.

[81] ADORNO, T., HORKHEIMER, M., *Dialektik der Aufklärung: philosophische Fragmente* (1947).

of thinking is characterised by multicentrism, veneration of differences and epistemological scepticism. Value or moral relativism is based on the presumption that it is not possible to make any value judgment in respect of cultures. Principles of justice, fairness or equity are nothing more than functions of moral practices.[82] Therefore all cultures and value systems are equally valuable and have to be respected as such.[83] Another basic aspect of relativist philosophy is epistemological scepticism, typified by mistrust in human cognitive ability and human communication. Its strongest form, so-called 'framework relativism',[84] suggests that since people of different cultural backgrounds communicate with each other within dissimilar intellectual frameworks, communication between cultures is fundamentally impossible.[85]

The relativist perspective has found a rather extreme expression in contemporary post-modernism.[86] Post-modernism repudiates the basic premises of Modernity so radically that it has rightly been called 'anti-Modernity'.[87] The universalism of Modernity is contrasted by the post-modernist embrace of disparity and difference.[88] The anthropocentrism of Enlightenment is replaced with a vision in which man is no longer the centre of things and 'the judge of the horizon of being'[89], but rather a 'derivative being',[90] 'preceded by the structure',[91] and representing no more than a 'bundle of relations'.[92] The view of Modernity philosophy that 'men act according to their values and judgments' is substituted by the idea that reality consists of objective structures lacking all conscious design and connection to human values.[93] Man's

---

[82] PETERS, A., SCHWENKE, H., 'Comparative Law Beyond Post-Modernism' (2000), p. 814.
[83] TOMESEN, L., 'Ideeënstelsels die ten grondslag liggen aan het Europese cultuurdebat' (1994), p. 9.
[84] Framework relativism is defined by Karl Popper as 'the doctrine that truth is relative to our intellectual background, which is supposed to determine somehow the framework within which we are able to think: that truth may change from one framework to another'. POPPER, K., *The Myth of the Framework. In Defence of Science and Rationality* (1994), p. 33, cited in: PETERS, A., SCHWENKE, H., 'Comparative Law Beyond Post-Modernism' (2000), at p. 815.
[85] TOMESEN, L., 'Ideeënstelsels die ten grondslag liggen aan het Europese cultuurdebat' (1994), p. 9.
[86] Jean-François Lyotard even suggested that the critique of Modernity is the central point unifying the very dissimilar views that are designated 'postmodernism'. LYOTARD, J-F., *Het postmoderne uitgelegd aan onze kinderen* (1987), p. 39.
[87] CASTILLO, M., 'The Dilemmas of Postmodern Individualism' (1997), p. 139.
[88] See also, for instance, Jacques Derrida, who claims that there is no culture and no cultural identity without difference. (DERRIDA, J., *The Other Heading. Reflections on Today's Europe* (1992), p. 9-10). Also Michel Foucault describes 'the archaeology of knowledge' as a method which 'task is to *make* differences: to constitute them as object, to analyse then, and to define their concept'. *The Archaeology of Knowledge* (1972), p. 205.
[89] NOWAK, L., 'On Postmodernist Philosophy: an Attempt to Identify Is Historical Sense' (1997), p. 125-126.
[90] Ibid, p. 126.
[91] Ibid.
[92] Ibid.
[93] Ibid, p. 127.

cognitive and creative potential as well as the technique and the possibility of progress are fundamentally disbelieved.[94] Reason is suspected as aggressive,[95] knowledge is claimed to be culturally, socially or economically determined,[96] and therefore not able to sustain any pretension of universal truth. The Kantian universal ethical approach is replaced by value relativism.

Harmonisation of law as a part of the 'unfinished Modernity project'

The Modernity/post-modernist discord clearly interacts with the harmonisation/cultural constraints debate. It is rightly observed that the idea of European unity as a whole,[97] and the endeavour of deliberate harmonisation of law as a part of it, is inspired by the 'Promethean' spirit of the 'Modernity project'. The ultimate objective of the harmonisation of law is not just approximation for the sake of uniformity, but rather the improvement of law via approximation.[98] It is justly noticed that harmonisation of law 'should not be considered as an end in itself, but as a mean towards the achievement of more obvious, more universal goals – "peace", "prosperity", "happiness", "justice", "freedom" or some combination of such things'.[99] Thus, the idea of harmonisation echoes the Modernity premise: that using the law of reason, a 'better' universally valid law can be elaborated. Although in present-day Europe conservative and progressive family values are simultaneously claimed to be universally valid, most of the proponents of harmonisation associate the 'better' law with the more modern law.[100] Therefore, it seems justified to consider the idea of 'better' harmonised law, which is based on universal values, and thus equally good for every European

---

94   LYOTARD, J.-F., *Het postmoderne uitgelegd aan onze kinderen* (1987), p. 88-89.
95   NOWAK, L., 'On Postmodernist Philosophy: an Attempt to Identify Is Historical Sense' (1997), p. 128. Michel Foucault has put in perspective the 'postulate of Western civilisation' that progress of knowledge is one of the most important safeguards of the liberation of man. He affirms that great systems of knowledge have fulfilled a function of domination and subjugation and that sometimes reason rolls freedom even further back. FOUCAULT, M., *Ervaring en waarheid* (1985), p. 58 and 85.
96   KENNEDY, E., 'Anticipations of Postmodernist Epistemology' (1997), p. 121.
97   TOMESEN, L., 'Ideeënstelsels die ten grondslag liggen aan het Europese cultuurdebat' (1994), p. 10.
98   René David named 'perfection of law' as the aim of its unification. DAVID, R., 'The International Unification of Private Law' (1971), p. 55.
99   DUN, F., van, 'Constitutional Choices For Europe: Integration vs. Unification' (1992), p. 662.
100   According to the founding fathers of the *Lando Commission*, their *Principles of European Contract Law* are intended to be 'progressive' (LANDO, O., BEALE, H., *Principles of European Contract Law*, (2000), p. xxii.). The members of the *European Group on Tort Law* plainly confess to 'equate "modern" with "best"'(SPIER, J, HAAZEN, O., 'The European Group on Tort Law' (1999), p. 480). The choices made by the *Commission on European Family* Law while drafting the *Principles on Divorce* witness a similar attitude. See the analysis of the CEFL *Principles on Divorce* in Part IV, Chapter 14, Section 14.5.4.

country, a part of the 'unfinished' Modernity project to make the human world better.[101]

Many arguments used by post-modernist critics against the 'Modernity project' are also employed by the opponents of harmonisation. The accusation of the 'Modernity project' 'of harbouring hidden despotic tendencies, the cosmopolitan and commercial mission of which was to homogenise the civilized world by merging the spirits, cultures, languages and intellectual productions of various nations',[102] often sounds in the harmonisation debate. So, Pierre Legrand rejects the idea of deliberate harmonisation as 'totalitarianism', 'an attack on pluralism, a desire to suppress autonomy, a blind attempt at diminishing of particularity and to eliminate '"other's" cultures'.[103] Others accuse harmonisation of being a 'part of a new interventionist political scheme'.[104] The suggestion of Jean-François Lyotard that one of the reasons for the failure of the Modernity project could be unbridgeable cultural differences,[105] strongly resembles the cultural constraints argument against harmonisation.

Post-modernist and Modernity arguments in the current comparative law debates

Presently, the adherence to the integrative and contrastive approach in comparative law is linked to the comparatist's conscious or unconscious affiliation with Modernity or post-modernist thought, respectively. Post-modernist comparative law tends to emphasise the differences and not the similarities between legal systems.[106] Under the influence of the relativist post-modernist approach, 'legal pluralism [became] the key concept in a post-modern view of law'.[107] The influence of post-modernist and Modern ways of thinking is clearly discernible in the discord between 'integrative' and 'contrastive' comparative law and the debate surrounding harmonisation and convergence. On the one hand, Pierre Legrand, who is rightly associated with postmodernism,[108] urges that '[…] the comparatist must learn to detect, to understand, to value, indeed, to cherish differences […]'.[109] Accordingly, convergence, which leads

---

[101] Jean-François Lyotard has described the final goal of the Modernity project as the emancipation of the whole of humanity. LYOTARD, J-F., *Het postmoderne uitgelegd aan onze kinderen* (1987), p. 33.

[102] CASTILLO, M., 'The Dilemmas of Postmodern Individualism' (1997), p. 145.

[103] LEGRAND, P., 'Against a European Civil Code' (1997), p. 53.

[104] FRANKENBERG, G., 'Stranger than Paradise: Identity and Politics in Comparative Law', *Utah Law Review* (1997), p. 265. Cited in: PETERS, A., SCHWENKE, H., 'Comparative Law Beyond Post-Modernism' (2000), at p. 824.

[105] LYOTARD, J-F., *Het postmoderne uitgelegd aan onze kinderen* (1987), p. 41.

[106] PINTENS, W., 'Accentenverschuiving in de rechtsvergelijking' (1998), p. 793.

[107] SAUSA SANTOS, B., DE, 'Law: A Map of Misreading. Towards a Postmodern Conception of Law' (1987), p. 297.

[108] See: ERP, S., VAN, *Europees Privaatrecht: Postmoderne dilemma's en keuzen*, p. 12.

[109] LEGRAND, P., *Fragments on Law-as-Culture* (1999), p. 10-11.

to the diminishment of differences, is being downplayed by all possible means and condemned as a threat to national cultural identities. On the other hand, scholars drawing on universalist Modernity premises,[110] tend to make the search for similarities an important task of comparative law. Thus, Zweigert and Kötz, introduce the *'praesumptio similitudinis'* as a useful 'working rule'[111] by performing comparative research. Rudolf Schlesinger postulates the existence of a common core of legal concepts and precepts shared by various legal systems.[112] Reinhard Zimmermann calls on the comparatist, dealing with civil and common law, 'to concentrate one's attention, for once, not so much on the distance and the difference between common and civil law as on their proximity and similarities'.[113] Illustrative in this respect is the aforementioned difference in the appreciation of the results of the Nordic harmonisation of family law in the framework of Nordic co-operation. While two prominent Scandinavian scholars estimate the Nordic family laws at the heyday of their harmonisation as 'almost identical',[114] David Bradley lays the emphasis on the remaining differences.[115]

The strong version of present-day 'contrastive' comparative law inclines to overlook any empirical evidence of convergence. Building on post-modernist 'epistemological scepticism'[116] and framework-relativism, the adherents of contrastive comparative law have erected an entire theory on the fundamental impossibility of convergence, harmonisation and even the very comparison of laws.[117] The best example of this theory is provided in the works of the same Pierre Legrand. Legrand postulates the fundamental impossibility for lawyers from different cultures to understand each other and each other's law. In his own words: 'what the common law lawyer can learn is not Italian-law-as-seen-by-an-Italian-lawyer but Italian-law-as-seen-by-a-common-law-lawyer.[118] The same, of course, applies to a comparatist. The comparatist only imagines

---

[110]   Paters and Schwenke remark that 'today, quite a few comparatists are openly universalists'. PETERS, A., SCHWENKE, H., 'Comparative Law Beyond Post-Modernism' (2000), p. 809.

[111]   ZWEIGERT, K., and KÖTZ, H., *An Introduction to Comparative Law* (1998), p. 40.

[112]   SCHLESINGER, R. et al, *Comparative law: cases, text, materials* (1998), p. 34 ff.

[113]   ZIMMERMANN, R., *The Law of Obligations. Roman Foundations of the Civilian Tradition* (1996), p. xi.

[114]   AGELL, A., 'Is There one System of Family Laws in the Nordic Countries' (2001), p. 314; SCHMIDT, T., 'The Scandinavian Law of procedure in Matrimonial Causes' (1984), p. 80.

[115]   BRADLEY, D., *Family Law and Political Culture* (1996). p. 12; BRADLEY, D., 'A Family Law For Europe? Sovereignty, Political Economy and Legitimation' (2003), p. 68 and 82-88.

[116]   PALMER, V., 'From Lerotholi to Lando: Some Examples of Comparative Law Methodology' (2005), p. 264.

[117]   For a general overview see: PETERS, A., SCHWENKE, H., 'Comparative Law Beyond Post-Modernism' (2000), p. 813 ff.

[118]   LEGRAND, P., 'Legal Traditions in Western Europe: The Limits of Commonality' (1995), p. 75.

that she analyses foreign law, in fact she merely 'becomes an observer of herself', because of the impact of her own experience on her perspective as observer.[119]

A general objection raised against this argument is that Legrand substitutes the notion of *understanding* of a foreign legal culture with the notion of *complete* understanding of a foreign legal culture.[120] His reasoning that because complete understanding of a foreign legal culture is not possible, no understanding thereof is possible, is evidently flawed. Applying the same line of reasoning to, for instance, the relations between men and women, one could say that because men and women will never be able to completely understand each other, they might just as well refrain from the futile effort all together. Legrand is rightly criticised for 'intellectual purism'[121] leading to an 'all or nothing'[122] epistemological approach; meaning that if we cannot reach a perfect understating of foreign legal systems we should not even strive for more profound communication.[123]

The strong correlation between the approach taken by an observer and the results of her comparative research allows the suggestion that if the proponents of framework relativism are right, perceiving differences or similarities, and consequently convergence or divergence in the same events, is just a matter of one's intellectual 'framework'. This would mean that the outcome of research cannot possibly reflect any objective truth, but is predetermined by the ideological and political inclinations (the 'framework') of the observer.[124] It is interesting to notice that if the post-modernist assumption that all intellectual 'frameworks' are equally valuable would be thought right through to its ultimate conclusion, any further debate on harmonisation or convergence seems rather pointless. Everyone would always have his own irrefutable truth on his side. This could make one wonder why the post-modernist opponents of convergence and harmonisation none the less keep trying to win the debate.

---

[119]   Ibid, p. 35-36.
[120]   It is interesting to notice a contradiction between Legrand's remark: 'while I am not saying that understanding is completely impossible, I argue that *complete understanding is impossible*' (LEGRAND, P., 'Legal Traditions in Western Europe: The Limits of Commonality' (1995), p. 82) and his conclusion, drawing on Nietzsche's paradigm 'Two neighbours never understand one another', that 'the structures of intelligibility embedded in discrete legal traditions can not be bridged. They *separate*' (LEGRAND, P., *Fragments on Law-as-Culture* (1999), p. 19).
[121]   VAN ERP, S., *Europees Privaatrecht: Postmoderne dilemma's en keuzen* (1998), p. 17.
[122]   Ibid, p. 25.
[123]   Ibid, p. 17-20.
[124]   VAN ERP, S., *Europees Privaatrecht: Postmoderne dilemma's en keuzen* (1998), p. 8.

2.3.2. THE FALLACY OF THE EXTREMES: THE NEED TO SEARCH FOR A MIDDLE WAY

The post-modernist's critiques of the Modernity modus of thinking often try to ridicule it by ascribing to the contemporary version the idealism and the radicalism of its 'strong' nineteenth-century versions.[125] The same is often done in order to deprecate the idea of harmonisation.[126] In turn, proponents of the Modernity ideas also tend to associate every version of post-modernist thought with the strongest versions of epistemological and value relativism. A similar tactic is often used by the proponents of harmonisation. Extreme viewpoints like those of Legrand facilitate them to dismiss all reservations about deliberate harmonisation for lack of credibility. For the true partisans of harmonisation, if there were no Legrand, it would be necessary to invent him.

This polarising approach is, however, not inevitable. There have always been scholars searching for a middle way between the extremes of relativism and universalism. An interesting example is the attempt made by Luciënne Tomesen. Tomesen suggests 'philosophical pluralism' as a possible remedy for reconciling both hostile viewpoints and helping to overcome their deficiencies.[127] She defines philosophical pluralism as a relatively young system of thought, based on two main premises: 'interaction' and 'diversity'.[128] Like Modernity, pluralism is an anthropocentric philosophy.[129] However, it sees man not as a closed, but rather as an open system.[130] Man is both a product and a producer of culture. The core of philosophical pluralism is the acknowledgement of the possibility of communication and (albeit limited) understanding between people

---

[125] It was rightly noticed that much critique on the Enlightenment is largely based on a subjective emotional perception of history. Moreover, it often aimed not at the real 'Enlightenment Project' with its fine distinctions and richness of different opinions, but at a crude and exaggerated version of it, 'invented by later commentators who needed a dead dog to kick with impunity, in order to blame it for a disease which they believe it had passed down to them'. WOKLER, R., 'The Enlightenment Project and Its Critics' (1997), p. 18.

[126] The idea of harmonisation is so often ridiculed by association with the eighteenth-century search for ideal law, based on the law of reason, that René David stressed that 'international unification of law in no way implies a return to the idealistic and universalist doctrines of the times past'. DAVID, R., 'The International Unification of Private Law' (1971), p. 26.

[127] According to Tomesen, philosophical pluralism only became discernible in the eighteenth century and acquired its place in the philosophy only at the end of the nineteenth century in the context of American Pragmatism. TOMESEN, L., 'Ideeënstelsels die ten grondslag liggen aan het Europese cultuurdebat' (1994), p. 13.

[128] Ibid.

[129] Ibid, p. 16.

[130] Ibid, p. 17.

with diverse cultural and ideological backgrounds.[131] Such interaction can occur without threatening diversity.[132]

Philosophical pluralism can provide a good theoretical foundation for modern harmonisation projects, namely 'unity in diversity'.[133] The idea of harmonisation as 'unity in diversity' has been put forward by Esin Örücü – a renowned Turkish-British comparatist. Örücü suggested that harmonisation only means bringing about harmony, which does not necessitate eradication of differences.[134] Only clear cut unification projects, pursuing top-down unification by means of imposing a universally valid 'better law', could be justifiably accused of disregarding cultural differences. Yet, modern harmonisation initiatives are as far away from their historical precursors, searching for the ideal universal law, as the modern vision of the world is distant from the mechanical model of Descartes. Almost none of the present-day harmonisation projects aspire to a straightforward, mechanical, top-down harmonisa-tion.[135] The modern, more cautious harmonisation initiatives, which go no further than encouraging voluntary bottom-up harmonisation, cannot be accused of the sins of their radical forbearers. Since the vast majority of scholars currently involved in harmonisation activities cautiously avoid the extremes of binding unification, reconciliation with their opponents seems not altogether impossible. Prudently putting forward the idea of harmonisation 'through appreciating differences and "transposi-tions", rather than pursuing creating plain "similars"'[136] may reassure the moderate opponents of harmonisation. This gives some hope for overcoming the polarising debate that aims to fight the ghosts of the extremes at the expense of the credibility and the academic quality of the arguments on both sides.

2.4. THE CULTURAL CONSTRAINTS ARGUMENT AND THE DIFFERENT THEORIES OF THE RELATION BETWEEN LAW AND SOCIETY

The second theoretical premise of the cultural constraints argument is the idea of the strong correlation between law and society. David Bradley, who made an enquiry into the theoretical roots of the convergence/divergence debate with relation to family

---

[131]   Ibid, p. 14.
[132]   Ibid.
[133]   Ibid, p. 17.
[134]   ÖRÜCÜ, E., *Critical Comparative Law: Considering Paradoxes for Legal Systems in Transition* (1999), p. 22.
[135]   See the brief analysis in Section 2.2.1. of this Chapter.
[136]   ÖRÜCÜ, E., 'Unde Venit, Quo Tendit Comparative Law?' (2002), p. 17.

law,[137] has delineated that the difference in perspective on the relations between law and society is crucial to the divergent positions taken in the convergence and harmonisation debate.[138]

The supporters of the cultural constraints argument consider law to be a deeply-rooted cultural phenomenon that can only develop by way of 'organic' growth. Their convictions are, to a lesser or greater degree, connected with the so-called 'mirror', or 'deterministic' theory of law, according to which, as William Ewald puts it, 'law is the mirror of some set of forces (social, political, economic, whatever) external to law'.[139] They therefore downplay the possibility of using law as a tool for social engineering and the feasibility of successfully transplanting law from one jurisdiction to another.[140] Consequently, they reject the possibility of deliberate harmonisation, which, according to them, would disturb the natural path of the evolution of law. One of their most prominent arguments against deliberate harmonisation is that the implantation of any newly engineered body of harmonised law will inevitably fail. They maintain that harmonised law will never take root in an alien cultural environment, and that a lasting gap between the uniform law in the books and the law in action would thereby be created. Family law is often used as a paradigmatic example of the strong embedment of law in society.

The opponents of the cultural constraints argument, on the contrary, generally adhere to the idea of the (relative) autonomy of law. The autonomist theories see law as a system that is (to a certain degree) insulated from the other systems and institutions of society.[141] They have no difficulty recognising instances of far-reaching convergence and acknowledging that law is often used as an instrument of regulation for human

---

[137]   See his insightful articles: 'Convergence in Family Law: Mirrors, Transplants and Political Economy' (1999), p. 128-150 and 'A Family Law For Europe? Sovereignty, Political Economy and Legitimation'(2003), p. 65-104.

[138]   BRADLEY, D., 'Convergence in Family Law: Mirrors, Transplants and Political Economy' (1999), p. 128-130

[139]   EWALD, W., 'Comparative Jurisprudence' (1995), p. 491.

[140]   LEGRAND, P., 'The Impossibility of "Legal Transplants"' (1997), p. 111-124. Legrand also denies the existence and the possibility of assimilation of the societal factors (mostly cultures) in which law is imbedded (LEGRAND, P., 'Legal Traditions in Western Europe: The Limits of Commonality' (1995), p. 68-69). Consequently, he also denies the existence of any past or present examples of convergence between the legal systems within Europe. LEGRAND, P., 'European Legal Systems are not Converging' (1996), p. 52-81.

[141]   EWALD, W., Social Structure and Law (1990), p. 32.

relations[142] and social change,[143] and that borrowing and transplantation is part of the reality of legal development all over the world.[144] They also generally think quite positively on the perspectives for deliberate harmonisation.

2.4.1. LAW AS A MIRROR OF SOCIETY: 'MIRROR' OR 'DETERMINISTIC' THEORIES OF LAW

'Mirror' or 'deterministic' theories vary according to their 'strength' and the societal factors that their adherents assume to be the determinants of law.[145] At present 'mirror' theories are rarely upheld in their pure or, using the terminology of Ewald,[146] 'strong' versions. Such 'strong' versions hold that 'nothing in law is autonomous, law is a mirror of society, and every aspect of the law is modelled by economy and society'.[147] The best-known historical examples of more or less 'strong' 'mirror' theories are the 'environmentalist' theory of Montesquieu,[148] Von Savigny's view of law as the reflection of the 'spirit of the people' (*Volksgeist*),[149] and Marxists' economic determinism.[150]

The 'strong' contemporary 'mirror' theory of Pierre Legrand: 'Law-as-culture'

Among modern scholars, Pierre Legrand, with his theory of 'law-as-culture', is probably the only representative of a 'strong' version of 'mirror' theory. The theory of Legrand deserves special attention, because his ideas come close to the core of the cultural constraints argument. Legrand's views, expressed in his main treatise *Fragments on Law-as-Culture* and a number of other works, lead him to the conclusion that 'if one forgoes surface examination at the level of rules and concepts to conduct

---

[142]   'Law, even embedded in our culture, is primarily an instrument to regularise human relationships and not a purpose in itself.' PINTENS, W., VANWINCKELEN, K., *Casebook. European Family Law* (2001), p. 15.

[143]   In the view of the moderate supporters of those ideas, law is seen as a 'product of change as well as the producer of change' and the relations between the legal and social change are not oversimplified. ÖRÜCÜ, E., 'A Theoretical Framework for Transfrontier Mobility of Law' (1995), p. 7.

[144]   The most drastic form of this view is presented in the works of Alan Watson, the principal one being *Legal Transplants. An Approach to Comparative law* (reprint 1993).

[145]   For an overview see: WATSON, A., *Society and Legal Change* (2001), p. 1-11; FREEDMAN, W., *Law in Changing Society* (1959).

[146]   EWALD, W., 'Comparative Jurisprudence (II): The Logic of Legal Transplants' (1995), p. 494.

[147]   Ibid, p. 492.

[148]   See MONTESQUIEU, C., *The Spirits of Laws*, Book 1, Chapter 3. 'On positive laws' (reprint 1977).

[149]   According to Von Savigny, positive law lives in the consciousness of the people; not in the individual consciousness, but rather in the collective legal consciousness of the whole of the people. This collective legal consciousness forms the *Volksgeist*. See: SAVIGNY, F., VON, *System des heutigen römischen Recht* (1840), p. 14.

[150]   See MARX, K., *The German Ideology* (reprint 1972), p. 270.

a deep examination in terms of legal *mentalités*, one must come to the conclusion that legal systems, despite their adjacency within the European Community, have not been converging, are not converging and will not be converging'.[151] Legrand regards law as an emanation of culture.[152] According to him, on a subjective level the legal culture takes the shape of a 'legal "*mentalité*" (a collective mental programme), also defined as an 'interiorised legal culture, within a given legal culture'.[153] Contrary to what Legrand's appeal to the 'historical, social, economic, political, and psychological context' of legal culture[154] might suggest, he actually reduces 'legal culture' to its formal elements at the expense of the ideological ones.[155]

Weak 'mirror theories' of the relation between law and society

Legrand's theory is rather an extreme that stands on its own. More influential are several 'weak' versions of 'mirror' or deterministic theories, which have recently been put forward in order to explain the developments of family law. Mary Ann Glendon emphasises that family structure has always been closely linked to economical structure.[156] Harry Willekens explains the evolution of family law during the last two hundred years of European history by changes of the social and economic functions of marriage and the family.[157] Otto Kahn-Freund and David Bradley both stress the paramount importance of political factors among the determinants of the developments of family law. It was suggested that Kahn-Freund's theory[158] can be seen as a variation on Montesquieu's 'environmentalist' theory, adjusted to modern circumstances.[159] Kahn-Freund states that with the ongoing economic, social and cultural assimilation and integration of the Western World, the geographical, economic and social factors, put forward by Montesquieu, have 'greatly lost, but that the political factors equally greatly gained in importance'[160] in determining differences between the laws. The predominance of political factors, put forward by Otto Kahn-Freund, is criticised by Gunther Teubner, who suggests that such overestimation of political factors at the expense of other social factors is no longer justifiable since 'all important

---

[151] LEGRAND, P., 'European Legal Systems Are Not Converging' (1996), p. 61-62.
[152] LEGRAND, P., *Fragments on Law-as-Culture* (1999), p. 5.
[153] LEGRAND, P., 'European Legal Systems Are Not Converging' (1996), p. 62.
[154] LEGRAND, P., *Fragments on Law-as-Culture* (1999), p. 5.
[155] This is rightly mentioned by Martijn Hesselink in his inauguration speech. HESSELINK, M., *The New European Legal Culture*, (2001), p. 70.
[156] GLENDON, M.A., *The New Family and the New Property* (1981), p. 1.
[157] WILLEKENS, H., 'Explaining Two Hundred Years of Family Law in Western Europe' (1997), p. 79-95.
[158] KAHN-FREUND, O., 'On Uses and Misuses of Comparative Law' (1974), p. 1-27.
[159] William Ewald called it 'a revised' and 'carefully nuanced' version of Montesquieu's theory. EWALD, W., 'Comparative Jurisprudence (II): The Logic of Legal Transplants' (1995), p. 495.
[160] Ibid, p. 8.

political differences of the Cold War' have disappeared.[161] This argument, however, seems to overlook that what Kahn-Freund means by 'political factors' is not merely the characteristics of different political regimes, but rather the balance of political power between various organised cultural, religious and other interest groups within each regime.[162] Those factors remain relevant within the more politically homogenous democratic societies of present-day Europe. Bradley shares Kahn-Freund's vision of political factors as the main determinants of family law. He suggests that 'family laws are unique to political culture',[163] and accentuates the function of family law as a 'component of political economy'.[164] Bradley has, however, carefully qualified his 'political determinism' by acknowledging a certain impact of economical factors and the imitation of foreign models.[165]

The following chapters will provide an abundance of empirical evidence in support of the importance of political factors. It will be shown that national differences in the balance of political power between the proponents and the adversaries of the modernisation of family law are the main determinant of the transformations of family law and the differences between the family laws across Europe. It is important to notice that despite his determinist inclinations, Otto Kahn-Freund is no irreconcilable opponent of convergence of family law. Although, he has called the idea of unification of family law 'a hopeless quest',[166] Kahn-Freund readily acknowledges that 'in hardly any legal field have we seen so intensive and so rapid an assimilation of ideas and institutions as in family law'.[167] Thereby Kahn-Freund actually sets an example of an appreciation of convergence in the light of a deterministic theory of law. He acknowledges convergence, but not primarily on the level of the institutions of family law, but rather on the level of the underlying ideas.[168] In contrast, David Bradley's assessment of the convergence tendency in family law is more negative. Bradley generally tends to reject the possibility of convergence rather firmly.

---

[161] TEUBNER, G., 'Legal Irritants: Good Faith in British Law or How Unifying Law Ends Up in New Divergences' (1998), p. 22.

[162] KAHN-FREUND, O., 'On Uses and Misuses of Comparative Law' (1974), p. 12.

[163] BRADLEY, D., 'Convergence in Family Law: Mirrors, Transplants and Political Economy' (1999), p. 128.

[164] BRADLEY, D., 'A Family Law For Europe? Sovereignty, Political Economy and Legitimation' (2003), p. 70.

[165] BRADLEY, D., 'Convergence in Family Law: Mirrors, Transplants and Political Economy' (1999), p. 148.

[166] KAHN-FREUND, O., 'Common Law and Civil Law – Imaginary and Real Obstacles to Assimilation' (1978), p. 141.

[167] KAHN-FREUND, O., 'On Uses and Misuses of Comparative Law' (1974), p. 14.

[168] Kahn-Freund rightly attributed the difference in the attitude towards divorce in Italy and Ireland and in the rest of Europe to the different structure of political power determined by the influence of the Catholic Church (Ibid). However, his doubts about whether divorce would be ever accepted in Italy or Ireland are refuted by history. We now know that both countries have introduced divorce, in 1970 and 1996 respectively.

2.4.2. LAW AS AN INSULATED SYSTEM: THEORIES OF THE (RELATIVE) AUTONOMY OF LAW

The theories of the autonomy of law are based upon two main presumptions. Their proponents, in the first place, regard the legal system to be autonomous from other systems and institutions constituting society.[169] In the second place, they consider law as a relatively 'closed system'.[170] This means that changes within this system 'are generated from within the legal system, not from without'.[171] The 'strong' versions of the autonomy theory are at present as uncommon as their 'strong' deterministic counterparts. In between the 'strong' versions of the theory of the autonomy of law and the 'mirror' or determinists' theories, lie theories that are based on the assumption of a 'relative autonomy of law'. Hugh Collins has rightly stressed the vagueness of the concept of the relative autonomy of law, as, in fact, it leaves the very question of a link between the law and the culture of a society more or less open.[172] These theories try to avoid the extremities of both deterministic and autonomist approaches. By doing so they come rather close to the weak versions of the 'mirror' theories. In the words of William Ewald, theories of the relative autonomy of law 'lay stress on the *complexity* of the phenomena, pointing out that the relationship between law and society is neither non-existent, nor a simple mirroring, but a subtle and intricate interrelationship that must be studied case by case'.[173] Modern scholars are more inclined to embrace these refined middle ground versions than the 'strong' versions of the autonomy theories.

The relative autonomy theories lay emphasis on the interrelation between law and society, rather than on the determination of law by society. Illustrative of this respect are statements like: 'the law with its own history and tradition shapes the values of the society in which it is embedded and in turn is shaped by them'.[174]

A 'strong' theory of the autonomy of law: Watson's theory of legal transplants

A well-known modern example of a 'strong' version of the theory of the autonomy of law is provided by Alan Watson's controversial theory of legal transplants.[175] The

---

[169] EWALD, W., *Social Structure and Law* (1990), p. 32.
[170] Ibid.
[171] Ibid.
[172] COLLINS, H., 'European Private Law and the Cultural Identity of States' (1995), p. 359.
[173] EWALD, W., 'Comparative Jurisprudence (II): The Logic of Legal Transplants' (1995), p. 504.
[174] CASSIDY, J., 'An Undergraduate Course in Comparative legal Studies' (1997), p. 104
[175] William Ewald warns that attributing Watson's theory to the 'strong' versions of the theory of autonomy of law requires a qualification (EWALD, W., 'Comparative Jurisprudence (II): The Logic of Legal Transplants' (1995), p. 491 ff). Ewald observes that the prudence of Watson's arguments varies sometimes quite significantly (Ibid). In polemical excitement he allows himself reckless remarks like: 'law is largely autonomous and not shaped by social needs' (WATSON, A., *The Evolution of Law*

essence of Watson's theory is that he considers legal borrowing as a major driving force of legal development and legal convergence.[176] Describing numerous examples of legal transplantation from Roman times to today leads Watson quite far in refuting the connection between law and society. According to Watson '[…] there does not exist a close, inherently necessary, relationship between existing rules of law and the society in which they operate'.[177] The issue is 'not that private law *fails* to mirror the needs and desires of society or its ruling élite, but that to a very considerable extent law is *out of step* with such needs and desires'.[178] Watson does not deny all together that 'the rules must have a connection with the society in some way and to some extent'.[179] However, he considers such relationship as unintelligible and 'impossible to define, perhaps because it varies from state to state and from one area of law to another'.[180] Watson applies his transplant thesis to family law without any reservations. He explicitly rejects the idea that family law is more resistant to change as a result of foreign influence,[181] and affirms that family law is very open to transplants.[182]

Watson's straightforward transplant theory was met with considerable criticism.[183] Pierre Legrand plainly stated that legal transplants are simply impossible,[184] as one can mechanically transplant a legal rule as such but its 'cultural-specific meaning' 'does not survive the journey from one legal system to another'.[185] Even commentators who generally see the merits of the transplant theory call for conceptual refinement and moderation.[186]

(1985), p. 119). But he often corrects himself by adding: that 'there is no *simple* relationship between a society and its law' (WATSON, A., *Legal Transplants. An Approach to Comparative Law* (1993), p.107. Emphasis added). These fluctuations in Watson's reasoning allowed Ewald to speak of 'weak' and 'strong' arguments by Watson. EWALD, W., 'Comparative Jurisprudence (II): The Logic of Legal Transplants' (1995), p. 491 ff.

[176]   This is affirmed in many places, for instance, in: WATSON, A., *Legal Transplants and European Private Law* (2000), p. 12.

[177]   WATSON, A., *Society and Legal Change* (2001) p. 130.

[178]   Ibid. Emphasis added.

[179]   Ibid, p. 134

[180]   Ibid.

[181]   WATSON, A., *Legal Transplants. An Approach to Comparative Law* (1993), p. 96.

[182]   Ibid.

[183]   E.g. LEGRAND, P., 'The Impossibility of Legal Transplants' (1997), p. 111-124. BRADLEY, D., 'Convergence in Family Law: Mirrors, Transplants and Political Economy' (1999), p. 130 ff; COTTERRELL, R., 'Is there a logic of legal transplants? (2001), p. 70-92.

[184]   According to Legrand: '[…] the transplant does not, in effect, happen: a key feature of the rule – its meaning – stays behind so that the rule that was "there", in effect is not itself displaced over "here". LEGRAND, P., 'The Impossibility of Legal Transplants' (1997), p. 118.

[185]   Ibid, p. 117.

[186]   E.g. TEUBNER, G., 'Legal Irritants: Good Faith in British Law or How Unifying Law Ends Up in New Divergences' (1998), p. 17; NELKEN, D., 'Legal Transplants and Beyond: Of Disciplines and Metaphors' (2002), p. 24 ff; ÖRÜCÜ, E., *The Enigma of Comparative Law* (2004), p. 100-105.

Watson himself does not work out any noteworthy explanatory scheme for the phenomenon of legal transplantation. Such schemes are later developed by other scholars. For instance, Rodolfo Sacco suggests two possible explanations for legal borrowing: imposition and prestige.[187] He rightly observes the inclination of every potent legal system to impose itself upon others.[188] Sacco stresses that the imposition by mere force mostly ends when the force is removed.[189] It should be added, however, that this depends on factors like the length and the profundity of such imposition, the perceived merits of the transplanted rule, and the question whether a legal transplant is still defined as something alien. For example, the influence of Soviet family law, imposed on the Eastern European countries after World War II, seems to persist in some of them, even after the force has been removed and the prestige of the donor has declined.[190] The incentive of prestige is described by Sacco as 'the desire to appropriate the work of the others' which one considers as 'prestigious'.[191] This was, for instance, the motivation behind the reception of Roman law in the Middle Ages.[192] Gianmaria Ajani highlights another important factor determining the choice of a source of borrowing: mere chance.[193] An example of borrowing by 'chance' is the adoption by Turkey of Swiss private law. Ugo Mattei suggests that there is a kind of market of competing legal models, which lend themselves for borrowing,[194] and that the selection of these models is largely based on the criteria of their efficiency.[195] Upon this 'efficiency' explanatory scheme, Jan Smits built up his already mentioned theory of spontaneous harmonisation of private law in Europe by way of 'free movement of legal rules'.[196]

In the following chapters the reader will come across various historical examples of transplantation of family law. I can already announce that a pure transplantation of rules without accepting social and ideological premises almost never happens. In most instances the transplantation of legal rules is preceded by the reception of the ideas on which these rules are based. Peter de Cruz rightly observes that 'the field of family

---

[187] SACCO, R., 'Legal Formants: A Dynamic Approach to Comparative Law' (1991), p. 398.
[188] Ibid.
[189] Ibid.
[190] Some of the Eastern European countries, e.g. Estonia, Latvia, have clearly chosen to part with this heritage, others, e.g. Bulgaria, Lithuania, Serbia, Poland, Czech Republic have preserved much of it.
[191] SACCO, R., 'Legal Formants: A Dynamic Approach to Comparative Law' (1991), p. 398.
[192] Ibid, p. 399.
[193] AJANI, G., 'By Chance and Prestige: Legal Transplants in Russian and Eastern Europe' (1995), p. 93-117.
[194] MATTEI, U., Comparative Law and Economics (1996), p. 130.
[195] Ibid, p. 129.
[196] See: SMITS, J., 'A European Private law as a Mixed Legal System. Towards a Ius Commune through the Free Movement of Legal Rules' (1998), p. 328-340 and SMITS, J., 'On Successful Legal Transplants in a Future Ius Commune Europaeum' (2002), p. 137-154.

law provides several examples of such transplant, primarily because of the universality and 'transferability' of some of its cornerstone principles'.[197] Thus, transplantation of legal ideas seems to be a more important phenomenon than transplantation of legal rules.[198] Ataturk's elite, firstly and paramountly, wished to import Western ideas and patterns into Turkey,[199] and the transplantation of the Swiss law was just a means to this end. More often, it's rather the ideas, and not the formal rules, that are adopted; the legal rules are not literally transplanted but drafted anew in the receiving country. Thus, Esin Örücü has rightly sketched a broader perspective of legal ideas, concepts, structures – and not only rules – moving across legal orders.[200]

Alan Watson himself does not lay a direct connection between his theory of legal transplants and the convergence and harmonisation debate. However, David Bradley justifiably locates the 'strong' version of the transplant thesis at the 'extreme end of convergence theories'.[201] If laws are not enrooted in the societies in which they operate, and 'the main type of relationship between systems arises because one system borrows from the other, or because both borrowed from the third',[202] legal borrowing can be seen as a major driving force of legal convergence.

Theories of the relative autonomy of law

Nuanced theories of the relative autonomy of law are at present more popular than the strong versions thereof. The theory of Gunther Teubner[203] gives a good impression of such theories. Teubner accepts some dependency of law from external factors, but refines the deterministic vision by suggesting that:

'(1) Law's contemporary ties to society are no longer comprehensive, but are highly selective and vary from loose coupling to tight interwovenness

---

[197]　DE CRUS, P.,'Legal Transplants: Principles and Pragmatism in Comparative Family Law' (2002), p. 118.

[198]　Otto Kahn-Freund admitted that 'even in relation to family, legal ideas are now moving freely around the world so as to influence legislation and pending law reform'. KAHN-FREUND, O., 'On Uses and Misuses of Comparative Law' (1974), p. 10.

[199]　ÖRÜCÜ, E., *Critical Comparative Law: Considering Paradoxes for Legal Systems in Transition* (1999), p. 86.

[200]　ÖRÜCÜ, E., 'Mixed and Mixing Systems: A Conceptual Search' (1996), p. 341.

[201]　BRADLEY, D., 'Convergence in Family Law: Mirrors, Transplants and Political Economy' (1999), p. 130.

[202]　WATSON, A., *Society and Legal Change* (2001) p. 141.

[203]　Gunther Teubner himself is quite unhappy with the term 'relative autonomy of law'. He hoped that the refinement of the strong deterministic and autonomist theories 'w[ould] not end up in the compromising formula' of relative autonomy. TEUBNER, G., 'Legal Irritants: Good Faith in British Law or How Unifying Law Ends Up in New Divergences' (1998), p. 17.

(2) They are no longer connected to the totality of the social but to diverse fragments of society.'[204]

At another place Teubner brings deterministic and autonomist theories even closer by suggesting that law is an 'autopoietic system' developing by way of an interrelated 'co-evolution' of legal and other social factors.[205] Teubner also submits that specific fields of law are predominately linked to different external factors.[206] He suggests that economic factors may be relatively more relevant for business-related areas of private law. Family law presents, in his view, the best example of the diminishing influence of environmental factors and increasing impact of political factors.[207]

As was already mentioned, the theories of the relative autonomy of law come rather close to 'weak' 'mirror or deterministic theories. Both theories try to 'get beyond juxtaposing cultural dependency and legal insulation or social context and legal autonomy'.[208] They admit some correlation between law and the societal factors external to it, but do not see such dependency as straightforward and linear.

2.4.3. THE RELATION BETWEEN LAW AND SOCIETY AND THE CONVERGENCE AND HARMONISATION DEBATE

In the preceding sections the theoretical background of the cultural constraints argument has been explored. This argument clearly rests upon a 'strong' version of a 'mirror' or determinist theory of the relation between law and society. Family law is supposed to be totally determined by one of the societal factors external to law, namely culture. The cultural constraints argument is built on the assumption that each country has just one culture, which determines the content of the national law. Further it is presupposed that each culture is unique to a particular country, and that national cultures are not moving closer to each other. The cultural constraints argument can be summarised as follows: due to their embedment in unique and unchanging national

---

[204] Ibid, p. 18.
[205] According to this idea: 'The environmental reference in evolution however is produced not in direct, causal production of legal developments, but in processes of co-evolution', characterised by a more 'mediatory' and 'indirect way' in which the social factors influence legal change. TEUBNER, G., *Autopoietic Law: A New Approach to Law and Society* (1988), p. 235-236 cited in: EWALD, W., *Social Structure and Law* (1990), at p. 45.
[206] TEUBNER, G., 'Legal Irritants: Good Faith in British Law or How Unifying Law Ends Up in New Divergences' (1998), p. 18.
[207] KAHN-FREUND, O., 'On Uses and Misuses of Comparative Law' (1974), p. 13.
[208] TEUBNER, G., 'Legal Irritants: Good Faith in British Law or How Unifying Law Ends Up in New Divergences' (1998), p. 17.

cultures, family laws in Europe are not converging spontaneously and cannot be harmonised deliberately.

These assumptions, after being subjected to an empirical scrutiny in the following chapters, will be revisited in the conclusion. At this place, however, it should be noted that it is only the combination of two extremes – a strong 'mirror' theory that considers law as an emanation of culture, and a strong form of framework-relativism á la Pierre Legrand – that necessarily leads to the far-reaching conclusion that convergence and harmonisation are fundamentally impossible. As the preceding sketch shows, such an uncompromising stance finds little support among contemporary scholars. Most of the proponents of the cultural constraints argument would not recognise themselves in this extreme. Much more common are intermediary positions like the weak 'mirror' theories, theories of the relative autonomy of law and moderate versions of relativism. Those theories do not necessarily support the thesis of the fundamental impossibility of harmonisation of law. Esin Örücü rightly notices that 'the relationship between a legal system and its socio-cultural context does not stand in the way of its relationship with other legal systems or even with other socio-cultural context'.[209] The moderate theories of the relation between law and society only deny that convergence and harmonisation can occur as easily as the unqualified version of the transplants theory alleges. In the light of these theories, convergence and deliberate harmonisation are principally possible, but must be grounded in preceding economic, social, cultural, political etc. approximation. The literature on convergence and harmonisation shows that plain harmonisation of rules alone is almost never considered a serious option. In contrast, it almost always links convergence and harmonisation to growing 'sharing of a certain conception of society',[210] 'political-cultural rapprochement',[211] 'building of common legal cultures' based on the 'acceptance of shared values',[212] 'import and export of ideas' and 'convergence of policy'.[213]

---

[209] ÖRÜCÜ, E., 'Looking at Convergence through the Eyes of a Comparative Lawyer'(2005), www.ejcl.org/92/art92-1.html
[210] KOOPMANS, T., 'Towards a New "Ius Commune"' (1992), p. 47.
[211] MERRYMAN, J., 'On the Convergence (and Divergence) of Civil Law and the Common Law' (1978), p. 212.
[212] ÖRÜCÜ, E., *The Enigma of Comparative Law* (2004), p. 126.
[213] ÖRÜCÜ, E., 'Looking at Convergence through the Eyes of a Comparative Lawyer'(2005), www.ejcl.org/92/art92-1.html.

PART II
FROM DIVERSITY TO UNIFORMITY: MEDIEVAL CANON LAW – THE *IUS COMMUNE* OF FAMILY LAW

INTRODUCTION TO PART II

In this Part, I will try to defend a controversial thesis: that family law is perhaps the only field of private law that in the past had an indisputable *ius commune*. This will help to qualify the perception that contemporary family law is a product and a part of national cultures; a perception that has been influenced by the a-historical notion that national family laws in Europe have always been different. This 'cultural' sentiment is largely rooted in the popular consciousness, yet it is also one to which jurists prove to be susceptible. For example, in England the belief that before the Reformation the position of England in respect to the application of canon law was different from the rest of the Catholic world had been widely cultivated until Frederic William Maitland proved the unsustainability of this view.[1] This perception stemmed from around the seventeenth century, when the unique and indigenous character of English law was cultivated; long after the Church of England actually separated from the Church of Rome.[2] Even today we can apply Rudolph Von Ihering's statement that 'legal science has degraded into the legal science of the particular countries'.[3] Thus, it is now difficult to imagine that the currently divergent national family laws found their origin in one and the same *ius commune* – the medieval canon law of the Roman Catholic Church – and that the entire concept of national culture most probably did not gain a real hold before the nineteenth century.[4]

Duly recognising that *ius commune* is an established concept that normally embraces both medieval canon law and received Roman law,[5] for the purposes of this book I have found it necessary to treat these two parts of the medieval *ius commune* separately. I will try to defend the premise that, unlike other areas of private law, the *ius commune* of family law was not received Roman law, but the medieval uniform canon family law of the Roman Catholic Church.[6] This *ius commune* of family law was equally pertinent for the whole of the Occident. The civil and common law countries, as well as the Nordic region and the Eastern European countries with a Catholic tradition, were all equal parties to it. The Orthodox Eastern European countries were, strictly

---

[1] See CAMERON, R., *Frederick William Maitland and the History of English Law* (1977), p. 62-81.
[2] Ibid, p. 65.
[3] VON IHERING, R., *Geist des römischen Rechts auf den verschiedenen Stufen seiner Entwicklung* (1891), p. 15.
[4] COING, H., *Die ursprüngliche einheit der Europäischen rechtswissenschaft* (1968), p. 164.
[5] See Section 3.5.2. of this Chapter, and particularly note 25 in Chapter 7.
[6] See Section 3.5.2. of this Chapter.

speaking, never part of this *ius commune*. However, despite the formal separation of the Orthodox Church from the West, very similar family laws developed throughout the Middle Ages in the Orthodox world. Therefore, it would even be possible to speak of two parts of one and the same medieval canon *ius commune* of family law: Catholic and Orthodox. A comparison of the development of these two similar systems is helpful for distinguishing mere historical incidents from regular historical patterns.

In its heyday the medieval canon law exclusively governed the core institutions of family law: marriage, divorce, illegitimacy, maintenance, child custody and sexual behaviour. It also had a significant impact on the regulation of other civil consequences of marriage. I will try to defend that this extensive scope of *ius commune* of family law does not merely include some institutions of canon family law, but comprises the complete canon family law.

In this Part, I will follow the formation of the medieval *ius commune* of family law that was started in the early Middle Ages and completed around the eleventh to twelfth centuries. The unity of the canon law part of the medieval *ius commune* in Europe lasted, strictly speaking, only until the Reformation. However, its influence in the field of family law long outlived not only the Reformation, but also the period of Enlightenment and beyond. Even contemporary laws on marriage, family relationships, inheritance, sexual behaviours 'often retain substantial elements of medieval church law at their core'.[7] Attempts to replace those core elements often resulted in bitter controversies. The history of divorce law-reforms in the nineteenth and twentieth centuries demonstrates this with particular clarity.[8]

For a number of reasons, a scrutiny of the medieval unification of family law is indispensable for the appreciation of the present debate surrounding the harmonisation of family law.

In the first place, the formation of the medieval *ius commune* of family law was, perhaps, the first and furthest significant attempt to deliberately unify family law in all of the history of Europe. It is also very possible that it was the first known attempt to deliberately unify private law as such.

In the second place, the issues surrounding the formation and the proliferation of – as well as the resistance to – the *ius commune* of family law offer a good example of the relative force of tradition and social engineering, cultural, ideological, political en economic factors. In order to estimate the importance of social engineering on behalf

---

[7]   BRUNDAGE, J., *Medieval Canon Law* (1995), p. 184.
[8]   Ibid.

of the Church, the formation of the medieval *ius commune* of family law will be contrasted with the evolution of matrimonial property law; this institution remained outside of and suffered little influence from canon law. Such scrutiny will provide interesting empirical material for the appreciation of the cultural constraints argument.

Thirdly, the examination of the medieval *ius commune* of family law could turn the argument of the proponents of the cultural embedment of family law around, by revealing the vast extent of the shared historical and cultural roots of the European family laws.

Finally, the analysis of the history of the medieval *ius commune* allows the delineation of the general lines of the convergence-divergence processes in the development of family law in Europe. Such analysis allows the outlining of a clear convergence tendency from the early Middle Ages till the formation of the *ius commune*, and a divergence tendency that is just as clear from the Reformation onwards. It is worthwhile to mention that setting down these general patterns does not predetermine the answer to the question of whether family laws in Europe are now converging.

This Part starts with an analysis of Roman and Germanic family law and the early Christian teaching; the historical precursors of the medieval canon *ius commune* family law, the background against which this *ius commune* has developed. Then I will focus on the formation of the medieval canon family law throughout the Carolingian period and the High Middle Ages in both parts of Europe. After that, the resistance to the enforcement of the *ius commune* will be sketched, as well as the way the gaps between 'the law in the books' and 'the law in action' that resulted from this resistance were overcome. In the end, the differences between the family law canon *ius commune* and the Roman *ius commune* of the rest of the private law will be analysed. Finally, I will address the implications of family law being, perhaps, the only area of private law which has had an undisputable *ius commune* in the past, on the contemporary debate surrounding the harmonisation of family law.

CHAPTER 3
HISTORICAL PRECURSORS OF THE
MEDIEVAL UNIFORM FAMILY LAW

3.1. INTRODUCTION

The historical precursors of the medieval uniform family law are being dealt with in this book not with the purpose of delineating convergence-divergence tendencies in classical and late Antiquity, but rather as a prelude to the examination of the medieval canon *ius commune* of family law. The medieval canon family law was developed by the Catholic Church against the background of, and often in contention with, pre-Christian family laws and customs, composed of remaining elements of Roman law mixed with the Germanic customary laws of the tribes that inhabited Europe over the course of the migration of nations. Thus, medieval uniform canon family law was partly a product of Roman-Jewish-Germanic tradition and partly a result of the Church's own family ideology that was developed during the Middle Ages. It has been noticed that 'the family of modern times is a historical product of the European Middle Ages, but it had its beginnings in a still earlier period'.[1] The gradual replacement of the Roman and Barbarian family laws with the new set of canon rules gives compelling examples of how the new Church ideology combined with instrumental legal change was capable of altering not only legal rules and practices but popular culture as well. In order to appreciate the scope and radicalism of the change the canon unification has brought about, it is necessary to set the unified canon law against its historical precursors: Roman and Barbarian family laws.

3.2. ROMAN FAMILY LAW

3.2.1. WHY START WITH ROMAN LAW?

Classical Roman family law is a logical starting point for any study of the development of European family law. First of all, both classical and postclassical Roman law are rather indispensable for the proper appreciation of the medieval canon family law. As I will try to defend in this chapter, the received Roman law was no *ius commune*

---

[1]   GIES, F., GIES, J., *Marriage and the Family in the Middle Ages* (1989), p. 16.

of family law,[2] and its influence is less traceable in modern family law than in the other areas of private law.[3] This is because between Roman and modern family law lies almost a half-millennium of dominance of medieval canon family law. Roman law did influence canon family law in such important aspects as monogamy, the consensual nature of marriage, ways of legitimating illegitimate children, and general methodology.[4] However, canon family law, with its highly institutionalised indissoluble marriage, was essentially different from Roman family law, with its informal private marriage and divorce. Thus the significance of the innovation brought about by canon law can only be truly appreciated through its comparison with Roman law. Since the Reformation, Roman law has become a continuous source of inspiration for those who tried to challenge the concepts vested in medieval canon law. The Renaissance, Enlightenment and Modern thinkers were fascinated that a European society with a developed and highly reputable law, regulated family affairs completely differently from the Europe of their days. The influence of Roman law is traceable in many episodes of the evolution of family law, such as the formation of the Reformation theory of marriage and divorce, the family ideology of the Enlightenment, the ideas of the nineteenth century liberals, the French revolutionary law,[5] the Bolshevik radical reforms of the 1920s, the Swedish liberal divorce reform of 1973 and the Spanish divorce reform of 2005.[6]

It is very imprecise, of course, to speak in this context of 'Roman law' without further qualifications, as it underwent substantial changes throughout the centuries. I will focus mainly on the classical[7] and postclassical[8] Roman law family, as they were the most relevant for the European developments. As previously announced, I will give an overview of marriage, concubinage, divorce, illegitimate children, and matrimonial property law.

3.2.2.   MARRIAGE IN ROMAN LAW: INFORMAL, SECULAR AND PRIVATE

According to Max Kaser, 'the Roman idea of marriage was fundamentally different from the modern one, which is determined by Christian motives'.[9] The informality

---

2   JOLOWICZ, H., *Roman Foundations of Modern Law* (1961), p. 155.
3   Ibid, p. 1.
4   See Section 3.2.3. of this Chapter.
5   ESMEIN, A., *Le mariage en Droit Canonique*, Part II (1929), p. 50.
6   GARCÍA CANTERO, G., 'Family Law Reform in Differing Directions' (2006), p. 433.
7   The period of *Principat*: 27 B.C. – 284 A.D.
8   The imperial period or *Dominat*: 284 A.D. until the end of the period of antiquity.
9   KASER, M., KNÜTEL, R., *Römische Privatrecht* (2003), p. 353; KASER, M., *Das Römische Privatrecht*, II (1975), p. 310.

of the Roman marriage and divorce of the classical period is striking, even in the eyes of a family lawyer of today. In the late Republican times, the ancient forms of marriage *cum manu,*[10] in which a wife was under the *manus* (power) of her husband or of his *pater familias,* rapidly came into disuse.[11] At the same time the free marriage *sine manu* became by far the prevailing form.[12] In a free marriage a wife did not come under the *manus* of her husband or his *pater familias* but remained under the power of her own father, or under no-one's power *(sui iuris).* Unlike the ancient *cum manu* marriage,[13] a marriage *sine manu* was a private, secular and formless act.[14] Free marriage, in the words of Max Kaser was 'not primarily a legal relationship, but rather a social fact, a "realised union for life"'.[15] The formation, dissolution and effects of the marriage were regulated not by law, but merely by morals and customs.[16] No state or religious authority was involved in the formation of such marriage.[17] According to John Crook 'marriage was not sacramental, [...] it was not thought to be maintained or sanctioned by anything beyond the will of those who were parties to it – or their heads of families'.[18] Marriage was often preceded by a betrothal *(sponsalia)* – a publicly made agreement to marry in the future. However, betrothal was not prerequisite to a valid marriage.[19] The genuine informality of Roman marriage did not mean that no marriage and betrothal rites existed in Roman times, but rather that these rites had no influence on the validity of marriage,[20] nor did the endowment. The consensual nature of Roman marriage implied that marriage was created not by a formal act or

---

[10]   See: VOLTERRA, E., *La conception du mariage d'après les juristes romains* (1940), p. 2 ff.

[11]   Corbett observes that: 'In the Rome of the classical jurists, manus is a matter of legal archaeology'. CORBETT, P., *The Roman Law of Marriage* (1969), p. 91.

[12]   Max Kaser observed that 'most marriages were still *manus* marriages down to the first century B.C.; later its frequency quickly decreased, so that by the end of the classical period manus marriage was completely displaced by "free marriage"'. KASER, M., *Roman Private Law* (1993), p. 286; KASER, M., KNÜTEL, R., *Römische Privatrecht* (2003), p. 355.

[13]   Marriage *cum manu* could be created in three forms, two of which, *confarreatio en coëmptio,* were formal and one, *usus,* informal. *Confarreatio* was in addition a religious ceremony. WATSON, A., *Rome of the XII Tables* (1975), p. 9-12.

[14]   According to Percy Corbett: 'Marriage in the classical period of Roman law is almost, if not entirely, a formless transaction'. CORBETT, P., *The Roman Law of Marriage* (1969), p. 68.

[15]   KASER, M., *Das römische Privatrecht,* I (1971), p. 310.

[16]   Ibid, p. 311.

[17]   CROOK, J., *Law and Life in Rome* (1984), p. 99.

[18]   Ibid.

[19]   'When free marriage became the norm, betrothals became informal and were not actionable. Either partner could renounce the engagement [...] A simple agreement, without formality, ceremony or added stipulations, was all that the law required for betrothal, and neither witness nor written testimony were necessary'. REYNOLDS, P., *Marriage in the Western Church* (1994), p. 4. Although since the time of the Christian Empire there has been evidence of a practice originating in Greece of bestowing the *arrha sponsalicia:* a wealth, that the bridegroom gave to the bride or to her parents, and that could be used as a sanction for breach of engagement. REYNOLDS, P., *Marriage in the Western Church* (1994), p. 6.

[20]   KASER, M., *Roman Private Law* (1993), p. 291.

consummation,[21] but rather by 'the intention of the parties to be man and wife coupled with *de facto* life as such'.[22] Therefore, the spouses' own mental attitude towards their relationship – regarding each other as husband and wife (*affectus maritalis*) – formed the essence of Roman marriage.[23] The view of Roman marriage as '*faktisches Verhältnis des sozialen Lebens*'[24] has, however, recently been challenged by authors who regard Roman marriage as a legal institution.[25]

Although written marriage contracts became rather common in Imperial times, they did not alter the informal character of Roman marriage. Such contracts did not function as a kind of 'marriage certificates',[26] but were merely agreements on financial matters.[27] As late as 533 A.D., Justinian (Eastern Roman Empire 527-569 A.D.) stated that 'marriages are contracted not by dowries but by affection'.[28] Only in 538 A.D. Justinian introduced *Novel* 74, which made the validity of marriages conditional upon a written document.[29]

Therefore, it is possible to conclude that in spite of a continuing trend to formalise the marriage ceremony,[30] the absence of marriage formalities persevered until the very end of the postclassical period. Thus, the sacraments and the formalisation associated with marriage in medieval canon law[31] cannot be traced back to Roman law.

The consensual character of Roman marriage has been compared with the consensual theory of marriage that came to prevail in canon law around the eleventh century.[32] There is, however, a very important difference. In canon law, marriage was always created by the sole consent of the parties themselves. In Roman law, on the contrary, marriage in the early period and in the first centuries of the classical period was created by the consent of *pater familias* and/or the parties to marriage.

---

[21] According to a statement ascribed to Ulpian: '*Nuptias enim non concubitus, sed consensus facit*'. (D. 35.1.15). See JOLOWICZ, H., *Roman Foundations of Modern Law* (1961), p. 144.

[22] Ibid, p. 145.

[23] VOLTERRA, E., *La conception du mariage d'après les juristes romains* (1940), p. 33.

[24] KASER, M., *Das römische Privatrecht, I* (1971), p. 310.

[25] See BÜRGE, A., *Römisches Privatrecht. Rechtsdenken und gesellschaftliche Varankerung* (1999), p. 162-167.

[26] GARDNER, J., *Women in Roman Law and Society* (1986), p. 49-50.

[27] Constitution enacted by Theodosius II (East Roman Empire reign 408-450 A.D.) and Valentinian III (West Roman Empire, reign 425-455 A.D.) in 428 A.D. confirmed the legal irrelevance of dotal documentation and ceremonies for the validity of marriage. REYNOLDS, P., *Marriage in the Western Church* (1994), p. 27.

[28] REYNOLDS, P., *Marriage in the Western Church* (1994), p. 28.

[29] WAL, N., VAN DE, *Manuale novellarum Justiniani: aperçu systématique du contenu des Novelles de Justinien* (1998), p. 69.

[30] NATHAN, G., *The Family in Late Antiquity* (2000), p. 45.

[31] See Chapter 4.

[32] Jolowicz remarked that 'in the general rules for contracting of marriage the continuality with Rome is strongest'. JOLOWICZ, H., *Roman Foundations of Modern Law* (1961), p. 156.

In the pre-classical time, if a bride was under power *(potestas)*, it was the consent of her father that created marriage.[33] The girl's own will was legally irrelevant.[34] If a bride was not under power *(sui iuris)*, the relevance of her consent is a matter of controversy.[35] If a bridegroom was in *potestate*, the consent of his father was necessary. The importance of the boy's own consent is debated; however, Corbett suggested that his consent was also irrelevant.[36] If a bridegroom was not under parental control, his sole consent was sufficient.[37]

In the classical period, the consent of a boy under power became necessary alongside the consent of his *pater familias*.[38] For a boy who was not under power, his own consent was sufficient.[39] The necessity of the consent of a bride under power is also a matter of controversy.[40] The same uncertainty applies to the relevance of the consent of girls not under power.[41] There is, at any rate, clear evidence of a gradual waning of the role of the consent of the *pater familias*. Parental consent was necessary for creating legal marriage, but a marriage created without it could not be dissolved on the ground of its absence.[42] Such marriages were considered improper but legally valid.[43] Since the times of Augustus (reign 27 B.C.-14 A.D.), a father who unreasonably refused to consent to the marriage of his child could be compelled to give consent by the consuls or provincial magistrates.[44] Jane Gardner suggested that 'in strict law' a father could always compel his children to marry, but it was not a common practice since the Late Republic.[45] At the time of Hadrian (reign 117-38 A.D.), a father 'dreamed neither of forcing a daughter's marriage nor opposing her determinate choice'.[46] From the time of Julian (circa 150 A.D.) the consent of the parties themselves

---

[33] WATSON, A., *Rome of the XII Tables. Persons and Property* (1975), p. 25-28.
[34] Ibid.
[35] Ibid.
[36] CORBETT, P., *The Roman Law of Marriage* (1969), p. 43.
[37] WATSON, A., *Rome of the XII Tables. Persons and Property* (1975), p. 28.
[38] KASER, M., *Das römische Privatrecht*, II (1975), p. 163.
[39] WATSON, A., *The Law of the Persons in the Later Roman* Republic (1967), p. 46.
[40] CORBETT, P., *The Roman Law of Marriage* (1969), p. 55. Alan Watson remarks that: 'It is certain that throughout our period [the late republic] the father had to agree to the marriage, and it seems that at one stage the agreement of the *filia familias* [a girl under paternal power] was not relevant, but there is no evidence whether or not this continued to be the case right up to the end of the Republic'. WATSON, A., *The Law of the Persons in the later Roman Republic* (1967), p. 45.
[41] Ibid, p. 46-47.
[42] GARDNER, J., *Women in Roman Law and Society* (1986), p. 42.
[43] KASER, M., *Das römische Privatrecht*, II (1975), p. 163.
[44] GARDNER, J., *Women in Roman Law and Society* (1986), p. 42.
[45] Ibid.
[46] GIES, F., GIES, J., *Marriage and the Family in the Middle Ages* (1989), p. 21.

became indispensable for the formation of marriage.[47] Justinian's Code[48] went further by clearly stating that 'no-one should be forced to marry'.[49] However, the possibility of a child to resist an arranged marriage was, in practice, always rather limited.

The conclusion is that throughout Roman history the children under power formally needed consent of their *pater familias* in order to create a valid marriage. Canon law, on the contrary, continued to insist that the consent of the parties themselves was sufficient for valid marriage.[50]

The absence of a formal marriage ritual did not mean that Roman marriage was of no concern to the State. Merely uninterested in how the marriage was performed, the law regulated in great detail *conubium:* 'the capacity to validly intermarry'.[51] *Conubium* existed between Roman citizens who were of a free state, had reached the marriageable age,[52] and were not related within prohibited degrees of consanguinity. Additionally, there were various requirements concerning the absence of impediments relating to differences in status. The rules in respect of age and the degree of relationship were generally not restrictive. The impediments relating to the difference in status were, on the contrary, rather rigid, reflecting the strict stratification of Roman society.

The extent of prohibited degrees experienced significant fluctuations over the time. The early Roman law prohibited marriages between ascendants and descendants, irrespective of the remoteness, and between collaterals up to the sixth degree (second cousins).[53] However, these prohibitions were gradually relaxed to the extent that marriages within the third degree (to a brother's daughter) became permitted during the Principat.[54] Later, the law again became more restrictive.[55] According to Percy Corbett, 'the rule that finally prevailed allowed collaterals to intermarry provided that neither was related in the first degree to the common ancestor,'[56] which amounts to

---

[47]   See. Iul. D. 23, 1, 11 and Ulp. D. 50, 17, 30. Cited in: KASER, M., KNÜTEL, R., *Römische Privatrecht* (2003), at p. 361.

[48]   Compiled in 534 A.D. in the Eastern Roman Empire, but designated for the whole of the Empire.

[49]   REYNOLDS, P., *Marriage in the Western Church* (1994), p. 23.

[50]   See Chapter 4.

[51]   KASER, M., *Das Römische Privatrecht*, II (1975), p. 164.

[52]   In the early period the marriageable age was determined by the actual onset of puberty, ascertained by the inspection of the body' (WATSON, A., *Rome of the XII Tables. Persons and Property* (1975), p. 25). Then the marriageable age for girls was set of twelve, at least from the time of Augustus, but the boys continued to be inspected until the time of Justinian when in 529 A.D. the inspection of the boys was abolished and their marriageable age was fixed at fourteen. CORBETT, P., *The Roman Law of Marriage* (1969), p. 52.

[53]   Ibid, p. 47-48.

[54]   Ibid, p. 48.

[55]   Marriages within the third degree were made a capital crime under Constantius (reign 293-306 A.D.) and Constans (reign 333-350 A.D.). Ibid, p. 49.

[56]   Ibid.

the fourth degree. In the end of the fourth century A.D., marriages between in-laws (step-children and brothers or sisters of the former spouse) were also forbidden.[57] Thus, the later canon law extension of the prohibited degrees went much further than Roman law.

The status prohibitions for marriage were extensive. Roman citizens, save for special privileges, could not marry foreigners.[58] Marriage between patricians and plebeians was, at least during a certain period, forbidden.[59] Soldiers, and provincial magistrates, at least at times, could not marry at all. Neither could slaves marry, even with each other.[60] Freemen could not marry slaves. From Augustus till Justinian, senators and their descendents could not marry freedwomen, nor women of dubious reputation.[61] However, the influence of Christianity led to the gradual waning of the status-related impediments.[62] At the same time, new faith-related impediments came to stage.[63]

Thus, under the influence of Christian ideas the legal regulation of marriage became stronger in the postclassical period.[64] However, as Max Kaser has put it, 'the fundamental character of marriage as a "realised union for life", resting on the continuing consent of the spouses, was maintained as much as was previously the case'.[65]

3.2.3. CONCUBINAGE IN ROMAN LAW: FROM BENEVOLENT NEUTRALITY[66] TO LEGAL RECOGNITION

Under concubinage, Romans understood 'a permanent sexual union between man and woman, not recognised as marriage'.[67] According to Alan Watson, only a woman with whom a man had set up house was a concubine.[68] If there were no impediments

---

[57]   Ibid, p. 50.
[58]   KASER, M., *Das römische Privatrecht*, Part. I (1971), p. 164. Marriage with Barbarians could in theory lead to a capital punishment. Ibid.
[59]   KASER, M., *Das Römische Privatrecht*, II (1975), p. 165.
[60]   Their union *contubernium* was no marriage. KASER, M., *Das römische Privatrecht*, Part. I (1971), p. 165.
[61]   According to the *Lex Papia Poppaea*. See: DIXON, S., *The Roman Family* (1992), p. 93.
[62]   VANDENBERGHE, H., *De juridische betekenis van het concubinaat* (1970), p. 13.
[63]   For instance impediments based on the vow of chastity and prohibition of intermarriage of Christians and Jews. KASER, M., *Das römische Privatrecht*, II (1975), p. 168.
[64]   Ibid, p. 158-159.
[65]   Ibid, p. 159.
[66]   After VANDENBERGHE, H., *De juridische betekenis van het concubinaat* (1970), p. 9.
[67]   KASER, M., *Das Römische Privatrecht*, II (1975), p. 328.
[68]   WATSON, A., *The Law of the Persons in the Later Roman Republic* (1967), p. 10.

to marriage, it was sometimes difficult to distinguish a legal marriage from concubinage, due to the informality of entering into marriage. In the absence of formalities the most important distinction was in the parties' own perception of their relationship: the presence or absence of *affectus maritalis*.

The position of concubinage in Roman law differed significantly from period to period. Historians agree that before Augustus it was a purely factual union neither prohibited nor recognised by law.[69] Concubinage was rather common,[70] and although it did not enjoy the dignity of marriage, it was considered as 'an honourable alternative to marriage'.[71] The social acceptance of concubinage did not yet provide a concubine with legal rights.[72]

The first legal regulation of concubinage was originated in the laws enacted by Augustus *Lex Iulia de maritandis ordinibus*,[73] *Lex Iulia de adulteriis* and *Lex Papia Poppaea*.[74] Legal historians are divided in their appreciation of the rationale of these rules.[75] Augustus's legislation provided for no private law regulation of concubinage, but rather made clear which kinds of concubinage were tolerated.[76] Incestuous concubinage, concubinage with girls under twelve, and concubinage by a married man[77] were not tolerated. The *lex Iulia de adulteriis* also prohibited concubinage with a married woman (regarded as adultery) and with a decent free-born woman (considered as *stuprum*: illicit sexual relationship).[78] Therefore, only concubinage with

---

[69] For an overview see: VANDENBERGHE, H., *De juridische betekenis van het concubinaat* (1970), p. 3.

[70] See also John Crook, who suggests that 'concubinage was regular and accepted in the life of Rome, and it was in no sense thought sinful. It did not carry the respect attended upon marriage, but this was because one of the partners was usually socially inferior; as Ulpian said, "The difference is only in dignity"'. CROOK, J., *Law and Life in Rome* (1984), p. 101.

[71] DIXON, S., *The Roman Family* (1992), p. 93.

[72] BECKER, H-J., 'Die nichteheliche Lebensgemeinschaft (Konkubinat) in der Rechtsgeschichte' (1978), p. 15.

[73] Promulgated in 18 B.C.

[74] Promulgated in 9 A.D.

[75] According to an older vision, the laws of Augustus gave concubinage the status of a second-rang marriage. For an overview of old sources see: (VANDENBERGHE, H., *De juridische betekenis van het concubinaat* (1970), p. 3). According to a more recent opinion, even after Augustus's laws concubinage remained a purely factual union tolerated, but not recognised by law. MEYER, P., *Der römische Konkubinat nach den Rechtsquellen und den Inschriften* (1895), p. 20.

[76] VANDENBERGHE, H., *De juridische betekenis van het concubinaat* (1970), p. 4-6.

[77] There is no clarity with respect to the possibility to keep more than one concubine or to have a concubine and a wife before Augustus. According to Suzanne Dixon this was impossible (DIXON, S., *The Roman Family* (1992), p. 94). John Crook proved, from the evidence of tomb inscriptions and marriage contracts, that it could sometimes be a possibility (CROOK, J., *Law and Life in Rome* (1984), p. 102). Alan Watson assumed that at least in the classical law it was no longer possible. WATSON, A., *The Law of the Persons in the later Roman Republic* (1967), p. 9.

[78] VANDENBERGHE, H., *De juridische betekenis van het concubinaat* (1970), p. 5-6.

or between freedmen, and with women of dubious reputation was officially tolerated.[79] At the same time, Augustus's laws in fact encouraged the further advance of concubinage by creating manifold status-related impediments to marriage. The only alternative for free persons who could not marry due to the lack of *conubium* was concubinage.[80]

In the beginning of the postclassical period, the first Christian Emperor Constantine (reign 306-337 A.D.), inspired by the Christian teaching that every sexual relationship outside marriage is immoral, passed extensive prohibitive legislation regarding concubinage.[81] Previously tolerated concubinage between a man of a high-standing and a low-class woman was then forbidden.[82] Donation in favour of a concubine was also invalidated.[83]

Later, under the law of Justinian, the pendulum swung back again, and concubinage became a virtual second rate-marriage (*inaequale coniugium*).[84] Previously existing restrictions regarding the status of persons who were able to live in concubinage were removed.[85] Concubinage was legally recognised only between parties who were able to legally marry each other.[86] Thus, concubinage lost its previous function as a marriage substitute for unequals and became mainly a resort for a widowed upper-class men with children, who did not wish to remarry.[87] If there were no lawful wife and legitimate children, a concubine had the right to inherit through intestate succession.[88]

The Roman tolerance for concubinage can be contrasted with the restrictive attitude from the part of canon law, which eventually resulted in the outlawing of concubinage.

---

[79] Ibid, p. 6.
[80] Alan Watson noticed: 'It is widely held that *concubinatus* in Rome owes its legal recognition to the restrictive legislation on marriage in the Empire, and that, from the social point of view, if it did not originate as result of that legislation, it became widespread in consequence of it'. WATSON, A., *The Law of the Persons in the later Roman Republic* (1967), p. 1. Also Suzanne Dixon contests the tendency 'to attribute widespread concubinage to moral decay,' and states that widespread concubinage was merely caused by the multiple status prohibition for marriage. DIXON, S., *The Roman Family* (1992), p. 90-93.
[81] KASER, M., *Das römische Privatrecht*, II (1975), p. 183.
[82] Ibid.
[83] VANDENBERGHE, H., *De juridische betekenis van het concubinaat* (1970), p. 13.
[84] Ibid.
[85] VOLTERRA, E., *La conception du mariage d'après les juristes romains* (1940), p. 676.
[86] KASER, M., *Das römische Privatrecht*, II (1975), p. 183.
[87] For instance emperors Vespasian (reign 69-70 A.D.) and Mark Aurelius (reign 161-180 A.D.) took concubines after the death of their wives. MEYER, P., *Der römische Konkubinat nach den Rechtsquellen und den Inschriften* (1895), p. 11.
[88] VANDENBERGHE, H., *De juridische betekenis van het concubinaat* (1970), p. 15.

3.2.4. DIVORCE IN ROMAN LAW: EASY AND PRIVATE

Roman society generally knew no 'religious or philosophical ban on divorce'.[89] However, there has always been disapproval of divorce and of a person liable for it. As with Roman marriage, Roman divorce was a factual, private process rather than a legal act.[90] The possibility of divorce in the classical period did not depend on fixed grounds, nor was it subjected to judicial control.[91] Until the end of the classical period, the freedom of divorce was perceived as an 'unavoidable principle', following from the very nature of marriage: *libera matrimonia* (freedom of marriage).[92] Accordingly, agreements not to divorce were rendered void.[93]

In ancient times, a wife could not divorce her husband, while a husband could repudiate his wife upon a number of specific grounds.[94] In order to terminate marriage *cum manu* special formalities were required.[95] One particular kind of *cum manu* marriage, a marriage by *confarreatio*,[96] was believed to be indissoluble approximately until the end of the Republic (first century B.C.).[97] The *pater familias* could terminate the marriage of a son or daughter who was under power, even against the child's will.[98]

In the classical period, a husband and wife *sui iuris* (not under power) could freely terminate their free marriage. If the spouses were under power, they needed the consent of their *pater familias*. According to Alan Watson, a father could still divorce children under his power against the child's wishes as late as the time of the Early Empire.[99] However, the power of a *pater familias* to terminate the marriage without consent of his child *in potestate* was later restricted.[100]

Since the late Republic (second-first century B.C.) women in free marriages 'could legally divorce as simply as their husband could'.[101] There were no longer any specific

---

[89] TREGGIARI S., 'Divorce Roman Style: How Easy and How Frequent Was It?' (1991), p. 40.
[90] KASER, M., *Das Römische Privatrecht*, II (1975), p. 326.
[91] Ibid.
[92] Ibid.
[93] Ibid.
[94] In case of divorce for any other reasons the husband has to forfeit his property partly to his wife and partly to the children of marriage. GARDNER, J., *Women in Roman Law and Society* (1986), p. 83.
[95] WATSON, A., *The Law of the Persons in the Later Roman Republic* (1967), p. 53.
[96] See note 13 in this chapter.
[97] GARDNER, J., *Women in Roman Law and Society* (1986), p. 84.
[98] KASER, M., *Das Römische Privatrecht*, II (1975), p. 327.
[99] WATSON, A., *The Law of the Persons in the Later Roman Republic* (1967), p. 52-53.
[100] GARDNER, J., *Women in Roman Law and Society* (1986), p. 85.
[101] TREGGIARI, S., *Roman Marriage Iusti Coniuges for the Time of Cicero to the Time of Ulpian* (1991), p. 443.

grounds for divorce.[102] However, Susan Treggiari suggested that 'it was still honourable to divorce only for serious reasons, so the initiator might need to declare a reason in order to protect his or her own reputation'.[103] The proof of matrimonial fault was also important for recovering the dowry.[104] In classical times, divorce became even easier and almost completely informal. A unilateral divorce was normally initiated by sending a formal notification (*repudium*) by a letter or messenger. The receipt of the notice of divorce by the other spouse was not legally relevant.[105] Divorce by mutual consent became common, and also required almost no formalities.[106] There were certain traditional words signifying divorce, but Percy Corbett is convinced that the variations in these wordings are incompatible with any sacramental or legislative origin.[107] Susan Treggiari stressed the significant contrast between the Roman divorce practices and the normal assumptions of modern Western society. The private character of Roman divorce was probably the most striking aspect of this difference. In Rome 'no ratification from an outside authority (such as Church or State) was necessary for divorce, any more than it was for marriage. No public record was kept for divorce. Also no private documentation (e.g. tablets witnessed by Roman citizens) was kept. This system was only slightly modified during the rest of the pagan period'.[108]

Augustus introduced strictly formal requirements for divorce from an adulterous wife and made them compulsory for a husband in his *Lex Iulia de adulteriis*. The presence of seven freeborn adult Roman witnesses was one of those requirements. However, it was argued that this formality was important not for the validity of divorce itself, but merely as evidence necessary for avoiding prosecution for not repudiating an adulterous wife.[109]

In the postclassical period, the regulation of divorce started to change under the influence of Christianity.[110] Freedom of unilateral divorce was for the first time questioned in 331 A.D. by the law of Constantine. Divorce by mutual consent,

---

[102]   GARDNER, J., *Women in Roman Law and Society* (1986), p. 84 and 89.

[103]   TREGGIARI S., 'Divorce Roman Style: How Easy and How Frequent Was It?' (1991), p. 38.

[104]   GARDNER, J., *Women in Roman Law and Society* (1986), p. 89-91.

[105]   TREGGIARI S., 'Divorce Roman Style: How Easy and How Frequent Was It?' (1991), p. 36-37.

[106]   A frequently cited case proving the informality of divorce was described by Cicero: A man has returned to Rome, leaving his pregnant wife in Spain. In Rome he started to cohabit with another woman, without sending a *repudium* to his wife in Spain. Both women gave birth to sons and the question was: which of them was legitimate. The disagreement among the jurists whether or not the first marriage could be dissolved simply by entering the second union proves that there was no prescribed form for dissolution of marriage. CICERO, *De Orat,* 1, 40, 183-4; 1, 56, 238. Cited in: CORBETT, P., *The Roman Law of Marriage* (1969), p. 225.

[107]   CORBETT, P., *The Roman Law of Marriage* (1969), p. 225.

[108]   TREGGIARI, S., 'Divorce Roman Style: How Easy and How Frequent Was It?' (1991), p. 36.

[109]   Ibid, p. 37.

[110]   KASER, M., *Das Römische Privatrecht*, II (1975), p. 175.

however, remained untouched. Constantine introduced a restrictive number of grounds upon which unilateral divorce could be effectuated. These grounds were different for a husband than they were for a wife.[111] The sanctions for illicit divorce provide even more apparent evidence of the different standards a husband and a wife were held to. If a wife repudiated her husband for an unlawful reason she forfeited her dowry ("down to a hairpin"),[112] suffered exile to an island and was forbidden to remarry. A husband liable for a similar fault was only forbidden to remarry.[113]

In the later period of the Christian Empire, the laws on divorce were changed many times,[114] gradually further restricting unilateral divorce. Divorce by mutual consent remained, however, largely untouched until 542 A.D., when it was banned by a law of Justinian.[115] However, this prohibition was short-lived, as it was repealed by his successor, Justin, in 566 A.D.[116] Therefore, as Pál Csillag has summed it up: in Rome 'the principle of dissolubility of marriage, though with certain limitations, survived in the time of the Christian emperors, even after Justinian'.[117]

3.2.5. ROMAN LAW ON ILLEGITIMATE CHILDREN: NO STATUS AT ALL

In the classical period, the position of illegitimate children under Roman law was certainly unfavourable. Children born out of wedlock were legally related only to their mother, and not to the father, and thus were under no-one's power.[118] The agnatic structure of the Roman familial system excluded the possibility of the *potestas* of the

---

[111] NATHAN, G., *The Family in Late Antiquity* (2000), p. 63.
[112] GRUBBS, J., *Law and Family in Late Antiquity* (1995), p. 230-131.
[113] Ibid.
[114] The most significant events were the following: The laws of Honorius and Constantius III in 421 reintroduced specific grounds for unilateral divorce. Theodisious II made by law of 439 A.D. sending of a *repudium* compulsory, but brought the unilateral divorce to the pre-Constantine's situation. Then in another law of 449 A.D. he created a new set of grounds for unilateral divorce. Women could be divorced, for instance, for attending the theatre of circus without a husband's permission. For the first time an equal possibility to divorce an adulterous spouse for men and women was introduced. These possibilities were however, in fact not equal, because of the definition of adultery: every married women having sex with a man other than her husband was a adulteress, but the husband was an adulterer only if he had sex with a married women. REYNOLDS, P., *Marriage in the Western Church* (1994), p. 122.
[115] Divorce remained valid, but the parties had to suffer punishment. Justinian himself, praising his restrictive legislation, quoted from Plato 'everything that is tied can be loosed'. Cited in: JOLOWICZ, H., *Roman Foundations of Modern Law* (1961), at p. 154.
[116] GRUBBS, J., *Law and Family in Late Antiquity* (1995), p. 237.
[117] CSILLAG, P., *The Augustan Laws on Family Relations* (1976), p. 128.
[118] KASER, M., *Das Römische Privatrecht*, II (1975), p. 351.

mother over them.[119] A father could adopt a male illegitimate child, but, until the second century A.D., not a female one.[120] In the pre-classical and classical period, illegitimate children could not be legitimated.[121] Illegitimate children had no right to inherit from or to be maintained by their father. However, from their mother they were entitled to maintenance and to take through intestate succession.[122] In the classical period, there was no distinction yet made between the children of a concubine, *liberi naturales*, and other illegitimate children.[123]

Constantine's legislation made the position of children of a concubine worse than that of other illegitimate children.[124] The former could not be adopted[125] and were not allowed to receive gifts from their father. The legitimisation of illegitimate children by subsequent marriage of the parents (*Legitimatio per subsequens matrimonium*) under rather restrictive grounds was first made possible under Constantine.[126] In 517 A.D. it became a general option for the *liberi naturales*.[127]

Inspired by Christian-humanitarian motivation,[128] Justinian's legislation greatly improved the position of children born to a concubine. The children acquired a limited right to take from their father in cases of intestacy and a right to be maintained by the father and his ascendants.[129] In addition to *Legitimatio per subsequens matrimonium*, the children of a concubine could from then on also be legitimated by an imperial decree (*legitimatio per rescriptum principis*).[130]

The Roman postclassical legislation regarding the position of illegitimate children had significant influence on medieval canon family law.[131] Thus, the forms of legitimisation were, in slightly modified form, taken over from the law of Justinian.[132]

---

[119] GARDNER, J., *Family and Familia in Roman Law and Life* (1998), p, 252.
[120] GARDNER, J., *Women in Roman Law and Society* (1986), p. 144.
[121] KASER, M., *Das römische Privatrecht*, I (1971), p. 352.
[122] Ibid.
[123] VANDENBERGHE, H., *De juridische betekenis van het concubinaat* (1970), p. 11.
[124] Ibid, p. 13.
[125] VOLTERRA, E., *La conception du mariage d'après les juristes romains* (1940), p. 676.
[126] KASER, M., *Das römische Privatrecht*, II (1975), p. 221.
[127] JOLOWICZ, H., *Roman Foundations of Modern Law* (1961), p. 198.
[128] KASER, M., *Das römische Privatrecht*, II (1975), p. 220.
[129] KASER, M., *Das römische Privatrecht*, II (1975), p. 220.
[130] GARDNER, J., *Women in Roman Law and Society* (1986), p. 143-144.
[131] See Chapter 4.
[132] JOLOWICZ, H., *Roman Foundations of Modern Law* (1961), p. 199.

3.2.6.   ROMAN LAW ON MATRIMONIAL PROPERTY: THE DOTAL SYSTEM

The classical Roman matrimonial property system could be described in modern terms as a system of separation of property,[133] mitigated by the institution of dowry (dotal system).[134] Marriage did not alter the property rights of the spouses or their *pater familias*. Moreover, Roman law forbad transferring property between husband and wife by way of donation.[135]

In the ancient marriage *cum manu,* the wife was not capable of owning or administering property. Therefore, the property she brought into marriage naturally became a part of the joint family holding owned by the husband or his *pater familias*.[136] According to Suzanne Dixon, 'the most significant development' of Roman matrimonial property law was a 'shift from a merged to a separate regime'.[137] This transformation took place with the advent of the free marriage, which did not affect the legal capacity of a woman; so, she remained the owner of her property.

From the early period of Roman history, it was conventional for a father to provide for his daughter by giving her a dowry (*dos*) when she was married, in order to compensate her for the loss of her inheritance rights.[138] However, the moral obligation to give a dowry was converted into a legal duty only in Justinian's law.[139] The functions of the dowry were to compensate a husband for his contribution to the 'burdens of marriage' and to provide for a wife in case of divorce or widowhood.[140] In both free marriage and marriage *cum manu,* the husband or his *pater familias* became the legal owner of the dowry. A marriage *cum manu* had the same effect because the wife did not have the required capacity. In free marriage, the rule to provide a dowry was maintained out of respect for the custom.[141] It was also common to stipulate that upon dissolution of marriage, the dowry would be returned to its giver.[142] In the second century B.C., when marriage *cum manu* almost disappeared and divorce became more common, a widowed or divorced wife was granted the possibility to reclaim her dowry for herself, even if no prior stipulation had been made.[143] The right of a wife to recover

---

[133]   KASER, M., *Das römische Privatrecht*, I (1971), p. 329.
[134]   JOLOWICZ, H., *Roman Foundations of Modern Law* (1961), p. 161.
[135]   This prohibition was aimed at preventing of favouring either the wife's or the husband's family at expense of the other's one. KASER, M., *Das römische Privatrecht*, I (1971), p. 331.
[136]   DIXON, S., *The Roman Family* (1992), p. 74.
[137]   Ibid.
[138]   JOLOWICZ, H., *Roman Foundations of Modern Law* (1961), p. 162.
[139]   KASER, M., *Das römische Privatrecht*, II (1975), p. 186.
[140]   KASER, M., *Das römische Privatrecht*, I (1971), p. 333.
[141]   JOLOWICZ, H., *Roman Foundations of Modern Law* (1961), p. 163.
[142]   Ibid, p. 164.
[143]   KASER, M., *Das römische Privatrecht*, I (1971), p. 337.

the dowry gradually came to be strengthened by far-reaching guarantees. In 18 B.C., Augustus's legislation forbad the husband to alienate dowered Italic lands without his wife's consent.[144] The law of Justinian extended this prohibition to all dowry lands, and deprived the wife of the right to sanction the alienation.[145] At the same time, the retrieval of the dowry came to be safeguarded by a general, privileged, tacit hypothec over the whole of the husband's property.[146] Thus, the obligation to return the dowry gradually left the husband with mere legal title to the property, while in fact his right more closely resembled that of the usufruct.[147] Originally, a surviving husband retained the dowry if his wife predeceased him.[148] A husband was also entitled to retain certain parts of the dowry on behalf of the children of the marriage,[149] and if divorce was caused by a wife's matrimonial offence.[150] In Justinian's times a wife could recover her dowry if she were widowed, or divorced without her fault.[151] If a husband outlived his wife, the legal ownership of the dowry passed to the children and the husband retained only a right of usufruct.[152]

Under Hellenistic influence, the institution of dowry was supplemented in the postclassical period by the institution of dower (*donatio ante nuptias*), a premarital gift of a husband to a wife.[153] The purpose of the dower was, like that of the dowry, to provide for the wife and the children if the marriage came to an end. Justinian transferred the dower in a mere counterpart of the dowry, subjected to the same legal regime and rules in respect of restoration and guarantees.[154]

Alongside the dowry and the dower, another part of a wife's property, called *parapherna*, came to be distinguished in the postclassical period. *Parapherna* included all those assets owned by a wife which were not given as dowry.[155] It could consist of anything from personal adornment to land.[156] *Parapherna* remained in the wife's legal

---

[144] CORBETT, P., *The Roman Law of Marriage* (1969), p. 180.

[145] Ibid. The consent to alienation on the part of the wife was only effective if it was repeated after two years and there was enough other property to satisfy the wife's claims. Nov. 61. Cited in: JOLOWICZ, H., *Roman Foundations of Modern Law* (1961), p. 170.

[146] KASER, M., *Roman Private Law* (1993), p. 303.

[147] KASER, M., *Das römische Privatrecht*, II (1975), p. 185.

[148] This right was, however, subjected to a few qualifications. KASER, M., *Roman Private Law* (1993), p. 301.

[149] 1/6th for each child, but not more than half of the dowry. Ibid.

[150] CORBETT, P., *The Roman Law of Marriage* (1969), p. 193.

[151] KASER, M., *Das Römische Privatrecht*, II (1975), p. 188.

[152] Ibid.

[153] KASER, M., *Das römische Privatrecht*, II (1975), p. 193. In the time of Justinian it became also possible to give dower during the marriage. JOLOWICZ, H., *Roman Foundations of Modern Law* (1961), p. 175.

[154] KASER, M., *Roman Private Law* (1993), p. 302-303;

[155] CORBETT, P., *The Roman Law of Marriage* (1969), p. 203.

[156] Ibid.

ownership, unless conveyed to the husband by specific agreement.[157] A wife could keep the administration of *paraphernal* property for herself, but it was more common to pass it to the husband.[158]

The influence of Roman matrimonial property law on the development of the family law in Europe can hardly be exaggerated. While the following chapters will show how Roman laws on marriage, divorce and concubinage were profoundly refashioned by the medieval canon law, matrimonial property law has never suffered considerable influence of canon family law. Therefore the Roman dotal system, save for a few modifications, survived in its entirety in the counters of the Mediterranean region – Byzantium, Italy, Spain, Portugal, Greece and South France – up to the nineteenth century and beyond.[159] In the time of the medieval reception of Roman law, it also, although to a much lesser extent, influenced German territories. Roman Byzantine law profoundly influenced Russia and some other Slavic countries.[160]

3.2.7. NO INTEREST IN UNIFICATION

At the end of this discussion of Roman law, it is interesting to notice that there were no attempts to submit the subjects of the ever-growing Roman Empire to uniform family law. Family law in Rome was merely the law of the Roman citizens; a question of personal status.[161] Other groups of the Empire's population were bound to their own territorial rules. In 212 A.D., Roman citizenship was granted to all free subjects of the Empire by Imperator Caracalla. In theory this meant that from then on the family relationships of these subjects would have to have been governed by Roman law. However, this seldom was a concern of the Roman authorities and nearly never happened in practice. Roman law did have some harmonising influence on Germanic tribes that came into the sphere of Roman influence. This influence mainly took effect after the West Roman Empire had already fallen under the pressure of the Barbarian invasions. Therefore, its influence should be ascribed to the persuasive authority of Roman law rather than to the political power of the Roman State. The same applies to the later influence of Roman family law upon canon family law.

---

[157] Ibid.
[158] Ibid, p. 203-204.
[159] For instance, in Napoleon's *Code Civil* the dotal regime became one of the contractual matrimonial property regimes for the whole of France.
[160] See Chapter 5.
[161] SPRUIT, J., *Enchiridium. Een geschiedenis van het Romeinse privaatrecht* (1994), p. 55.

3.3. BARBARIAN FAMILY LAW

3.3.1. WHAT IS 'BARBARIAN' LAW?

In addition to Roman family law, the formation of the medieval *ius commune* of family law was significantly influenced by the customary family law of various Barbarian tribes,[162] whose invasions changed the face of Europe at the dawn of the Middle Ages. In Western Europe 'the Barbarians' were predominantly Germanic tribes[163] and in Eastern Europe the Slavonic peoples. The most important codifications of customary law, so-called *leges barbarorum,* were made between the fifth and the ninth centuries. The most important among them are the Germanic *Leges Burgundionum* (attributed to Gundobad 471-516),[164] the Visigothic Code *Lex Visigothorum* (476),[165] the Code of the Salic Francs *Lex Salica* (*c.* 510), the Code of Ripuarian Franks *Lex Ribuaria* (eighth century) and *Leges Alamannorum* (seventh-eighth century),[166] and the Anglo-Saxon Code of King Æthelberht of Kent (early seventh century). Due to a certain delay in the development of North-Eastern Europe, the early eleventh century Russian Code *Russkaia Pravda* can also be treated among these Barbarian laws. Customary Barbarian family law, with its patriarchal male-dominated character, more resembled early Roman family law than the Roman law of that time.[167] However, it is important to remember that the early medieval Barbarian family laws have not, for the most part, reached us in their pure original forms but rather at a stage after they had been already influenced by late Roman law; so, it is often difficult to distinguish the original Barbarian customs from the traces of Roman influence. Illustrative is the history of the Visigothic Code. Around 476 the customary law of the Germanic tribe of Visigoths was codified. Some forty years later a codification of Roman law, *Breviary,* was promulgated by King Alaric for the use of the Roman population of the Visigoth Kingdom. In 654 the *Breviary* was repealed and the Visigoth Code, heavily revised under influence of Roman law, became equally applicable to both Visigoth and Romans.

---

162 DREW, K., *Law and Society in Early Medieval Europe* (1988), VII, p. 2-4.
163 The Lombards invaded Gaul in the end of the sixth century.
164 The Burgundians founded their Kingdom in the corridor between the valleys of the Rhône and the Saône in the middle of the fifth century. The Burgundian Kingdom was conquered by the Franks in the middle of the sixth century.
165 The Visigoths settled in the beginning of the fifth century A.D. in the French Aquitaine. In the course of this century they build up a Kingdom that also came to include Provence and the Iberian Peninsula. The Visigoths lost Provence and Aquitaine to the Franks in the sixth century, and Spain to the Arabs in the early eighth century.
166 The Allemanni inhabited Alsace in the fifth century and were overpowered by the Franks in the middle of the sixth century.
167 GIES, F., GIES, J., *Marriage and the Family in the Middle Ages* (1989), p. 33 and 93.

This paragraph will be dealing with Barbarian family laws from approximately the fifth till the eight century. I will again discuss marriage, divorce, concubinage, non-marital children and matrimonial property law.

3.3.2. BARBARIAN LAW ON MARRIAGE: PATRIARCHAL AND FORMAL

Germanic marriage was much more formal than Roman marriage has ever been. Entering a valid Germanic marriage generally required the presence of three formal elements: the petition; the betrothal, which included the promise of the dowry by the bride's family and the promise of the dower by the groom; and finally the marriage proper, which entailed the delivery of the bride and the dowry. The consent of the parties and their families alone was not sufficient; dowry, dower and other formalities were essential for the validity of the marriage. Those formal elements, later supplemented by a benediction, would form the background of the Church requirements for a proper marriage. Although canon law would, contrary to Germanic law, consider a marriage, concluded without observing these requirements, improper, but not invalid.[168] Marriage, at least for upper class Franks, was not entirely monogamous up to the eighth century.[169] The Frankish King Chlotar I (reign 511-561) had at least two, but more probably even four wives at the same time. Dagobert I (reign 629-639) married three wives simultaneously.[170] Slavic customs also allowed polygamy,[171] which persisted even after Christianisation.[172]

A close relationship was considered an impediment to marriage. However, marriages with close in-laws were rather common among Frankish nobility.[173] The Visigothic Code contained the most extensive list of prohibited degrees: up to the sixth degree of consanguinity.[174]

Betrothal was a formal contract between the groom and the holder of the *mundium* (power) over the bride. The holder was usually the father or the guardian of the bride

---

[168] See Chapter 4.
[169] GIES, F., GIES, J., *Marriage and the Family in the Middle Ages* (1989), p. 53.
[170] Ibid.
[171] SOLOV'EV, C., *Rus' iznachal'naia* (2001), p. 71.
[172] Ibid, p. 73.
[173] Chlotar I married his brother's widow and later his wife's sister. The Visigothic King Leuvigild (†
       586) married his brother's widow. GIES, F., GIES, J., *Marriage and the Family in the Middle Ages* (1989),
       p. 52.
[174] REYNOLDS, P., *Marriage in the Western Church* (1994), p. 75.

and/or in some instances the bride herself.[175] A girl 'was the object of this agreement rather than a party to it, and her consent was not always required'.[176] Betrothal could take place years before the marriage proper. Betrothal was itself a binding legal contract, and the betrothed parties were almost equated to a married couple in respect of fidelity.[177] The formalities of the marriage proper included the delivery of the bride, the transfer of the *mundium* to the groom and the endowment.

Alongside the full marriage with the transfer of *mundium*, Germanic customs allowed a *mundium*-free marriage: *Friedelehe*.[178] This marriage, resembling the Roman marriage *sine manu*, was formed upon consent of the parties themselves and not of their families. The formalities consisted of the bringing of the bride into the groom's house and donation of the morning gift[179] by the groom.[180]

The marriage customs of the Slavonic tribes bore the traces of more ancient practices, such as abduction and purchase of the bride,[181] although the regular form of marriage resembled the Germanic customs. Marriage was arranged by the relatives of the bride and the groom and/or his relatives. The bride was brought into the house of the groom and the next morning her family brought the dowry.[182] Consent of the bride was not of much relevance, although the *Russkaia Pravda* already contained a provision prohibiting forcing daughters into marriage.[183]

---

[175] Under Anglo-Saxon law betrothal was a transaction between the groom and the woman's father or other protector (POLLOCK, F., MAITLAND, F., *The History of English Law before the Time of Edward I*, Vol. II (1952), p. 365). Under Lombard law, betrothal was a contract between the prospective husband and the relatives of the bride. The prospective husband paid or promised to pay a bride price (*meta*) and the father or another *mundward* of the woman promised to hand over the *mundium* of her on the day of marriage. If the *mundward* was someone other than a father or a brother, the woman's consent was required (DREW, K., *Law and Society in Early Medieval Europe* (1988), IV, p. 59). According to the *Lex Burgundionum* (circa 474-516). Marriage was a contract between the groom and the relatives of the bride (Ibid, V, p. 7). Betrothal included the payment of a bride price (*wittimon*) and handing over of the *mundium* of the bride. Visigoth law provided that the betrothal had to be arranged by the groom (or his guardian if he was under the age of 20) and the father (or another relative) of the bride. The agreement should be in writing and symbolised by the exchange of the rings. Only the Frankish law allowed Katherine Fischer DREW the careful suggestion that 'betrothal seems to have been arranged by the man and the woman in the presence of their relatives'. Ibid, VI, p. 5.

[176] REYNOLDS, P., *Marriage in the Western Church* (1994), p. 76.

[177] DREW, K., *Law and Society in Early Medieval Europe* (1988), IV, p. 59.

[178] See OGRIS, W., 'Friedelehe' (1971), No. 1293-1296.

[179] See Section 3.3.6.

[180] BECKER, H-J., 'Die nichteheliche Lebensgemeinschaft (Konkubinat) in der Rechtsgeschichte' (1978), p. 19.

[181] ZAGOROVSKII, I., *Kurs semeinogo prava* (2003), p. 101-102.

[182] NEVOLIN, K., *Istoria rossiiskikh grazhdanskikh zakonov*, V. 1 (1851), p. 456.

[183] ZAGOROVSKII, I., *Kurs semeinogo prava* (2003), p. 214.

3.3.3. CONCUBINAGE IN BARBARIAN LAW: AN ACCEPTED PRACTICE

Concubinage, so-called *Kebsehe*, was a union not prohibited by law because of close relationship or other impediments, but just missing formalities necessary for the formation of a legal marriage. James Brundage suggested that other than in Roman law, the Germanic customs did not recognise concubinage as a legal institution alongside marriage.[184] This standpoint is contested rather persuasively. Katherine Fischer Drew notices in this respect that: 'Although only the Lombard laws specifically recognised that a man might have more than one conjugal partner at a time, what we know about Merovingian and Carolingian Gaul suggests that such multiple unions not only occurred there also but that the offspring there likewise enjoyed a protected place in the inheritance'.[185] Thus, although Lombard law allowed a man to enter only one legitimate marriage, he could simultaneously enter another union or unions which had a quasi-marital status.[186] Visigothic law recognised a concubine (*barragana*) as a kind of a second-rate wife and entitled her to a half of the wife's legitimate portion after his death.[187] This attitude was common also for the other Germanic peoples, except for the Burgundians, who did not recognise any permanent unions except legitimate marriage.[188]

The sexual practises of the Frankish Merovingian kings support the view that concubinage had some legal standing in Germanic society. When the Frankish King Childebert II (reign 575-595) married at the age of fifteen, he already had a concubine and a son. A half-century later, Dagobert I, famous for his sexual laxity, had so many concubines alongside his multiple wives that a contemporary chronicler noted that he 'could not spare space to name them all'.[189]

The same social practices were noticed among the Slavic peoples. The historians agree that keeping multiple concubines alongside one or more legal wives was rather common among them.[190] Even much later, Prince Vladimir (reign 980-1015), under

---

[184] According to James Brundage, 'only marriage with full legal consequences was considered a legitimate union. Other unions had no real standing in Germanic law; consequently concubinage was not legal institution in Germanic society'. BRUNDAGE, J., 'Concubinage and Marriage in Medieval Canon Law' (1975), p. 3.

[185] DREW, K., *Law and Society in Early Medieval Europe* (1988), VIII.

[186] HOYER, E., VON, *Die Ehen minderen Rechts in der fränkischen Zeit* (1926), p. 200.

[187] WEBER, M., *Ehefrau und Mutter in der Rechtsentwicklung* (1907), p. 246.

[188] DREW, K., *Law and Society in Early Medieval Europe* (1988), V, p. 9.

[189] GIES, F., GIES, J., *Marriage and the Family in the Middle Ages* (1989), p. 53.

[190] ZAGOROVSKII, I., *O razvode po russkomy pravy* (1884), p. 7-25.

whose rule Russia embraced Christianity, 'had as many concubines as King Solomon'.[191]

3.3.4. DIVORCE IN BARBARIAN LAW: MORE EASY FOR MEN

The Germanic divorce laws were rather restrictive and male oriented, and in that respect came close to the early Roman law. The canon law idea of indissolubility of marriage was definitely not of Germanic origin. However, the suggestion that divorce under Barbarian law was easy for a husband and impossible for a wife[192] seems to be an oversimplification. In the majority of the Germanic laws, unilateral divorce, even on the part of a husband, was only possible if a wife was guilty of a serious crime.[193]

Visigothic law, although probably the only exception among Germanic laws, allowed a wife to divorce her husband unilaterally if she could prove that her husband had participated in homosexual acts or allowed someone to fornicate with her against her will.[194] Fault was not an indispensable prerequisite of Germanic divorce, however. A woman was also allowed to remarry in case of a long-lasting absence of her husband. Some Germanic laws allowed a husband to leave his wife if he was prepared to surrender to her the children and the property.[195] According to Katherine Fischer Drew, Visigothic law was also the only one that provided for divorce by mutual consent. Such consent had to be confirmed by a written agreement made in the presence of witnesses.[196] However, Pollock and Maitland pointed to the wording of the Anglo-Saxon Code of King Æthelberht of Kent, that stated: 'if she [the wife] wishes to go away with the children, she is to have half the goods'. This wording allows the suggestion 'that the marriage might be dissolved at the will of both, or even at the will of one of the parties to it'.[197] This widespread interpretation of the provision of the King Æthelberht's code[198] has been, however, persuasively contested.[199]

---

[191] SOLOV'EV, C., *Rus' iznachal'naia* (2001), p. 166.
[192] GIES, F., GIES, J., *Marriage and the Family in the Middle Ages* (1989), p. 34.
[193] The most frequently mentioned crimes were: adultery, witchcraft, violation of graves, plotting against the husband's life.
[194] DREW, K., *Law and Society in Early Medieval Europe* (1988), VII, p. 9.
[195] Ibid, VIII.
[196] DREW, K., *Law and Society in Early Medieval Europe* (1988), VII, p. 9.
[197] POLLOCK, F., MAITLAND, F., *The History of English Law before the Time of Edward I*, Vol. II (1952), p. 393.
[198] FELL, C. et al, *Women in Anglo-Saxon England and the Impact of 1066* (1984), p. 57.
[199] Carole Hough believed that the aforementioned provision dealt not with a divorce but with a widow. HOUGH, A., 'The early Kentish "divorce laws": a reconsideration of Æthelberht, chs. 79 and 80' (1994), p. 34.

Although Burgundian law formally recognized no legal divorce, Katherine Fischer Drew is certain that the Burgundians could have also repudiated their wives for adultery, witchcraft and violation of graves.[200] Under the Celtic Brehon Laws, which were in force in Ireland during almost the whole of the first millennium A.D., marriage was dissoluble upon the initiative of a husband as well as that of a wife.[201] Divorce among the Slavs was rather free, including divorce by mutual consent, and possibly, even upon the wife's initiative.[202]

3.3.5. NON-MARITAL CHILDREN IN BARBARIAN LAW: AN INTERMEDIATE POSITION

The Barbarian attitude towards children from a concubine was more tolerant than that of the Romans. As opposed to the children of illicit (for instance, incestuous) unions, the children of a concubine were not called illegitimate, but natural children. Such children were not under the power (*mundium*) of their father, but in *mundium* of their maternal grandfather.[203] However, if a father recognised his natural children, they came to belong to his household and his family, 'along with his legitimate children'.[204] Under Lombard and Visigothic law, natural children could inherit from their father, but their rights were inferior compared to those of the full-born children.[205] In the clan system of Celtic Ireland, illegitimate birth was a rather common event.[206] Illegitimate children were not disadvantaged under Brehon Law and enjoyed equal inheritance rights.[207]

According to Pollock and Maitland: 'It must be remembered that our medieval law did not consistently regard the bastard as *filius nullius*'.[208] In the words of Bishop Gregory of Tours: 'the children of the Frankish kings were king's sons irrespective of the position of their mother'.[209] This is illustrated by the fact that when the founder of the Frankish Merovingian dynasty, Clovis (481-511), died in 511, his three sons by a legitimate wife and the oldest son by a concubine inherited equal shares of his

---

[200]   DREW, K., *Law and Society in Early Medieval Europe* (1988), V, p. 9.
[201]   O'HALLORAN, K., 'Ireland: The Family and the Law in a Divided Land' (1998), p. 116.
[202]   ZAGOROVSKII, I., *Kurs semeinogo prava* (1909), p. 103.
[203]   HUEBNER, R., *History of Germanic Private Law* (1918), p. 671.
[204]   Ibid.
[205]   REYNOLDS, P., *Marriage in the Western Church* (1994), p. 109.
[206]   O'HALLORAN, K., 'Ireland: The Family and the Law in a Divided Land' (1998), p. 116.
[207]   Ibid.
[208]   POLLOCK, F., MAITLAND, F., *The History of English Law before the time of Edward I*, Vol. II (1952), p. 382.
[209]   GREGORY OF TOURS, *Historia francorum*, V 20. Written between 573 and 594. Cited in: WOOD, I., 'Kings, Kingdoms and Consent' (1979), p 15.

kingdom.[210] The Slavs had a rather similar attitude. Thus, illegitimate birth did not preclude Prince Vladimir from becoming a prince and inheriting a share of the princedom, and finally becoming the Grand Prince of Russia.[211]

3.3.6. BARBARIAN LAW ON MATRIMONIAL PROPERTY

Germanic laws have often been seen as the source of the community property in Europe.[212] The community property system has played as significant a role in European history as the Roman dotal system. It would not be an exaggeration to say that the interaction of these two systems has actually determined the further development of the matrimonial property systems in Europe. However, the origin of the community property in Europe is still a matter of controversy.[213] Various hypotheses thereof have been put forward in different times.[214] The fact that the community had been founded in many territories that were affected by Roman civilisation led some sixteenth-century scholars[215] to suggest that the community property in Europe was of Roman origin. This hypothesis was somehow revived in the nineteenth century,[216] but had been completely abandoned by the beginning of the twentieth century.[217] At that time, it became rather clear that Roman law at the time of the Germanic invasions definitely knew no community of matrimonial property. Other theories sequentially attributed the origins of the community of property in Europe to Celtic[218] or Gallic[219] peoples. According to another hypothesis, the community of property was an inherent

---

[210]   WOOD, I., 'Kings, Kingdoms and Consent' (1979), p 6.

[211]   Vladimir was born from King Sviatoslav and the housekeeper of his mother Olga. NEVOLIN, K., *Istoria rossiiskikh grazhdanskikh zakonov* (1851), p. 312.

[212]   OLIVERCRONA, K., D', 'Précis historique de l'origine et du développement de la communauté de biens entre époux' (1865); LOBINGIER, C., 'The Matrimonial Community: Its Origin and Diffusion' (1928), p. 212 ff, HUEBNER, R., *History of Germanic Private Law* (1918), p. 621, ff; THIELEN, J., *Oude en nieuwe opvattingen over het ontstaan van de algehele gemeenschap van goederen* (1965), p. 46-58.

[213]   Charles Lobingier remarks that although the first elements of community property can be foreshadowed in the ancient Babylonian, Greek and, perhaps, early Roman law, none of those systems could possibly have influenced the laws of early Medieval Europe. LOBINGIER, C., 'The Matrimonial Community: Its Origin and Diffusion' (1928), p. 211.

[214]   For an overview see: THIELEN, J., *Oude en nieuwe opvattingen over het ontstaan van de algehele gemeenschap van goederen* (1965), p. 26-95, and WYK, A., VAN, 'Theories on the Historical Origins of the Community of Property Between Spouses' (1979), p. 279-293.

[215]   For an overview see: THIELEN, J., *Oude en nieuwe opvattingen over het ontstaat van de algehele gemeenschap van goederen* (1965), p. 26-27.

[216]   By two French authors: M. GIRAUD and E. BIMBINET. See THIELEN, J., *Oude en nieuwe opvattingen over het ontstaan van de algehele gemeenschap van goederen* (1965), p. 27.

[217]   LOBINGIER, C., 'The Matrimonial Community: Its Origin and Diffusion,' (1928), p. 211-112.

[218]   See DE FUNIAK, W., VAUGHN, M., 'Why Community Property is so Misunderstood – Knowing its Origins is the Key' (1974), p. 94.

[219]   See THIELEN, J., *Oude en nieuwe opvattingen over het ontstaan van de algehele gemeenschap van goederen* (1965), p. 33-46.

Germanic 'Teutonic'[220] institution. One more theory saw the origins of community in Christian influence, mainly in the concept of the unity of the spouses *in carne una* (two in one flesh).[221]

Due to the general legal incapacity of a Germanic married woman under power (*mundium*) and the right of her husband to administer the entire family property, it is extremely difficult to describe the old Barbarian property laws using modern concepts of 'community' or 'separation' of property. However, it is possible to see that in the course of the early medieval period certain features of the community became more and more distinguishable in some Germanic matrimonial property systems.[222]

Analysing the Germanic folk-laws, Rudolf Hübner came to the conclusion that the traces of the community property system do not go back to the beginnings common to all Germanic tribes.[223] Hübner suggested that in the early times, of which we have hardly any solid evidence, the husband was the sole owner of the whole of the family property,[224] as was the case in the Roman marriage *cum manu*. Only later in the time of folk-laws, did a wife become the separate legal owner of her estate, consisting of the dowry, the dower and the morning gift.[225] These three core stones of Germanic matrimonial property law were discernable in the matrimonial property law of the non-Romanised parts of Europe well into the early modern times.

The **dowry** was provided by the bride's family and, other than in Roman law, served primarily as a source of the wife's property.[226] The **dower** was a 'bride price' that was paid, or was promised to be paid, by the groom at the time of the betrothal. At the time of marriage proper, the whole or part of the dower went to the bride and became a

---

[220] On the so-called 'Teutonic theory' see: D'OLIVERCRONA, K., 'Précis historique de l'origine et du développement de la communauté de biens entre époux' (1865); LOBINGIER, C., 'The Matrimonial Community: Its Origin and Diffusion,' (1928), p. 212 ff, HÜBNER, R., *History of Germanic Private Law* (1918), p. 621, ff; THIELEN, J., *Oude en nieuwe opvattingen over het ontstaan van de algehele gemeenschap van goederen* (1965), p. 46-58.

[221] THIELEN, J., *Oude en nieuwe opvattingen over het ontstaan van de algehele gemeenschap van goederen* (1965), p. 68-85.

[222] The ideas as to from which period of time it is appropriate to speak of community property vary considerably. Thus, Van Wyk suggested the existence of community from the eighth century (WYK, A., VAN, 'Theories on the Historical Origins of the Community of Property Between Spouses' (1979), p. 289), while Charles Donahue referred to 'the trend in modern scholarship which would place the institution of community property, at the earliest, in the fourteenth century, when the word "community" was first used in the context of matrimonial property'. DONAHUE, C., 'English and French Marriage Cases in the Later Middle Ages: Might the Difference be Explained by Differences in the Property Systems?' (1992), p. 350.

[223] HÜBNER, R., *History of Germanic Private Law* (1918), p. 622.

[224] Ibid.

[225] Ibid, p. 623.

[226] DREW, K., *Law and Society in Early Medieval Europe* (1988), VI, p. 6.

part of her property. This institution resembled, to some extent, the Roman *donatio ante nuptias*.[227] The **morning gift** was the property added by a groom after the consummation of the marriage.[228] The morning gift also constituted a part of the wife's property.

As a Germanic woman in general had no legal capacity[229] and had to be represented by the holder of the *mundium* (power) over her, she could not, as a rule,[230] administer her property.[231] Thus, in the original folk-laws, the wife's property was owned by the wife but administered during the marriage by the husband, as the wife's *mundium-holder*.[232] The husband had a kind of 'seisin in mundium' of the wife's estate.[233] By virtue of this position he enjoyed the right of possession, usufruct and administration of his wife's property, but was not allowed to alienate it without her consent.[234] The surviving spouse did not take the deceased spouse's property.[235] In case of divorce or the death of the husband, the wife's property returned to her.[236] A widow was also entitled to the usufruct of a certain portion of her husband's property.[237] If the husband predeceased his wife, her property went to her heirs.[238] During the marriage, therefore, although legal ownership was kept apart, the property of husband and wife was accumulated into a kind of community of administration under the control of the husband. According to Rudolf Hübner, this community of administration[239] was, nonetheless, not yet a real community, as there was only physical and administrative unity of the property, while the legal titles remained separate.[240]

It is difficult to say exactly when and where this ancient Germanic system grew into a real community property system.[241] The earliest traces of the real community were

---

[227] See Section 3.2.6.

[228] Originally a gift of a bridegroom to a bride, meant as a price for her virginity. HÜBNER, R., *History of Germanic Private Law* (1918), p. 625-626.

[229] BRISSAUD, J., *A History of French Private Law* (1912), p. 163 ff.

[230] It is maintained that under the Frankish law a wife may have administered her own property. DREW, K., *Law and Society in Early Medieval Europe* (1988), VI, p. 5.

[231] Ibid, VIII, p. 22.

[232] Married woman under Germanic law had, as a rule, no capacity to dispose of property. HÜBNER, R., *History of Germanic Private Law* (1918), p. 623.

[233] HÜBNER, R., *History of Germanic Private Law* (1918), p. 627.

[234] DREW, K., *Law and Society in Early Medieval Europe* (1988), VIII, p. 19.

[235] Ibid.

[236] HÜBNER, R., *History of Germanic Private Law* (1918), p. 628

[237] DREW, K., *Law and Society in Early Medieval Europe* (1988), VIII, p. 19.

[238] Ibid.

[239] HÜBNER, R., *History of Germanic Private Law* (1918), p. 623.

[240] Ibid, p. 626-627.

[241] Jean Brissaud has rightly mentioned 'that the transition from one system to another was scarcely perceptible' and that because the 'old texts are not very precise' it was a rather 'embarrassing question to decide whether or not they have in view the community system'. BRISSAUD, J., *A History of French Private Law* (1912), p. 813.

found, according to Olivecrona, in the Visigothic Code, the Law of Ripuarian Franks and the Saxon law.[242] It fair to add to this list the Anglo-Saxon Æthelberht's Code.[243] Rudolf Hübner suggested that 'some of the legal systems of the Frankish period had already departed from the principle of distinct estates to the extent of recognising a true legal community in respect of the so-called *acquiests*'.[244] The distinctive feature of a true community is that during the marriage it comes to be treated as the undivided property of both spouses, and each of them is entitled to a share if there is to be a dissolution of the marriage.[245] From that point onwards, the property came to be devised in case of death or divorce, rather than the wife having the right to recover 'her own' property. This criterion allows the majority of the Germanic matrimonial property systems to be classified as forms of community. The rules on division of these communities were, however, different. Æthelberht's code provided for equal division of property if the wife was taking the children.[246] This was interpreted as a token of the existence of the universal community of property.[247] Universal community is also supposed to have been developed in Holland, Flanders and Westphalia.[248] The division of property among the Franks was different. For instance, among the Ribuarian Franks under the *lex Ribuaria* a widow received one-third of the property that had been commonly acquired by the spouses during the marriage.[249] This type of division appears to be a precursor to the community of *acquiests*.[250] The Frankish community of *acquiests* became a dominant rule in Thuringia, parts of Swabia, Bavaria and Austria.[251] Another example of community of *acquiests* can be found in the Visigothic Code, which provided for a division of *acquiests* in proportion to the spouses' fortunes.[252] However, not all Germanic laws were evolving towards community; the matrimonial property regime under the *leges Alamannorum* remained that of separation of property, as no division of matrimonial property took place there.[253]

---

[242]   D'OLIVERCRONA, K., 'Précis historique de l'origine et du développement de la communauté de biens entre époux' (1865), p. 254.

[243]   WORMALD, R., *The Making of English Law: King Alfred to the Twelfth Century*, Vol. 1 (1999), p. 93-101.

[244]   HÜBNER, R., *History of Germanic Private Law* (1918), p. 627.

[245]   This division of acquiests upon dissolution of marriage is generally considered as an evidence of true community. For instance: HÜBNER, R., *History of Germanic Private Law* (1918), p. 627; THIELEN, J., *Man en vrouw hebben geen gedeeld goed* (2001), p. 132 ff.

[246]   POLLOCK, F., MAITLAND, F., *The History of English Law before the time of Edward I*, Vol. II (1952), p. 393.

[247]   THIELEN, J., *Man en vrouw hebben geen gedeeld goed* (2001), p. 131.

[248]   LOBINGIER, C., 'The Matrimonial Community: Its Origin and Diffusion' (1928), p. 113.

[249]   BRISSAUD, J., *A History of French Private Law* (1912), p. 762-763

[250]   Ibid, p. 763-764.

[251]   LOBINGIER, C., 'The Matrimonial Community: Its Origin and Diffusion' (1928), p. 113.

[252]   'When persons of equal rank marry one another, and, while living together, either increase or waste their property, where one is more wealthy than the other; they shall share in common the gains and losses, in proportion to the amount which each one holds. [...]' Visigothic Code, book IV, title II, law XVI.

[253]   THIELEN, J., *Man en vrouw hebben geen gedeeld goed* (2001), p. 133.

It is claimed that the matrimonial property relations of the Slavonic peoples were more like the Roman dotal system than the Germanic community of property.[254] It is rather certain that a Slavic wife could own separate property,[255] but it is not completely clear who was entitled to administer it.[256] A bride received a dowry from her father, her kin, or (perhaps, if she was a widow) determined for herself which part of her property would constitute her dowry.[257] The legal regime of the rest of the wife's property probably resembled the Roman *paraferna*. Dowry was most probably administered by the husband,[258] but could not be alienated without consent of the wife.[259] In case of the husband's death, a wife could recover her dowry[260] together with the part of the husband's property that was promised by him as her dower.[261] No division of property took place in case of a spouse's death or divorce.

3.4. CONCLUDING REMARKS

The preceding sketch shows that the difference between the Roman and the Barbarian family law was, in spite of the Roman law influence, still very substantial. Other than the Roman law, the Barbarian rules on formation of marriage were strictly formal. The upcoming canon law attempts to formalise marriage drew on the Germanic, rather than on the Roman tradition. As in classical and postclassical Rome, Barbarian marriage was neither a religious matter nor a sacrament. Divorce, at least on the part of the husband, was easily attainable. The Catholic doctrine of indissolubility of marriage would, therefore, be as alien to Germanic peoples as it would be to Romans. Concubinage and illegitimate birth in Germanic law had no less definite social and legal standing than it did in Roman law. The Church's campaign for outlawing concubinage and illegitimate birth[262] was, accordingly, rooted neither in Germanic nor in Roman tradition.

---

[254]   Nevolin claimed that separation of property was a core element of Russian as well as Greco-Roman law. NEVOLIN, K., *Istoria rossiiskikh grazhdanskikh zakonov* (1851), p. 94.

[255]   There is evidence that in the tenth-century Queen Olga, mother of Vladimir under whose reign Russia was Christianised in 988, had her own town, villages and hunting grounds. NEVOLIN, K., *Istoria rossiiskikh grazhdanskikh zakonov* (1851), p. 94.

[256]   ZAGOROVSKII, I., *Kurs semeinogo prava* (2003), p. 197.

[257]   NEVOLIN, K., *Istoria rossiiskikh grazhdanskikh zakonov* (1851), p. 110-111.

[258]   An early medieval written monument *Voproshenie Kurikovo* named squandering of wife's property by a husband a reason for divorce. Cited in: ZAGOROVSKII, I., *O razvode po russkomy pravy* (1884), p. 185. This sanction for ill administration implies that a husband had the capacity of administration.

[259]   NEVOLIN, K., *Istoria rossiiskikh grazhdanskikh zakonov* (1851), p. 117.

[260]   ZAGOROVSKII, I., *Kurs semeinogo prava* (2003), p. 198.

[261]   NEVOLIN, K., *Istoria rossiiskikh grazhdanskikh zakonov* (1851), p. 110-111.

[262]   See Chapter 4.

With respect to matrimonial property law, it is possible to say that regardless of the true origin of the community of property in Europe, the developments of Germanic matrimonial property law definitively inserted the element of community into the European legal tradition.

CHAPTER 4
FORMATION OF THE MEDIEVAL
CANON *IUS COMMUNE* OF
FAMILY LAW

4.1. INTRODUCTION

The process of the creation of medieval uniform canon family law evolved over centuries. In the area of Western Christendom, three more or less distinctive periods can be delineated within this process.

The initial period lasted approximately from the second to the eight century A.D. In Church history this period is called 'patristic', as Christian teaching was mainly developed in the oeuvres of the Church Fathers. During the patristic period the Christian view on marriage and the family started to be elaborated by the Church Fathers, and the first Christian rules were formulated as a part of the Church's moral teaching. Christian ideas progressively influenced Roman family law since Constantine (middle fourth century A.D.), and even more the early medieval laws. However, in spite of this influence there was always a clear distinction and significant difference between the Church moral norms and the rules of secular law. At that stage the Church did not yet demand that secular family law should strictly conform to Christian moral teaching. Although Eastern and Western Christendom had already started to grow apart by the end of this period, there were not yet significant differences with relation to family law.

The second period of the formation of the *ius commune* of family law more or less coincided with the Carolingian times (eighth to tenth century). In the course of this period, the Church acquired broad jurisdiction in family matters and tried to crystallise its own concepts of marriage, divorce, concubinage and related matters. In both parts of Europe, the Church tended to be absorbed by the State. In the Orthodox world, Church and State were merged, under the sceptre of the Emperor, into one theocratic system. Here the expansion of the Church's jurisdiction in family matters and the crystallisation and systemisation of the canon family law already reached an advanced stadium. In the heyday of the Carolingian period, the theocratic regime of Charlemagne started to resemble the Byzantine practices of the Emperor embodying both temporal and spiritual power.

The third period is the High Middle Ages (eleventh-thirteenth centuries), during which the Roman Catholic Church defeated the worldly rulers in the Investiture struggle. As a result, the Church grew into in a kind of highly centralised, supranational 'quasi-state' with its own legislative, enforcement and adjudication system. It acquired exclusive competence in the bulk of family matters, which allows one to speak of an entire canon family law. Thus, in the West, the formation of the medieval canon family law was completed in this period and this law acquired the character of *ius commune*. The Orthodox Church formally separated from the West in the mid-eleventh century. The accession to Orthodoxy of Russia and other Slavic peoples was accompanied by the extension of Byzantine canon family law. This allows one to speak of the Orthodox world as the second part of the European *ius commune* in the field of family law, substantially very similar to its Western counterpart.

The periods outlined above will be discussed successively in the paragraphs below.

4.2. EARLY CHRISTIAN TEACHING: PAVING THE WAY FOR CANON FAMILY LAW

4.2.1. CHURCH JURISDICTION: *LEX DIVINA* AND *LEX HUMANA*

A comparison of the concepts of the medieval *ius commune* of family law with its worldly precursors, Roman and Barbarian family laws, makes it clear that it must have been the Church's own teaching that was responsible for the significant differences between them. In the first centuries of its existence, the Christian Church did not aim to provide extensive legal regulation to the family; it merely considered the moral dimension of family relationships as an object of its pastoral attention. The Church regarded marriage mainly as a civil institution and therefore as a subject of secular law. However, as the Church's ideas about marriage and the family crystallised, it became clear that the secular laws were not always in agreement with the ideas of the Church. For instance, both Roman and Jewish law allowed divorce for a number of causes, while the Christian teaching on this matter was much more restrictive. Thus, during the fourth century, Western bishops and theologians developed the view that the Church had its own marriage law, and drew a distinction between the secular law of marriage and the family (*lex humana*), and the divine law on these subjects (*lex divina*).[1] With the Christianisation of the Roman Empire, starting with Constantine in the fourth century A.D., the secular marriage law 'was gradually modified in a Christian sense. [But] it must not be supposed, however, that the Christian rule was even approximately identified with the imperial law'.[2] The Latin Fathers rarely contested this situation; they only made it clear that the divine law to which they adhered was superior.[3] For example, they recognised the applicability of Roman marriage law to the Christians[4] and did not protest against the fact that this law permitted divorce.

By the fifth century, however, the contradictions between the secular law and the Church's teaching resulted in the establishment of a dual, secular-divine regime. According to Reynolds, marriage must have been subject to both regimes. The bishops applied the rules of divine law using ecclesiastic sanctions, while the civil judges applied civil law using civil sanctions. Although divine law was already clearly distinguishable by then, Reynolds warns that 'it would be inappropriate to speak of canon law in the patristic period, for the law of the Church was not yet a distinct science with its own scholars. [...] What served instead, as well as the Bible itself, was a gradually accumulating quantity of decisions by Popes and councils'.[5] The divine family law had its own means of enforcement using ecclesiastic penances and excommunication. For instance, in the third century the Church had already started to excommunicate adulterers and remarried divorcées.[6]

During the first centuries of Christianity there was hardly any difference in attitude towards marriage and the family between Eastern and Western Christendom.[7] However, in the East the rules of divine law were systematised much earlier than in the West. The *Nomocanon*[8] of John the Scholastic, Patriarch of Constantinople (565-577), digested all known canons of Councils, supplemented with the sentences of the Fathers, as early as the sixth century.[9] Thus, Eastern Christendom at this early stage had already been supplied with a systematic treatise of a kind for which the Western world had to wait until the twelfth-century Gratian's collection.[10]

---

[1]   REYNOLDS, P., *Marriage in the Western Church* (1994), p. 121.
[2]   LACEY, T., *Marriage in Church and State* (1947), p. 102.
[3]   REYNOLDS, P., *Marriage in the Western Church* (1994), p. 151.
[4]   SCHILLEBEECKX, E., *Het huwelijk: aardse werkelijkheid en heilsmysterie* (1963), p. 169.
[5]   REYNOLDS, P., *Marriage in the Western Church* (1994), p. 146.
[6]   Thus the Council of Elvira (ca. 300 A.D.) determined that women who left their husbands and married again, even if their husbands were adulterers, were to be excommunicated. REYNOLDS, P., *Marriage in the Western Church* (1994), p. 145.
[7]   SCHILLEBEECKX, E., *Het huwelijk: aardse werkelijkheid en heilsmysterie* (1963), p. 229.
[8]   From Greek *νομος* and *κανων*: a collection of Imperial statutes and Church canons.
[9]   CYPIN, V., 'O kanonakh s tolkovaniami episkopa Nicodima (Milosha)' (1996), p. VII.
[10] LACEY, T., *Marriage in Church and State* (1947), p. 106.

4.2.2. FIRST CHRISTIAN RULES ON MARRIAGE: MARRIAGE AS SECOND BEST

The early Church initially did not pay much attention to marriage and the family due to the eschatological spirit holding sway among the first Christians. This attitude was based upon the belief that the Second Coming of Christ was near. The Christians of the first centuries felt that they had to release everything that connected them to this world in order to prepare themselves for the next one. Their ascetic mistrust of sexuality also contributed to the undervaluation of marriage.[11] Against this eschatological, ascetic background, the belief of the St. Apostle Paul that a celibate state is better than marriage, becomes more understandable. St. Paul taught that it is better to await the Second Coming in chastity, but if a man cannot remain content, 'it is better to marry than to burn'.[12] Thus, 'He who marries his betrothed does well, and he who refrains does better'.[13]

As far as the Church paid attention to marriage at that early period, it concentrated not on its worldly dimension, but rather on the importance of the spiritual bond between husband and wife, the importance of love and the personal nature of their relationships. Hence, the main difference between the Roman and the Christian attitude to marriage manifested itself from the outset. Geoffrey Nathan observes that unlike Roman law, St. Paul's teaching enjoined upon the man a specific duty 'to love his wife as his own body, since husband and wife were one'.[14] According to Nathan: 'Roman marriage was [...] the beginning of the family, not a goal or end in itself'.[15] In contrast, the joining between a man and a woman, and the manner of that joining, was the most important human relationship to the early Christians. 'The essential pairing for the Christians was thus husband and wife, not husband and familia'.[16] The early fathers condemned the double standards with which secular law threaded male and female infidelity.[17]

---

[11]   Later, it was settled that sexuality must be permitted 'only between a man and a woman who were legitimately married to one another, and then only if done for the sake of procreation.[...] All other forms of sexual contacts must be considered forbidden'. PAYER, P., *Sex and the Penitentials* (1984), p. 115.

[12]   1 Cor. 7:8.

[13]   'It is well for a man not to touch a woman'. 1 Cor. 7:1.

[14]   NATHAN, G., *The Family in Late Antiquity* (2000), p. 41.

[15]   Ibid, p. 39.

[16]   Ibid.

[17]   See, for instance, Basil the Great (†379) *Pravila Provoslavnoi Cerkvi*, Vol II (1996), p. 387-391.

Due to the focus on the spiritual dimension of marriage, there were no specific Christian rules on marriage in the first centuries of Christianity.[18] Marriage was seen as a mere worldly matter.[19] The Christians kept following traditional nuptial rites of the folks to which they belonged, as far as they did not involve sacrifices to pagan gods or idols. The Synod of Elvira (306) expressly noticed that Christians marry in the same way as pagans.[20]

The lack of attention to marriage started to change in the fourth century, when Christianity became the state religion of the Roman Empire. The first Christian teaching on marriage was formulated by St. Augustine[21] in the West and by St. John Chrysostom[22] in the East, some fifty years after Constantine's death.[23] However, the change of attitude did not manifest itself in the immediate enactment of legal rules. Even after the Church's attitude towards marriage became more positive, the early fathers were still more concerned with the spiritual aspects of Christian marriage, and its value as 'Christian virtue in a pagan world', than with its legal aspects.[24]

The teaching of St. Augustine endorsed marriage, but still bore a great deal of suspicion towards sexuality. According to St. Augustine, marriage was not connected with the fall and had already been established in Paradise, but lust was connected with the first sin. Accordingly, Augustine followed the Pauline tradition that placed virginity and widowhood above marriage.[25] At the same time, he stressed that marriage was not only an honourable status,[26] but also a sacrament.[27]

The Church expressed its endorsement of marriage by starting to grant it a priestly benediction. The first evidence of benediction by a priest came no earlier than in the fourth century.[28] In the fourth and the fifth centuries, the Church in the Western Roman Empire prescribed that a clerical marriage should have a nuptial benediction. From the fourth century, a liturgical celebration of marriage began to develop in the

---

[18] RITZER, K., *Formen, Riten und religiöses Brauchtum der Eheschliessung in den christlichen Kirchen des ersten Jahrtausends* (1962), p. 39.
[19] SCHILLEBEECKX, E., *Het huwelijk: aardse werkelijkheid en heilsmysterie* (1963), p. 171-172 and 229.
[20] Ibid, p. 169.
[21] Born in 354, died in 430.
[22] Archbishop of Constantinople. Born in 347, died in 407.
[23] GRUBBS, J., *Law and Family in Late Antiquity* (1995), p. 65.
[24] MCNAMARA, J., WEMPLE, S., 'Marriage and Divorce in Frankish Kingdom' (1976), p. 97.
[25] NATHAN, G., *The Family in Late Antiquity* (2000), p. 76.
[26] Ibid.
[27] According to St. Augustine, marriage symbolises the mystic bond between Christ and the Church. For more on the Augustine theology of marriage see: REYNOLDS, P., *Marriage in the Western Church* (1994), p. 241-315.
[28] SCHILLEBEECKX, E., *Het huwelijk: aardse werkelijkheid en heilsmysterie* (1963), p. 172.

East.[29] A priestly benediction of a lay marriage was at that time a sign of Church appreciation of the parties' good behaviour, a sign which was not granted to everyone. Only the first marriage could acquire benediction, a second marriage was excluded.[30] The nuptial liturgy was developed a century later in the middle of the fifth century.[31] Neither the benediction nor the liturgy was required for the validity of the marriage. In order to be valid, the marriage had to be celebrated according to the secular personal laws of the parties.

Around the sixth century, the Church began a campaign against marriages between close relatives. Such marriages were previously quite common among the Germanic nobility. The Church was initially content with the Roman prohibition of marriages between partners closer than the fourth degree of consanguinity, prohibiting marriage with aunts, uncles, nephews and nieces, but allowing marriages between first cousins. The Council of Agde (506), however, extended the prohibition to marriages between first cousins and even their children (second cousins).[32] During the sixth century, these rules were extrapolated to the in-laws and were gradually incorporated into secular law. In line with the Church policy, Frankish King Childebert II (reign 575-595) introduced the death penalty for a man who married his father's widow or his wife's sister, or for a widow who married her husband's brother. At the beginning of the seventh century another Frankish King, Chlotar II (reign 584-629), 'whose own grandfather had married his living wife's sister, pronounced the death penalty against a noble who married his stepmother'.[33]

4.2.3. EARLY CHURCH ATTITUDE TOWARDS CONCUBINAGE

As we have seen, concubinage was rather accepted both in Roman and Germanic societies. Christopher Brook suggested that following this tradition, the Church also accepted concubinage, although not without prevarication, down to the twelfth century.[34]

In patristic times it was rather common for a young man to take a concubine before he legally married. A well-known depiction of such a relationship was left by St. Augustine in his *Confessions,* where he described his own experience before his

---

29   Ibid, p. 229.
30   Ibid, p. 176-182.
31   Ibid, p. 180.
32   GIES, F., GIES, J., *Marriage and the Family in the Middle Ages* (1989), p. 56.
33   Ibid, p. 52.
34   BROOKE, N., *The Medieval Idea of Marriage* (1989), p. 67.

conversion to Christianity.[35] Concubinage, sanctioned by Roman social conventions, was tolerated by the Church provided that a man had only one concubine at the time.[36] A canon of the 1st Council of Toledo (400), later included in the Gratian's *Decretum*,[37] provided that 'an unmarried man who had a concubine should not be forbidden to receive communion, as long as he was content to limit himself to one women'.[38] The early Germanic kingdoms witnessed even greater tolerance in respect of concubinage from the part of the Church.[39]

4.2.4.   FIRST CHRISTIAN RULES ON DIVORCE: CAN CHRISTIAN MARRIAGE BE DISSOLVED?

Christian ideas about the dissolubility of marriage were at variance with those of the Romans, Jews and Barbarians from the very beginning. The Christian teaching was primarily based on the interpretation of the few instances in the Scripture where Jesus addressed the subject of divorce. Jesus' most general statement regarding divorce is that 'what God has joined together, let no men put asunder'.[40] Further, Jesus comments that the right to divorce his wife was given to a man by Moses 'because of the hardness of men's hearts',[41] and that a man who divorced his wife and remarried committed adultery.[42] In Matthew's gospel, however, Jesus makes an exception for a man who divorces his wife due to adultery.[43] This exception became known as the 'Matthean Exception'.

---

[35]   This emotive description is very illustrative: 'In those years I knew a girl who was my comrade, not in that kind of marriage which is called lawful, but one whom I had found by wandering passion, empty of wisdom [...] in whom I experienced in my own person the distance between the restraint of the marriage alliance, a treaty made for the sake of procreation, and the contract of love based on lust, where a child is born against the parents' wish'. [Then the Christian mother of Augustine found for him a suitable bride and he had to leave his concubine.] 'Meanwhile my sins were multiplying, and she with whom I had been living was ripped from my side as a hindrance to my marriage. She was still a part of me and my heart was torn and wounded; her loss drew blood from me. She had to return to Africa, vowing to you, O God, not to know any other man, leaving with me my natural son by her'. Augustine, *Confessions*, vi. 2, 2., written in 397-398. Cited in: BROOKE, N., *The Medieval Idea of Marriage* (1989), p. 65-66.

[36]   BROOKE, N., *The Medieval Idea of Marriage* (1989), p. 66.

[37]   However, it has been argued that Gratian quite misunderstood the intent of this canon. BRUNDAGE, J., 'Concubinage and Marriage in Medieval Canon Law' (1975), p. 4.

[38]   BRUNDAGE, J., 'Concubinage and Marriage in Medieval Canon Law' (1975), p. 4.

[39]   GIES, F., GIES, J., *Marriage and the Family in the Middle Ages* (1989), p. 53.

[40]   Matt. 5.31-32, 19:3-19; Luke 16: 18; Mark 10; 2-12.

[41]   Matt. 19.8.

[42]   REYNOLDS, P., *Marriage in the Western Church* (1994), p. 173.

[43]   Matt. 19.9.

The interpretation of these words was a subject of continuing controversy in the early and medieval Church.[44] A rigid interpretation finally led the Catholic Church to formulate the doctrine of the indissolubility of marriage, which became an important part of the medieval family *ius commune*.[45] A less rigid interpretation of the same words led the Orthodox,[46] and later the Reformation theologians,[47] to a restrictive admission of divorce. A true appreciation of these contradicting readings is impossible without placing the words of Jesus in the context of the Jewish divorce situation of his days.

Mosaic Law allowed a husband to repudiate his wife whenever he pleased and for whatever reasons.[48] The severity of this law was gradually tempered by numerous restrictive measures.[49] In the time of Jesus' sermon, the extent of the husband's right to repudiate his wife was a subject of controversy. According to the rigorist school, a man could divorce his wife only for adultery.[50] A more moderate school held the position that a husband did not 'need not assign any reason whatever for his divorce'.[51] The view of the latter school eventually prevailed. It is important to notice that this discussion concerned only repudiation, as neither of the schools attempted to restrain divorce by mutual consent.[52] The right to repudiate was an exclusive right of the husband and the wife had no counterpart.[53] Women never acquired a formal right to repudiate their husbands at Jewish law.[54] That can explain why Jesus mentioned only a man repudiating an adulterous wife, and did not speak of a woman divorcing an adulterous husband.

---

[44] For more on the interpretation of the Matthean Exception see: REYNOLDS, P., *Marriage in the Western Church* (1994), p. 173-227.

[45] See Sections 4.3.4. and 4.4.5

[46] See Sections 4.3.4. and 4.4.5

[47] See Part III, Chapter 8, Section 8.2.3.

[48] 'At the very beginning, or at least, as far back as the history of this institution can be traced, the husband's right to divorce was absolutely unlimited'. AMRAM, D., *The Jewish law of Divorce According to Bible and Talmud* (1968), p. 24.

[49] Ibid. For instance, neither a man who had falsely accused his wife of antenuptial incontinence, nor a man who had raped a virgin had the right to divorce his victim. Ibid. p. 28. The 'oral law' forbade a divorce from an insane wife, a wife who had been taken into captivity or a minor wife who was so young that she could not understand the meaning of the bill of divorce – the *get*. Ibid. p. 45-46.

[50] Ibid, p. 33.

[51] Ibid, p. 33.

[52] Ibid, p. 39.

[53] Such an act, according to Amram, 'would have been in opposition to the fundamental theory that divorce was the exclusive right of the husband, and although, as was shown above, this exclusive right was modified in favour of the wife, the old forms were always used and the idea of the bill of divorce given by the wife to her husband was impossible to the Jewish legal mind'. Ibid, p. 60.

[54] A wife could only ask the court to compel her husband to give a bill of divorce in case of the husband 's falsely accusing his wife of antenuptial incontinence, the husband's impotency, or suffering from leprosy or involvement in a disgraceful business, his desertion, or restricting the wife's liberty, apostasy and in some other instances. Ibid, p. 28.

Against this background, the words of Jesus that the right of a man to divorce his wife was given by Moses 'because of the hardness of men's hearts', and restricting the right of repudiation to the cases of adultery could also be read as merely a plea for protecting an innocent wife against repudiation without a cause. Interpretations of the 'Matthean exeption' given by the early and later Church, however, were made without regard of their historical context. The Catholic theology tended to refuse seeing it as a qualification to the statement that divorce was no part of the original, God-given order of things, and that man should not separate what God has joined together.[55]

The proposition that the words of Jesus regarding divorce were open to more than one interpretation was reinforced by the fact that the admissibility in principle of divorce became controversial in Christian teaching from the very beginning. The position of the Western Church on this matter did not become uniform for centuries. The notion of the absolute inadmissibility of divorce was supported by such authorities as Tertullian,[56] St. Clement of Alexandria in the second and third centuries and later by St. Ambrose,[57] St. Jerome[58] and St. Augustine in the fourth and fifth centuries. Their strict position was adopted by various Church councils.[59] The rigorists tried to reconcile the absolute rejection of divorce with the Matthean Exception by treating it merely as a permission to separate from an adulterous wife, without the possibility to remarry.[60] However, several other councils[61] allowed remarriage after divorce for reasons of adultery.[62] Eighth-century councils even extended valid grounds for divorce and remarriage beyond adultery.[63] Although the Matthean Exception literally permitted only a husband to dismiss his adulterous wife, the Western Patristic finally unanimously rejected double standards for men and women. It was 'declared that what was not allowed to women in Christian law was equally illicit for men'.[64] The Council of Cartage (407 A.D.) even passed a canon explicitly demanding the same standards for men and women.[65]

---

55   REYNOLDS, P., *Marriage in the Western Church* (1994), p. 173.
56   Born *c.* 155/160, in Carthage, died after 220.
57   Bishop of Milan born in 339, died in 397.
58   Born *c.* 347, died in 419/420.
59   Among them those of Arles (314), Mileve (416), and Hereford (673). PHILLIPS, R., *Putting asunder* (1988), p. 20.
60   PHILLIPS, R., *Putting asunder* (1988), p. 21.
61   For instance, that of Vanner (465).
62   PHILLIPS, R., *Putting asunder* (1988), p. 21.
63   GIES, F., GIES, J., Marriage and the Family in the Middle Ages (1989), p. 57.
64   MCNAMARA, J., WEMPLE, S., 'Marriage and Divorce in Frankish Kingdom' (1976), p. 97.
65   GRUBBS, J., *Law and Family in Late Antiquity* (1995), p. 250.

It is worth noticing that in the early period, the adherents of the strict indissolubility of marriage made few efforts to combat the existence of divorce in secular law.[66] Rather, they accepted that divorce may be prohibited by divine law but allowed by civil law. According to Augustine and the majority of the patristic tradition, the indissolubility of marriage was not a legal, but rather a moral, imperative. Differing from the twelfth and thirteenth century theologians who developed the doctrine that marriage *cannot* be dissolved, the Fathers held that marriage *may* not be dissolved.[67] This can in some way explain why the Christian teaching on divorce was never implemented in the legislation of the Christian Roman emperors. The Christian Roman Emperors were eager to bring the law on divorce in line with Christian teaching.[68] However, they did not feel called upon to legally enforce the indissolubility of marriage, which was perceived at their time as a moral virtue and not as a legal prohibition.[69] The same applies to the early Germanic kingdoms. Nonetheless, as time passed the moral principle of indissolubility of marriage, except perhaps for adultery, became more and more an imperative.[70] Thus, already in this period the signs point to impending discord between Church teaching and secular law on divorce.

4.2.5. CONCLUDING REMARKS

As we have seen, important differences between the Church rules and the secular laws regarding marriage, divorce and concubinage were discernible from the outset. In this first period, however, the Church was not yet insisting on the implementation of its teaching in the secular law. It was, rather, content with the formulation of clear moral imperatives, and did not hasten to enforce them. As a result, the gap between the Christian ideal on the one hand, and secular law and social practises on the other, increased inch by inch. By the end of this period, Germanic 'kings and nobles of the

---

[66]   The few attempts to do so provided no result. The Synod of Cartage (405 A.D.) provides one of the earliest, albeit unsuccessful, examples of the Church's attempts to influence secular family law. This Synod not only forbad divorce and remarriage, but also requested Emperor Honorius to incorporate the prohibition of remarriage into the secular law. The emperor did not follow this call. (SCHILLEBEECKX, E., *Het huwelijk: aardse werkelijkheid en heilsmysterie* (1963), p. 169). The Council of Agde (506) ruled that a man could not repudiate his wife without submitting the case to the Bishop's court. The canon went largely ignored. (GIES, F., GIES, J., *Marriage and the Family in the Middle Ages* (1989), p. 57).

[67]   SCHILLEBEECKX, E., *Het huwelijk: aardse werkelijkheid en heilsmysterie* (1963), p. 195.

[68]   REYNOLDS, P., *Marriage in the Western Church* (1994), p. 64.

[69]   Ibid.

[70]   Reynolds summarises that: 'What is crucial here is not whether persons who remarried were excommunicated, but rather what they had to do to satisfy for their crime and to be taken back into the Church. (Ibid, p. 148). To this end, remarried persons had to terminate cohabitation with the second spouse, and the second marriage was invalid in the eyes of the Church and considered as adultery. 'From this point of view, penance looks more like a legal sanction than a means of atonement'. Ibid.

sixth and seventh centuries [still] kept concubines, maintained multiple wives, and repudiated one wife to take another with no more formality than a word or a gesture'.[71] As Geoffrey Nathan has put it: 'the grains of Christian thought were only sown in late antiquity; they had not yet blossomed. They took root and grew stronger later'.[72]

4.3. THE CAROLINGIAN TIME: A CRUCIAL MOMENT

The Carolingian time (eighth to tenth centuries) was a rather crucial period for the formation of the medieval canon *ius commune* of family law. Church jurisdiction in family matters was largely extended. The Church began to claim a more prominent role in the formation of marriage and in the assessment of its validity. The indissolubility of marriage became a rule of both secular and ecclesiastical law, but was not yet a part of the actual social practice.

4.3.1. EXTENSION OF THE CHURCH JURISDICTION

Under the 'theocratic regime of the Carolingians',[73] Western Europe became for some time an arena of developments typical of the Byzantine Empire. Christopher Dawson suggested that the Carolingian Empire 'was to an even greater extent than the Byzantine Empire a *church-state*',[74] as Charlemagne (reign 768-814, in 800 crowned Emperor) was not only 'the governor of the Church as well as of the state', but also 'the lawgiver of the Church' and therefore 'held two swords of spiritual and temporal authority'.[75] The sharp distinction between secular and divine marriage law started to erode under Charlemagne's rule. Charlemagne summoned Church councils and made Church law,[76] including the rules governing the conduct of the clergy and the regulation of doctrine and rituals.[77] The decisions of the Church councils were

---

[71] GIES, F., GIES, J., *Marriage and the Family in the Middle Ages* (1989), p. 53.
[72] NATHAN, G., *The Family in Late Antiquity* (2000), p. 189.
[73] REYNOLDS, P., *Marriage in the Western Church* (1994), p. 153
[74] DAWSON, C., *The Making of Europe: an Introduction to the History of European Unity* (1956), p. 190-193.
[75] According to Christopher Dawson: '[Kings'] legislation laid down the strictest and most minute rules for the conduct of the clergy and the regulation of doctrine and ritual'. DAWSON, C., *The Making of Europe: an Introduction to the History of European Unity* (1956), p. 190.
[76] BERMAN, H., *Law and Revolution. The Formation of the Western Legal Tradition* (1983), p. 66.
[77] DAWSON, C., *The Making of Europe: an Introduction to the History of European Unity* (1956), p. 190.

promulgated by the Royal Capitularies.[78] Marriage was still a subject of both jurisdictions;[79] the bishops did not yet claim the sole jurisdiction in matrimonial matters. Matrimonial trials still took place in the general assembles where the bishops and the laity came together. The bishops did not contest the competence of the lay courts in marital cases.[80] However, they started to insist that the *lex divina*[81] should be the only law applicable in matrimonial cases, irrespective of which court was to hear the case.[82] In the ninth century, the Church acquired the exclusive right to punish incest. However, Church officials had to seek the assistance of the secular powers in enforcement of their judgments.[83] The first King of Carolingian Dynasty, Pippin III the Short (reign 751-768), added worldly punishments to the Church penalties for the violation of the Church rules on marriage.[84] The Carolingian period also witnessed the Church's first attempts to gain more competence in the process of celebration of marriage. According to Edward Schillebeeckx, these attempts failed because Church solemnisation was at that time not a requirement for the validity of marriage.[85]

The process of transfer of jurisdiction in matrimonial matters to the Church in the Carolingian time was not part of any power struggle. The Carolingians conveyed jurisdiction to the Church rather indeliberately, and probably without much concern. This seems quite understandable, given the fact that in their heyday the Carolingians held almost all secular and ecclesiastical power. The weakening of the royal power after Charlemagne's death contributed to the same process, yet for opposite reasons.[86] Thus, Church competence in matrimonial matters continued to gradually extend during

---

[78]   When in 802 A.D. Charlemagne had become Emperor he implemented into practice the old wish, expressed already at the synod of Carthage of 407 A.D., that the Church rules should be promulgated by an imperial law. REYNOLDS, P., *Marriage in the Western Church* (1994), p. 154.

[79]   REYNOLDS, P., *Marriage in the Western Church* (1994), p. 152.

[80]   STUARD, S., *Women in Medieval Society* (1976), p. 104. A good example thereof is the well-known case of a noble lady called Northilda who complained at the synod of bishops and laity at Attigny in 822 about the shameful practices of her husband. The bishops refused to judge the case on the ground that laymen, 'being more familiar with marriage and with secular laws, were better qualified to handle the case'. Ibid.

[81]   Reynolds submits that 'the question of any discrepancy between the precepts of human and of divine law hardly arose. [...] In deciding whether a marriage was valid, it was ultimately God's law alone that counted'. REYNOLDS, P., *Marriage in the Western Church* (1994), p. 153.

[82]   Hincmar Archbishop of Reims, one of the most important Church officials of that time, noticed that both secular and ecclesiastical courts had to apply in marriage cases the same 'Christian laws, that is secular and ecclesiastical laws'. Cited in: REYNOLDS, P., *Marriage in the Western Church* (1994), p. 153.

[83]   MCNAMARA, J., WEMPLE, S., 'Marriage and Divorce in the Frankish Kingdom' (1976), p. 104.

[84]   RITZER, K., *Formen, Riten und religiöses Brauchtum der Eheschliessung in den christlichen Kirchen des ersten Jahrtausends* (1962), p. 259.

[85]   SCHILLEBEECKX, E., *Het huwelijk: aardse werkelijkheid en heilsmysterie* (1963), p. 185.

[86]   Ibid, p. 189.

the Carolingian times.[87] How far this process actually reached is still a matter of controversy among the scholars. Some assert that even at the end of this period, 'one can still find no notion of the exclusive competence of the ecclesiastical courts'.[88] Others hold that the exclusive competence of the Church courts in matters of marriage, illegitimacy and sexual behaviour had already been well established by the tenth century.[89]

4.3.2. MODIFICATION OF THE LAW ON MARRIAGE IN THE CAROLINGIAN TIME

At the beginning of the Carolingian era, both Church and secular activity in the field of marriage increased. Church and State put more and more emphasis on the publicity of the celebration of marriage. In 755 the Synod of Verneuil, convened by Pippin the Short, made public celebration of marriage compulsory.[90] Another Synod, held in Bavaria between 740 and 750, stated that the benediction of marriage should be given only after the announcement of marriage and the priestly enquiry in the prohibited degrees of relationships.[91] The *Capitulare* of Charlemagne of 802 made such announcement and the priestly enquiry compulsory throughout the whole Empire.[92]

In 845, the Pseudo-Isidorian Decretals[93] were brought to stage in order to justify the Church's aspirations to regulate matrimonial matters. Both these false Decretals and one of the most prominent clergymen of that time, Hincmar of Reims,[94] tried to give an ecclesiastical flavour to the Germanic requirements regarding marriage formalities.[95] According to Hincmar, a marriage was valid only if the formalities prescribed by both the Germanic and Church law were fulfilled. In this respect he mentioned the betrothal, the endowment and the delivery of the bride, required by Germanic custom,

---

87   For more on this process see: DAUDET, P., *Études sur l'histoire de la juridiction matrimoniale: les origines carolingiennes de la compétence exclusive de l'Église (France et Germanie)* (1933).

88   SCHILLEBEECKX, E., *Het huwelijk: aardse werkelijkheid en heilsmysterie* (1963), p. 190.

89   BRUNDAGE, J., *Medieval Canon Law* (1995), p. 72.

90   However, this Synod was more concerned with the publicity of celebration according to the requirements of various Germanic laws than with the publicity of the Church celebration. RITZER, K., *Formen, Riten und religiöses Brauchtum der Eheschliessung in den christlichen Kirchen des ersten Jahrtausends* (1962), p. 259.

91   Ibid, p. 260.

92   Ibid, p. 261.

93   They were falsely attributed to, among others, Pope Evaristus (around 99-107), who succeeded St. Peter. They were considered authentic until the 13th century and influenced the *Decretum Gratiani.* Ibid, p. 275-277.

94   Archbishop of Reims. Born *c.* 806, died in 881.

95   RITZER, K., *Formen, Riten und religiöses Brauchtum der Eheschliessung in den christlichen Kirchen des ersten Jahrtausends* (1962), p. 265.

and the benediction, promoted by ecclesiastical law.[96] However, the benediction could not at that time become a firm requirement for a valid marriage. The problem was that the benediction was still a privilege reserved only for 'perfect' marriages. It could not be given to a second marriage, or to a marriage of parties who had already started to cohabit. Those 'imperfect' marriages had to be celebrated solely according to the rules of civil law.

Although there had not yet been a formal schism between the Orthodox and the Catholic Churches, family law in Eastern and Western Europe had already developed quite independently. The vanishing of institutional links makes the similarities in the development of canon rules on marriage all the more striking. The *Eklogé* of Leo III (reign 717-741) described two alternate forms of marriage: a religious one – celebrated before the priest during liturgy,[97] and a civil one – celebrated before two witnesses.[98] Retention of the secular form was indispensable because before the end of the eighth century in Byzantium, as in the West, only a first marriage could be celebrated in the Church.[99] A difference is that the power struggle of the Byzantine emperors with the Church authorities led to a much earlier uniformity of marriage formation than was the case in the West. Already by the end of the tenth century, Emperor Leo VI, also known as Leo the Wise (reign 867-886), had managed to compel the Church to bless his second marriage with Zoi Karbonopsina.[100] After this precedent, the road to Church celebration of subsequent marriages was open. In 893 Leo the Wise made Church celebration a necessary requirement for the validity of marriage.[101] However, the Church kept resisting this innovation, and it took another two centuries before compulsory Church celebration was generally accepted in Byzantine.[102]

In the same period, the impediments to marriage were made rather severe in both parts of the Christian world. Two councils of Rome (721 and 744) ruled that a man could not marry those to whom he was related in the third and fourth degree, Roman style (niece or first cousin).[103] In the mid-eighth century, the prohibited degree of consanguinity was extended to the seventh degree and the prohibition became a part

---

[96]   SCHILLEBEECKX, E., *Het huwelijk: aardse werkelijkheid en heilsmysterie* (1963), p. 187.
[97]   Since Emperor Basilius I (867-886) the nuptial liturgy has had to be celebrated in public. SCHILLEBEECKX, E., *Het huwelijk: aardse werkelijkheid en heilsmysterie* (1963), p. 243.
[98]   Ibid, p. 242.
[99]   RITZER, K., *Formen, Riten und religiöses Brauchtum der Eheschliessung in den christlichen Kirchen des ersten Jahrtausends* (1962), p. 103. According to the rules of Nikifor the Confessor († 818), Patriarch of Constantinople, a second marriage should not be blessed but should be punished by deprivation of the Holy Communion for two years. *Pravila Provoslavnoi Cerkvi*, Vol II (1996), p. 574-575.
[100] RITZER, K., *Formen, Riten und religiöses Brauchtum der Eheschliessung in den christlichen Kirchen des ersten Jahrtausends* (1962), p. 103.
[101] TROITSKII, S., *Khristianskaia filisofia braka* (1995), p. 192.
[102] Ibid.
[103] GIES, F., GIES, J., *Marriage and the Family in the Middle Ages* (1989), p. 84.

of the secular Frankish law. The Church equally extended this prohibition to the spiritual kinship created by baptism or confirmation.[104] In the early ninth century, on the basis of the Pseudo-Isidorian Decretals, the Roman method of calculating degrees was substituted by the Germanic one, which resulted in the doubling of prohibited degrees.[105] Peculiarly enough, at the same time the Eastern Church independently extended the impediments up to the seventh degree of consanguinity, affinity and spiritual kinship.[106]

The consequences of this new system of impediments for the feudal society of that time were so dramatic that it is suggested that 'if it were actually adhered to, hardly anyone within the narrow circle of the aristocracy could marry at all'.[107] The motives for these excessive prohibitions are still a mystery and have no satisfactory explanation.[108] The anthropologist Goody suggested that the Church extended the list of impediments in order to render itself the power to interfere with the marriage strategies of feudal families by granting and denying dispensations and annulling incestuous marriages.[109] Goody's theory has been, however, convincingly criticised.[110]

4.3.3. CONCUBINAGE IN THE CAROLINGIAN TIME: NO STRICT MONOGAMY

The polygamy, that was rather common among the Merovingian aristocracy, disappeared completely in the Carolingian period. However, there was not yet a strict monogamy in the modern sense of this word. It remained a common practice among the Frankish aristocracy to have one or more[111] concubines alongside a lawful

---

[104]   GOODY, J., *The European Family* (2000), p. 28.

[105]   'The Roman method of computing kinship, heretofore invariably used by the Church, reckoned back from the person to the common ancestor, than forward to the proposed spouse. The Germanic method, in contrast, counted back only to the common ancestor. Thus, where in Roman reckoning first cousins were related in the fourth degree, in Germanic they were related only in the second'. GIES, F., GIES, J., *Marriage and the Family in the Middle Ages* (1989), p. 87.

[106]   In fact these restrictions went less far as the Eastern Church kept counting according to the Roman method.

[107]   GIES, F., GIES, J., *Marriage and the Family in the Middle Ages* (1989), p. 87.

[108]   Ibid, p. 83.

[109]   GOODY, J., *The Development of the Family and Marriage in Europe* (1983), p. 44-45 and 145.

[110]   'Any such Machiavellian policy presupposes a wholly indemonstrable capacity for secret, concerted action on the part of the medieval Church. It ignores the way Church policy was actually formed, openly, and typically with two steps forward and one back: the debate of a council, the declaration of a synod, the decision of a Pope'. GIES, F., GIES, J., *Marriage and the Family in the Middle Ages* (1989), p. 84.

[111]   TOUBERT, P., 'The Carolingian Moment' (1996), p. 398.

wife.[112] In the Carolingian time, the Church's attitude towards concubinage became less tolerant. A number of local Church councils[113] proclaimed concubinage immoral and illicit.[114] The Church also sought to promulgate punishments against adulterous, incestuous, and clerical concubinage.[115] Byzantine law had already forbade concubinage altogether in 887.[116] After its accession to Christianity, Russia imported this prohibitive attitude towards concubinage as a part of its transplanted Byzantine law.

4.3.4. DIVORCE IN THE CAROLINGIAN TIME: INDISSOLUBILITY PREVAILS IN THEORY

Indissolubility of marriage became a very central issue at the time of the Carolingians. Unlike before, it is peculiar that during this time the Church displayed a readiness to alleviate its pressure for indissolubility.[117] The State, on the contrary, took the lead in the struggle to outlaw divorce. The prologue was Pippin the Short's law, promulgating the decree of the Council of Soissons (744), which prohibited remarriage during a divorced spouse's lifetime. The only exception to this prohibition was for a man who repudiated his wife due to adultery.[118] It is, however, assumed that in practice the effect of this prohibition was negligible. It is submitted that 'the formulas of the period amply demonstrated that the practice of divorce by mutual consent was as popular as ever'.[119] In the last half of the eighth century a number of Church councils[120] showed a tendency towards less rigorous divorce laws by extending the grounds for unilateral divorce, with a possibility of remarriage, beyond adultery. The admitted grounds were: the servile status of one of the spouses, leprosy, lack of consent, impotence, and the spouse's choice for religious life.[121] Divorce by

---

[112] Charlemagne himself is a good illustration of the matrimonial practices of his time. 'In his early years, Charlemagne had dismissed a concubine in order to contract a political marriage with a Lombard princess; a year later he divorced the princess, apparently because she was barren. But in the 780s and 790s, he enacted rigorous legislation prohibiting divorce on any grounds. He then set the example, contracting three more marriages and living with each wife until her death (but comforting his old age with four concubines)'. GIES, F., GIES, J., *Marriage and the Family in the Middle Ages* (1989), p. 88.

[113] Of Rome (826), of Mainz (851), of Rome (853).

[114] VANDENBERGHE, H., *De juridische betekenis van het concubinaat* (1970), p. 19.

[115] Ibid.

[116] VOLTERRA, E., *La conception du mariage d'après les juristes romains* (1940), p. 676.

[117] Roderick Phillips notices that the church in this period 'was moving towards a less rigorous interpretation of the biblical divorce texts'. PHILLIPS, R., *Putting Asunder* (1988), p. 24.

[118] MCNAMARA, J., WEMPLE, S., '*Marriage and Divorce in Frankish Kingdom*' (1976), p. 102.

[119] Ibid, p. 103.

[120] Compiègne in 757, Verberie in 758 or 768.

[121] GIES, F., GIES, J., *Marriage and the Family in the Middle Ages* (1989), p. 57.

mutual consent, although still a rather common practice at the time, was resolutely rejected.[122]

The final victory of the principle of indissolubility of marriage was largely the result of Charlemagne's efforts to strengthen marriage law; a policy that went directly against the aforementioned trend within the Church itself. In 789, the Ninth Synod of Carthage, conveyed by Charlemagne, prohibited the remarriage of any person who had been repudiated by his or her spouse for whatever reason. Eight years later, the Council of Friuli (797) ruled that not even adultery can dissolve marriage, but only justify a separation *a mensa et thoro*.[123] This rule was incorporated in Charlemagne's Capitulary in 802, and thus became the law of the whole Empire. Later, the Roman Synod of 826 allowed an innocent party a divorce with remarriage in case of adultery. This decision reveals that the Church continued to hesitate about the dissolubility of marriage in cases of adultery. However, three years later the son of Charlemagne, Louis I the Pious (reign 814-840), reversed the decision of the Synod. Four Frankish councils convened in 829 ruled that adultery did not dissolve the marriage bond. In the same year Louis introduced a public penance for a man who repudiated his wife.[124] By the end of the ninth century, a consensus on indissolubility of marriage was reached in both the secular and the ecclesiastical codes of the Western world.[125] As Susan Stuart summed up, 'for three hundred years, after Augustine had enunciated the absolute indissolubility of marriage, the Church had hesitated on the question, but now a secular law upheld it for all Christians'.[126]

The winning outcome of indissolubility in the Western Church was by no means an 'inevitable deduction from Jesus' teaching'.[127] As Philip Reynolds stated '[o]ne should not suppose that Jesus' words in themselves determined the Western Church's strict prohibition of divorce and remarriage'.[128] The Church was always quite selective in endorsing Biblical commandments as binding law or deeming them no more than moral premises.[129] It is not easy to explain why the medieval Catholic Church finally decided to totally prohibit divorce, ambiguously dealt with in the Scripture, and almost

---

[122] Ibid, p. 88.
[123] ('From bed and board') PHILLIPS, R., *Putting Asunder* (1988), p. 24.
[124] Ibid.
[125] Ibid.
[126] STUARD, S., *Women in Medieval Society* (1976), p. 104.
[127] Indeed interpretation of the same words led the Eastern Church and later the Protestants to the restrictive admission of divorce. REYNOLDS, P., *Marriage in the Western Church* (1994), p. 148.
[128] Ibid.
[129] Reynolds also noticed that: 'While the Western Church rigorously applied Jesus' condemnation of divorce and remarriage in Matthew 5:31-32, the Church failed to apply his categorical prohibition of oaths in Matthew 5:33-37'. Ibid, p. XXIV.

at the same time developed the theory of a 'just war', clearly running against the rather clear-cut commandment that one shall not kill.

The Byzantine example demonstrates that indissolubility of marriage was not the only conclusion that could be derived from the scripture. The Orthodox law on divorce was finalised in the *Nomocanon* of XIV Titles,[130] which became binding throughout the Orthodox Church in the tenth century. The indissolubility of marriage was not a part of this law. The grounds for divorce were partly derived from Justinian's *Novellae* and included adultery, some offences considered analogical to it,[131] as well as the commitment of a crime punishable by capital punishment, impotence, and the choice for a monastic life.[132] This *Nomocanon* became the leading document of the medieval canon law of all Orthodox Churches.[133] After the Christianisation of Russia in 988, the Byzantine canon law was received in Russia, and the *Nomocanon* also became applicable there.[134] However, the grounds for divorce under Russian canon law, identical to the Byzantine ones in the books, were not the same in practice.[135]

4.3.5. ILLEGITIMATE CHILDREN IN THE CAROLINGIAN TIME: A TRANSITORY PERIOD

Under the influence of the Church, which tried to eliminate every form of sexual intercourse outside marriage, the position of illegitimate children worsened.[136] As the Church was not favouring concubinage, the earlier distinction between the children of concubines and other illegitimate children was not maintained.[137] Instead, the term 'natural' children came to be applied to the simple illegitimate children in order to distinguish them from children born from adulterous and incestuous unions. Natural children by a free-born mother, who were recognised by their father, could still inherit from him, but only by default of legitimate offspring.[138] Even succession to the throne

---

[130] Collection finalised in 883 by the Byzantine Patriarch Photy.

[131] ZAGOROVSKII, I., *Kurs semeinogo prava* (2003), p. 107.

[132] *Pravila Provoslavnoi Cerkvi*, Vol I (1996), p. 580-581.

[133] For instance, it was also the main source of canon law of Serbia and Bulgaria.

[134] ZAGOROVSKII, I., *Kurs semeinogo prava* (2003), p. 103.

[135] For instance, divorce for wifely adultery, compulsory under Byzantine law, was only compulsory for priests under Russian law. Some grounds, like a wife's attendance at a theatre or circus without her husband's consent, were never applied in Russia due to the absence of both theatres and circuses. At the same time, divorce on the ground of a choice for monastic life became very popular in Russia and acquired rather excessive forms, as for the purposes of divorce the wives were often forced by their husbands into nunneries against their will. ZAGOROVSKII, I., *Kurs semeinogo prava* (2003), p. 105-110.

[136] HÜBNER, R., *History of Germanic Private Law* (1918), p. 672.

[137] JOLOWICZ, H., *Roman Foundations of Modern Law* (1961), p. 199.

[138] HÜBNER, R., *History of Germanic Private Law* (1918), p. 671-672.

was not impossible for a 'bastard'. Thus, the illegitimate Arnulf[139] could succeed his uncle to the German Throne,[140] and the 'bastard' William the Conqueror[141] could inherit the Duchy of Normandy.[142]

Illegitimate children were also still heirs in Russia, albeit of the second rank. Thus Art. XXXVII of the most important source of Russian medieval secular law, *Russkaia Pravda*,[143] provided that only 'the children born from a slave-mother were excluded from the succession, but gained instead freedom together with their mother'.[144] With the advent of Christianity, Russian law also adopted the notion of children born of an adulterous union. Thus, a son of King Vladimir and the King's brother's wife was called an 'issue of adultery'.[145]

Denying illegitimate children the rights of full born children, both Catholic and Orthodox canon law made the father liable for alimentation of the illegitimate children.[146]

4.3.6. MATRIMONIAL PROPERTY LAW IN THE CAROLINGIAN TIME

Contrary to its involvement in marriage, divorce, concubinage and illegitimacy, the Church maintained almost no interest in matrimonial property. Thus, matrimonial property law remained entirely within the domain of the secular law. However, this area also underwent considerable evolution due to the economic and political consolidation that came up in the framework of the 'Carolingian Renaissance'.

The rudimental forms of matrimonial property law from the period of the Germanic folk-laws crystallised in the Carolingian time into two distinctive property regimes: that of the community of administration and that of the community of property.[147] Some parts of the Empire clung to the old folk-law tradition and preserved the distinct separation between the estates of husband and wife. The only elements of community

---

[139] Arnulf, in 887, deposed his uncle Charles the Fat, the last Carolingian Emperor. This act led to the definite disintegration of the Carolingian Empire, as many parts of it refused to recognise Anulf's rule.
[140] BURGE, W., *Commentaries on Colonial and Foreign Laws*. V. II (1908), p. 330.
[141] Duke of Normandy (1035–87) and King of England (1066–87).
[142] HÜBNER, R., *History of Germanic Private Law* (1918), p. 671–672.
[143] In all probability compiled during the reign of the King Jaroslav (1019–1054).
[144] KARAMZIN, N., *The History of the State of Russia* (2003), p. 108.
[145] NEVOLIN, K., *Istoria rossiiskikh grazhdanskikh zakonov* (1851), p. 306.
[146] ZHISHMAN, J., *Das Eherecht der orientalischen Kirche* (1864), p. 724.
[147] HÜBNER, R., *History of Germanic Private Law* (1918), p. 629.

were the community of possession, usufruct and administration, exercised by the husband.[148] Other principalities had already developed a genuine system of community of property. In these areas a single collective estate of husband and wife was created under the administration of the husband.[149] The scope of this common estate differed, however, from place to place. Thus, it is possible to distinguish different forms of community, stretching from limited community to universal community.[150]

Despite the emerging division of regimes, the general developments in the field of matrimonial property were the same everywhere in Carolingian Europe and were fairly independent of the type of matrimonial property regime. One of the sources of the wife's property, the ancient Germanic morning gift from husband to wife, merged almost everywhere with the dower.[151] The dower, 'formerly an outright transfer of property from husband to wife, was restricted to her lifetime possession, received by her only when the husband died, and in the absence of children reverting to the husband's family'.[152] Dowry received by a wife from her parents, which formerly was an independent property of the wife, became part of the family estate in the Carolingian times, inheritable by the husband and the children.[153] The husband acquired even stronger rights to possess, administer and enjoy the fruits of the wife's estate. Therefore, the community of administration on the part of the husband became a common feature of all property systems of that time.[154]

4.4. THE HIGH MIDDLE AGES: THE *IUS COMMUNE* COMPLETED

4.4.1. THE VICTORY OF THE CHURCH OVER THE WORLDLY POWERS

In the course of the eleventh to thirteenth centuries, the formation of the medieval family canon *ius commune* of family law in Western Europe was actually completed. Marriage, divorce, illegitimacy and many other family matters definitively passed into

---

[148] Ibid.
[149] Ibid.
[150] Ibid.
[151] BRISSAUD, J., *A History of French Private Law* (1912), p. 755.
[152] GIES, F., GIES, J., *Marriage and the Family in the Middle Ages* (1989), p. 88. That meant, among others, that a wife could no longer bequeath to the children of a second marriage the lands of her first husband that were received as a dower. Ibid.
[153] Ibid.
[154] Ibid.

the exclusive jurisdiction of the Roman Catholic Church.[155] By this time, the Church had all but finalised the elaboration of a system of canon family laws, largely based on the Church's own principles regarding marriage, divorce and the family. This law exclusively and uniformly governed the bulk of family relationships everywhere from the British Islands in the West to Poland in the East, and from Scandinavia in the North to Italy in the South.

Such development became possible in the first place due to important changes in the position and the structure of the Church itself. These changes came about as a result of the Pope's victory in the Investiture Struggle and the Gregorian Reform. The significance of the Investiture Struggle went far beyond the mere question of who had the authority of investiture of the bishops, the Pope or a worldly sovereign. Some two hundred years before, Charlemagne 'regarded the Pope as his chaplain, and plainly told Leo III that it is the King's business to govern and to defend the Church and that it is the Pope's duty to pray for it'.[156] In 1075, Pope Gregory VII (pontificate 1073–85) claimed political and legal supremacy of the papacy not only over the entire Church, but also over the worldly rulers.[157] This claim cost the Church fifty years of war with the German Emperor. In 1122, during the Concordat of Worms, Church supremacy was recognised in most of continental Europe.[158] In 1170 the Pope's claim was also imposed on England.[159] As result of the Gregorian Reform, the Church not only acquired independency from the secular powers, but also obtained a firm structural unity. At the beginning of this period the ecclesiastical courts still remained 'ad hoc affairs and had not yet developed a systematic structure',[160] while near the end a complete system of professional Church courts had been developed.[161] The Pope

---

[155] The main events of this period were accurately summarised by Michael Sheehan: 'As the first millennium came to an end [...] marriage, hitherto essentially an institution regulated by family custom and, to a certain extent, by Roman and Barbarian civil law, passed more and more into the jurisdiction of the bishop. The older pastoral attitude towards marriage, one involving instruction, blessing, exhortation, and the occasional excommunication when abuse became intolerable, was no longer considered adequate. Instead, as part of a general re-examination of Christian life by canonists and theologians, marriage was analysed in detail: the creation of the marriage bond, the role of consent, the qualifications of the principles of the relationship, the ends and the qualities of the married state all were subject to careful scrutiny. A collecting and sorting, ordering an interpretation of patristic literature went through the late eleventh end twelfth centuries. [...] By the 1150s, the first syntheses, the one canonistic, the other theological, were available in the *Decretum Gratiani* and the *Libri IV Sententiarum* of Peter Lombard'. SHEEHAN, M., *Marriage, Family, and Law in Medieval Europe* (1996), p. 91.

[156] DAWSON, C., *The Making of Europe: an Introduction to the History of European Unity* (1956), p. 191.

[157] BERMAN, H., *Law and Revolution. The Formation of the Western Legal Tradition* (1983), p. 87.

[158] Ibid.

[159] Ibid.

[160] BRUNDAGE, J., *Medieval Canon Law* (1995), p. 120.

[161] For a synopsis on the development of the system of ecclesiastical courts see: BRUNDAGE, J., *Medieval Canon Law* (1995), p. 120-126.

definitively became the supreme ecclesiastical legislator and the supreme judge of the system of the ecclesiastic courts.[162] Around 1140, the canon law was 'harmonised' in Gratian's *Decretum*,[163] which provided the Church courts with a methodical compilation of canon law. These developments made the Church capable to enact, promulgate and enforce uniform legislation upon the whole of Western Christendom.

After simmering for centuries, the schism between the Orthodox Church and the Roman Catholic Church became final in 1054. In the Orthodox world, the early Russian Kingdom had almost eclipsed Byzantium as the most important centre of Eastern Christianity. Although until the fifteenth century the Russian Church was formally dependent from the Patriarchat of Constantinople,[164] this dependency became more and more nominal during the High Middle Ages.[165] Thus, while the Catholic Church consolidated its power, the Orthodox Church exemplified the tendency to partition. The Russian translation of the *Nomocanon*, supplemented by the rulings of the Russian kings, was incorporated into the *Kormchia Kniga*,[166] which became the main source of Russian family law. The substance of the Orthodox canon law was, however, almost identical in all Orthodox countries and very similar to its Western counterpart.

4.4.2. CHURCH JURISDICTION IN FAMILY MATTERS: ALL BUT EXCLUSIVE

In the High Middle Ages the applicability of canon law was extended so far[167] that it became possible to speak of an entire canon family law.[168] The Church had indisputably acquired the exclusive jurisdiction in respect of most of matrimonial matters, as well as over the civil consequences of marriage.[169] The ecclesiastical courts primarily decided questions involving the formation, the validity, the nullity, and the dissolution of marriage and the separation of the spouses. At the same time, their competence was extended to such marriage-related issues as legitimacy of the children, maintenance,

---

[162] BERMAN, H., *Law and Revolution. The Formation of the Western Legal Tradition* (1983), p. 99.
[163] Or *Decreta*, the full name of the compilation is: *Concordantia discordantium canonum*, which literally means 'Harmonising of Divergent Texts'.
[164] Metropolitan MAKARIY, *The History of the Russian Church*, book IV, part I (1996), p. 11.
[165] Ibid, p. 11-21.
[166] A 13th century Slav collection of canons officially adopted in Russia, Serbia and Bulgaria. For more details see: ibid, p. 80-81.
[167] BRUNDAGE, J., *Medieval Canon Law* (1995), p. 71.
[168] 'If there is one area of western law where the influence of the canon law is unquestionable, it is marriage law, and through it a significant part of family law'. MARTÍNEZ-TORRÓN, J., *Anglo-American Law and Canon Law. Canonical Roots of the Common Law Tradition* (1998), p. 93.
[169] SCHILLEBEECKX, E., *Het huwelijk: aardse werkelijkheid en heilsmysterie* (1963), p. 190.

child support, and custody.[170] Marital property remained, however, in the competence of the lay courts.[171] The extension of the ecclesiastic competence affected the whole of Europe. England was no exception;[172] however, there the boundaries between the secular and the ecclesiastical jurisdictions were defined in a bitter confrontation.[173] Since a definite separation between the ecclesiastic and the lay courts was made by William the Conqueror in the early eleventh century,[174] those two jurisdictions had to make clear-cut rules to divide their competence. Eventually a state of 'symbiotic competition' was achieved.[175] If a King's secular court, while hearing a civil case came across, for instance, a question of the legitimacy of the heir, or of the validity of the marriage, according to Glanvill, the secular court respected the exclusive competence of the ecclesiastical court in these matters. In such cases the King's court normally suspended the case and asked the Court Christian to decide upon these issues first.[176] There was, therefore, a necessary close cooperation between the lay and the Church courts.

In the Orthodox East, the competence of the Church in matrimonial matters also expanded. Many developments in East and West during the High Middle Ages were surprisingly similar. In Russia, Vladimir's Charter, a document that was in all probability false,[177] was invoked to justify the Church's claim of exclusive competence in family matters.[178] This episode strikingly resembles the role of the Pseudo-Isidorian Decretals in the West in the ninth century to justify the Papacy's claims of exclusive competence in matrimonial matters. In Russia the competence of the ecclesiastical authorities in family matters became even broader than in Western Europe. The Church law came to govern not only marriage, divorce, nullity of marriage and illegitimacy, but also all matrimonial property disputes.[179] Matrimonial property cases

---

170   BRUNDAGE, J., *Medieval Canon Law* (1995), p. 74.

171   Ibid, p. 71-72.

172   For example, Frederic William Maitland clearly states that since the 11-12 century the marriage law of England was the canon law. POLLOCK, F., MAITLAND, F., *The History of English Law before the Time of Edward I*, Vol. II (1952), p. 370.

173   HELMHOLZ, R., '*Conflicts Between Religious and Secular Law: Common Themes in the English Experience*' (1991), p. 707-728.

174   POLLOCK, F., MAITLAND, F., *The History of English Law before the Time of Edward I*, Vol. II (1952), p. 367.

175   BRUNDAGE, J., *Medieval Canon Law* (1995), p. 97.

176   POLLOCK, F., MAITLAND, F., *The History of English Law before the Time of Edward I*, Vol. II (1952), p. 367.

177   The Charter attributed the bestowing of the Church with the competence to govern matrimonial matters to King Vladimir, who Christianised Russia in 988. KARAMZIN, N., *The History of the State of Russia* (2003), p. 84.

178   In the fourteenth century, another false document, the Church Charter of Jaroslav, was made in order to reinforce the ecclesiastical claims. KARAMZIN, N., *The History of the State of Russia* (2003), p. 108.

179   ZAGOROVSKII, I., *Kurs semeinogo prava* (2003), p. 198.

were dealt with by special Church courts. Those courts applied canon law, but their judges were mainly recruited among the laymen.[180]

4.4.3.   MARRIAGE LAW IN THE HIGH MIDDLE AGES: VICTORY OF THE CONSENSUAL THEORY

The main events of the period in the field of marriage law were the contest between the consensual and the coital theories of marriage and the development of the doctrine of marriage as a sacrament. The consensual theory evolved under the influence of the revival of Roman law in the eleventh century.[181] The consensual theory in its purest form emphasised the contractual elements of marriage and did not regard sexual intercourse between the spouses as constitutive for the creation of a valid marriage.[182] The main proponents of the consensual theory were the theologians.[183] The coital theory, by contrast, held that it was sexual intercourse which made a man and a woman 'one flesh'. Therefore, consummation was, in the view of its adherents, of more importance for the creation of the marriage bond than the consensus of the parties.[184] This theory was mainly elaborated by canonists.[185]

At the beginning of the twelfth century, Gratian summarised in his *Decretum* the main ideas of the proponents of the coital theory. Almost simultaneously, Peter Lombard[186] recapitulated in his *Libri IV Sententiarum* the concepts of the consensual theory. Gratian's abridgment, however, was in a way an attempt to reconcile both rivalling standpoints.[187] According to Gratian, marriage was created in two stages. During the first stage the parties declared their intention to marry each other; during the second stage they 'sealed' their marriage by sexual intercourse. Although after the first stage they were already held to be married, only after the second did they become 'two in one flesh'.[188] Thus, consensus constituted marriage but consummation made it indissoluble. Gratian also tried to reconcile the Church's emphasis on the personal position of the prospective spouses and the social custom that required the parental

---

[180]   Metropolitan MAKARIY, *The History of the Russian Church*, book IV, part II (1996), p. 106.

[181]   Hugo of St. Victor based the consensual theory on the definition ascribed to Ulpian: '*nuptias non concubitus sed consensus fecit*' (see note 21 in Chapter 3).

[182]   BRUNDAGE, J., 'Marriage and Sexuality in the Decretals of Pope Alexander III' (1986), p. 61.

[183]   In the period of the early scholastics, such authorities as Isidor of Seville supported the consensual theory. SCHILLEBEECKX, E., *Het huwelijk: aardse werkelijkheid en heilsmysterie* (1963), p. 198-199.

[184]   BRUNDAGE, J., 'Marriage and Sexuality in the Decretals of Pope Alexander III' (1986), p. 61-62.

[185]   Prominent scholars, like Hinkmar of Reims and later Ivo of Chartres, held that only the consummation made marriage indissoluble. SCHILLEBEECKX, E., *Het huwelijk: aardse werkelijkheid en heilsmysterie* (1963), p. 198-199.

[186]   Bishop of Paris. Born in 1100, died in 1160.

[187]   BRUNDAGE, J., 'Marriage and Sexuality in the Decretals of Pope Alexander III' (1986), p. 65.

[188]   Ibid.

consent to marriage. Therefore, Gratian, on the one hand, opposed forced marriages because, 'where there is to be union of bodies there ought to be union of spirits, and therefore no unwilling person is to be joined to another'.[189] At the same time he stated that marriage without parental consent was valid, but illicit.[190]

According to the consensual theory, digested by Peter Lombard, even an unconsummated marriage was final and indissoluble.[191] Lombard distinguished two forms of marital consent. The consent *de futuro,* was formulated in the future tense and expressed the intent to marry in the future. This kind of consent was often exchanged by the parties during the betrothal. The other form of consent, the consent *de presenti,* was formulated in the present tense and expressed the intent to enter into marriage from that very moment on. In Lombard's view, the consent *de presenti* alone was sufficient for the creation of a marriage bond.[192] Moreover, Lombard taught that the consent of the parties was all that was necessary for the creation of a valid marriage. In his consensual theory, 'no essential role was reserved for third parties, be they family or lord'.[193]

Through the legislation of Pope Alexander III (pontificate 1159–81), a mitigated version of the consensual theory of Peter Lombard acquired the status of the official doctrine of the Catholic Church.[194] However, the consensual theory that was finally adopted as the official doctrine was heavily influenced by the compromise view suggested by Gratian. Consent was rendered crucial for the formation of marriage, as without it no marriage could be created. It had to be given freely. No special formula for expressing it was prescribed. Consent *de presenti* already constituted a valid marriage. Consent *de futuro* was enough for creating legal marriage, even if no formalities were observed, provided that the parties had sealed it by consummation.[195] More importantly, although a purely consensual marriage had already been rendered indissoluble, the Church still had the power to terminate it under certain very limited circumstances. Only after consummation was every possibility of divorce definitively ruled out.[196] Thus, while stressing the importance of consent, Alexander in fact 'also laid major emphasis upon consummation, because it was required if the marriage was to become in strict sense indissoluble'.[197]

---

189   Cited in: SHEEHAN, M., *Marriage, Family, and Law in Medieval Europe* (1996), p. 96.
190   SHEEHAN, M., *Marriage, Family, and Law in Medieval Europe* (1996), p. 96-97.
191   SCHILLEBEECKX, E., *Het huwelijk: aardse werkelijkheid en heilsmysterie* (1963), p. 201-202.
192   BRUNDAGE, J., 'Marriage and Sexuality in the Decretals of Pope Alexander III' (1986), p. 62-63.
193   SHEEHAN, M., *Marriage, Family, and Law in Medieval Europe* (1996), p. 98.
194   SHEEHAN, M., *Marriage, Family, and Law in Medieval Europe* (1996), p. 96.
195   BRUNDAGE, J., 'Marriage and Sexuality in the Decretals of Pope Alexander III' (1986), p. 62-63.
196   SCHILLEBEECKX, E., *Het huwelijk: aardse werkelijkheid en heilsmysterie* (1963), p. 203-204
197   BRUNDAGE, J., 'Marriage and Sexuality in the Decretals of Pope Alexander III' (1986), p. 76.

However, assenting to Gratian's compromise in respect of consummation, the official doctrine uncompromisingly ruled out the requirement of parental consent. This aspect constitutes the main difference from the Roman concept of consensual marriage. Although the consensual theory was based on Roman law, pre-classical and early classical Roman law primarily required the consent of the *pater familias* of the parties under power, and only then of the parties themselves,[198] while the consensual theory that came to prevail in medieval canon law required the consent of only the parties themselves.

Church policy in the High Middle Ages with regard to marriage was to some extent contradictive. On the one hand, giving priority to the free will of the parties, the Church adopted the consensual theory leading to the recognition of purely consensual clandestine marriages entered into without any formalities. On the other hand, the Church took great pains to reinforce ecclesiastic control over marriage and to strengthen the rules requiring Church solemnisation of marriage. In the framework of these efforts at the beginning of the twelfth century, the secular marriage ceremony was gradually replaced by the ecclesiastical ritual including the nuptial mass and priestly benediction.[199] The parish priest was granted a more prominent role in the marriage ceremony; he took the place of the father in the ceremony of delivering the bride to the groom.[200] Therefore, as Michael Sheehan puts it, the marriage solemnisation 'was removed from the family circle to a public forum, the place of meeting of the local community considered in its religious capacity. Leadership in the proceedings had been assumed by the head of that community, the parish priest. Thus an important element in the family control of marriage was diminished'.[201] In order to strengthen the ecclesiastical discipline of marriage, the Fourth Lateran Council (1215) extended the requirement of the publication of the banns of marriage to the whole of Western Christendom. The banns were supposed to be published with the purpose to call upon everyone to make public any impediment to marriage he or she might know. Amplifying the enquiry into the marriage impediments, the Church, however, simultaneously made the substantive rules regarding the impediments less rigid. The excessive system of prohibitions introduced in the Carolingian period turned to be absolutely impractical. Therefore the same Fourth Lateran Council brought the prohibited degrees back from the seventh to the fourth degree.[202]

---

[198] At least that of the groom. See Chapter 3, Section 3.2.2.
[199] SHEEHAN, M., *Marriage, Family, and Law in Medieval Europe* (1996), p. 111.
[200] RITZER, K., *Formen, Riten und religiöses Brauchtum der Eheschliessung in den christlichen Kirchen des ersten Jahrtausends* (1962), p. 333.
[201] SHEEHAN, M., *Marriage, Family, and Law in Medieval Europe* (1996), p. 112.
[202] GIES, F., GIES, J., Marriage and the Family in the Middle Ages (1989), p. 140.

Any marriage that was not publicly solemnised in the Church after publication of the banns was regarded a clandestine marriage. The consensual theory made it valid but illicit, and the Church tried to discourage it by a system of ecclesiastical punishments. The Fourth Lateran Council took special efforts to discourage clandestine marriages and to forbid the priests to officiate them.[203] The application of sanctions differed from place to place, however. In France for instance, the parties to a clandestine marriage were often automatically excommunicated.[204] In England, a clergyman who participated in such marriage risked suspension from office.[205] Still, in spite of all discouragements the number of clandestine marriages continued to rise.[206] Charles Donahue sums up the paradoxical situation that resulted from the acceptance of the consensual theory: 'The proper way to get married, as Alexander and innumerable councils both local and general emphasised, was publicly and in the face of the Church with the blessing of the parish priest, following the publication of the banns, which called upon anyone to declare any impediment which might prevent the union. But according to Alexander's rules, marriages which had none of those characteristics were valid'.[207]

The contradiction between adherence to the consensual theory and the aspiration to strengthen ecclesiastic control over marriage also marked the Western doctrine of marriage as a sacrament. Although marriage had already been called a sacrament by St. Augustine in the sixth century, it was only in the High Middle Ages that this doctrine acquired systematic theological expression.[208] In line with the consensual theory, it was considered that it was not the priests, but the parties themselves that gave sacrament to each other. According to the influential theologian Hugo of St. Victor, even a marriage of two pagans was therefore sacral. Marriage was seen as a sacral symbol of the unification of Christ and the Church.[209]

In the Orthodox East, the consensual theory never managed to prevail. As the Orthodox Church of the Byzantine Empire had already become completely independent of Rome by 1054, the reforms of Alexander III did not reach it. As was mentioned above, the efforts of the Byzantine Emperors to make Church solemnisation

---

[203]   BRUNDAGE, J., 'Concubinage and Marriage in Medieval Canon Law' (1975), p. 8.
[204]   DONAHUE, C., 'The Canon Law on the Formation of Marriage and Social Practice in the Later Middle Ages' (1983), p. 153.
[205]   Ibid.
[206]   One of the best examples is a fifteenth-century legend of Romeo and Juliet, which constituted the plot of the famous Shakespeare's tragedy.
[207]   DONAHUE, C., 'The Canon Law on the Formation of Marriage and Social Practice in the Later Middle Ages' (1983), p. 145.
[208]   SCHILLEBEECKX, E., Het huwelijk: aardse werkelijkheid en heilsmysterie (1963), p. 233.
[209]   Ibid, p. 219. 'The marital love is the sacrament of the spiritual love between God and the soul; the sexual relationship is the sacrament of the bodily (carnal) unity between Christ and the Church. Also without sexual relationship the images of Christ and the Church can be found in the marital affection itself'. Ibid. p. 222.

compulsory for all marriages achieved its goal around the twelfth century.[210] Consensus was regarded as an indispensable element of the formation of marriage, but unlike in the Catholic West, it was not the consensus but the priestly blessing that made the marriage a sacrament. The tendency to attribute the sacral character of marriage to the benediction was also present in the West, but the dominance of the consensual theory of marriage prevented it from prevailing.[211] Therefore, in the Orthodox law the priestly blessing acquired the status of the second constitutive element of marriage alongside the consensus.[212] In Russia, however, the law in action differed from the law in the books. Although the Russian Church always insisted on the free consent of the parties to a marriage, it was unable to implement this rule in practice.[213] By having already made Church celebration a firm requirement of the validity of marriage from an early stage, the Orthodox Church did not go through the period of ambiguity that is characteristic for the Western canon law of that period. It can be therefore concluded that the Orthodox Church straight away developed the rigid rules on formation of marriage that were introduced in the West only by the Council of Trent in the sixteenth century.

4.4.4. CONCUBINAGE IN THE HIGH MIDDLE AGES

Concubinage persisted through the High Middle Ages. Compared to the Carolingian times, the situation was, however, changed. It was no longer acceptable to have multiple concubines, or both a wife and a concubine,[214] but it was widely believed that an unmarried man was allowed to comfort himself with a concubine.[215] Christopher Brooke suggested that difference in social standing between a legal wife and a concubine grew sharper in the eleventh century.[216] However, the victory of the consensual theory of marriage made it extremely difficult to distinguish between a pure

---

[210] TROITSKII, S., *Khristianskaia filisofia braka* (1995), p. 192.

[211] SCHILLEBEECKX, E., *Het huwelijk: aardse werkelijkheid en heilsmysterie* (1963), p. 216-217.

[212] NEUHAUS, P. et al, 'The Family in Religious and Customary Laws' (1983), p. 16-17.

[213] The practice of arranged marriages was facilitated by the usage of betrothing children in their infancy and the custom that a groom should not see a bride before wedding. ZAGOROVSKII, I., *Kurs semeinogo prava* (2003), p. 214.

[214] BECKER, H.-J., 'Die nichteheliche Lebensgemeinschaft (Konkubinat) in der Rechtsgeschichte' (1978), p. 22.

[215] Gratian included in his *Decretum* a text from the canon of the Council of Toledo (400 A.D.) that allowed an unmarried man who had a concubine to receive communion, so long as he was loyal to one woman, be she wife or concubine. 'It has been argued that Gratian quite misunderstood the intent of this canon and probably in fact he did. But, misunderstood or not, the canon was included in the *Decretum* and thenceforth stood as a witness that concubinage was tolerated by the Church and that it might in fact be considered the functional equivalent of marriage' BRUNDAGE, J., 'Concubinage and Marriage in Medieval Canon Law' (1975), p. 4.

[216] BROOKE, N., *The Medieval Idea of Marriage* (1989), p. 64.

consensual informal marriage and a concubinage.[217] The term 'concubine' was also rather ambivalent. On the one hand, the word concubine was used for a temporary, non-marital union without the intention of continuance. In this sense concubinage was no more than a particular a kind of fornication. On the other hand, the word 'concubine' was used for a durable informal union, characterised by permanence and even by marital affection.[218] Gratian saw concubinage in the latter sense 'as an imperfect, informal marriage, marriage which lacked legal formalities and full legal consequences, but which was nonetheless a true and valid marriage'.[219] It is very possible that concubinage with marital affection was even rendered as indissoluble as marriage. Hence, in the late eleventh century Ivo of Chartres argued 'that if a man treated a concubine as a wife, their union was indissoluble. They could obtain separation for "carnal reasons", but could not remarry'.[220] Other canonists suggested that concubinage was allowed only by civil law, and was illicit according to ecclesiastical law.[221] In the aftermath of the Gregorian reforms that firmed clerical celibacy, in the thirteenth century clerical concubinage was forbidden under pain of excommunication.[222] Lay concubinage was also condemned by various regional French councils in the thirteenth century;[223] however, there was still no general prohibition. Concubinage became definitively outlawed only during the Council of Trent in 1563.[224]

4.4.5. DIVORCE IN THE HIGH MIDDLE AGES: INDISSOLUBILITY PREVAILS ALSO IN PRACTICE

Although indissolubility of marriage had generally prevailed in theory both in ecclesiastical and secular law in the Carolingian period, the actual practises were still rather different. As Christopher Brooke puts it: 'the kings sought marriage above all to provide themselves with male heirs and for personal satisfaction; if the wife was unsatisfactory she was changed'.[225] Robert the Pious (reign 996-1031) was divorced twice and every French King from Philip I (reign 1060-1108) to Philip II Augustus (reign 1180-1223) had at least one divorce.[226] Two of these divorces became famous

---

217   BRUNDAGE, J., 'Concubinage and Marriage in Medieval Canon Law' (1975), p. 8.
218   Gratian went so far that he even attributed to concubinage in the latter sense the quality of marital affection which Roman jurists applied only to marriage. BRUNDAGE, J., 'Concubinage and Marriage in Medieval Canon Law' (1975), p. 3-4.
219   Ibid.
220   PHILLIPS, R., Putting asunder (1988), p. 30.
221   BRUNDAGE, J., 'Concubinage and Marriage in Medieval Canon Law' (1975), p. 5.
222   BECKER, H-J., 'Die nichteheliche Lebensgemeinschaft (Konkubinat) in der Rechtsgeschichte' (1978), p. 23.
223   Ibid, p. 24.
224   BRUNDAGE, J., 'Concubinage and Marriage in Medieval Canon Law' (1975), p. 10.
225   BROOKE, N., The Medieval Idea of Marriage (1989), p. 120.
226   Ibid.

historical anecdotes. In 1092 Philip I's repudiation of his first wife Bertha of Holland and his subsequent marriage to Bertrada, the wife of the count of Anjou, led to a culmination of the Church's efforts to enforce indissolubility in practice.[227] The King, however, kept Bertrada in spite of dire consequences, such as his excommunication in 1094, followed by the papal interdict in 1100, and a bitter conflict with the most influential cleric of France of his days, Ivo of Chartres, and the Pope, that lasted for decennia.[228] Louis VII (crowned in 1131, reign 1137-1180) married in 1137 the legendary Eleanor of Aquitaine. In 1152 Eleanor managed to persuade the Pope to get that marriage annulled because the spouses were related as third cousins. Three months later she remarried to Henry II of England although she was also related to him within a prohibited degree.[229]

As Roderick Phillips observed, 'it has often been argued that the Church circumvented its own doctrine of marital indissolubility by using annulments as if they were divorces, so that many annulments in name were divorces in intent and effect'.[230] Georges Duby for instance, cites a letter of a twelfth century knight to support this interpretation. The knight remarked about his prospective wife:

> 'Without any doubt she is related to me within the third degree. That is not close enough to stay away from her. But if I want, and if she does not suit me, I can, on the basis of this relationship, obtain a divorce.'[231]

However, more recent research on the case law of the ecclesiastical courts has shed new light on the actual practices of annulment and has taken the edge off this interpretation. Helmholz's study of marriage litigation in England from the thirteenth to the fifteenth centuries shows that annulment of marriage was rather seldom.[232] The same was also true for Paris.[233] Roderick Philips notices that 'the relative paucity of suits for annulment does nothing to enhance the view of the Catholic ecclesiastical courts as crypto divorce mills. What is more, the courts demanded rigorous proof before they would declare a marriage null'.[234]

---

[227] The course of this affaire has been extensively described by Georges Duby in: DUBY, G., *Ridder, vrouw en priester* (1985), p. 19-36.
[228] BROOKE, N., *The Medieval Idea of Marriage* (1989), p. 123.
[229] BROOKE, N., *The Medieval Idea of Marriage* (1989), p. 123.
[230] PHILLIPS, R., *Putting asunder* (1988), p. 5.
[231] DUBY, G., Ridder, vrouw en priester (1985), (translation mine) p. 221.
[232] HELMHOLZ, R., *Marriage Litigation in Medieval England* (1978), p. 72-73.
[233] PHILLIPS, R., *Putting asunder* (1988), p. 10-11.
[234] Ibid, p. 9-10.

The Orthodox Church also rendered marriage indissoluble as a rule, but nonetheless allowed divorce and remarriage in case of adultery,[235] a choice for a religious life, and a few other instances. The Orthodox example shows that the development of the concept of marriage as a sacrament did not necessitate rendering marriage indissoluble. The Byzantine theologians managed to reconcile the sacred character of marriage with a limited admissibility of divorce.[236] Still, divorce in the Orthodox countries was almost as seldom as annulment in the Catholic part of Europe.

4.4.6. ILLEGITIMACY IN THE HIGH MIDDLE AGES

The children of a concubine, who made no claim to marital status, were still treated as natural children.[237] However, due to the Church's efforts to discourage concubinage, natural children definitively lost their previously privileged status and were equated with children born of simple fornication.[238] Instead of the earlier distinction between the legal position of privileged natural children and the rest of the illegitimate children, canon law made a new distinction between the specifically deprivileged *spurii,* and the rest of the illegitimate children. *Spurii* were the children born from unions where marriage was not possible: mainly children of adulterous or incestuous unions.[239] In canon law, all illegitimate children were regarded as *filius nullius,* being legally related to neither father nor mother.[240] Private recognition by the father was definitively ruled out. In place thereof came two forms of legitimisation developed by the canon law on the basis of Roman law. Legitimisation was possible by an Act of the Pope, the medieval substitute of the Roman *legitimatio per rescriptum principis*, and by the subsequent marriage of the parents. Legitimisation by an Act of the Pope was introduced in the 1100s.[241] Legitimisation by subsequent marriage of the parents was allowed by Pope Alexander III in the second decennia of the twelfth century.[242] The

---

[235]   It is interesting to notice that the double standards regarding male and female adultery that developed in Roman law came to prevail in Russian canon law over the teaching of the Church regarding the equality of spousal duty of fidelity. ZAGOROVSKII, I., *Kurs semeinogo prava* (2003), p. 104.

[236]   Their reasoning was that marriage was a gift of God's grace and not a magic action. Being only human, the parties to a marriage could make mistakes and ask for this grace while they were not yet ready to receive it. Therefore the Church accepted that the sacrament could in exceptional cases be regarded as not properly received and the Church authorities could dissolve such marriages. TROITSKII, S., *Khristianskaia filisofia braka* (1995), p. 244.

[237]   BRUNDAGE, J., 'Concubinage and Marriage in Medieval Canon Law' (1975), p. 10.

[238]   HÜBNER, R., *History of Germanic Private Law* (1918), p. 672.

[239]   MAYALI, L., 'Note on the Legitimization by Subsequent Marriage from Alexander III to Innocent III' (1986), p. 65-67.

[240]   BAKER, J., *An Introduction to English Legal History* (2002), p. 400.

[241]   HÜBNER, R., *History of Germanic Private Law* (1918), p. 675.

[242]   MAYALI, L., 'Note on the Legitimization by Subsequent Marriage from Alexander III to Innocent III' (1986), p. 61-63.

possibility of legitimisation was altogether excluded in respect of the *spurii*. In England legitimisation by subsequent marriage of the parents was possible, as it was everywhere in Europe. The only difference was that the English common law denied it any civil consequences, most importantly the right to inherit.[243] Orthodox canon law allowed legitimisation by subsequent marriage and maintained the old Roman legitimisation *per rescriptum principis*.[244]

---

[243] As the barons refused in 1235 to recognise legitimisation by subsequent marriage, such children were treated as legitimate in canon law but illegitimate at common law (so-called 'special bastardy') and thus could not inherit land at common law. POLLOCK, F., MAITLAND, F., *The History of English Law before the time of Edward I*, Vol. II (1952), p. 375-377.

[244] ZHISHMAN, J., *Das Eherecht der orientalischen Kirche* (1864), p. 724-725.

CHAPTER 5
MATRIMONIAL PROPERTY LAW
IN THE HIGH MIDDLE AGES:
BEYOND THE CANON LAW
UNIFICATION

5.1. MATRIMONIAL PROPERTY LAW AT THE FRINGES OF CANON LAW

The development of matrimonial property law during the High Middle Ages was determined by the interaction of three factors: local rules rooted in old Germanic folk-laws; interventions of the Church authorities; and the influence of the newly discovered Roman law. An account of the rules of the local folk-laws has been already given in Chapter 3.[1]

The issue of the influence of canon law on matrimonial property is not without controversy. Matrimonial property law, save for some minor and temporal exceptions, remained in the realm of secular law even in the time of the great expansion of medieval canon law. Nonetheless, it also suffered its influence. Some nineteenth century authors have tended to exaggerate the extent of the influence of canon law on matrimonial property law.[2] Charles Lefebvre even attributed the emergence of the institution of the total community of property to it.[3] The influence of canon law, especially with regard to the endorsement of the property rights of women,[4] cannot be denied. But on the whole this influence was of a rather sporadic character and of secondary importance. The crucial difference, as compared to marriage, divorce, concubinage and illegitimacy, was that the Church never developed its own ideology in respect of matrimonial property. Therefore matrimonial property law was spared

---

[1]   See Chapter 3, Section 3.3.6.
[2]   THIELEN, J., *Oude en nieuwe opvattingen over het ontstaat van de algehele gemeenschap van goederen* (1965), p. 68-85.
[3]   LEFEBVRE, C., *Cours de doctorat sur l'histoire du droit matrimonial français. Le droit des gens mariés* (1908), p. 222 ff.
[4]   According to Rudolf Hübner, 'The Church always energetically championed in this the matter of the equality of the sexes, but struggled along in vain before it was able to enforce its view, which was morally far the higher'. HÜBNER, R., *History of Germanic Private Law* (1918), p. 618.

the heavy ideological connotation that was imposed upon the other family law institutions when they were made part of the canon law doctrine. This ideological dimension appears to be so obstinate that it still exerts considerable influence on present day debates surrounding marriage, divorce and extramarital cohabitation. This probably explains why matrimonial property law always distinguished itself as a fairly ideology-neutral 'technical' area of family law.[5]

In the heydays of canon law, the ecclesiastical authorities nonetheless did lodge a claim on the regulation of matrimonial property relations. Their pretensions were based on the fact that the adjudication of separation and annulment cases was in the competence of the ecclesiastical courts. According to the canonists, the subsequent division of property was logically 'accessory to the main cause and, as such pertained to their jurisdiction'.[6] The secular courts, however, were not eager to relinquish their authority. The contest between the two jurisdictions led to many controversies. The compromises that were finally reached on the division of authority varied from country to country. In England, matrimonial property law was 'cut in twain' around 1200 A.D.[7] Frederic William Maitland submits that due to this particular fact England rejected the system of community property and developed instead its own, peculiar *common law* matrimonial property system.[8]

The influences of folk law, canon law and Roman law were rather contradictory. Traditional local rules mostly entailed either the community of property or the community of administration. In both cases the administration of property was solely in the hands of the husband, and the wife was progressively excluded from the decision making. The canonists, by contrast, persistently defended married women's property rights during and after marriage.[9] Roman law brought in the concept of separation of spousal property and the right of the wife to administer her own estate.

---

[5]   See: PINTENS, W., VANWINCKELEN, C., *Casebook. European Family Law* (2001), p. 21; ANTOKOLSKAIA, M., 'Enkele gedachten over de harmonisatie van het familierecht in Europa' (2002), p. 8; PINTENS, W., 'Europeanisation of Family Law' (2003), p. 12, note 45.

[6]   SHEEHAN, M., Marriage, Family, and Law in Medieval Europe (1996), p. 35.

[7]   POLLOCK, F., MAITLAND, F., *The History of English Law before the time of Edward I*, Vol. II (1952), p. 402.

[8]   Ibid.

[9]   SHEEHAN, M., *Marriage, Family, and Law in Medieval Europe* (1996), p. 16. Among others, the canonists defended the idea that the widow was free to chose to remarry or to remain single (Ibid, p. 18.). The Church courts gave effect to the wills of married women, although their capacity to make a will was resolutely denied at common law (ibid, p. 29).

5.2. DIVERSITY OF MATRIMONIAL PROPERTY REGIMES

5.2.1. OVERVIEW OF MATRIMONIAL PROPERTY REGIMES

The interrelation of the influences of folk law, canon law and Roman law, set forth the further differentiation of matrimonial property regimes that started during Germanic times and continued through the Carolingian era. As a result, systems that incorporated quite dissimilar combinations of Germanic, Roman and canon law elements took shape all over Europe. Within this diversity it is possible to distinguish certain types of matrimonial property systems, such as universal community, limited community, separation of property with community of administration, the common law system and the dotal system. However, it is rightly pointed out that any attempt to group the matrimonial systems of that period can be no more than a generalisation. In reality there existed in the Middle Ages 'an infinite number of legal systems of matrimonial property'.[10] It is rightly noticed that at that time the fundamental division between the systems with and without community had not yet clearly crystallised.[11] It is also justly pointed out that 'under medieval conditions characterised by absence of clear cut legal concepts',[12] it is sometimes extremely difficult to determine whether a certain law provided for a community of administration or for a real community, and in the latter case, what particular type of community that was. The endless debates about the qualification of the medieval property systems provided by the *Sachsenspiegel* and about the system of medieval Russian law can support this view. Nonetheless, the following schematic differentiation could be of some use:

---

[10] HÜBNER, R., *History of Germanic Private Law* (1918), p. 631.
[11] HOLDSWORTH, W., *A History of English Law*, Vol. 3 (1945), p. 522.
[12] GRAUE, E., 'German Law' (1972), p. 115.

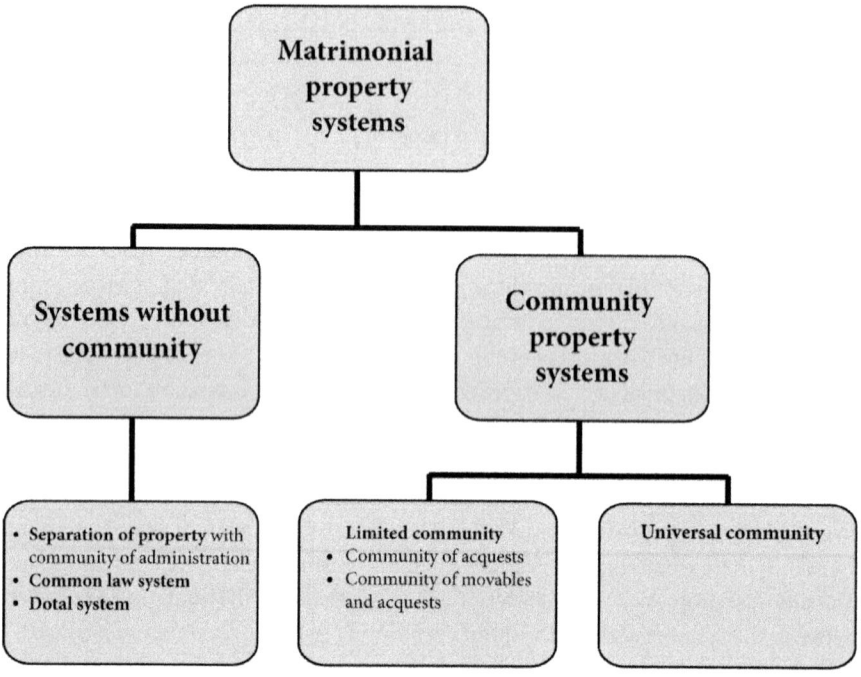

5.2.2. COMMUNITY PROPERTY SYSTEMS

Universal community

The idea of matrimonial community found its most profound expression in the system of the universal community. Under this regime the whole of the movable and immovable property of the spouses, acquired both before and during the marriage, merged into one collective matrimonial estate, equally belonging to both spouses. During the marriage, this collective estate was administered by the husband. The husband could solely dispose of chattels but needed the concurrence of his wife for disposition of land.[13] If no child was born to the marriage and the marriage was terminated by death, the property was divided between the surviving spouse and the heirs of the deceased spouse. In most territories, the surviving spouse was entitled to a larger portion, often two thirds.[14] If a child was born to the marriage, the most common situation was that the surviving spouse took the whole of the property.[15]

---

[13]   HÜBNER, R., *History of Germanic Private Law* (1918), p. 644.
[14]   Ibid.
[15]   Ibid, p. 645.

However, the right of the surviving spouse in respect of land was limited by a right of sequestration of that land belonging to the children.[16] Therefore the survivor's right in respect of land was merely a kind of usufruct.[17] Universal community was first developed in some Flemish[18] and Dutch provinces.[19] It was not, however, confined to a certain geographical region or to a certain populace. The area of its spread included territories as diverse as Sicily, Denmark, Portugal, parts of Switzerland, some German territories,[20] and some parts of Northern France[21] and of Spain.[22]

Limited community

Yet, it was not the universal, but the limited community of property that became the most widespread community property system in the Middle Ages. This community primarily took one of two forms: the community of acquests or the community of movables and acquests. Under the system of community of acquests, only the property acquired during the marriage became common. The community of acquests was the common regime in various German territories,[23] in Castile[24] and Navarre,[25] in Friesland,[26] and in the Franche-Comté.[27] By far the most widespread limited community regime however, was the community of movables and acquests. Under this regime not only all property acquired during marriage, but also all premarital movable property was regarded common. This system came to prevail in most parts of Northern France, in Austria[28] and in Aragon.[29] It was also popular in Germany West of the Rhine, in Baden and in parts of Holstein.[30]

---

16 Ibid.
17 Ibid.
18 Brissaud, J., *A History of French Private Law* (1912), p. 822.
19 Gelderland (Fockema Andreae, S., *Bijdragen tot de Nederlandsche Rechtsgeschiedenis* (1888), p. 91-97); Utrecht (Ibid, p. 97-109); Holland and Zeeland (Ibid, p. 109-119); as well as in some parts of Overijssel. (Feenstra, R., 'Family, Property and Succession in the Province of Holland during the Sixteenth, Seventeenth and Eighteenth Century' (1992), p. 39.). In Brabant and Groningen the universal community initially existed on the condition that a child was born into the marriage. Fockema Andreae, S., *Bijdragen tot de Nederlandsche Rechtsgeschiedenis* (1888), p. 121-122.
20 Like Westphalia, Thuringia, Silesia, Prussia, Bohemia, Moravia and the areas of the cities of Hamburg and Lübeck. Hübner, R., *History of Germanic Private Law* (1918), p. 643.
21 Brissaud, J., *A History of French Private Law* (1912), p. 822-823.
22 Perez-Bustamante, R., 'La communauté de biens en histoire du droit espagnol' (1992), p. 549-550.
23 Parts of Bavaria and of Hessen, Hannover, Thüringen and Holstein, Massfeller, F., 'Matrimonial Property Law in Germany' (1955), p. 370.
24 Perez-Bustamante, R., 'La communauté de biens en histoire du droit espagnol' (1992), p. 543-544.
25 Ibid, p. 546.
26 Feenstra, R., 'Family, Property and Succession in the Province of Holland during the Sixteenth, Seventeenth and Eighteenth Century' (1992), p. 39.
27 Brissaud, J., *A History of French Private Law* (1912), p. 823, note 2.
28 Hübner, R., *History of Germanic Private Law* (1918), p. 640.
29 Perez-Bustamante, R., 'La communauté de biens en histoire du droit espagnol' (1992), p. 545.
30 Massfeller, F., 'Matrimonial Property Law in Germany' (1955), p. 370.

Northern France (*les pays coutumier*)[31] provides a good example of how the limited community system operated. This form of community presupposes a distinction between three types of assets. Firstly, the husband's *propres*: land passed to him by his family through inheritance,[32] gift or bequest. Secondly, the wife's *propres*: land passed to her by her family through inheritance, gift, bequest or endowment. Thirdly, the collective estate of husband and wife, composed of the movables irrespective of the time of acquisition, and the land acquired after marriage (*acquêrs* or *conquêts*) other than by donation or inheritance from the spouses' families.[33] The husband was regarded as the 'lord and master' (*seigneur et maître*) of the common property.[34] He had a right of usufruct and could freely alienate the community assets without the concurrence of his wife.[35] The husband equally administered the wife's separate estate,[36] but according to de Beaumanoir,[37] the alienation of land was only possible with the wife's consent.[38] During the thirteenth century, even the alienation of the husband's own land started to require the wifely consent.[39] This was a kind of guarantee of the wife's right to receive the dower, bestowed on her by custom should she be widowed.[40] This customary dower included the right of the surviving wife to a usufruct of a portion of all her husband's land.[41] This customary dower was supplemented by the legal dower, established by the ordinance of Philippe-Auguste in 1214.[42] Legal dower included a usufruct of half of the husband's land. If the marriage ended through death or annulment, the division of property differed from province to province. If there were no children, the surviving spouse sometimes acquired the entire common fund[43] and sometimes obtained the whole of the movables and a share of the immovables.[44] If there were children, the right of the survivor was often limited to a usufruct because of the right of sequestration belonging to the children.[45]

---

[31]   With the exemption of Normandy and a few territories where universal community came to prevail.
[32]   BURGE, W., *Commentaries on Colonial and Foreign Laws*, V. III (1910), p. 495.
[33]   BART, J., *Histoire du droit privé de la chute de l'Empire romain au XIXe siècle* (1998), p. 300.
[34]   Ibid, p. 304.
[35]   Ibid, p. 304.
[36]   BRISSAUD, J., *A History of French Private Law* (1912), p. 83.
[37]   Phillippe de Remy de Beaumanoir, c. 1250-1296. A distinguished medieval North French scholar and jurist, author of *Livres des coutumes et des usages de Clermont et Beauvoisins*.
[38]   BART, J., *Histoire du droit privé de la chute de l'Empire romain au XIXe siècle* (1998), p. 301.
[39]   TERRÉ, F., SIMLER, P., *Droit civil. Les régimes matrimoniaux* (1994), p. 17.
[40]   BART, J., *Histoire du droit privé de la chute de l'Empire romain au XIXe siècle* (1998), p. 304-310.
[41]   TERRÉ, F., SIMLER, P., *Droit civil. Les régimes matrimoniaux* (1994), p. 17.
[42]   BART, J., *Histoire du droit privé de la chute de l'Empire romain au XIXe siècle* (1998), p. 302.
[43]   BRISSAUD, J., *A History of French Private Law* (1912), p. 857.
[44]   Ibid, p. 857.
[45]   HÜBNER, R., *History of Germanic Private Law* (1918), p. 645.

5.2.3. SYSTEMS WITHOUT COMMUNITY

Separation of property with community of administration

The ancient Germanic separation of property with community of administration (*Verwaltungsgemeinschaft*) prevailed in Northern Germany, as well as in some parts of Southern Germany and contemporary Switzerland.[46] Later, it independently emerged in Russia. Franz Massfeller believes that this regime is of a purely Germanic origin and was not significantly affected by the reception of Roman law.[47] He asserts that the features of the Germanic System of separation of property are clearly traceable in such influential German medieval compilations of customary law as the 1215-1235 *Sachsenspiegel*, the 1265 *Schwabenspiegel* and the 1275 *Deutschenspiegel*.[48] Other scholars question this hypothesis because it is doubtful whether, for instance, the *Sachsenspiegel* really provided for separation of property with community of administration.[49] This system of separation of property with community of the administration combined the elements of separation and community. Husband and wife remained the sole legal owners of their respective estates (separation element).[50] But as the wife had no legal capacity, the husband had the right of usufruct and administration (*'seisin in mundium'*) of his wife's property (community element).[51] However, he could not alienate his wife's land without her consent.[52] On the termination of marriage each spouse took his or her own property.[53] Thus, this system was characterised by separate legal ownership combined with (physical and) administrative community.

The Russian late medieval system resembled the Germanic community of administration. The property of husband and wife remained separate. The husband acquired the right to administer his wife's property and to use it for the needs of the family. However, he could not dispose of the wife's estate without her consent.[54] If the husband died first, the dowry returned to the widow and passed from her to her

---

[46] MASSFELLER, F., 'Matrimonial Property Law in Germany' (1955), p. 369-370.

[47] Ibid, p. 370-371.

[48] Ibid, p. 369.

[49] Its wording: 'when a man takes a wife he shall be seized and possessed of all her property as lawful guardian' (*Sachsenspiegel* I, 31 § 2.), and 'husband and wife have no common property during their life' (*Sachsenspiegel* I, 31 § 1.) have been understood to support both the system of universal community by PLANTZ, H., (*Deutsche Rechtsgeschichte* (1981), p. 201), as community of movables by THIELEN (*Man en vrouw hebben geen gedeeld goed* (2001), p. 135-136) and as separation of property community of administration by Hübner (*History of Germanic Private Law* (1918), p. 632).

[50] HÜBNER, R., *History of Germanic Private Law* (1918), p. 635.

[51] Ibid, p. 634.

[52] Ibid, p. 636.

[53] Ibid.

[54] ZAGOROVSKII, I., *Kurs semeinogo prava* (2003), p. 198.

children or, in the absence of children, to those who had given the dowry or their heirs.[55] Russian scholars have qualified this system in various ways. The nineteenth century author Nevolin believed that during the marriage the 'dowry was the husband's property'.[56] He was obviously mistaken, as the husband did not posses the right to dispose of the dowry. Zagorovskii comes closer to the truth, supposing that the dowry became a kind of 'common familial property'.[57] However, an important element of the community system, the division upon death, was missing. That is why in my view the Russian system most resembled the community of administration.

Dotal system

The Roman *dotal system* existed since Roman times in the Southern French area of written law (*pays de droit écrit*),[58] in Normandy, Italy, Hungary,[59] and in the Mediterranean fringe of Spain.[60] In the twelfth century, it also penetrated, albeit in a modified form,[61] into some parts of Germany as a result of the reception of Roman law.[62] Under the dotal system, three patrimonies could be distinguished: the dowry given to the wife by her family, the separate property of the wife (*paraphernalia*),[63] and the property of the husband.[64] Unlike in Rome, the medieval husband was not the legal owner, but only the administrator of his wife's dowry.[65] Therefore, the wife remained the legal owner of her dowry.[66] The dotal land formed a type of 'reserved fund' for the family[67] and gradually became unalienable even by both spouses acting together.[68] During the marriage, the husband could freely dispose of the movable part of the dowry and of the revenues of its immovable part.[69] Later, the

---

[55]   NEVOLIN, K., *Istoria rossiiskikh grazhdanskikh zakonov* (1851), p. 117.
[56]   Ibid.
[57]   ZAGOROVSKII, I., *Kurs semeinogo prava* (2003), p. 198.
[58]   BART, J., *Histoire du droit privé de la chute de l'Empire romain au XIXe siècle* (1998), p. 314.
[59]   BURGE, W., *Commentaries on Colonial and Foreign Laws,* V. III, (1910), p. 609.
[60]   PEREZ-BUSTAMANTE, R., 'La communauté de biens en histoire du droit espagnol' (1992), p. 550-551.
[61]   HÜBNER, R., *History of Germanic Private Law* (1918), p. 655.
[62]   However, Franz Massfeller believes that the purely Roman dotal system was not widely accepted in Germany. Even at the eve of the Codification of 1900 the dotal system affected no more than 3 million people. MASSFELLER, F., 'Matrimonial Property Law in Germany' (1955), p. 370-371.
[63]   BART, J., *Histoire du droit privé de la chute de l'Empire romain au XIXe siecle* (1998), p. 315.
[64]   RODOTÀ, S., 'Le regime matrimonial en droit Italien' (1972), p. 224.
[65]   TERRÉ, F., SIMLER, P., *Droit civil. Les régimes matrimoniaux* (1994), p. 19.
[66]   The ideas on the legal ownership of the dowry changed over the time. The Glossators attributed it either to the husband or to the wife. Later, the husband was considered to be a titular owner, while the wife was supposed to keep the true ownership. More recent authors treat the husband as a mere usufructuary. BRISSAUD, J., *A History of French Private Law* (1912), p. 803.
[67]   BRISSAUD, J., *A History of French Private Law* (1912), p. 801.
[68]   ANCEL, M., 'Matrimonial Property Law in France' (1955), p. 5.
[69]   TERRÉ, F., SIMLER, P., *Droit civil. Les régimes matrimoniaux* (1994), p. 19.

application[70] of the misinterpreted[71] late Roman *Senatus consultum Velleianum* contributed to the extrapolation of the inalienability of the movable part of the dowry as well.[72] Yet, the wife had a statutory hypothec over the husband's land as a safety for the recovery of the movable part of her dowry.[73] The separate property of the wife (*paraphernalia*) was originally administered by the wife alone.[74] However, again due to incongruous application of the *Senatus consultum Velleianum*, which forbad women to bind themselves in respect of third parties, the wife was deprived of the power to alienate her *paraphernalia*.[75] In the German territories the husband could administer both dowry and *paraphernalia*, which diminished the difference between the two.[76] In case of termination of the marriage, the husband or his heirs were obliged to restore the dowry to the wife or to her heirs.[77]

A rather peculiar variety of the dotal system evolved in Normandy. The Normandian system was different from that of the South of France. As in the English common law system, the husband could administer, enjoy and dispose of all movable and immovable property of his wife.[78] Moreover, contrary to the rest of France, no other regime could be chosen by way of ante-nuptial agreement.[79]

Common law system

A fairly distinct common law system of matrimonial property emerged in England after the Norman Conquest. William Holdsworth follows the opinion of Jean Brissaud in regarding it as a species of the dotal system.[80] However, the differences between the common law system and the continental dotal systems are so significant that the English system deserves separate examination. As was mentioned above, a peculiar feature of England lay in the division of the competence, in respect of matrimonial

---

[70] It was applied in the French *pays de droit écrit* and in Italy through the Middle Ages. It was officially repealed in France by the Edict of 1606, but was de-facto kept in the *pays de droit écrit* until the Napoleonic *Code Civil.* BRISSAUD, J., *A History of French Private Law* (1912), p. 805.

[71] In Post-Classical Rome the immovable part of the dowry could be alienated and the *Senatus consultum Velleianum* was not brought in connection with the inalienability of dowry. JOLOWICZ, H., *Roman Foundations of Modern Law* (1961), p. 171.

[72] JOLOWICZ, H., *Roman Foundations of Modern Law* (1961), p. 171.

[73] BART, J., *Histoire du droit privé de la chute de l'Empire romain au XIXe siècle* (1998), p. 316.

[74] BRISSAUD, J., *A History of French Private Law* (1912), p. 802.

[75] Ibid, p. 805. In the times of Justinian, the general rule that a woman must not bind herself with respect of third parties became comparatively easy to evade. In contrast, the provision that a wife must not make herself answerable for the debts of her husband was firmly observed. JOLOWICZ, H., *Roman Foundations of Modern Law* (1961), p. 171.

[76] HÜBNER, R., *History of Germanic Private Law* (1918), p. 655.

[77] BURGE, W., *Commentaries on Colonial and Foreign Laws,* V. III, (1910), p. 553.

[78] BRISSAUD, J., *A History of French Private Law* (1912), p. 787 and 790.

[79] BART, J., *Histoire du droit privé de la chute de l'Empire romain au XIXe siècle* (1998), p. 316-319.

[80] HOLDSWORTH, W., *A History of English Law,* Vol. 3 (1945), p. 522.

property, between the lay and the ecclesiastical courts. The Royal courts retained the complete control of pleas on land, while the division of movable property and the succession of movable goods came to resort under the courts Christian.[81] Consequently, the succession of movables came to be governed by the canon law, while the succession of immovables was regulated by common law. This divide had far reaching consequences for the consistency of the system of matrimonial property as a whole.[82] At common law, a single woman (*feme sole*) enjoyed full legal capacity while a married woman (*feme covert*) was totally deprived of it. Therefore she could neither administer her property nor make a will, nor could she interfere in her husband's transactions in regard of her own property.[83] Accordingly, the common law considered husband and wife, for most purposes of private law, as 'one person', represented by the husband.[84] At the same time the Church courts undermined the concept of *coverture* by giving effect to the wills of married women, although their capacity to make such a will was resolutely denied at common law.[85]

As the regulation of land was in the sole domain of common law, the system of matrimonial real property was quite consistent. The husband acquired an interest in his wife's freehold land as long as the marriage lasted.[86] Pollock and Maitland assume that it was no more than a usufructuary interest,[87] while others suggest that this interest finally grew into a kind of temporary ownership.[88] If a child was born to the marriage, the husband's interest became lifelong (so called 'tenancy by curtesy'[89]).[90] If no child

---

[81] SHEEHAN, M., *Marriage, Family, and Law in Medieval Europe* (1996), p. 33.

[82] Ibid, p. 25.

[83] KIRALFY, A., 'The English Law' (1972), p. 182.

[84] As summarised in Blackstone's *Commentaries on the Laws of England*, 'By marriage, the husband and wife are one person in law: that is, the very being of legal existence of the women is suspended during the marriage, or at least is incorporated and consolidated into that of the husband' Book, 1, Ch. 15, cited in: KAHN-FREUND, O., 'Matrimonial Property Law in England' (1955), p. 272.

[85] In the fourteenth century the power of married women to make a will became a matter of controversy between the clergy and the laity. A provincial council held at London in 1342 threatened excommunication to anyone who would impede the free testation of a married woman. The Commons complained to the Parliament. The Church lost this struggle as the lay courts kept refusing the execution of such wills and even ecclesiastical courts 'were brought to a reluctant admission that the wife has only such testamentary power as her husband is pleased to allow her'. POLLOCK, F., MAITLAND, F., *The History of English Law before the Time of Edward I*, Vol. II (1952), p. 429.

[86] The legal position of a wife in respect of leasehold land was less favourable, as her husband could retain them upon her death and a surviving wife could not reclaim them if they were disposed off. KIRALFY, A., 'The English Law' (1972), p. 182-183.

[87] POLLOCK, F., MAITLAND, F., *The History of English Law before the Time of Edward I*, Vol. II (1952), p. 404.

[88] KIRALFY, A., 'The English Law' (1972), p. 182.

[89] For more details see: POLLOCK, F., MAITLAND, F., *The History of English Law before the Time of Edward I*, Vol. II (1952), p. 416-418 and HOLDSWORTH, W., *A History of English Law*, Vol. 3 (1945), p. 185-189.

[90] KAHN-FREUND, O., 'Matrimonial Property Law in England' (1955), p. 273.

was born and the wife predeceased her husband, the freehold land passed to the wife's heirs.[91] The wife could not alienate her land during her husband's lifetime.[92] A husband administered his wife's land and was able to alienate his interest in it (but no more than just that) without his wife's concurrence.[93] The husband did not have the right to convey the property of the wife's freehold land. But if, nonetheless, he did so, the wife had no remedy as long as he lived. However, if the husband died first, the freehold land returned to the widow. Her title and legal capacity revived and she or her heirs could recover the land from the purchaser to whom the land had been conveyed by the husband during the *coverture*.[94] Thus the husband's interest in the wife's land, and the rights of anyone to whom the husband might have conveyed his interest, ended with the husband's death. Consequently, the only way to alienate the freehold land of a married woman was through the making of a conveyance by fine, during the levying of which the wife had to be examined separately from her husband.[95]

The wife had the right to a dower from her husband's lands.[96] In was customary in the twelfth century to specify in a contract made at the time of marriage which land was set apart to provide for the wife in case of widowhood.[97] The *Magna Carta* of 1217 set this dower at one-third of all of the husband's land, unless less was stipulated by the endowing.[98] Later this portion, which used to be an upper limit, changed into a minimal 'common law dower'.[99] Therefore, the wife could be entitled by contract to more than one-third, but not less. Since the thirteenth century, the husband has not been able to alienate the dower land without his wife's consent, given by means of a fine.[100]

One of the specific features of the common law system was that the movables of the wife became the property of the husband, and he could do with them as he pleased.[101] According to Pollock and Maitland, by granting the husband this right, the thirteenth

---

[91]   HOLDSWORTH, W., *A History of English Law*, Vol. 3 (1945), p. 525.
[92]   POLLOCK, F., MAITLAND, F., *The History of English Law before the Time of Edward I*, Vol. II (1952), p. 404.
[93]   Ibid.
[94]   HOLDSWORTH, W., *A History of English Law*, Vol. 3 (1945), p. 525.
[95]   Ibid), p. 526.
[96]   For further details see: HOLDSWORTH, W., *A History of English Law*, Vol. 3 (1945), p. 189-198.
[97]   KIRALFY, A., 'The English Law' (1972), p. 183.
[98]   POLLOCK, F., MAITLAND, F., *The History of English Law before the Time of Edward I*, Vol. II (1952), p. 421.
[99]   Ibid.
[100] HOLDSWORTH, W., *A History of English Law*, Vol. 3 (1945), p. 193.
[101] POLLOCK, F., MAITLAND, F., *The History of English Law before the Time of Edward I*, Vol. II (1952), p. 427.

century lawyers made a definitive step in the rejection of the concept of community.[102] The community notion was however, still traceable in the widow's right to a legitimate portion of one-half of her husband's movable goods if the marriage had not produced children, and of one-third of these goods if children had been born into the marriage.[103] Pollock and Maitland suggest that the right of the wife to a dower and to a legitimate portion in movables indicates that England was not very far from embracing a kind of community property system. They attribute the rejection of the community to the division of competence that resulted from the extension of the ecclesiastical jurisdiction to movable property.[104]

5.3. DIVERSITY IN TOOLS, SIMILARITY IN FUNCTION

As was discussed above, after obtaining the exclusive competence to govern and adjudicate marriage, divorce, concubinage and illegitimacy matters, the Catholic Church achieved an almost total unification of the relevant laws. The Church's interventions into the regulation of matrimonial property were, by contrast, just one factor in addition to customary and Roman law influencing matrimonial property laws. This interference of the ecclesiastical authorities not only produced no harmonising effect, but rather contributed to an even greater diversity of matrimonial property regimes in Europe. For instance, in the view of Pollock and Maitland, the Church's interference should be held responsible for the emergence of the separate English common law system.

It is rather interesting that, contrary to what might be expected on the basis of the proposition that there always is a strong correlation between law and society, in many areas of Europe the various matrimonial property regimes formed a real patchwork, of which it seems impossible to attribute any particular patch to specific ethnical, tribal, geographical, economic, urban or rural factors.[105] One of the possible explanations

---

[102]   Ibid, p. 432. Following this opinion, Holdsworth explained the rejection of the community by the fact that in the thirteenth century, after the Royal courts, and therefore the common law, lost its competence in respect of succession of movables to the ecclesiastical courts, the common law lost sight of the redistribution of chattels by death of the husband. It looked at it only as long as marriage lasted, and in the Middle Ages the family chattels were under absolute control of a husband under all property systems. Thus, the common law 'naturally tended to magnify the control of the husband to such degree that literally gave him the chattels of the wife, and denied the wife any right own them'. HOLDSWORTH, W., *A History of English Law*, Vol. 3 (1945), p. 524.

[103]   KIRALFY, A., 'The English Law' (1972), p. 183.

[104]   POLLOCK, F., MAITLAND, F., *The History of English Law before the Time of Edward I*, Vol. II (1952), p. 432.

[105]   MASSFELLER, F., 'Matrimonial Property Law in Germany' (1955), p. 370-371.

could be that all medieval matrimonial property systems, no matter how divergent they seemed to be, were functionally serving the same needs of feudal society. Frederic William Maitland suggests that 'underneath this superficial variety, there was during the Middle Ages a substantial uniformity about some main matters of practical importance'.[106] The main concern of the feudal families of course was land: the absolute paramount object of value in that period. A family's prime interest was that land given to a daughter as dowry would pass to her children or return to her blood family. Therefore, in all property systems (the separation of property, the dotal system, the common law system, and the various forms of community), land brought into the marriage by a wife was protected from unilateral alienation by her husband. All systems also involved a mechanism for the protection of dower land. Another common feature was that, irrespective of the title of legal ownership, the property of husband and wife was physically united in a 'community of administration'. Due to the legal incapacity of married women, husbands everywhere had a right of usufruct and a right of administration in respect of the property brought into marriage by their wives.[107] Therefore as long as marriage went on, the differences between the common law system, the systems of community of property and the systems of separation of property were rather unimportant.[108] The main differences between these regimes concerned the status of movables, a significantly less important asset in feudal times. Another difference lay in the legal techniques employed to ensure the rights of the surviving spouse to share in the matrimonial property.

It seems clear that, in spite of a notable functional similarity, the assortment of matrimonial property regimes not only did not diminish, but actually increased during the High Middle Ages. As Maitland puts it, 'at the end of Middle Ages we see a perplexing variety of incongruous customs for which it is very difficult to account'.[109] This diversity persisted until the national codification movement in the nineteenth century reduced it to a calculable number of systems. The fact remains that, contrary to the law of marriage, divorce, concubinage and illegitimacy, matrimonial property law never had a *ius commune* in the past. This absence of a common starting point probably explains the conceptual and technical diversity that is typical for the matrimonial property law of the Europe of today.

---

[106] POLLOCK, F., MAITLAND, F., *The History of English Law before the Time of Edward I*, Vol. II (1952), p. 400.
[107] HÜBNER, R., *History of Germanic Private Law* (1918), p. 632.
[108] POLLOCK, F., MAITLAND, F., *The History of English Law before the Time of Edward I*, Vol. II (1952), p. 400.
[109] Ibid, p. 399.

CHAPTER 6
MEDIVAL CANON *IUS COMMUNE* OF FAMILY LAW: CONTINUANCE AND RADICAL CHANGE

6.1. THE SCOPE OF THE CHANGE

It possible to say that the unification of the medieval family canon law in the West was generally achieved sometime around the twelfth to thirteenth century.[1] This *ius commune* of family law remained almost unchanged for four centuries, until the Council of Trent. The Orthodox Church, despite its definite separation from the West in 1054 and the ensuing multiplicity of Orthodox Churches, developed a surprisingly similar set of canon family law rules at around the same time. The preceding chapters have shown that in Western Europe the unification represented a final point in the gradual replacement of a wide spectrum of Roman and Barbarian laws by a set of uniform Roman Catholic canon law, developed according to the Church's own principles. The rules of canon *ius commune* of family law differed from its predecessors so radically that, although the unification process was no part of any revolution in the narrow meaning of this term,[2] it can be perceived as a kind of a revolutionary change. This change was deliberately brought about by the Roman Catholic Church, which used the canon law as an instrument of social engineering in order to bring family practice in line with the newly developed ecclesiastical concept of a strictly monogamous, exogamous, indissoluble sacramental marriage. The following comparative table could illustrate the extent of the differences between the uniform canon family law, on the one hand, and its historical precursors, on the other hand:

---

[1]   However, Richard Helmholz rightly warns that 'we must see the process by which the Church vindicated its control over marriage as a longer and more gradual process than has hitherto been thought. It did not come with the definite formulation of the classical canon law in the twelfth century. Rather it was the product of slow growth and acceptance, which was almost imperceptible to contemporaries but is apparent in the records of the Church courts'. HELMHOLZ, R., *Marriage Litigation in Medieval England* (1978), p. 72-73.

[2]   Yet, Harold Berman called the Gregorian consolidation of the Church that made unification possible a 'Gregorian Revolution'. BERMAN, H., *Law and Revolution. The Formation of the Western Legal Tradition* (1983), p. 85-115.

Classical Roman family law	Barbarian family law	Roman Catholic canon family law (before Trent)	Orthodox canon family law
Family matters were the competence of the family itself	Family matters were the competence of the family itself	Ecclesiastical authorities acquired exclusive competence in family matters	Ecclesiastical authorities acquired exclusive competence in family matters
Marriage was a private, secular matter	Marriage was a private, secular matter	Marriage came to be regarded a sacrament	Marriage came to be regarded a sacrament
Consent of the parties *sui iuris* alone and the consent of the parties in *potestate* and their *pater familias* was required for marriage	Consent of the bridegroom and the father of the bride was required for marriage	Consent of the parties alone was sufficient for valid marriage	Consent of the parties alone was sufficient for marriage in theory, but not in practice
No compulsory procedure existed for the celebration of marriage	A secular procedure of solemnisation of marriage was compulsory	Church solemnisation of marriage was required, but purely consensual marriage was illicit, not invalid	Consensus and Church solemnisation were both constitutive for the validity of marriage
Concubinage was tolerated	Concubinage was tolerated	Durable concubinage almost amounted to informal marriage	Concubinage was not accepted
Natural children were part of the family structure	Natural children were part of the family structure	Illegitimate children were excluded from the family structure	Illegitimate children were excluded from the family structure
Divorce upon mutual consent and upon a unilateral declaration by one of the spouses was possible	Unilateral divorce for cause was possible. Consensual divorce was sometimes possible	Marriage became indissoluble	Divorce before ecclesiastical courts was possible for a limited amount of mainly fault grounds
Double standards for men and women regarding the duty of marital fidelity	Double standards for men and women regarding the duty of marital fidelity	Equality of men and women regarding the duty of marital fidelity	Double standards for men and women regarding the duty of marital fidelity prevailed in practice

This table is, of course, no more than a simplified sketch. Different Barbarian family laws certainly varied a great deal between one another. It is also difficult to compare the sophisticated classical Roman law with the rather undeveloped Barbarian laws. However, the table may still help to delineate certain features common to all of them, and thus enable comparisons among them and the Catholic and the Orthodox canon law rules.

Several authors have shown dissimilar appreciation of the magnitude of continuance and radical change in the formation of medieval uniform family canon law. On the one hand, some authors have maintained that the Christian ideal of moral behaviour, on the basis of which canon law was developed, was 'fully identical with the general social and moral duties and virtues that would have been expected of any upright citizen of the time'.[3] It is of course true that, for instance, denunciation of divorce was not an entirely new idea. Romans, Jews and the Germanic peoples considered divorce as morally wrong, although none of those people sought to prohibit it by law. The idea that marriage should be indissoluble other than by death, and the appreciation of *univera* had always been a deeply rooted Roman ideal, although this ideal was neither implemented in Roman law and nor realised in practice.[4] On the other hand, it has been claimed that 'the Middle Ages brought large transformations, essential to preparing the way for the modern family. Both Romans and Barbarians would have found marriage and the family in 1500 radically different from what they had known'.[5] John Crook has even proposed that in order to understand the Roman marriage it is necessary 'to make a clean break with all the Christian notions of marriage'.[6] In my view, both stances have their merits, as a radical departure from the past does not necessarily mean an overall break with it. Canon family law was built extensively upon Roman and Germanic ideals about marriage and family, but it also uncompromisingly modified everything that contradicted the Church doctrine.

The victory of the consensual theory of marriage, attributed to the influence of Roman law, is often used to underline the Roman foundations of canon family law. However, as I have already pointed out, even at this point there was a great deal of difference. The individualistically orientated canon law required no more than the consent of the parties alone. The more family-orientated Roman law, by contrast, required consent of the *pater familias* (if the parties were under power) and/or the parties themselves. Herbert Jolowicz has pointed out that 'as soon as we leave the subject of the conclusion of marriage, it becomes plain that the two systems [Roman and canon family laws] are radically different'.[7] Roman marriage law knew no general right to marry, limited only by impediments. The 'Roman *conubium*[8] was a positive requirement, which normally existed only among persons belonging to the same legal order',[9] and the same class. Even though feudal society was highly class conscious, canon law generally allowed marriage between all Christians. Canon law also went significantly further

---

3   Koester, H., *Introduction to the New Testament* (1982), p. 302.
4   Treggiari, S., *Roman Marriage Iusti Coniuges for the Time of Cicero to the Time of Ulpian* (1991), p. 228.
5   Gies, F., Gies, J., *Marriage and the Family in the Middle Ages* (1989), p. 295.
6   Crook, J., *Law and Life in Rome* (1984), p. 99.
7   Jolowicz, H., *Roman Foundations of Modern Law* (1961), p. 159.
8   Capacity to marry.
9   Jolowicz, H., *Roman Foundations of Modern Law* (1961), p. 146.

than both Roman and Germanic law in placing marriage and the family under public control. Thereby, marriage was turned from a private, secular and dissoluble contract, subjected to family control, into an indissoluble sacral bond, subjected to exclusive Church jurisdiction and control.

It would, however, be unfair to picture medieval canon family law as a regress, as compared to its 'liberal' precursors. The canon law period was no Dark Ages of family law. The canon concept of marriage based on the primacy of the spiritual dimension[10] paved the way for the recognition of personal freedom, individual choice[11] of a marriage partner, and equality of men and women,[12] unimaginable in the Antiquity and the early Middle Ages.[13] The individualistic orientation of the medieval canonists, which led to the victory of the consensual theory of marriage, 'reflected their more general views on individual human rights'.[14] It has been suggested that the very concept of the human rights 'usually ascribed to the inventive genius of seventeenth and eighteenth-century writers'[15] had already begun to surface in the beginning of the thirteenth century.[16] One should also be cautious with seeing the struggle of the medieval Church against divorce in the light of present day discourses. Medieval

---

[10] 'Christianity as a whole was developing the innovative concept of marriage as a spiritual bond which might, in its highest form, eliminate sexual relations altogether. The principle of spiritual equality between men and women was basic to Christian thought'. MCNAMARA, J., WEMPLE, S., 'Marriage and Divorce in Frankish Kingdom' (1976), p. 97.

[11] 'Not only was the consent of the spouses necessary for valid marriage, but in time it became evident that the consent of no other persons was required. However much theologians and canonists stressed the importance of the social controls and support of marriage, they had launched a new set of ideas whereby marriage would be considered from the point of view of the couple rather than from that of the extended family. The potential for an individualistic view of marriage in these ideas might not have been realized if the situation had permitted social controls to intervene later and force withdrawal from the union. But since the consensual theory was linked with the teaching that a valid marriage was indissoluble, the possibilities were immense. It meant that medieval society had developed a theory of matrimony which enabled the individual to escape the control of the family, feudal lord, and even the King in the choice of marriage partner'. SHEEHAN, M., *Marriage, Family, and Law in Medieval Europe* (1996), p. 39-40.

[12] There is an interesting, albeit controversial, study shedding a new light on the issue of the female equality in the New Testament, in general, and in the letters by St. Apostle Paul, in particular. (BRISTOW, J., *What Paul Really Said About Women. An Apostle's Liberating View on Equality in Marriage, Leadership, and Love* (1991).) It suggests that Paul has been unjustly reputed as 'the Great Christian Male Chauvinist towards women' (Ibid, p.1), while in fact he was 'the great champion of sexual equality' (Ibid, p. xi). The alleged misconception of Paul's views occurred through the interpretation of Paul's teaching by his Hellenist followers in the light of the Greek notion of female inferiority. This tendency to interpret the Scripture from the viewpoint of the Greek philosophy became canonised in the works of Thomas Aquinas in the thirteenth century. (Ibid, p. 29).

[13] Richard Helmholz stresses that this concept of marriage 'was no part of the legacy of Christian antiquity'. HELMHOLZ, R., *The Spirit of Classical Canon Law* (1996), p. 239.

[14] BRUNDAGE, J., *Medieval Canon Law* (1995), p. 81.

[15] Ibid.

[16] Ibid, and TIERNEY, B., 'Villey, Ockham and the origin of individual rights' (1988), p. 1-31. Cited in: ibid at p. 81.

prohibition of divorce was not about precluding the partners from dissolving their marriage when love has come to an end and to marry a new love. In the medieval context, the indissolubility of marriage merely improved the position of women by protecting them from repudiation at their husband's will.[17]

The emphasis on the spiritual dimensions of marriage forced the Western Church to give more importance to the consensual aspect of marriage than to the solemnisation[18] and the interests of the families. In order to live up to this ideal, the Western Church undermined its own policy towards enforcing the Church solemnisation of marriage. The Church's concern with the equal duty of marital fidelity[19] also witnesses of this attitude. It could be suggested that medieval Western Church law 'conveyed an ideal that was directly opposed to the view of marriage of these days,'[20] and, instead, belonged to the future.[21] Allowing marriage without parental consent is one of the best examples thereof. By not requiring such a consent, the Church 'put tremendous trust in human choice',[22] clearly running against the interest of the feudal families to be able to arrange strategic marriages between the noble clans.[23] This way 'a giant democracy,

---

[17] Such an unsusceptible writer as John Stuart Mill has ascertained that: 'There can be no doubt that for a long time the indissolubility of marriage acted powerfully to elevate the social position of women. The state of things to which in almost all countries it succeeded, was one in which the power of repudiation existed on one side but not on both: in which the stronger might cast away the weaker but the weaker could not fly from the yoke of the stronger'. MILL, J.S., 'On Marriage' (1995), p. 5-6.

[18] Edward Schillebeeckx stressed that: 'The early scholastic has worked out a concept, that marriage is a *personal* decision of two marriage partners self. Their mutual "yes" word is the valid solemnisation of marriage [...]. All the rest is collateral: the parental consent, the formal marriage proposition, the betrothal, the endowment, etc end *even* a benediction by the priest. There is no formal difference between a clandestine and a public marriage'. SCHILLEBEECKX, E., *Het huwelijk: aardse werkelijkheid en heilsmysterie* (1963), p. 206-207.

[19] 'Before God the two parties to marriage were equal and this doctrine of equality was first taught by Christianity. In practice it meant, above all, the obligations, especially that of fidelity, were mutual'. LE BRAS, G., 'Canon law' (1951), p. 348.

[20] SHEEHAN, M., *Marriage, Family, and Law in Medieval Europe* (1996), p. 100.

[21] [...] Alexander's rules were more than a synthesis of previous views on marriage; they represented a vision of what marriage ought to be. It was a vision, which was far from social reality of the time in which Alexander lived. In the late twelfth century, marriage as a matter of customary law, and also as a matter of social fact, was not the exclusive concern of the marriage partners. At all the level of society, family, financial, and feudal concerns, and at the upper level of society, political and military concerns as well dictated marriage choices in many instances. There is evidence that the choice of partners, particularly that of the woman, was hardly considered in many marriages'. DONAHUE, C., 'The Canon Law on the Formation of Marriage and Social Practice in the Later Middle Ages' (1983), p. 146.

[22] DONAHUE, C., 'The Policy of Alexander III's Consent Theory of Marriage' (1975), p. 277.

[23] Goody has suggested that the reasons for recognising consensual marriage stemmed from the wishes of the Church to gain more control over marriage (GOODY, J., *The Development of the Family and Marriage in Europe.* (1983), p. 44-45 and 145). His explanation seems to be unsustainable: defending purely consensual marriage, the Church actually denied any claim of control of marriage, as it was valid without a supervision of the Church. The same reasoning applies equally to the indissolubility of marriage: by its promulgation the Church forfeited its own power to grant and refuse divorce.

in which everyone might marry anyone'[24] was created. Neither Roman nor Jewish nor Germanic laws ever went so far in respecting the individual freedom of choice of the marriage partners.

The Eastern Church shared the ideals of its Western counterpart in theory. However, being more dependent on secular power, it often 'went hand in hand with secular law, and therefore changed and adjusted itself to the requirements of social reality'.[25] This dependence made the Orthodox Church compromise its own ideals. Thus, it appeared unable to enforce the conception of consensual marriage and the equal standards of fidelity for husband and wife in practice.

In order to implement its principles into practice, the Roman Catholic Church had to launch an unprecedented venture of social engineering aimed at promoting its 'impractical' ideals.[26] The preceding Roman, Jewish and Germanic laws were much more 'practical',[27] following the requirements of established social reality. Thus, those laws enforced the parental control of the choice of marital partner, allowed the possibility of 'correction' of the marital choice by divorce, and sanctioned male dominance and different standards for man and women. This venture of the Western medieval canon family law not only influenced the mores of its day, but also set an 'overall tendency [...] in the direction of the individual's freedom'.[28] Canonists 'elevated the individual choice of the marrying couple above any familial and communal approval'.[29] According to Schillebeeckx, it led to the 'desocialisation of marriage, its liberalisation from its cultural-historical, social framework, and on the other side, at least in principle, has contributed to more personal application of marriage'.[30] The individualistic tendency set up by the Western medieval canon law became an important part of the Western heritage. However, after the Reformation, the Counterreformation and the Enlightenment, the Church ideologists fairly renounced this legacy, which was taken over by the secular humanistic thought.[31]

---

[24]   John Noonan, cited in: HELMHOLZ, R., *The Spirit of Classical Canon Law* (1996), at p. 239.

[25]   ZAGOROVSKII, I., *Kurs semeinogo prava* (2003), p. 56.

[26]   REYNOLDS, P., *Marriage in the Western Church* (1994), p. 148.

[27]   '[Roman] concordia might have had little to do with love. What it did require from both partners was an understanding: in the case of the husband, of a woman's foibles and, in the case of the wife, of man's need'. NATHAN, G., *The Family in Late Antiquity* (2000), p. 20.

[28]   SHEEHAN, M., *Marriage, Family, and Law in Medieval Europe* (1996), p. 39-40.

[29]   HARRINGTON, J., *Reordering Marriage and Society in Reformed Germany* (1995), p. 58.

[30]   SCHILLEBEECKX, E., *Het huwelijk: aardse werkelijkheid en heilsmysterie* (1963), p. 206.

[31]   See: Part III of this book.

6.2. RESISTANCE TO MEDIEVAL CANON FAMILY LAW: LAW IN THE BOOKS VERSUS LAW IN ACTION

6.2.1. THE GAP BETWEEN THE LAW IN THE BOOKS AND THE LAW IN ACTION

One of objectives of this book is to explore the pro's and contras of harmonisation of modern family law in Europe. The modern proponents of the cultural constraints argument hold that any top-down harmonisation of family law would end up in a cultural alienation of the imposed harmonised law, and thus produce a lasting gap between the law in the books and the law in action. The example of the medieval top-down unification of family law provides us with a chance to subject this argument to empirical proof; by finding whether the first attempt to unify family law in Europe was able to penetrate into social reality, or merely remained the 'law in the books'.[32]

Although the way for the replacement by the medieval uniform canon family law of its historical precursors had been paved for centuries, the climax of this process still involved a rather dramatic social change. A transformation of such calibre required an unprecedented level of social engineering on the part of the Church, one which induced a considerable resistance.[33] As result of this resistance, a certain discord between the law in the books and the law in action was manifest everywhere, although this discrepancy was more persistent in some regions than in the others. The overcoming of this discord took the Church a great deal of time and effort. The resistance was particularly strong in the periphery of Western Europe, which had been Christianised relatively late.[34] Thus, in East Germany and Poland, which wasn't Christianised until the tenth century, and in Scandinavia, which became Christian as

---

[32] Michael Sheehan writes that: 'by the middle of the thirteenth century the uniform canon family laws "in the books" were practically completed. The question is whether they succeeded in permeating European Society and, if so by what means and at what rate'. SHEEHAN, M., *Marriage, Family, and Law in Medieval Europe* (1996), p. 100.

[33] According to Michael Sheehan, the canon family law 'was slowly incorporated in the local law of the Western Church among peoples of widely varied traditions. Some of these traditions had contributed to the formation of the general law; others were more or less seriously threatened by its application. The process of adjustment was continuous and sometimes marred by bitter conflicts'. SHEEHAN, M., *Marriage, Family, and Law in Medieval Europe* (1996), p. 39.

[34] 'Diversity in marriage practices in medieval Europe was influenced by social level and geography. Although the Catholic Church was nominally universal, its doctrines and legislation respecting matrimonial matters were only weakly felt by some of its distant faithful'. PHILLIPS, R., *Putting Asunder* (1988), p. 33.

late as the eleventh to twelfth centuries,[35] the population kept clinging to the old pre-Christian traditions. Max Rheinstein even suggests that the whole medieval canon unification never completely reached Scandinavia.[36] Lars Tottie observes that the papal edicts on the indissolubility of marriage were never fully enforced in Sweden.[37] In Norway until 1276[38] the local 'district laws' allowed both husband and wife to dissolve their marriage freely and without stating any ground.

One of the strongest examples of this delay was Iceland. Christianity was established there in 1000, but 'on the Icelandic terms'.[39] Although the canon law of marriage was officially received in Iceland in the thirteenth century, the earliest attempts to enforce it date from 1429. Before then, the Icelandic collection of indigenous laws (*grágás*)[40] continued to regulate marriage. These laws diverged from the Church law in a great number of respects. One example is that, 'whereas the Catholic Church emphasized that a valid marriage required the freely given consent of both spouses, in Icelandic law (*grágás*) the consent of the women was not necessary'.[41] Icelandic clerics married or lived in concubinage, and their sons often inherited their office. Moreover, a rather liberal divorce was maintained by the *grágás*[42] at the time when the doctrine of indissolubility had already been implemented in the bulk of Europe. A unilateral divorce was possible if, for instance, the economic situation of the other spouse had suddenly deteriorated[43] or the spouses had caused each other 'large wounds'.[44] At the same time adultery was not sufficient ground for divorce![45] There was evidence that the Church tolerated those deviations, as the bishop's permission for divorce was required (and presumably given) if the divorced spouses wanted to remarry.[46]

Not only the latecomers, but even some countries with a long-standing Christian tradition had problems with the internalisation of the new Church law. For instance, it is believed that in Ireland, the Gregorian reformation had not yet begun in the

---

[35]   It is suggested that in Scandinavia paganism remained significant until well into the sixteenth century. BRADLEY, D., *Family Law and Political Culture* (1996), p. 5.
[36]   RHEINSTEIN, M., *Marriage Stability, Divorce, and the Law* (1972), p. 153.
[37]   TOTTIE, L., 'The Elimination of Fault in Swedish Divorce Law' (1980), p. 131.
[38]   In this year the 'district laws' were replaced by the uniform law of the King Magnus Lagabøte.
[39]   JACOBSEN, G., 'Sexual Irregularities in Medieval Scandinavia' (1982), p. 73.
[40]   The Codification of Icelandic indigenous law, in force from 1118 till 1264. JACOBSEN, G., 'Sexual Irregularities in Medieval Scandinavia' (1982), p. 73.
[41]   PHILLIPS, R., *Putting asunder* (1988), p. 33.
[42]   JACOBSEN, G., 'Sexual Irregularities in Medieval Scandinavia' (1982), p. 73.
[43]   Ibid.
[44]   Ibid.
[45]   Ibid.
[46]   Ibid.

fourteenth century.[47] 'Gaelic Ireland took no notice of Church marriage or of the canonical rules of consanguinity: cousins married cousins, and unions were easily dissoluble, leading to serial polygamy'.[48] Kerry O'Halloran maintained that 'the looseness of the marriage tie' persisted in Ireland at least until Elizabethan times'.[49]

Spanish law also displayed essential deviations from the canon law standards. In line with the canon law, the important thirteenth century Spanish Code, *Las Siete Partidas*, did not mention divorce in the normal sense of this word.[50] However, the *Partridas* provided for the possibility of the annulment of a marriage upon 'non-canonical' grounds. Such annulment was possible, for instance, if one of the spouses wanted to enter a monastic order, had committed adultery, or had turned heretic, Moor, or Jew. In case of adultery, the innocent spouse could be granted permission to remarry. Thus, this provision on annulment was 'a divorce in all but name'.[51]

There is evidence that in Germany the rules on the legitimating of illegitimate children by subsequent marriage of their parents initially met an 'exceedingly hostile reception'.[52]

England was a case apart. The acceptance of the uniform canon law there was not a problem as such. According to Michael Sheehan, the uniform canon family law was implemented in England with a delay of as much as a generation.[53] However, Javier Martínez-Torrón has less optimistically suggested that it took considerably longer before the canon laws really took root:

> 'Certainly, the ecclesiastical ideas on marriage were to some extent a novelty and they were not easily accepted by English society. While ecclesiastical matrimonial jurisdiction gained control quite rapidly, control was not sufficient. The real issue was changing the pre-Christian vision, which considered it a private union not necessarily indissoluble, into a new concept which understood matrimony as a binding legal contract, whose essential ties were set forth by public norms of *ius cogens*, and which was inescapably subject to judicial power. The task was achieved slowly, in a process that may be considered complete by the late fifteenth century'.[54]

---

[47] BURGUIERE, A. et al. (eds.), *A History of the Family*. Volume I. Distant Worlds, Ancient Worlds (1996), p. 435.
[48] BRESC, H., 'Europe: Town and Country' (1996), p. 435.
[49] O'HALLORAN, K., 'Ireland: The Family and the Law in a Divided Land' (1998), p. 116, note 2.
[50] VAN KLEFFENS, E, *Hispanic Law Until the End of the Middle Ages* (1968), p. 199.
[51] PHILLIPS, R., *Putting Asunder* (1988), p. 34.
[52] HÜBNER, R., *History of Germanic Private Law* (1918), p. 675.
[53] SHEEHAN, M., *Marriage, Family, and Law in Medieval Europe* (1996), p. 102.
[54] MARTÍNEZ-TORRÓN, J., *Anglo-American Law and Canon Law. Canonical Roots of the Common Law Tradition* (1998), p. 97.

Modern historians believe that towards the middle of the thirteenth century it was accepted in England that consent alone without any formalities could create a valid marriage.[55] The peculiarity of England was not because of the late or more difficult internalising of the uniform canon family law, but rather in the fact that there was a long period in English history when it was widely believed that the English clergy had never accepted the consensual theory of marriage. Frederic William Mainland was the first to challenge this view. He convincingly demonstrated that:

'It would have been as impossible for the courts Christian of this country to maintain about this vital point a schismatical law of their own as it would be for a judge of High Court to persistently disregard the decisions of the House of Lords: there would have been an appeal from every sentence, and reversal would have been a matter of course.'[56]

The unsustainable belief that the English canon law kept aloof from the uniform canon law, was provoked by the fact that the English secular common law never really came to terms with canon law. Thus, at common law a woman was entitled to dower only if she was, according to the custom, endowed at the church doors. If the marriage was a clandestine one, there was no church ceremony and therefore no proper endowment. The secular law did not question the validity of such marriage: validity was the domain of canon law. But it denied the clandestine wife a right to dower.[57] In a similar way, the common law denied the inheritance rights of the children legitimated by subsequent marriage.[58] The secular courts did not contest the legitimacy of those children as such, but denied them the right to inherit land, as disputes dealing with the inheritance of land were within the secular jurisdiction.[59] At the Council of Merton in 1236, 'the bishops, anxious to bring English law into accord with what they conceived to be the clear dictates of religion, reason and civil law, urged upon the baronage the proposition that children born before the marriage of their parents should be counted as legitimate at English [secular] law. The barons refused'.[60]

Comparable contradictions between the secular and the canon laws were noticeable in Spain. It was accepted that the bride's consent was rendered necessary for betrothal, as the Church law demanded it. However, the secular law provided that a father could disinherit his daughter, if she refused to accept a suitor chosen by him.[61]

---

[55] SHEEHAN, M., *Marriage, Family, and Law in Medieval Europe* (1996), p. 101.
[56] POLLOCK, F., MAITLAND, F., *The History of English Law before the Time of Edward I*, II (1952), p. 373.
[57] Ibid, p. 377-375.
[58] Ibid, p. 375-377.
[59] HELMHOLZ, R., *Canon Law and the Law of England* (1987), p. 190-191.
[60] Ibid, p. 187.
[61] STONE, M., *Marriage and Friendship in Medieval Spain* (1990), p. 36-37.

In Orthodox Russia the requirements of the Orthodox canon law were for a long time obeyed only by the nobility. In Northern Russia where Christianisation was weaker, instances of polygamy among common people were recorded even in the thirteenth century. The population also continued to marry according to pagan customs, considering the Church solemnisation only relevant for 'princes and barons'.[62]

6.2.2. HOW THE DISCREPANCY WAS ENDED

The analysis of the further process of the implementation of canon family law allows the conclusion that the first attempt to unify family law in Europe was successful both on the level of the 'law in the books' and on the level of 'the law in action'.[63] The question, however, is: 'What was the price of this success?' No matter how slow and difficult the implementation evolved in some countries, 'on the long run [...] the canonical concepts prevailed, both in the British Isles and on the Continent'.[64] The Church had enough power to impose its new vision of the family on the society: the history of the effectuation of the medieval uniform canon family law is a history of excommunications, interdicts and bitter clashes. The implementation of the medieval canon family law was not restrained by any notion of democracy or respect for ideological pluralism.[65] 'Medieval churchmen [...] believed that they had not merely the right but the duty to repress any religious or moral ideas that departed from orthodox norms'.[66] Thus it is possible to conclude that it is quite feasible to achieve an infringing reformation of traditional family patterns and traditional family ideology by means of a radical instrumentalist legal change. And this even when the ideology of the reform is initially quite alien to the society and runs somewhat against its practical interests. The price of such success is, however, a persistent ideological pressure and the readiness to use unrestrained coercion.

---

[62] SOLOV'EV, C., *Istoria Rissii 1054-1462* (2001), p. 89.
[63] The opposite view has been expressed by Wolfram Müller-Freienfels, who suggested that '[...} although certain provisions of the canon law of marriage entered the secular system of law, they had no practical impact' and that some provisions of canonic law '[...] produced grievances that were significant in the Reformation' MÜLLER-FREIENFELS, W., 'The Unification of Family Law' (1968-69), p. 182.
[64] MARTÍNEZ-TORRÓN, J., *Anglo-American Law and Canon Law. Canonical Roots of the Common Law Tradition* (1998), p. 98.
[65] BRUNDAGE, J., *Medieval Canon Law* (1995), p. 70.
[66] Ibid.

CHAPTER 7
THE MEDIEVAL *IUS COMMUNE* OF FAMILY LAW AND THE CURRENT HARMONISATION DEBATE

7.1. INTRODUCTION

After the foregoing account of the formation of the Western medieval uniform canon family law, it is time to analyse its significance for the current debate concerning harmonisation of family law in Europe. The relevance of the Roman law part of the medieval *ius commune* for the assessment of the perspectives of the harmonisation of private law in general has attracted considerable attention.[1] However, the specific relevance of the canon law part of the *ius commune* in the context of contemporary harmonisation of family law has not yet acquired appropriate attention.[2]

It may come as a surprise that the common-legal-past argument has been used as frequently in favour for, as against, the deliberate harmonisation of contemporary private law. The proponents of the so called 'Neo-Pandectism', as for instance Reinhard Zimmermann, assert the relevance of the *ius commune* for the Europe of today. They hold that the old *ius commune* 'provides the intellectual and doctrinal framework within which a new European legal unity may one day emerge'.[3] Most of the proponents of the *ius commune* argument are, however, quite cautious not to overestimate its direct utility for the present-day European legal integration. In the words of Franz Wieacker, the historical models '[...] cannot be offered as guidelines for the concrete solution of contemporary problems [...] primarily because of the unrepeatability of the original conditions'.[4] Nonetheless, Wieacker submits that '[...] the reception of Roman law [...] represents a model of progressive unification of a

---

[1]   For a brief overview of the literature and the discussion see, for instance: LUIG, K., 'The History of Roman Private Law and the Unification of European Law (1997), p. 405-427; Smits, J., The *Making of European Private Law. Towards a Ius Commune Europaeum as a Mixed legal System* (2002), p. 43-45.

[2]   For the relevance of the *ius commune* for family law see my contribution 'Geschiedenis van het familierecht: gelijke ontwikkelingen' to ANTOKOLSKAIA, M., DE HONDT, W., STEENHOFF, G., *Naar een Europees Familierecht* (1999), p. 33-62.

[3]   ZIMMERMANN, R., *The Law of Obligations. Roman Foundations of the Civilian Tradition* (1996), p. X.

[4]   WIEACKER, F., 'Historical Models for the Unification of European Law' (1994), p. 297.

profusion of individual tribal, territorial and city laws'.[5] The value of such models for the present-day situation is that they 'may suggest common patterns in comparable constellations, and may thus indicate a framework for contemporary action'.[6] The proponents of the *ius commune* argument see the common legal past more as a source of inspiration for the creation of a common European science and a common European education than as a direct model for the elaboration of a uniform law for the whole of Europe.[7] The approach of Govaert Van den Bergh is also illustrative in this respect. On the one hand, he considers the *ius commune* as a 'valuable asset for a Europe making its way towards unification'. On the other hand, he does not 'believe that the *ius commune* can be revived in the united Europe of the future'.[8] Reinhard Zimmermann goes a bit further, as he seems not to completely exclude the possibility of unification by means of legislation. In his view, the new *ius commune* 'will have to be shaped by judges, legislators, and professors, acting in cooperation with each other',[9] building upon the common roots of the modern legal systems inherited from the times of the old *ius commune*. This cautious approach contrasts the voices that boldly suggest that 'a new *ius commune* is taking shape before our eyes, […] but we are not completely aware of it'.[10]

Ius commune sceptics like Pierre Legrand, in the first place, reject the suggestion that the *ius commune* ever had pan-European relevance. Legrand submits 'that there never was an *ius* that was truly *commune*', as some European countries were never part of it.[11] In the second place, the opponents of the *ius-commune* argument hold that even if a true *ius commune* ever existed in the past, that does not in any way favour the harmonisation of private law in the present. According to Legrand, even if one considers that 'the common law lawyers and civilian jurists possibly once thought alike in the era of the *ius commune*,'[12] this hardly matters now. What does matter is how they think now and how they would think in the face of a new common European law. And now, there exists a 'fundamental' and 'irreducible'[13] difference between common and civil law legal thinking, '[T]his difference is not at all mitigated by the fact that there may once have been a time when these lawyers thought more closely like each

---

5   Ibid, p. 303.
6   WIEACKER, F., 'Historical Models for the Unification of European Law' (1994), p. 297.
7   See, for instance: KÖTZ, H., 'A Common Private Law for Europe: Perspective for the Reform of European Legal Education' (1992), p. 34; COING, H., 'European Common Law: Historical Foundations (1978), p. 42-44.
8   VAN DEN BERGH, G., '*Ius Commune*, A History with a Future' (1992), p. 605.
9   ZIMMERMANN, R., 'Roman Law and the Harmonisation of Private Law in Europe' (2004), p. 39.
10   KOOPMANS, T., 'Towards a New "*Ius Commune*"' (1992), p. 49.
11   LEGRAND, P., 'European Legal Systems Are Not Converging' (1996), p. 61, note 40. See also: BRAUNEDER, W., 'Europäisches Privatrecht; aber was ist es?' (1993), p. 225-235.
12   LEGRAND, P., 'Legal Traditions in Western Europe: The Limits of Commonality' (1995), p. 68.
13   Ibid.

other'.[14] The verdict of Pierre Legrand is that 'the era of the *ius commune* must be seen to belong to a past that will not be re-enacted on the European stage'.[15] Mart?n Hesselink has remarked that the proposition that the new common law for Europe should be based on the old *ius commune* 'does not seem more obvious than to suggest Latin as the official language for the Internet'.[16] A more far reaching criticism accuses the 'Neo-Pandectists' of cherishing a reactionary nostalgia for the good old *ius commune* days.[17] It has been suggested that they interpret the progressive developments that put an end to the *ius commune* as merely 'historical accidents', and thereby fail to appreciate their proper social and political significance.[18]

Remarkably enough, even scholars who consider the common legal past of Europe as a factor favouring a possible future harmonisation of private law, stop short of extrapolating this appreciation to family law. Some of them do not even seem to be aware of the existence of *ius commune* of family law. Thus, Kurt Lipstein, describing the existence of the *ius commune* up until the era of national codifications, remarks that 'family law and the law of succession have always retained their local characteristics'.[19] Others, like Govaert Van den Bergh, doubt the bearing of the *ius commune* argument in respect of the possibility to harmonise family law, as 'people tend to cling tenaciously to their old laws in matters of family and inheritance'.[20] This attitude is quite remarkable given the fact that, irrespective of the outcome of the debate surrounding the existence of the *ius commune* in the other areas of private law, the preceding recapitulation clearly shows that if any area of private law in Europe ever had an irrefutable *ius commune* in the past, it was family law.

7.2. FAMILY *IUS COMMUNE* DIFFERENT FROM THE REST OF PRIVATE LAW?

7.2.1. TWO PARTS OF MEDIEVAL *IUS COMMUNE*

Family law, with the exception of matrimonial property law and a few other parts, has its roots in a different *ius commune* or, at least, a different part of the common *ius*

---

[14]   Ibid.
[15]   LEGRAND, P., 'Legal Traditions in Western Europe: The Limits of Commonality' (1995), p. 65; See also: GAIRO, T., 'Römisches Recht, Romanistik und Rechtsraum in Europa' (1995), p. 1-16.
[16]   HESSELINK, M., *The New European Legal Culture* (2001), p. 66.
[17]   For an overview see: HESSELINK, M., *The New European Legal Culture* (2001), p. 66-98.
[18]   HESSELINK, M., De redelijkheid en billijkheid in het Europese privaatrecht (1999), p. 15.
[19]   LIPSTEIN, K., 'European Legal Education in the Future: Teaching the "Common Law of Europe"' (1992), p. 255.
[20]   VAN DEN BERGH, G., '*Ius Commune*, A History with a Future' (1992), p. 605.

commune than the economically-related areas of private law. This *ius commune* of family law was the uniform medieval canon family law, developed by the canonist of the Catholic Church. In contrast, the *ius commune* of most other fields of private law was the medieval Roman law, developed at the European universities from the eleventh century[21] on the basis of re-discovered Roman law.[22] Matrimonial property law actually fell outside the scope of both *ius communes*. It was not part of the canon *ius commune*, and was also much less influenced by the Roman *ius commune*.

The issue of the composition of the medieval *ius commune* is not without controversy.[23] The *ius commune* is often seen as one integral *ius utrumque* ('the one and the other law'[24]): the medieval Roman-canon law embracing both the canon and the Roman law.[25] John Merryman submits, for instance, that 'just as Roman civil law was the universal law of the temporal empire [...], so the canon law was the universal law of the spiritual domain, directly associated with the authority of the Pope'.[26] This universal law grew into a complete legal system, 'based on Roman foundations from a technical standpoint, and based on spiritual, theological and philosophical foundations from the perspective of principle'.[27] The appreciation of Roman and canon law as a unity is often reinforced by the fact that the study of canon law was, together with the study of Roman civil law, an integral part of the curriculum of the Italian universities. '[T]he degree conferred on a student who had completed the full course of study was *Juris Utriusque Doctor*, or Doctor of Both Laws, referring to the civil and

---

[21] For a brief account of the process see, for instance, WIEACKER, F., *A history of private law in Europe* (1995), p. 28 ff.

[22] The term 're-discovery' should be used with some qualifications. Some incomplete copies of the last original of the sixth century Justinian compilation, unknown and considered unimportant, survived through the Middle Ages. In the eleventh century they started to attract the academic interest. (BELLOMO, M., *The Common Legal Past of Europe 1000-1800* (1995), p. 60-61.) The critical version of *Digest* came into sight in the late eleventh century in North Italy. (WIEACKER, F., *A history of private law in* Europe (1995), p. 28.) The re-discovery actually started with the work of Irnerius (died around 1130), who 'was the first to have the courage to recompose and restore' the Justinian's texts. BELLOMO, ibid., p. 61.

[23] WIJFFELS, A., 'A New Software-Package for an Outdated Operating System?' (2000), p. 104-105.

[24] BELLOMO, M., *The Common Legal Past of Europe 1000-1800* (1995), p. 74.

[25] For instance, Helmut Coing maintained that: '[...] Roman-Canon law has become a Ius Commune, the Common Law of the continent'. COING, H., 'European Common Law: Historical Foundations' (1978), p. 33. Reinhard Zimmermann refers to Roman-Canon *ius commune* as the foundation of the European legal unity. ZIMMERMANN, R., 'Roman Law and the Harmonisation of Private Law in Europe' (2004), p. 29. In the same sense, see also his *The Law of Obligations. Roman Foundations of the Civilian Tradition* (1996), p. ix-xi. Thomas Lacey stated: 'from the tenth century onward there was one law, fully digested in the *Corpus Iuris* and in the books of the canonists, for the whole Western Christendom'. LACEY, T., *Marriage in Church and State* (1947), p. 123.

[26] MERRYMAN, J., *The Civil Law Tradition* (1969), p. 12.

[27] MARTÍNEZ-TORRÓN, J., Anglo-*American Law and Canon Law. Canonical Roots of the Common Law Tradition* (1998), p. 26.

the canon law'.[28] Within this dual *ius commune* the canon law was sometimes perceived as an inferior part,[29] not more than merely an 'offspring' of the Roman law.[30]

There are many good reasons to treat, at least for some purposes, the medieval Roman and canon law as the parts of one and the same *ius commune*. Both laws were certainly closely interrelated.[31] The canon and the Roman law have often influenced one another.[32] There is an opinion that the methodology of the canonists was possibly influenced by the methods of the early Glossators.[33] The canonists and the civilists often used the same conceptual language,[34] especially after the Church had obtained competence in such purely civil law matters as, for instance, ecclesiastical corporations and foundations.[35] There are equally good reasons however, to make a clear distinction between these two parts of the medieval *ius commune*. It is even suggested that treating the Roman and the canon law as one *ius commune* is merely a fiction.[36] Harold Berman argues that 'the idea that canon law was somehow modelled on Roman law involves serious misconceptions'.[37]

It is worth noticing that the distinction between the Roman and the canon parts of the *ius commune* has always been maintained by the medieval scholars themselves.[38]

---

[28] MERRYMAN, J., *The Civil Law Tradition* (1969), p. 12.

[29] Illustrative in this respect is Maitland's portrayal of the medieval Roman and Canon law as 'imperial mother and her papal daughter'. POLLOCK, F., MAITLAND, F., *The History of English Law before the Time of Edward I*, Vol. I (1898), p. 116.

[30] Harold Berman regrets that the statement of Sherman, who maintained: 'The great problems of law and jurisprudence were thought out once and for all by the Roman lawyers, and their labours are recorded in the Corpus Juris Canonici, and with them saved civilization in Europe'. (SHERMAN, C., 'A Brief History of Medieval Roman Canon Law' (1919), p. 649.) 'is still shared by many, although convincingly refuted by virtually all contemporary specialists in the field'. BERMAN, H., *Law and Revolution. The Formation of the Western Legal Tradition* (1983), p. 605, note 12.

[31] Harold Berman notices that 'the canonists used Roman law abundantly, [...] just as they used Biblical law, and just as they used Germanic law; they used them all as sources. Thus one may speak, in a qualified sense, of the "Romano-canonical" legal system'. BERMAN, H., *Law and Revolution. The Formation of the Western Legal Tradition* (1983), p. 204.

[32] WIEACKER, F., *A History of Private Law in Europe* (1995), p. 53-54.

[33] Franz Wieacker notices that Gratian himself was probably influenced by the methods of the Glossators, but 'detailed proof' of that is very difficult. WIEACKER, F., *A History of Private Law in Europe* (1995), p. 50.

[34] As Reinhard Zimmermann puts it: 'The Popes could not, and did not want to, develop an intellectually independent legal system. Instead they developed to a large extent upon Roman legal rules and concepts [...]'. ZIMMERMANN, R., 'Roman Law and the Harmonisation of Private Law in Europe' (2004), p. 30.

[35] BERMAN, H., *Law and Revolution. The Formation of the Western Legal Tradition* (1983), p. 85-115 and 225 ff.

[36] BRAUNEDER, W., 'Europäisches Privatrecht; aber was ist es?' (1993), p. 228.

[37] BERMAN, H., *Law and Revolution. The Formation of the Western Legal Tradition* (1983), p. 204.

[38] '*Ius civile* and *ius canonicum*, the work of the legist and the canonist, remained in principle distinct in the mind of the time'. WIEACKER, F., *A History of Private Law in Europe* (1995), p. 53.

The two sets of laws were incorporated into different collections: the *Corpus Iuris Canonici*[39] and the *Corpus Iuris Civilis*. These laws were applied by different courts: the uniform system of ecclesiastical courts and the national civil courts, respectively. The ecclesiastic judges habitually applied canon law even if they had to deal with a secular case.[40] Likewise, the secular judges normally did not apply canon law.[41] Spiritual and secular courts applied, however, the Roman and the canon law, respectively, on the ground of mutual principle of subsidiarity, in the absence of law of their own.[42] The study of the canon law was awarded with the title *Doctor iuris,* while the students in Roman law acquired the title of *Doctor Legum*.[43] The fact that the papal *Decretale* of 1219 prohibited the University of Paris to organise regular education in Roman law alongside education in canon law,[44] shows that the university curricula were not necessarily combining the studies of both laws. The *Corpus Iuris Civilis* of Justinian and the *Vulgate* of Irnerius (1060-1125) gave rise to the school of Glossators, commenting on Roman law. The *Decretum Gratiani* gave rise to the different school of *Decretists*, commenting on the canon laws collected in the *Decretum.*[45] Not only did Roman law influence canon law, influence also went the other way around.[46] Other differences between the two parts of the medieval *ius commune* relate to the methods of their formation, the level of 'commonality' and their territorial scope. Because of the particular importance of these matters for the purposes of this study, they will be treated more extensively below.

7.2.2. DELIBERATE UNIFICATION VERSUS SPONTANEOUS HARMONISATION

A notable difference between the canon and the Roman *ius commune* lies in the way they were achieved. The canon *ius commune* was, in general, the result of a top-down unification. It was brought about by deliberate efforts on the part of the Roman Catholic Church in general, and of the Papal Curia in particular. It was imposed upon states and dioceses; resistance to it was rigorously suppressed. The Roman *ius commune*

---

[39] Unofficial name of the collection of canon law from *Decretum Gratiani* to the Clement V (1305-1414). This name became official in the end of the sixteenth century, when an official addition appeared in 1582. WIEACKER, F., *A history of private law in Europe* (1995), p. 51.

[40] WIEACKER, F., *A History of Private Law in Europe* (1995), p. 52.

[41] ZIMMERMANN, R., 'Roman-Dutch Jurisprudence and its Contribution to European Private Law', (1992), p. 1691.

[42] WIEACKER, F., *A history of private law in* Europe (1995), p. 54.

[43] BRAUNEDER, W., 'Europäisches Privatrecht; aber was ist es?' (1993), p. 228.

[44] WIEACKER, F., *A history of private law in* Europe (1995), p. 53.

[45] *Ibid,* p. 51.

[46] WOLTER, U., *Ius canonicum in jure civili: Studien zur Rechtsquellenlehre in der neueren Privatrechts-geschichte* (1975).

was, by contrast, a result of spontaneous harmonisation, a kind of 'free movement of legal rules'.[47] This process has been often described as the voluntary reception of Roman law due to the irresistibility of its persuasive authority. It is true that the expansion of Roman law has also been depicted as a 'centuries-long struggle [of Roman law] with indigenous law'.[48] But this does not diminish the fact that the Roman part of the *ius commune* came about in a completely different way than the canon law part of the *ius commune*. This difference had at least two consequences that are relevant here. In the first place, the level of 'commonality' of the medieval canon family law was considerably higher that that of the Roman law. In the second place, the territorial scope of application of the canon law covered the whole of Western Christendom, while the scope of application of the Roman law was significantly more modest. Both aspects will be addressed in the next two sections.

7.2.3. DIFFERENT LEVEL OF 'COMMUNALITY'

The difference in the level of 'commonality' between the canon law and the Roman law parts of the medieval *ius commune* and Roman law part thereof is easily discernible. The unification of the canon law in the West was, from around the eleventh century until the Reformation, virtually total. As Raoul van Caenegem has pointed out, 'medieval canon law was the first common law of the whole of Western Europe, as it was administered, taught and studied in the whole of Latin Christendom without any regard for political, ethic or linguistic frontiers'.[49] Medieval canon law was more or less a coherent hierarchical system of imperative laws, which consisted of generally applicable canons and decrees and the locally applicable laws of the local ecclesiastic authorities. The 'top level' of the system, the generally applicable rules, was uniform for the whole of the Catholic world and formed the canon law part of the *ius commune*. The level of 'commonality' of the Roman law, by contrast, was so low that it allows the suggestion that 'there has never been a Roman "*ius commune*" conceived as one

---

47   A modern theory of spontaneous harmonisation of private law in Europe by means of 'free movement of legal rules', for instance a free choice made by judges among different competing models represented in different legal systems, has been developed by Jan Smits. (SMITS, J., 'A European Private Law as a Mixed Legal System. Towards a Jus Commune Through the Free Movement of Legal Rules' (1998), p. 328-340 and The *Making of European Private Law. Towards a Ius Commune Europaeum as a Mixed legal System* (2002), p. 60-71). For more on the theory of the 'free movement of legal rules', see Part I, Chapter 2, Section 2.2.1. Jan Smits rightly suggests that the old *ius commune* was partly created by way of 'free movement of legal rules and 'not by way of binding imposition by a centralist government'. The *Making of European Private Law. Towards a Ius Commune Europaeum as a Mixed legal System* (2002), p. 62.

48   KOSCHAKER, P., *Europa en het Romeinse recht* (1995), p. 142.

49   CAENEGEM, R., *European Law in the Past and the Future: Unity and Diversity of Two Millennia* (2002), p. 14.

single legal system'.[50] Instead, the Roman '*ius commune*' was no more than 'a legal tradition which was scattered and divided by privileges and diverse jurisdictions in Europe'.[51]

The difference in the level of community of the two parts of the medieval *ius commune* reflected the different status of the uniform canon family law and the received Roman law in medieval Europe. Canon law was the positive law of the Roman Catholic Church: the greatest supranational political entity of the Middle Ages, while 'Roman law was not the positive law of any specific policy in the West' during the Middle Ages.[52] Thus the canon law was developed by or under the auspice of the Church legislative hierarchy, headed by the Pope as the supreme lawgiver. In contrast, the Roman *ius commune* was developed through the unstructured and non-hierarchical mechanisms of teaching, opinions and academic writings of the Glossators and Post-Glossators or Commentators.[53] The standing of the medieval uniform canon law as the positive law of the Catholic Church gave it the status of imperative law, enforced by the political and judicial power of the Church. The Church courts applied canon law prior to any local or national laws or customs. Therefore, the indigenous family law rules all but disappeared in the fields where the Church had exclusive jurisdiction.[54] As Roman law had no political authority behind it and owed its application merely to its persuasive authority,[55] it never reached the status of the primary applicable law. Roman law was applied by the secular courts merely as a subsidiary source,[56] resorted to when the primary applicable law, the *ius proprium* (local laws and customs),

---

[50] CHAMBOREDON, A., 'Form v Substance? An Ideological Venture beyond the Dichotomy in European Law of Contracts' (2000), p. 246.
[51] Ibid.
[52] BERMAN, H., *Law and Revolution. The Formation of the Western Legal Tradition* (1983), p. 204.
[53] WIEACKER, F., *A History of Private Law in Europe* (1995), p. 54-61.
[54] LACEY, T., *Marriage in Church and State* (1947), p. 123. It was virtually impossible to maintain any divergent local canon rule, as any judgment based on it would not outlive the appeal. There were however some cases when the secular law provided a solution divergent from that of canon law. For instance, as was already mentioned, English secular law denied inheritance rights of the children legitimated by the subsequent marriage according to the canon law. (POLLOCK, F., MAITLAND, F., *The History of English Law before the Time of Edward I*, Vol. II (1952), p. 375-377.) The secular law did not question their legitimacy, subjected to the canon law, but it did not qualify them as lawful heirs. HELMHOLZ, R., *Canon Law and the Law of England* (1987), p. 190-191. The existence of two separate jurisdictions made such contradictions possible.
[55] Franz Wieacker noticed that, 'the whole authority of Roman law rested on its being *ratio scripta*. WIEACKER, F., *A history of private law in Europe* (1995), p. 35.
[56] However, Manlio Bellomo has convincingly argued that the *ius proprium* itself and the practice of its application was deeply influenced by the conceptual language and underlying values of Roman law. (BELLOMO, M., *The Common Legal Past of Europe 1000-1800* (1995), p. 79-159). Therefore, in spite of the hierarchy of sources, 'in every important practical act the *ius commune* was the basis of every decision'. Ibid. p. 154.

provided no solution.[57] The fact that the Roman part of the medieval *ius commune* was not developed by any hierarchal entity[58] explains why there was no strict mechanism to find out which source of medieval Roman law was more authoritative. The uniform common opinion of learned jurists (*communis opinio doctorum*)[59] was a much too feeble mechanism to ensure uniform application. As to the canon law, the situation was quite different: the Church had the papal curia as the supreme lawmaker and the structured hierarchal system under it. Accordingly the hierarchy of the canon law sources was determined by this system. Not being connected to any particular state, Roman law was applied by the autonomous secular courts of different states and principalities without any uniform system of judicial revision that could safeguard the uniformity of its application. As a result, 'the outcome of disputes would not necessarily be the same everywhere'.[60] By contrast, the hierarchical system of the ecclesiastic courts,[61] with 'a complete system of appeal, first to a provincial court with the authority of the metropolitan, and thence to the court of Rome',[62] together with the common academic training of the principal officers in all of these courts ensured a fundamental uniformity in the application of the canon family law.[63]

Thus, the level of commonality of the Roman part of the medieval *ius commune* was not only lower than that of the canon law part, but its commonality was of a quite different nature. While the canon law was a set of imperative, uniform and uniformly applicable rules, the harmonising effect of the Roman law was, rather, that of creating a common legal tradition, and a 'common *lingua franca* in the field of private law.[64] This effect was achieved not only through the subsidiary application of received Roman law, but also via the centuries-long influence that the Roman law executed upon the applicable primary local laws: the *ius proprium*. As a result of this influence, 'a common stock of legal solutions, rules and concepts'[65] was developed. Thereby Roman law managed to create a common legal science, a common legal education and a common conceptual framework of private law[66] whose hold is perceptible even today.

---

57 According to the doctrine of hierarchy of sources, the secular court applied firstly Royal and feudal law of the particular principality, secondly, customary law and thirdly Roman law, as a kind of residual law. BELLOMO, M., *The Common Legal Past of Europe 1000-1800* (1995), p. 151.

58 See: KOSCHAKER, P., *Europa en het Romeinse recht* (1995), p. 142.

59 COING, H., 'Die europäische Privatrechtsgeschichte der neueren Zeit als einheitliches Forschungsgebiet' (1967), p. 1-33.

60 ZIMMERMANN, R., 'Civil Code and Civil Law' (1994-1995), p. 82.

61 See BRUNDAGE, J., *Medieval Canon Law* (1995), p. 120-126.

62 LACEY, T., *Marriage in Church and State* (1947), p. 124.

63 DONAHUE, C., 'The Canon Law on the Formation of Marriage and Social Practice in the Later Middle Ages' (1983), p. 147.

64 Ibid.

65 COING, H., 'European Common Law: Historical Foundations (1978), p. 34.

66 Ibid.

Hence, two lessons for the modern harmonisation debates could be derived from the comparison of the two parts of the medieval *ius commune*. Firstly, it appears rather clear that even during times when local private law was primal and undeveloped, a much superior Roman law could not, by virtue of 'the free movement of legal rules', develop itself into anything more than a vague set of subsidiary applicable rules. The ambiguity of the Roman law part of the medieval *ius commune,* as compared to the canon law part, suggests that the creation of a coherent uniform legal system is not possible other than by way of a top-down unification. Unification appears to be unattainable without a political power that is determined to take deliberate efforts to develop and enforce the uniform law. The case of matrimonial property law, which fell outside the medieval canon family law, demonstrates the causality of deliberate efforts on the part of a political power.[67]

The second lesson that can be derived from the comparison of the two parts of the medieval *ius commune* is that without a hierarchical judicial system and the possibility of appeal, the level of consistency of application of the uniform law will never be high enough to truly maintain its uniformity.

7.2.4.   DIFFERENT TERRITORIAL SCOPE

Another important difference between the two parts of the medieval *ius commune* is the differing territorial scope of application of the medieval canon and the medieval Roman law. The reception of Roman law took a considerable period of time. One reason for the slow pace of this reception is that the 'free movement of legal rules' was not the most efficient vehicle of proliferation.[68] The reception started in Italy in the twelfth century, then stretched to Spain, South France and Holland in the thirteenth century, affected Northern France in the fourteenth century and carried on in Germany from the thirteenth to the sixteenth century.[69] England, in spite of all justified efforts to put this into perspective,[70] strictly speaking never really took part in this

---

[67]   In the same period that the law on marriage, divorce and illegitimacy was unified, matrimonial property law experienced further diversifications. See Chapter 5.

[68]   Franz Wieacker remarks that 'further developments were required before the *ius commune* could oust native law or replace its unlearned representatives'. WIEACKER, F., *A History of Private Law in Europe* (1995), p. 61.

[69]   COING, H., *Europäisches Privatrecht*, V. I (1985), p. 13-14; KOSCHAKER, P., *Europa en het Romeinse recht* (1995), p. 139-143.

[70]   The impact of the Roman law on English law was persuasively delineated by Zimmermann in a number of works: ZIMMERMANN, R., 'Der europäische Character des englishen Rechts. Historische Verbindungen zwischen civil law und common law' (1993), p. 4-51; ZIMMERMANN, R., 'Civil Code and Civil Law. The "Europeanization" of Private Law Within the European Community and the Re-emergence of a European Legal Science'(1994-1995), p. 63-105; ZIMMERMANN, R., 'Savigny's Legacy Legal History, Comparative Law, and The Emergence of A European Legal Science' (1996),

reception, nor in the Roman part of the medieval *ius commune*.[71] Scandinavia[72] and Orthodox Eastern European countries like Russia, Bulgaria, Romania and Greece, were not a part of medieval Roman *ius commune* as such. Later, the Roman law reached them indirectly via other countries (mainly Germany and France).

The process of unification of the canon law of the Roman Catholic Church had commenced much earlier, but proceeded rather slowly until the time of the Gregorian Reform. From then on, canon law started to spread more rapidly, as it was carried into every Catholic Church province by such efficient vehicles as the Church officials and the Church courts.[73] As a result, the canon law penetrated into northern Europe well before Roman law was received there.[74] In France, Italy and what is now Germany, the process of internalisation of canon law went faster; in other places slower.

England, before Henry VIII, was part of the Roman Catholic Church, as was every other Western European country. It is a peculiarity of English legal historical thought that the status of canon law in medieval England was for a long time believed to have been different. Until Frederic William Maitland shed new light on this issue in the nineteenth century,[75] for almost two centuries it had been widely held that the English ecclesiastical courts paid no more respect to the canon law of Rome than 'nowadays an English Court will pay to an American or Irish decision'.[76] This autarchic view found its most profound expression in the writings of William Stubbs,[77] who was Bishop of Chester and then of Oxford and professor of Modern History at Oxford University, and a contemporary of Maitland and his main opponent in the discussion of that time. The report of the 1883 Ecclesiastical Court Commission,[78] actually written by Stubbs, stated that in medieval England, 'The papal law-books were regarded as manuals, but not as codes or statutes'.[79] The same report held that 'attempts to force on the church and nation the complete canon law of the Middle Ages were always unsuccessful'.[80] It was also stated, 'that the English courts Christian held themselves

---

p. 587-596; ZIMMERMANN, R., 'Roman Law and the Harmonisation of Private Law in Europe' (2004), p. 37-41.

[71] In respect of England see: MERRYMAN, J., 'On the Convergence (and Divergence) of Civil Law and the Common Law' (1978), p. 198.

[72] Scandinavia was also influenced by Roman law, but it never acquired the status of subsidiary applicable law there. COING, H., *Europäisches Privatrecht*, V. 1 (1985), p. 14.

[73] WIEACKER, F., *A History of Private Law in* Europe (1995), p. 61.

[74] Ibid.

[75] CAMERON, R., *Frederick William Maitland and the History of English Law* (1977), p. 63.

[76] MAITLAND, F., *Roman Canon Law in the Church of England* (1968), p. 2.

[77] 1825-1901.

[78] Reports of The Commissioners into the Constitution and Working of The Ecclesiastical Courts (Great Brittan 1883).

[79] Cited by MAITLAND, F., in: *Roman Canon Law in the Church of England* (1968), at p. 52.

[80] Cited by MAITLAND, F., in: *Roman Canon Law in the Church of England* (1968), at p. 52.

free to accept or reject, and they did in some cases reject, the canon law of Rome'.[81] Bishop Stubbs also suggested that the papal canon law required ratification by an English church council in order to become authoritative in England.[82]

Frederic William Maitland attributed this opinion to a twofold misconception. In the first place, the jurisdictional conflicts between the lay courts and the canonical courts of the English Church that took place in the Middle Ages, were presented as internal church conflicts between the papal curia and the English Catholic Church. According to Maitland, the fallacy of this allegation can be derived from the fact that such internal conflict between the church courts was quite inconceivable before the Reformation.[83] Secondly, the relations between the Roman Catholic Church and the Church of England after the Reformation were a-historically extrapolated to pre-Reformation times.[84] Maitland pointed out the unsustainability of the assertion that generally applicable canon texts were not authoritative in medieval England.[85] He persuasively demonstrated that 'in all probability large portions [...] of the "canon law of Rome" were regarded by the courts Christian of this country as absolutely binding statute law'.[86] According to Maitland, there was no doubt that 'from the middle years of the twelfth century until the Council of Trent, the marriage law of England was the canon law of the Catholic Church'.[87] Although England was an independent State, the English Church was just a part of the universal Roman Catholic Church and was subjected to its ecclesiastical laws.[88] The English ecclesiastic courts were part of a uniform European system of courts Christian, subjected to the papal curia, and were administering the uniform canon law.[89] Moreover, 'the canon law of marriage was also the law of England. It was not a foreign law that imposed itself with greater or lesser force, and for a more or less prolonged period. It was rather an integral part – and an important one – of English law'.[90] Maitland also stressed that 'to say that the English Church received and adopted the Catholic law on marriage would be untrue; the rulers never conceived that they were free to pick and chose their law'.[91] Today, Maitland's

---

[81]   MAITLAND, F., *Roman Canon Law in the Church of England* (1968), p. 51.
[82]   STUBBS, W., *Seventeen Lectures on the Study of Medieval and Modern History and Kindred Subjects* (1990), p. 354-357.
[83]   MAITLAND, F., *Roman Canon Law in the Church of England* (1968), p. 54 ff.
[84]   Ibid, p. 81-90.
[85]   CAMERON, R., *Frederick William Maitland and the History of English Law* (1977), p. 64.
[86]   MAITLAND, F., *Roman Canon Law in the Church of England* (1968), p. 2.
[87]   POLLOCK, F., MAITLAND, F., *The History of English Law before the Time of Edward I*, Vol. II (1952), p. 372.
[88]   CAMERON, R., *Frederick William Maitland and the History of English Law* (1977), p. 69.
[89]   MILSOM, S., *Historical Foundations of the Common Law* (1981), p. 23.
[90]   MARTÍNEZ-TORRÓN, J., Anglo-American Law and Canon Law. Canonical Roots of the Common Law Tradition (1998), p. 96-97.
[91]   POLLOCK, F., MAITLAND, F., *The History of English Law before the Time of Edward I*, Vol. II (1952), p. 373.

position is generally accepted in England.[92] Recent research in the records of the Church courts has largely confirmed his views.[93]

Until the Reformation, the uniform canon family law was imposed throughout the whole of Western Christendom. The uniformity of the canon law part of the medieval *ius commune* was, however, not lasting. Protestant countries parted with the canon *ius commune* at the time of the Reformation. In the countries that stayed Catholic, the emergence of national secular family legislation weakened the uniformity of the canon law from about the same time onwards. But the fact remains that, contrary to the Roman *ius commune*, the uniform canon family law had been equally shared for at least 500 years by Western European countries with common and civil law traditions.[94] The influence of Roman law, by contrast, 'varied from close to nil (in the case of the English common law) to massive (in the case of the German Pandectists of the nineteenth century), with various shades in between'.[95] The fact that English common law had no share in the Roman law part of the medieval *ius commune* has always been an important impediment for the common legal past as an argument in favour of the harmonisation of the economically-related areas of private law in Europe. For instance, Merryman argued, 'there is something incongruous in urging a return to *ius commune* for nations that never were part of it'.[96] No matter what one may think of this argument in respect of the economically-related areas of private law, this reasoning is obviously not valid in regard of most parts of family law.

7.3. CONCLUDING REMARKS

It is time to evaluate the bearing of the argument that 'family law had an undisputable *ius commune* in the past and could have it again today' for the cultural constraints argument and the present-day debate that surrounds the harmonisation of family law. It goes without saying that the reference to the *ius commune* argument does not include an appeal to restore the substance of the medieval canon family *ius commune* in present-day Europe. Even ultra-conservatives would not wish to go that far. As the following chapters will illustrate, the whole subsequent history of family law is a story of gradual liberalisation from the rigid dogmas that were vested in that period. Any

---

[92] For an overview of developments after Maitland see: DONAHUE, C., 'Roman Canon Law in the Medieval English Church: Stubbs Vs. Maitland Re-examined After 75 Years in the Light of Some Records From The Church Courts' (1974), p. 650-653.
[93] Ibid, p. 653-708.
[94] BRUNDAGE, J., *Medieval Canon Law* (1995), p. 188.
[95] CAENEGEM, R., *European Law in the Past and the Future: Unity and Diversity of Two Millennia* (2002), p. 25.
[96] MERRYMAN, J., 'On the Convergence (and Divergence) of Civil Law and Common Law' (1978), p. 198.

new common family law for Europe could not and should not be built upon the medieval law as it stood in those days. If there is to be a new common family law, than this can only be appropriately developed upon the pan-European spirit of innovation and liberalisation that was the driving force behind the centuries of gradual breaking through the constraints imposed by the medieval *ius commune*.

The *ius commune* argument seems to be relevant for the current debate surrounding the harmonisation of family law in two main respects. Firstly, the common legal past of family law puts the cultural constraints argument into perspective. Secondly, the medieval unification could be presented as historical evidence that a top-down unification of family law is possible in principle.

The medieval uniform canon family law of the Roman Catholic Church was the common cradle from which all Western European countries started their evolution. Due to the overriding similarities between the Western medieval uniform canon family law and Eastern canon family law, the period of medieval uniformity of family law could be regarded as the starting point from which all European jurisdictions, East and West, commenced their development towards modern family law. Each country proceeded through this development following its own path and in its own pace until the medieval uniformity was replaced by the present day diversity. However, as I will try to show in the following chapters, the common starting point predetermined the basic similarity and the common direction of the subsequent evolution of the family law in Europe. Moreover, medieval *ius commune* is not only our common history, but, to the frustration, perhaps, of the proponents of modernisation, still remains part of our common present. Many medieval dogmas continue to endure in the background of current family law.[97] Most of the basic concepts of modern family law (marriage as a monogamous, heterosexual, life-long union; full divorce, separation of bed and board, illegitimacy and so on.) have been shared by the whole of Europe for centuries because they were inherited from the medieval *ius commune*. The influence of this heritage becomes readily apparent if one compares the common conceptual language of marriage and divorce law with the disparity of legal concepts in the area of matrimonial property law, which has never been part of the *ius commune*. And if one takes a closer look, it becomes obvious that we owe to the medieval *ius commune* much more than just a common legal language. Many values and ideological concepts that were developed as part of this *ius commune* have been influencing family law for centuries, and up to the present day they refuse to leave the stage without a

---

[97]   In the same way as the Roman *ius commune* still manifests itself in the 'common systematic, conceptual, doctrinal and ideological foundation' of modern private laws of different European countries. ZIMMERMANN, R., 'Roman Law and European Legal Unity' (1998), p. 39.

fight.[98] A clear example of the persistence of the medieval canon law concepts is the struggle for divorce. In the Catholic European countries and Anglican England there was a centuries-long struggle against the medieval canon doctrine of indissolubility of marriage. In Portugal, Spain, Italy and Ireland this struggle lasted until well beyond the second half of the twentieth century. In Malta the indissolubility of marriage is still the law today. This makes the suggestion that modern family laws are rooted in 'common European history' and 'common European culture' not less justifiable than the claim that contemporary family laws are embedded in 'unique national history' and 'unique nation cultures'.

The second way in which the medieval unification of canon law seems to be relevant for the present-day harmonisation debate is that, in a way, it supports the view that deliberate harmonisation is, in principle, possible. It could be presented as undeniable historical evidence, as such harmonisation has already once been realised in practice. However, this argument is obviously rather problematic. The political, ideological and legal conditions of medieval Europe are of course incomparable to the modern ones. Whatever view one would take on the relevance of the opinions of the populace for the medieval Church authorities, it is abundantly clear that present day democratic imperatives simply rule out any attempt to introduce whatever rule of family law by whatever means that cannot count on sufficient support from the electorate within the European Union and its individual member states. As pointed out above, the implementation of the medieval canon family law was not restrained by any notion of democracy or respect for ideological pluralism. But since the fundamental unfeasibility of deliberate harmonisation of family law, even apart from the undisputed necessity of democratic legitimacy, forms an important element of the present day argument against harmonisation, it remains nonetheless interesting to analyse what conditions made it possible for the medieval Church to accomplish its grand unification project.

The preceding discussion suggests that there were at least three vital preconditions: the homogeneous ideology; the supranational power of the Church, and the fact that the Church was hardly constrained in its means to enforce the uniform law. Firstly, the unification of the medieval canon family law was part of a vast process of legal and ideological consolidation of the Catholic Church, culminating in the Gregorian reform.[99] 'A common idea of marriage, common theoretical rules on consent, common tables of consanguinity, common control by the Church over families and individual

---

[98]   After the canon law finally prevailed, 'it influenced Western thought so deeply that it was able to resist even the push of post-revolutionary secularisation in the nineteenth century'. MARTÍNEZ-TORRÓN, J., *Anglo-American Law and Canon Law. Canonical Roots of the Common Law Tradition* (1998), p. 98.
[99]   BRESC, H., 'Europe: Town and Country' (1996), p. 432-433.

consciousness'[100] can be only understood in the context of this overall ideological consolidation. Such ideological unity is, of course, out of the question in modern pluralistic Europe. Still, the shared notion of human rights could in principle provide for some ideological common ground. As will be discussed in the following chapters,[101] however, the differences in interpretation of human rights, especially in relation to family law, impede the development of an ideological basis required for harmonisation.

Secondly, the unification of the medieval canon family law became possible due to the 'characteristic religious and political unity of medieval Europe'.[102] It was not the ideological unison alone, but also the political power of the Church that provided an indispensable precondition to this successful unification. As has been noted above, the medieval Catholic Church was in some respects a 'quasi-state' that 'comprised the nations of the present European Union'.[103] Although it had to share its power with the secular states, it possessed an enormous supranational political authority. Such concentration of supranational political power is also not present at the moment. The European Union is the only entity that could be considered in this respect. The EU capacity to enact and enforce binding law is based on the voluntary transfer of power by the Member States, and therefore is auxiliary to them. The medieval Church, by contrast, gained its power in struggle with the secular rulers. It did not depend on the consent of the states and was free to impose its law upon them whether they liked it or not.

Thirdly, the Church not only succeeded in developing a whole body of uniform family law, but also managed to implement it into real life. As described above, this effectuation entailed excommunications, interdicts and even wars. Although this suggests that the enforcement of far-reaching and difficult to digest reform is not altogether impossible, it is clear that the methods the medieval Church had to resort to are unthinkable in present day circumstances. As a matter of theory, one could nonetheless conclude that all it takes to implement fundamental family law change is sufficient political power, effective coercion and time. As will be discussed in the following chapters, the twentieth century Bolshevik and Attaturk reforms[104] are able to illustrate that the medieval family law unification was not the only historical occasion to provide this theory with empirical proof.

---

[100]   Ibid.
[101]   This issue will be discussed at length in the Part IV.
[102]   MARTÍNEZ-TORRÓN, J., *Anglo-American Law and Canon Law. Canonical Roots of the Common Law Tradition* (1998), p. 26.
[103]   CAENEGEM, R., *European Law in the Past and the Future: Unity and Diversity of Two Millennia* (2002), p. 1
[104]   See Part III, Chapter 11, Section 11.2.

It seems relevant here to note that the triumph of the Church in implementing its far-reaching reforms provides a strong argument not to overestimate the power of tradition, as stressed by the proponents of the cultural constraints argument. History shows that once the canon vision of marriage had finally overpowered older traditions, it became itself the tradition, and the same inertia mechanism that previously obstructed it started to work in its favour. This allows the suggestion that in the modern harmonisation debate the power of tradition should not be exaggerated. Tradition will always play an important part and will always take considerable time to be overcome, but it never constitutes an absolute obstacle as such.

Thus, the history of the medieval unification of family law offers a perhaps somewhat cynical insight for those who are searching for the outer limits of effectiveness of instrumentalist methods, indispensable in any successful top-down unification. The experience of the medieval unification allows suggesting that once one has sufficient political power, all that remains are the limits of an ethical nature. The question seems not to be whether it is possible in principle to impose certain changes using law as an instrument of social engineering, but, rather, how far one is able and prepared to go. The true limitations of a top-down implementation of harmonised family law in the Europe of today would not be constituted by the inherent inflexibility of its divergent national family cultures and traditions. Long before the possibilities to manipulate these would have dried up, barriers of another kind would prevail. Those are the contemporary imperatives of democracy and the protection of human rights that would obstruct any top-down harmonisation attempt. These values are fundamentally shared by the European countries of today. From an instrumentalist point of view, the real 'cultural constraints' for the harmonisation of family law in Europe are the common values of democracy and human rights, not the peculiarities of national family culture and tradition.

PART III
MODERN TIMES –FROM UNIFORMITY
TO THE CURRENT DIVERSITY

Similar developments: difference in timing, resemblance in substance

INTRODUCTION TO PART III

In this Part, I will deal with the developments of family law in Modern Europe[1] from the sixteenth century Protestant Reformation till the radical reforms of the second part of the twentieth century. In the previous Part, it was shown how the diversity of pre-Christian family law was replaced by the uniformity of medieval canon family law. The current Part will deal with a tendency that is rather the opposite; the movement away from the medieval uniformity to the diversity of our time. Facilitated by the Roman Catholic Church, the development of medieval family law was clearly dominated by the tendency towards more similarity. In contrast, in the following Modern period, that commenced after the Reformation, family law became the playground of two opposing tendencies: one that moved towards diversity, the other towards convergence. The Modern time was also characterised by the 'Westernisation' of Eastern Europe;[2] thus, Eastern Europe came to be influenced by the same developments and ideas as Western Europe.

The tendency toward divergence, which became predominant in the Modern time, was instigated by the diffusion of legislative power and religious diversity that arose after the Reformation. In contrast to Medieval Catholic Europe, the Protestant and the Orthodox countries knew neither a supranational legislative authority in family matters, nor a supranational hierarchical judicial system for adjudicating family cases. Even in Catholic countries, secular claims to authority that commenced during the Counter-reformation began to undermine the Church's legislative monopoly in the field of family law. As a result, the development of family law followed its own path in each European county. Europe became divided into a Catholic, a Protestant and an Orthodox part, each characterised by a multiplicity of family law sources and doctrines. The Enlightenment added ideological diversity to the religious and legislative mix. From the Enlightenment on, the aspiration to emancipate man and to improve the world according to the law of reason took shape into what could be called the 'Modernity project'.[3] From this time onwards, an ideological discord between 'conservative' and 'progressive' camps divided each European country. Family law became an important battleground of their clashes.

---

[1] Unless it is explicitly stated otherwise, in this Part the terms 'Modern Europe', 'Modern times' and 'Modernity' refer to the post-medieval period of European history.
[2] Starting with the reforms of Peter the Great in Russia in early eighteenth century and ending with the reforms of Kemal Atatürk in Turkey in the 1920s.
[3] For more on the 'Modernity project' see Part I, Chapter 2, Section 2.3.

The tendency toward similarity, albeit less prominent in the Modern time, did not entirely disappear. It remained rooted in the overall unity of European economical and political history. The family law of every European country was influenced by such pan-European events as the Reformation, the decline of the *Ancien Régime*, the industrialisation, the political democratisation occurring in the nineteenth century, and the sweeping modernisation at the end of the twentieth century. The fact that the family law of all Western European countries came from the same cradle, the medieval *ius commune*, predetermined the general similarity in family law's response to those events. The medieval period was, with some qualifications, characterised by the development from a less institutionalised and more lenient family law towards a more institutionalised and less permissive family law. The Modern period, by contrast, is clearly typified by the gradual evolution towards a less institutionalised and more permissive law. Phillips has justly pointed out that, 'for the most part, the history of divorce since the sixteenth century has been one movement away from the Roman Catholic doctrines of marriage'.[4] The same is equally true for the history of marriage, concubinage and illegitimacy. Differing from what one would perhaps imagine, the real liberalisation of family law actually did not start with the Reformation, but with the Enlightenment.[5] During the period from the Reformation till the middle of the twentieth century, all European countries underwent more or less the same changes. During the Modern period, the development of family law was generally typified by a great deal of stability and conservatism. Save some sweeping but temporary breakthroughs after the French, Portuguese and Russian revolutions, changes were for the most part steady, evolutional developments. On the eve of the dramatic reforms of the 1960s-1970s, a sixteenth century family lawyer would still have been able to recognise the ideas of his own time in the family laws of many European countries.

The main changes in the Modern period can be summed up as follows:

The exclusive ecclesiastical authority in most family matters gave way to secular legislation. Marriage more or less lost its religious character. The position of illegitimate children evolved from *filius nullius* to a hesitant, piecemeal improvement of their position. Concubinage, which lost its legal standing at the beginning of the period, remained in the shadow of the law at the end of it. Divorce law, evolving during the Modern period through several generations of divorce laws,[6] underwent perhaps

---

[4]   PHILLIPS, R., *Putting Asunder* (1988), p. 1.

[5]   As Glendon has put it 'Only with the Enlightenment did a true antithesis to traditional Christian attitudes towards marriage begin to appear'. GLENDON, M.A., *The Transformation of Family Law* (1989), p. 31.

[6]   For instance, Philips distinguishes three generations of divorce laws: the Protestant laws of the sixteenth century (first generation), 'the widespread legalisation and liberalisation of divorce legislation in the latter half of the nineteenth century' (second generation), and the no-fault divorce

the most spectacular move forwards. The first generation[7] fault-based 'divorce-as-sanction' appeared in Western Europe during the Protestant Reformation.[8] The second and third generation: divorce, based on the irretrievable breakdown of the marriage ('divorce as remedy or failure') and divorce by mutual consent of the spouses (divorce as an autonomous decision by the spouses themselves), were first introduced during the Enlightenment. The fourth and last generation divorce on demand ('divorce-as-a-right') granted upon the unilateral request of one of the spouses first came briefly upon the stage in Post-Revolutionary Russia, in the early twentieth century.

The general similarity of the development of family law along with the overall similitude of the European history of ideas predetermined the continuing similarity of the subject matter of the ideological debates between the proponents and opponents of the modernisation of family law in the whole of Europe. Every period of European history is typified by its own pan-European ideological developments: Reformation theology, the ideology of the Enlightenment, nineteenth-century liberalism, feminism, the sexual revolution, and so on. All these ideological trends generated their own ideas about the family and its legal regulation. Each new ideological trend of course was met with resistance from conservative forces and gave new content to the ideological divide between the 'conservative' and 'progressive' camps. The process of the modernisation of family law was part of an ideological battle in which every bit of liberalisation had to be fought for. Conservative thought combined medieval dogmas, such as the indissolubility of marriage and the casting out of illegitimate children, with the patriarchal dogmas of parental and male dominance. Several canon law concepts were taken over and upheld by secular law for a considerable period of time, much longer than other medieval political and religious dogmas. However, with the differentiation within the Church after the Reformation and the ideological breakthrough of the Enlightenment, ideological pluralism increased and it became more and more difficult for the State to justify the concepts that it had uncritically taken over from canon law. The proponents of modernisation invoked the ideas of anthropocentrism, humanism, individualism, equality and emancipation in order to challenge the old dogmas.

---

law from the 1960s onwards (third generation). The fist generation is mainly based on theological arguments, the second on 'moralistic and fault based precepts,' the third 'was motivated mainly by pragmatic reasons: 'growing awareness of, and objection to, the gap between appearance and reality, by perception that restrictive laws forces wives, husbands, witnesses, lawyers, and judges into a network of collusion, perjury, and hypocrisy, and that laws could be circumvented by migration'. (PHILLIPS, R., *Putting Asunder* (1988), p. 571.) In this book I draw on a somewhat different systematisation.

[7]   The designation 'first' is only appropriate from a West-European perspective, as it implies that one starts counting from the medieval prohibition of divorce by the canon Law of the Western Church onwards. In Eastern Europe the existing tradition of divorce was not discontinued.

[8]   The Eastern canon law of this period was based on a similar concept of divorce.

The most important characteristic of this period of 'movement away' from the concepts and dogmas of the medieval canon *ius commune* could perhaps be described as the gradual switch from the old transpersonalistic, to a modern personalistic appreciation of the relations between society, family and family members.[9] The struggle between the transpersonalistic and the personalistic ways of family law thinking remained undecided until the reforms of the second part of the twentieth century. The medieval heritage survived the attacks of the Enlightenment and the French Revolution. After the Restoration, old dogmas again became part of the conservative status quo and the emancipation project of Enlightenment remained 'unfinished'.[10] The beginning of the twentieth century witnessed several breakthroughs in the liberalisation of family law, undertaken in countries as different as Portugal, Bolshevik Russia and in the Nordic Region. In the politically divided Europe of the interwar period, the attitude towards the modernisation of the family became coupled with the political colour of the regimes. The liberal ideas of the Enlightenment did not acquire a durable and profound hold on family law until the era of the 'family revolution', commencing in the 1960's. Only then the ideas of the Enlightenment found their true and durable implementation.

The overall similarity of the ideological and political controversies in Europe after the Reformation did not mean that these events and ideas had the same effect in every country. Although the same developments are more or less explicitly visible in the evolution of the family law of all countries, they did not come about at the same time, nor were they everywhere equally profound. These pace and profundity dissimilarities in the evolution of family law have everything to do with the differences in the balance of political power between 'conservative' and 'progressive' forces.[11] As a result of these dissimilarities, various European countries entered into the period of radical reforms at the end of the 20th century with quite different baggage. It is these dissimilarities that constitute the main source of diversity that typifies the current family law in Europe; and it is these dissimilarities that made divergence, not convergence, the most dominant tendency of the Modern time, although both tendencies can clearly be discerned.

In this Part, I will follow the course of the development of family law in Europe from the Reformation until the 'family revolution' that started in the 1960s, trying to delineate the convergence and divergence tendencies throughout each of the successive periods of the Modern time: the Reformation, the Enlightenment and the French

---

[9] For more on transpersonalism and personalism see Chapter 9, Section 9.1. and Part I, Chapter 2, Section 2.2.2. For an example see Part III, Chapter 11, Section 11.3.3.
[10] See Part I, Chapter 2, Section 2.3.1.
[11] KAHN-FREUND, O., 'On Uses and Misuses of Comparative Law' (1974), p. 12;

Revolution, the 'conservative modernisation' of the post-Restoration nineteenth century, the radical reforms of the early twentieth century, and the interwar period.

CHAPTER 8
DEVELOPMENT OF FAMILY LAW
IN THE TIMES OF THE
PROTESTANT REFORMATION

8.1. INTRODUCTION: THE BREAKING OF THE UNIFORMITY OF THE MEDIEVAL CANON LAW

The period that commenced in the early sixteenth century with the Protestant Reformation is first and foremost characterised by the breaking of the uniformity of the medieval Roman Catholic family law. The wrongs and abuses of the Renaissance Papacy period exposed Roman canon family rules and practices to the accusation of vagueness and laxity.[1] Both Catholic and Reformed critics were concerned with 'the widening gap between the marriage in law and in practice'.[2] The Reformation theologians attacked the Catholic concept of marriage as a sacramental and indissoluble union. The family laws inspired by the Protestant teaching did away with the ambiguity of the canon rules regarding the solemnisation of marriage, but at the same time made marriage again dissoluble in principle. The Roman Catholic Church reacted to the same critique with the Counter-Reformation movement. Some canon law concepts, such as the indissolubility and sacramental character of marriage, were buttressed. Others, such as purely consensual marriage, had to be relinquished in the name of the orderliness of the marriage law. Consequently, the Catholic Church carried out rather similar reforms, culminating in the decisions of the Council of Trent. The secular reforms of family law in Orthodox Russia generally followed the same pattern. Thus, during the period of Reformation, the formal uniformity of family law in Western Europe disappeared. However, the common objective of reinforcing marriage discipline led different reformers in Western and Eastern Europe 'to some similar conclusions, despite important confessional and political differences'.[3]

---

[1]   See: OZMENT, S., *When Fathers Ruled: Family Life in Reformation Europe* (1983).
[2]   HARRINGTON, J., *Reordering Marriage and Society in Reformed Germany* (1995), p. 33.
[3]   Ibid, p. 47.

8.2. THE PROTESTANT DOCTRINE OF MARRIAGE AND DIVORCE

8.2.1. CHURCH JURISDICTION. HESITANT SECULARISATION OF MARRIAGE AND DIVORCE LAW

In contrast with the Roman Catholic and the Orthodox Church, Reformed theology did not consider marriage a sacrament or matrimonial affairs a matter of exclusive ecclesiastical competence. However, recent research[4] has persuasively shown that none of the actors of the Reformation pleaded for the complete secularisation of matrimonial legislation and a purely lay jurisdiction in matrimonial matters.[5] This constitutes an important qualification of a classical view set up by Jean Esmein at the end of the nineteenth century,[6] according to which the Protestant Reformation is perceived as a 'turning point' in the process of the secularisation of family law and family jurisdiction.[7]

Marriage was for Luther 'a divine and holy estate of life'. However, according to Luther's theory of 'two kingdoms', marriage belonged to the earthly, political kingdom and not to the heavenly, spiritual one.[8] Marriage was therefore completely subject to Divine law, but the administration of this law belonged to secular arms.[9] Calvin's early writings followed Luther in maintaining that marriage and the family belonged to the earthly kingdom alone.[10] However, in his later theology Calvin applied the biblical doctrine of covenant – an agreement between God and humanity – to the horizontal relationship between husband and wife.[11] According to this teaching, it is God who draws man and woman into a marriage covenant and appoints the husband as its head.[12] Like Luther, the late Calvin also attributed marriage to the civil order, but in his view, the whole of the civil order was subjected to God's law.[13] In line with this theory, the *Ecclesiastical Ordinances of Geneva*, drafted by Calvin in 1541, created two authorities for dealing with matrimonial matters. The first, the *Central Consistory*, was

---

[4]   HARRINGTON, J., *Reordering Marriage and Society in Reformed Germany* (1995), p. 202 ff.
[5]   PHILLIPS, R., *Putting Asunder* (1988), p. 195.
[6]   ESMEIN, A., *Le mariage en droit canonique*, Part I (2nd edtion 1929), p. 3-4.
[7]   HARRINGTON, J., *Reordering Marriage and Society in Reformed Germany* (1995), p. 201-202.
[8]   WITTE, J., *From Sacrament to Contract* (1997), p. 49.
[9]   Ibid, p. 52.
[10] CALVIN, J., *Ioannis Calvini Institutio Religionis Christianae*, (1536), cited in WITTE, J., *From Sacrament to Contract* (1997), p. 79.
[11] WITTE, J., *From Sacrament to Contract* (1997), p. 94.
[12] Ibid, p. 95.
[13] LACEY, T., *Marriage in Church and State*, p. 148.

an ecclesiastical authority, and the second, the *Small Council*, was a secular one.[14] Thus Calvin's doctrine resulted in a mixed ecclesiastical and lay jurisdiction in family matters.

Although England, like every other Protestant country, had formally broken with Rome, English family law remained somewhere between the Catholic and the Reformed traditions. As a result, the jurisdiction of the ecclesiastical courts in matrimonial matters was almost entirely preserved.[15]

8.2.2. PROTESTANT DOCTRINE AND LEGISLATION OF MARRIAGE

The Protestant teaching on marriage

The Protestant reformers accused the Roman Catholic canon law of marriage of being 'confusing, inequitable, impractical, arbitrary and easily abused'.[16] This 'common enemy' brought about a general similarity of the ideas regarding marriage, divorce and the family, introduced by the main actors of the Reformation. All Protestant reformers rejected, albeit not unqualifiedly,[17] the notion of the supremacy of the celibate state above marriage and the requirement of clerical celibacy. Thus they definitely abandoned the concept of 'marriage as second best', as a mere remedy against sinful lust.[18] Differing from the Catholics and the Orthodox, marriage for Protestants was no longer 'a second choice, [...] but the only choice'.[19] Thus, although neither Lutheran nor Calvinist theologians considered marriage a sacrament,[20] the dignity of marriage was in fact elevated.

---

[14] WITTE, J., *From Sacrament to Contract* (1997), p. 81.
[15] In 1533, the Parliament Act in Restraint of Appeals withdrew English cases from appeal to the Pope and thus also from the jurisdiction of the Catholic Church. Therein it was declared that 'all the cases of matrimony and divorce were now exclusively in the jurisdiction of the King of England', who was proclaimed as the 'supreme head of the Church of England' by the Supremacy Act of 1534. WITTE, J., *From Sacrament to Contract* (1997), p. 154.
[16] HARRINGTON, J., *Reordering Marriage and Society in Reformed Germany* (1995), p. 28.
[17] Only Bucer consistently rejected the sinfulness of sex within marriage. The other reformers 'refused both to absolve marital sex of all sins and to dismiss or condemn chastity altogether'. HARRINGTON, J., *Reordering Marriage and Society in Reformed Germany* (1995), p. 67.
[18] BRUNDAGE, J., *Law, sex, and Christian society in medieval Europe* (1987), p. 574-575.
[19] HARRINGTON, J., *Reordering Marriage and Society in Reformed Germany* (1995), p. 73.
[20] PHILLIPS, R., *Putting Asunder* (1988), p. 195.

Protestant doctrine did away with the ambiguities of purely consensual marriage. The demands of social reality were met by making parental consent[21] and Church celebration in the presence of witnesses indispensable requirements of a valid marriage. This change has been interpreted as a 'thoroughly conservative' revision of the consensual character of marriage.[22] It was also depicted as a partial return to the situation that existed in classical Roman law; marriage was still created by consent, but this was extended to the consent of 'not just the couple, but their parents [...] as well'.[23]

The Protestants initially intended to reduce the marriage impediments to the Mosaic prohibition of intermarrying within the second degree of consanguinity.[24] Later on however, only Bucer held on to this intent.[25] Others, including Luther, readily extended the prohibition to the third degree.[26] Calvin even proposed to keep the fourth-degree prohibition that existed in the Catholic canon law of his day.[27]

Implementation of Protestant doctrine of marriage into law

The legal impact of the Protestant teaching on marriage was almost immediate. Lutheran theology mostly influenced the Nordic region and the territory of present day Germany. The first marriage laws based on Lutheran thought appeared as early as 1523 and rapidly spread through the German states in the following decades.[28] Although inspired by the same teaching, these laws were not identical. The requirements in respect to the formalities regarding the solemnisation of marriage were in some Lutheran countries less strict than the doctrinal teaching. Some Lutheran marriage laws were comparable to those prescribed by the Catholics at the Council of Trent,[29] but didn't go as far as in the countries influenced by Calvin's teaching. For example, although Church solemnisation of marriage was prescribed by the official Church doctrine in Sweden, a marriage concluded informally in the presence of witnesses and with the consent of the parents was also regarded valid.[30]

---

[21] However forcing children into unwanted marriage was explicitly prohibited in Calvin's Marriage Ordinance for Geneva of 1545. WITTE, J., *From Sacrament to Contract* (1997), p. 83.
[22] HARRINGTON, J., *Reordering Marriage and Society in Reformed Germany* (1995), p. 90.
[23] Ibid, p. 92.
[24] *Leviticus*, 18.
[25] HARRINGTON, J., *Reordering Marriage and Society in Reformed Germany* (1995), p. 85.
[26] Ibid.
[27] Ibid.
[28] WITTE, J., *From Sacrament to Contract* (1997), p. 55.
[29] See: Section 8.3.
[30] According to Ordinance of Västerås of 1527 and Church Constitution of 1572. SELLIN, J., *Marriage and Divorce Legislation in Sweden* (1922), p. 10.

The first family law based on Calvin's doctrine was the *Marriage Ordinance for Geneva*, drafted in 1545.[31] Calvin's teaching on marriage influenced the French Huguenots, the Dutch Pietists, the Scottish Presbyterians, and the English Puritans, as well as various smaller religious communities.[32] As the marriage laws of those communities were made by autonomous legislatures, there were considerable differences between them. The first rules on marriage in the Dutch provinces dated from the 1580s.[33] The provinces generally followed a similar pattern; along with betrothal and the reading of the banns, three requirements were essential for the formation of a valid marriage: the consent *de praesenti,* the solemnisation by a priest or a magistrate, and the consummation.[34] However, the legal consequences of the omission of Church solemnisation varied from province to province.[35] In Friesland, Zeeland, Drente and Utrecht, such omission was punishable but did not render the marriage invalid.[36] By contrast, in Gelderland and Holland an unsolemnised marriage was regarded invalid.[37] Parental consent was required in all Provinces.[38] In Scotland, marriages *per verba de praesenti* alone, and *per verba de futuro* followed by consummation, continued to be recognised as valid even after the Reformation, even if they were concluded without any formalities.[39]

In England, in the first part of the sixteenth century after the partition from Rome that was instigated by Henry VIII's matrimonial aspirations, Parliament made a few important alterations to the canon law on marriage. It reduced the prohibited degrees of consanguinity and affinity, allowed priests to marry, and denied marriage a sacramental character.[40] But there was neither a sweeping change in the substance of the law,[41] nor a real disruption with the past.[42] In a way, England got stuck between the Catholic and the Protestants worlds. It missed not only the profound changes

---

[31] WITTE, J., *From Sacrament to Contract* (1997), p. 83.
[32] Ibid, p. 126.
[33] E.g. the Political Ordinance of Holland of 1580 and the Ordinance of Utrecht of 1584.
[34] APELDOORN, L., *Geschiedenis van het Nederlandsche huwelijksrecht* (1925), p. 92-100.
[35] The Catholic marriages were not recognised by secular law in the whole of the North Netherlands. The Catholic Church showed some tolerance by recognising the civil marriages, concluded by the Catholics, and even allowing a Catholic to marry before a minister of the Reformed Church in case of a mixed protestant-catholic marriage.
[36] APELDOORN, L., *Geschiedenis van het Nederlandsche huwelijksrecht* (1925), p. 101-110.
[37] Ibid.
[38] In Gelderland this requirement was not limited to children under a certain age and its violation made marriage invalid. In other provinces, parental consent was a requirement for valid marriage only if the children were under age (mostly under twenty-five). APELDOORN, L., *Geschiedenis van het Nederlandsche huwelijksrecht* (1925), p. 153-155.
[39] THOMSON, J., *Family Law in Scotland* (1996), p. 14.
[40] WITTE, J., *From Sacrament to Contract* (1997), p. 156.
[41] MARTÍNEZ-TORRÓN, J., *Anglo-American Law and Canon Law. Canonical Roots of the Common Law Tradition,* (1998), p. 99.
[42] HELMHOLZ, R., *Marriage Litigation in Medieval England,* (1978), p. 3.

initiated by the continental Protestant reformers, but also the mild modifications introduced by Council of Trent in the Catholic counties.[43] As a result, the pure consensual marriage, which in the sixteenth century almost disappeared everywhere else in Europe, remained formally valid in the ecclesiastical law of the Church of England until the late eighteenth century. The growing hostility of the ecclesiastical courts had by the end of the seventeenth century almost eradicated marriages concluded by the parties alone.[44] However, clandestine marriages concluded by a clergyman in violation of the requirements of ecclesiastical law regarding the publication of the banns or the place of solemnisation[45] flourished until 1753.[46] It was not until then that Hardwicke's Marriage Act made marriages concluded in violation of these formal requirements null and void.[47] Thus, these requirements, very much resembling those introduced in Catholic Europe by the *Tametsi* decree of the Council of Trent in the sixteenth century, were introduced in England after a delay of two centuries.[48]

8.2.3. PROTESTANT TEACHINGS AND LEGISLATION ON DIVORCE. DIVORCE-AS-SANCTION

The Protestant teaching on divorce

The Lutheran reformers rejected the Catholic doctrine of the indissolubility of marriage. This denunciation was based on arguments from Scripture, history and utility.[49] The Lutheran theologians tried to reconcile the liberal Roman and Biblical divorce laws with the words of Christ: 'what God has joined together, let no men put asunder'.[50] The Lutheran reformers regarded Christ's command as 'an absolute moral standard for Christians,' which was the law of the chaste heavenly kingdom, but with which the sinful earthly kingdom was unable to comply.[51]

---

[43]   WITTE, J., *From Sacrament to Contract* (1997), p. 131.
[44]   See: STONE, L., *Road to Divorce* (1990), p. 67-79.
[45]   Ibid, p. 96.
[46]   See: ibid, p. 97-120
[47]   JAMES, M., 'The English Law of Marriage' (1957), p. 26.
[48]   That made Martínez-Torrón believe that England kept looking to Rome for the inspiration long after the formal bands with Catholicism were broken. MARTÍNEZ-TORRÓN, J., *Anglo-American Law and Canon Law. Canonical Roots of the Common Law Tradition*, (1998), p. 100.
[49]   WITTE, J., *From Sacrament to Contract* (1997), p. 65.
[50]   Matt. 5.31-32, 19:3-19; Luke 16: 18; Mark, 10; 2-12.
[51]   WITTE, J., *From Sacrament to Contract* (1997), p. 67.

All Protestant reformers unanimously accepted adultery as a ground for divorce.[52] Malicious desertion was the second widely accepted ground. However, in Calvin's thought, desertion was perceived not so much as a separate divorce ground, but rather as a virtual form of adultery.[53] More liberal Lutheran reformers, notably Bucer and Zwingli, pleaded for an even wider scope of divorce grounds, for instance impotence, grave incompatibility, sexually incapacitating illnesses, felonies, deception, and one spouse's serious threats against the life of the other spouse.[54] As a rule, Protestant doctrine gave husbands and wives an equal right to seek divorce.

The Protestant teaching gave rise to what Phillips has called the 'first generation'[55] of divorce laws.[56] This generation of laws was based on the idea of divorce-as-sanction, and rooted in the belief that the State and/or the Church, as guardians of universal morality, were entitled to impose this sanction. Some scholars interpret this re-introduction of divorce as a sign of the personalistic aspiration to promote the empathic ideal of loving, sharing and companionate marriages.[57] Others more plausibly maintain that although during the Protestant Reformation the formal dissolution of marriage became possible, it is difficult to ascribe to the Protestant theologians any intention to liberalise family law.[58] On the contrary, the main point of the Protestant stance was the 'laxity' of the Roman Catholic law of marriage.[59] Thus it was quite defendable for the Protestant countries to introduce divorce on the basis of the transpersonalistic premise of the protection of the interests of the social order, and of marriage discipline having preference above the interests of the individuals concerned.[60] Unlike in the Lutheran communities, divorce was not made easier in the Calvinist territories, as compared to the Catholic annulment practices. On the contrary, it was made extremely difficult.[61] Divorce was allowed merely because the Calvinist reformers held that a spouse guilty of the crime of adultery was to be rendered 'spiritually dead'.[62] In contrast with the merciful treatment of an adulteress

---

[52]   Ibid, p. 68.
[53]   Ibid, p. 102.
[54]   WITTE, J., *From Sacrament to Contract* (1997), p. 69.
[55]   Starting count after the prohibition of divorce by the canon Law of Western Church.
[56]   PHILLIPS, R., *Putting Asunder* (1988), p. 571.
[57]   OZMENT, S., *When Fathers Ruled: Family Life in Reformation Europe* (1983), p. 99.
[58]   Harrington noticed that 'it would be difficult to characterise [the Protestant reformers'] overwhelming concern with sexual order and discipline as " progressive," yet this has all too often been the case among scholars of the Reformation when referring to the reintroduction of divorce'. HARRINGTON, J., *Reordering Marriage and Society in Reformed Germany* (1995), p. 90. For an opposite view see: OZMENT, S., *When Fathers Ruled: Family Life in Reformation Europe* (1983), p. 99 ff.
[59]   Luther declared in his sermon of 1522 that 'The estate of marriage has fallen into awful disrepute'. LUTHER, M., 'Vom eelichen leben', cited in: WITTE, J., *From Sacrament to Contract* (1997), p. 47.
[60]   HARRINGTON, J., *Reordering Marriage and Society in Reformed Germany* (1995), p. 90.
[61]   LACEY, T., *Marriage in Church and State*, p. 149.
[62]   HARRINGTON, J., *Reordering Marriage and Society in Reformed Germany* (1995), p. 88.

by Christ himself, Calvin regarded capital punishment the only suitable sentence for adultery.[63] Calvin complained that because of the laxity of his days adultery cases had become unnecessarily complicated. He reasoned that it was only because adulterous wives were being spared their well-deserved death punishment that the whole divorce issue had become necessary.[64]

Thus, the Protestant theorists saw the dissolution of marriage not a as remedy for the breakdown of marriage, but rather as a punishment for matrimonial offence.[65] The principle of recrimination, precluding a guilty spouse from seeking divorce, was one of the cornerstones of this concept of divorce-as-sanction. Accordingly, only a demonstrably innocent spouse could seek the remedy of divorce. Moreover, many divorce laws permitted remarriage only for an innocent spouse.[66] The guilty spouse had to be severely punished, if not by death, than by banishment, fine, or imprisonment.[67] However, not even adultery constituted an absolute ground for divorce, proof of which would lead to the automatic granting of divorce. The adulterous spouse had to first seek forgiveness and the innocent had to be forgiving.[68] Divorce was granted only if it was proven that reconciliation was not achievable.[69] This double fault-breakdown test made obtaining divorce very difficult. The petitioning spouse had to prove not only that a matrimonial offence had taken place, but also that it had led to the irreconcilable breakdown of marriage. Later, making adultery an absolute ground for divorce and releasing the petitioner from the obligation to prove the resulting breakdown of marriage became one of the first tokens of the liberalisation of divorce law.

Implementation of Protestant teaching on divorce into law

Lutheran thought inspired the promulgation of the first Nordic laws on divorce. Divorce was first introduced in Sweden by the *Church Ordinance* of 1571, and then

---

[63] According to Calvin, 'the punishment of death was always awarded to adultery. This is all the more base and shameful that Christians do not emulate Gentiles at least in this. Adultery is punished no less severely by Julian [i.e., Roman] law than by the law of God. Yet those who boastfully call themselves Christians are so tender and remiss that they punish this execrable offence only with a very light reproof." Calvin's Commentary to Lev. 20.10, 22-27. Cited in: WITTE, J., *From Sacrament to Contract* (1997), p. 100.

[64] In the words of Calvin, 'today it is the perverted indulgence of magistrates that makes it necessary for man to divorce their impure wives, inasmuch as that is a punishment for adultery'. CALVIN, J., *A harmony of the Gospels, Mathew, Mark and Luke,* Vol. II, p. 247. Cited in: PHILLIPS, R., *Putting Asunder* (1988), p. 53.

[65] PHILLIPS, R., *Putting Asunder* (1988), p. 90.

[66] Ibid.

[67] LACEY, T., *Marriage in Church and State*, p. 149.

[68] WITTE, J., *From Sacrament to Contract* (1997), p. 68.

[69] For that reason Phillips assumed that the 'protestant doctrines went further than setting the course of Western divorce on its path of matrimonial fault'. PHILLIPS, R., *Putting Asunder* (1988), p. 92.

reaffirmed by the *Church Law* of 1686. Both laws allowed divorce on the grounds of adultery and malicious desertion.[70] In Denmark, divorce was introduced in 1582 by *The Articles of Marriage*, which also applied in Norway and Iceland. In 1687 Norway adopted its own rather similar rules on divorce.[71] The Danish law provided for divorce in case of adultery, desertion and impotence.[72] In line with the earlier Swedish ecclesiastical laws, the *Swedish General Code* of 1734[73] also contained adultery and malicious desertion in the 'canonical' grounds for divorce.[74] The rigidity of the ecclesiastical divorce grounds was, however, mitigated by the introduction of the possibility of divorce by Royal dispensation. From the early eighteenth century, the Swedish[75] and the Danish[76] Kings started to grant full divorce upon a wider range of grounds than those provided for by judicial divorce.[77] This led to the emergence of the dual administrative-judicial system of divorce in the Nordic countries.

Calvin's teaching on divorce influenced the legislation in Scotland and in the Dutch provinces. In Scotland, divorce for adultery was recognised at common law from the beginning of the Reformation. Divorce for desertion was introduced by the Statute of 1573.[78] The first divorce laws in the Dutch provinces date from the 1580s.[79] Divorce for adultery was allowed from the outset,[80] while the ground of malicious desertion was added by the *Marriage Law* of 1656.[81] A peculiarity of Dutch law was that the preservation of such Catholic canon law institutions as the separation of bed and board

---

[70]   SELLIN, J., *Marriage and Divorce Legislation in Sweden* (1922), p. 34.

[71]   These rules were part of the 1687 *Norwegian Code*.

[72]   PHILLIPS, R., *Putting Asunder* (1988), p. 51-52.

[73]   *Sveriges Rikes Lag.*

[74]   SELLIN, J., *Marriage and Divorce Legislation in Sweden* (1922), p. 35.

[75]   This practice emerged in Sweden and Finland, that was at that time part of it, from 1734 onwards (SELLIN, J., *Marriage and Divorce Legislation in Sweden* (1922), p. 36.) The procedure was, however, rather complicated and involved mediation by the clerical authorities. Divorce could be granted upon a number of fault grounds 'and in case of a serious conflict between the spouses which had 'transferred their relationship into mutual hate and loathing'. In the latter case, the spouses first had to undergo mediation by the clerical authorities, and divorce was granted only after a one-year judicial separation had expired. JÄNTERÄ-JAREBORG, M., *Swedish Report concerning the CEFL Questionnaire on Grounds for Divorce and Maintenance Between Former Spouses* (2003) http://www.law.uu.nl/priv/cefl > working field 1 > Sweden.

[76]   This practice also applied in Norway.

[77]   At the beginning, dispensation was granted only in cases of grave hardship. But from about 1770 on, the number of grounds for dispensation started to expand. Dispensation became possible even on the ground of incompatibility. Since 1790, dispensation has been possible in Denmark if there had been a judicial separation for three years. SCHMIDT, T., 'The Scandinavian Law of procedure in Matrimonial Causes' (1984), p. 74.

[78]   THOMSON, J., *Family Law in Scotland* (1996), p. 98.

[79]   E.g. Political Ordinance of Holland of 1580 and Ordinance of Utrecht of 1584.

[80]   APELDOORN, L., *Geschiedenis van het Nederlandsche huwelijksrecht* (1925), p. 184.

[81]   *Echtreglement* of the *Staten-Generaal* of 1656. HEIJDEN, M., *Huwelijk in Holland* (1998), p. 53.

and the annulment of marriage. Therefore the Dutch law of this period is rightly perceived as a 'blend of Catholic and Calvin's teaching'.[82]

England: a case apart

The theologians of the Church of England were initially rather inclined to admit divorce.[83] The theological opinion on this subject remained divided far into the seventeenth century.[84] In 1552, a mixed clergy and lay *Reform Commission*, set up by Henry VIII, produced a draft *Reformatio Legum Ecclesiasticarum*.[85] The draft promised to bring about sweeping liturgical, doctrinal and canonical changes. One of the intended changes was to grant both spouses equal rights to sue for divorce and to remarry thereafter. The proposed grounds for divorce – adultery, desertion, deadly hostility and prolonged ill-treatment[86] – were rather liberal for the Protestant standards of those days. Parliament also considered the proposal too liberal and refused to promulgate it in 1553, and again in 1571.[87] Thereafter, the momentum for reform was lost. Subsequently, a number of political coincidences, like Queen Mary's Catholicism and Queen Elizabeth's reluctance to introduce profound ecclesiastical reforms, took England back in time to the situation that existed in pre-Tridentine Catholic Europe. By the early seventeenth century, it became the prevailing theological opinion that full divorce was not accepted by the Church of England.[88] Oddly enough, England, where the break from Rome was instigated by Henry VIII's wish to repudiate his Queen and to remarry,[89] remained the only Protestant country that retained the doctrine of the indissolubility of marriage and did not introduce a full judicial divorce after the Reformation.[90]

However, as in the Nordic Region, the strictness of the ecclesiastical doctrine was softened by the emergence of extra-judicial practices. In 1670, the *Roos* case made a start at what came to be called Parliamentary divorce. This peculiar form of divorce was in each particular case granted by means of an individual private act of Parliament. Parliamentary divorce was originally designated as a rare exception to the principle

---

[82]   WITTE, J., *From Sacrament to Contract* (1997), p. 129.
[83]   Several influential theologians proposed a limited legalisation of divorce in the late sixteenth – early seventeenth century. STONE, L., *Road to Divorce* (1990), p. 303.
[84]   STONE, L., *Road to Divorce* (1990), p. 308.
[85]   PHILLIPS, R., *Putting Asunder* (1988), p. 83.
[86]   WITTE, J., *From Sacrament to Contract* (1997), p. 157-158.
[87]   PHILLIPS, R., *Putting Asunder* (1988), p. 85.
[88]   STONE, L., *Road to Divorce* (1990), p. 305.
[89]   For more details see: KELLY, H., *The Matrimonial Trials of Henry VIII* (1976), p. 21-241.
[90]   Partly due to historical accident, partly due to 'the tortuous and zig-zag path by which it moved from the Catholic into the Protestant camp'. STONE, L., *Road to Divorce* (1990), p. 301.

of the indissolubility of marriage.[91] However, it later grew into a rather regular practice[92] and the number of petitions rose considerably.[93] Parliamentary divorces were initially granted only to a husband on the ground of a wife's adultery. Later, a few divorces were also granted to wives on the ground of adultery on the part of the husband, aggravated by incest or bigamy.[94] By the institution of Parliamentary divorce, full divorce, that had been kicked out through the front door was allowed through the back one. Such practice was, in the words of Lawrence Stone, logically quite untenable, as the same spiritual lords who resolutely upheld the indissolubility of marriage in theory and in the practice of the ecclesiastical courts, voted in Parliament for the passage of private divorce acts.[95] After the English colonisation of Ireland in the seventeenth century, Parliamentary divorce by the act of the Irish Parliament in this thoroughly Catholic country also became possible.[96]

8.2.4. THE PROTESTANT ATTITUDE TOWARDS CONCUBINAGE

The Protestant attitude towards concubinage was very negative. During the early Reformation this rigorous stance gave rise to a whole campaign against informal unions. The State and the Church worked together to eradicate this 'evil'.[97] In various European principia, concubinage became forbidden under the pain of criminal punishments.[98] In line with the Church doctrine, authoritive professors of civil law taught that a concubine and her children had no right to inherit.[99]

8.2.5. THE POSITION OF ILLEGITIMATE CHILDREN IN PROTESTANT LAW

The difference between the position of legitimate and illegitimate children remained sharp both in the private and public law of the Protestant countries. An illegitimate

---

[91] STONE, L., *Road to Divorce* (1990), p. 146.
[92] It has been observed that the procedure became more judicial than legislative and the Parliament in fact acted as a court. Ibid, p. 323
[93] Ibid.
[94] From about 3 per decade in the 1710s to 12 in 1799. Ibid, p. 325-326.
[95] Ibid, p. 350.
[96] SHATTER, A., *Family Law in the Republic of Ireland* (1986), p. 237.
[97] BECKER, H-J., 'Die nichteheliche Lebensgemeinschaft (Konkubinat) in der Rechtsgeschichte' (1978), p. 29-30.
[98] For and overview see: Ibid, p. 30.
[99] Ibid, p. 29-30.

child was legally related only to its mother, as it was generally[100] held that a 'mother makes no bastards'.[101] An illegitimate child shared its mother's status, and, with some exceptions,[102] was entitled to inherit from her.[103] At the same time, an illegitimate child was not legally related to his or her father, and, with a few minor exceptions,[104] had no right to inherit from him. In some jurisdictions an illegitimate child could be acknowledged by the father, but such acknowledgement did not create a legal filiaton link between them.[105] Nonetheless, an acknowledged child was entitled to maintenance and in some countries[106] could even share in the father's status and bear his name. Another way of acquiring maintenance was by proof of paternity, upon the request of the mother. Legitimisation by subsequent marriage of the parents, as before, was open only to those natural illegitimate children whose parents were not prohibited from marrying one another.[107] This form of legitimisation mainly gave the children all the rights of the full-born. England and Ireland (occupied by England), however, continued to refuse to admit legitimisation by subsequent marriage.[108] Legitimisation *per rescriptum papae* was replaced in the Reformed countries by the legitimisation *per rescriptum principis.*[109] However, this form of legitimisation did not give illegitimate children all the benefits of legitimate children.[110]

8.3. THE TRIDENTINE REFORMS OF ROMAN CANON LAW: MOVEMENT IN THE SAME DIRECTION

8.3.1. COUNTER-REFORMATION – THE CATHOLIC RESPONSE

The Catholic Church of Rome responded to the Protestant Reformation with the series of reforms known as the Counter-Reformation, or the Catholic Reformation. In the

---

[100] At common law illegitimate children were not related to both of the parents and could not inherit from them. JAMES, M., 'The Illegitimate and Deprived Child' (1957), p. 43.

[101] HUEBNER, R., *History of Germanic Private Law* (1918), p. 673.

[102] For instance Saxon law denied them this possibility. HUEBNER, R., *History of Germanic Private Law* (1918), p. 673.

[103] Ibid.

[104] For instance, Saxon law and English common law denied them this possibility. HUEBNER, R., *History of Germanic Private Law* (1918), p. 673; CRETNEY, S., *Family Law in the Twentieth Century* (2003), p. 545-546.

[105] BURGE, W., *Commentaries on Colonial and Foreign Law*, vol. II, (1908), p. 332.

[106] For instance, under Roman-Dutch law. Ibid, p. 352.

[107] Ibid, p. 350.

[108] Regarding Russian law see: ZAGOROVSKII, I., *Kurs semeinogo prava* (2003), p. 333.

[109] In England, such legitimisation was only possible by private Act of Parliament. JAMES, M., 'The Illegitimate and Deprived Child' (1957), p. 43.

[110] BURGE, W., *Commentaries on Colonial and Foreign Law*, vol. II, (1908), p. 364.

framework of these reforms, the canon family law of the Roman Catholic Church was modified almost simultaneously with the transformations that took place in the Reformed countries. The Counter-Reformation adjustment of family laws culminated in the decisions of the Council of Trent. Its *Tametsi* Decree (1563) eliminated most of the ambiguities of canon marriage. This was in a way a response to two centuries of humanist critique and two decades of Protestant attacks.[111]

8.3.2. THE TRIDENTINE REFORMS OF MARRIAGE AND DIVORCE

Some measures taken at Trent were mere declarations of the intent to stick to vested doctrines. In this fashion the principle of the indissolubility of marriage,[112] the sacramental character of marriage[113] and the superiority of virginity and celibacy above marriage[114] were confirmed and formally became part of the canon law.[115] Other measures were very similar to those introduced in the Reformed countries. Thus, clandestine marriage was also made invalid in the Catholic parts of Europe. Public church solemnisation became a legal requirement for the validity of marriage.[116] Concubinage was altogether formally forbidden.[117]

It is, however, interesting to notice that the Roman Catholic officials, even under the threat of the disintegration of the Catholic camp, refused to go any further in curtailing consensual marriage. During the Council, the French and Spanish delegations pressed to make parental consent a requirement for a valid marriage.[118] The preliminary drafts of the *Tametsi* Decree did incorporate this requirement; however, in the text of the Decree the Council returned to 'what we might call the spirit of Alexander's rules'.[119] Parental consent was not made a condition for the validity of marriage. The Council's reluctance in respect to parental consent ran so much against the dominant spirit of the power of patriarchal authority that it became a threat to the uniformity of marriage law within the Catholic domain. The *Tametsi* decree was 'inconsistently applied' in

---

[111] WITTE, J., *From Sacrament to Contract* (1997), p. 37.
[112] Canons 5, 7 and 8 of *Tametsi* Decree.
[113] Canon 1 of *Tametsi* Decree.
[114] Canons 6 and 10 of *Tametsi* Decree.
[115] PHILLIPS, R., *Putting Asunder* (1988), p. 27. However, an unconsummated marriage might still be dissolved in case of a choice for religious life by one of the spouses. Ibid. p. 35.
[116] ESMEIN, A., *Le mariage en droit canonique*, Part I (1929), p. 202.
[117] Concubinaries had to be admonished by the church minister who demanded them to separate. If they disobeyed they had to undergo heavy punishment, up to excommunication. BECKER, H-J., 'Die nichteheliche Lebensgemeinschaft (Konkubinat) in der Rechtsgeschichte' (1978), p. 28-29.
[118] HARRINGTON, J., *Reordering Marriage and Society in Reformed Germany* (1995), p. 95.
[119] BURGUIÈRE, A., LEBRUN, F., 'Prince, Priest and Family' (1996), p. 108.

most of Catholic Europe.[120] The French Royal Council even refused to promulgate the decisions of the Council of Trent as the laws of France and did not submit them to the *Parlements* for registration.[121] Instead, amended provisions of the *Tametsi* decree were promulgated in France by Royal Acts.[122] Even before the Council of Trent, the French secular law obliged sons up to the age of thirty and daughters up to the age of twenty-five to obtain parental consent to marriage under the treat of disinheritance.[123] Case law went even further and determined that every marriage of a minor without parental consent was presumed to be based on abduction and therefore void.[124] French jurists proudly presented the making of parental consent a requirement for the validity of marriage as a return to the principles of classical Roman law.[125]

It can be suggested that the Counter-Reformation reforms of the Council of Trent have transformed the flexible and ambiguous rules of the medieval canon family law into a system of rigorous imperatives. Consequently, it was not the individualistic spirit of the medieval canon law but the more rigid Tridentine attitude[126] that 'set the basic theological and legal tone of the Catholic contribution to the Western tradition of marriage'[127] until the Second Vatican Council of 1962-1965. It was this post-Tridentine system that came to be perceived by the modern jurists as 'the Catholic family law'.

8.4. ORTHODOX FAMILY LAW: REMARKABLE SIMILARITY

8.4.1. CHURCH JURISDICTION

After the fall of Byzantium in 1453, Russia became by far the most important country of Orthodox Christendom. Until the eighteenth century, the Russian Orthodox Church enjoyed exclusive jurisdiction in an even broader scope of family matters than the Roman Catholic Church during its hey day. This came to an end in the early eighteenth

---

[120]   HARRINGTON, J., *Reordering Marriage and Society in Reformed Germany* (1995), p. 97.
[121]   BURGUIÈRE, A., LEBRUN, F., 'Prince, Priest and Family' (1996), p. 108.
[122]   Ordinance of Blois (1579), Edict of Henry IV (1606) and Declaration of Louis XIII (1639). BRISSAUD, J., *A History of French Private Law* (1912), p. 109.
[123]   By Edict of Henry II of February 1556 and Ordinance of Blois. BURGUIÈRE, A., LEBRUN, F., 'Prince, Priest and Family' (1996), p. 108.
[124]   BRISSAUD, J., *A History of French Private Law* (1912), p. 116-117.
[125]   ESMEIN, A., *Le mariage en droit canonique*, Part I (1929), p. 188.
[126]   McSweeney characterised the post-Tridentine Church as 'a bureaucratic machine intended to counter ideas and attitudes which deviated from official orthodoxy'. MCSWEENEY, B., *Roman Catholicism. The Search for Relevance* (1980), p. 16.
[127]   WITTE, J., *From Sacrament to Contract* (1997), p. 37.

century when Peter the Great transformed the half-oriental Russia into the westernised Russian Empire. The impact of Peter's reforms on family law was fairly comparable to that of the Protestant Reformation. Peter the Great's ecclesiastical reforms were clearly inspired by the State churches of the Reformed countries. He did away with the independency of the Russian Church and abolished the position of the Patriarch. Consequently the Russian Orthodox Church became a kind of State Church with the Tsar as its head and the *Holly Synod* as its highest authority. The ecclesiastical jurisdiction in family matters was diminished, and secular laws replaced some parts of the canon family law.

8.4.2. ORTHODOX MARRIAGE LAW

As was mentioned before, Orthodox marriage law around the twelfth century had already established parental consent and public Church solemnisation as requirements for the validity of marriage. The Church continued to insist on the free consent of the parties, but in Russia before Peter this was no more than fiction.[128] From the High Middle ages till the times of Peter the Great, a Russian upper class woman would spend her life under conditions resembling those of a harem, hardly ever seeing any man that did not belong to her close family.[129] Marriages were arranged by the parents, and the future spouses often did not even see each other before the day of wedding.[130] Peter the Great, eager to 'westernise' Russia, reformed family law in line with contemporary European trends. He forced the nobility to let their wives and daughters take part in courtly life.[131] Secular law reinforced the canon law requirement of free consent of the parties to a marriage.[132] At the same time, family control over the marriages was strengthened. Although the absence of parental consent did not make marriage invalid, children of any age married without consent of their parents could be punished through disinheritance.[133] As everywhere in Europe, the requirements for the solemnisation of marriage became stricter. After due announcement, the solemnisation of marriage had to be conducted in public in the presence of the parties and witnesses. From 1775 on, the solemnisation had to be performed in the parish church of the bride or the groom. Other innovations were also similar to those in Western Europe. For

---

[128] ZAGOROVSKII, I., *Kurs semeinogo prava* (2003), p. 214.
[129] SOLOV'EV, C., *Istoria Rossii 1463-1584* (2001), p. 197.
[130] KARAMZIN, N., *The History of the State of Russia* (2003), p. 593.
[131] Ibid, p. 999.
[132] A short-lived Ukase of Peter the Great required a sworn statement of the parents that they had not forced their children into marriage. Later Art. 12 of the *Svod Zakonov* repeated the requirement of 'free and unforced' consent of the parties to a marriage.
[133] Art. 6 of the *Svod Zakonov*.

instance, the degrees of consanguinity and affinity impeding marriage were limited to the fourth degree.[134]

8.4.3. ORTHODOX DIVORCE LAW

As was explained in the preceding chapters, Orthodox law has, albeit under rigid conditions, always allowed divorce. The reforms of Peter the Great did not make divorce easier. Divorce by mutual consent was explicitly forbidden.[135] The number of grounds for divorce was diminished,[136] but even so, they were still more numerous than in the Protestant countries.[137] Granting divorce remained the prerogative of the ecclesiastical courts. Divorce by Royal dispensation, resembling the Nordic practice, was briefly introduced during the reign of Peter the Great.[138] As everywhere in the Europe of those days, divorce remained rare and very difficult to obtain due to the intricate procedure and the notorious reluctance of the ecclesiastical courts.[139]

8.4.4. CONCUBINAGE IN ORTHODOX LAW

Concubinage had legal standing neither in the ecclesiastical law[140] nor in the secular legislation enacted since the time of Peter the Great.[141] A good example of this approach can by found in *The Military Statute* of 1716, which threatened a bachelor who had a child by an unmarried girl with imprisonment and Church penance, 'unless he lawfully marries her'.[142]

---

[134] Ukas of the Synod of 1810.
[135] Art. 46 *Svod Zakonov.*
[136] ZAGOROVSKII, I., *Kurs semeinogo prava* (2003), p. 114.
[137] Except for the canonical ground of adultery, divorce was possible in case of bigamy, impotence, some incurable diseases, disappearance for five years, attempt on the spouse's life, choice for monastic life, long-term imprisonment and exile, and some others. (Ibid, p. 111-114.) It is interesting to notice that, differing from before, the adultery of husband and wife began to be treated equally. Ibid. p. 111.
[138] Ibid.
[139] The special ecclesiastical courts of Duhovnaia Consistoria were competent in marriage and divorce cases.
[140] ZAGOROVSKII, I., *Kurs semeinogo prava* (2003), p. 329 ff.
[141] Ibid, p. 334-336.
[142] Art. 176 of the *Military Statut.* ZAGOROVSKII, I., *Kurs semeinogo prava* (2003), p. 336.

8.4.5. ILLEGITIMATE CHILDREN IN ORTHODOX LAW

Differing from Byzantine law, Russian canon and secular law did not allow legitimisation by the subsequent marriage of the parents.[143] Due to the reforms of Peter the Great, the adjudication of the illegitimacy cases passed into secular hands. Legitimisation by subsequent marriage and *per rescriptum principis* became possible. Illegitimate children followed the status of their mother, unless she was of nobility.[144] The mother was obliged to maintain her unlawful children, but could not pass property to them upon death.[145] The establishment of paternity was possible under a criminal procedure, with the sole purpose of claiming 'damages': maintenance for the child and the mother.[146]

8.5. DID THE *IUS COMMUNE* OF FAMILY LAW SURVIVE THE REFORMATION?

How the evolution of family law in Europe in the time of Reformation should be appreciated, in terms of divergence or convergence, is a matter of controversy. On the one hand, several reputable scholars tend to underplay the divergence between the Protestant and the Catholic marriage and divorce laws and hold that the Protestant doctrine of marriage, and even the admissibility of divorce, was not a radical break from the doctrine of Rome.[147] Some academics even defend the idea that the medieval family *ius commune* continued to exist in spite of the Reformation. Thus, John Witte affirms that 'canon law remained part of the common law *(ius commune)* of Protestant and Catholic Europe until the legal reforms and codification movement of the later eighteenth and nineteenth centuries'.[148] Thomas Safley goes as far as alleging that both the Protestant and the post-Tridentine Catholic marriage and divorce laws 'were isolated elements in a far larger marital code, which remained unchanged upon both

---

[143]   It was explicitly forbidden in an important 1648 Code (Vol. X, 280). See: Ibid, p. 333.

[144]   Ibid, p. 419.

[145]   Ibid, p. 346.

[146]   Idid, p. 336-338, 345-350. Russian law knew no civil maintenance claim on behalf of an illegitimate child. Instead a begetter had to pay 'damages' caused by the crime of illicit cohabitation. Ibid, p. 348.

[147]   Jean Esmein proposed in his standard work that the Catholic notion of marriage was reused in the protestant countries 'like a twig being detached from the trunk and planted in the soil'. (ESMEIN, A., *Le mariage en droit canonique*, Part I (second edition 1929), p. 34). Many Ann Glendon assumed that 'secular government simply took over much of the ready-made set of the canon law'. (GLENDON, M.A., *The Transformation of Family Law* (1989), p. 31). Thomas Safley stressed the important role of the canon law in the formation of the Protestant marriage doctrine. SAFLEY, T., 'Canon Law and Swiss Reforms: Legal Theory and Practice in the Marital Courts of Zurich, Bern, Basel and St. Gall' (1992), p. 188.

[148]   WITTE, J., *From Sacrament to Contract* (1997), p. 44.

sides of the religious division of the period'.[149] Considering the similarity of the Orthodox law, one could extend this reasoning by suggesting that this 'code' covered the whole of Western and Eastern Europe.

On the other hand, it has been suggested that the early Modern period was clearly dominated by a tendency towards divergence. The main event of the period was the transformation from the uniformity of the Roman Catholic canon law to the Protestant/Catholic dichotomy. This primary divide was accompanied by the growing diversity of family law in the Protestant countries and the commencement of disintegration within the Catholic camp. In this respect it is quite clear that divergence advanced with the coming of the Reformation. This can be illustrated by the following examples. Regardless of how similar the Catholic and Protestant attitude was towards divorce, the Protestants in Western Europe made divorce possible again after centuries of dominance of the Catholic indissolubility doctrine. This is a substantial difference that should not be taken too lightly. In addition, the post-Tridentine Catholic and Orthodox law required parental consent but did not make it conditional for the validity of marriage. The Protestant laws by contrast, regarded marriage entered into without consent of the parents as invalid.

The authors that stress the differences between the Protestant and Catholic family law sometimes go further than emphasising differences between the rules of positive family law and search for a deeper, ideological dimension of this difference. The Protestant attacks on canon family law are sometimes presented as 'progressive', while the Catholic Tridentine counter-reform is perceived as a 'conservative, even reactionary, reaffirmation of the same medieval tradition both in ideal and practice'.[150] Joel Harrington has rightly highlighted the dubiousness of this perception.[151] She convincingly stressed the fundamentally conservative nature of the Protestant marriage reform.[152] According to her, 'protestant reformers of marital doctrine made several initial attempts to return to a purely biblical standard, yet they eventually ended up with a model based overwhelmingly on medieval canonical principles'.[153] Reformation was not the beginning of the liberalisation of family law. Quite the opposite, Protestants attacked the Catholic canon law on marriage and divorce not for its rigidity and departure from the humanistic spirit of the Scripture, but for its laxity. It has been noticed that the 'true nature of all sixteenth-century marriage reform

---

[149] SAFLEY, T., *Let No Man Put Asunder* (1984), p. 38. The 'Striking similarity' of these 'codes' was also stressed by Harrington. *Reordering Marriage and Society in Reformed Germany* (1995), p. 98.

[150] For an overview, see: HARRINGTON, J., *Reordering Marriage and Society in Reformed Germany* (1995), p. 48-49.

[151] Ibid, p. 48 ff.

[152] Ibid, p. 70.

[153] Ibid, p. 47.

[…was] improvement of enforcement rather than rejection of legal and theological heritage'.[154]

From this perspective, to stress the similarities between the family laws in the Catholic, Protestant and Orthodox parts of Post-Reformation Europe certainly has its merits. One can even suggest that the *ius commune* continued after the Reformation, provided that one does not perceive this *ius commune* as the uniform medieval canon family law of Roman Catholic Church, but rather as the general commonality of European family law on the level of underlying values. The conservative urge for discipline was indeed not confined to the Protestant camp. After the Reformation, the whole of Europe experienced similar economic changes and was inspired by the shared desire of strengthening patriarchal stability.[155] Common challenges determined the general similarity of family law responses. Notwithstanding the bitter confrontation between the Reformation and Counter-Reformation, both responded very much alike to the growing complaints about the 'laxity and ambiguity' of the canon family law and the resulting 'relaxation of morals'. The Catholic Church responded to this critique by the introduction of rigid rules and a further replacement of individual responsibility with obedience and discipline. Consequently, both the Catholic and the Protestant parts of Safley's 'marital code' modified the rather lenient medieval institution of marriage into a closed, highly institutionalised bond. In many aspects, the period of the Reformation constitutes the low point in respect to permissiveness and the high point in respect to the institutionalisation of family law on both sides of the Protestant-Catholic divide. Inspired by the same ideas, the secular reforms of Peter the Great instigated similar changes in Orthodox Russia. The 'unpractical' ideal of purely consensual marriage was abandoned in every part of Europe. The requirement of public Church solemnisation in the presence of witnesses, the insistence on parental consent,[156] and the concept of marriage as a life-long and, in principle, indissoluble union can be regarded as parts of a 'marital code' that was equally common to the Catholic, the Protestant and the Orthodox countries.

As was already mentioned, the fundamental difference between Catholic and Protestant theologies regarding the dissolubility of marriage does not preclude some scholars from emphasising similarities rather than differences between the Catholic and the Protestant marriage doctrine. It is claimed that despite the Protestant rejection of the Catholic doctrine of indissolubility of marriage, the Protestant attitude towards divorce has not been as radically different from Catholic practice as it used to be

---

[154]   Ibid, p. 39.
[155]   Ibid.
[156]   WITTE, J., *From Sacrament to Contract* (1997), p. 61.

suggested.[157] Phillips noticed that 'the Protestant attitudes toward divorce, and the Protestant laws dealing with it, broke significantly with their Roman Catholic precedents, yet were informed by many of the same values and some of the same fundamental moral orientations'.[158] He has a good point, as the admissibility of divorce in the Orthodox and the Reformed countries was by no means a token of the recognition of an individual's liberty to escape from an unhappy marriage. It was also not an acknowledgment of an individual's right to decide when his or her marriage had failed. Divorce was highly controlled and extremely difficult to obtain.[159] It could be added that the Orthodox attitude and practices of divorce also perfectly fit this picture.

Comparing both perceptions, it is possible to appreciate the merits of both. On the one hand, both family ideology and family law remained quite similar long after the medieval uniformity of family law in Western Europe was broken. This had to do with the common starting point: the medieval *ius commune* and the steady general similitude of European history. Moreover, both the Reformation and the Counter-Reformation were extra-national phenomena and provided for a certain accord between the national family laws in the respective camps. Thus, the states influenced by the same denomination of Orthodox or Reformed thought often developed similar family law. On the other hand, the same examples illustrate that the same ideas can have a very different impact in terms of the intensity and pace of reforms, and therefore produce very different laws. For instance, the reform of marriage law in England in the spirit of the Reformation was much slower and far less radical than on the continent.[160] Therefore, it can be suggested that in the early Modern period the Reformed, the Catholic and the Orthodox countries underwent rather similar changes, but each in its own peculiar pace and fashion. The best examples are the institutionalisation of marriage and the tendency towards the secularisation of family

---

[157]   PHILLIPS, R., *Putting Asunder* (1988), p. 93.

[158]   Ibid, p. 85.

[159]   Philips illustrates his view by noticing that, similar to the attitude of the Catholic Church, the main concern of the Protestant authorities 'was to preserve the integrity of individual marriages. If it was not possible, then they sought to preserve the integrity of marriage as an institution, by providing a second marriage as replacement for that which had been dissolved. In this respect the discontinuity between Roman Catholic and Protestant doctrines of marriage becomes less distinct than the nondissolubilist–dissolubilist dichotomy might suggest. To be sure, there was an important difference in the means employed, but the reluctance of the Catholic Church's courts to act in a separation *a mensa et thoro* and in annulments of marriages, which has been documented by scholars such as Helmholz, is strongly reminiscent of the policy the courts of the Protestant states apparently applied in respect of divorce'. Ibid, p. 93.

[160]   HELMHOLZ, R., *Marriage Litigation in Medieval England*, (1978), p. 3.

law, noticeable not only in the Protestant countries but also in the Catholic domain,[161] and later in Orthodox Russia.[162]

The conclusion is that it cannot be maintained that the *ius commune* in the narrow sense of this word (a set of rules of canon law common the whole of Catholic Europe) survived the Reformation. What did outlive the disintegration brought about by the Reformation is a general similarity of development of family laws in Europe.

8.6. MATRIMONIAL PROPERTY LAW: SIMILAR CHANGES

Because in Western Europe matrimonial property law was traditionally the domain of secular law, it was not directly affected by the Reformation. However, the general tendency towards secularisation rolled back the modest influence the canon law had accrued in this area in the High Middle Ages. For instance, in Russia, where matrimonial property had previously been regulated by canon law, Peter the Great passed competence in this area to the secular authorities. Starting with the Renaissance, new economic developments necessitated changes in the regulation of matrimonial property in the whole of Europe. In feudal times, only land was of real economic importance. Consequently, medieval matrimonial property law developed tools to safeguard the wife's land from being lost to her kin due to the irresponsible behaviour of her husband.[163] In the early Modern period, as the importance of chattels, and especially of capital, greatly increased, the law did not provide enough facilities to protect the inheritable immovables of the wife. This deficiency instigated a general trend involving a husband's limitation of power over his wife's immovables. Functionally similar legal means were developed within almost every European matrimonial system. The most common form of the new protective measures was to grant the wife the contractual possibility of obtaining a separate estate. The problem with a separate estate was that during the early Modern period, married women almost everywhere in Europe did not have legal competency.[164] Therefore, irrespective of the statutory property regime, the property of the wife as well as the rest of the familial

---

[161] Tokens thereof were the above mentioned refusal of the French Royal Council to acknowledge the decisions of the Council of Trent as the law of France, and the subsequent extension of the jurisdiction of the Royal courts in family matters. BRISSAUD, J., *A History of French Private Law* (1912), p. 91.

[162] In Russia, the intervention of the secular authorities in matrimonial affairs started with Peter the Great, who introduced important changes and additions into the ecclesiastical family law. BURGE, W., *Commentaries on Colonial and Foreign Laws,* vol. III, (1910), p. 61.

[163] KAHN-FREUND, O., 'Matrimonial Property Law in England' (1955), p. 273.

[164] BURGE, W., *Commentaries on Colonial and Foreign Law,* Vol. III, (1910), p. 320-325.

property was administered solely by the husband.[165] Thus, the creation of a separate estate had to be accompanied by granting a married woman some legal capacity over her separate property.

In common law countries, the problem was resolved through the system of equity. From the sixteenth century, property could be conveyed to trustees for a married woman's 'separate use'.[166] A wife's 'separate estate' could be created through the equitable machinery of trusts and ante-nuptial agreements.[167] Therefore, the wife became the equitable owner of her separate property. Equity also recognised her contractual, procedural and testamentary capacity over this property.[168] In the eighteenth century, an additional measure to safeguard the wife's separate estate was introduced. This measure, called 'restraint on anticipation' was deemed to protect the wife from being induced during the coverture[169] to alienate or charge her property on behalf of her husband.[170]

In France, the wife was at first granted the possibility to obtain a separate estate by judicial decision only if her husband became insolvent.[171] In this case, she escaped the power of her husband and was treated as a widow.[172] In the sixteenth century, Du Moulin suggested that such a woman could administer and freely dispose of her property.[173] His view did not find much support, however. According to the opinion that eventually prevailed, a woman with a separate estate could only administer and dispose of her chattels.[174] In respect to the disposition of movables, such women still needed the authorisation of either their husbands or of the court.[175] In France, the establishment of a separate estate by contract became possible only at the end of the *Ancien Régime*, and even then remained extremely rare.[176]

German customary law had a long-standing tradition of separate property of the wife (*Sondergut*).[177] Such a separate estate could be established either by contract or

---

[165]   HUEBNER, R., *History of Germanic Private Law* (1918), p. 648.
[166]   HOLDSWORTH, W., *A History of English Law*, vol. 5, (1945), p. 312.
[167]   Ibid, p. 310-315.
[168]   KAHN-FREUND, O., 'Matrimonial Property Law in England' (1955), p. 274.
[169]   See Part II, Chapter 5, Section 5.2.3.
[170]   BAKER, J., *An Introduction to English Legal History* (2002), p. 486.
[171]   BRISSAUD, J., *A History of French Private Law* (1912), p. 550.
[172]   Ibid.
[173]   Ibid.
[174]   Ibid.
[175]   Ibid, p. 838.
[176]   Ibid, p. 778-779.
[177]   Initially this involved only things for pure personal use (*Nadelgeld*), but later it could include any kind of property. Ibid, p. 778-779.

stipulated to by a testator or donator.[178] In Russia, the reforms of Peter the Great gradually led to the establishment of a statutory regime of separation of marital property.[179] A peculiarity of Russia was that a married woman, although under power of her husband, enjoyed legal capacity in patrimonial matters and could administer and alienate her own property without the authorisation of her husband.[180] Similar developments took place in Hungary. In 1514, the *Tripartitum* established a statutory regime of separation of property, combined with the unrestrained power of administration and disposition of property on the part of a married woman.[181]

Thus, granting the wife the right to a separate estate resulted in the pan-European recognition of the capacity of a married woman to manage her separate property. It should be born in mind, however, that the reason for this development was the urge to protect the family interests in the wife's immovables rather than concern over the rights of married women themselves.[182]

---

[178]   Ibid, p. 779.
[179]   ZAGOROVSKII, I., *Kurs semeinogo prava* (2003), p. 198-199.
[180]   In 1753, the Senate (the highest judicial instance in Imperial Russia) explained that a married woman is free to dispose of her property without the authorisation of her husband. Ibid, p. 199.
[181]   BURGE, W., *Commentaries on Colonial and Foreign Laws*, vol. III, (1910), p. 609.
[182]   KAHN-FREUND, O., 'Matrimonial Property Law in England' (1955), p. 274.

CHAPTER 9
THE ENLIGHTENMENT: THE CRADLE OF THE MODERN IDEAS ON MARRIAGE AND THE FAMILY

9.1. ENLIGHTENMENT IDEOLOGY ON MARRIAGE AND THE FAMILY

The patriarchal family of the *Ancien Régimes* on the eve of the Enlightenment in the Catholic, Orthodox and Protestant countries has often been compared to absolute monarchy.[1] The power of the paterfamilias was seen as God-given and indisputable.[2] In his apologetic work *Patriarcha*, Robert Filmer, a fervent proponent of absolutism, derived a legitimation of the absolute power of the monarch over his country from Adam's 'natural' God-given patriarchal power over his family.[3] This patriarchal family model was build upon the transpersonalistic premises of communitarianism and patriarchy. Marriage and family were seen as ends in themselves rather than as means to the well-being of their members.[4] Family members were perceived as subservient to the family. The family in its turn was seen as subservient to the society at large. To perform the role of spouse, child or parent was understood to be the fulfilment of a social and religious duty. The authority bestowed upon the paterfamilias was supposed to be granted to enable him to enforce the performance of those duties. Therefore the patriarchal family of the *Ancien Régimes* was characterised by the far-reaching marital power of the husband and the concentration of the parental power in the hands of the father alone. A rather extreme example of this patriarchal attitude can be found

---

[1]   Such comparison of the family and the State was also employed by John Milton, Thomas Hobbes and Jean Bodin. For a short account, see: ZWAAN, T., *Familie, huwelijk en gezin in West-Europa* (1993), p. 150 ff.

[2]   Joel Harrington noticed that 'the ancient ideological identification of the authority of the head of the household with that of the head of the government' became a commonplace. HARRINGTON, J., *Reordering Marriage and Society in Reformed Germany* (1995), p. 41.

[3]   FILMER, R., *Patriarcha or the natural power of kings* (1680).

[4]   The well-known poet and critic of the patriarchal family John Milton noticed that: 'To enjoy the indissoluble keeping of a marriage found unfit against the good of man both soul and body [...] is to make an idol of marriage' MILTON, J., *The Doctrine and Discipline of Divorce* (1959), p. 282.

in the influential Russian sixteenth-century handbook *Domostroy,*[5] which contained detailed instructions for the chastening of wives and children. Russia was no exception; everywhere in Europe the paterfamilias had a broad spectrum of chastising measures at hand. If his own measures were insufficient, he could often invoke the authority of the State to punish disobedient family members. For example, in France and Imperial Russia, the paterfamilias could have his children (in France even his wife) imprisoned without any investigation by simply issuing an Order of Arbitrary Arrest (*Lettres de cochet*).[6]

The ideology of the Enlightenment disparaged many aspects of the patriarchal family and in fact inspired the revolt against both royal and household tyrants.[7] The Enlightenment period can truly be regarded as the cradle of modern family law ideology. It seems justified to suggest that the century-long process of gradual liberalisation of family law actually only started with the Enlightenment. After centuries of discussing family law on the basis of theological arguments, the actors of the Enlightenment, most of whom were deists,[8] undercut 'the traditional notion that God was somehow a necessary party to every marital contract, or that the church was a necessary agent in every scheme of marital governance'.[9]

The first step in this direction was made by such precursors of the Enlightenment, like John Locke and the famous English poet John Milton.[10] These thinkers based their plea for a more liberal attitude to marriage, divorce and parental power on a mixture of natural law and theological arguments. Milton regarded marriage as a 'covenant', one of the most important parts of which was 'soul love'.[11] He derived the natural right of an individual to escape from a failed marriage on the same premises that justified the natural right of a citizen to revolt against a despotic sovereign.[12] Locke launched a full-scale attack on Robert Filmer's theologically- historical apologia of the

---

[5]   The literal meaning of this title is: 'how-to-build-up-a-household'. The second part of this handbook contained guidelines on how 'to live in peace with wife, children, and servants' according to the patriarchal ideal, and 'how to punish and to teach them'. So 'a wife should submit herself to her husband, and do everything that he orders her with fear and love' (Chapter 29). Next followed the advice to punish the wife without witnesses. The oldest known version of *Domostroy* was compiled in the first half or the sixteenth century. Later this popular manual was re-edited and amended many times. For more details see: Metropolitan MAKARIY, *The History of Russian Church,* book IV, part I (1996), p. 445-449.

[6]   See for France: VIOLLET, P., *Précis de l'histoire du droit français* (1886), p. 425-426, and for Russia: ZAGOROVSKII, I., *Kurs semeinogo prava* (2003), p. 242-244.

[7]   PHILLIPS, R., *Family Breakdown in Late Eighteenth Century France* (1980), p. 15.

[8]   Deism is based on the premise that God does not habitually interfere in man's daily affairs.

[9]   WITTE, J., *From Sacrament to Contract* (1997), p. 197.

[10]   MILTON, J., *The Doctrine and Discipline of Divorce, Restored to the Good of Both Sexes, from the Bondage of Canon Law* (1644).

[11]   Ibid, p. 256-269.

[12]   Ibid, p. 229.

-

patriarchal family.[13] Locke maintained that the true basis of marriage was not the God-given authority of the paterfamilias, but rather 'a voluntary compact'[14] which 'gives the husband no more power over [the wife's life] than she has over his life'.[15] According to Locke such contract could, in principle, be ended at the will of the spouses when its purpose, the nurturing of the children, had been fulfilled.[16] Locke's further reasoning brought him to the idea that the parental power belonged equally to the mother and the father. Also, parental power was not, in his view, an absolute power, but rather an authority subject to the purpose of the education of the children.[17] In spite of these open-minded ideas, Locke remained, however, 'a man of a pious Puritan stock'.[18] This constraint made him compromise his ideas when it came to a woman's equal right to divorce.[19]

The thinkers of the Enlightenment actually started where John Locke stopped and made Locke's contractarian model of marriage the starting point of secular theory of marriage.[20] Although the term 'Enlightenment thought' assembles such dissimilar philosophers as Voltaire and Jean-Jacques Rousseau, it is quite possible to discern certain common features of the Enlightenment attitude towards the family. The cornerstones of this attitude were personalism, individualism, and rationalism. Man was supposed to be able to understand and to master the causal order of the world with the help of reason. Therefore it was held possible to emancipate man and to improve human life according to universally valid values.[21] One of the main events of the Enlightenment was the initiation of a general shift from the traditional transpersonalistic[22] perception of marriage and family to the personalistic attitude towards them.[23] Man started to be seen as the centre of the order of things. For the first time, marriage began to be seen not as a social and religious duty encompassing an end in itself, but rather as an asset for man: a means to achieving personal happiness. The French Philosophers sensed marriage as a union based on the

---

[13] LOCKE, J., *Two Treatises of Government* (1978).
[14] Ibid, p. 155.
[15] Ibid, p. 157.
[16] Ibid, p. 156.
[17] Ibid, p. 141 ff
[18] WITTE, J., *From Sacrament to Contract* (1997), p. 190.
[19] Locke was often criticised by feminists for stating that in case of impossibility to reach an agreement 'the last determination [...] naturally falls to the man's share as the abler and stronger' (Ibid, p. 156). For the feminists critic see, for instance, OKIN, S., *Women in Western Political Thought*, (1979), p. 199-200.
[20] WITTE, J., *From Sacrament to Contract* (1997), p. 196.
[21] TOMESEN, L., 'Ideeënstelsels die ten grondslag liggen aan het Europese cultuurdebat' (1994), p. 6.
[22] However, the terms 'transpersonalism' and 'personalism' came into use in legal lexis only by the end of the ninetheeth century.
[23] As Phillips put it 'family was no longer thought of as a cooporative unit to which the interests of the individual members were subordinated, but more as a union of individuals whose separate interests were considered important in themselves'. PHILLIPS, R., *Putting Asunder* (1988), p. 180.

sentiment of love,[24] rather than as a conventional social and economical relationship'.[25] The idea of marriage as a merely private law relationship, a civil contract, became a true antithesis to the patriarchal theological perception.[26] The right to dissolve an unhappy marriage was a logical result of the vision of marriage as 'one of the avenues open to man in his pursuit of happiness'.[27] From this personalistic point of view, the 'state had no right to prevent its citizens from pursuing such happiness' and 'to make impossible or cumbersome the exercise of the natural right of divorce'.[28]

In line with these ideas, the period of Enlightenment became the cradle of the next two generations of divorce laws: divorce on the ground of irretrievable breakdown of marriage (divorce as remedy or failure), and divorce by the mutual consent of the spouses (divorce as an autonomous decision of the spouses). The theorists of the French Enlightenment employed against the Catholic notion of indissolubility of marriage the models from classical antiquity and contemporary examples of indigenous and European (Protestant and Orthodox) nations.[29] The Philosophers revealed that the doctrine of indissolubility was of a relatively recent origin, and was not adhered to by the early Church.[30] From the Enlightenment perspective, divorce was no longer seen as a punishment for a matrimonial offence, but rather as a remedy for marital breakdown.[31] Accordingly, it was suggested that it should also be possible to dissolve a failed marriage, even when its failure could not be attributed to the fault of one of the spouses. For instance, Morelly advocated divorce by mutual consent – even on the ground of a unilateral application.[32]

Some of the Philosophers also saw divorce as a means to improve the position of women, 'as the ability of women to divorce would be a useful counterweight to male authority'. Thus, Montesquieu proposed to grant the right of unilateral repudiation only to women.[33] He also scorned the power of the husband as 'a creation of despotic government'.[34] Women's equality was, however, only a marginal and hesitant theme

---

[24] TRAER, J., *Marriage and the Family in the Eighteenth-Century France* (1980), p. 70-71.
[25] Ibid, p. 49.
[26] MÜLLER-FREIENFELS, W., 'Family Law and the Law of Succession in Germany' (1967), p. 433-434.
[27] RHEINSTEIN, M., *Marriage Stability, Divorce, and the Law* (1972), p. 25.
[28] Ibid, p. 196.
[29] TRAER, J., *Marriage and the Family in the Eighteenth-Century France* (1980), p. 53-57.
[30] PHILLIPS, R., *Putting Asunder* (1988), p. 167.
[31] Ibid, p. 172.
[32] Ibid, p. 166.
[33] Ibid, p. 171.
[34] MONTESQUIEU, C., *The Spirits of Laws* (1914) (Harmony between the political system and the conditions of the family).

in the palette of the Enlightenment.[35] Still, the picture of the ideology of the Enlightenment would not be complete without the names of three prominent proponents of the emancipation of women: de Condorcet,[36] Olympe de Gouges[37] and Mary Wollstonecraft.[38]

Enlightenment thought lays at the beginning of the process of the liberalisation of the family. However, it has been rightly warned that although the Enlightenment brought a lot of change in family ideology, it would be erroneous to picture it as a deliberate radical break with tradition. It is rightly mentioned that the Enlightenment actors 'sought to improve the Western legal tradition of marriage rather than to abandon it'.[39] They generally shared the conventional ideal of marriage as a monogamous and, as a rule, life-long union as well as the traditional definition of the goods and goals of marriage: mutual love and affection, mutual protection and the nurturance of children.[40] Therefore, 'the primary goal of these Enlightenment reformers was to purge the traditional household and community of its excessive paternalism, patriarchy, and prudishness, and thus to render the ideal structure and purpose of marriage a greater reality for all'.[41]

As was explained in Chapter 2, the appeal to universal values and the craving for emancipation gave the Enlightenment ideology the character of what could be called a 'Modernity project'.[42] The realisation of this emancipation project started in the late eighteenth century and still continues in our day.

---

[35] Jean-Jacques Rousseau considered that inequality of man and woman within a family is not a human invention or a prejudice, but is founded in reason (ROUSSEAU, J-J., *Emile* (1969), p. 697). A man should be able to control his wife in marriage because 'it is essential for him to be certain that the children, whom he is compelled to recognise and maintain, belong to no one but himself' (ROUSSEAU, J-J., *Third Discourse on Political Economy* (1969), p. 241-242. Cited in: OKIN, S., 'Are Our Theories of Justice Gender-Neutral?' (1986), p. 130). For en extensive examination from a feminist perspective of Rousseau's ideas on family and women's equality see: OKIN, S., *Women in Western Political Thought*, (1979), p. 99-197.

[36] In 1792 Condorcet wrote his famous treatises 'On the admission of women to the rights of the citizen'.

[37] Gouges passionately vindicated in her pamphlet 1791 'the Rights of woman', the extension to women of the 'right of Man and the Citizen'. Her pamphlet was composed in the form of an appendix to the Declaration of the Rights of Man and of the Citizen adopted by the National Assembly in 1789. See: WILLIAMS, D., *The Enlightenment* (1999), p. 36-38.

[38] An English late eighteenth-century feminist, author of 'A vindication of the rights of woman' (1792). For more about her works see: WILLIAMS, D., *The Enlightenment* (1999), p. 38-40 and 329-330.

[39] WITTE, J., *From Sacrament to Contract* (1997), p. 208

[40] Ibid.

[41] Ibid.

[42] See Part I, Chapter 2, Section 2.3.

9.2. IMPLEMENTATION OF ENLIGHTENMENT IDEOLOGY INTO LAW

9.2.1. AN OVERVIEW OF SOURCES

The Enlightenment thought inspired a whole wave of family law reforms coming from sources as different as the codifications of enlightened monarchs, French Revolutionary legislation and Napoleon's *Code Civil*. The most important examples of the attempts on the part of the enlightened monarchs to cautiously implement the new ideas into law were the Prussian *Allgemeines Landrecht für die Preussischen Staaten* of 1794 and the Austrian *Allgemeines Bürgerliches Gesetzbuch* of 1811. The Enlightenment ideas clearly found their zenith in the French revolutionary legislation. This legislation sought a profound revision of the patriarchal family; comparable to the revolutionary change brought to the political institutions of the *Ancien Régime*. The 'household Capets had to be stripped of the despotic aspects of their power',[43] in the same radical way as the royal ones. The individuals within the family became the focus of the new law. In Napoleonic times the pendulum partially swung back. The emphasis was again no longer on the individual within the family, but on the communitarian aspect of the family.[44] Some aspects of the revolutionarily legacy, especially secularism, were preserved, however.[45] Others were countermanded by a new urge for order and discipline, which found its expression in the enforcement of parental and marital power and the protection of legitimate families only.[46] The nineteenth century started with the triumphal spread of family law inspired by the Enlightenment ideas, albeit in the moderate form of the Napoleonic *Code Civil*, throughout Europe. The export of the Code Civil provides one of the first examples of a harmonisation of family law in modern Europe, although not particularly a peaceful one. This expansion, however, abruptly gave way to the conservative Restoration after the defeat of Napoleon.

9.2.2. ENLIGHTENMENT LAWS ON MARRIAGE

Even before the Enlightenment, the influence of natural law ideas and the desire to put an end to the ambiguity of the ecclesiastical rules governing the solemnisation of marriage led to several attempts to institute civil marriage. Thus, in the framework

---

[43] PHILLIPS, R., *Family Breakdown in Late Eighteenth Century France* (1980), p. 15.
[44] Ibid, p. 186.
[45] Although it was rightly stressed that despite the principle of secularisation, the *Code Civil* 'remained profoundly marked by the canonical conception of marriage and the family'. FOYER, J., 'The Reform of Family Law in France' (1978), p. 77.
[46] Ibid.

of the English revolution, the Barebone's Parliament passed an Act in 1653[47] that replaced the Church wedding with a civil marriage ceremony before a Justice of the peace.[48] This law, however, appeared to be rather fleeting, as it had already been repealed in 1660, shortly after the Restoration of the Monarchy.[49]

By the Law of 1783 of Emperor Joseph II, civil marriage[50] was introduced in the Austrian Empire,[51] including Lombardy[52] and the Austrian Netherlands.[53] The Austrian *Allgemeines Bürgerliches Gesetzbuch* of 1811 took over this innovation.

The French revolutionary legislation was by far the most uncompromising example of the implementation of the Enlightenment contractarian idea of marriage into law. The Constitution of 1791 declared that marriage was no more than a civil contract.[54] The law of 20 September 1792 replaced the Church rituals, prescribed for marriage, birth and death, with civil registration. Civil marriage had to be solemnised in public in a town hall in the presence of the parties and four witnesses. Parental consent was required only for children under the age of twenty-one.[55] Married women were granted equal rights[56] within the family and obtained full legal capacity.[57] The ill-famed *Lettres de cochet* were abolished in 1789.[58] Instead of a *paterfamilias* making his own justice, new family courts were introduced in order to resolve family disputes.[59]

Napoleon's *Code Civil* retained the secular control over family matters and the obligatory civil registration of marriage. However, the authority of the parents over their children and of the husband over his wife was largely restored. Marriage of sons under 25 and daughters under 21, entered without parental consent, was rendered

---

[47] 'Act touching Marriages and the registering thereof'.
[48] DURSTON, C., *The Family in English Revolution* (1989), p. 69.
[49] Ibid, p. 71.
[50] Civil marriage was an alternative form confined to those who did not belong to any recognised religious denomination. BURGE, W., *Commentaries on Colonial and Foreign Laws*, vol. III, (1910), p. 165.
[51] HALLER, M., 'Austria' (1977), p. 212.
[52] SGRITTA, G., TUFARI, P., 'Italy' (1977), p. 254.
[53] Currently Belgium.
[54] PHILLIPS, R., 'Remaking the Family: The Reception of Family Law and Policy during the French Revolution', (1992), p. 65.
[55] TRAER, J., *Marriage and the Family in the Eighteenth-Century France* (1980), p. 95.
[56] It is interesting to notice that Maximilien Robespierre, a faithful adherent of Jean-Jacques Rousseau, was against the emancipation of women. BRISSAUD, J., *A History of French Private Law* (1912), p. 150.
[57] PHILLIPS, R., *Putting Asunder* (1988), p. 181.
[58] Ibid.
[59] *Tribunaux de famille* were composed of family members and friends of the litigants in order to resolve family disputes within the family framework. The experiment proved not to be a success and the competence of the family courts was transferred to the regular courts in 1796. See: PHILLIPS, R., *Family Breakdown in Late Eighteenth Century France* (1980), p. 17-43.

void. Even after this age children were obliged to ask for parental permission in so-called '*actes respectueux*'.[60] It is observed that the *Code Civil* treated married women as 'minors or lunatics'.[61] A husband owed his wife a duty of protection, while a wife owed her husband a duty of obedience and respect, and had to follow her husband anywhere he decided to make his home.[62]

Napoleon's victorious armies brought civil marriage into various parts of Europe.[63] Thus, the obligatory civil registration of marriage was introduced in the Southern Netherlands[64] and Luxemburg in 1895,[65] in the Kingdom of Holland[66] in 1809,[67] and in various Italian states between 1804 and 1810.

9.2.3. ENLIGHTENMENT LAWS ON DIVORCE

The ideas of the precursors to the Enlightenment, Milton and Locke, had little influence on the divorce situation of the England of their days.[68] Even Cromwell's secular revolutionary government did not introduce divorce into English law. Instead, it 'solved' the problem of failed marriages by passing the 1650 Adultery Act,[69] which established capital punishment[70] for adultery.[71] The influence of the ideology of the Enlightenment first manifested itself in the divorce provisions of the codifications that

---

[60] BÉNABENT, A., *Droit civil: La Famille* (2001), No 100.

[61] COLIN, A., CAPITANT, H., *Traité de droit civil*, Vol. 1 *Introduction générale. Institutions civiles et judiciaires, personnes et famille* (1957), p. 612.

[62] Art. 213 and 214. These provisions matched Napoleon's personal patriarchal vision of the position of women, which he expressed so brusquely: '*Le mari a le droit de dire à sa femme: Madame, vous ne sortirez pas, Madame, vous n'irez pas à la comédie, Madame, vous m'appartenez corps et âme*'. THIBEAUDOT, A-C., *Mémoires sur le Consulat, 1799 à 1804* (1827), p. 426.

[63] For a fine synopsis, see the recent reprint of Jean Carbonnier's piece: CARBONNIER, J., 'Le Code Civil' (reprint 2004), p. 17-37.

[64] At that time the Austrian Netherlands, currently Belgium.

[65] The Austrian Netherlands were formally integrated into Revolutionary France in 1895, so the *Code Civil* was from the outset equally applicable there.

[66] Currently The Netherlands. In 1795, the French revolutionary army inspired a revolt as a result of which the Republic of the Seven Provinces was replaced by the Batavian Republic (1795-1806). In 1806 Napoleon transformed this Republic into the Kingdom of Holland with his brother Louis Bonaparte as King. In 1811, this marionette kingdom was annexed by France and made into a French province called Pays-Bas.

[67] APELDOORN, L., *Geschiedenis van het Nederlandsche huwelijksrecht* (1925), p. 123-125.

[68] WITTE, J., *From Sacrament to Contract* (1997), p. 186.

[69] 'Act for suppressing the detestable sins of Incest, Adultery and Fornication'.

[70] The Act was based on a double standard attitude: only a married woman who committed adultery, and her accomplice, were subjected to capital punishment. A married man fornicating with an unmarried woman was punished only by a three-month imprisonment. PHILLIPS, R., *Putting Asunder* (1988), p. 130.

[71] DURSTON, C., *The Family in English Revolution* (1989), p.153.

were commenced by enlightened monarchs. In 1751, Frederick the Great of Prussia issued a Rescript, encouraging the civil courts to grant a divorce if the marriage was irreconcilably disturbed by dreadful and notorious enmity.[72] The 1794 *Allgemeines Landrecht für die Preussischen Staaten* (ALP) secularised the law on divorce and allowed divorce for a large number of causes.[73] A true innovation allowed childless couples to dissolve their marriage upon mutual consent[74] and upon an irretrievable breakdown of marriage, manifested by such 'fierce and deep hatred' of one spouse towards the other 'that there was no hope of reconciliation or achieving the goals of marriage'.[75] The ALP's liberal approach of divorce can, however, only partially be attributable to the influence of the ideas of the Enlightenment. The other influence was the pragmatic demographic policy of Frederick the Great. In line with this policy, Frederick considered it more practical to enable the spouses to end a broken marriage from which no children could be expected, in order to enable them to enter a new union capable of producing children.[76] It is notable that, unlike ecclesiastical law, this new secular divorce law introduced 'double standards' to deal with adultery on the part of the husband and the wife.[77]

The French revolutionary law of 20 September 1792, enacted during the zenith of the Revolution, has rightly been characterised as 'one of the most liberal and permissive divorce laws to have ever been applied' on a national basis in the Western society'.[78] Divorce was made possible on the ground of matrimonial fault and other specific fault grounds. Revolutionary innovations were the almost unrestrained admission of divorce by mutual consent and the allowance of easy divorce upon an irretrievable breakdown of marriage resulting from 'incompatibility of temperament'.[79]

The Liberal revolutionary divorce law was attacked immediately after the Termidorian seize of power in July 1794.[80] At the time of Directory,[81] divorce became 'a political

---

[72]   Circular Rescript of 27 September 1751.
[73]   Paragraphs 669-718b of the ALR provided, among others, for the following divorce grounds: adultery, malicious desertion, refusal to fulfil marital duties, sexual incapacity, madness, change of religion, drunkenness, attempt on the spouse's life, refusal of the husband to support the family, condemnation for a dishonourable crime. See also: VON BÔNÉ, E., 'Comparaison entre le droit au divorce dans la République Batave (1798-1806) et dans l'Allgemeines Landrecht für die der Preussischen Staaten' (2001), p. 173-186.
[74]   MÜLLER-FREIENFELS, W., *Ehe und Recht* (1962), p. 22.
[75]   Para. 718a of the ALR.
[76]   WEBER, M., *Ehefrau und Mutter in der Rechtsentwicklung* (1907), p. 336.
[77]   Ibid, p. 336.
[78]   PHILLIPS, R., *Putting Asunder* (1988), p. 159.
[79]   Ibid, p. 11-12.
[80]   TRAER, J., *Marriage and the Family in the Eighteenth-Century France* (1980), p. 167-168.
[81]   1795-1799.

symbol'[82] for both its republican defenders and its conservative adversaries. Napoleon's *Code Civil* made divorce law considerably more restrictive. Unilateral divorce for reasons of incompatibility of temperaments was abolished. Divorce by mutual consent was retained in the *Code Civil* due to the personal insistence of Napoleon,[83] but became 'nearly a dead letter'[84] because it came to be surrounded with many restrictions.[85] The number of specific causes for divorce was drastically diminished; adultery on the part of a husband started to be treated more leniently than adultery committed by a wife.[86] Napoleon's expansion made the divorce provisions of the *Code Civil* a pan-European event. The rules of *Code Civil* became the law of the Netherlands, Belgium, Luxemburg, Sweden, Italy and large parts of Germany.

9.2.4. ENLIGHTENMENT LAWS ON CONCUBINAGE

The ideology of Enlightenment did not bring much change in the attitude towards concubinage. As before, concubinage largely remained outside the law. The only notable exception was a still-born attempt to regulate concubinage under the name of 'left-hand marriage'[87] in the 1791 *Allgemeine Gezetsbuch für die Preussischen Staten* and the 1794 *Preussisches Allgemeines Landrecht*.[88] The necessity of such regulation was explained in the comments by the frequency of the situation that a man of high standing did not want to re-marry after the death of his wife, but was not able to remain celibate and thus resorted to concubinage.[89] The attitude toward concubinage of the *Code Civil* is exemplified by the often cited expression of Napoleon: '*Les concubins se passent de la loi, la loi se désintéresse d'eux*', which could be freely translated as: 'concubines do without the law, the law is not interested in them'. This position became the paradigm of the way concubinage was dealt with in the nineteenth century and beyond.

---

[82]   TRAER, J., *Marriage and the Family in the Eighteenth-Century France* (1980), p. 129.
[83]   Ibid, p. 175-176.
[84]   GLENDON, M. A., 'The French Divorce Reform Law of 1976' (1976), p. 227.
[85]   Rheinstein has rightly noticed that 'Napoleon's Code hides breakdown behind consent', as mere consent was not sufficient for divorce. One had to be able to prove 'that life in common has become unbearable to the spouses' (art. 233 CC). RHEINSTEIN, M., *Marriage Stability, Divorce, and the Law* (1972), p. 212.
[86]   TRAER, J., *Marriage and the Family in the Eighteenth-Century France* (1980), p. 177-178.
[87]   '*Ehe zur linken Hand*' or *matrimonium ad morganaticam*. See: 'Die Ehe zur linken Hand', *Berliner iur. Diss.*, 1915. Refered to by BECKER, H-J.,'Die nichteheliche Lebensgemeinschaft (Konkubinat) in der Rechtsgeschichte' (1978), at p. 35, note 105.
[88]   Ibid, p. 34-35.
[89]   Ibid, p. 34.

9.2.5. ENLIGHTENMENT LAWS ON THE POSITION OF ILLEGITIMATE CHILDREN

The first sight of a more favourable attitude towards illegitimate children became visible in the *Preussisches Allgemeines Landrecht*. A mother's oath was admitted as proof of paternity, irrespective of her conduct and in disregard of the *exceptio congressus cum pluribus*.[90] The obligation to maintain an illegitimate child was imposed not only on the father but also on his ascendants.[91]

French revolutionary law[92] abolished the rights of the first-born, and bestowed upon children of both sexes equal rights of succession. These rights were shortly extended even to illegitimate children during the Jacobin period.[93] Under the *Code Civil*, the position of illegitimate children became in many respects even worse than it was during *Ancien Régime*. The judicial establishment of paternity (*la recherche de la paternité*) was, save for a few exceptions, explicitly forbidden by Art. 340 CC.[94] An illegitimate child had affiliation neither with the father nor the mother unless it was formally[95] acknowledged by one or both of them.[96] A married father was not allowed to acknowledge his extramarital child.[97] Acknowledgement was only possible in respect of natural illegitimate children; so-called adulterous or incestuous children could neither be acknowledged nor legitimised,[98] and had almost no rights.[99] Acknowledgment placed an illegitimate child in a position close to that of a legitimate issue in respect of the mother,[100] but created no legal ties with her relatives.[101] In respect of the father, acknowledgement produced only a limited right to maintenance and succession,[102] and in some respects, to parental custody.[103] This approach, in which the legal status of an illegitimate child depended on the acknowledgement of the

---

[90] WEBER, M., *Ehefrau und Mutter in der Rechtsentwicklung* (1907), p. 340.

[91] ibid.

[92] Statute of November 2, 1993.

[93] Only 'adulterous' children were still disadvantaged. TRAER, J., *Marriage and the Family in the Eighteenth-Century France* (1980), p. 158.

[94] Except for cases of abduction and rape. Art. 335, 342 *Code Civil*. FOYER, J., 'The Reform of Family Law in France' (1978), p. 95.

[95] If a child was not acknowledged in it's birth certificate it could be later acknowledged only by a public 'authentic act'. Art. 334 CC.

[96] Art. 336 CC.

[97] TRAER, J., *Marriage and the Family in the Eighteenth-Century France* (1980), p. 189.

[98] Art. 335 CC. See also: FOYER, J., 'The Reform of Family Law in France' (1978), p. 93.

[99] Except for a very limited right to maintenance. Art. 762 CC.

[100] BURGE, W., *Commentaries on Colonial and Foreign Laws*, vol. II, (1908), p. 332-333.

[101] Art. 757 CC.

[102] Only acknowledged children could inherit after their parents, but not after their family. An illegitimate child was no heir but a '*successeur irrégulier*' and his or her share was less than that of the legitimate children (art. 757 CC).

[103] BURGE, W., *Commentaries on Colonial and Foreign Laws*, vol. II, (1908), p. 337.

parents, is sometimes not quite accurately referred to as 'Romanic'.[104] The Napoleonic rules in regard to illegitimate children had lasting effect in Belgium, Luxemburg, The Netherlands, Italy, Spain, Portugal, some parts of Germany and some Swiss cantons.[105]

9.2.6. ENLIGHTENMENT LAWS ON MATRIMONIAL PROPERTY

The statutory matrimonial property regime under the Austrian *Allgemeines Bürgerliches Gesetzbuch* of 1811 was that of separation of property.[106] The spouses were allowed to modify this regime by a marriage settlement.[107] A married woman enjoyed legal capacity, however her husband could declare her legally incompetent upon the allegation of poor management of her property.[108] A wife was entitled to administer her own property; however, there was a legal presumption that she had transmitted this right to her husband.[109]

During the French revolution, attempts to equalise the property rights of spouses went no further than drafts.[110] One of the most important achievements of the *Code Civil* was the unification of French matrimonial property law; traditionally divided into the dotal separate property system in the South and the community of movables and acquests in the North. The model finally adopted in the Code was one of the varieties of the Northern system laid down in the influential *Coutume* of Paris. Under this regime (art. 1401 CC), all movable property of husband and wife, together with immovables acquired by onerous title after the marriage as well as all the fruits, incomes, interests and products of work of both spouses, constituted their common property.[111] Pre-marital movables of husband or wife, together with the movables acquired after marriage by way of inheritance or donation by each of them, were the separate property of husband or wife respectively. Therefore three patrimonies could be distinguished: the common fund, the separate property of the husband and the separate property of the wife.[112] All three sets of assets stood under the administration

---

[104] ZAGOROVSKII, I., *Kurs semeinogo prava* (2003), p. 325-328. For more on the 'Romanic' and 'Germanic' approaches of illegitimacy, see Chapter 10, Section 10.3.2.

[105] BURGE, W., *Commentaries on Colonial and Foreign Laws*, vol. II, (1908), p. 335-337.

[106] Para. 1237 ABGB.

[107] For more details see: WEBER, M., *Ehefrau und Mutter in der Rechtsentwicklung* (1907), p. 344-345.

[108] Para. 1241 ABGB.

[109] Para. 1238 ABGB.

[110] The Project of the *Code Civil* of 1793 drafted by Condorcet provided for equal rights of the spouses in respect of the administration of their property and required the joint consent of the spouses for the alienation of family property. BRISSAUD, J., *A History of French Private Law* (1912), p. 166.

[111] COLOMER, A., 'The Modern French Law' (1972), p. 81.

[112] ANCEL, M., 'Matrimonial Property Law in France' (1955), p. 13.

of the husband,[113] who had also a right of enjoyment in respect to the personal property of the wife.[114] The wife was legally incompetent[115] and could not enter into a contract[116] or litigate without the authorisation of her husband.[117] However, she was allowed to freely make a testament.[118] The administrative power of the husband in respect to the common fund was not limited by any accountability towards the wife.[119] But in respect to the wife's personal property, the husband had no power of disposition without her consent.[120]

9.3. THE INFLUENCE OF ENLIGHTENMENT AND THE CONVERGENCE OF FAMILY LAW

9.3.1. THE COMMENCEMENT OF THE CONSERVATIVE-PROGRESSIVE DISCORD

The age of Enlightenment reveals a more prominent tendency towards convergence than the preceding period of the Reformation. Like the Reformation, the Enlightenment was a pan-European phenomenon. Although the Enlightenment thought did not directly affect the marriage and divorce law in every European country, its ideas had political impact even in countries where they did not induce legislative change. As was already mentioned, the Enlightenment ideal of marriage and family found its most profound implementation in the family legislation of the French Revolution. Moreover, at the zenith of the Revolution, French family law went further than most of the Enlightenment theorists had ever dreamed of. The revolutionary legislators endeavoured to bring the ideas of Enlightenment to their logical end. They essentially extended the principles of liberty and equality to family matters, which the ideologists of the Enlightenment had proclaimed in respect to the relations between the individual and the State.[121] Thus, the 'modern' concepts of marriage[122] and family, based on

---

113 COLOMER, A., 'The Modern French Law' (1972), p. 81.
114 Ibid, p. 82.
115 Art. 1124 *Code Civil.*
116 Art. 217 *Code Civil.*
117 FOYER, J., 'The Reform of Family Law in France' (1978), p. 79.
118 BAETEMAN, G., 'The Original System of the Code Napoleon in Belgium and Holland' (1972), p. 2.
119 ANCEL, M., 'Matrimonial Property Law in France' (1955), p. 13.
120 Ibid.
121 PHILLIPS, R., 'Remaking the Family: The Reception of Family Law and Policy during the French Revolution', (1992), p. 65.
122 Witte rightly mentioned that 'It is this Enlightenment contractarian model of marriage that has helped to drive the twentieth-century revolution of Western marriage'. WITTE, J., *From Sacrament to Contract* (1997), p. 198.

equality, free choice and affection,[123] were born in the turmoil of the Jacobin terror, destined to inspire and to horrify generations to come. It is important to notice that the French revolutionary legislators, like the theorists of the Enlightenment, never intended to 'destroy' the family, but rather attempted to modify it and to make it fit the newly designed social order.[124]

The widely divergent appreciation of the ideas of Enlightenment generated a major change: the basic ideological consensus concerning marriage and family issues that was typical for the medieval religious unity, and which managed to survive the confessional division of the Reformation,[125] made place for modern ideological diversity. From the period of the Enlightenment onwards, Western family law would be an arena of competition between two value systems, roughly labelled to consist of either 'progressive' or 'conservative' family ideology. One or the other of these systems would prevail from time to time in certain places but neither of them has become universally dominant.[126] The principal players of this drama also assumed a certain political colour.[127] From this time onwards, a common tendency to associate political liberalism with an adherence to 'progressive' family law and political conservatism with the adherence to the traditional patriarchal model of marriage and family is, with a few qualifications,[128] clearly traceable up to the present day.[129] As a result of this ideological pluralisation, each European State became to be divided into these two competing ideological clusters, each living in its own mental world[130] and having great difficulties understanding the other.

Another remarkable change that manifested itself from the Enlightenment onwards is the reversal of the role of the churches. After almost a millennium of leadership, the churches lost the lead in both the development of the ideology of marriage and the family, and the promotion of legal change. The churches-as-institutions, Catholic,

---

123 TRAER, J., *Marriage and the Family in the Eighteenth-Century France* (1980), p. 166.
124 PHILLIPS, R., *Family Breakdown in Late Eighteenth Century France* (1980), p. 14.
125 As was discussed in the previous chapter, the confessional division did not bring about a radical difference of family values.
126 STONE, L., *Road to Divorce* (1990), p. 22.
127 Thus Phillips, although warning against generalisations, suggested that 'In general [...] the associations of political liberalism with positive attitude towards divorce, and political conservatism with negative attitudes towards divorce, are a useful rule of thumb'. PHILLIPS, R., *Putting Asunder* (1988), p. 534.
128 Philips warns that this is a generalisation and that it's easy to point out exceptions. 'In general, though, the associations of political liberalism with positive attitude towards divorce, and political conservatism with negative attitudes towards divorce, are a useful rule of thumb'. PHILLIPS, R., *Putting Asunder* (1988), p. 534.
129 For more on the relation between the various political denominations on the one hand, and 'progressive' or 'conservative' ideas on the family and family law on the other, see Chapter 10, Section 10.1.
130 STONE, L., *Road to Divorce* (1990), p. 22.

Protestant and later also Orthodox, distanced themselves from the humanistic movement and progressive ideology and became merely opponents of the changes instigated by their secular adversaries.[131] In this new role, the churches' hierarchy eventually compromised many of the humanistic principles of Christianity for 'strict disciplinary laws and precepts'.[132] This move has ultimately resulted in the 'moral and devotional austerity' of many institutionalised churches.[133] The results of this development are traceable well into the twenty first century. This is the main reason why the Christian attitude of our time towards family law is commonly associated with rigidity, conservatism and transpersonalism. This association has become so self-evident that many of our contemporaries will find it difficult to imagine that the churches' role was quite different for many centuries.

9.3.2. UNIFICATION OF FRENCH LAW AND THE HARMONISING EFFECT OF THE EXPORT OF THE *CODE CIVIL*

Throughout Europe, the French *Code Civil* inspired a tendency to unify family law on a national level as part of the general process of the formation of nation states. Within France itself, however, the unifying effect of the *Code Civil* was far less significant than, for instance, that of the German BGB within Germany or the Swiss Federal Civil Code within Switzerland.[134] This was because France, unlike Germany and Switzerland, was a centralised state long before its law was unified in single Codes. It already had a uniform marriage and divorce law. The unification effect of the *Code Civil* was largely limited to matrimonial property law, which had previously been regulated by various *coutumes* in the North and by the *droit écrit* in the South.

Napoleon's dream was 'one European system, one European Code, one European Cassation Court'.[135] Persistently exporting his *Code Civil*, Napoleon nearly managed to implement his ideal of uniformity throughout a large part of Europe. Napoleon's insistence upon the introduction of the original form of the *Code Civil* in the Kingdom of Holland,[136] in spite of the fact that this country had just prepared it own up to date

---

[131]   Duffy notices that Catholicism 'grew progressively negative and defensive' in regard to modernity. DUFFY, S., 'Catholicism's Search for a New Self-Understanding' (1984), p. 9.

[132]   These characterisations, used by Dillon (DILLON, M., *Debating Divorce. Moral Conflict in Ireland.* (1993), p. 14) in respect to nineteenth century Catholicism, seem more or less equally applicable to all Post-Reformation Churches-as-institutions in Europe.

[133]   Ibid.

[134]   See Chapter 10, Section 10.2.

[135]   *Propos tenus a Sainte Hélène,* cited by Baron Silvercruys in his speech during his inauguration as President of the French Constitutional Court. *Bull.,* 1930, p. 7.

[136]   See: HUUSSEN, A., *De codificatie van het Nederlandse huwelijksrecht 1795-1838* (1975), p. 199.

draft-code,[137] suggests that legal uniformity within the Empire was more important to Napoleon than the substance of the law.

The expansion of the *Code Civil* is repeatedly used by the proponents of convergence as one of the strongest historical examples of the successful transplantation of legal rules. However, in the field of family law this event provides quite conflicting evidence regarding the transplantation theory.[138] Some of the innovations, like the introduction of the obligatory civil marriage, had enduring influence and largely survived the defeat of Napoleon and the conservative backlash of the Restoration. The imposed civil marriage survived the Restoration in Belgium, The Netherlands[139] and Luxemburg. In Italy, the secularisation of marriage was less successful. After the French occupation it remained in force only with regard to the non-Catholic populace of the Lombard-Venetian region, which after the Restoration fell under Austrian reign.[140]

The export of Napoleonic divorce law provides a good example of both the impact of cultural constraints and the potential of instrumentalist change. Divorce matters were considered so culturally and politically sensitive that even Napoleon refrained from enforcing this part of his law everywhere in the Empire.

In Protestant countries, divorce itself was not an issue, but no-fault divorce, as allowed by the *Code Civil*, was a far-reaching innovation. In the Kingdom of Holland, an adapted version of the *Code Civil*[141] that did not contain divorce by mutual consent was introduced.[142] This concession was made because the Dutch considered divorce by mutual consent to be contrary to good morals.[143] Thus, divorce by mutual consent reached the Northern Netherlands only after the marionette Kingdom of Holland was absorbed by France in 1811. The Kingdom of Holland was turned into a French province, and this entailed the introduction of the authentic version of the *Code Civil*.[144] Enforced divorce by mutual consent was formally abandoned in The

---

137 For more information about the history of this Dutch draft see: HUUSSEN, A., *De codificatie van het Nederlandse huwelijksrecht 1795-1838* (1975), p. 143-198 and VON BÓNÉ, E., 'Comparaison entre le droit au divorce dans la République Batave (1798-1806) et dans l'Allgemeines Landrecht für die der Preussischen Staaten' (2001), p. 173-186.

138 See on this theory Part I, Chapter 2, Section 2.4.2.

139 Alter the Restoration, the Southern (Austrian) and Northern Netherlands temporarily (from 1815-1830) became one country. The *Code Civil* remained in force during this period. After the separation of North and South in 1830, The Netherlands enacted its own Civil Code in 1838, while Belgium stayed faithful to the *Code Civil*. The *Code Civil* also remained in force in Luxemburg.

140 SGRITTA, G., TUFARI, P., 'Italy' (1977), p. 254-255.

141 Entitled '*Code Napoleon* adapted for the Kingdom of Holland'.

142 HUUSSEN, A., De codificatie van het Nederlandse huwelijksrecht 1795-1838 (1975), p. 201.

143 VON BÓNÉ, E., 'Comparaison entre le droit au divorce dans la République Batave (1798-1806) et dans l'Allgemeines Landrecht für die der Preussischen Staaten' (2001), p. 186.

144 HUUSSEN, A., De codificatie van het Nederlandse huwelijksrecht 1795-1838 (1975), p. 216.

Netherlands in 1838.[145] However, bills proposing its elimination, as it was considered contrary to 'the spirit of the people', began to appear shortly after Napoleon's fall.[146]

For Catholic countries, the introduction of Napoleon's rules on divorce meant a genuine revolution. Spain was skipped over; officially because divorce was considered to be manifestly contrary to its tradition and practices.[147] However, the true explanation may be that Napoleon never felt strong enough to enforce divorce upon rebellious Spain. This explanation becomes all the more plausible if one considers that although divorce was no less alien to the tradition and practices of an equally Catholic Italy, Napoleon did not hesitate to introduce it there, in spite of the persistent resistance of the populace.[148] This alien legal transplant proved unable to change Italy's long-standing tradition and offset the influence of the Catholic Church. The number of reported divorces 'could be counted on one hand'.[149] Unsurprisingly, Napoleon's divorce law was repealed immediately after the Restoration.[150] However, even in Italy the brief introduction of divorce produced some enduring effect; the dissolubility of marriage has remained on the political agenda ever since.[151] For Belgium and Luxemburg,[152] which had been part of Revolutionary France since 1795,[153] Napoleon's rules on divorce were perhaps a mere balm on the wounds struck by the revolutionary law of 20 September 1792. For one reason or another, divorce lived on in these Catholic countries, even after it was repealed in France itself in 1816.

As was mentioned above, the Napoleonic rules regarding illegitimate children had, by contrast, a lasting effect in many European countries. These rules were probably the most successful export in the whole of the Napoleonic family law. This may be explained by the fact that the idea of protecting the legitimate family at the expense of the illegitimate one was very much in line with the economic policies and the conservative spirit of nineteenth century Europe. The export of the French legislation

---

[145] See: VON BÓNÉ, E., 'Der Einfluß des französischen Scheidunsrechts im Vereinigten Königreich der Niederlande (1815-1830)' (1998), p. 267-276.

[146] The Council of State carted off consensual divorce from a 1816 Bill. The explanatory note to the divorce Bill of 1820 explicitly referred to the fact that 'in no other subject is considering the spirit of the people so important as in divorce matters'. Cited in: DUMON, W., KOOY, G., *Echtscheiding in België en Nederland* (1983), p. 25.

[147] PHILLIPS, R., *Putting Asunder* (1988), p. 405.

[148] SGRITTA, G., TUFARI, P., 'Italy' (1977), p. 255

[149] Ibid.

[150] Ibid.

[151] Twelve divorce bills were presented to the Parliament between 1878 and 1965. Ibid, p. 255-526.

[152] NEYENS, M., 'Entwicklungen in der Luxemburger Familienrechtspolitik' (2000), p. 616-617.

[153] DUMON, W., KOOY, G., *Echtscheiding in België en Nederland* (1983), p. 13-14. The Austrian Netherlands (the current Belgium) were annexed by Revolutionary France in 1795. Thus, the French revolutionary law was equally applicable there. After the fall of Napoleon, the Northern and the Southern Netherlands formed one state from 1815 till 1830.

led to the extension of the co-called 'Romanic' approach of the regulation of the position of illegitimate children.[154] According to this system, the position of an illegitimate child was largely dependant on an acknowledgement by the child's parents, not biological facts. The prohibition of acknowledgement by a married man, in conjunction with the far-reaching restrictions on the judicial establishment of paternity upon the initiative of a child or the child's mother, made this system perfectly safe for the legitimate family. It is noteworthy that the successful transplantation of Napoleonic law on the status of illegitimate children provides an example of harmonisation that was a success in terms of convergence, but at the same time had a clearly negative effect in terms of the progressive development of family law.

The less ideologically-sensitive matrimonial property law of the *Code Civil* was only a relatively successful export article. The French system of matrimonial property law took roots in Belgium,[155] and some parts of Rhineland. In Italy[156] and The Netherlands,[157] it was abolished after the fall of Napoleon. In Italy, the French community system was customarily excluded by marriage contract, even when Italy was still under Napoleon's rule.[158] After independence was regained, the community system could still be adopted by marriage contract in some Italian Principia, but it enjoyed no popularity.[159]

Thus, when it comes to harmonisation, Napoleon's legal expansionism had a very mixed effect in the long run. The most significant converging influence of the Enlightenment did not emanate from the legislation that was spread over Europe on the bayonets of Napoleon's armies, but from the emergence of a modern, progressive pan-European family law ideology that became part of the political discourse of every European country for the centuries to come.

---

[154] For more on the 'Romanic' and 'Germanic' approaches of illegitimacy, see Chapter 10, Section 10.3.2.
[155] BAETEMAN, G., 'The Modern Belgian Law' (1972), p. 18.
[156] BURGE, W., *Commentaries on Colonial and Foreign Laws*, vol. III (1910), p. 578.
[157] DE BLÉCOURT, A, *Kort begrip van het oud-vaderlands burgerlijk recht* (1950), p. 76.
[158] BURGE, W., *Commentaries on Colonial and Foreign Laws*, vol. III (1910), p. 578.
[159] Ibid.

CHAPTER 10
THE NINETEENTH CENTURY: FAMILY LAW IN THE MIDDLE OF THE CONSERVATIVE-PROGRESSIVE DISCORD

10.1. STRUGGLE BETWEEN TWO IDEOLOGIES

The conservative Restoration significantly delayed the implementation of the Modernity ideas into law. The progressive ideology of the Enlightenment suffered a great setback, but was far from disappeared from the scene. As a result, the watershed between the transpersonalistic-conservative and the personalistic-progressive ways of thinking became even more apparent than before. The whole of the nineteenth century is epitomized by the discord between conservative and 'liberal-individualistic'[1] attitudes towards marriage and divorce. These subjects became 'a major battleground for competing ideologies'.[2] The metaphor of Max Rheinstein, that ever since the Revolution France was split up into '*les deux Frances*' – one progressive and one conservative – and his account that 'French history has been characterised by the struggle between two camps',[3] are more or less applicable to almost every European country. Yet, the political climate of the age, except for two rather short episodes around the revolutionary years of 1830 and 1848, was predominantly conservative, especially during the 1820s and the last three decades of the century.

10.1.1. CONSERVATIVE FAMILY IDEOLOGY

The conservative camp after the Restoration appeared as a 'heterogeneous group'[4] of those who wanted to buttress the 'traditional' family. They opposed divorce, the emerging ideas of gender equality and the growing urge for individual freedom. All conservatives took a transpersonalistic and communitarian stance by placing the

---

[1]   RHEINSTEIN, M., *Marriage Stability, Divorce, and the Law* (1972), p. 195.
[2]   TAYLOR, B., *Eve and the Jerusalem: Socialism and Feminism in the Nineteenth Century* (1983), p. 183.
[3]   RHEINSTEIN, M., *Marriage Stability, Divorce, and the Law* (1972), p. 195.
[4]   PHILLIPS, R., *Putting Asunder* (1988), p. 487.

interests of the community above of the interests of individuals. Marriage was seen as a cornerstone of society and was thus 'regarded not, or not so much, as an avenue to individual satisfaction and happiness, but as an institution to serve the society'.[5] Max Rheinstein abridged the essence of the transpersonalistic stance in the following assertion: 'better let an individual suffer from the consequences of a poor choice of partner or from the harshness of fate than to undermine the firmness of the institution'.[6] All conservatives shared this communitarian ideal of marriage, but they differed on how it was to be achieved. There were the true reactionaries who simply wanted to turn the clock back and restore the ideal family of the good old days.[7] Others more pragmatically considered that some minor improvements in family law and the reluctant admission of divorce were better ways to help save marriage as an institution[8] than the unqualified rejection of all reform.

The political conservatism of the Restoration clearly coincided with conservatism in family matters. Divorce and the modernisation of family law were irredeemably associated with the secularism and libertarianism of the French Revolution.[9] Illustrative is a statement made by the French conservative deputy Bonald, under whose guidance divorce was abolished after the Restoration. He stated that divorce, by promoting 'veritable domestic democracy', allows the weaker party to marriage – the wife – 'to rebel against marital authority' in the same fashion as 'political democracy allows the people, the weak part of the political society, to rise against the established authority'.[10] Thus, 'in order to keep the state out of the hands of the people, it is necessary to keep the family out of the hands of wives and children'.[11] The Catholic Church grew increasingly conservative and proclaimed a genuine crusade against modernity and progress. Pope Pius IX announced that 'if anyone thinks that the Roman Pontiff can and should reconcile and accommodate himself to progress, liberalism and modern civilization, let him be anathema'.[12] While the liberal camp built upon the legacy of the great *Philosophers* of the Enlightenment, the conservatives relied on such eminent

---

[5] RHEINSTEIN, M., *Marriage Stability, Divorce, and the Law* (1972), p. 197.
[6] Ibid.
[7] PHILLIPS, R., *Putting Asunder* (1988), p. 487.
[8] O'NEILL, W., *Divorce in the Progressive Era* (1973), p. 89.
[9] Dicey noticed that for England, 'the French Revolution worked nothing but evil; it delayed statutory changes for forty years, and rendered reforms, when at last they came, less beneficial than they might have been if gradually carried out as natural result of undisturbed development'. DICEY, A., *Relations Between Law and Public Opinion* (1963), p. 123-124.
[10] Archives parlementaire, 2me série, XV, p. 612. Cited in: PHILLIPS, R., *Putting Asunder* (1988), at p. 189.
[11] Ibid.
[12] *Syllabus of Errors*, 1864, cited in: MCSWEENEY, B., *Roman Catholicism. The Search for Relevance* (1980), p. 22.

thinkers as Jean-Jacques Rousseau and Immanuel Kant.[13] Their conservative posture towards family matters was pursued by the French philosopher Auguste Comte, who pleaded for the indissolubility of marriage[14] and the retention of gender inequality.[15] The most extreme view was promoted by Arthur Schopenhauer, who even launched an attack against monogamous marriage[16] and the right of women to inherit.[17] According to his opinion, these institutions were wrong because they 'bestow upon the women an unnatural position of privilege, by considering her throughout as the full equivalent of the man'.[18] Schopenhauer saw the source of all evil in the concept of the *lady*. This concept, 'the monster of European civilisation and Teutonic-Christian stupidity',[19] elevated the European woman to 'an object of our honour and veneration',[20] instead of retaining her 'to her natural position as subordinate being'.[21] In similar fashion, Friedrich Nietzsche discarded the women's rights movement as the 'stupidity of this moment',[22] and called for the adoption of an 'Oriental' view of the woman, namely to 'conceive her as a possession, as confinable property, as being predestined for service'.[23]

The conservative ideology had a profound influence on the legal policies within eighteenth century Europe. As the Roman Catholic Church held on to an irreconcilable position in respect of divorce and the reform of family law, countries where its influence was strong, like Italy, Spain and Portugal, began to display a persistent delay in the modernisation of family law. On the secular side of the conservative spectrum,

---

[13] Kant unromantically defines marriage as 'the union of two persons of different sex for long-life reciprocal possession or their sexual facilities' (KANT, I., *The Philosophy of Law* (1887), p. 110). Although Kant considers that the 'relation of married persons to each other is a relation of equality as regards the mutual possession of their persons' (ibid. p. 111), he holds that the 'law says in any way of the husband in relation to the wife, "he shall be the muster" [... as] such legal supremacy is based only upon the natural superiority of the facilities of the husband compared with the wife' (ibid. p. 111). Kant's ideas of the natural inequality of woman are based on his opinion that a woman is not a rational creature and therefore 'has nothing of ought, nothing of must, nothing of due' and is hardly 'capable of principles', (KANT, I., *Observations on the Feeling of the Beautiful and Sublime* (reprint. 1979), p. 156-157). These assumptions lead Kant to the general conclusion that women lack political and civil reason and are unable to encompass universal morality. PATEMAN, C., *The Sexual Contract* (1988), p. 168-169.

[14] MILL, J.S., *Auguste Comte and Positivism, Essays on Ethic, Religion, and Society* (1994), p. 34.

[15] Following Kant in his footsteps, Comte considers the subordination of women in marriage the true consequence of 'their inborn [intellectual] inferiority'. COMTE, O., *Letter to John Stuart Mill from 5 October 1843* (1995), p. 189.

[16] SCHOPENHAUER, A., 'Studies in Pessimism' (reprint. 1979), p. 217-220.

[17] Ibid. p. 220.

[18] Ibid. p. 218.

[19] Ibid. p. 219.

[20] Ibid. p. 217.

[21] Ibid. p. 219.

[22] NIETZSCHE, F., *Beyond Good and Evil* (reprint 1979), p. 233.

[23] Ibid, p. 232.

in Victorian England, a new 'moral code' was developed on the premises of the permanency of marriage, the sacredness of the home, and civilised life's dependence on the family.[24] In Prussia, an unsuccessful attempt to restrict divorce law was made in the 1840s, inspired by the conservative thought of Friedrich Karl von Savigny.[25]

10.1.2.   PROGRESSIVE FAMILY IDEOLOGY

The conservative camp was continually opposed by an equally heterogeneous progressive bloc. The issue of the modernisation of family law brought together such unusual allies as the liberals and the socialists, later joined by the feminists.[26] What they had in common was the desire to uphold the progressive legacy of the Enlightenment and the personalistic perception of marriage and the family.[27] For all participants of the progressive cluster, the starting point in family issues was the individual within the family, not the family as a cornerstone of society. Another common point of reference was the attempt to diminish State control over marriage and divorce.[28] On top of that, 'a late descendant of the enlightenment',[29] the equality of women, became programmatic for all nineteenth-century progressively minded circles.

The political diversity of the progressive camp involved, of course, profound ideological differences. The liberals advocated much less far-reaching family law reforms than the Marxists and the radical feminists. They had no intention of making marriage and divorce totally informal and private, but rather argued for a shift from rigid State regulation to more individual responsibility.[30] As a rule, liberal thought did not discard the communitarian idea of marriage and family all together, but tried to reconcile it with the notion of individual freedom. The reasoning of Jeremy Bentham, one of the most renowned representatives of utilitarian liberalism of the first part of the century, is quite illustrative. Bentham considered marriage for life as 'the most

---

[24]   O'NEILL, W., *Divorce in The Progressive Era* (1973), p. 89.
[25]   PHILLIPS, R., *Putting Asunder* (1988), p. 429.
[26]   However the two latter groups were not unanimous in their support for divorce.
[27]   For instance John Stuart Mill believed that it is 'wrong [...] on every view of morality [...] that there should exist any motives to marriage except the happiness which two persons who love one another and feel in associating their existence'. MILL, J.S., *Essay on Equality, Law, and Education* (1994), p. 7.
[28]   Different trends within liberal thought agreed in their 'general concern for the achievement of individual happiness and a common aversion to external interference in matters of personal life. Such believes easily and logically led liberals to support marriage and divorce polices that maximalised individual freedom, and they approached social issues from the perspectives of the individuals directly concerned rather than with the social impact uppermost in their minds'. PHILLIPS, R., *Putting Asunder* (1988), p. 487.
[29]   MÜLLER-FREIENFELS, W., 'Equality of Husband and Wife in Family Law' (1959), p. 251.
[30]   PHILLIPS, R., *Putting Asunder* (1988), p. 487.

natural marriage, best adapted to the wants and the circumstances of families, and in general, the most favourable to individuals'.[31] However, he was prepared to compromise this ideal of lifelong marriage for the sake of the happiness of the individuals involved in it. Bentham acknowledged that 'marriage presents to the generality of men the only means of satisfying fully and peaceably the imperious desire of love'.[32] The logical conclusion than was 'that mere humanity requires that a marriage should be dissoluble if such love comes to turn into hatred'.[33] Thus Jeremy Bentham dubbed the indissolubility of marriage an 'absurd and cruel clause,' that was not determined by the spouses themselves, but imposed by law which 'comes in between the contractors' and says, 'you are entering a prison of which the gate will never open'.[34]

Bentham's thought was pursued in the second part of the century by the eminent liberal feminist John Stuart Mill. Mill passionately condemned the marriage of his days as a 'worse description of slavery'.[35] John Stuart Mill's position on divorce was, like the view of Jeremy Bentham, not without ambiguity. On the one hand Mill maintained that husband and wife should be able to get a divorce at any time if they discovered their marital love had come to an end.[36] On the other hand, Mill called upon spouses to act with 'moral responsibility' and 'restraint' when considering divorce, as the disintegration of marriage made children suffer. He also envisaged that the initiator of divorce would often attribute his or her discontent with the marriage to the failures of the other spouse, while in fact these disappointments had to do with the initiator's own 'scanty capabilities of happiness'.[37]

Feminist ideas on marriage and divorce were far from uniform. There was the influence of liberal thought like that of Mill, but also a more conservative stance which gained influence in the second half of the nineteenth century. As more women were drawn into industrial production, unmarried cohabitation became more common among working class women. Friedrich Engels idealistically acclaimed such a relationship to be a 'proletarian' marriage – the prototype of the free marriage of the future, when marriage would be liberated from the jerk of economic determination.[38] In reality, as soon as children were born into such an informal union, the woman had to stay at home and came into a position of dependency and uncertainty. She was in

---

[31]   BENTHAM, J., *The Theory of Legislation* (1950), p. 223.
[32]   Ibid, p. 224.
[33]   Ibid.
[34]   Ibid.
[35]   MILL, J.S., *The Subjection of Women* (1974), p. 32.
[36]   MILL, J.S., *Article on Henry Saint-Simon* (1994), p. 23.
[37]   MILL, J.S., *Essay on Equality, Law, and Education* (1994), p. 15.
[38]   ENGELS, F., *The Origin of the Family, Private Property and the State* (1985), p. 103.

fact left at the mercy of the man, who could continue their relationship or abandon her penniless. This experience made women more interested in 'enforcing the obligations of marriage than in abolishing them'. Thus working class women were more inclined to seek 'safer relationships, rather than freer ones'.[39] At the same time, radical feminists, like for instance Mona Caird, proclaimed rather extreme views. In her article 'The Practice of Marriage', published in 1895 Caird not only condemned the inequality within marriage, but also pleaded against marital intimacy and devotion.[40]

The Marxists criticised the contemporary marriage much more militantly than the liberals. The classical[41] Marxist idea of marriage and the family took shape in the works of Friedrich Engels. Engels claimed that a 'bourgeois' marriage often amounted to legalised prostitution on the part of the women, whereby the woman 'sells [her body] once and for all into slavery'.[42] Therefore he advocated free love and divorce at volition as stepping-stones to the free unions of the future. He further believed that only with the abolition of capitalist production would marriage become a truly free union. It would still be an individual marriage, but truly monogamous on both parts and free from any dominance of the husband. This marriage would also be dissoluble at the will of the parties, as soon as affection had come to an end. His conclusion was that 'if only the marriage based on love is moral, than also only the marriage is moral in which love continues'.[43] It goes without saying that the liberals and the vast majority of feminists neither supported the Marxist idea of the abolition of marriage, nor anticipated its withering away in the future.

---

[39] TAYLOR, B., *Eve and the Jerusalem: Socialism and Feminism in the Nineteenth Century* (1983), p. 203-205.

[40] CAIRD, M., 'The Practice of Marriage', *18 Current Literature* (1895), p. 317, cited in: O'NEILL, W., *Divorce in the Progressive Era* (1973), p. 106.

[41] In his early works, Karl Marx, following the footsteps of Hegel, seemed to prop up a communitarian rather than an individualistic position is respect of the family. In his early and not widely known 1842 reaction on a proposed divorce Bill, Marx wrote that individualists think only of rights and not of duties, and therefore advocate easy divorce, forgetting 'that they are dealing, not with *individuals*, but with *families*'. Further on he claimed that the laws of marriage 'cannot be subordinated to [...] arbitrary wishes; on the contrary [...] arbitrary wishes should be subordinated to marriage'. MARX, K., 'On Divorce Bill' in: MARX, K. and ENGELS, F., *Collected Works*, vol. 1 (1975), p. 307-310. Cited in: ELSHTAIN, J., *Public Man, Private Woman* (1981), p. 186 and 257.

[42] ENGELS, F., *The Origin of the Family, Private Property and the State* (1985), p. 102.

[43] Ibid, p. 113-114.

10.2. LEGISLATIVE CHANGE: THE 'CONSERVATIVE MODERNISATION' OF FAMILY LAW

As mentioned earlier, family law policy came to be one of the principal fields where the progressive and conservative forces of the nineteenth century competed. After the rebound brought about by the Restoration, family law in Europe hesitantly returned to the path of modernisation. However, the predominantly conservative political spirit of Post-Reformation Europe made this modernisation, which Roderick Phillips rightly dubbed 'conservative',[44] particularly reluctant and piecemeal. The last part of the nineteenth century was characterised by the overall rise of nationalism and the unification of numerous Principia in the territory of Germany, Italy and Switzerland into powerful national states. The urge for political unification gave a strong impetus to the unification of law within the newly emerged national states. However, the conservative climate, which grew even stronger as the century was approaching its end, deeply affected the character of the uniform national laws. As a consequence, the net result of the national unification was often a step back for the modernity of family law.

10.2.1. THE PROLIFERATION OF CIVIL MARRIAGE IN THE NINETEENTH CENTURY

As was explained above, the civil registration of marriage that was introduced by Napoleon survived the Restoration in France, Austria, Belgium, The Netherlands, and Luxemburg. In spite of the general dominance of conservative forces, the nineteenth century witnessed a European-wide proliferation of civil marriage. In 1836, civil marriage was introduced in **England**. The peculiarity of England was that, differing from the countries influenced by the *Code Civil*, it did not institute an obligatory civil marriage.[45] Instead, England opted for a two-track system, allowing a choice between civil or religious marriage. Civil marriage had to be conducted by a State official and was considered to be a civil contract only. Religious marriage was conducted by a Church minister and was regarded as a 'sacred religious ceremony'.[46] In **Denmark**, civil marriage was introduced in 1851 for those who did not belong either to the State Anglican Church or any other recognised Church.[47] As was already mentioned, in **Austria** the 1811 *Allgemeines Bürgerliches Gesetzbuch* allowed civil marriage for the non-Catholic populace. However, after 1848, conservative pressure was so strong that

---

[44]   PHILLIPS, R., *Putting Asunder* (1988), p. 494.
[45]   DICEY, A., *Relations Between Law and Public Opinion* (1963), p. 346.
[46]   STONE, L., *Road to Divorce* (1990), p. 133.
[47]   Danish State Archive www.sa.dk

in 1855, a Concordat with Rome restored Church authority over marriage.[48] Civil marriage was no longer possible even for non-Catholics.[49] This backward move was opposed by progressive forces with such persistence that in 1868 civil marriage for non-Catholics was restored.[50]After **Italy** was united, the Italian Civil Code of 1865 introduced civil marriage as the only form of valid marriage.[51] In **Spain,** obligatory civil marriage was introduced in 1870[52] during a short lived Republic. The new law was met with considerable resistance, as the vast majority of the population clung to the long established tradition of the Church marriage.[53] After the restoration of the monarchy in 1874, the law on civil marriage was repealed, and Church marriages that had been concluded during its application were validated with retroactive effect.[54] However, in 1875 civil marriage was again made possible, but this time only for those who could prove to be non-Catholic.[55] In **Switzerland,** the Federal Law on Civil Status and Marriage of 14 December 1874 made civil marriage the only valid form of marriage.[56] The *Schweizerischen Zivilgesetzbuch (ZGB)* of 1907[57] took over this provision. In **Germany,** obligatory civil marriage, which already existed in several states,[58] was first introduced for the whole of the newly formed Empire in 1875,[59] and retained in the BGB. On the whole, the regulation of marriage in the BGB was generally built upon conservative communitarian ideas.[60] In conservative fashion the emphasis was laid on 'the unity of the family and the predominance of the husband'.[61] The husband retained the right to 'decide all matters of matrimonial life'.[62] In **Hungary,** obligatory civil marriage was introduced in 1894 by the new Marriage Law.[63] The thoroughly conservative *Ancien Régime* of **Russia** resolutely rejected even the possibility

---

[48] HALLER, M., 'Austria' (1977), p. 212.
[49] Ibid.
[50] Ibid.
[51] PHILLIPS, R., Putting Asunder (1988), p. 407.
[52] By law of 18 July 1870.
[53] LANGNER, D., *Eheschließung und Ehescheidung nach spanischem Recht* (1984), p. 4.
[54] Ibid, p. 5
[55] By Decree of 27 February 1875.
[56] BURGE, W., *Commentaries on Colonial and Foreign Laws*, vol. III, (1910), p. 172.
[57] Came into force in 1912.
[58] In Frankfurt in 1850, in Baden in 1869 and in Prussia in 1874. HUEBNER, R., *History of Germanic Private Law* (1918), p. 610.
[59] The Imperial Act of Personal Status of February 6, 1875.
[60] GLENDON, M. A., 'Power and Authority in the Family: New Legal Patterns as Reflection of Changing Ideologies' (1975), p. 7.
[61] Para. 1354 I BGB. See: GLENDON, M. A., 'Power and Authority in the Family: New Legal Patterns as Reflection of Changing Ideologies' (1975), p. 7.
[62] GLENDON, M. A., 'Power and Authority in the Family: New Legal Patterns as Reflection of Changing Ideologies' (1975), p. 7.
[63] BURGE, W., *Commentaries on Colonial and Foreign Laws,* vol. III, (1910), p. 166.

216

of introducing civil marriage.[64] A married woman was under the power of her husband, who was considered the sole head of the family.[65] Throughout the whole of the nineteenth century, parents still had the legal ability to imprison disobedient children by means of *Lettres de cochet*. Eventually this measure became so much at odds with the common perception of the personal rights of children[66] that by the end of the century the magistrates refused to enforce such requests.[67]

10.2.2. THE NINETEENTH CENTURY LAW OF DIVORCE

The conservative wave of the Restoration wiped away divorce in France, Italy, and (temporarily) in Austria. Throughout the century the divorce issue remained a primary focal point of legislative and political clashes between conservative and progressive forces.

France provides a clear example. Divorce was abolished there in 1816, immediately after the restoration of the monarchy. The abolition of this 'evil of the Revolution' was done 'in the interest of religion, of morality, of the monarchy, of families'.[68] From then on, 'passionate propaganda' for the reinstatement of divorce, resulting in various bills, met 'equal[ly] passionate counterattacks'.[69] Divorce was finally reintroduced only in 1884. This divorce law, sponsored by the Socialist member of parliament Alfred Naquet,[70] was much less liberal than the divorce provisions of Napoleon's *Code Civil*. The new law provided for two absolute fault grounds,[71] adultery and condemnation

---

[64] Even the Legislative Commission in charge of the drafting of the Russian Civil Code that worked, with some interruptions, from 1882 until the Bolshevik revolution, considered the introduction of Civil Marriage as a 'rush and dangerous innovation'. WAGNER, W., *Marriage, Property, and Law in Late Imperial Russia* (1994), p. 160.

[65] Illustrative is Article 107 of the *Svod Zakonov*, which stated that: 'the wife should unconditionally obey the husband as the head of the family, love him, be devoted to him, and serve him as he is the chief of the household' (translation mine).

[66] SHERSHENEVICH, G., *Russkoe grazgdanskoe pravo* (1995), p. 458.

[67] ZAGOROVSKII, I., *Kurs semeinogo prava* (2003), p. 243.

[68] PHILLIPS, R., *Putting Asunder* (1988), p. 189.

[69] RHEINSTEIN, M., *Marriage Stability, Divorce, and the Law* (1972), p. 214.

[70] Naquet first introduced a Bill that 'aimed simply to revive the liberal legislation of 1792. After this Bill failed, he introduced another much more moderate one'. PHILLIPS, R., *Putting Asunder* (1988), p. 423.

[71] Just to remind the reader that the 'absolute grounds' are the grounds the mere proof of which is sufficient for obtaining divorce. If the existence of such ground is proven, the court does not have the discretion to dismiss a divorce petition.

to infamous punishment, and a number of relative grounds[72] including cruelty and the infliction of grave or renewed bodily harm.[73]

In **England,** the *Divorce and Matrimonial Causes Act* of 1857 abolished Parliamentary divorce[74] and introduced a judicial one. The divorce jurisdiction of Church courts was also put to an end, and a secular *Court for Divorce and Matrimonial Causes* was established to hear divorce cases.[75] Albert Dicey assessed these events as a 'triumph of individualistic liberalism and common justice',[76] while John Baker sees it as a rather modest change.[77] Nonetheless, even this modest innovation was vigorously opposed by the conservatives.[78] As with Parliamentary divorce, the sole ground for divorce remained adultery.[79] Unlike husbands, wives could still obtain divorce only in a case of adultery aggravated by particular circumstances.[80] However, the list of these aggravating circumstances was extended beyond the previously accepted bigamy and incest, and now also included cruelty and wilful desertion.[81]

In **Ireland,** after the unison of the Kingdom of Ireland and the Kingdom of Great Britain into the United Kingdom of Great Britain and Ireland, followed by dissolution of the Irish Parliament in 1801, the capacity to grant a Parliamentary divorce was transferred from the Irish Parliament to the Imperial Parliament.[82] The English 1857 *Divorce Reform Act* did not apply to Ireland, so even after that the only possibility to dissolve marriage in Ireland remained the Parliamentary divorce.[83]

In **Austria,** the 1811 ABGB allowed non-Catholics to divorce. This possibility was abolished after the signing of the *Concordat* in 1855,[84] but was soon restored again.[85] An important peculiarity of Austrian law was the presence of no-fault grounds for

---

[72] 'Relative grounds' are the grounds which alone are not sufficient for obtaining divorce. The court grants a divorce only if, in addition to proving the relative grounds, the petitioner also manages to prove that due to these circumstances the marriage has irretrievable broken down.
[73] FOYER, J., 'The Reform of Family Law in France' (1978), p.102-103.
[74] By that time Parliamentary divorces had turned from rare exceptions into a 'convenient collusive agreement between a rich husband and his wife for a divorce by mutual consent'. STONE, L., *Road to Divorce* (1990), p. 146.
[75] BAKER, J., *An Introduction to English Legal History* (2002), p. 496.
[76] DICEY, A., *Relations Between Law and Public Opinion* (1963), p. 347.
[77] BAKER, J., *An Introduction to English Legal History* (2002), p. 496.
[78] See: STONE, L., *Road to Divorce* (1990), p. 371-283.
[79] BAKER, J., *An Introduction to English Legal History* (2002), p. 496.
[80] Ibid.
[81] STONE, L., *Road to Divorce* (1990), p. 376
[82] SHATTER, A., *Family Law in the Republic of Ireland* (1986), p. 237.
[83] Ibid.
[84] HALLER, M., 'Austria' (1977), p. 212.
[85] Ibid.

divorce alongside the fault ones.[86] Thus, after a period of separation, Austrian law allowed divorce in a case of irremediable aversion between the spouses.[87] In **Hungary**, the Marriage Law of 1894 provided for divorce on the basis of fault grounds.[88]

When **Germany** was unified in 1871, a uniform divorce law had to be made for the newly established state. That was a tricky task, as the level of modernity of the various German Principia's divorce law was quite uneven. A rather liberal legislation, inspired by the *Code Napoléon*, had survived the Restoration in the Rheinland and a few other provinces. In Prussia, the liberal divorce law of one of the most notable Enlightenment codifications: the *Preussisches Allgemeines Landrecht*, had remained in force. At the same time marriage was still indissoluble in the Catholic states of Southern Germany. Although Germany was united under strong Prussian domination, Prussian liberal divorce law did not become the uniform law. The first imperial divorce law was passed as part of the Personal Status Act of 1875.[89] According to this Act the separation of bed and board was abolished and divorce also became available to the Catholic parts of the Empire. For the most part the new divorce law was based on the Prussian model, but the divorce by mutual consent, that was allowed in Prussia, was excluded from the uniform law.[90] This law became the basis of the divorce provisions of the BGB. The result was clearly a step back; no-fault divorce, with the sole exception of insanity, was abolished.[91]

In **Switzerland**, divorce law was unified by the Federal Law on Civil Status and Marriage of 1874. Divorce could be granted for insanity and on a number of fault grounds: adultery, wilful desertion, the sentence of a degrading punishment. A notable particularity of this Law was that no-fault divorce by mutual consent was allowed. Such divorce was possible if the judge came to the conclusion that the continuation of married life was incompatible with the nature of marriage.[92] Divorce by mutual consent disappeared, however, from Swiss law in 1912 when the *ZGB* came into force.[93]

In **The Netherlands,** the Civil Code *(Burgerlijk Wetboek)* of 1838 added two new grounds, a conviction with a dishonouring punishment, and life-endangering violence against the spouse, to the classical Protestant grounds of adultery and malicious

---

[86] Paragraphs 115-116 ABGB.
[87] PHILLIPS, R., *Putting Asunder* (1988), p. 432.
[88] BURGE, W., *Commentaries on Colonial and Foreign Laws,* vol. III (1910), p. 848.
[89] Ibid, p. 430.
[90] Ibid.
[91] Para. 1564 -1569 BGB. See: MÜLLER-FREIENFELS, W., 'Family Law and the Law of Succession in Germany' (1967), p. 434.
[92] BURGE, W., *Commentaries on Colonial and Foreign Laws,* vol. III (1910), p. 848.
[93] Ibid, p. 843.

desertion.[94] Divorce by mutual consent was explicitly forbidden.[95] Nonetheless, in 1883 the Dutch Supreme Court (*Hoge Raad*) made a fundamental decision that allowed for divorce on the ground of adultery without scrutiny, provided that the allegation was not contested by the other party.[96] This opened the gates to consensual divorce by collusion (nicknamed in Dutch literature 'the great lie').[97] The result was a growing gap between the law in the books, prohibiting consensual divorce, and the law in action, where most divorces were in fact consensual.

Nordic divorce law was rather modern for European standards. No fault divorce, exceptional in the rest of Europe, existed in the Nordic countries along with divorce on fault grounds. The law also provided for both judicial and administrative divorce. The number of divorce grounds for judicial divorce was extended. Divorce by Royal dispensation[98] could be granted even when no fault was involved, for instance in a case of a 'difference of temperament and opinion, which [...] turned into disgust and hatred' between the spouses.[99] In **Denmark**, after three years of judicial separation, administrative divorce was granted without the allocation of fault.[100] In **Sweden,** administrative divorce on no-fault grounds was allowed after a special warning and mediation procedure involving clerical authorities, followed by one year of judicial separation and, if it was proven that the differences between the parties had 'transferred their relationship into mutual hate and loathing'.[101] In **Norway,** divorce was possible, among other possibilities, after three year of unjustified desertion.[102]

In the Catholic South of Europe, divorce still did not exist. In conformity with Roman Catholic canon law, only separation from bed and board without the possibility of remarriage was allowed. In **Spain,** divorce remained equally impossible both for Catholics and non-Catholics. Even the liberal republican law of 1870 reaffirmed the indissolubility of marriage.[103] Similarly, no divorce existed in **Portugal**[104] or **Malta.** In

---

[94] HUUSSEN, A., *De codificatie van het Nederlandse huwelijksrecht 1795-1838* (1975), p. 216.

[95] Art. 263 Civil Code. DE BLÉCOURT, A., *Kort begrip van het oud-vaderlands burgerlijk recht* (1950), p. 72.

[96] HR 22 juni 1883.

[97] BRIËT, C., 'De grote leugen' (2006).

[98] There were no fixed grounds for divorce by Royal dispensation. Therefore it could be granted 'for any cause deemed sufficient by the King,' although certain grounds were specifically listed in the decree. SELLIN, J., *Marriage and Divorce Legislation in Sweden* (1922), p. 36.

[99] Ibid, p. 36-37.

[100] BURGE, W., *Commentaries on Colonial and Foreign Laws,* vol. III (1910), p. 853.

[101] JÄNTERÄ-JAREBORG, M., *Swedish Report concerning the CEFL Questionnaire on Grounds for Divorce and Maintenance Between Former Spouses* (2003) http://www.law.uu.nl/priv/cefl > working field 1 > Sweden.

[102] BURGE, W., *Commentaries on Colonial and Foreign Laws,* vol. III (1910), p. 855.

[103] LANGNER, D., *Eheschließung und Ehescheidung nach spanischem Recht* (1984), p. 4.

[104] BURGE, W., *Commentaries on Colonial and Foreign Laws,* vol. III (1910), p. 840.

Italy, divorce, introduced by Napoleon, was abolished in most territories in 1815. Its reinstatement, however, was the subject of continual debates, leading to persistent, albeit unsuccessful, attempts to instigate legal change.[105]

Divorce in **Russia** was possible for Russian Orthodox Christians (by far the largest religious denomination) on fault grounds such as adultery, bigamy, desertion for more than five years, attempt on the life of the other spouse, and certain no-fault grounds, such as impotency and the choice of a religious life.[106] Divorce by mutual consent was explicitly forbidden.[107] In other Orthodox countries, the divorce situation was not much different. With the exception of **Rumania**, which allowed divorce by mutual consent,[108] divorce grounds for the Orthodox population of the Eastern European countries were more or less the same as in Russia.[109] For Catholics, who constituted the great majority of the **Polish** population,[110] marriage was indissoluble.

10.2.3. THE POSITION OF ILLEGITIMATE CHILDREN IN THE NINETEENTH CENTURY: NO SIGNIFICANT CHANGE

This area of Family Law remained basically almost unchanged over the course of the century.

In **France,** the position of illegitimate children was slightly improved by the amendment of the *Code Civil* of March 1896. By virtue of this amendment illegitimate children were treated as heirs instead of *successeurs irréguliers*, they acquired the right to a legitimate portion, and it became possible for them to receive more by will than through intestacy.[111]

---

[105]   SGRITTA, G., TUFARI, P., 'Italy' (1977), p. 255-526.
[106]   For a comprehensive account see: ZAGOROVSKII, I., *Kurs semeinogo prava* (2003), p. 115-127.
[107]   Art. 46 *Svod Zakonov*.
[108]   BURGE, W., *Commentaries on Colonial and Foreign Laws,* vol. III, (1910), p. 842.
[109]   In Serbia, there were, among others: adultery, attempt on the spouse's life, desertion for seven years and long-term imprisonment. In Greece, divorce was still governed by the slightly amended Novels of Justinian, which was based on double standards for wife and husband. BURGE, W., *Commentaries on Colonial and Foreign Laws,* vol. III, (1910), p. 842-843.
[110]   The Kingdom of Poland was at that time part of the Russian Empire.
[111]   They became heirs (art. 724 and 756 CC new), their share was increased (art.758-760 CC new) and they acquired the right to a legitimate portion (art 913 Para. 2 CC new), and the testamentary increase of their share was made possible (art. 908 new).

The unification of law in the BGB was based on the so-called 'Germanic' approach[112] towards the status of illegitimate children. Under the **German** BGB, children born outside marriage were regarded as legitimate in respect to their mother and her family,[113] but were not considered to be legally related to their father.[114] An unmarried mother, however, was not granted with parental power[115] so an extramarital child had to be assigned a guardian.[116] Accordingly, illegitimate children inherited after the mother and her family on an equal footing with legitimate issue, but they were not heirs of their father.[117] A paternity suite was possible, but it created no filiation link between a child and the child's biological father; the purpose of such a suit could only be to obtain maintenance. A putative father was allowed the *exceptio congressus cum pluribus* in order to deny his paternity.[118] Once paternity was established, a father was considered to be responsible for the primary maintenance of his illegitimate issue. If the father died, this obligation passed to his heirs.[119] The only way to establish a legal relationship between an illegitimate child and its father was through acknowledgment and legitimisation. The BGB provided for both forms of legitimisation by subsequent marriage (*Legitimation durch nachfolgende Ehe*)[120] and *per rescriptum principis* (*Ehelichkeitserklärung*).[121] Yet, *Ehelichkeitserklärung* legitimisation worked only in respect to the father; it created no legal link of filiation between the child and the child's paternal family.[122]

The position of illegitimate children in **Austria** resembled that under the BGB. Both voluntary acknowledgement and establishment of paternity were possible.[123] The most significant difference was that in Austria illegitimate children were not only considered legally unrelated to their father, but, with some exceptions, to their mother as well.[124] As in Germany, illegitimate children had the right to be maintained by their father and his heirs.[125] The inheritance rights of the child and the provisions on legitimisation resembled the German ones.[126]

---

[112]   ZAGOROVSKII, I., *Kurs semeinogo prava* (2003), p. 320.
[113]   Para. 1705 BGB.
[114]   Para. 1705 and 1589 II BGB. See also: HUEBNER, R., *History of Germanic Private Law* (1918), p. 674.
[115]   Para. 1707 BGB.
[116]   HUEBNER, R., *History of Germanic Private Law* (1918), p. 674.
[117]   Para. 1705 BGB.
[118]   Para. 1720 BGB.
[119]   Para. 1712 BGB.
[120]   Para. 1719 BGB.
[121]   Para. 1723 BGB.
[122]   Para. 1737 I BGB.
[123]   Para. 163 ABGB.
[124]   Para. 165 ABGB.
[125]   Para. 167-171 ABGB.
[126]   Sie: Para. 161 and 162 and Para. 753 ABGB.

The provisions of the 1865 **Italian** Civil Code on illegitimate children were largely based on the example of the French *Code Civil*.[127] Illegitimate children were considered not to be legally related to either father or mother, unless voluntarily acknowledged by him or her.[128] Adulterous and incestuous children could not be acknowledged[129] and had no rights whatsoever, with the exception of the right to a modest maintenance allowance. Judicial establishment of maternity was possible, but following the French *Code Civil*, no judicial search for paternity[130] was allowed.[131] Acknowledgment entitled illegitimate children to name, guardianship, and maintenance from the father,[132] but did not equate them with legitimate children. Their succession rights remained limited.[133]

Swiss law regarding illegitimate children was a mixture of the 'Romanic' and the 'Germanic' systems.[134] It allowed both acknowledgement and *la recherche de la paternité*. However, a paternity search could result in the establishment of paternity only if the biological father had either promised to marry the mother of the child, or had raped or abused her.[135] The *ZGB* of 1907 replaced full legitimisation by subsequent marriage and limited legitimisation by *per recsriptum principis* by a single judicial legitimisation procedure, which granted a child all the rights of a full born.[136]

Russian legislation regarding illegitimate children underwent considerable changes back and forth over the course of the nineteenth century. Legitimisation by subsequent marriage and *per recsriptum principis* were possible at the beginning of the century,[137] abandoned in 1828,[138] and de-facto allowed again in a limited form in 1857.[139] Finally, legitimisation by subsequent marriage was again legalised in 1891.[140] It was only in 1902 that the position of illegitimate children was slightly improved.[141] Under this law

---

[127]   See: Section 9.2.5. of this Part.
[128]   Art. 182 LIBRANDO, V., 'The Reform of Family Law in Italy' (1978), p. 161.
[129]   Art 180 of Italian Civil Code. Ibid, p. 162.
[130]   *'La recherche de la paternité'*.
[131]   Art. 340 of Italian Civil Code. This except in the case of abduction and rape (Art. 189 of the Italian Civil Code). Ibid, p. 161.
[132]   BURGE, W., *Commentaries on Colonial and Foreign Laws*, vol. II, (1908), p. 337.
[133]   The succession rights of illegitimate children were limited to inheritance from their parents (Art. 749 of Italian Civil Code). Their share was less than that of the legitimate issues (Art. 745-757 of Italian Civil Code).
[134]   ZAGOROVSKII, I., *Kurs semeinogo prava* (2003), p. 320. For more on the 'Romanic' and 'Germanic' approaches of illegitimacy, see Chapter 10, Section 10.3.2.
[135]   ZAGOROVSKII, I., *Kurs semeinogo prava* (2003), p. 321.
[136]   HUEBNER, R., *History of Germanic Private Law* (1918), p. 676.
[137]   For a general overview see: ZAGOROVSKII, I., *Kurs semeinogo prava* (2003), p. 339ff.
[138]   By Royal Ordinance of Emperor Nicolas II of 2 January 1829.
[139]   By Royal Ordinances of Emperor Alexander II of 1858 and 1860.
[140]   By Law of 12 March 1891.
[141]   By law of 3 July 1902.

children born outside wedlock were legally related only to their mother. Acknowledgement by the father was still not possible.[142] The paternity suit became a civil, instead of a criminal action. Parental power over illegitimate children was executed by the mother.[143] A father, who provided maintenance, could be appointed as a guardian.[144] The obligation to maintain the child rested primarily with the mother and only subsidiarily on the father.[145] An illegitimate child was not an heir to its biological father. It could inherit from its mother, but only the assets she had acquired during her life, not her heritable property.[146]

10.2.4. THE NINETEENTH CENTURY MATRIMONIAL PROPERTY LAW

The developments in the field of matrimonial property law were mainly influenced by three factors: the export of Napoleonic law, the women's struggle for more equal treatment, and the unification of law at the national level.

In **The Netherlands,** the legal regime of community of movables and acquests, introduced during the French rule, was replaced in the Civil Code of 1838 by the universal community of property, which was the traditional regime for most of the Provinces.[147]

In **England** during the second half of the century, step by step innovations took place in the field of matrimonial property law that owed their enactment to persistent efforts of several generations of women's movement. As was mentioned above, the possibility to mitigate the community property system by means of equitable adjustments was created in the early Modern Times for the sake of protection of the patrimonial interests of the wife's family.[148] The nineteenth-century reforms, however, were inspired by the desire to protect the patrimonial rights of the wife herself. In the middle of the nineteenth century, the medieval common law system of matrimonial property was no more than scarcely mitigated by the operation of equitable instruments. As equitable arrangements were commonly made only by the wealthy few at the top of the society, the common law system still remained the law for the majority of the

---

[142] ZAGOROVSKII, I., *Kurs semeinogo prava (2003)*, p. 252.
[143] Art. 132¹ *Svod Zakonov.*
[144] Art. 132¹¹ *Svod Zakonov.*
[145] Art. 132⁴ *Svod Zakonov.*
[146] Art. 132¹² *Svod Zakonov.*
[147] DE BLÉCOURT, A., *Kort begrip van het oud-vaderlands burgerlijk recht* (1950), p. 76.
[148] See Chapter 8, Section 8.6.

English population.[149] Since the medieval doctrine of *coverture* still remained in force, a married woman had no legal personalia.[150] The husband administered all community assets, including the personal belongings of the wife. More importantly, the husband retained the right to administer his wife's property even if the spouses separated.[151] The first reform of 1857 had to do with this matter, and was triggered, among other things, by the publicity around the case of Caroline Norton. This lady of letters and considerable political influence managed to draw political attention to the troubles she encountered due to the position in which the common law system placed a separated wife.[152] The 1857 *Matrimonial Causes Act* gave a wife who had obtained a judicial separation the legal position of *femme sole* in respect of her property.[153] The 1870 *Married Women's Property Act* was curtailed in Parliament to such an extent that it retained no more than a list of exceptional cases in which married women could enjoy a separate estate in addition to those provided in equity.[154] Relief came only with the *Married Women's Property Act* of 1882. This Act introduced, albeit ambiguously, the regime of separation of property. It did not grant married women the full legal capacity of a *femme sole*, but it extended the regime of separate estates to the whole of the wife's property, thus from then on, equity recognised a married woman's legal capacity over all her assets.[155]

The formation of the **German** national State placed the unification of matrimonial property law on the agenda. It was not an easy task, as at that time about a hundred different modifications of various regimes of matrimonial property operated simultaneously in Germany.[156] Under these circumstances, a 'rush and total unification' was considered unfeasible.[157] Therefore the draftsmen of the BGB tried to achieve no more than the 'cautious reduction of existing patterns to a limited number of prototypes';[158] the next step being to acclaim one of those prototypes as the statutory regime, while the others would become contractual regimes.[159] Although the various

---

[149]   As Otto Kahn-Freund put it: 'until late 19ᵗʰ century there existed two *"regimes matrimoniaux"*: the common law for the many, the equity for the few'. KAHN-FREUND, O., 'Matrimonial Property Law in England' (1955), p. 276.

[150]   THOMSON, J., 'The Reform of Family Law in England' (1978), p. 43.

[151]   SHANLEY, M., *Feminism, Marriage and the Law in Victorian England, 1850-1895* (1989), p. 25-26.

[152]   She drew public attention to the shortcomings of the system of that time in a series of passionate pamphlets: 'A Plain Letter to the Lord Chancellor on the Infant Custody Bill' (1939), 'English Law for Women in the Nineteenth Century' (1854), and 'A Letter to the Queen on Lord Chancellor Granworth's Marriage and Divorce Bill' (1855). SHANLEY, M., *Feminism, Marriage and the Law in Victorian England, 1850-1895* (1989), p. 23-29.

[153]   LOWE, N., DOUGLAS, G., *Bromley's Family Law* (1998), p. 110.

[154]   Ibid, p. 110-111.

[155]   KAHN-FREUND, O., 'Matrimonial Property Law in England' (1955), p. 277.

[156]   MASSFELLER, F., 'Matrimonial Property Law in Germany' (1955), p. 371.

[157]   GRAUE, E., 'German Law' (1972), p. 115.

[158]   Ibid.

[159]   Ibid.

forms of community regimes were most common in the German territories, separation of property with the community of administration (*Verwaltungsgemeinschaft*)[160] became the new statutory regime under the BGB. The wife retained the title of legal owner to all her movable and immovable property, but the husband enjoyed the right of administration and usufruct (*Nutznießung*) with respect to the non-reserved property of the wife (*eingebrachtes Gut*).[161] For alienation of this property the husband generally needed the cooperation of his wife.[162] The wife, however, retained the right to administer her reserved property (*Vorbehaltsgut*).[163] This reserved property consisted of the assets for the purely personal use of the wife and the means of her professional work, as well as any other assets, stipulated to be of such nature by marriage contract, an act of donation, or a Will.[164]

The **Swiss** *ZGB* of 1907 unified the matrimonial property law of the cantons. The new legal regime of separate property with the administration and usufruct of a husband resembled the statutory regime under the BGB.[165]

The matrimonial property regime in **Hungary** had already been separation of property for a long time. In the end of the nineteenth century this regime has evolved in the direction of the system of deferred community of property. During the marriage the wife and the husband were entitled to administer and dispose of her/his assets independently from her husband.[166] However, at the time of termination of marriage each of the spouses (and/or their hairs) were intituled to share in the increase of each others property.[167]

As was mentioned above, the draftsmen of the 1865 **Italian** Civil Code decided to drop the community of movables and acquests that had been introduced by the *Code Napoléon*. This legal regime was not considered to be in line with Italian tradition.[168] Thus, the statutory regime under the Italian Code became Italy's traditional dotal regime of separation of property.[169] According to this regime, the property of the wife was divided into the dowry and the paraphernalia. The wife remained the legal owner

---

[160]   Para. 1363 et seq. BGB. See: MASSFELLER, F., 'Matrimonial Property Law in Germany' (1955), p. 372.
[161]   Para. 1373 et seq. BGB. See: GRAUE, E., 'German Law' (1972), p. 115.
[162]   In case of refusal, the wife's consent could be substituted by a decision of the Guardianship Court (para. 1379 BGB). See: MASSFELLER, F., 'Matrimonial Property Law in Germany' (1955), p. 373.
[163]   Para. 1365, 1371 BGB. See: Ibid, p. 372.
[164]   Para. 1366-1369 BGB.
[165]   GRAUE, E., 'German Law' (1972), p. 115.
[166]   BURGE, W., *Commentaries on Colonial and Foreign Laws,* vol. III (1910), p. 609.
[167]   WEISS, E., 'Remarks on Certain Aspects of the Codification of Family Law' (2002), p. 185-186.
[168]   RODOTÀ, S., 'Le regime matrimonial en droit Italien' (1972), p. 225.
[169]   Ibid.

of the dowry, but the husband had the right of administration and usufruct.[170] Alienation of the dowry was generally not possible.[171] Paraphernalia were owned and administered by the wife herself. However, due to her legal incapacity a married woman could not perform legal acts without her husband's consent.[172]

In **Spain,** the 1889 Spanish Civil Code introduced the system of limited community of property.[173]

An important peculiarity of **Russia,** as compared to most of Western Europe, was a long-standing tradition of separation of marital property.[174] The right of the wife to administer and alienate her own property without the intervention of her husband[175] had been vigilantly preserved by the courts[176] and remained unchanged up to 1926.

10.3. CONVERGENCE AND DIVERGENCE: SIMILAR IDEAS, DIFFERENT BALANCES OF POWER

It is difficult to assess whether a convergence tendency was more apparent during the nineteenth century than in the preceding period of the Enlightenment. The main legislative events of the nineteenth century were the advance of civil marriage and the creeping liberalisation of divorce.[177] The conservative political spirit of the age is masterly portrayed by Roderick Phillips in his *magnus opus, 'Putting Asunder'.* The peculiarity of this period is that the reforms that brought about a reluctant modernisation of family law were most often designed and performed by moderate, pragmatic conservatives.[178] These conservative reformers 'had little or nothing to do with the liberal doctrines in any meaningful sense'.[179] They considered the modernisation of family just an inevitable compromise that had to be made for the sake of buttressing the stability of marriage and the family.

---

[170] Art. 1399 of the Italian Civil Code.
[171] Art. 1404-1407 of the Italian Civil Code.
[172] Art. 1427-1434 of the Italian Civil Code
[173] CHECA MARTINEZ, M., National Report 'Spain' (2001), p. 4.
[174] Art. 109 *Svod Zakonov.*
[175] Art. 114 *Svod Zakonov.*
[176] The Civil Cassation Department always resisted any attempt to derive a right for the husband to administer wifely property from the nature of the marriage union and the subordinate position of the wife. See: WAGNER, W., *Marriage, Property, and Law in Late Imperial Russia* (1994), p. 66.
[177] PHILLIPS, R., *Putting Asunder* (1988), p. 571.
[178] Ibid, p. 494.
[179] Ibid, p. 495.

10.3.1. THE CONSERVATIVE UNIFICATION IN THE NEW NATIONAL STATES: SOME OBSERVATIONS

In respect of the convergence of positive law, the main event of the nineteenth century was the unification of family law on the national level in Germany, Italy and Switzerland. The stories of these unifications can provide us with interesting information regarding the prerequisites, the dilemmas, the techniques, the cultural and political connotations and the effects of deliberate unification. Cultural constraints do not seem to have played a significant role, as these unifications were carried out within more or less culturally homogeneous regions. What was clearly of considerable influence on these unification projects, however, was the predominantly conservative mindset of the age.

This was even so in unified Italy, where the unification of law was to a large extent in the hands of liberal and anticlerical intellectuals and statesmen.[180] Their liberalism however, was limited to political issues and 'did not cover family law'.[181] The drafters of the uniform law were not interested in the introduction of divorce, the improvement of the position of illegitimate children, women's emancipation or equality within the family.[182] They were just building a new, national State. The introduction of a compulsory civil marriage was more a step in their anticlerical policy than a measure of liberalisation of family law.

A strong example of 'conservative' unification is provided by the uniformisation of family law in Germany. The most significant political dilemma was the reconciliation of the liberal divorce law of Prussia and the indissolubility of marriage in the south of Germany.[183] The drafters of the BGB were generally inspired by the ideals of nationalism, as well as by such conflicting ideas as the progressive legacy of the Enlightenment and the French Revolution, on the one hand, and 'the empirical-conservative scholarship of the Historical School',[184] on the other hand. In the field of family law, the conservative ideas clearly prevailed. The family law provisions of the BGB were based upon a communitarian, rather than an individualistic, vision of the family. Despite the political dominance of Prussia and the eagerness of Bismarck to roll back the influence of the Catholic Church (*Kulturkampf*), the final draft of the BGB 'favoured the conservative-Christian view rather than the liberal-individualistic tradition'.[185] The obligatory civil marriage and the introduction of divorce in the

---

[180]   RHEINSTEIN, M., *Marriage Stability, Divorce, and the Law* (1972), p. 186.
[181]   Ibid.
[182]   Ibid.
[183]   MÜLLER-FREIENFELS, W., 'Family Law and the Law of Succession in Germany' (1967), p. 434.
[184]   Ibid.
[185]   Ibid.

Catholic territories can probably be best understood as elements of Bismarck's *Kulturkampf*, rather than as part of liberal policies, as had been the case in France and England.[186]

The nineteenth-century examples of deliberate unification of family law offer the present-day surveyor some interesting observations. In the current debates surrounding the harmonisation of family law, deliberate harmonisation is often associated as a matter of course with modernisation. The nineteenth-century experience illustrates that harmonisation as such is nothing more than a tool to bring about the approximation of laws that can have a positive, as well as negative, effect on the level of modernity of family law. The present-day harmonisation projects are carried out by self-appointed groups of scholars not bound by a political mandate and therefore able to work under rather ideal conditions. There is nothing to prevent them from composing whatever they consider to be the very best and most advanced. The nineteenth-century examples illustrate that when a harmonisation project is carried out under the guidance of politicians in a real-life situation, the outcome will probably be severely influenced by political considerations. The case of the BGB demonstrates that in such ideologically sensitive areas as the law of divorce, the level of modernity of the harmonised law would most likely correspond to some sort of common denominator, rather than be inspired by the most modern and advanced precedents. For the regions with the most modern law, as was the case with Prussia, such a compromise necessarily results in a step back in their own historical development. Thus, the harmonisation of ideologically laden fields of family law appears to be very much a political exercise that can most likely only succeed at the expense of the modernity of the law of the most advanced regions.

Another interesting observation is that this phenomenon is clearly less prominent in the less ideologically-sensitive areas of family law, like, for instance, matrimonial property law. Although on the threshold of unification, the diversity of matrimonial property laws in France, Germany, Italy and Switzerland was even greater than in the field of divorce law,[187] the unification of matrimonial property law was nowhere carried out at the expense of modernity. A first explanation is that matrimonial property law is much more politically neutral, so that it is hardly possible to say that one system (for instance community) is more modern than the other (for example separation with community of administration in the hands of the husband). Secondly, compared to the law of divorce, the unification of matrimonial property law did not involve such

---

[186]   Phillips proposed this view in respect of the provisions of divorce of the law of 1875. PHILLIPS, R., *Putting Asunder* (1988), p. 431.

[187]   Before the introduction of the *BGB* there existed about one hundred matrimonial property regimes in Germany. MASSFELLER, F., 'Matrimonial Property Law in Germany' (1955), p. 371.

difficult political considerations. A third explanation is that, differing from marriage and divorce law, matrimonial property law allows contractual freedom. This non-mandatory character of matrimonial property law granted the drafters of the uniform law in all the aforementioned countries the opportunity to retain, alongside the statutory regime of matrimonial property, the old customary regimes of matrimonial property as contractual regimes.[188] This allowed the possibility of a gradual 'democratic' internalisation of the new unified law, by permitting the population a choice between the old and the new models.

10.3.2. CONVERGENCE / DIVERGENCE ON THE LEVEL OF POSITIVE LAW

The most important occurrence in the field of the nineteenth century marriage law was the proliferation of civil marriage. At the beginning of the century, the European countries allowing civil marriage could be counted on the fingers of one hand. By the end of the century, the countries that did not provide for some possibility of civil marriage formed only a small minority. This is undeniably a token of modernisation, but could hardly be dubbed convergence, as the level of uniformity at the beginning of the century was no less than at the end.

A common feature of the development of divorce law was the absence of significant change. In most of Europe, divorce law at the end of the century was hardly more permissive than it had been at the beginning. On the contrary, in many countries divorce law clearly took a step backwards. A common element of this backward development was the almost unanimous rejection of divorce by mutual consent. The spouses' autonomous right to decide about the termination of their marriage, hesitantly recognised in the first decade of the century in some parts of Europe under the influence of the Enlightenment and the export of the *Code Napoléon*,[189] was discarded almost everywhere.[190] Another common denominator was that divorce was allowed only upon specific grounds, listed in the law.[191] Fault grounds clearly dominated the picture. Where no-fault grounds existed, they were no more than exceptions, anxiously curtailed by cumbersome restrictions. The piecemeal reforms

---

[188] For example, the contractual regimes under the *BGB* were: separation of property (*Gütertrennung*); general community of property (*Allgemeine Gütergemeinschaft*); and community of movables (*Fahrnisgemeinschaft*).

[189] In 1810, divorce by mutual consent existed in Prussia, France, The Southern and Northern Netherlands, Luxemburg, Italy, Rheinland, and some Swiss Cantons.

[190] In 1900, divorce by mutual consent had survived only in Belgium, Luxemburg and Switzerland (in the last country it was to be abolished in 1912).

[191] NEUMAYER, K., 'General Introduction' (1978), p. 5.

that were carried out during the century typically amounted to no more than the addition of a few new specific (usually fault) grounds to the already existing ones. Roderick Phillips rightly qualified such reforms not as the liberalisation of divorce, but rather as 'divorce extension'.[192] On the pan-European scale, the gap between the most permissive and the most restrictive divorce laws remained quite significant. On the one side of the spectrum, there were of course countries that did not allow divorce at all, followed by England with adultery as the only ground for divorce. On the other side were the Nordic countries, whose laws provided for a broad number of fault and no-fault divorce grounds.

The legal position of illegitimate children in nineteenth-century Europe was characterised by the co-existence of two different approaches, the 'Germanic' and the 'Romanic'. There was a clear proliferation of the 'Romanic' approach, resulting from the export of the *Code Civil*. The 'Germanic' approach was not only typical for Germany but also for other jurisdictions; for instance, those of the Nordic region and Britain. According to the 'Romanic' system, the position of an illegitimate child was largely dependant on an acknowledgement by the child's parents, not on the biological truth. A distinctive feature of this approach was that the judicial establishment of paternity (*la recherche de la paternité*) was, as a rule, impossible. The 'Germanic' approach, in contrast, gave more weight to the biological truth than to the acknowledgement. Little difference was made between the status of acknowledged and unacknowledged illegitimate children. The judicial establishment of paternity was generally allowed. However, under the 'Germanic' system, illegitimate children enjoyed significantly less rights in respect of their father than acknowledged children under the 'Romanic' system.[193]

Harry Willekens rightly noticed that despite the differences in approach, 'the treatment of illegitimate children in Romanic and non-Romanic systems looks, roughly speaking, functionally equivalent'.[194] The common element of both systems was that the claims of illegitimate children with regard to their natural fathers were very limited. In the 'Romanic' system these claims were in the first place conditional on the volition of the father. But on top of that, acknowledgement by a married man was excluded, as well as the acknowledgement of so-called 'adulterous' and 'incestuous' children. In the 'Germanic' system almost all illegitimate children were given more or less the same rights in respect of the father, but the scope of these rights was restricted to no more than a maintenance claim.[195] Obviously, because of these limitations the position of

---

[192] PHILLIPS, R., *Putting Asunder* (1988), p. 494.
[193] ZAGOROVSKII, I., *Kurs semeinogo prava* (2003), p. 224-328.
[194] WILLEKENS, H., 'Explaining Two Hundred Years of Family Law in Western Europe' (1997), p. 63.
[195] Ibid.

illegitimate children in both systems differed significantly from that of legitimate children.

In general, the family pattern in nineteenth-century Europe still remained rather traditional and patriarchal. A legitimate family was based solely upon marriage, and everywhere remained the only legally recognised form of family. Cohabitation outside marriage had no standing in law. In all European jurisdictions the husband remained the head of the family.[196] All important issues, such as the choice of the family domicile, were decided by the husband. In the majority of European countries a wife had no legal capacity.[197] The husband's power to administer the assets of his wife remained uncontested almost everywhere.[198]

10.3.3. CONVERGENCE / DIVERGENCE ON THE LEVEL OF IDEOLOGY

Convergence was more apparent on the ideological level than on the level of positive law. As discussed above, the argumentation, the political and moral discourses, and the political colour of the opponents and the advocates of the liberalisation of family law displayed abundant similarity. The intellectual unity of Western and Eastern Europe became even closer than before. The late-nineteenth century family law reforms in Russia were conducted in the atmosphere of the same ideological confrontation[199] that divided public opinion in Western Europe. As was typical for the whole of Europe ever since the Restoration, conservatives held the initiative in the field of family law, and the progressive forces were generally on the defence. More similarity on the ideological level, however, did not lead to significant approximation of the positive laws. The main ideas were the same everywhere, but the political compromises between their proponents and opponents varied from country to country. This predetermined dissimilar outcomes of the family law reforms carried out in the various European jurisdictions.

---

[196] Art. 213 of the French *Code Civil* and the Belgian Civil Code, Art. 144 of the Italian Civil Code; Art. 160 of the Swiss Civil Code; Para. 91 of the Austian *Allgemeines Bürgerliches Gesetzbuch*; Art. 160 of the Dutch Civil Code; Art. 107 of the Russian *Svod Sakonov*, etc.

[197] For instance, in France, Italy, Belgium, and The Netherlands. In Russia, Hungary and, since 1882, also in England, a married woman was legally capable with respect to her separate property. German and Austrian law did not contain any general provisions on the legal capacity of married women.

[198] Only Hungary and Russia allowed married women to freely administer their property. England was a pioneer among the Western European countries by granting married women the right to administer their property.

[199] WAGNER, W., *Marriage, Property, and Law in Late Imperial Russia* (1994), p. 138 ff.

CHAPTER 11
THE TWENTIETH CENTURY
UNTIL THE SIXTIES

11.1. INTRODUCTION

In the twentieth century, Europe broadened its borders as several countries situated on its geographical fringes acceded to Europe in regard to culture, ideology and politics. The Russian Revolution implemented, albeit not without 'Asiatic' flavour, the ideas of the Western European socialists. The countries of the Balkan region, liberated from the Ottoman Empire, celebrated their return into the European family. Turkey itself chose for Europe and commenced an unprecedented cultural transformation under the leadership of Kemal Atatürk.

The developments of family law in the twentieth century can be divided into four distinctive periods: the first two turbulent decades, the polarisation of the interwar period, the lull before the storm after World War II, and the veritable family law revolution that commenced in the 1960s. The beginning of the century displayed anything but convergence. In the first two decades, Portugal, Nordic Region and Russia underwent radical breakthroughs in the modernisation of family law, while the rest of Europe remained in the ban of creeping reforms. The interbellum is typified by movements back and forth in the reform of family law, which were closely related to the rise and fall of political regimes. After the war, the family law waters became quieter. The radical reforms of the 1960s started a new era in the modernisation of family law and will therefore be dealt with in the following Chapter.

11.2. THE RADICAL REFORMS AT THE BEGINNING OF THE CENTURY

The beginning of the twentieth century witnessed radical family law reforms in Portugal, Nordic Region, the Soviet Union and Turkey. These regions differed in almost every respect: religious and cultural, economical and social. For the purpose of this study, the reforms of the early twentieth century are of special interest for several reasons. Portugal and the Soviet Union exemplify pioneering reforms, which prefigured the developments in other countries. The Nordic Region provides an appealing example of a successful forward-looking harmonisation of family law. The Soviet Union and Turkey represent compelling cases for the study of the potential and limits of instrumentalist change and social engineering. And Atatürk's reforms offer one of the best examples of successful cross-cultural legal transplantation.

11.2.1. CONTENT OF THE REFORMS

Radical family law reforms in agrarian Catholic Portugal

The first of the radical reforms of family law in the twentieth century occurred, of all places, in agrarian Catholic Portugal in the framework of the 'anticlerical revolution' of 1910.[1] On the eve of the revolution, Portuguese law was altogether in line with Catholic doctrine. Marriage was regarded a sacrament, divorce was not allowed. In 1910, the King was overthrown and the First Republic was proclaimed. The new Republican government proclaimed the liberalisation of family law a matter of high priority. Accordingly, it promptly introduced obligatory civil marriage, equalising husband and wife before the law,[2] and enacted a liberal divorce law.[3] In addition to the traditional fault grounds, the new law allowed divorce by mutual consent, and in case of desertion, absence of one of the spouses for four years, and de-facto separation for five years.[4] For the European standards of the time, this was truly progressive.

Coordinated modernisation of family law in the Nordic region

The Nordic region was the second area where family law was profoundly liberalised at the beginning of the twentieth century (1909-1927). Unlike Portugal, the Soviet Union and Turkey, the Nordic reforms were not the result of political revolution, but were rather the product of a gradual, evolutionary process of modernisation. Many scholars still seek to explain why the Nordic region was the first European region to modernise family law in a 'natural' fashion. The Nordic case puzzles both those who consider economic developments to be the major factor of legal change, as well as those who hold that ideology is the crucial factor in legal development. At the time of the reforms, the Nordic countries had neither the most developed economy, nor the strongest influence of liberal ideology.[5] Several scholars have suggested a relatively high

---

[1]   SOTTOMAYOR, M., 'The Introduction and Impact of Joint Custody in Portugal' (1999), p. 247.
[2]   The superior position of the father above the mother was retained, however. SOTTOMAYOR, M., 'The Introduction and Impact of Joint Custody in Portugal' (1999), p. 248.
[3]   Decree 3 of November 1910 'Divorce Law'.
[4]   SOTTOMAYOR, M., 'The Introduction and Impact of Joint Custody in Portugal' (1999), p. 247.
[5]   See WILLEKENS, H., 'Explaining Two Hundred Years of Family Law in Western Europe' (1997), p. 87.

level of secularisation as one of the explanations.[6] Another possible explanation has been sought in a long-standing tradition of relatively liberal family law; at the time of the reforms, Nordic family law was already rather permissive for the European standards of the day. Although the grounds for judicial divorce were fairly restrictive, the alternative system of divorce by Royal dispensation provided for divorce, not only on the ground of fault, but also on the basis of prolonged discord.[7]

The reform of family law was conducted in the framework of close legislative co-operation. In 1910, Law Commissions were simultaneously appointed in Norway, Sweden and Denmark.[8] The basis of this cooperation lay in the long history of political and legal ties between the Nordic countries.[9] Although the Nordic region was united in a personal union under one King only for a very brief period in the distant past from 1397 till 1520,[10] the common links of the Nordic countries go far beyond this period. From about 1100 until 1809, Sweden and Finland formed one Kingdom,[11] and after Finland became a Grand Duchy under the Russian Tsar in 1809, Swedish civil and family law remained in force there. Norway, which also included Iceland, and Denmark, was united into one Kingdom from 1380 until 1814.[12] Therefore, the legislation in the two countries was strongly related. Norway was united with Sweden under the personal union which was imposed on it in 1814 and lasted until 1905.[13]

Civil marriage was introduced in 1908 in Sweden,[14] in 1917 in Finland,[15] in 1923 in Denmark,[16] and in 1918 in Norway.[17] Unlike the countries influenced by the French *Code Civil*, the Nordic countries did not make civil marriage the only form of valid

---

[6]   BRADLEY, D., *Family Law and Political Culture* (1996), p. 5. TOTTIE, L., 'The Elimination of Fault in Swedish Divorce Law' (1990), p. 131. RHEINSTEIN, M., *Marriage Stability, Divorce, and the Law* (1972), p. 153.

[7]   SCHMIDT, T., 'The Scandinavian Law of procedure in Matrimonial Causes' (1984), p. 81.

[8]   On the course of this Nordic cooperation see: DAVID, R., 'The International Unification of Private Law' (1971), p. 181- 185.

[9]   WENDT, F., *The Nordic Council and Co-operation in Scandinavia* (1959), p. 11ff.

[10]   The Kalmar union united Nordic countries under one King. WENDT, F., *The Nordic Council and Co-operation in Scandinavia* (1959), p. 12-13.

[11]   Ibid, p. 10 and 17.

[12]   Ibid, p. 12 and 18.

[13]   In 1814 Bernadotte's army forced Norway to accept the Swedish monarch as their King (Ibid, p. 12 and 18). Iceland and some other Norwegian territories remained, however, under the Danish crown. Ibid, p. 22.

[14]   The possibility for civil marriage between Christians and Jews had existed in Sweden from 1863. SCHMIDT, F., 'The Prospective Law of Marriage' (1971), p. 191.

[15]   BRADLEY, D., 'Antecedents of Finnish Family Laws: Legal Traditions, Political Culture and Social Institutions' (1998), p. 97- 98.

[16]   From that time it was possible to choose freely between religious and civil marriage. Before then, civil marriage had only been open to those who belonged to neither the State Church nor to another recognised Church (see: Danish State Archive www.sa.dk).

[17]   By the 1918 Norwegian Marriage Act.

marriage. The Nordic system more closely resembled the British two-track system, attaching legal consequences to both civil and religious marriage.

The need to reform divorce law was particularly felt in connection with a manifest discrepancy between the law in the books and the law in action that was exemplified in the so-called 'Copenhagen' or 'Haparanda' divorce. The Nordic countries were in fact the first to respond to the problem of divorce by collusion, a problem that was clearly manifest in several other countries as well. In many countries the phenomenon of divorce by collusion would sooner or later become one of the main reasons for the further liberalisation of divorce law. As soon as the courts were no longer inclined to or capable of scrutinising proof of matrimonial fault, a forged 'fault-based' divorce by collusion of consenting spouses would become the 'shortest road' to divorce. In the Nordic region, these divorces were called 'Copenhagen' or 'Haparanda' divorces. As Nordic law did not allow divorce by consent, a consensual divorce had to be presented as a divorce due to desertion. Part of this work around was that one of the spouses went to the closest foreign city – the Swedish to Copenhagen, and the Finnish to Haparanda – in order to allow the other spouse to apply for divorce on the ground of desertion.[18] Typical of the time is the statement of the Swedish Minister of Justice, who said that with the 'Copenhagen' divorce 'we have an abuse to be countered, but also a need which should be recognised'.[19] The new divorce law was the result of a compromise between two opposing paradigms. The first was the liberal belief in the right of the spouses to decide for themselves whether and when their marriage has come to an end.[20] The other was the belief that divorce should not to be made too easy, as the primary purpose of divorce law was to buttress the institution of marriage.[21] Divorce law was reformed in Norway in 1909, in Sweden in 1915, in Denmark in 1922, in Iceland in 1923 and in Finland in 1929. The new Acts have been depicted as very similar, if not identical.[22] Their common core was the introduction of the irretrievable breakdown as a ground for divorce. The conditions under which divorce could be obtained were, however, not exactly the same.[23] The irretrievable breakdown was presupposed in the case of a mutual application for divorce, submitted after a relatively short period of separation (for instance, one year in Sweden, and a year and a half in

---

[18] SCHMIDT, T., 'The Scandinavian Law of procedure in Matrimonial Causes' (1984), p. 79-80.
[19] SELLIN, J., *Marriage and Divorce Legislation in Sweden* (1922), p. 38-39.
[20] According to Sellin, if the spouses agreed that their marriage has failed 'the court has no right to inquire into the nature of the "discord", which brought the marriage to such an unhappy end', as "[n]o one knows the condition better than the spouses themselves." Ibid, p. 79.
[21] The Swedish Minister of Justice expressed the hope that the liberalisation of divorce would diminish cohabitation outside marriage and would serve to protect of the family. Ibid, p. 55.
[22] 'Almost identical', according to Schmidt and Agell. SCHMIDT, T., 'The Scandinavian Law of procedure in Matrimonial Causes' (1984), p. 80; AGELL, A., 'Is There one System of Family Laws in the Nordic Countries' (2001), p. 314.
[23] BRADLEY, D., *Family Law and Political Culture* (1996), p. 12.

Denmark).[24] In case of unilateral application, a longer period of separation was required. Alongside the irretrievable breakdown, traditional fault-based grounds were preserved. The dual judicial and administrative divorce system was retained in Denmark and Norway, but abolished in Sweden and Finland.

Another common feature of the Nordic reforms was a benevolent attitude towards illegitimate children.[25] There were significant differences however, between the most progressive Norwegian (1915) and Danish (1937) legislation on children born out of wedlock, on the one hand, and the less far reaching Swedish law (1917),[26] and the relatively conservative Finish (1922)[27] and Icelandic (1947)[28] Acts, on the other hand. None of these Acts completely abolished the difference between legitimate and illegitimate children. Norwegian, Danish and Swedish law granted extramarital children the possibility to be recognised by their natural fathers.[29] Paternity suits were also permitted.[30] A rather comprehensive right of a natural child to inherit was introduced in Norway in 1915,[31] in Iceland in 1921 and in Denmark in 1937.[32] More limited inheritance rights of natural children were introduced in Sweden in 1917.[33]

The traditional legal regime of matrimonial property – the community property with the right of the husband to administer the community – no longer answered the emancipation ambitions of the Nordic women.[34] The introduction of a new regime of deferred universal community of property in Sweden in 1920, Denmark in 1925,

---

[24]   RHEINSTEIN, M., *Marriage Stability, Divorce, and the Law* (1972), p. 141.
[25]   SUNDBERG, J., 'Marriage or no Marriage' (1971), p. 226.
[26]   BRADLEY, D., *Family Law and Political Culture* (1996), p. 36-37.
[27]   BRADLEY, D., 'Comparative Family Law and Political Process: Regulation of Sexual Morality in Finland' (1999), p. 178.
[28]   BJÖRGVINSSON, D., 'General Principles and Recent Developments in Icelandic Family Law' (1995), p. 216.
[29]   BRADLEY, D., *Family Law and Political Culture* (1996), p. 37-38.
[30]   In Norway, if an unmarried father used the *exceptio congressus cum pluribus,* all putative fathers were held responsible for the support of the child. Ibid, p. 210
[31]   If parentage was established by recognition or court decision, illegitimate children had the same inheritance rights with regard to the father as legitimate ones. The only exceptions were the special rights to inherit land *'oldelsrett'* and *'asetesrett'*. LÖGDBERG, A., 'The Reform of Family Law in the Scandinavian Countries' (1978), p. 219.
[32]   Danish law granted children full inheritance rights with regard to the father and his family. Ibid, p. 217.
[33]   Only children born during betrothal or children in respect of whom the father issued a declaration of inheritance could inherit after their father in Sweden. Ibid, p. 212.
[34]   This regime had already been gradually mitigated during the course of the nineteenth century. For instance, in Sweden in 1862 a wife obtained the right to apply, under certain conditions, for separation of property; in 1874, the right to opt for separation by pre-nuptial agreement; and in the same year the right to dispose of her own earnings. In Denmark, a wife obtained, in 1899, the same rights to dispose of her property as a *femme sole.* FAURHOLT, J., FEDERSPOEL, P., *Recent Danish Legislation on the Relations of Husband and Wife* (1927), p. 9.

Norway in 1927, Iceland in 1923 and Finland in 1929 gave women equal rights to the family assets.[35] The common feature of the matrimonial property systems of all Nordic countries could be roughly summed up as follows: As long as a marriage lasted, the property of the spouses was not united in a community. Each of the spouses retained legal title and had the right to administer the property that he or she had brought into the marriage. In a case of dissolution of the marriage, the premarital property, together with the property acquired during the marriage, had to be equally divided between husband and wife.[36]

Radical reforms in the Soviet Union: back to the future

The scope and radicalness of the family law reforms carried out in the Soviet Union were without precedent, even in the first two decades of the twentieth century. These innovations could be seen as an early herald of the pan-European 'family law revolution' that would take place at the end of the twentieth century. In Imperial Russia, marriage and divorce law had been neither uniform nor secular. The population was subordinated to the ecclesiastical rules of different religions and confessions. This diversity was swiftly replaced by a uniform civil law of unprecedented libertarianism; for the first time since the days of classical Rome, marriage and divorce were completely deformalised. The reform of family law was a matter of the highest priority for the Bolshevik government. As part of the general progressive attitude towards sexual morality, Soviet Russia introduced the most liberal law in Europe in regard to same-sex relationships. Neither the criminal code of 1922 nor of 1926 contained sanctions for same-sex acts between consenting adults. The age of consent was set at 16 for both homo- and heterosexual acts.[37]

Just two months after the *coup d'état* of October 1917, civil marriage was made the only valid form of marriage.[38] The first Russian Family Code of 1918[39] proclaimed the total equality between a man and woman within the family and in public life.[40] The Second Family Code of 1926[41] gave de-facto durable cohabitation the legal status of

---

[35] For an overview of literature see: BRADLEY, D., *Family Law and Political Culture* (1996), p. 10-11.
[36] MALMSTRÖM, Å., 'Matrimonial Property Law in Sweden' (1955), p. 411.
[37] ALEKSEEV, N., *Pravovoe regulirovanie polozgenia sexual'nikh men'shinstv* (2002), p. 197.
[38] Decree of 18 December 1917 *O grazhdanskom brake, detiakh. u vedenii knig aktov grazhdanskogo sosnoiania* (On Civil Marriage, Children and the Act of Civil Status).
[39] *Kodeks Zakonov ob Aktah Grazhdanskogo Sostoiania, Brachnom, Semeinom i Opekynskom Prave* (Code on Civil Status, Marriage, Family and Guardianship) of 22 October 1918.
[40] Art. 100-132 Family Code of 1918.
[41] *Kodeks zakonov o brake sem'e i opeke* (Code on Marriage, Family and Guardianship) of 19 November 1926.

marriage.[42] For the first time since it was banned in the High Middle Ages, concubinage returned to the European legal stage. The reasons for this far-reaching innovation were manifold. In the first place, the deformalisation of marriage simply followed from the consensual theory of marriage, which again came to the surface after marriage was released from its theological straight-jacket. The registration of marriage was preserved,[43] but no longer treated as a constitutive element of the formation of marriage.[44] As in Roman and pre-Tredintine Europe, consent alone was sufficient for creating a valid marriage. Marriage therefore became a private informal transaction, as it had been in classical Roman law. Another, rather utopian motive behind the deformalisation was the urge to enter the communist future, where marriage was supposed to 'die out'. A more down-to-earth incentive to equate registered and unregistered marriage was the aim of protecting 'proletarian' de-facto wives from 'exploitation' by their usually more economically powerful de-facto husbands.[45]

Divorce law was simultaneously liberalised with the law on marriage.[46] In 1917, the fault grounds for divorce were abolished. An administrative procedure without inquiry was established for divorce by mutual consent. Until 1926, judicial divorce was retained for contested cases, but even in the court procedure, no proof of the irretrievable breakdown of marriage was required.[47] The deformalisation of marriage in 1926 drastically affected the law on divorce. Formal divorce was preserved, but came to be regarded as just a subsidiary means of termination for both registered and unregistered marriage.[48] There was a general consensus that spouses could not be kept in a marriage, even if only one of them wanted out of it. The State declined to decide upon the dissolution of marriage, leaving the floor to the autonomous decisions of the spouses themselves. Marriage was dissolved upon the demand of one or both of the spouses; the registration of divorce was, therefore, merely a formality. In light of this approach, the administrative procedure without any inquiry was extended to all divorce cases. The deformalisation of divorce went so far that the presence of a contesting spouse at the time of the registration was not considered essential. In the light of the fact that his or her defence was of no relevance anyway, this was only logical. The absent spouse was then to be informed by a letter, which caused the procedure to be nicknamed

---

[42]   The Code as such did not treat both institutions as equal, but this result was reached by virtue of case law.

[43]   The registration of marriage was regarded by one of the drafters of the Code as 'a remnant of the past that is doomed to disappear, but at the moment is temporally maintained largely as a measure against church marriages'. BRANDENBURGSKII J., Presentation at the dispute on the family in the House of Soviets (1925), p. 1504 (translation mine).

[44]   RAEVICH, S., 'Brarnoe i semeinoe pravo' (1927), p. 426.

[45]   GENKIN, D. et al, *Istoria sovetskogo grazhdanskogo prava 1917-1947* (1949), p. 443.

[46]   Decree of 19 December 1917 'O rastorzhenii braka' (On divorce).

[47]   SEMIDVORKIN, N., *Sozdanie pervogo brachno-semeinogo kodeksa* (1989), p. 50.

[48]   Art. 19 Family Code of 1926.

'divorce by postcard'.[49] This was the birth of a 'new' generation of divorce law: divorce on demand. It the Europe of those days, which had almost forgotten its own history on this matter, this mode of divorce was experienced as a shocking extremity. In reality, it was no more than an unintended return to the unilateral divorce by divorce letter *repudium* of Classical Roman law.[50]

Illegitimate children were equalised with legitimate issue in every legal aspect. The very concept of illegitimacy was done away with. The voluntary recognition of paternity and the winning of a paternity suit against a reluctant biological father became extremely easy. The Family Code of 1918 (Art. 140-141) introduced the so-called 'establishment of paternity by registration'. Accordingly, a mother during her pregnancy could declare before the civil servant that a certain man was the father of her child. The putative father could deny his paternity before the court during a short period of two weeks. If the paternity was not denied in time, it was presumed to be established. The Code of 1926 (Art. 32) went even further. The putative father was no longer allowed to evoke the *exceptio congressus cum pluribus*. The Ukrainian legislature was even more creative. If a man evoked this *exceptio,* the most probable biological father was declared the legal father, while all the other 'suspects' were obliged to contribute to maintenance payments in shares. This rule was supposed to disencourage men to act out of male solidarity as witnesses to the promiscuity of the mother.[51] This rather unbalanced character of the paternity legislation became the subject of justified criticism.[52] The reasons for these 'woman-friendly' rules were partly the influence of feminist ideology, and partly the Bolshevik's urge to protect unmarried mothers who were often of humble origin and therefore considered as an 'exploited class' whose weak position could be abused by socially more privileged men.[53]

The existing matrimonial property regime of separate property was initially preserved after the Revolution. However, as divorce became easier, separate property came to work to the disadvantage of women, the majority of whom at that time did not have any independent income. Thus, in 1926 a limited form of community property, the community of acquests, replaced the separate property regime.[54] Two features distinguished the newly introduced Russian community from those in Western Europe. First, the community in Russia was administered by both husband and wife

---

[49]   GENKIN, D. et al, *Istoria sovetskogo grazhdanskogo prava 1917-1947* (1949), p. 441.
[50]   For more on Roman divorce see: Section 3.2.4. of the Part II.
[51]   GENKIN, D. et al, *Istoria sovetskogo grazhdanskogo prava 1917-1947* (1949), p. 443.
[52]   Ibid.
[53]   Ibid.
[54]   Ibid, p. 433-440.

on an equal basis.[55] Secondly, Russian law did not allow any contractual deviation from the legal matrimonial property regime.

Turkey westernises family law: a remarkable example of successful legal transplantation

The reforms of family law that were conducted after the foundation of the Turkish Republic in 1923 are very interesting for the purpose of this work, not so much because of their liberalism, as by European standards they were not particularly liberal, but because they represent a most successful case of the trans-cultural transplantation of law. Through these reforms, Islamic, oriental Turkey was to embrace European culture, the European way of life and European family patterns.[56] The westernisation and secularisation of family law was considered to be of paramount importance for the success of the entire design. Using law as an instrument, the nationalistic elite led by Kemal Atatürk endeavoured to bring about far-reaching social change. First and foremost the reformers wished to roll back the influence of their ideological rival, the Islamic clergy, to break up the traditional family, and to insert secularisation and modernisation deep into the pattern of family life.

Like the Russian Empire, the Ottoman Empire did not have a uniform secular family law. The family relations of the multiethnic population were governed by the rules of the various streams of the Islamic faith (for the majority of population), Jewish rules, the rules of the Orthodox Church, and the rules of other Christian convictions.[57] Because Westernisation was one of the principal aims, it was decided to copy the Swiss Civil Code (*ZGB*) of 1907 *in toto*.[58] Although the *ZGB* was not the epitome of liberal family law, its transplantation into Islamic Turkey in 1926 involved a genuine revolution.

Marriage, previously considered a religious institution, was secularised and the civil registration of marriage became compulsory.[59] Polygamous Islamic marriages were forbidden.[60] The new Code put an end to the absolute authority of the husband and

---

[55]   Ibid, p. 439-439.
[56]   The goal of the Turkish reformers was to change the 'family life and the way of living' of the entire population according to the 'common practice of civilized nations'. ÖRÜCÜ, E., 'The Impact of European Law on the Ottoman Empire and Turkey' (1992), p. 51-52.
[57]   ÖRÜCÜ, E., 'Turkey: Change Under Pressure' (1996), p. 90.
[58]   ÖRÜCÜ, E., 'Turkish divorce law' (1996), p. 27.
[59]   In Islamic law marriage was a consensual contract, completed through consent alone. The religious celebration was not required for its validity. ÖRÜCÜ, E., 'Turkey: Change Under Pressure' (1996), p. 96.
[60]   ÖRÜCÜ, E., 'Turkey: Reconciling Traditional Society and Secular Demands' (1987-1988), p. 222.

proclaimed, albeit qualified,[61] a general equality of rights and duties between the spouses.

Paradoxically, the restriction of divorce was regarded in the Turkish setting as a progressive measure. Due to this restriction, a husband lost his unilateral right to repudiate his wife at volition. The new Code introduced judicial divorce for severe incompatibility, insanity and a number of fault grounds.[62] Because it was feared that this would lead to the revival of repudiation, divorce by mutual consent was not allowed until 1988, and even then it was alleged that 'in a country where on the whole the will of the husband prevails, divorce by mutual consent can be regarded as a return to the old Islamic practices'.[63]

The legal regime of matrimonial property became the regime of separate property, with the administration and usufruct of the husband.

11.2.2. DO RADICAL INSTRUMENTALIST REFORMS NECESSARILY LEAD TO A GAP BETWEEN THE LAW IN THE BOOKS AND THE LAW IN ACTION?

As mentioned above, the radical reforms from the beginning of the twentieth century in Portugal, the Nordic region, Russia and Turkey are, for several reasons, of special interest to the purpose of this study. Their importance goes beyond an appreciation in the context of the search for convergence-divergence tendencies. They represent empirical evidence of the workability of certain methods that could come into play if one considers deliberate harmonisation: bottom-up and top-down harmonisation, the use of law as a means of social engineering and legal transplantation. These historical precedents are of great value for the assessment of the theoretical questions concerning the merits of legal transplantation, instrumentalist change and deliberate harmonisation that were discussed in Chapter 2. If the proponents of the 'mirror theory of law'[64] are right, all these radical reforms would have produced and irremediable gap between the law in the books and the law in action. For this reason I shall take a closer look at the actual effects of these reforms.

---

[61] Among other things, the husband had the right to choose the place of residence, and to represent the family as the head of the conjugal union. Ibid, p. 223-224.
[62] ÖRÜCÜ, E., 'Turkish Family Law: a New Phase' (1991-1992), p. 431-432.
[63] ÖRÜCÜ, E., 'Turkey: Change Under Pressure' (1996), p. 90.
[64] See Part I, Chapter 2, Section 2.4.1.

The Nordic region: success in almost every aspect

The Nordic reforms seem to have been a success in almost every aspect. Although the reforms did not, of course, proceed without resistance,[65] to my knowledge there were no reports of any significant discrepancies between the law in the books and the law in action. If anything, it was the other way around; the reforms could be considered as the response to a discord between the outdated pre-reform law in the books and the changing social practices. They were more a response to pressing social needs than an attempt to reshape society according to the vision of some minority *élite dirigeante,*[66] as was the case in Turkey and the Soviet Union. Although in some ways the Nordic reforms could also be considered to be the result of the efforts of an elite.[67] In the Nordic region, at least in Norway, Denmark and Sweden,[68] the reforms were the result of the co-operation between the two dominant political movements of the day: the liberal and the social democratic.[69] Nonetheless, one could rightly say that in the Nordic region the reforms were in line both with the social needs and the wishes of the population.

This can explain why the modernisation of family law in the Nordic region was so successful, but it does not explain why the reforms were developed in close co-operation between the countries concerned. René David explains this by the fact that the need to modernise the existing family law was felt everywhere in the Nordic region, and that the relations between the Nordic countries were such that it was considered desirable for this revision to result in uniform rules.[70] At the beginning of the twentieth century, nationalism was still in vogue in Europe and the Nordic people felt united by the 'bonds of language, law, religion and, in part, by common origin'.[71] Although the early-twentieth century period of the Nordic co-operation would turn out to be the most fruitful,[72] this cooperation as such is generally considered a great success.[73]

---

[65] For the opposition to the reforms see: BRADLEY, D., *Family Law and Political Culture* (1996), p. 22-24.

[66] I am indebted to Esin Örücü for this term. See her *Critical Comparative Law: Considering Paradoxes for Legal Systems in Transition* (1999), p. 86.

[67] For instance, the introduction of the new property regime, strongly influenced by the feminist movement, was 'principally an upper class concern'. BRADLEY, D., *Family Law and Political Culture* (1996), p. 24.

[68] In Finland, the reforms were mainly the result of conservative policy. See BRADLEY, D., 'Equality and Patriarchy: Family Law and Sate Feminism in Finland' (1998), p. 197-212 and 'Antecedents of Finnish Family Laws: Legal Traditions, Political Culture and Social Institutions' (1998), p. 98-110.

[69] GAUNT, D., NYSTRÖM, L., 'The Scandinavian Model' (1996), p. 480. For a more extensive analysis, see: BRADLEY, D., *Family Law and Political Culture* (1996), p. 34- 63.

[70] DAVID, R., 'The International Unification of Private Law' (1971), p. 187.

[71] WENDT, F., *The Nordic Council and Co-operation in Scandinavia* (1959), p. 11.

[72] LOGDBERG, A., 'The Reform of Family Law in the Scandinavian Countries' (1978), p. 201. The co-operation actually continued until the 1960s. Today the legislative co-operation mainly takes shape of mutual consultations and exchange of information on ongoing legislative projects. However, after the turn of the millennium, the Committee of Ministers of the Nordic Council initiated a

Åke Malmström has even suggested that legal co-operation has become a tradition of the Nordic countries and 'a part of the daily life of the Nordic people'.[74]

The role of elites in Portugal, Turkey and the Soviet Union

There are considerable parallels between the reforms of family law in Portugal, the Soviet Union and Turkey. In all these countries, the reforms were the result of revolutionary political change and instigated by a determined *élite dirigeante*. In Portugal, the enactment of liberal family law could be largely attributed to the activities of the women's movement led by the Republican League of Portuguese Women.[75] In Turkey, the reforms were driven by the secular, nationalistic party of Kemal Atatürk. In the Soviet Union, the reforms were carried out by the Bolshevik dictatorship, although in regard to the liberalisation of family law and the emancipation of women, the Bolsheviks shared the ideals of the whole of the progressive elite of the Russian Empire. In all three countries, a vast gap existed between the great majority of the traditional, religious, illiterate, rural population and a small, Westernised, secular and modern elite. In Russia and Turkey this divide was so notable that both countries could, in a way, be said to be inhabited by two different 'peoples'.[76] The elite and the peasantry could hardly understand each other, and had a different mentality and different ideas about family, marriage and divorce. As often occurs at the time of social disruption, both in Russia and in Turkey the elites were engulfed in a kind of instrumentalist fanaticism.[77] They did not hesitate to impose their vision of the future on the rest of the population,[78] whether it liked it or not. Despite their eliterian and top-down character, the reforms did produce lasting social change.

---

comprehensive comparative study of the family law of the Nordic countries. The background of this initiative was 'a general feeling that the developments in recent years had broken down the results of the close Nordic cooperation during the first 70 years of' the last century.' LØDRUP, P., 'Comparative Studies of Nordic Law', *The ISFL Family Letter* (2004), p. 1.

[73]   According to Åke Malmström, 'nowhere in the world have efforts for the unification of law, made on a regional scale, been so successful as in Scandinavia'. MALMSTRÖM, Å., 'Die Zusammenarbeit der nordischen Staaten auf dem Gebiete der Gesetzgebung' (1955), p. 18.

[74]   Ibid, p. 27.

[75]   PHILLIPS, R., *Putting Asunder* (1988), p. 505.

[76]   In Russia this divide goes back to the reforms of Peter the Great, who actually Westernised Russia in the early eighteenth century much in the same manner as Atatürk did in Turkey in the beginning of the 1920s.

[77]   Esin Örücü described the spirit of Atatürk's reforms as 'optimistic normativism'. This implied the 'political belief' in the potential of the large-scale use of law as an instrument of 'social engineering'. ÖRÜCÜ, E., *Critical Comparative Law* (1999), p. 87.

[78]   Esin Örücü concisely dubs this phenomenon the 'paternalistic imposition of purposes'. ÖRÜCÜ, E., 'Turkey: Change Under Pressure' (1996), p. 97.

Portugal: not just a leftist experiment

In Portugal, the reforms did not appear to be just an unsuccessful example of leftist social engineering.[79] Although divorce remained rare even after the liberal law of 1910 came into force, the new legislation grew such roots in Portuguese society that even the right-wing regime of Salazar was not able to repeal it altogether.[80]

Turkey: to a success through lasing discord

In Turkey, a certain discord between the newly transplanted laws and the social practices appeared from the very beginning and has persisted until the present day.[81] The traditional rural population largely ignored the requirement of compulsory registration and continued to live in informal *imam* marriages that were not recognised as legal marriage.[82] The minimum age for marriage was not respected in the rural areas.[83] The State was reluctant to resort to coercion in order to enforce the adherence to marriage law.[84] The judiciary also demonstrated considerable respect for the traditional habits of the population.[85] As a consequence, even today some 32% of all Turkish children are born to informal marriages.[86] Such children were considered illegitimate in respect of their fathers, and had to encounter all the disadvantages of their illegitimate status.[87] The response of the State to these problems was rather flexible. In several instances the transplanted legislation was adapted to the persisting social customs. For example, the minimum age for marriage, originally set at 18 for men and 17 for women, was lowered to 17 and 15, respectively.[88] Such compromise was out of the question with regard to other parts of family legislation, like the total secularisation of marriage, as these were considered 'a monument of fundamental legal and social reform'.[89] Here, the discord between the law in the books and the law in action was smoothed over in a rather inventive manner. The secular legislation remained unamended, but so-called *Amnesty acts* were enacted about

---

[79] PHILLIPS, R., *Putting Asunder* (1988), p. 542.
[80] Ibid.
[81] ANSAY, T., WALLACE, D., *Introduction to Turkish Law* (1996), p. 110.
[82] As a result, even nowadays 'one in twelve marriages are union in the sociological sense alone and not in the legal sense'. ÖRÜCÜ, E., 'Turkey: Change Under Pressure' (1996), p. 97
[83] ÖRÜCÜ, E., 'Turkish Family Law: A New Phase' (1991-92), p. 437.
[84] The punishment that existed for the conclusion of an unregistered marriage was almost never imposed. ÖRÜCÜ, E., 'Turkey: Change Under Pressure' (1996), p. 96-98.
[85] ÖRÜCÜ, E., Critical *Comparative Law: Considering Paradoxes for Legal Systems in Transition* (1999), p. 91.
[86] ÖRÜCÜ, E., 'Turkey: Change Under Pressure' (1996), p. 97
[87] Although for inheritance purposes there has been no difference between the two categories since 1990. ÖRÜCÜ, E., 'Turkish Family Law: A New Phase' (1991-92), p. 437.
[88] ÖRÜCÜ, E., 'Turkey: Change Under Pressure' (1996), p. 98.
[89] Ibid.

every ten years, which legitimised all children born from the traditional informal marriages.[90]

In spite of some remaining discrepancies between the written law and actual social practice, the appreciation in present day Turkey of the effect of the transplanted family legislation is generally very positive. Statistics show that dramatic changes have been brought about even in rural areas.[91] It has been claimed that 'the determination of the Turkish leaders to succeed in their objectives, finally caused the desired alteration of the existing socio-economic structure by the imported legal system'.[92] The slow pace of the implementation of the positive law into social practice could in a way be seen as a compliment to the level of democracy in Turkey. Its rulers did not want to (or perhaps just could not) shape social life by the means of repression. The ultimate success of the reform allowed Esin Örücü to conclude that: 'it cannot be claimed that only trans-cultural and morally neutral rules can be successfully received. The Turkish experience challenges this claim'.[93]

The Soviet Union: progressive family legislation by means of oppression

The Soviet Union stands for a case of radical social engineering by means of family legislation undertaken by a dictatorial regime that knew little, if any, restraint when it came to the use of coercion. The social impact of the Soviet reforms differed depending on the particular area of family law. Some long awaited and broadly supported changes, like the emancipation of women and easy divorce, were an immediate success. The effect of the divorce reform was as if the prison gates had suddenly been opened: during the first months in Moscow alone some 5,000 divorce petitions were filed.[94]

The abolition of Church marriages did not initially take root. The majority of the population was deeply religious. Reading between the lines of the manipulated statistics of that time, it is possible to discern indications that the rural population continued to solemnise marriages in the Church, ignoring the prescribed civil registration.[95] The Bolsheviks considered the secularisation of marriage an important weapon in the battle

---

[90]   Ibid, p. 69.
[91]   STARR, J., POOL, J., 'The impact of the revolution in Rural Turkey'; 8 Law and Society Review (1974), p. 533. Cited by Örücü, in Critical Comparative Law: Considering Paradoxes for Legal Systems in Transition (1999), p. 116.
[92]   BANAKAS, E., 'Some thoughts on the methods of comparative law: the concept of law revised', 67 Archiv für Recht und soziale Philosophie (1981), p. 16694, cited by ÖRÜCÜ, E., in: Critical Comparative Law (1999), p. 116.
[93]   ÖRÜCÜ, E., 'The Impact of European Law on the Ottoman Empire and Turkey' (1992), p. 56.
[94]   GENKIN, D. et al, Istoriia sovetskogo semeinogo prava (1949), p. 419.
[95]   NETCHAEVA, A., Semeinoe prevo (1998), p. 74.

with their ideological opponents. They did not hesitate to use terror and repression against the clergy and the religious population in order to implement civil marriage. The extent of the pressure can be illustrated by the fact that by the end of the 1920s there was hardly any church to go to for the solemnisation of marriage, and hardly any priest left to bless it. After this successful 'social engineering', the risk had disappeared that as soon as the requirement of State registration of marriage was relaxed, the population would resort to Church ceremonies. The communists proudly announced their victory over the 'religious superstition of the population'. This opened the gates for further experiments, and in 1926 informal marriage was given the status of legal marriage.[96] This innovation soon turned into a custom; in the 1920s and 1930s it became the fashion of the day not to go through a marriage ceremony. Marrying was considered something for backward peasants; the communist establishment lived in free unions.

This rather peculiar combination of progressive family legislation and dictatorial methods of its implementation made it difficult to properly appreciate the place of the Soviet radical reforms in the overall development of family law in Europe. Some scholars, such as for instance Max Rheinstein, consider these reforms merely excesses of the revolutionary period with rather limited importance.[97] Others, like Roderick Phillips, are of the view that the Soviet reforms had 'an immediate and enduring impact in social and political thought in Western Europe'.[98] This because these reforms were 'the first translations into law of the ideas of the Western socialists on marriage, divorce, women, and the family'.[99]

In my view, the Soviet reforms were indeed of enduring significance for European family law, not so much because they 'translated' socialist ideology into positive law, but rather because they implemented the ideas of the broad Western progressive movement as a whole.[100] It is possible to delineate three distinctive components of the ideological background of the reforms: radical secularism,[101] liberal individual-

---

[96] RAEVICH, S., *Brachnoe i semeinoe pravo* (1927), p. 426.
[97] RHEINSTEIN, M., *Marriage Stability, Divorce, and the Law* (1972), p. 231-243.
[98] PHILLIPS, R., *Putting Asunder* (1988), p. 534.
[99] Ibid, p. 514.
[100] Phillips acknowledges this: 'Soviet family policy [...] found support – qualified and unqualified – across the liberal and socialist spectrum in Europe and America. It responded to liberal and socialist hostility to the oppressive character of bourgeois marriage, and complemented the socialist feminist critiques of Western family institutions and practices. In this sense the Soviet experiments [...] reinforced the individualistic tendencies of the Lefts' analysis of the family'. PHILLIPS, R., *Putting Asunder* (1988), p. 538.
[101] The secularisation of family law as such was broadly desired across the socialist and liberal spectrum. Of course, the Bolsheviks turned it into an excessive and bloody exercise that few would have stood for.

ism[102] and the idea of the 'withering away' of the 'bourgeois' family. Only the later element was of purely socialist origin.[103] As I have argued elsewhere,[104] although some of the Soviet innovations could rightly be called excessive,[105] the essence of the reforms was exactly in line with the general evolution of family law in Europe. Because of these reforms, Soviet family law had already, in the 1920s, attained a level of modernity that several European countries have not yet reached today. In my view, the Soviet reforms of the 1920s could best be appreciated as the same kind of radical modernisation breakthrough as the French revolutionary legislation of 1792. The reforms of the 1920s, even after their partial repeal by Stalin in 1944, were of lasting influence to the development of family law, not only in Eastern Europe but also in the West.[106]

Cultural and other restraints revisited

As was already announced at the end of Chapter 7, the early twentieth century reforms in Turkey and the Soviet Union can add empirical proof to the proposition, made on the basis of the history of the unification of family law by the medieval Catholic Church.[107] This proposition was that cultural constraints do not necessarily preclude a radical family law reform from being successful on the level of actual social practices. As with the medieval unification, both Turkish and Soviet reforms suggest that there are few limits to what is feasible, provided one is not restrained by the rules of democracy and the respect of human rights.[108] The rapid implementation of the reforms in the Soviet Union was obviously to a large extent the result of large-scale

---

[102]   Liberal individualism was generally alien to Bolshevist ideology. It was, however, temporarily borrowed from liberal thought and employed in the reform of family law.

[103]   Some young communists from the first 'romantic' generation, led by prominent feminists such as Inesse Armand and Alexandra Kollontay, who held important positions in the Bolsheviks' government, believed that under communism marriage would completely die out and make place for free sexual relationships (KOLLONTAY, A., *Sem'ia i kommunisticheskoe gosudarstvo* (1918), p. 9 and ELWOOD, R., *Inesse Armand: Revolutionary and Feminist* (1992). A more moderate group, which was supported by Lenin, suggested, in accordance with the writings of Engels, that only 'bourgeois' marriage and family would die out in order to be replaced by a 'higher form of the family,' freed from financial considerations and male dominance. See: LENIN, V., *Letter to I.F. Armand of 24 January 1915* (1964), p. 56. For a synopsis of this discussion see: MATWEEV, G., *Semeinoe pravo* (1985), p. 25-29.

[104]   ANTOKOLSKAIA, M., 'De ontwikkeling van het Russische familierecht vanaf de Bolsjewistische revolutie: een poging tot verklaring' (2002), p. 137-171.

[105]   For instance, the judicial establishment of paternity that offered the putative father no realistic opportunity to deny his fatherhood.

[106]   According to Sundberg, the early Soviet reforms served as one of the models for the Swedish law of 1973 that introduced divorce on demand. SUNDBERG, J., 'Marriage or no Marriage. The Directives for the Revision of Swedish Family Law' (1971), p. 233.

[107]   See Section 7.3.

[108]   It should be added that, as Wolfram Müller-Freienfels correctly points out, results produced by compulsion are often 'Pyrrhic victories'. MÜLLER-FREIENFELS, W., 'The Unification of Family Law' (1968-69), p. 183.

coercion. The totalitarian Soviet State simply employed as much repression as was needed to achieve its goals. Where the Turkish authorities preferred to hold back at a certain point, the Bolsheviks did not hesitate to press on all the way. But in the end, the Turkish reforms seem to have been hardly less successful. Again, it is suggested that the outer limits of instrumentalist methods are merely of an ethical and political nature. The question is not whether it is possible to impose certain changes using law as an instrument, but rather how far one is able and prepared to go. At the same time, the positive example of the Nordic region shows that the radical reform of family law does not necessarily entail such dubious assessments. Provided that such is in line with the developments of society and that there is sufficient support from the population, a far reaching change of family law is quite attainable without compromising the imperatives of democracy and human rights.

11.3. FAMILY LAW DURING THE INTERBELLUM, WORLD WAR II, AND AFTER THE WAR

11.3.1. CORRELATION BETWEEN THE POLITICAL COLOUR OF THE REGIMES AND THEIR FAMILY POLICY

The family law policies of the 1930s closely followed the vicissitudes of the political developments of this dark age. During the interwar period, almost half of Europe came under dictatorial rule. Roderic Philips suggests a strong correlation between the political orientation of the regimes and their legislative policies towards marriage and divorce.[109] He associates restrictive family law policies with fascist and reactionary regimes, and a liberal approach with regimes, inspired by the socialist movement and the example of the Soviet Union.[110] In reality, however, the picture was somewhat more complicated than this simple opposition suggests. If one would like to draw a general line, it seems more correct to suggest a correlation between reactionary policies in family law and all dictatorial regimes, no matter whether they were rightist-fascists or leftist-communists.

In **Portugal,** a reactionary ultra-Catholic dictatorship was established in 1926. Immediately, two unsuccessful attempts were undertaken to repeal the liberal revolutionary divorce law altogether. After these failed, the Catholics, who formed the vast majority of the population, were deprived of the right to divorce after the

---

[109]   PHILLIPS, R., *Putting Asunder* (1988), p. 534.
[110]   Ibid.

Government signed the Concordat of 1940.[111] They were obliged to renounce their civil right of divorce when entering into a Catholic marriage.[112] Dictatorship in Portugal survived long after World War II. As late as in 1966 the new Civil Code abolished divorce by mutual consent, which had still been possible for non-Catholics, and replaced it with a fault-based divorce.[113]

In **Spain,** the Republic was proclaimed in 1931. The Republican Constitution contained the right to divorce.[114] The promulgation of the law on divorce, however, resulted in a bitter controversy between progressive republicans and conservative Catholics.[115] In 1932, the Republican government managed to adopt a liberal divorce law.[116] Divorce was permitted upon, among others,[117] mutual consent, two years of de-facto separation, if both spouses applied for divorce, and three years of de-facto separation, if only one of them did.[118] The law of 28 July 1932 reintroduced obligatory civil marriage,[119] and proclaimed the 'equality of rights of both spouses'. The fascist government of Franco, which seized power in 1938, immediately suspended the divorce law,[120] and a year later[121] abrogated it with retroactive effect.[122] As in Portugal, the dictatorship also survived World War II and lasted until the death of Franco in 1975. Thus, divorce disappeared from Spanish law for over 40 years.[123] Obligatory civil marriage was also abolished.[124] In 1941, Church marriage was made de-facto

---

[111] Article 24.
[112] OLIVEIRA, G., DE, *National Report for Portugal* (2003), p. 47.
[113] SOTTOMAYOR, M., 'The Introduction and Impact of Joint Custody in Portugal' (1999), p. 248.
[114] Art. 43 stated that: 'marriage is based upon equality of right of both sexes and can be dissolved by mutual consent, or upon the petition of any of both spouses pleading the existence of a ground'. MARTÍN-CASALS, M., *Spanish Report concerning the CEFL Questionnaire on Grounds for Divorce and Maintenance Between Former Spouses,* http://www.law.uu.nl/priv/cefl, p. 5.
[115] LANGNER, D., *Eheschließung und Ehescheidung nach spanischem Recht* (1984), p. 7-8.
[116] Divorce law of 2 March 1932. It is interesting to notice that the draft of Article 43 of the Republican Constitution originally contained a kind of 'positive discrimination' provision granting a wife the possibility to divorce her husband 'through free volition' while a husband could divorce his wife only 'with assertion of just cause'. The reason for this provision was that 'many women were too timid to present the proofs required in a divorce case' and the only way to enable them to use the facility of divorce was to allow them to divorce without alleging a cause. This proposal did not scrape through and in the final version the spouses were granted an equal right to divorce each other. GLICK, T., 'Sexual Reforms, Psychoanalysis, and the Politics of Divorce in Spain in the 1920 end 1930s' (2003), p. 89.
[117] Divorce was also possible upon thirteen specific grounds listed in article 3.
[118] LANGNER, D., *Eheschließung und Ehescheidung nach spanischem Recht* (1984), p. 9.
[119] Ibid, p. 8.
[120] By decree of 2 March 1938.
[121] By the law of 23 September 1939.
[122] PHILLIPS, R., *Putting Asunder* (1988), p. 541.
[123] MARTÍN-CASALS, M., *National Report for Spain* (2003), p. 51.
[124] By law of 12 March 1938.

obligatory, as the civil marriage remained open only to the small minority of population who could prove not to have been baptised Catholic.[125]

In **Italy,** the fascist regime of Mussolini replaced obligatory civil marriage with a dual system introduced by the Concordat of 1929.[126] The jurisdiction over separation of bed and board and marriage annulment was partly transferred from the secular to the ecclesiastical courts.[127] Max Rheinstein has rightly concluded that thereby, the secularisation of marriage was in part undone.[128] Divorce was abolished even in the former Austrian territories that had been annexed after World War I, where it was previously allowed for non-Catholics.[129] The Code of 1942 'faithfully reflected the ideological vision, embraced by the Fascist regime',[130] and was characterised by a 'family strongly structured by the Fascist regime, the principle of parental control taking precedence within it over that of individual autonomy'.[131]

In **Austria,** the pseudo-fascist government, that came into power after the February Uprising of 1934, the same year signed a Concordat, which fully restored Church authority in matrimonial matters.[132] In 1941,[133] the Vichy government of **France** prohibited application for divorce during the first three years of marriage.[134] In **Greece,** a drafting committee, appointed by the dictatorial regime of General Metaxas, revised in a conservative fashion the provisions on family law that were part of the previously prepared liberal draft of the Civil Code. The conservative draft was promulgated in 1940, but due to the occupation did not come into force. After the liberation of Greece a new, more progressive Code was drafted and enacted under a liberal government in 1945. But after the installation of a conservative government in 1946, the code of 1945 was repealed and the conservative Code of 1940 was re-enacted.[135]

In the **Soviet Union,** Stalin's regime substantially turned back the liberal reforms of the 1920s. Homosexual acts between consenting adults were made a criminal offence

---

[125]   LANGNER, D., *Eheschließung und Ehescheidung nach spanischem Recht* (1984), p. 15.
[126]   RHEINSTEIN, M., *Marriage Stability, Divorce, and the Law* (1972), p. 163.
[127]   PHILLIPS, R., *Putting Asunder* (1988), p. 546.
[128]   RHEINSTEIN, M., *Marriage Stability, Divorce, and the Law* (1972), p. 167.
[129]   SGRITTA, G., TUFARI, P., 'Italy' (1977), p. 258.
[130]   POCAR, V., RONFANI, P., 'Family Law in Italy: Legislative Innovations and Social Change' (1978), p. 608.
[131]   POCAR, V., RONFANI, P., 'Family Law in Italy: Legislative Innovations and Social Change' (1978), p. 608.
[132]   HALLER, M., 'Austria' (1977), p. 212.
[133]   Law of 2 April 1941. Carbonnier connected this Law with the increase of Catholic influence during the Vichy regime. CARBONNIER, J., *Droit civil: La famille, l'enfant, le couple* (2002), p. 536.
[134]   FOYER, J., 'The Reform of Family Law in France' (1978), p.103. This provision was repealed in 1945. Ibid.
[135]   ARGYRIADIS, A., 'Reform of Family Law in Greece' (1978), p. 140-141.

in 1934.[136] Marriage and divorce law became less permissive[137] in 1944.[138] Obligatory civil registration of marriage regained its importance, and informal marriage lost its legal standing. Church celebration was not formally forbidden, but those who resorted to it risked their life and freedom. The easy administrative divorce procedure was replaced by a cumbersome judicial procedure in which courts of two instances were involved. The court of first instance could merely act as a conciliator. Only the court of second instance was entitled to grant a divorce, after a thorough inquiry as to whether the marriage had indeed been irretrievably broken down. The position of illegitimate children deteriorated dramatically. The acknowledgement of children, born outside wedlock, as well as the judicial establishment of paternity, was altogether forbidden. Even maintenance claims on behalf of natural children were no longer rendered possible. The libertarian spirit of the 1920s gave way to unlimited State interference, justified by the official propaganda of the day as 'strengthening the socialist family as a basic cell of socialist society'. The spirit of the Soviet family law of those days is perhaps best epitomised by the following statement of Sverdlov, one of the most influential scholars of that time: 'the Socialist State rejects the interpretation of the relationships between the sexes as individualistic, personal and neutral for society and the State. The State dictates the rules and determines these relationships in order to safeguard the interests of the society and to enforce the fulfilment of the duties in regard of society'.[139] In Portugal, Spain, Italy, Austria and France, restrictive family policy was related to the rightist governments' aspirations to conform to the doctrines of the Catholic Church. In the Soviet Union, by contrast, the conservative backlash had nothing to do with religion. The association of conservative family policy with religion is so strong, that Max Rheinstein was inclined to search for the roots of Stalin's counter-reform in the 'survival of Christian tradition'.[140] In my view, this was not the case at all. Stalin's conservative policy can be explained perfectly in terms of 'purely secular statism', the second underlying motive suggested by Rheinstein.[141] The communists' brief flirt with individual freedom in family matters was over. As the desire of the totalitarian regime grew to bring all corners of society under its control, 'the socialist family' had to submit to the needs of society as defined by the State.[142] Thus, the focal point of family law policy shifted from the individual to the communitarian.

---

[136]   ALEKSEEV, N., *Pravovoe regulirovanie polozgenia sexual'nikh men'shinstv* (2002), p. 198.
[137]   This was a step back in relation to the Law of 1926, but compared to the average European standard of those days, what remained was still a very liberal divorce law.
[138]   Ukase of 8 July 1944.
[139]   SVERDLOV, G., *O predmete i sisteme sotsialisticheskogo semeinogo prava* (1941), p. 58.
[140]   RHEINSTEIN, M., *Marriage Stability, Divorce, and the Law* (1972), p. 236.
[141]   Ibid.
[142]   See ANTOKOLSKAIA, M., 'De ontwikkeling van het Russische familierecht vanaf de Bolsjewistische revolutie: een poging tot verklaring' (2002), p. 137-151.

Nazi **Germany** was to some extent a case apart. The Marriage and Divorce Act (*Ehegesetz*) of 1938[143] liberalised divorce law and introduced, alongside the old fault grounds, divorce on the ground of the irretrievable breakdown of marriage. The German circumstances in some ways resembled the Soviet reforms of the 1920s; in both instances a totalitarian regime instigated a liberal divorce reform. Just as early Soviet divorce policy was not the product of communist ideology alone; neither was the German divorce reform a product of Nazi ideology alone. One of its principle sources was the 'reform ideas developed during the 1920s not least of all by modern social investigations, undogmatic secular value judgements and comparative reference to the Nordic countries and Switzerland'.[144] Nonetheless, the typically Nazi preoccupation with racial purity and eugenics was also traceable in the new German law, as it was also to facilitate divorce from a non-Arian spouse.[145] How much the concept of no-fault divorce was at odds with the conservative family ideology of the time can be illustrated by the fact that in 1946 the Allied Control Council restricted the application of the German provisions on divorce upon the irretrievable breakdown of marriage by a hardship clause.[146]

Another special case was **Ireland**. A highly restrictive family law was introduced there, not by a totalitarian dictatorship but by a nationalistic democratic government. After the liberation from British rule in 1922, it was formally still possible to obtain divorce in Ireland by a private act of the *Oireachtas*, the newly established Irish Parliament.[147] However, the Government 'expressly disregarded' any divorce bill brought before the Parliament and thereby effectively banned divorce without changing the legislation.[148] The 1937 Constitution prohibited not only divorce as such, but even the future enacting of any divorce law.[149] Its creator Eamon De Valera[150] – the 'father of modern Ireland'[151] – could in some respects be seen as an antipode of Kemal Atatürk. His role in shaping the free Irish State was comparable to that of Atatürk in respect of Turkey. But, while Atatürk devoted himself to turning Turkey into a modern, open, Western

---

[143] Also applicable in Austria after it had become part of Germany by the *Anschluss* of 1938.

[144] MÜLLER-FREIENFELS, W., 'Family Law and the Law of Succession in Germany' (1967), p. 412.

[145] PHILLIPS, R., *Putting Asunder* (1988), p. 550.

[146] Divorce upon this ground could be granted only 'if the proper interests of any minor children of the marriage does not require the denial of the divorce petition'. MÜLLER-FREIENFELS, W., 'Family Law and the Law of Succession in Germany' (1967), p. 441.

[147] SHATTER, A., *Family Law in the Republic of Ireland* (1986), p. 238-239.

[148] JAMES, C., 'Cead Mile Failte. Ireland Welcomes Divorce: The 1995 Irish Divorce Referendum and the Family (Divorce) Act of 1996' (1997), Lexis.

[149] According to the art. 41.3.2. 'No law be enacted providing for the grant of a dissolution of marriage'.

[150] The Constitution of 1937 is reputed to be written by De Valera 'almost single-handedly'. De Valera was the President of Ireland of that time and the founder of Fianna Fail – Ireland's largest party. Ibid, note 1.

[151] Ibid, note 1.

secular State, the ambition of the 'staunch Catholic and Nationalist'[152] De Valera was to make independent Ireland an autarchic[153] 'Catholic state for Catholic people'.[154] Atatürk borrowed Western family law in an attempt to create a new cultural identity for the Turkish people. De Valera, by contrast, built his Constitution upon the 'socio-religious mores of the country'.[155] The colonial submission to Protestant Britain had turned Catholicism for Ireland into a 'force of mythic impact'.[156] This made Catholicism a much more prominent part of the national identity[157] than was the case in other predominantly Catholic countries like Italy or Spain.[158] Accordingly, the new Constitution represented 'a synthesis of Catholic social principles',[159] including the prohibition of divorce, the recognition of the paramount importance of the family, special care for the institution of marriage,[160] and the desire to confine married women to home.[161] The State prohibition of divorce was even more drastic than that of the Roman Catholic Church itself.[162] The ban on divorce was criticised for imposing the Roman Catholic teaching on marriage on the non-Roman Catholic minority. The 1937 Constitution successfully delayed the modernisation of Irish family law, until the very end of the twentieth century.[163]

---

[152] BURLEY, J., REGAN, F., 'Divorce in Ireland: the Fear, the Floodgates and the Reality' (2002), p. 204.

[153] Self-sufficiency became one of the 'dominant objectives' of Irish policy. Dillon, M., *Debating Divorce. Moral Conflict in Ireland* (1993), p. 22.

[154] BURLEY, J., REGAN, F., 'Divorce in Ireland: the Fear, the Floodgates and the Reality' (2002), p. 204.

[155] JAMES, C., 'Cead Mile Failte. Ireland Welcomes Divorce: The 1995 Irish Divorce Referendum and the Family (Divorce) Act of 1996' (1997), Lexis. In De Valera's own words 'there is a stage in the life of every community in which its customs as well as its philosophy of life pass into laws. A system of law which is divorced from the convictions, the beliefs and spiritual character of a people is in no sense a national code'. Ibid.

[156] Ibid.

[157] According to Dillon, 'Catholicism and Irishness thus became intertwined as synonyms and gave the Irish people an inflated sense of social value grounded in a collective, rigorously Catholic identity'. DILLON, M., *Debating Divorce. Moral Conflict in Ireland* (1993), p. 14.

[158] PRICE, C., 'Finding Fault with Irish Divorce Law' (1997), lexis.

[159] DILLON, M., *Debating Divorce. Moral Conflict in Ireland* (1993), p. 23.

[160] Art. 41.3.1.

[161] Art. 41.3.2.

[162] It did not allow the few instances of divorce admitted by the Catholic Church: the so-called *Pauline* and *Petrine* privileges. Also it was more rigid than the Church in proclaiming a marriage null and void. For mote details see: SHATTER, A., *Family Law in the Republic of Ireland* (1986), p. 140-142.

[163] As Dillon has put it: 'As Irish society became more "backward" relative to its modern, industrialised neighbours, the superiority of rural life and traditional values [...] became the cultural paradigm venerated by political and Church leaders'. DILLON, M., *Debating Divorce. Moral Conflict in Ireland* (1993), p. 22.

11.3.2. LAW IN THE BOOKS VERSUS LAW IN ACTION: DIVORCE BY COLLUSION

A notable development in many European countries during the interwar period was the growing de-facto accessibility of divorce. This was brought about by a combination of the de-stigmatisation of divorce and the creeping relaxation of statutory and, especially, case law. Even countries with a relatively restrictive divorce law, solely providing for divorce upon matrimonial offence, found themselves confronted with the emergence of large-scale consensual divorce by collusion. As a result, a sharp discrepancy occurred between the restrictive divorce law in the books and the effects of its application in practice.[164] Max Rheinstein called this situation a 'democratic compromise',[165] although perhaps one could more appropriately call it a 'hypocritical compromise'. The conservatives were content with the restrictive laws in the books and the liberals with the permissive law in action.[166]

In **France**, case law was mainly responsible for this change. The statutory divorce grounds remained unaltered, but the courts started to interpret these grounds, such as 'injury' or 'bodily harm', more extensively.[167] The courts were more inclined to consider these relative grounds sufficient for proof that a marriage had become intolerable for the spouses. As adultery was an absolute ground for divorce, it presented the easiest way to divorce by collusion. A consenting couple simply agreed that the wife would falsely accuse the husband (as male adultery was socially more acceptable) and that he would not oppose her claim.[168]

In **England**, where adultery also constituted an absolute ground for divorce, the situation started to resemble the French one from 1923 onwards. In that year, a wife was allowed to seek divorce on the ground of non-aggravated adultery by the husband. As Lawrence Stone had put it, this 'made it easy for the rich to divorce by mutual consent'.[169] The reform of 1937, which introduced some additional fault grounds, like three-year desertion and cruelty, along with a no-fault divorce for insanity; only

---

[164] As Glendon has put it: 'in fact, the revolution in divorce law was already under way well before [...the] legislatures began to change the law in the books'. GLENDON, M.A., *Abortion and Divorce in Western Law* (1987), p. 65.

[165] RHEINSTEIN, M., *Marriage Stability, Divorce, and the Law* (1972), p. 247 ff.

[166] GORECKI, J., 'Moral Premises of Contemporary Divorce Laws: Western and Eastern Europe and the United States' (1980), p. 125.

[167] FOYER, J., 'The Reform of Family Law in France' (1978), p. 103.

[168] 'Spouses agreed on divorce, they then invented fictitious grievances, wrote letters about false injuries, sometimes dictated by their respective lawyers, and the judges closed their eyes to the comedy'. Ibid.

[169] 'The way it was done was for the husband to provide his wife with evidence of his adultery by a procedure known as a "hotel bill case"'. STONE, L., *Road to Divorce* (1990), p. 397.

reinforced the tendency towards consensual divorce by collusion.[170] The Church of England expressed its disapproval of divorce by forbidding divorced persons to remarry before the Church.[171]

As described above, **Germany** had, since 1938, a mixed system of fault grounds and divorce on the basis of irretrievable breakdown. However, divorce upon the irretrievable breakdown of marriage without allegation of fault was far more time-consuming than a fault-based divorce.[172] Divorce upon mutual consent could be granted only after three years of separation, while a fault divorce could be obtained without delay. It appeared that when the spouses agreed upon divorce, they preferred not to wait for three years, but resorted to an immediate, easy divorce on the ground of some 'trumped-up matrimonial offence'.[173] It has been emphasised that 'the fact that 80 to 90 percent of divorce actions brought on the ground of adultery or some other matrimonial offence resulting from such collusion emphasises the wide gap between law and reality'.[174]

11.3.3. AFTER WORLD WAR II: THE FINAL DAYS OF THE TRADITIONAL FAMILY

After the Second World War, the century-old canon law doctrines and the concept of the authoritarian patriarchal family still largely formed the ideological basis of family laws. The opponents of modernisation continued to rely on transpersonalistic argumentation. In line with a centuries old way of thinking, they tended to give the abstract interests of society as envisaged by the old dogmas priority over the interests of the individuals. An illustrative example is the following statement of the Dutch Minister of Justice, made during a debate on the position of illegitimate children in 1947:

> The acceptance of monogamous marriage as the only socially recognised form of cohabitation of man and woman logically entails that a difference must be made between children born in and out of wedlock [...]. Not because the legislator does not have any compassion with these indeed innocent children [...] *but because the*

---

[170]   Ninety percent undefended petitions allowed strong suggestion of collusion. STONE, L., *Road to Divorce* (1990), p. 401.

[171]   A.P. Herbert's Act 1937. BAKER, J., *An Introduction to English Legal History* (2002), p. 497.

[172]   However, matrimonial offences were not absolute grounds for divorce and it was necessary to prove matrimonial breakdown irrespective of whether divorce was sought on fault grounds or objective ones, the courts were not very strict with the proof in not contested cases. MÜLLER-FREIENFELS, W., 'Family Law and the Law of Succession in Germany' (1967), p. 436.

[173]   Ibid, p. 441.

[174]   GIESEN, D., 'Divorce Reform in Germany' (1973), p. 353.

interest of society as a whole in the preservation of the respect for the institute of marriage, has priority over the individual interests of those persons.[175]

As one can see, an unequivocal manifestation of transpersonalism *pur sang*. It is exactly this way of thinking about the position of the family and the individual that was still completely conventional right after the war, but would soon lose its self-evident character forever.

The family law of most of Europe was, at least on paper, hardly more permissive than it had been at the time of the Reformation. The popularity of marriage as such had only been growing; in the 1950s, the marriage 'had not been so close to universal [...] in Western Europe for at least two centuries'.[176] Extramarital sex was still more or less taboo. Concubinage had no legal standing, and illegitimate children, despite some improvements of their position, suffered many social and legal disadvantages. There had been a significant improvement in the position of women in public life, which was generally reflected in public law. Women were entitled to vote and had proven to be able to substitute men in the work place during two wars. But this emancipation hardly touched the position of women in private life. In most of Europe,[177] a married woman was still under the authority, albeit somewhat moderated, of the 'head of the family', her husband.[178] Divorce law, at least the law in the books, had in most countries become hardly more lenient than the first-generation divorce laws introduced during the Reformation. Fault-based divorce existed in thirteen Western European countries, divorce upon the irretrievable breakdown of marriage in seven, divorce upon mutual consent in six, and four countries allowed no divorce at all.[179]

Thus, on the eve of the boisterous sixties, only one family form – legitimate family based on a monogamous life-long marriage – and only one uniform set of traditional family values were accepted, the rest was considered dissidence. Nothing seemed to threaten this status quo. But this was merely the quiet before the storm.

---

[175] ASSER-WIARDA (1957), p. 496-497 (translation mine, emphasis added).
[176] FESTY, P., 'On the New Context of Marriage in Western Europe. Data and Perspectives' (1980), p. 311.
[177] Generally only the Nordic and Eastern-European countries and West Germany had already equalised the rights of the spouses.
[178] MÜLLER-FREIENFELS, W., 'Equality of Husband and Wife in Family Law' (1959), p. 254.
[179] PHILLIPS, R., *Putting Asunder* (1988), p. 570.

PART IV
CURRENT FAMILY LAW:
SWEEPING MODERNISATION

Breakthrough of uniformity
or self-reproducing diversity?

CHAPTER 12
THE BACKGROUND OF THE REFORMS

12.1. INTRODUCTION

12.1.1. RADICAL CHANGES IN FAMILY PATTERNS

The storm came in the last half of the twentieth century. The family revolution of the 1960s and 1970s brought about cultural and legislative changes comparable with the family law reforms that followed the French and Russian revolutions.[1] Consequently, by the end of the millennium the monopoly of the traditional marriage-based family, which seemed to have been so universal and everlasting, had all but gone[2] – a situation that is considered almost as self-evident today as it had been unthinkable for centuries. The society dominated by traditional values gave way to a pluralistic society, one in which different family forms and different sets of family values co-exist alongside each other.[3] Divorce and serial monogamy began to be considered normal. In this general atmosphere of tolerance, men and women became more and more free to choose between marriage or some other form of affective relationship. Extramarital sex, non-marital cohabitation and birth outside wedlock lost their stigmatic character. Non-marital cohabitation (concubinage) made its re-entrance on the legal stage after more than thousand years of disdain. Moreover, same-sex relationships became first decriminalised, then legalised, and then, in some countries, even equated with marriage. Due to the fact that more and more children were born outside marriage, it became increasingly unacceptable for the legal status of these children to differ from that of children born in a marriage. Thus, eventually illegitimate children were granted a truly equal place alongside their legitimate brothers and sisters. This equalisation stripped marriage of one of its greatest advantages above cohabitation, that of

---

[1] Mary Ann Glendon sums up that 'not one of the basic assumptions [...]' of the traditional Western family law has survived this period unchanged. '[...] most have been eliminated and some have been replaced by opposite principles'. GLENDON, M.A., *The New Family and the New Property* (1981), p. 101.

[2] For instance in the Netherlands, in 2000, only 27% of the population still saw the traditional family as their ideal. LIEFBROER, A., 'Het gezinsideaal: Van traditioneel naar modern' (2002), p. 8.

[3] Mary Ann Glendon emphasises that 'Modern family law has recognised both the family behaviour of groups it previously ignored and the diversity in the family behaviour of its traditional clientele'. GLENDON, M.A., *The New Family and the New Property* (1981), p. 109.

providing children with the status of legitimacy,[4] and made cohabitation all the more an equal alternative. The women's rights movement managed to overcome the centuries-long dominance of the man within the family. As result of these developments, the family acquired a new structure: 'more horizontal and more equal, more contractual [and], more centred on the production of identities than around transmission of goods'.[5] The 'conservative camp' experienced these changes as a token of an overall crisis of the family: a symptom of decline, decadence, triumph of individualism and egoism.[6] The 'progressive camp' welcomed the changes as a sign of emancipation, freedom and tolerance.[7] They submitted that the 'crisis' was only 'a legal one'[8] and resulted not from the relaxation of morals, but rather from unsatisfactory legal means. According to them, the nuclear family (if one also included informal cohabitation) 'was flourishing as never before'.[9]

12.1.2. THE INFLUENCE OF HUMAN RIGHTS LAW

European Convention on Human Rights: Article 8 – 'A whole code of family law'

Another important aspect of the discussed period is the gradual increase of the harmonising influence of the growing body of human rights law on the family law of the European States. By far the most important among the human rights instruments was the 1950 European Convention for Human Rights and Fundamental Freedoms. The European Court of Human Rights (ECHR) was both accused and praised for deriving 'a whole code of family law'[10] from its Article 8, which initially contained no more than a negative obligation on the part of the State to refrain from arbitrary interference in the family.[11] In developing the concept of family rights, the ECHR had to use the so-called 'dynamic interpretation' of the Convention. Because the text of all three articles relating to family rights (8 (protection of family life), 12 (right to marry and to found a family) and 14 (prohibition of discrimination)) did not always provide relief, the Court, in deciding cases, had to involve factors which were external to the Convention, and considered that 'the Convention must be interpreted in the

---

4   GLENDON, M.A., *The Transformation of Family Law* (1989), p. 285.
5   MARTIN, C., THÉRY, I., 'The PACS and Marriage and Cohabitation in France' (2001), p. 155.
6   Ibid.
7   Ibid.
8   ANDRUP, H., BUCHHOFER, B., ZIEGERT, K., 'Formal Marriage Under the Crossfire of Social Change' (1980), p. 32.
9   Ibid.
10   Dissenting opinion of Judge Sir Gerald Fitzmaurice in *Marckx v. Belgium*. ECHR (1979).
11   On the drafting and the initial meaning of the ECHR see the excellent work of Deirdre Van GRUNDERBEECK. VAN GRUNDERBEECK, D., *Beginselen van personen- en familierecht. Een mensenrechtelijke benadering* (2003), p. 22-28 and 37-51.

light of present-day conditions'.[12] Since the political mandate of the Court was indubitable only within the margins of the Convention, it needed an additional source of authorisation every time it employed an extensive or even contra-legal interpretation of the original provisions. In seeking such authorisation, the ECHR generally referred to the consensus or the 'common European standard' among the Contracting States.[13] Naturally, an overall consensus almost never existed; if such unanimity had existed, the case probably would never have been brought before the Court.[14] Neither should one forget that the Court had to decide its cases in a Europe divided by conservative and progressive family ideologies, nor that the composition of the judges, representing the Contracting States, reflected this divide. As a result of this ideological controversy, when the Court was called to make a value judgment it often had no 'standard that enable[d] it to prefer one system to another, so that it could not do much more than check whether the national authorities' decision was a reasonable one'.[15] Furthermore, the international protection of human rights under the Convention is considered subsidiary to the national protection offered by the sovereign states.[16] One thing or another obliged the Court to be cautious in using its power. One of the vehicles that balanced the need for a gradual extension of the protection of family rights and the self-restraint of the Court's power was the doctrine of 'margin of appreciation'.[17] The case law of the ECHR shows that the Court as a rule tended to grant the Contracting States a wide margin of appreciation in cases where no or little consensus between the Member States was established and, as a broader consensus was found, the Court would narrow the scope of the margin.[18] The innovative force of the decisions of the ECHR was significantly weakened by the fact that the ECHR normally vested the rank of 'common ground' just above the lowest common denominator. The ECHR was also accused of misusing the margin of appreciation doctrine in order to avoid difficult political dilemmas.[19]

---

[12]   *Marckx v. Belgium*. ECHR (1979), para. 41
[13]   CAROZZA, G., 'Propter Honoris Respectum: Uses and Misuses of Comparative Law in International Human Rights: Some Reflections of the Jurisprudence of the European Court of Human Rights' (1998), p. 1231-1232.
[14]   Ibid. p. 1228.
[15]   SAPIENZA, R., 'Sul margine d'apprezzamento statale nel sistema della Convenzione Europea dei Diritti de' Uomo', (1991), *Rivista di Diritto Internazionale*, p. 605-606, cited in BREMS, E., *Human Rights: Universality and Diversity*, Nijhoff, the Hague (2001), at p. 361.
[16]   MACDONALD, R. et al (eds.) *The European System for the Protection of Human Rights* (1993), p. 87; MAHONEY, P., 'Marvellous Richness of Diversity or Invidious Cultural Relativism?'(1998), p. 2.
[17]   Ibid, p. 3–4.
[18]   See also: MACDONALD, R. et al (eds.) *The European System for the Protection of Human Rights* (1993), p. 84 and 123; ARAI, Y., 'The Margin of Appreciation Doctrine in the Jurisprudence of Article 8 of the European Convention on Human Rights' (1998), p. 57.
[19]   MAHONEY, P., 'Marvellous Richness of Diversity or Invidious Cultural Relativism?' (1998), p. 1.

One thing is clear: as long as the ECHR seeks support for its innovative solutions in the broad consensus between the Contacting States, the level of the protection of family rights developed this way will never become a true vehicle of modernisation. The 'narrow and traditional' concept of the family developed this way by ECHR case law was rightly stressed by Claire McGlynn.[20] As the following analysis will show, all of the most far-reaching decisions have been passed by the ECHR when it dared to abandon the safe ground of common core and to support the progressive standpoint of the vanguard of the European countries. Because the scope of protection of family rights under the Convention has been developed by the Court on an unsystematic case-by-case basis, the level of protection that is actually attained in various fields of family law is also quite uneven. As the further examples will show, it varies from the lowest common denominator in respect of the right of divorce, to a high degree of protection with regard to the equality of marital and extramarital children and the right to marry on the part of post-operative transsexuals.

European Union protection of family related human rights

A great deal of the above analysis with respect to the case law of the European Court of Human Rights could be equally applied to the case law of the European Court of Justice (ECJ). The long road towards the recognition of EU capacity in respect of human rights,[21] especially those related to family law and the subjection of the protection of the family to the economic goals of the Union, had its impact on the development of EU policy regarding family rights.[22] The ECJ is also restrained by the subsidiarity principle and often seeks additional authorisation in the consensus argument.[23] The low level of protection offered to family rights in some areas has more than once been criticised.[24]

The 2000 non-binding EU Charter,[25] which has been incorporated into the unratified EU Constitution[26] as a Human Rights Chapter, is important for our purposes because it is alleged to present 'a fully up-to-date *Ius Commune Europaeum* of human rights

---

[20]   McGlynn, C., 'Families and the European Union Charter of Fundamental Rights: progressive change or entrenching the status quo?' (2001), p. 587-593.

[21]   See for instance: Alston, P. (ed.), *The EU and Human Rights* (1999), p. 9-11; Bogdandy, A., von, 'The European Union as a Human Rights Organisation? Human Rights and the Core of the European Union' (2000), p. 1317.

[22]   Neuwahl, N., Rosas, A., *The European Union and Human Rights* (1995), 221-230; McGlynn, C., 'A Family Law for the European Union' (2000), p. 229-232.

[23]   On the use of this argument see, for example: McGlynn, C., 'A Family Law for the European Union' (2000), p. 226.

[24]   See for instance: Ibid. p. 224 –229.

[25]   [2000] O.J. C364/1.

[26]   The future of the EU Constitution is very uncertain since the populations of France and The Netherlands voted against it in the referenda of 2005.

protection in Europe'.[27] The purpose of the Charter is 'to strengthen the protection of fundamental rights in the light of the changes in society, social progress and scientific and technological developments by making those rights more visible in the Charter'. Therefore, in contrast to the more than 50-year old Convention upon which it is built, the Charter could be reasonably expected not only to reflect the current level of protection, but also to upgrade it. It could also be expected to systematically fill all the gaps which have arisen from the piecemeal development of case law. Yet, as the following chapters will illustrate, at least with respect to family rights almost all these expectations have remained unjustified.

12.2. TWO WAVES OF REFORMS

Within the period of sweeping modernisation of family law that was commenced after the 1960s, two basic waves of family law reforms can be distinguished. The first wave generally entailed the introduction of no-fault divorce grounds, basic equalisation of the rights of the spouses, and granting equal status to illegitimate children. In most of Western Europe this phase was accomplished during the radical climate of the 1960s-70s. The second wave of reforms, dated after the 1980s, by and large contained attempts to altogether eradicate fault divorce, institutionalise unmarried cohabitation and same-sex relationships, and clean up the last remnants of discrimination in respect of married women and illegitimate children. This second phase took place during the less favourable political climate that emerged after the 'New-Right' conservative wave of the 1980s.

12.2.1. THE RADICAL 1960S AND 1970S

The eventual triumph of Enlightenment ideas

The first wave of reforms, which can be roughly estimated to have taken place from 1965 until 1980, was characterised by sweeping social and legal change, instigated by radical ideological and cultural transformations. It would be no exaggeration to say that these two decades, with their optimistic spirit, both in terms of economical optimism and political and moral reformism, were in fact a first unrestrained attempt 'to finish' the 'unfinished Modernity project'[28] started after the Enlightenment, in the

---

27 WOUTERS, J., 'The EU Charter of the Fundamental Rights – Some Reflections on its External Dimension' (2001), p. 3.
28 See Part I, Chapter 2, Section 2.3.

field of family law. It is during this time that the ideas of the Enlightenment,[29] refined and enhanced during the two hundred years of struggle against conservative opposition, finally came to prevail over the dogmas inherited from the medieval uniform canon law and the patriarchal tenets.[30] The last stronghold of traditionalism, the private domain of the family, was finally 'democratised'.[31] The idea of equality and the rights approach, already having been accredited in political and economic life in the first part of the century, were fully extended to the private and family life. As it has been summarised:

> 'The contractual model which prevails in today's' society and which rests in free will and personal autonomy, has now also become a model for family. Family has, thus, become a free association of persons and area for freedom and equality. It is the move towards the protection of individual's rights, made at the expense of traditional family values, which has allowed married women and children to be emancipated from patriarchy.'[32]

In the same period, the modern personalistic attitude finally overcame the old transpersonalistic approach. Regard for the feelings and aspirations of individual family members became so self-evident that people were no longer willing to endure personal suffering in the name of such abstract concepts as legitimate family, heterosexual marriage or indissolubility of marriage.

Modernisation affects the churches

The ethical transformations with regard to family law were also a success because the changes in the 1960s affected even the greatest opponents of modernisation of family law during the last four centuries: the official churches. The epitome of the

---

[29]   Mary Ann Glendon suggests a direct connection between the profundity of liberalisation of divorce and the influence of the ideas of the Enlightenment. In her view, a more profound influence of Enlightenment ideas was responsible for a uncompromising introduction of no-fault divorce in America. On the European continent 'these ideas were softened, deflected, and counterbalanced to a greater extent by classical and customary notions of law', which made 'pure no-fault divorce with a short waiting period' politically unacceptable in the Western Europe. GLENDON, M.A., *Abortion and Divorce in Western Law* (1987), p. 75 and 131.

[30]   Only in the course of the twentieth century the Enlightenment contractual model of marriage 'slowly eclipsed Protestant and Catholic models of marriage and the ideas and institution that those models have introduced into the Western legal tradition'. WITTE, J., *From Sacrament to Contract* (1997), p. 196.

[31]   COMMAILLE, J., 'Les métamorphoses de la gestion politique de l'univers privé des individus' (2002), p. 21.

[32]   MOUTOUH, H., 'Le question de la reconnaissance du couple homosexuel: entre dogmatisme et empirisme' (1998), p. note 6. Cited in: STEINER, E., 'The spirit of the new French registered partnership law – promoting autonomy and pluralism or weakening marriage' (2000), at p. 4.

personalistic attitude materialised at that time in a number of dissident attempts to bring the official Christian ethics back to its humanistic roots. Perhaps the ultimate example is presented in 'Honest to God'; a ground-breaking theological treatise, published in 1963 by John Robinson – a Church of England Bishop of Woolwich.[33] In this brilliant piece, Robinson embraced the earlier attempts[34] to reformulate Christian ethics on the basis of a personalistic approach. The thus redefined ethics appear to be situational, rather than regulative,[35] prescriptive ethics, based on the imperative that 'nothing [is] prescribed – except love'.[36] According to this personalistic ethical system, compassion for *persons* should override all laws.[37] Consequently, defining divorce or sexual relations before marriage as good or wrong must be done 'situationally, not prescriptively'. Such definition must not depend upon some abstract rule or dogma, but on the principle of love, demanding that 'the deepest welfare of these particular persons in this particular situation matters more than anything else in the world'.[38] The main advantage of the situational 'love' ethic over the prescriptive ethics of the law is that 'love's casuistry must cut deeper, and must be more searching, more demanding, than anything required by the law, precisely because it goes to the heart of the individual personal situation'.[39] Consequently, 'if the emotional and spiritual welfare of both parents and children in a particular family can be served best by a divorce, wrong and cheapjack as divorce commonly is, then love requires it'.[40] Dissident voices like these neither represented official churches, nor were able to change the face of the official Church ethical doctrines. However, they showed that churches-as-institutions were not immune to the spirit of the time and were also searching for renovation. Maybe they were the first signs of longing for reunification of the official Christian doctrines with progressive humanistic ideology.[41]

The modernity spirit of the 1960s was so compelling that even its greatest adversary came to pay it homage. The Roman Catholic Church, which a century ago had solemnly proclaimed never to reconcile with 'progress, liberalism and modern

---

[33]   ROBINSON, J., *Honest to God* (reprint 1967).

[34]   FLETCHER, J., 'The New Look in Christian Ethics' (1959), p. 7- 18.

[35]   'It is love which is the constitutive principle [of this ethic] – and law, at most, is only the regulative one'. FLETCHER, J., 'The New Look in Christian Ethics' (1959), p. 17.

[36]   ROBINSON, J., *Honest to God* (reprint 1967), p. 116.

[37]   Ibid.

[38]   Ibid, p. 118.

[39]   Ibid.

[40]   FLETCHER, J., 'The New Look in Christian Ethics' (1959), 15.

[41]   It has been suggested at the end of Section 9.3.1. that the Churches-as-institutions have parted with humanistic and progressive thought around sixteenth century. The following quotation from Bishop Robinson illustrates how far they had moved from each other by the second part of the twentieth century: 'Not infrequently, as I watch or listen to a broadcast discussion between a Christian and a humanist, I catch myself realizing that most of my sympathies are on the humanist's side'. ROBINSON, J., *Honest to God* (reprint 1967), p. 8.

civilization',[42] now made an attempt 'to come to terms with modernity'.[43] Vatican II, the historic Council of the Roman Catholic Church held in 1962-1965, proclaimed the policy of *aggiornamento*,[44] which shifted the course that Catholicism had steered ever since the Council of Trent.[45] It should be born in mind that Vatican II has never gone so far as to alter the main Catholic family law dogmas,[46] such as the indissolubility of marriage, procreation as the goal of marriage,[47] or the prohibitive attitude towards contraception and homosexuality. Nonetheless, the Council indirectly opened the way to modernisation of secular family law in Catholic countries. These new opportunities were a result of the general acknowledgement of religious freedom,[48] the pluralistic character of the modern society,[49] the autonomy of the 'political community'[50] and secular culture.[51] An important step was made in the direction of reintegrating the Catholic Church with humanistic thought. The Church 'borrowed from personalistic philosophy'[52] the concept of an integral, autonomous, responsible human person,[53]

---

[42]   *Syllabus of Errors*, 1864, cited in: MCSWEENEY, B., *Roman Catholicism. The Search for Relevance* (1980), p. 22.

[43]   DUFFY, S., 'Catholicism's Search for a New Self-Understanding' (1984), p. 9. According to Stephen Duffy the Council manifested a shift from a static backward-looking perspective to an Enlightenment forward-looking perspective on the movement of history, which is expressible in the general word "progress". Ibid. p. 19.

[44]   *Aggiornamento* (literal meaning: 'bringing up to date') was appreciated as a real 'revolution in the Catholic history of idea of reform'. MCSWEENEY, B., *Roman Catholicism. The Search for Relevance* (1980), p. 19.

[45]   DUFFY, S., 'Catholicism's Search for a New Self-Understanding' (1984), p. 10.

[46]   On Catholic doctrine of marriage as synthesised at Vatican II see: 'The Dignity of Marriage and the Family ' in: *Pastoral Constitution of the Church in the Modern World* (7 December 1965), art 48, 50. During the Council there was a sharp split between the 'conservatives (or traditionalists)' who wished to reinforce the old dogmas and the 'progressives (or liberals)' who wished to update the Catholic teaching on marriage. ALBERIGO, G., KOMONCHAK, A. (eds.), *History of Vatican II*, Vol. IV, (2003), p. 308 ff.

[47]   See: 'The Dignity of Marriage and the Family', in: *Pastoral Constitution of the Church in the Modern World*, art 48, 50, 7 December, 1965. At the same time there was a powerful plea from Cardinal Suenens to give 'the communion of the spouses' equal status with procreation as an end of marriage. He warned that the ability to modernise the Church notion of marriage is very crucial and called to 'avoid another "Galileo Case": one is enough for the Church'. ALBERIGO, G., KOMONCHAK, A. (eds.), History of Vatican II, Vol. IV (2003), p. 310.

[48]   In its *Declaration on Religious Liberty* (7 December 1966) the Council not only recognised religious liberty, but also acknowledged the right of the civil society to protect itself against possible abuses of this freedom and condemned the 'unfair principle of favouritism'. Ibid, Art. 7. These statements were of paramount importance for the modernisation of family law in the predominantly Catholic countries where the Catholic Church enjoyed a privileged status.

[49]   DUFFY, S., 'Catholicism's Search for a New Self-Understanding' (1984), p. 76.

[50]   'The Political community and the Church', in: *Pastoral Constitution of the Church in the Modern World* (7 December 1965), art 76.

[51]   DUFFY, S., 'Catholicism's Search for a New Self-Understanding' (1984), p. 16.

[52]   BOEVE, L., '*Gaudium et Spet* and the Crisis of Modernity: The End of the Dialogue with the World?' (2002), p. 84.

[53]   Ibid.

and acknowledged the personal moral responsibility of individual Catholics.[54] This revolutionary change made it possible for the Irish hierarchy to not only remain officially neutral during the Irish divorce campaigns, but even to acknowledge the right of its flock 'to vote in good conscience in favour of divorce'.[55] This same influence is traceable in 2002 in the position of the Flemish Christian Democrats, who, although in opposition, supported the Governmental Bill on the introduction of the same-sex marriage in Belgian Parliament under the motto: *misericordia et iustitia.*[56]

The progressive/conservative discord remains

It should not, however, be forgotten that the political polarisation between progressive and conservative forces did not disappear even in this predominantly progressive period. The conservatives were just holding the line, waiting for the right moment to switch from defence to offence. The 1973 Swedish situation in which a new-radicalist socialist government managed to conduct an unrestricted reform of such ideology-sensitive areas as marriage and divorce, remained a rare exception. In the vast majority of European countries, the existence of the conservative opposition necessitated compromises that influenced the profundity of modernisation of family law. The balance of political power in the 'big three', Britain, France and Germany, as well as in many other Western European countries, compelled the proponents of reform to seek a compromise even when they were in office.

12.2.2. THE NEW-CONSERVATIVE WAVE: THE 1980S AND BEYOND

The conservatives got a new chance with the New Right (or New Conservative) 'pro-family' backlash of the 1980s. Although the conservative governments of Thatcher in Britain and Reagan in the US were only in office in the 1980s, their ideology deeply influenced the political and intellectual climate of the late twentieth century and thereafter.[57] Thus, the second phase of the late twentieth century reforms took place under much less favourable circumstances than the first one. The neo-conservative

---

[54] As McSweeney has noticed that the personalistic approach to morality has replaced 'a legalistic system of morality and a casuistic approach', which dominated Catholicism ever since the Council of Trent. MCSWEENEY, B., *Roman Catholicism. The Search for Relevance* (1980), p. 146 and 18 ff. In its *Declaration on Religious Liberty* the Council stated that 'everyone has the duty and consequently the right, to seek the truth in religious matters so that, through the use of appropriate means, he may prudently form judgements of conscience which are sincere and true' Ibid, Art. 3.

[55] DILLON, M., *Debating Divorce. Moral Conflict in Ireland* (1993), p. 97.

[56] 'Compassion is justice'. Senator Vandenberghe (Flemish Christian Democrat (CD&V)) Senate, 2002/2002, 2-246, p. 38.

[57] ABBOT, P., WALLACE, C., *The family and the New Rights* (1992), p. 1.

wave was not strong enough to turn back the tide, but the reformist modernity spirit of the 1960s-70s had to give way to post-modernist scepticism and pro-family traditionalism.[58] The New Right saw a good chance to launch an attack on the permissive sexual climate of the 1960s, the rising divorce and illegitimacy rates, and especially, the success of the sexual minorities rights movement.[59] However, after the all-embracing changes of the 1960s, the conservative camp was no longer the same. On top of the old, nostalgic, traditional, pro-family communitarian argumentation, the conservative developed a new kind of ideology.[60] This ideology was devised upon a liaison of the conservative critique of the permissiveness of the 1960s and the post-modernist critique of modernity.[61] The new conservative argument can be more or less accurately labelled as 'humanistic' conservatism. In the same fashion as the post-modernists accused the Modernity project of failing to keep its promises 'of freedom, welfare, happiness for all',[62] the conservative critics of the modernisation of family law accused it of failing to benefit all family members. The post-modernist, 'humanistic' conservatives stressed the disadvantages that the liberalisation of family law brought to abandoned spouses, children of divorce, and other victims. Therefore the conservatives opposed liberalisation of family law from a personalistic position and emphasised the fact that freedom, which brings benefits for one family member, can easily be detrimental to the other. Thus, the humanistic conservative argument appeared to be a much more nuanced, cultured, and up to date remedy than traditional, transpersonalistic conservative rhetoric.[63] Through this approach, the credibility and effectiveness of the conservative critique was significantly improved.

The neo-conservative wave also affected the churches. In the Roman Catholic Church, the reformist spirit of Vatican II gave way to the conservatism of Johannes Paul II and his 2005 successor. The neo-conservative Catholic theorists readily embraced post-modernism. The basis of this '"unholy alliance" between post-modernist and neo-

---

[58]   The pro-family movement advocated a traditional role of women in the family, male authority and non-intervention of the state within the family. Ibid, p. 11.

[59]   Ibid, p. 5-6.

[60]   See for example: REGAN, M., *Family law and the Pursuit of Intimacy* (1993) and *Alone Together and the Meaning of Marriage* (1999).

[61]   For this critique see: Part I, Chapter 2, Section 2.3.1.

[62]   BOEVE, L., '*Gaudium et Spet* and the Crisis of Modernity: The End of the Dialogue with the World?' (2002), p. 86.

[63]   Transpersonalistic communitarian arguments were still employed by more old-fashioned conservatives, especially in order to justify the discrimination of same-sex couples.

conservative philosophers and theologians'[64] was a shared negative attitude towards the accomplishments of modernity.[65]

In the 1990s, the conservative trend in family law was, ironically enough, to a certain extent reinforced by the fall of the Soviet Block. After the liberation, some parts of the Soviet block threw away the Soviet tradition of liberal family law together with rest of the Soviet heritage.

Since the new conservative wave, save for few exceptions, compromise became an even more indispensable precondition to the reform of marriage, divorce and partnership law in most European countries, irrespective of the political colour of the government in office. However, the general nature of this compromise changed. The conservative advance shifted the balance of political power and allowed the conservatives to exert heavy influence on compromises surrounding the reforms of family law. The 1996 reform of divorce law in England and Wales, and the French PACS and 2004 divorce reform provide good illustrations of such compromises with a strong conservative flavour. On the other hand, the examples of unrestricted reforms in particularly sensitive fields also became more common. In the 2000s, the Dutch and Belgian socialist-green-liberal coalitions and the Spanish socialist Government managed to introduce same-sex marriage without paying much regard to conservative opposition.

The reasons for the necessity of compromise in most European countries, on the one hand, and the possibility of uncompromising reforms, on the other hand, have a lot to do with the particularities of the progressive camps in different European countries, especially in regard of the social-democrats. Conservative/progressive divides with respect to family law always go along the lines of division between the Christian-democrats and the liberals, but in many European countries this line does not always coincide with the divide between the Christian-democrats and the social-democrats. While the liberals have always been on the forefront of the modernisation of family law, the social-democrats in many European countries are internally divided upon these matters. This division often reflects the difference with regard to family values between the more emancipated and more traditional parts of the socialists' grassroots support. This analysis is equally valid for the above discussed progressive period of the 1960s -1970s. A good example from the 1970s is the concern the Italian socialists

---

[64] BOEVE, L., 'Gaudium et Spet and the Crisis of Modernity: The End of the Dialogue with the World?' (2002), p. 89-90.

[65] The conservative critics of Vatican II claimed that 'the efforts of reconciling the modern world with Christian faith, as carried out by progressive Christians and theologians who claimed to be the real heirs of Vatican II, have proved themselves illusory: modernity did not succeed in keeping its promises'. BOEVE, L., 'Gaudium et Spet and the Crisis of Modernity: The End of the Dialogue with the World?' (2002), p. 86.

had with their Catholic grassroots' support, which predetermined the reticent position of the socialists in the debate surrounding the introduction of divorce in Italy. A more recent example from the 1990s is the regard that the French socialists had to pay to the anti-homo feelings on the part of their grassroots' support in the PACS debates. In contrast, in some other European countries the social-democrats proved to be consolidated around the modernisation of family law. In the countries where the social-democrats are internally divided upon the issue of modernisation of family law, family law reforms are generally doomed to be a compromise. In the countries where they are consolidated around the modernisation of family law, a uncompromising reform is sometimes possible. Thus, the Swedish social-democrats, inspired by the so-called 'new radicalism' in the 1970s, introduced the most sweeping marriage and divorce reform in Western Europe. Some thirty years later the Governing Spanish socialist democrats of Rodríguez Zapatero were so resolutely in favour of the radical modernisation of family law, that their Government was able to introduce same-sex marriage and divorce on demand within one and the same year. These examples suggest that the internal consolidation of a progressive camp around the modernisation of family law sometimes empowers it to disregard the conservative opposition altogether[66] and to carry out uncompromising reforms.

It should be mentioned that during both the soaring 1960s-70s and the more restraint period that commenced in the 1980s, the reformation of some institutions of family raised more controversy than the modification of the others. The reformation of matrimonial property law has always been less ideologically sensitive and more informed by a pragmatic attitude.[67] Marriage and divorce law have at all times remained a battleground between the zealots of conservative and progressive ideologies. However, controversy has shifted from one subject of marriage law to another. While the issue of the equality of the spouses and of legitimate and illegitimate children gradually lost its controversial character, since the 1990s the legal recognition of same-sex unions has grown into the main new field of heated controversy. To a large extent, this has been due to the influence of the international human rights instruments. The equality of spouses, and of marital and extramarital children, have acquired the status of fundamental human rights and can count on a more or less general consensus within each European country. The issue of the equality of sexual minorities, however, is far from reaching this stage.

---

[66]   With regard to Spain, Gabriel García Cantero points at the 'lack of parliamentary debate' with those opposing the introduction of same-sex marriage. GARCÍA CANTERO, G., 'Family Law Reform in Differing Directions' (2006), p. 434.

[67]   GLENDON, M.A., *Abortion and Divorce in Western Law* (1987), p. 108.

CHAPTER 13
'DEATH OF MARRIAGE' OR SEARCH FOR A NEW CONCEPT OF MARRIAGE?

13.1. A NEW CONCEPT OF MARRIAGE

In spite of a steady decrease in the number of marriages over the last decennia,[1] and the fact that cohabitation and divorce have already 'eroded the primacy of marriage as the basis of family life',[2] marriage is still seen by many as the crown of the affective relationships.[3] However, in present-day Europe it is no longer possible to speak of a concept of marriage that is equally adhered to by everyone. On the contrary, the contemporary notion of marriage embraces a whole variety of different concepts of marriage (for instance, a traditional marriage with a male breadwinner and a housewife, a modern marriage with an equal division of labour in and outside the household, an intentionally childless marriage, a same-sex marriage, and so on),[4] incorporated under the same term 'marriage'.[5]

Since the 1960s, marriage has undergone such important transformations that not only those who associated marriage with its traditional patriarchal form, but even those who agreeingly watched marriage becoming indistinguishable from the other forms of cohabitation, started talking about the 'death of marriage'.[6] Although the way for

---

[1]   See: VAN NIMWEGEN, V., BEETS, G., VAN DER ERF, R., 'De bevolking in Europa', p. 47.

[2]   KIERNAN, K., 'The State of European Unions: an Analysis of Partnership Formation and Dissolution' (2002), p. 75

[3]   SCHRAMA, W., *De niet-huwelijkse samenleving in het Nederlandse en Duitse recht* (2004), p. 39. A recent Dutch survey shows that ¾ of the population still wants to marry, albeit after having first cohabited for some time. LIEFBROER, A., 'Het gezinsideaal: Van traditioneel naar modern' (2002), p. 2.

[4]   Changes in the popularity of the traditional and the modern ideal of marriage have recently been surveyed in The Netherlands. In 1990, 51% of the population stated to cherish the ideal of traditional marriage, in 2000 this number had decreased to 27%. In the same period, the number of the population with preference for the modern ideal of marriage increased from 35% to 60%. LIEFBROER, A., 'Het gezinsideaal: Van traditioneel naar modern' (2002), p. 8.

[5]   Mary Ann Glendon speaks in this respect of 'different marriage models'. GLENDON, M.A., *The Transformation of Family Law* (1989), p. 144.

[6]   The possible disappearance of marriage as a legal concept has been discussed, among others, in: CLIVE, E., 'Marriage: An Unnecessary Legal Concept' (1980), p. 71-72; HOGGERTT, B., 'Ends and Means: The Utility of Marriage as a Legal Institution' (1980), p. 94-103 and more recently in the inaugural speech by Frederik Swennen. SWENNEN, F., *Het huwelijk afschaffen?* (2003).

these changes had been paved for a long time, the 1960s were the turning point, after which progressive ideology came to dominate the developments in the law of marriage.[7] Since then, both the social function of marriage and its ideological connotation have changed.[8] The importance of the procreative function of marriage drastically diminished as marriage ceased to be the only union through which children were bestowed full legal rights in respect of the parents and their families.[9] The relationships between the spouses have evolved from the wife's dependency and subordination to that of the spouses' legal,[10] and, gradually, also economic equality. Due to women's emancipation, increasing female employment and the progress of social welfare, the function of the family as provider of financial means and security has diminished. This development has contributed to an attitudinal shift in the emphasis of marriage, from communitarian to personalistic.[11] In line with the Enlightenment ideal, the main function of marriage became to provide spouses and children with companionship, personal fulfilment, love and happiness.[12]

However, this 'hedonistic' function of marriage appeared to have its shadow sides. Marriage based on affection and free commitment, rather than on economic necessity and duty, proved to be less stable and durable.[13] The disturbing side of love-based marriage is that love often comes to an end only by one of the loving ones, rather than by both of them. As the hedonistic function of marriage came more to the foreground, the partners' expectations as to the quality of their relationship grew higher and higher. Economically independent spouses tend to disregard the maxim that 'you become responsible, forever, for what you have tamed',[14] and to leave the other behind as soon as she or he feels that their relationship no longer satisfies him or her 110%. Under

---

[7] Mary Ann Glendon emphasises that 'the reforms that began in the 1960 did not destroy the traditional family. What that mainly did was to consolidate and, sometimes increase the power of several movements that were already going forward'. GLENDON, M.A., *The Transformation of Family Law* (1989), p. 311.

[8] See: Ibid, p. 144 ff.

[9] SWENNEN, F., *Het huwelijk afschaffen?* (2003), p. 1. WILLEKENS, H., 'Explaining Two Hundred Years of Family Law in Western Europe' (1997), p. 69.

[10] SWENNEN, F., *Het huwelijk afschaffen?* (2003), p. 1.

[11] In other words: 'the passage from family to individual'. MARTIN, C., THÉRY, I., 'The PACS and Marriage and Cohabitation in France' (2001), p. 154.

[12] According to Alan Bénabent the new concept of marriage involves that marriage is a means to the fullest possible development of a person (BÉNABENT, A., 'Le Liberté individuelle et le mariage' (1973), p. 480). The pre-eminence of affective and sexual relationships within marriage is also stressed by VAN GRUNDERBEECK, D., *Beginselen van personen- en familierecht. Een mensenrechtelijke benadering* (2003), p. 183.

[13] Mary Ann Glendon notes that modern marriage law simultaneously expresses the closeness and intensity as well as the instability of the modern marriage based on emotional rather than economic ties. GLENDON, M.A., *The New Family and the New Property* (1981), p. 29.

[14] 'Tu deviens responsable pour toujours de ce que tu as apprivoisé'. Antoine de SAINT EXUPÉRY, *Le petit prince* (1946), p. 72.

---

the influence of these transformations, the modus of marriage has generally shifted from life-long monogamy to serial monogamy. These negative side-effects of liberalisation gave rise to justified criticism from the side of the 'humanistic' conservatives.

The evolution of the concept of marriage was reflected, with some delay, in the European human rights law. It is common knowledge that the initial variant of the Convention on Human Rights anno 1950 was based upon the traditional vertical concept of marriage as a durable, heterosexual, male-dominated union, aimed at procreation.[15] Article 9 of the EU Charter of the Fundamental Rights,[16] and the identical provision of the Article II-69 of the unratified EU Constitution, have slightly modernised this concept by making the right to create a family independent of the right to marry.

The main events of the last half of the twentieth century in the field of the law of marriage in every West European country were the secularisation and de-ideologisation of marriage law, the acceptance of the right to marry as a fundament human right,[17] the diminishment of marriage impediments, the lowering of the age of capacity to marry, and the grant of equal legal rights to spouses. Another important transformation, noticed by Glendon already by the end of the 1980s,[18] was the diminishing State intervention in some areas of marriage law (such as the regulation of the personal rights and duties of spouses), and the simultaneous increase of the State's interference in an ongoing marriage in order to protect a weaker party. However, the profundity of these transformations depended on the compromise reached between the conservative and progressive forces, and therefore varied essentially from one State to another. Yet the period in question also witnessed a number of uncompromising breakthroughs in the field of marriage law. In the early 1970s, the Swedish new radical socialist government managed to carry out a far-reaching non-constraint reform in every aspect of marital law. In the early 2000s, the progressive camps in The Netherlands, Belgium and Spain succeeded in introducing same-sex marriage. These breakthroughs have generally determined the selection of the countries to be analysed in the following Sections in addition to the standard 'big three', England and Wales, France and Germany.

---

[15] For more details and an overview of literature see: VAN GRUNDERBEECK, D., *Beginselen van personen-en familierecht. Een mensenrechtelijke benadering* (2003), p. 198-199.

[16] [2000] O.J. C364/1.

[17] On the development of this right see: VAN GRUNDERBEECK, D., *Beginselen van personen- en familierecht. Een mensenrechtelijke benadering* (2003), p. 185-195.

[18] GLENDON, M.A., *The Transformation of Family Law* (1989), p. 293-296.

13.2. GRADUAL MOVEMENT FORWARDS: ENGLAND, FRANCE, AND GERMANY

13.2.1. ENGLAND AND WALES: INFLUENCE OF THE ESTABLISHED CHURCH

With regard to marriage law, England and Wales provide an example of respect for tradition and enduring ecclesiastical influence. The core of the problem was that, as the Law Commission acknowledged in 1973, 'reform in this particular field is a topic on which personal views and religious opinion influence decisions'.[19] Considering the lack of political consensus on this issue, every step in the direction of reform required a difficult compromise. Even the radical spirit of the 1960s did not enable the proponents of profound modernisation and simplification of marriage law to reach their goals. The chain of the piecemeal reforms that followed continually reflected uneasy compromises between the different players: the Church of England, the secular conservatives, and the proponents of reforms. However, at the moment, important changes to marriage law are expected.[20]

Secularisation and de-ideologisation of the law of marriage

A peculiarity of English law is that its civil law on marriage is even now to a significant extent dominated by the Canons of the Church of England. The present English definition of marriage as 'the voluntary union of a man and a woman, solemnised in public according to law, and based upon mutual commitment and intended to last for life, to the exclusion of all others',[21] barely diverges from the classical definition given by Lord Penzance in 1866.[22] Monogamy and heterosexuality, at least as far as same-sex marriage is concerned, are still considered corner stones to the concept of marriage.[23] The requirement of (genetic) heterosexuality was, however, recently removed, after it failed the test of conformity to the European Convention on Human

---

[19]   LAW COMMISSION, *Solemnisation of Marriage in England and Wales* (1973), para. 34. Cited in: CRETNEY, S., *Family Law in the Twentieth Century* (2003), p. 28.

[20]   These changes have been proposed in the government's 2003 consultation paper *Civil Registration: Delivering Vital Change*. For an analysis of the proposed changes see: PROBERT, R., 'Lord Hardwicke's Marriage Act – Vital Change 250 Years On?' (2004), p. 595-589.

[21]   This definition has been proposed at a symposium held in 1994. LOWE, N., DOUGLAS, G., *Bromley's Family Law* (1998), p. 23.

[22]   *Hyde v. Hyde*, L.R. 1 P&D 130, 1866.

[23]   In 1996 a judge of the Court of Appeal, Ward L.J., said that despite the fact that Lord Penzance's classical definition of marriage 'may have been eroded, bigamy and single-sex unions remain proscribed as fundamentally abhorrent to this notion of marriage'. *J v. S–T (Formerly J)* [1997] 1 *FLR* 402. Cited in: FREEMAN, M., 'Some Reflections on Gay Marriages at the Beginning of the Twenty-First Century' (2002), p. 359.

Rights.[24] It is also suggested that the life-long character of marriage can now only be interpreted to mean that 'the marriage must last for life unless it is previously terminated by a decree or some other act of dissolution'.[25] The old common law concept of *consortium*, the right of the spouses to one another's society, assistance, comfort and protection,[26] is now interpreted in such a way that the consortium and duty to cohabit exist as a legally unenforceable symbol of the marital community between the spouses.[27] The duty of cohabitation was abolished already in the nineteenth century.[28] The right of a husband to claim damages for enticement, harbouring and adultery was abolished in 1970.[29] In 1981[30] the liability of a third party in tort for depriving a husband of the services and society of his wife was abolished.[31] Nonetheless, a breach of the duty to consummate the marriage is still actionable under the law of England and Wales. A marriage unconsummated due to incapacity or wilful refusal can be declared void.[32] The duty of fidelity is also (indirectly) legally enforceable as adultery still constitutes a ground for divorce.

The two-tier system of alternative civil and religious celebration of marriage, introduced in England and Wales in 1836, is still in effect. It has been asserted that current marriage law, the Marriage Act 1949,[33] still largely reflects the pattern established in 1936.[34] The wedding and pre-wedding formalities differ significantly,[35] depending on the type of ceremony chosen by the parties.[36] At present, English law provides for four basic categories of marriage ceremony: according to the rites of the Church of England, the rites of non-Anglican religious ceremony, Quaker or Jewish rites, and through a civil registration.[37] The Established Church – the Church of England – still occupies a privileged position. It is allowed to use its own ecclesiastical

---

[24] See below.

[25] LOWE, N., DOUGLAS, G., *Bromley's Family Law* (1998), p. 24.

[26] CRETNEY, S., MASSON, J., BAILEY-HARRIS, R., *Principles of Family Law* (2003), p. 71.

[27] GLENDON, M. A., 'Power and Authority in the Family: New Legal Patterns as Reflection of Changing Ideologies' (1975), p.11.

[28] By the *Matrimonial Causes* Act of 1884,

[29] By the 1970 *Law Reform (Miscellaneous Provisions)* Act.

[30] By the 1982 Administration of Justice Act.

[31] CRETNEY, S., MASSON, J., BAILEY-HARRIS, R., *Principles of Family Law* (2003), p. 72.

[32] Sec. 12 (a) and (b) of the *Matrimonial Causes* Act 1973.

[33] The Act underwent a number of amendments, the most important of which were made by the Marriage Act 1994. CRETNEY, S., MASSON, J., BAILEY-HARRIS, R., *Principles of Family Law* (2003), p. 12, note 20.

[34] CRETNEY, S., MASSON, J., BAILEY-HARRIS, R., *Principles of Family Law* (2003), p. 12.

[35] See: LOWE, N., DOUGLAS, G., *Bromley's Family Law* (1998), p. 38 ff.

[36] For details on these formalities see: CRETNEY, S., MASSON, J., BAILEY-HARRIS, R., *Principles of Family Law* (2003), p. 12-34.

[37] Ibid, p. 22.

preliminaries for marriage (banns and common licence), while other denominations must observe the preliminaries prescribed by civil law.[38]

In general, the law governing the celebration of marriage has been characterised by Stephen Cretney as being '[n]either simple or easy to understand'.[39] The attempts of the last four decades to simplify and unify the law of marriage are very illustrative of the implications that the conservative/progressive controversy has had on marriage law in England and Wales.[40] The Government itself has acknowledged that 'many of the procedures are unnecessarily complex and restrictive and reflect the needs and social customs of the early nineteenth century rather than those of the late twentieth century'.[41] In 1969, the Joint Working Party set up by the Law Commission concluded that 'the "simplest and most effective" solution would be to enact [...] the Continental model'.[42] Such a radical change was considered impossible by the Working Party itself as it was expected to trigger strong opposition both from the churches and from the general public'.[43] A less far-reaching proposal to introduce uniform civil preliminaries for all forms of marriage was put forward by the Law Commission in 1973.[44] However, even this modest innovation was opposed by the Standing Committee of the General Synod of the Church of England 'as a "diminution of the centuries old responsibilities of the Church" in relation to marriage'.[45] Twenty years later the government acknowledged that 'fundamental change' in such a 'sensitive area' as marriage law could not be made without 'a wider consent',[46] so the reform was put on the back burner for another decade. However, at the moment it finally looks as though a radical change to the law of the celebration of marriage is about to be made. New proposals for reform are laid down in 2002 in the Government's White Paper,[47] *Civil Registration: Vital Change.* Surprisingly enough this reform is intended to be carried out by

---

[38]   PROBERT, R., 'Lord Hardwicke's Marriage Act – Vital Change 250 Years On?' (2004), p. 587.

[39]   CRETNEY, S., *Family Law in the Twentieth Century* (2003), p. 37.

[40]   For a comprehensive account see: CRETNEY, S., *Family Law in the Twentieth Century* (2003), p. 4-89.

[41]   Green Paper *Registration: A Modern Service*, Cm. 531 (1988), para. 3.2. Cited in: CRETNEY, S., MASSON, J., BAILEY-HARRIS, R., *Principles of Family Law* (2003), p. 31.

[42]   PWP 35 para. 5; LAW COMMISSION, *Solemnisation of Marriage in England and Wales* (1973), Annex, para. 6 cited in: CRETNEY, S., *Family Law in the Twentieth Century* (2003), p. 26.

[43]   Ibid.

[44]   LAW COMMISSION, *Solemnisation of Marriage in England and Wales* (1973), see also CRETNEY, S., MASSON, J., BAILEY-HARRIS, R., *Principles of Family Law* (2003), p. 14. In the meantime uniform civil preliminaries have been introduced in Northern Ireland by the *Marriage (Northern Ireland)* Order 2003.

[45]   Working Party established by the Standing Committee of the General Synod of the Church of England in 1988. An Honourable Estate (1988) para. 188. Cited in: CRETNEY, S., *Family Law in the Twentieth Century* (2003), p. 28.

[46]   White Paper *Registration: Proposals for Change*, Cm. 939 (1990), para. 3.2-3. Cited in: CRETNEY, S., MASSON, J., BAILEY-HARRIS, R., *Principles of Family Law* (2003), note 35 at p. 15.

[47]   OFFICE FOR NATIONAL STATISTICS, *Civil Registration: Vital Change. White Paper* (2002).

delegated legislation,[48] without much political debate. In 2003 the White Paper was followed up by the Consultation Paper, *Civil Registration: Delivering Vital Change,*[49] in which the Government proposes the introduction of uniform preliminaries for all forms of marriage.[50] Other than in the 1970s, in 2002 the General Synod of the Church of England approved this new system of joint State and Ecclesiastical preliminaries.[51] The expected reform is also aimed at removing existing restrictions on the time and place of marriage celebrations.[52]

Another important innovation has to do with de-ideologisation and de-formalisation of marriage ceremony. Although current law does not prescribe it, the celebrants of a civil marriage sometimes consider it their duty to remind the couple of the 'solemn and binding character of the vows they are about to take', and that marriage is a union for life.[53] Under the new regulation the ceremonial requirements of the new marriage ceremony will be reduced to a minimum.[54] Instead of the wording currently prescribed by law,[55] the parties will be free to choose their own form of declaration stating that they accept each other as husband and wife.[56]

Capacity to marry

The persistent influence of the Church of England is most explicit in the law governing the impediments to marriage. In 1955, a Church of England report noted that, 'with limited exceptions, Church and civil law on capacity [to marry] are compatible',[57] and the situation has not changed much since that time. The present law[58] prohibits marriage between the following persons related by blood: children and parents, grandchildren and grandparents, brothers and sisters, nephews and aunts or nieces and uncles.[59] Certain degrees of affinity also constitute an impediment to marriage,

---

[48]   Under the *Regulatory Reform Act* 2001. See: PROBERT, R., 'Lord Hardwicke's Marriage Act – Vital Change 250 Years On?' (2004), p. 588.

[49]   OFFICE FOR NATIONAL STATISTICS, *Civil Registration: Delivering Vital Change. Consultation Paper* (2003)

[50]   PROBERT, R., 'Lord Hardwicke's Marriage Act – Vital Change 250 Years On?' (2004), p. 585.

[51]   Ibid.

[52]   Ibid.

[53]   CRETNEY, S., *Family Law in the Twentieth Century* (2003), p. 36.

[54]   PROBERT, R., 'Lord Hardwicke's Marriage Act – Vital Change 250 Years On?' (2004), p. 586.

[55]   The current wording is: 'I call upon those persons to witness that I, [name] do take thee, [name] to be my lawful and wedded wife [or husband]'. *Marriage Act* 1949, s. 44 (3). The parties are also entitled to use an alternative formula "I [name] take you [or thee] [name] to be my wedded wife [or husband]", introduced by s. 44 (3A) of the *Marriage Ceremony (Prescribed Words) Act* 1996.

[56]   PROBERT, R., 'Lord Hardwicke's Marriage Act – Vital Change 250 Years On?' (2004), p. 586.

[57]   *The Church and the Law of Nullity of Marriage*, cited in: BRADLEY, D., 'Comparative Law, Family Law and Common Law' (2003), p. 130.

[58]   *Marriage Act* 1949 (with amendments) and *Marriage (Prohibited Degrees of Relationship) Act* 1986.

[59]   See: CRETNEY, S., MASSON, J., BAILEY-HARRIS, R., *Principles of Family Law* (2003), p. 43-44.

although this impediment can be lifted except in the case that one of the protective spouses has been a 'child of the family' of the other prospective spouse.[60] An attempt to dispense with the impediments to marriage based on affinity failed due to the opposition of the clergy.[61] The prohibited degrees of affinity were reduced and qualified in 1960[62] and 1986. In 2005, the European Court of Human Rights held that the prohibition to marry ones daughter in law as long as both the former spouse of the father in law and the former spouse of the daughter in law are still alive, violates Article 12 of the European Convention on Human Rights.[63] In 2002, the ECHR declared in *Goodwin v. the United Kingdom* and *I. v. the United Kingdom,* that the English rules on marriage capacity, prohibiting post-operative transsexuals to marry a person of the opposite gender to that of their new gender, were incompatible with the European Convention on Human Rights.[64] This decision of the Strasburg Court was instantly followed by a decision of House of Lords in *Bellinger,*[65] in which the House of Lords declared the same provisions incompatible with the Human Rights Act 1998. In response to these developments the Government initiated the promulgation of the Gender Recognition Act (GRA) 2004,[66] which allows post-operative transsexuals to marry in their acquired gender.[67] The abandonment of the requirement of genetic heterosexuality as a precondition for marriage, implemented by the GRA, could be considered one of the most significant recent reforms of English marital capacity law. The age of marriage without parental consent is reduced from 21 to 18 in 1969.[68] The minimum age of marriage with parental consent is stated at 16,[69] with no possibility of dispensation.[70]

Equality of the spouses

In England and Wales, granting spouses with equal rights involved a rather peculiar process of piecemeal deterioration of the common law notion of unity of the

---

[60]   See: ibid.

[61]   The Marriage (Enabling) Bill was introduced for this purpose into Parliament in 1979 and defeated in the House of Lords among others due to the strong opposition of the Bishops. CRETNEY, S., *Family Law in the Twentieth Century* (2003), p. 53, note 106.

[62]   The 1960 Marriage Enabling Act relaxed the prohibited degrees of affinity in cases where there had been a divorce or decree of nullity.

[63]   *B. and L. v. U.K.* ECHR (2005).

[64]   *Goodwin v. the United Kingdom.* ECHR (2002) and *I. v. the United Kingdom.* ECHR (2002). For more on this development see Section 13.4.3.

[65]   *Bellinger v. Bellinger* [2003] *2 FLR,* p. 1048.

[66]   *Gender Recognition Act* (received Royal assent on 2 July 2004 and came into force on 4 April 2005).

[67]   See WELSTEAD, M., 'Reshaping Marriage and the Family – The Gender Recognition Act 2004 and the Civil Partnership Act 2004' (2006), p.185-197.

[68]   By the *Family Reform Act* 1969.

[69]   *Marriage Act* 1949, s. 2.

[70]   However, marriages concluded under this age abroad may be valid. CRETNEY, S., MASSON, J., BAILEY-HARRIS, R., *Principles of Family Law* (2003), p. 46, note 62.

spouses,[71] which actually meant the disappearance of the legal person of the wife in the legal person of the husband.[72] In the course of the nineteenth and twentieth centuries, the doctrine of legal unity 'has been eroded by the judges'[73] and 'cut down by statute after statute',[74] so that 'little of it remains'.[75] Nonetheless, very much an English tradition, the concept as such has never been abolished. The concept of *consortium*, previously interpreted in such a way that only the husband had an enforceable right to society and company of his wife, also underwent transformations that lean towards the equality of sexes.[76] By the 1970s, the interpretation of *consortium* evolved enough to acknowledge that 'both spouses are joint, co-equal heads of the family'.[77]

Another peculiarity of English law is that the rights of married women were equalised not with those of their husbands, but with those of single women. The property rights of married women had been equalised with those of unmarried ones in 1882.[78] In 1935, a married woman was granted contractual capacity of *femme sole*.[79] A statute of 1973 abolished the rule that provided for a married woman to automatically have the same legal domicile as her husband.[80] The duty to provide maintenance, which at common law traditionally rested with the husband, is now equally attributed to both spouses.[81] In 1973, the Guardianship Act stated that a mother should have the same rights and authority as the law attributed to a father, and that the rights of the parents should be equal.[82]

Concluding remarks

Thus, in spite of a generally felt need for a more coherent and comprehensive marriage law,[83] the ideological sensitivity of the matter precluded the various proposals from producing anything more than piecemeal changes,[84] which only increased

---

[71] On the doctrine of unity see Part II, Chapter 5, Section 5.2.3.
[72] See CRETNEY, S., MASSON, J., BAILEY-HARRIS, R., *Principles of Family Law* (2003), p. 71.
[73] Ibid.
[74] Ibid.
[75] Ibid.
[76] GLENDON, M. A., 'Power and Authority in the Family: New Legal Patterns as Reflection of Changing Ideologies' (1975), p. 10-11.
[77] BROMLEY, P., *Family Law* (1971), p. 94.
[78] See Part III, Chapter 10, Section 10.2.4.
[79] By the *Married Women and Tortfeasors* Act 1935.
[80] *Domicile and Matrimonial Proceedings* Act 1973.
[81] Sec. 27 of the *Matrimonial Causes* Act 1973.
[82] For more on this Act see: CRETNEY, S., *Family Law in the Twentieth Century* (2003), p. 574 ff.
[83] Ibid, p. 28.
[84] Ibid, p. 30-32.

incoherency.[85] Considering the 'close if not symbiotic relationship'[86] between the State and the Established Church, the general adherence to tradition[87] and the divide of public opinion on the matters concerning the secularisation of marriage law, the reform of marriage law has been successfully postponed up until the present day. There is, however, a good chance that the pending reform will bring English law more in line with other European countries in respect of the secularisation and coherency of marriage law.

13.2.2. FRANCE: LIBERTÉ, ÉGALITÉ, LAÏCITÉ

Secularisation and de-ideologisation of the law of marriage

It has been asserted that the evolution of French family law since 1804, and especially since 1965, has been 'one continuous promotion of two principles: liberty and equality'.[88] This could also be said of marriage law, even though French marriage law has shown remarkable stability over the last two centuries. According to Carbonnier, one of the persons behind the major reforms of family law of the 1960s and 70s, 'the winds of change that have blown on family law have left marriage intact, governed, with minor exceptions, by the original texts of the *Code Napoleon*'.[89] At the beginning of the third millennium, marriage, at least in appearance, has remained very much the same as it had been before.[90] This apparent stability did not mean the absence of tension. The sharp polarisation between the conservative and the progressive camps in France has generated a century-long controversy. The conservative camp, strongly influenced by Catholicism, supported the hierarchical model of marriage, while progressive circles contested this model in the name of 'individual liberty, secularism and equality'.[91]

The legislation inherited from the *Code Civil* remains, despite the obligatory civil marriage and the principle of secularisation, profoundly marked by the canonical concept of marriage.[92] 'Marriage retains its status as a fundamental institution, of

---

[85]   Ibid, p. 28.
[86]   BRADLEY, D., 'Comparative Law, Family Law and Common Law' (2003), p. 132.
[87]   Bradley remarked that 'If the starting point in the United Sates is, "how can limitations on the right to marry be justified?" the English approach has been, "why should existing restrictions on marital capacity be modified?"' Ibid, p. 131.
[88]   DEKEUWER-DÉFOSSEZ, F., 'Codifier le droit de la famille?' (2004), p. 229
[89]   Cited in: RUBELLIN-DEVICHI, J., 'How Matters Stand Now in Relation to French Law Reform' (2000), p. 152.
[90]   Ibid.
[91]   MARTIN, C., THÉRY, I., 'The PACS and Marriage and Cohabitation in France' (2001), p. 154.
[92]   CARBONNIER, J., 'Terre et ciel dans le droit français du mariage' (1950), p. 329.

unique nature in contrast to other forms of living together'.[93] The spouses are obliged to maintain a *communauté de vie* which includes a mutual obligation of fidelity, cohabitation and assistance.[94] The duty of cohabitation traditionally included the obligation to maintain a sexual relationship and a community of life which presupposed sharing a household.[95] Because a married woman has been allowed to have a separate domicile since 1975,[96] the community of life is now interpreted as maintaining an effective bond, without necessarily living under the same roof.[97] Most of the personal duties of the spouses, including the duty of fidelity, are still rendered legally enforceable, albeit indirectly, as their culpable violation constitutes a ground for divorce.[98] The duty of the spouses to maintain a sexual relationship is, however, no longer enforceable at law.[99] Civil marriage, first introduced in the Revolutionary law, is still perceived as one of the pillars of the *laïcité*: separation of Church and State, secularized society, and equality of the citizens before the law.[100] This 'unique and exclusive character of civil marriage'[101] is still reinforced by a criminal prohibition against celebrating a religious marriage before the civil registration has taken place.[102]

Capacity to marry

The impediments to marriage preclude marriage between descendents and ascendants,[103] siblings[104] and their descendents and ascendants related by affinity (parents and children in law, step-parents and step-children).[105] However, a dispensation can be obtained for a marriage between the collaterals and for those related by affinity, if the spouse, who created the affinity is deceased.[106] The question of opening up marriage to same-sex couples was a collateral issue in the discussion introducing the PACS.[107] It has been reported that the majority of French scholars neither support

---

[93] FERRÉ-ANDRÉ, S., 'A Pause in the Reform of French Family Law' (2004), p. 186.

[94] The original wording of the *Code Civil* imposing on the spouses the duty of mutual fidelity, help and assistance is still preserved: (*'Les époux se doivent mutuellement fidélité, secours, assistance'*). Art. 212 *Code Civil.*

[95] BÉNABENT, A., *Droit civil : La Famille* (2001), No. 161.

[96] Law of 11 July 1975. CARBONNIER, J., *Droit civil: La famille, l'enfant, le couple* (2002), p. 489.

[97] BÉNABENT, A., *Droit civil : La Famille* (2001), No. 162.

[98] The necessity to maintain this sanction is often used as an argument against abolition of the fault-based divorce. FERRÉ-ANDRÉ, S., H. et al, 'A Pause in the Reform of French Family Law' (2004), p. 186.

[99] RUBELLIN-DEVICHI, J., *Droit de la famille, 2001-2002* (2001) nr. 25, p. 51.

[100] MARTIN, C., THÉRY, I., 'The PACS and Marriage and Cohabitation in France' (2001), p. 154.

[101] THÉRY, I., 'La contrat d' union sociale en question' (1997), p. 170.

[102] Art. 433-21 of the Criminal Code. See also CORNU, G., *Droit Civil, La famille* (2003), No. 162.

[103] Art. 161 *Code Civil.*

[104] Art. 162 *Code Civil.*

[105] See CORNU, G., *Droit Civil, La famille* (2003), No. 181.

[106] BÉNABENT, A., *Droit civil : La Famille* (2001), No. 50-52 and 54-55.

[107] On the *Pacte civil de solidarité (PACS)* see Chapter 15, Section 15.6.2.

the idea of same-sex marriage nor feel restrained from expressing their negative attitude openly.[108] It has also been observed that the issue of same-sex marriage is perceived by its opponents neither as a question of minority rights nor as an issue of individual human rights.[109] It is rather presented as an issue of a minority's dissenting values and practices. It is therefore argued that the law must not always have to recognise such practises and values when they conflict with those upheld by the society as a whole.[110]

The age of marriage for women (15 years old) was different than that for men (18 years old) until 2006.[111] In line with the general European trend, this has been changed in 2006,[112] when the marriage age was equalised at 18 years old (the age of majority) for both sexes. If there are serious reasons, it is also possible for a marriage to occur below this age after obtaining a dispensation.[113]

Equality of the spouses

The controversy between the conservative and the progressive forces with regard to reforming the hierarchical model of marriage established in the *Code Civil* continued to persist deep into the 1970s.[114] As late as 1965, an attempt to remove the legal definition of the husband as the head of the family was successfully defeated.[115] Only by Law of 4 June 1970 was this provision replaced by the statement that spouses have an equal duty to ensure the moral and material guidance of the family, and to choose the matrimonial home.[116] Since then, the equality of the spouses has been rendered one of the fundamental principles of French family law.[117] However, even in the beginning of the new millennium the last remains of inequality were still traceable

---

[108] STEINER, E., 'The spirit of the new French registered partnership law – promoting autonomy and pluralism or weakening marriage' (2000), p. 10.
[109] Ibid, p. 12.
[110] Ibid.
[111] Art. 144 *Code Civil.*
[112] Act no 2006-399 of 4 April 2006. The new Article 144 of the *Code Civil* states that: "*L'homme et la femme ne peuvent contracter mariage avant dix huit ans révolus*".
[113] Art. 145 *Code Civil.*
[114] CARBONNIER, J., *Droit civil: La famille, l'enfant, le couple*, (2002), p. 489.
[115] GLENDON, M. A., 'Power and Authority in the Family: New Legal Patterns as Reflection of Changing Ideologies' (1975), p. 6.
[116] Glendon attributed this change of attitude to the revolts of 1968: 'it can be hardly doubted that the events of 1968 had an effect in causing the legislature so resistant to change only five years earlier to recognize this evolution'. GLENDON, M. A., 'Power and Authority in the Family: New Legal Patterns as Reflection of Changing Ideologies' (1975), p. 16. She suggested further that this change did not reflect the fact that a majority of the French society had rejected the traditional hierarchical structure of marriage, but rather that it was 'the "young people's" view that the new law responded to'. Ibid. p. 17-18.
[117] FOYER, J., 'The Reform of Family Law in France' (1978), p. 81.

in French marriage law, only to finally be removed in the 2000s. Thus, in 2002 the spouses acquired the right to choose either one of their names as the family name for their children. However, a 'trace of inequality did survive',[118] as, due to a last minute compromise with the Senate, a child will acquire the father's family name if the parents fail to agree.[119]

13.2.3. (WEST) GERMANY: MARRIAGE UNDER PROTECTION OF THE CONSTITUTION

Secularisation and de-ideologisation of the law of marriage

German marriage law is heavily influenced by two constitutional principles: that of the special State protection of marriage, laid down in Article 6 paragraph 1 of the German Constitution (*Grundgesetz, GG*), and that of the equality of man and woman, laid down in Article 3 paragraphs 2 and 3 *GG*. According to legal doctrine, the constitutional protection of marriage includes the general value guideline that the State should protect family and marriage,[120] the protection of marriage as an institution (*Institutsgarantie*), and the classical liberal protection of fundamental freedoms in marital matters.[121] These freedoms include the freedom over the decision to marry and the choice of a future spouse,[122] and the freedom to build a marital life according to the wishes of the spouses.[123] The *Institutsgarantie* is aimed at preserving the fundamental core features of the institution of marriage.[124] These fundamental features were delineated by the Federal Constitutional Court (*Bundesverfassungsgericht*) in its definition of marriage as 'an all-embracing, in principle indissoluble union between one man and one woman'.[125] The characterization of marriage as 'in principle indissoluble' does not involve a prohibition against divorce. Indeed, the 1976 West German Divorce Law, oddly enough, added a paragraph to the BGB proclaiming that

---

[118]   FERRÉ-ANDRÉ et al, 'Work in Hand for the Reform of French Family Law' (2003), p. 182.

[119]   Law of March 2002. See: FERRÉ-ANDRÉ et al, 'Work in Hand for the Reform of French Family Law' (2003), p. 182-183.

[120]   SCHLÜTER, W., HECKES, J., STOMMES, S., 'Die gesetzliche Regelung von außerehelichen Partnerschaften gleichen und verschiedenen Geschlechts im Ausland und die deutschen Reformvorhaben' (2000), p. 1-18.

[121]   Ibid, p. 8.

[122]   JARASS, H., PIEROTH, B., *Grundgesetz für die Bundesrepublik Deutschland: Kommentar*, Art. 6 (2002).

[123]   See: STINTZING, H., Constitutional Values and Social Change – The Case of German Marital and Family Law' (1999), p. 133.

[124]   SCHIMMEL, R., *Eheschliessungen gleichgeschlechtlicher Paare?* (1996), p. 133 ff.

[125]   This definition has been repeated in decisions of the BVerfG of 29 July 1959, *NJW* (1959), p. 1489-1490. 11 October 1978, *NJW* (1979), p. 595-596, 28 February 1980, *NJW* (1980), p. 689-690 and 30 November 1982, *NJW* (1983), p. 511-512. See: STRICK, K., 'Gleichgeschlechtliche Partnerschaft – Vom Straftatbestand zum Status?' (2000), p. 83.

'marriage is concluded for life'. This was part of a last-minute compromise enforced by the Christian Democrats on the ruling coalition Government.[126] This provision was later amended, following a decision of the Federal Constitutional Court, so that now the spouses have to demonstrate no more than the aspiration to stay together during their lifetime.[127] The heterosexual character of marriage was first explicitly mandated by the Federal Constitutional Court in 1993.[128] The appreciation of heterosexuality as fundamental to marriage boiled down to a constitutional ban on the introduction of same-sex marriage in Germany.[129] The Federal Constitutional Court confirmed as late as in 2002 that monogamy and the heterosexual character are still among the fundamental features of marriage.[130] The *Institutsgarantie* certainly does not mean that the concept of marriage is not open to change.[131] On the contrary, the general provisions dating from 1946 have constantly been adapted to social change through a kind of 'dynamic interpretation' by the Federal Constitutional Court.[132] However, the function of the *Institutsgarantie* is to create an additional barrier to adapting the ethical substance of marriage to social changes and transformations of moral views.[133] This barrier has more than once made modernisation of German marriage and cohabitation law more difficult than in other countries.[134]

German law imposes an obligation on the spouses to maintain a conjugal community of life.[135] This obligation has been interpreted to include a duty of fidelity and joint care of common tasks.[136] The spouses also owe each other mutual support and respect.[137] Since the Marriage Formation Act of 1998, the rules on the formation of marriage have been reincorporated into the BGB.[138] As in France, civil celebration of marriage is compulsory in Germany, and no religious marriage may be celebrated prior

---

[126] GLENDON, M.A., *Abortion and Divorce in Western Law* (1987), p. 109.

[127] STINTZING, H., 'Constitutional Values and Social Change – The Case of German Marital and Family Law' (1999), p. 139 and note 45 on p. 145.

[128] BVerfG, 4 October 1993, *NJW* (1993), p. 3058. See: SCHIMMEL, R., *Eheschliessungen gleich-geschlechtlicher Paare?* (1996), p. 133 ff.

[129] BVerfG, 17 July 2002, *NJW* (2002), p. 2543-2548.

[130] BVerfG, 17 July 2002, *NJW* (2002), p. 2543-2548.

[131] STRICK, K., 'Gleichgeschlechtliche Partnerschaft – Vom Straftatbestand zum Status?' (2000), p. 83.

[132] See: STINTZING, H., Constitutional Values and Social Change – The Case of German Marital and Family Law' (1999), p. 132-146.

[133] STRICK, K., 'Gleichgeschlechtliche Partnerschaft – Vom Straftatbestand zum Status?' (2000), p. 83.

[134] It was complained that 'marriage in Germany at the beginning of the twenty-first century enjoys the same protection as marriage in 1949, the founding year of the German Constitution – regardless of the many demographic and social changes'. OSTNER, I., 'Cohabitation in Germany – Rules, Reality and Public Discourses' (2001), p. 100.

[135] Para. 1357 I BGB. See: MARTINY, D., 'Family Law' (2005), p. 254.

[136] GOTTWALD, P., SCHWAB, D., BÜTTNER, E., *Family and Succession Law in Germany* (2001), p. 52.

[137] Ibid.

[138] The Eheschießungsrechtsgesetz of 4 May 1998 repealed the separate Marriage Law *Ehegesetz* of 1938.

to the civil celebration.[139] The exclusiveness of the civil ceremony is seen as a necessary aspect of the separation between Church and State.[140]

Capacity to marry

The rules on the capacity to marry were relaxed by the 1998 Marriage Formation Act. Affinity ceased to be an impediment to marriage.[141] The impediments based on consanguinity were reduced to descendents, ascendants and siblings.[142] In 1995, the political party Alliance 90/Greens proposed a Bill aimed at opening up marriage for same-sex couples.[143] The Bill, however, shattered against the constitutional ban of same-sex marriage. The fate of the 1995 Bill provides a good illustration of the conservative effect of the *Institutsgarantie*. The constitutional ban of same sex marriage, derived from the interpretation of Article 6 paragraph 1 *GG* by the Federal Constitutional Court, is, of course, no absolute impediment as the last word is always reserved for the legislature. However, this ban makes the introduction of same-sex marriage a more difficult job, as compared to the other countries. Such introduction is only possible in Germany through a preceding amendment of the constitutional law, which requires a qualified majority of the votes.[144] Considering the highly controversial nature of same-sex marriage, the requirement of a constitutional amendment creates a hefty impediment.

The age of marriage (18 years old) is the same as the age of majority under German law. The parties can seek a dispensation of the family court, provided that at least one of them has reached the age of majority and the other is at least 16 years old.[145] The party under age generally needs the consent of his or her legal representative. However, if such consent in rejected without reasonable grounds, the family court can allow the marriage without consent.[146]

---

[139]   Article 13 III Introductory Act to the *BGB* (with exceptions for international cases), see: MARTINY, D., 'Family Law' (2005), p. 254.

[140]   According to Müller-Freienfels the German law on civil ceremony still bears the mark of the *Kulturkampf*: Bismarck's struggle with the Catholic Church. MÜLLER-FREIENFELS, W., 'Family Law and the Law of Succession in Germany' (1967), p. 423.

[141]   GOTTWALD, P., SCHWAB, D., BÜTTNER, E., *Family and Succession Law in Germany* (2001), p. 49.

[142]   Ibid.

[143]   Bill *On Introduction of the Right to Conclude a Marriage for the Persons of the Same Sex* of 24 October 1995.

[144]   SCHLÜTER, W., HECKES, J., STOMMES, S., 'Die gesetzliche Regelung von außerehelichen Partnerschaften gleichen und verschiedenen Geschlechts im Ausland und die deutschen Reformvorhaben' (2000), p. 9.

[145]   Para. 1303 II BGB. MARTINY, D., 'Family Law' (2005), p. 254.

[146]   Para. 1303 III BGB. MARTINY, D., 'Family Law' (2005), p. 255.

Equality of the spouses

Other than the complex Article 6 paragraph 1, Article 3 paragraph 2 of the Constitution has, from the outset, served as a vehicle to modernise the law regarding equality of the spouses. While this was a matter of gradual piecemeal reforms in other West European countries, all of the legislation violating the equality of sexes in West Germany was in principle emasculated at once by Article 3 *GG*. However, legal provisions conflicting with the equality of sexes remained in force until 31 March 1953.[147] After some hesitation the 1957 'Law on Equal Rights of Man and Women in the Field of Civil Law' ('Equality Act')[148] formally altered most of the legal provisions in the spirit of equality.[149] The last remnants of inequality were cleaned up by the joint efforts of the legislature and the Federal Constitutional Court in the following years. Thus, in 1976 the husband's name ceased to be the family name by operation of law. In 1991, the Federal Constitutional Court declared the priority of the husband's name unconstitutional.[150] Following this decision, the Act of 1993[151] allowed the spouses to keep their own names unless they choose the name of one of them as a common family name.[152]

13.3. ENTERING THE 'ZONE OF HORROR': SWEDEN AND THE NETHERLANDS

13.3.1. SWEDEN: BREAKING WITH TRADITION

Secularisation and de-ideologisation of the law of marriage

As with other Swedish family law reforms, the reform of marriage law in Sweden was the most far-reaching and uncompromising in Europe. This reform was heavily influenced by the 'new radicalism'[153] that came to dominate Swedish politics in the

---

[147] Art. 117 para 1 *GG*.
[148] *Gesetz über die Gleichberechtigung von Mann und Frau auf dem Gebiete des Bürgerlichen Rechts* of 1 July 1957.
[149] GIESEN, D., 'The reform of Family Law in Germany' (1978), p. 115 ff.
[150] BVerfG, 5 March 1991, *NJW* (1991), p. 1602.
[151] *Gesetz zur Neuordnung des Familiennamensrechts* of 16 December 1993 amended on the 6th of February 2005. See: DETHLOFF, N., KROLL, K., 'The Constitutional Court as Driver of Reforms in German Family Law' (2006), p. 227.
[152] Ibid. p. 225-227.
[153] GYLLENSTEN, L., 'Swedish Radicalism in the 1960s: An Experiment in Political and Cultural Debate' (1972), p. 281.

mid-1960s.[154] In 1969, the Swedish Minister of Justice outlined the Guidelines for The Committee on Family Law, the group of experts appointed to prepare the new law on marriage and divorce.[155] These Guidelines became well-known, as they first formulated the famous Swedish 'neutrality policy'.[156] This policy was based on two fundamental political choices – the respect of ideological pluralism and the non-privileged legal treatment of marriage as compared to unmarried cohabitation. According to the neutrality policy, 'the legislation on marriage should not contain laws of specified, ethical nature, since ethical viewpoints could vary and couples should be allowed to develop their relationship within their own individual assumptions and values'.[157] The Guidelines stated that marriage should retain its central place within family law;[158] but at the same time, the law should not 'create unnecessary difficulties' for those who decide to build up a family without marrying'.[159] Marriage was defined as 'a form of voluntary cohabitation by independent persons'.[160] In line with these Guidelines, in 1972 the Committee on Family Law made its first proposals containing some far-reaching innovations. The Committee proposed to replace both civil and religious marriage ceremonies with a simple registration of civil status.[161] Further it was suggested that the duty of faithfulness should be omitted from the law 'as [an] expression of an ethical value'.[162] Although both of these proposals were rejected,[163] the new law of 1973, now incorporated in the 1987 Marriage Code, was still very innovative. As David Bradley rightly pointed out, it was felt that 'legal rules and norms [...] no longer reinforce[d] traditional values'.[164] Swedish law preserved the freedom of choice between civil or religious ceremony, but religious values no longer had any

---

[154]   SUNDBERG, J., 'Marriage or no Marriage. The Directives for the Revision of Swedish Family Law' (1971), p. 232.

[155]   See: Official Reports Series of Swedish Legislative and Investigative Commission, 1972, No. 41 *Family and Marriage*. For an English translation see: *Abstract of protocol in justice department matters*, 15 Augustus 1969.

[156]   See: AGELL, A., 'Should and Can Family Law Influence Social behaviour?' (1998), p. 127-129.

[157]   Ibid, p. 127.

[158]   *Abstract of protocol in justice department matters*, 15 Augustus 1969, p. 4.

[159]   Ibid.

[160]   Ibid, p. 5.

[161]   Report of the Committee on Family Law. *Official Reports Series of Swedish Legislative and Investigative Commission*, 1972, No. 41 'Entering into and Dissolving of Marriage', p. 257-259. One of the critics of the proposal – Sundberg connected this attempt to de-formalise marriage with the fact that in his mind 'socialist ideology in Sweden always took a negative view of the bourgeois church marriage and favoured, as a matter of principle, the *de facto* marriage or free partnership based on conscience. Greatly encouraged by the Bolshevik developments in Russia of the 1920s making the *de facto* marriage the mainstay of Russian married life, this attitude took a deep hold among the Swedish Socialists and survived the later twists and turns in Communist ideology'. SUNDBERG, J., 'Marriage or no Marriage. The Directives for the Revision of Swedish Family Law' (1971), p. 230.

[162]   AGELL, A., 'Should and Can Family Law Influence Social behaviour?' (1998), p. 127.

[163]   The current Swedish marriage law states that spouses owe each other fidelity and respect. Ibid.

[164]   BRADLEY, D., *Family Law and Political Culture* (1996), p. 66.

influence on the civil law of marriage.[165] The civil marriage ceremony was stripped of ideological adornments to the extent that couples were allowed to choose not to exchange life-long vows.[166] At the moment, the introduction of obligatory civil marriage is being discussed in Sweden in connection with the debate surrounding the opening up of marriage for same-sex couples. As it is considered inappropriate to impose a duty on the Church to provide a Church registration of same-sex marriages, replacing the dual system with obligatory civil marriage has been suggested as a solution to this problem.[167] Considering, however, that a general inquiry held in 2006 showed that a vast majority of respondents wants to maintain the present double-track system,[168] it seems unlikely that this system will be changed.[169]

Capacity to marry

The impediments to marriage are reduced in Sweden 'to an absolute minimum';[170] even a marriage between half-brother and half-sister is possible with a dispensation.[171] The legislature dealt with the reform of marriage law in a personalistic and pragmatic fashion, refusing to make concessions to abstract religious or moral principles.[172] Also, the classical canon vision of marriage as a union aimed at procreation, lost its place in Swedish law as post-operative transsexuals were allowed to marry.[173] At the same time, the Swedish legislature fell short of introducing same-sex marriage in 1984 as the public opinion was not ready yet to accept it.[174] Since 2002, the public debate on opening up marriage for same-sex couples has been revived.[175]

---

[165] As Bradley has rightly concluded, the Swedish law dispensed with 'a religious code as the foundation for the institution of marriage'. Ibid.

[166] AGELL, A., 'The Swedish Legislation on Marriage and Cohabitation: A Journey Without a Destination' (1980), p. 13.

[167] JÄNTERÄ-JAREBORG, M., SÖRGJERD, C., 'The Experiences with Registered Partnership in Scandinavia' (2004), p. 586.

[168] The enquiry was carried out in 2006 by the Committee on Marriage and Partnership of The Swedish Statistical Bureau among a selected portion of Swedish population. See: Undersökning om kyrklig och borgerlig vigsel, 2006. Uppdragsgivare: Äktenskaps- och partnerskapsutredningen, Statistics Sweden 2006.

[169] Letter by Professor Maarit JÄNTERÄ-JAREBORG to the author.

[170] BRADLEY, D., *Family Law and Political Culture* (1996), p. 67.

[171] Ibid.

[172] Report of the Committee on Family Law. *Official Reports Series of Swedish Legislative and Investigative Commission*, 1972, No. 41 'Entering into and Dissolving of Marriage', p. 257. Cited in: Ibid.

[173] Ibid, p. 67-68.

[174] Ibid, p. 68.

[175] Since, 2000, several motions advocating introducing same-sex marriage have been submitted to the Swedish Parliament. JÄNTERÄ-JAREBORG, M., SÖRGJERD, C., 'The Experiences with Registered Partnership in Scandinavia' (2004), p. 582.

Equality of the spouses

The problem of the formal equality of the spouses was not an issue in Sweden at the time of the reform of marriage law in 1973; it had already been introduced in 1920. In the period after the 1960s, Sweden proceeded to the next stage: achieving de-facto equality of women in the family and in the public sphere.[176]

13.3.2. THE NETHERLANDS: ALLOWING SAME-SEX COUPLES INTO THE TEMPLE OF MARRIAGE

Secularisation and de-ideologisation of the law of marriage

The Dutch marriage law of today in general is rather modern compared to other European countries. This is the result of a sweeping liberalisation from the 1970s onwards that radically changed the face of the, until that time, traditionally conservative Dutch family law.

The obligatory civil marriage ceremony introduced in Holland by the *Code Civil* was retained in the subsequent codifications. Celebration of a religious marriage prior to a civil marriage is prohibited under pain of criminal prosecution.[177] This prohibition has been the subject of legislative discussion more than once, but has thus far remained untouched.[178]

Dutch marriage law is profoundly purged of ideology. The definition of a marital bond as a life-long union has given way to the perception of marriage as a 'durable community of two natural persons'.[179] The law still states that the spouses owe each other fidelity, help and assistance;[180] however, in line with modern trends, reproduc-

---

[176] One of the important steps in this field was the 1979 Law *Concerning Equality between Men and Women at Work*. For more on the path to de-facto equality in Sweden, see: BRADLEY, D., *Family Law and Political Culture* (1996), p. 79- 95.

[177] Art. 1:68 Dutch *Civil Code (Burgerlijk wetboek)* and Art. 449 Dutch *Criminal Code*.

[178] In 1992, the Ministry of Justice was working on a Bill abolishing the prohibition of preceding religious ceremony. As late as 2001 this prohibition was challenged in the Parliament as violating religious freedom and interfering in religious affairs (Proceedings of the Second Chamber, 2001 p. 19-1428-19-1431). The Secretary of Justice, in a report, concluded after excessive scrutiny that the current situation should be maintained in the name of 'legal certainty, carefulness and publicity'. Second Chamber, 2001/2002, 28 078, No. 1. Also, diverse suggestions ranging from allowing preceding religious ceremony to the introduction of a dual system of marriage celebration have recently been made in the legal doctrine. See WESTERHOF, L., 'Civiel effect voor het kerkelijk huwelijk?' (2002), p. 80-81.

[179] ASSER – DE BOER, *Personen- en familierecht* (2002), No. 105.

[180] Art. 1:81 Dutch *Civil Code*.

tion and sexual relationships are no longer considered to be essential elements of marriage.[181] Since 2001 the spouses are no longer under legal obligation to cohabit.[182]

Capacity to marry

Dutch rules on capacity to marry were liberalised in 1970. Since then only a close degree of consanguinity (descendents, ascendants, and siblings) forms an impediment to marriage.[183] In 1983, all persons related by affinity were allowed to intermarry.[184] Since 1985, post-operative transsexuals have been able to marry a person of the gender opposite to that of their new gender.[185]

In 1985, the difference in the marital age between men (18 years old) and women (16 years old) was replaced by a uniform marital age of 18 for both sexes.[186] In case of serious reasons, parties can seek dispensation by the Minister of Justice.[187] If a girl is pregnant or has given birth to a child and both parties have reached the age of 16, marriage is possible without dispensation.[188] In order to marry, parties under the age of majority (18 years old) need the consent of their parents.[189] Such consent can be substituted by the consent of the district judge.[190]

By far the most interesting development of Dutch marriage law was that the Netherlands became the first country in the world to open up marriage for same-sex couples. It took almost thirty years before the Netherlands was able to make this step after the Swedish had considered it too far-reaching in 1973. On 1 April 2001, same-sex couples were allowed to enter into civil marriage. The introduction of same-sex marriage in the Netherlands had a relatively long prehistory.[191] This story started rather undramatically. Dutch law, as with most European legal systems, did not explicitly

---

[181]   ASSER – DE BOER, *Personen- en familierecht* (2002), No. 105.
[182]   Law of 13 May 2001.
[183]   Art. 1: 41 (1) Dutch *Civil Code*.
[184]   Law of 15 June 1983. ASSER – DE BOER, *Personen- en familierecht* (2002), No. 124.
[185]   This is a consequence of the legal recognition of gender reassessment by the law of 24 April 1985.
[186]   Art. 31 part 1 of the Book one of the Dutch Civil Code.
[187]   Art. 31 part 2 of the Book one of the Dutch Civil Code.
[188]   Art. 31 part 3 of the Book one of the Dutch Civil Code.
[189]   Art. 35 part 1 of the Book one of the Dutch Civil Code.
[190]   Art. 36 of the Book one of the Dutch Civil Code.
[191]   The prehistory of same sex marriage is comprehensively described in English by Caroline Forder in: *The International Survey of Family Law*: 'An Undutchable Family Law: Partnership, Parenthood, Social Parenthood, Names and Some Article 8 ECHR Case Law' (1997), p. 264-268; 'Opening Up Marriage to Same Sex Partners and Providing Adoption by Same Sex Couples, Managing Information on Sperm Donor, and Lots of Private International Law' (2000), p. 247-251; 'To Marry or Not to Marry: that is the Question' (2004), p. 301-304.

forbid same-sex marriage;[192] no one thought of such a possibility at the time of its drafting. In the early 1990s this lacuna inspired two same-sex couples to start legal proceedings in order to be allowed to marry. In 1990, the Dutch Supreme Court rejected their claim,[193] but allowed for 'a possibility that there is no sufficient legitimation for the fact that some legal consequences are attributed to marriage, and not to a durable cohabitation of two same-sex persons'.[194] This decision gave an important impetus to the preparation of legislation on institutionalising same-sex relationships.[195] The intent at that time was to create a legal institution that would be clearly different from marriage, but would provide same-sex partners with certain rights.[196] The tide started to change only when, for the first time since 1918, a Government without the participation of a confessional party was formed in 1994.[197] The coalition liberal-socialist Government ('Purple I') was formed by two large parties: the VVD (liberals) and the PvdA (social democrats), together with D66, a small progressive liberal party which was to play a crucial role in the introduction of same-sex marriage. On 16 April 1996, the Second Chamber[198] of the Dutch Parliament accepted a resolution calling for the removal of the legislative bar on same-sex marriage.[199] The same year, the Government formed a *Commission On the Opening of Civil Marriages for Persons of the Same Sex* (*Kortmann Commission II*) to advise on this matter. In 1997 this Commission completed its report in which all arguments pro and contra were summed up.[200] The majority of the *Kortmann Commission II* (five members) advised to open up marriage to same-sex couples,[201] and the minority suggested an 'separate but equal' solution by proposing equating same-sex partners with spouses, without granting them the right to marry.[202] The Government was initially more inclined to go on with the Bill on Registered Partnership rather than to follow the advice of the majority of the Commission to introduce same-sex

---

[192] For an extensive analysis of this issue see: WAALDIJK, C., 'Beantwoording rechtsvraag Homohuwelijk' (1987), p. 645.

[193] See: WAALDIJK, C., 'De heteroseksuele exclusiviteit van het huwelijk na Hoge Raad 19 oktober 1990' (1981), p. 47-56.

[194] Hoge Raad, 19 October 1990, *NJ* (1992), no. 129.

[195] For more details see: WAALDIJK, C., 'Partnerschapsregistratie en huwelijk: toenemende rechtsgelijkheid voor geslachtsgelijke partners en hun kinderen' (2000), p. 128-130.

[196] WORTMANN, S., 'Zo zijn we niet getrouwd. De openstelling van het huwelijk voor personen van hetzelfde geslacht' (2001), p. 83.

[197] http://www.parlement.com. Kabinetten per tijdvak. Periode 1994 – 2002: Paars.

[198] The Lower Chamber of the Dutch Parliament.

[199] The resolution stated that 'there was no objective justification' for such a bar. Second Chamber, 1995/1996, 22 700, No. 18.

[200] *The Report of the Kortmann Commission On the Opening of Civil Marriages for Persons of the Same Sex*, Ministry of Justice, The Hague, 1997, p. 14-16. Further referred to as Report Commission Kortmann II. For an account in English see: FORDER, C., 'Un Undutchble Family Law: Partnership, Parenthood, Social Parenthood, Names and Some Article 8 ECHR Case Law' (1997), p. 264-268.

[201] Report Commission Kortmann (1997), p. 22.

[202] Ibid, p. 23.

marriage.[203] Consequently, in January 1998, the Law on Registered Partnership[204] introduced a marriage-like partnership[205] which virtually equalised same-sex couples with spouses in nearly all aspects, except for the status of the marriage, the presumption of legal parentage on the part of the partner of the mother of the child, the right to adopt children, and some less important points.[206] However, neither the legislature nor the gay community were content with this 'separate but equal' solution. The Second Chamber reacted by accepting another resolution in favour of same-sex marriage.[207] A survey among the lesbian and gay community pointed out that 80% of respondents among same-sex registered partners said that had same-sex marriage existed, they would have opted for it.[208] In the summer of 1998, a second coalition Government of the same political parties was formed (Purple II). This time D66 had managed to elevate the question of same-sex marriage to one of the items of the coalitional agreement.[209] It was agreed that a Bill opening up marriage for same-sex couples should be enacted no later than 1 January 1999.[210] The Government nearly kept this promise; the Bill was introduced in the Second Chamber on 8 July 1998, in spite of negative advice from the Council of State.[211] It was supported in the Second and First Chambers[212] by all parties except the Christian Democrats and small religious parties, and became law on 1 April 2001.[213]

One may wonder why the Netherlands became the first country in the world to allow same-sex marriage. It had neither a century-long tradition of liberal family law, like Scandinavia, nor experienced a radical break with religion, like the Soviet countries. Part of the explanation may lie in the fact that the transformations of the 1960s and 70s were, in the Netherlands, perhaps more sweeping and far reaching than in the most of Western Europe. Tolerance for homosexuality was part and parcel of this change. The secularisation of Dutch society went so far that in the whole discussion surround-

---

[203]   Second Chamber, 1997/1998, 22 700, No. 26.
[204]   Law of 5 July 1997, entered into force on 1 January 1998.
[205]   For more on the Dutch Registered Partnership see: Section 15.7.3. of the Chapter 15.
[206]   Kees Waaldijk has estimated the level of equalisation at 93%. (WAALDIJK, C., 'Partnerschapsregistratie en huwelijk: toenemende rechtsgelijkheid voor geslachtsgelijke partners en hun kinderen' (2000), p. 136). For a detailed comparison of legal consequences of marriage and registered partnership see: Ibid. p. 132-154.
[207]   Second Chamber, 1997/1998, 22 700, No. 26.
[208]   SCHERF, Y., Registered Partnership in the Netherlands. A quick scan (1999), p. 28.
[209]   In the Dutch context, such coalitional agreement forms the basis of Governmental policy and is binding in so far as that non-performance could result in the fall of the Government.
[210]   Second Chamber, 1997/1998, 26 024, No. 9.
[211]   The Counsel of State considered that 'the time was not yet ripe' for such innovation. Second Chamber, 1998/1999, 26 672, B.
[212]   The Upper Chamber of the Dutch parliament.
[213]   Act of 21 December 2000 On the Opening Up Marriage for the Persons of the Same Sex. Came into force on 1 April 2001.

ing same-sex marriage only secular and rational arguments were brought into play.[214] Once the idiom of religion was dismissed, it became very difficult to reject same-sex marriage on the basis of rational arguments.[215] It is difficult to say whether a majority of the Dutch population supported the idea of same-sex marriage, but it was definitely not against it. There were no heated debates either in Parliament or in Dutch society in general.[216] The absence of commotion was attributed to the 'indifference' of the majority of the Dutch population,[217] but it could also be seen as a manifestation of tolerance.

As the Law on Registered Partnership had already almost equalised same-sex couples with spouses, it was rightly concluded that introducing same-sex marriage was a purely ideological undertaking and not a matter of practical or legal need.[218] The main arguments in favour of same-sex marriage in all stages of discussion remained equality and non-discrimination. However, both supporters and opponents[219] of same-sex marriage felt very clearly that the central issue was the ultimate approval of same-sex relationships.[220] In the explanatory note that accompanied the Bill to the Parliament, the Government cited the report of the *Kortmann Commission II*, which stated that because of the 'symbolic and emotional value of marriage', the inaccessibility of marriage for same-sex couples could be interpreted to mean that their relationships were regarded as being of lesser value.[221]

Complete equality was not reached even by the introduction of same-sex marriage, as according to the new law the legal presumption of parentage is not applicable for

---

[214] For a concise analysis of the argumentation, see: BOELE-WOELKI, K., SCHRAMA, W., 'Die Rechtsstellung von Menschen mit homosexueller Veranlagung im niederländischen Recht' (2000), p. 79-80.

[215] For the motives behind the introduction see also: WAALDIJK, C., 'De voorgestelde Wet openstelling huwelijk' (1999), p. 199.

[216] The issue was really debated only in media with a specific religious affiliation. WORTMANN, S., 'Zo zijn we niet getrouwd. De openstelling van het huwelijk voor personen van hetzelfde geslacht' (2001), p. 84.

[217] Ibid.

[218] Ibid, p. 83.

[219] Thus, Van Mourik, a committed opponent of same-sex marriage, wrote that: 'the homosexual couples wished not just a public recognition of their union but merely a kind of recognition which is coupled on the very institution which is century long open only for heterosexual couples'. MOURIK, M., VAN, 'Turbulentie in het familierecht' (1997), p. 398.

[220] Differing from the discussion in the USA, the Dutch discussion was never held from the position that marriage should be made available to same-sex couples because it is one of the fundamental rights to which homo- and heterosexual people must have access without discrimination, but rather from the position that 'the state must remain neutral on whether homosexuality is a normative good'. On the American case see: FELDBLUM, C., 'The Limitations of Liberal Neutrality Arguments in Favour of Same-Sex Marriage' (2001), p. 55-60.

[221] Explanatory note. Second Chamber, 1998/1999, 26 672, No. 3.

same-sex spouses.[222] At the same time, adoption was opened up for same-sex couples.[223] The legislature chose to institutionalise the social parentage between a child, born within homosexual relationships with the aid of artificial procreation techniques, and the same-sex partner of the child's parent, not by amending paternity law, but via adoption law.[224] This allowed opponents to speak about the creation of 'two types of marriage', one with and one without the presumption of parentage,[225] and even to deny same-sex marriage the quality of marriage.[226] But this was considered not so important as long as same-sex couples obtained access to the status of marriage and the marital 'decency' which it radiated. The recognition of same-sex marriages abroad was seen as a far more serious problem.[227]

As has already been mentioned, the opponents of same sex marriage appeared to be unable to present convincing rational arguments against it. In general they came with not much more than the habitual appeal to 'history, tradition, social reality, quantitative predominance of heterosexuality and the fact that only a heterosexual couple can procreate a child'.[228] It was rightly counter-argued that a history and tradition of discrimination and exclusion is more an argument in favour than against complete equalisation.[229] The procreation argument was one of the few rational arguments brought about. This argument allowed to maintain that the different treatment of same-sex couples was not discrimination, as they were not naturally equal to heterosexual coupes in respect of procreation. However, the Government discharged this argument referring to the changes which marriage, as a worldly institution, has undergone. It was noticed that the importance of procreation as an attribute of

---

[222] In the Report by the Kortmann Commission II this limitation was justified by the argument that '[…] otherwise the gulf between reality (there is no parentage) and the law (there is a legal filiation link) […]' would be too great. Report Commission Kortmann II, p. 5.

[223] Act of 21 December 2000 *On the Opening Up Adoption for the Persons of the Same Sex*. Came into force on 1 April 2001. See also: ANTOKOLSKAIA, M., 'Recent Developments in Dutch Filiation, Adoption and Joint Custody Law' (2002), p. 793-796.

[224] Although under Dutch law a female spouse or partner of the mother of the child is deprived of the possibility to recognise that child, she can adopt it according to a simplified procedure. ANTOKOLSKAIA, M., 'Recent Developments in Dutch Filiation, Adoption and Joint Custody Law' (2002), p. 795. The easiness of such adoption allowed Sylvia Wortmann to suggest that the very boundaries between adoption and the establishment of paternity are fading away. WORTMANN, S., 'Kroniek van het personen- en familierecht' (2001), p. 1543.

[225] This was one of the main counter-arguments of the Christian Democratic Party during the parliamentary debates. Second Chamber, 1999/2000, 26 672, No. 4.

[226] Thus, Andre Nuytinck was convinced that marriage with no consequences for parentage is no marriage. NUYTINCK, A., 'De Wet openstelling huwelijk en de Wet adoptie door personen van hetzelfde geslacht' (2000), p. 214.

[227] See: PELLIS, L., 'Het homohuwelijk: een bijzonder nationaal product' (2002), p. 162-168; BOELE-WOELKI, K., 'De prijs van het homohuwelijk' (1999), p. 113.

[228] DE BOER, J., 'A whole code of family law: boek 1 BW getoetst aan het EVRM' (1987), p. 11.

[229] WAALDIJK, C., 'Beantwoording rechtsvraag. Homohuwelijk' (1987), p. 645.

marriage has significantly diminished in the course of the years, while the characteristic of marriage as an affective bond aimed at mutual care and care for children has grown in importance.[230]

The most used argument against same-sex marriage was rather tautologous; it claimed that marriage is a heterosexual union that, if it were to be opened up to same-sex couples, would cease to be a marriage. Some were convinced that 'when naming same-sex marriage a 'marriage' we are sticking the label 'marriage' to something that is not a marriage and can never be a marriage'.[231] Others went a step further and claimed that the introduction of same-sex marriage would boil down to the 'abolition of marriage'.[232] This vision was based upon the transpersonalistic assumption that a considerable group of individuals should suffer in the name of the abstract notion of 'marriage as a heterosexual institution'. The Government has, however, chosen a personalistic approach, based on the supposition that marriage is made for man and not man for marriage.

It is notable that during the parliamentary debates even the Christian Democrats kept within the secular rational discussion and did not put forward any theological arguments. Only the small, strictly Protestant parties that are represented in Dutch Parliament did so. They referred to the fact that 'marriage is founded in the creation' and that same-sex marriage would conflict with their religious beliefs.[233] These complaints presented a very sensitive choice for the Government. The Government could either pay respect to the right of same-sex couples to equally share the symbolic and emotional meaning of marriage, or pay respect to the feelings of those for whom the symbolic and emotional value of marriage was inseparable from its heterosexual character.[234] The law professor Van Mourik, one of the most fervent opponents of same-sex marriage, had even announced that if the Netherlands would open up marriage for same-sex couples, he would dissolve his marriage in The Netherlands and conclude it again in Belgium or Germany[235]– not anticipating at the time, that Belgium would become the second European country to open up marriage for same-

---

[230]   First Chamber, 2000/2001, 26 672, No. 92a.
[231]   NUYTINCK, A., 'De Wet openstelling huwelijk en de Wet adoptie door personen van hetzelfde geslacht' (2000), p. 214.
[232]   VAN MOURIK, M., 'Wettelijke en contractuele vormgeving van affectieve relaties' (1999), p. 67-68.
[233]   Second Chamber, 1999/2000, 26 672, No. 4.
[234]   This choice was delineated by the Council of State in its report on the Bill. Second Chamber, 1998/1999, 26 672, B.
[235]   Public conversation between Van Mourik and an editor of the Gay magazine (*Homokrant*) during the annual meeting of the Royal Organisation of Public Notaries (*KNB*) held in Maastricht on 29 September 2000.

sex couples in 2003.[236] However, the appeals of some conservative heterosexuals against same-sex marriage because they wanted their marriage to be a part of a solely heterosexual institution were taken no more seriously than were the appeals to deny the possibility of divorce because some wanted to be a part of an indissoluble marriage. The Government acknowledged that it is painful to hurt the feelings of some parts of the population, but stressed that the new law concerned only marriage as a worldly institution, not marriage as a religious, God-given establishment.[237] Very much in the Dutch tradition, a 'practical' solution was found in response to a particular civil servant who claimed to have conscientious objections to administrating same-sex marriages. According to the Minister of Justice, civil servants with conscientious objections should be substituted by their colleges or not scheduled to officiate same-sex marriages.[238]

Equality of spouses

In the Netherlands, married women were granted legal capacity only in the late 1950s.[239] In 1958, the definition of the husband as the head of the family 'disappeared in the museum of legal curiosities'.[240] In 1984, the majority of the remaining legal provisions that violated the equality between spouses were altered.[241] However, as in most of Europe, some remnants of inequality are still visible in Dutch law. Thus, although since 1998 parents are free to choose the name of the father or of the mother as the family name of their children, in the absence of such agreement the child will be given the name of the father.[242] This situation has been widely considered by the legal community as discrimination against the mother.[243]

13.4. CONVERGENCE OF THE LAW OF MARRIAGE?

13.4.1. DE-IDEOLOGISATION OF THE LAW OF MARRIAGE

The suggestion made by Mary Ann Glendon in the late 1980s, that the main differences in marriage law in Europe could be structured along two lines: '(1) the extent to which

---

[236] Law of 13 February 2003 *On Opening up Marriage for the Same Sex Persons.* Came into force on 1 July 2003.
[237] First Chamber, 2000/2001, 26 672, No. 92a.
[238] Second Chamber, 1999/2000, 26 672, No. 12.
[239] By Law of 14 June 1956.
[240] ASSER – DE BOER, *Personen- en familierecht* (2002), No. 181.
[241] Law of 30 August 1984.
[242] Art. 1: 5 (5) Dutch *Civil Code.*
[243] For instance: BOOR, E., 'Blijft vaders wil wet?' (2003), p. 54-60; BOELE-WOELKI, K., 'Het WODC rapport: De gekozen achternaam' (2003), p. 37.

marriage rituals, religious or customary in origin, have been appropriated by the State, secularized, and made uniform for all groups of the population, and (2) the ideology of marriage being communicated by the legal system',[244] remain true to this day. In spite of the secularisation and liberalisation of marriage law during the 1960s and 70s, for the conservatives marriage retained a symbolic ethical and ideological meaning, inherited from the times when marriage was considered a holy estate. The present state of affairs is that the level of de-ideologisation of marriage remains quite different throughout Europe. Two opposing tendencies with regard to the de-ideologisation of marriage law are apparent in Europe through the discussed period. On the one hand, avoiding ideological declarations both in the definition of marriage and during the civil marriage ceremony can be considered as one of the general trends of marriage law. On the other hand, many European countries are quite reluctant to strip marriage law completely of its traditional ideological décor.

In the Western European countries the tendency towards the de-ideologisation of marriage comes down to stressing the contractual nature of marriage and extending the release of marriage law from the remnants of the canonical concept of marriage and traditional marriage values. In the Eastern European countries the same tendency is apparent, but here it is rather a reaction to communist marriage ideology, according to which spouses were taught to strengthen marriage and the family as 'a basic cell of socialist society'. This detested piece of the past makes post-communist legislatures quite allergic to ethical declarations.[245] In both cases the de-ideologisation tendency reflects the growing awareness that the law is unable to regulate feelings and moral convocations, and that there can be no legal sanction for lack of marital affection[246] or disregard of the duty of fidelity.[247] It is for these reasons that many countries have chosen to avoid declarative rules that cannot be enforced and at best are only able to provide some educational effect. Another incentive to avoid ethical declarations has to do with the difficulty of finding shared ethical values with regard to marriage in a

---

[244] GLENDON, M.A., *The Transformation of Family Law* (1989), p. 66.

[245] For example, post-socialist Russian law contains no definition of marriage, and even scholarly definitions say nothing about fidelity, life-long commitment and other ethical dimensions of marriage. See the comments on the provisions on marriage of the 1996 Russian Family Code by KHAZOVA O., 'Conclusion of Marriage' (2000), p. 51.

[246] E.g. the French Cassation Court ruled in 1972 that the fact that a wife acknowledged to her husband that she never felt any affection for him is no ground for divorce, as 'the law imposes an obligation of fidelity and not of feelings'. (Cass. fr. (2e civ), 2 February 1972, D. 1972, jur., 295). According to Dutch law the absence of affection is of no influence on the validity of marriage. ASSER – DE BOER, *Personen- en familierecht* (2002), No. 108.

[247] Under German law one of the spouses can bring an action before the court asking for fulfilment of the personal duties including the duty of fidelity (*Herstellungsklage*). However, the court order may only state that the duty has been violated: the personal nature of the duty precludes the legal enforceability of such order. GOTTWALD, P., SCHWAB, D., BÜTTNER, E., *Family and Succession Law in Germany* (2001), p. 52.

modern pluralistic society.[248] The tendency towards de-ideologisation is for instance overtly manifest in Dutch marriage law, which deliberately avoids dealing with 'ethical and religious'[249] aspects of marriage and limits itself to regulation of its 'practical civil aspects'.[250] The same applies to Russian law.[251] Swedish law deliberately allows spouses to avoid vows for life.

At the same time, many European countries continue to preserve the traditional ideological message of the law of marriage. Jean Carbonnier had already explained this thirty years ago by the fact that, 'even though secularised, marriage has a sort of religious gravity which is peculiar to it and which separates it from the free union – a gravity based on the idea that man's binding himself until death is an aspect of his intimation of mortality and his struggle against the ephemeral nature of existence'.[252] This appreciation is still an appealing argument for retaining the vows for life and the duty of fidelity as part of marriage ceremony. Of course in a time of widespread divorce, a promise of commitment for life is more an expression of intent than the reflection of a future reality. However, as everyone who drives a car, knowing that accidents happen every day, still hopes that he or she will be spared, so almost every marrying couple hopes that their love will be everlasting and that they will stay married 'until death do us part'. This way, by promising eternal commitment, the future spouses try to challenge the imperfection of human efforts and pay homage to the 'secular religion of love'.[253] The fact that marriage has become only one of many socially accepted forms of cohabitation has largely relieved the tension surrounding the ideological message of marriage. Today, when people are more or less free to choose marriage as one of several forms of cohabitation, some prospective spouses opt for marriage mainly because of the romance of eternal commitment and the solace of tradition.[254] This suggestion is supported by the fact that in the countries with obligatory civil marriage (for instance the Eastern European countries), even non

---

[248] Thus, it quite accepted in post-Soviet Russia that 'the ethical assessment of their marriage is strictly the personal business of the spouses, depending exclusively upon their religious, philosophic and ethical views. Imposing such views from above is nothing else than interference in the freedom of ideology'. ANTOKOLSKAIA, M., *Semeinoe pravo*, (1999), p. 105.

[249] ASSER – DE BOER, *Personen- en familierecht* (2002), No. 108.

[250] Ibid.

[251] As I have written in my monograph on Russian family law: 'law has to limit itself to the regulation of the civil dimension of marriage, as the ethical and religious dimensions of marriage lie outside the scope of secular marriage law'. ANTOKOLSKAIA, M., *Semeinoe pravo* (1999), p. 105.

[252] CARBONNIER, J., *Flexible droit: textes pour une sociologie du droit sans rigueur* (1971), p. 137, Cited in: GLENDON, M.A., *The Transformation of Family Law* (1989), at p. 71.

[253] LEWIS, J., 'Debates and Issues Regarding Marriage and Cohabitation in the British and American Literature' (2001), p. 179.

[254] Recent surveys show that the most important reasons to opt for marriage rather than cohabitation are: religious observance (KIERNAN, K., 'The State of European Unions: an Analysis of Partnership Formation and Dissolution' (2002), p. 65-66) and the birth of a child. SCHRAMA, W., *De niet-huwelijkse samenleving in het Nederlandse en Duitse recht* (2004), p. 86.

religious couples often wish to have a subsequent Church wedding, out of a certain dissatisfaction with a down-to-earth civil ceremony that is stripped of all romance and ambience.

Considering the tension between the two aforementioned trends, it seems realistic to predict that the diversity in respect to the ideological message of marriage law will not disappear in the near future. It is rather unlikely that the countries with far-reaching de-ideologisation of marriage law will make a step back and re-introduce ideological statements into marriage law. It seems also improbable that all countries retaining ideological messages in their marriage law will be willing to abandon these anytime soon. Another important political aspect of ideological differences in the law is the position that various European states have taken in respect of the institution of marriage. These positions vary from the Swedish ideology of 'neutrality' to the German constitutional protection of the institution of marriage and the English choice for State support of the institution of marriage.

13.4.2. SECULARISATION OF THE LAW OF MARRIAGE

The secularisation of marriage law has gone so far that presently there is no European State that does not provide for the civil registration of marriage. It is here, however, that the 'common core' ends. Europe continues to be divided into those countries with obligatory civil marriage and those with a two-tier system of civil and religious marriage.

A majority of European jurisdictions[255] provide for a dual system of civil and religious marriage. Such a solution could be characterised as half-hearted secularisation, but it could be also attributed to respect for pluralism and religious tolerance. The latter interpretation is reinforced by the presence of countries with the most liberal family law, for instance the Scandinavian countries, among the countries with a dual system of marriage celebration. Two tendencies, perhaps at first glance contradictory, can be traced with respect to the development of the dual system of marriage registration in Europe. On the one hand, predominantly Catholic countries, like Malta and Spain, have democratised the choice between civil and religious marriages. Thus, in Spain, proof of the absence of an affiliation with the Catholic Church as a precondition to entering a civil marriage was abolished in 1977.[256] On the other hand,

---

[255]   The Czech Republic, Denmark, England and Wales, Finland, Greece, Croatia, Iceland, Ireland, Italy, Latvia, Lithuania, Malta, Norway, Northern Ireland, Poland, Portugal, Scotland, Sweden.

[256]   By Royal Decree of 1 December 1977.

in Latvia,[257] Lithuania,[258] Poland,[259] the Czech Republic[260] and Croatia,[261] where the compulsory civil registration of marriage was associated with the militant atheism of the Soviet domination, alternative religious celebration of marriage was introduced in the framework of the post-communist restoration of democracy. This was perceived as a reaction to 'the Soviet aversion to religion',[262] and 'a partial compensation for the repression experienced by the church during the Soviet regime'.[263] The two aforementioned tendencies complement each other in the way that they provide individuals with free choice with regard to the form of the celebration of their marriage.

There are, however, certain pre-conditions necessary to regard a dual system as modern and democratic, and not every country yet satisfies these conditions. The first requirement is that admitting religious celebration of marriage should not privilege one dominant religious denomination to the detriment of the others. This is the case with the new Croatian law, where the possibility to solemnize marriages is reserved for the Roman Catholic Church alone.[264] The second condition is that there must be uniform, State-determined, minimal preconditions for the celebration of both civil and religious marriage. This can be illustrated by the Lithuanian example; right after the country regained independence, the 1992 Constitution proclaimed the unconditional recognition of religious marriage. 'Unconditional' meant among other things that not even subsequent reporting to a civil register was required, and civil conditions for a valid marriage were no longer applicable.[265] Unsurprisingly, this did not prove to work well. Therefore, the 2000 Lithuanian Civil Code made the recognition of religious marriage conditional upon the subsequent reporting of the marriage to the civil register and upon conformity with the civil requirements for a valid marriage.[266] Another point is that the churches should, of course, be free to make further

---

257 Introduced in 1993 by the restored Latvian *Civil Code* of 1937. VEBERS, J., 'Family Law in Latvia: From Establishment of the Independent State of Latvia in 1918 to Restoration of Independence in 1993' (1997), p. 212.

258 By the 1992 Constitution. KASERAUSKAS, Š., 'Moving in the Same Direction? Presentation of Family Law Reforms in Lithuania' (2004), p. 322

259 Introduced in 1998 in line with the Concordat with the Holy See of 1993, ratified in 1998. SMYCZYNSKI, T., 'Das Polnische Familienrecht im Reformprozeâ der staatlichen Ordnung' (1999), p. 138.

260 Introduced in 1992. HADERKA, J., 'A Half-Hearted Family Law Reform of 1998' (2000), p. 122.

261 Introduced by the Croatian *Family Act* of 1999. TOMLIJENOVIC, V., 'The Canonic Marriage – Revision of Croatian Family Law and Its Conflict of Laws Implication' (2003), p. 109.

262 KASERAUSKAS, Š., 'Moving in the Same Direction'? Presentation of Family Law Reforms in Lithuania' (2004), p. 322.

263 Ibid.

264 TOMLIJENOVIC, V., 'The Canonic Marriage – Revision of Croatian Family Law and Its Conflict of Laws Implication' (2003), p. 109.

265 KASERAUSKAS, Š., 'Moving in the Same Direction'? Presentation of Family Law Reforms in Lithuania' (2004), p. 322, note 32.

266 Ibid, p. 322.

restrictions for entering into religious marriages, but it is quite undesirable that these restrictions come to also dominate the civil registration of marriage, as is the case in England and Wales. It seems reasonable to expect a further convergence between the countries concerned on both of these preconditions, i.e. the indiscriminate access to religious marriage if such marriage is recognised by law, and the imposition of a least some minimal preconditions for this recognition.

In Scandinavia, the suggestion to introduce an obligatory civil marriage is presently being brought up as part of the debate on the opening up of marriage for same-sex couples that is going on in Sweden and Denmark. As the State will not, nor cannot impose a duty on the Church to provide a Church registration of same-sex marriage, only a one-track system, based on obligatory civil marriage, can be equally applicable to both same- and opposite-sex couples.[267]

A minority of European jurisdictions recognise only civil marriage as a legal marriage.[268] Some, while refusing religious marriage's civil consequences, do not prohibit its celebration prior to civil registration. Others[269] are more strict and do prohibit the celebration of religious marriage prior to civil celebration. Several Eastern European countries have recently broken with this tradition and have removed criminal sanctions for undergoing prior religious celebrations.[270] All of these countries adhere to a strict separation of Church and State and consider that, as the religious celebration of marriage is allowed as such, religious freedom is sufficiently safeguarded without the attribution of legal consequences to such celebration.

The unitary system is undoubtedly simpler and easier in operation than the dual. Some countries attribute important symbolic and political meaning to it. France was the cradle of obligatory civil marriage in Europe. Civil marriage is still considered by the French as part of the 'unwritten constitution of France',[271] and one of the corner stones of the *laïcité*. In Turkey, the importance of compulsory civil marriage as 'the fundamental building block in the bridge to a contemporary and secular legal system' has been recently reaffirmed by the Constitutional Court.[272] Furthermore, the recent

---

[267] JÄNTERÄ-JAREBORG, M., SÖRGJERD, C., 'The Experiences with Registered Partnership in Scandinavia' (2004), p. 586.

[268] Austria, Belgium, Bulgaria, Estonia, France, Germany, Luxemburg, Moldova, The Netherlands, Romania, Russia, Turkey and Serbia.

[269] France, Belgium, Luxemburg, Switzerland, The Netherlands, Germany, Austria and Turkey.

[270] Serbia has removed criminal prohibition in 1994. (KOVACEK STANIC, G., 'Legal Reforms Concerning the Family' (1995), p. 534-535).

[271] CARBONNIER, J., 'Pas de droits si l'on refuse le droit,' in: KALTENBACH, P. (ed.), *La famille contre les pouvoirs,* Nouvelle Cité, Paris, 1985, cited in: GLENDON, M.A., *The Transformation of Family Law* (1989), at p. 263.

[272] ÖRÜCÜ, E., 'Family Law Enters the New Century' (2004), p. 469-482.

discussion in The Netherlands suggests that even the countries, where exclusive civil marriage is not so much a matter of principle, but merely a matter of 'practical reasons'[273] will be reluctant to give up obligatory civil ceremony.

The conclusion seems to be that the division between countries with a unitary and with a dual system of celebration of marriage will probably continue to exist, and that neither of these systems will prevail in the foreseeable future as a result of spontaneous convergence.

13.4.3. CAPACITY TO MARRY

Under the influence of progressive ideology, national laws on capacity to marry became increasingly devoid of remnants of religious concepts of marriage and related legal restrictions. The right to marry assumed the status of a fundamental human right in 1950, when it was incorporated into Article 12 of the European Convention on Human Rights. However, neither Article 12 nor the case law of the European Court of Human Rights and later international human rights instruments like Article 9 of the EU Charter and the corresponding Article II-69 of the not-ratified EU Constitution, present the right to marry as an absolute and unconditional right. The determination of restrictions to the right to marry is left to the national laws of the Member States.[274] This capacity on the part of the national states is rather broad, albeit not unrestricted.[275] Thus, the national states are not allowed to implement restrictions affecting the fundamental essence of the right to marry.[276] Such violation of a right to marry is, however, not easily acknowledged.[277] As a result, the international human rights instruments did not initiate any developments in this area, but rather codified the common core that had already been achieved through the progressive development of the substantive laws of the national states.

Nonetheless, the status of the right to marry as a fundamental right influenced the nature of the controversies on the remaining marriage impediments. These impediments, originating from religion and tradition, obstructed the claims to marriage of homosexuals, transsexuals, and other groups, traditionally deprived of the right to

---

[273] WESTERHOF, L., 'Civiel effect voor het kerkelijk huwelijk?' (2002), p. 80.
[274] VAN GRUNDERBEECK, D., *Beginselen van personen- en familierecht. Een mensenrechtelijke benadering* (2003), p. 201 ff.
[275] Ibid, p. 202.
[276] Ibid, p. 202-203.
[277] Thus, for instance, the impossibility to dissolve a broken marriage in order to enter another did not constitute such violation. See: *Johnston v. Ireland*. ECHR (1986).

intermarry. Exposed as merely a matter of ideology,[278] these impediments were no longer taken for granted and were put to the test of secular rationalism.[279] This resulted in the present heated controversy on the issue of the capacity of same-sex couples and transsexuals to marry. Before these recent developments occurred, the twentieth century witnessed a general trend towards the diminishing and lessening of marriage impediments, so that one could rightfully speak of spontaneous convergence of the national laws on marriage capacity. This convergence tendency was, however, disturbed by the new discord surrounding the marriage capacity of homosexuals and transsexuals.

The laws governing the age of marriage display a similar tendency towards coupling the age of marriage to the age of majority. This development is clearly supported by the lowering of the age of majority as part of the overall emancipation of the youth after the 1960s. At present a vast majority of European countries have coupled the age of marriage to the age of majority which is set at 18 years. Only in a few countries is the general age of marriage still below the age of majority.[280] A second tendency that can be observed, is a trend towards equating the age of marriage for both sexes and lifting the minimum age of marriage. This transformation has to do with the later socialisation of the youth in industrialised countries and the equalisation of the social roles of men and women. It has also been held that differing ages of marriage for males and females falls within the scope of unjustified discrimination on the ground of sex, prohibited by the international human rights instruments.[281] Most countries allow the marriage of persons under the general marriage age, provided a dispensation by a competent authority is granted.[282] Some countries allow a dispensation only for a person who has reached a certain age,[283] others do not have an age limit. In most of the countries concerned, persons under age who wish to marry must first acquire the consent of their parents or guardians. If parental consent is refused without good reason, it can be substituted by the consent of the competent authority.

---

[278] GLENDON, M.A., *The Transformation of Family Law* (1989), p. 75 ff.

[279] As Bradley has put it: 'development of enlightenment values is in evidence, in particular, the advance of secular rationalism and [...] recognition of claims to rights and empowerment'. BRADLEY, D., 'Comparative Law, Family Law and Common Law' (2003), p. 144.

[280] E.g.: 16 years old for both partners in Portugal, England and Wales and in Scotland. HAMILTON, C., PERRY, A., *Family Law in Europe* (2002), p. 524, 102, 549, respectively.

[281] For an overview of literature and case on this subject see: VAN GRUNDERBEECK, D., *Beginselen van personen- en familierecht. Een mensenrechtelijke benadering* (2003), p. 218, particularly note 922.

[282] Exceptions are, for instance, England and Wales, and Scotland, where no dispensation is possible.

[283] This minimum age of dispensation is often 16 years old (Austria, Germany, Italy). In Greece, however, it is as low as 10 years old. HAMILTON, C., PERRY, A., *Family Law in Europe* (2002), p. 5, 296, 408 and 329, respectively.

There is also a clear tendency to diminish the number of marriage impediments that are based on consanguinity and affinity. A marriage between descendents and ascendants is prohibited all over Europe. The same applies to a marriage between brothers and sisters.[284] Some countries have limited the number of impediments to these closest blood-relatives.[285] However, the majority of European countries provide for a more extensive list of impediments based on consanguinity and affinity. These prohibitions are often mitigated by the possibility to seek dispensation.

As was already mentioned, the traditional requirement that the marriage partners must be of opposite sexes has become a matter of a sharp discord. Many European countries have of their own initiative hesitantly granted transsexuals the right to marry in their new gender.[286] The issue of transsexual's right to marry remained nonetheless controversial. The process of piecemeal recognition of the rights of transsexuals to marriage was brought to an end through the intervention of the European Court of Human Rights. The matter has more than once been a subject of scrutiny by this Court. The Court has long been trying to find a proper balance between innovation and feasibility by combining the doctrine of margin of appreciation with the consensus argument. In *Rees* (1986), the court ruled that the State had a broad margin of appreciation regarding the possibility to change a birth certificate after gender reassignment surgery because 'there is at present little common ground between the Contracting States'.[287] Fourteen years later the persistent absence of sufficient common ground was again invoked in order to justify a similar decision concerning transsexuals' rights in *Cossey* (1990).[288] In 1996, in *X, Y. and Z. v. the United Kingdom*, the Court found that the State enjoys a wide margin of appreciation regarding the legal recognition of paternity in the case of a female-to-male transsexual with respect to his non-biological child because of the absence of 'any generally shared approach amongst the High Contracting Parties'.[289] In 1998, in *Sheffield and Horsham*,[290] the Court found that the absence of legal recognition of gender reassignment under British law does not constitute a violation of Articles 8 and 12; again, because no sufficient common ground was found. Only in 2002, in the two very similar cases of *Goodwin*

---

[284] Only Sweden has made marriage of half-brothers and sisters possible upon dispensation.

[285] E.g. Germany, The Netherlands, Norway, Russia, Sweden.

[286] According to research submitted by the non-governmental organisation 'Liberty' to the ECHR in connection to the *Goodwin* case, 54% of the Contracting States (Austria, Belgium, Denmark, Estonia, Finland, France, Germany, Greece, Iceland, Italy, Latvia, Luxembourg, the Netherlands, Norway, Slovakia, Spain, Sweden, Switzerland, Turkey and Ukraine) permitted post-operative transsexuals to marry a person of the sex opposite to their acquired gender. 14% (Ireland and the United Kingdom, Moldova, Poland, Romania and Russia) did not permit such marriage. The legal position in the remaining 32% was unclear. *Goodwin v. the United Kingdom*. ECHR (2002).

[287] *Rees v. the United Kingdom*. ECHR (1986), para. 37.

[288] *Cossey v. the United Kingdom*. ECHR (1990), para. 44.

[289] *X, Y. and Z. v. the United Kingdom*. ECHR (1997), para. 44.

[290] *Sheffield and Horsham v. the United Kingdom*. ECHR (1998).

v. the United Kingdom[291] and *I. v. the United Kingdom*,[292] the European Court of Human Rights finally acknowledged that the refusal to provide legal recognition to the new gender of post-operative transsexuals violates both Article 8 and Article 12 of the European Convention on Human Rights.[293] Thus, in spite of the continuing absence of consensus, the Court withdrew the issue of the legal recognition of post-operative transsexuals from the scope of the Contracting States' margin of appreciation and imposed on them the obligation to grant transsexuals the right to marry in their new gender. This decision manifested the willingness of the Court to renounce its disinclination to act as a modernising force with regard to the law of marriage and acknowledged the right of transsexuals to marry in their new gender. The significance of this decision can hardly be overestimated.[294] It will have an indefectible unifying impact on the marriage laws of all European countries. The activism of the European Court of Human Rights on behalf of transsexuals disproves David Bradley's suggestion that if harmonisation on issues of marital capacity for transsexuals were achieved, it would 'be influenced by domestic political considerations'.[295]

Of course, a highly controversial issue of marriage capacity remains the marriage of persons of the same sex. With the ECHR's abandonment of the old canon law notion that procreation is one of the indispensable characteristics of marriage,[296] one of the most important arguments against same-sex marriage seems to have been removed. Also, the definition of the right to marry in Article 9 of the Charter and Article II-69

---

291   *Goodwin v. the United Kingdom.* ECHR (2002).

292   *I. v. the United Kingdom.* ECHR (2002).

293   The reasoning of the Court was as follows: 'In the later case of Sheffield and Horsham, the Court's Judgment laid emphasis on the lack of a common European approach as to how to address the repercussions which the recognition of a change of sex may entail for other areas of law such as marriage, filiations, privacy or data protection. While this would appear to remain the case, the lack of such a common approach among forty-three Contracting States with widely diverse legal systems and traditions is hardly surprising. In accordance with the principle of subsidiarity, it is indeed primarily for the Contracting States to decide on the measures necessary to secure Convention rights within their jurisdiction and, in resolving within their domestic legal systems the practical problems created by the legal recognition of post-operative gender status, the Contracting States must enjoy a wide margin of appreciation. The Court accordingly attaches less importance to the lack of evidence of a common European approach to the resolution of the legal and practical problems posed, than to the clear and uncontested evidence of a continuing international trend in favour not only of increased social acceptance of transsexuals but of legal recognition of the new sexual identity of post-operative transsexuals'. *Goodwin v. the United Kingdom*, para 85.

294   On the significance of the *Goodwin* decision see: VAN GRUNDERBEECK, D., *Beginselen van personen-en familierecht. Een mensenrechtelijke benadering*, (2003), p. 234-240.

295   BRADLEY, D., 'Convergence in Family Law: Mirrors, Transplants and Political Economy' (1999), p. 135.

296   The Court observed that 'Article 12 secures the fundamental right of a man and woman to marry and to found a family. The second aspect is not however a condition of the first and the inability of any couple to conceive or parent a child cannot be regarded as *per se* removing their right to enjoy the first limb of this provision'. *Goodwin v. the United Kingdom*, ECHR. (2002).

---

of the not-ratified EU Constitution contains some promising alterations, compared to the corresponding Article 12 of the Convention. In contrast to the Article 12, the Charter does not use the words 'men and women' in respect to this right. However, the Explanatory note reveals that 'this Article neither prohibits nor imposes the granting of the status of marriage to unions between people of the same sex. This right is thus similar to that afforded by the ECHR, but its scope may be wider when national legislation so provides'.[297] Nevertheless, this alteration has already had a clear impact on the practices of the European Court of Human Rights.[298] However, at the moment the majority of European jurisdictions, with the exception of The Netherlands, Belgium and Spain – and perhaps in the near future also of Sweden and Denmark – are reluctant to open up marriage for same-sex couples.

The political context and the discussion surrounding the introduction of same-sex marriage in Belgium in many ways resembled the above-described Dutch situation. In 1999, a coalitional socialist-liberal-green Government ('purple green') came into office.[299] The coalition agreement did not contain a provision for same-sex marriage, but promised to introduce a proper legal framework for same-sex partners.[300] As in The Netherlands, some problems of the institutionalisation of same-sex relationships had already been solved in Belgium by the Law of 23 November 1998,[301] which introduced an institution of statutory cohabitation. However, this Act gave Belgian same-sex partners significantly less equality than their Dutch counterparts when their legal rights were compared to spouses.[302] Thus, the pressure for equalisation remained, giving the Belgian legislature two choices: grant same-sex couples, through partnership legislation, almost all rights of spouses,[303] or open up marriage to include them.[304] The Bill was supported by all the governmental parties and by an oppositional Flemish Christian-Democratic Party (CD&V), which decided to support the Bill during a party congress.[305] As was mentioned above, one of the senators of this party expressed its

---

[297] Explanatory Note to the Charter. 11 October 2000, Charter 4473/00, p. 12.

[298] For instance the ECHR invoked this alteration in support of its decision to recognise transsexuals' right to marry in their new gender in the *Goodwin* case. *Goodwin v. the United Kingdom*, Decision of 11 July 2002, para. 101.

[299] This Government allied Walloon Socialists (PS), Walloon Greens (ECOLO), Walloon Liberals (PRL), Flemish Socialists (SP), Flemish Greens (AGALEF) and Flemish Liberal-Democrats (VLD).

[300] Coalitional agreement 7 July 1999 'A bridge to the twenty-first century'.

[301] Came into force on 1 January 2000.

[302] VERSCHELDEN, G., DEVOS, S., 'Kroniek van het Belgisch familierecht (1993-2001)' (2002), p. 318.

[303] This option was advocated by Patrick Senaeve. See: SENAEVE, P., COENE, E., 'Geregistreerd partnership. Pleidooi voor de institutionalisering van de homoseksuele tweerelatie' (1998), p. 129-256.

[304] PERTEGÁS SENDER, M., 'Huwelijk tussen personen van hetzelfde geslacht in België: internrechtelijke en internationaal-rechtelijke implicaties' (2003), No. 554.

[305] Senate, 2002/2002, 2-246, p. 16.

genuinely Christian position in the wording *misericordia et iustitia*.[306] Against the Bill voted a awkward coalition of Walloon Liberals, Walloon Christian-Democrats and the Flemish Extreme Right. It was noticed that 'this was a new split' between the advocates of progress and the conservatives.[307]

The Spanish case was somewhat different. At the time marriage was opened for same-sex couples, Spanish federal law provided no regulation for same-sex couples, although much had been done on the level of the Spanish Autonomous Communities.[308] Federal partnership legislation became a matter of bitter controversy between the social democrats and the conservative *Partido Popular*. When the Socialist Party won the election in 2004, it kept the promise made during its election campaign[309] to open up marriage and adoption to same-sex couples.[310] The Spanish legislature explicitly connected the introduction of same-sex marriage with two fundamental human rights, guaranteed by the Spanish Constitution: the right to develop one's personality freely; and the right to non-discriminatory treatment.[311] The Spanish example is particularly important as a radical breakthrough;[312] it occurred in a South European country with a vast majority of Catholic population. However, in spite of the success of the socialist Government, mass demonstrations of Catholics against the same-sex marriage and the opposition of some scholars[313] illustrate that in Spain, both the general populace and the academic community remain split on this issue. Perhaps it is also part of the highly polarised political climate in present day Spain that a parliamentary majority shows no hesitation to push through legislation that a significant minority of the electorate passionately opposes. The oppositional *Partido Popular* instantly challenged the constitutionality of the new law before the Spanish Constitutional Court.[314] The new law also provoked an immediate reaction from the Vatican. Same-sex marriage was labelled as 'wrong, destructive and dehumanising'.[315] Spanish Catholic civil

---

[306] 'Compassion is justice'. Senator Vandenberghe (Flemish Christian Democrat (CD&V)) Senate, 2002/2002, 2-246, p. 38.

[307] Senator Van Quickenborne (Flemish Liberal-Democrat (VLD)) Senate, 2002/2002, 2-246, p. 42.

[308] See Chapter 15, Section 15.6.4.

[309] MARTÍN-CASALS, M., 'Same-Sex Partnerships in the Legislation of Spanish Autonomous Communities' (2002), p. 57.

[310] Law 13/2005, of 1 July 2005.

[311] GONZÁLEZ BEILFUSS, C., 'Private international law aspects of homosexual couples', Spanish National Report (2006), p. 2.

[312] Gabriel García Cantero depicted this change as 'revolutionarily'. GARCÍA CANTERO, G., 'Family Law Reform in Differing Directions' (2006), p. 431.

[313] See: GARCÍA CANTERO, G., 'Family Law Reform in Differing Directions' (2006), p. 431ff.

[314] See: GONZÁLEZ BEILFUSS, C., 'Private international law aspects of homosexual couples', Spanish National Report (2006), p. 2. At the time this book was completed the decision of the Constitutional Court was still awaited.

[315] The standpoint of the new Pope has been expressed by Cardinal López Trujillo in his Interview to the Italian newspaper *Corriere della Sera*, cited in *NRC Handelsblad*, 25 April 2005, translation mine.

servants were called on to not collaborate with the new law and, if necessary, even give up their jobs.[316]

For the time being there are only three countries which allow same-sex marriage; Sweden and Denmark are likely to join this group in the near future. However, the proliferation of same-sex marriage has also provoked a counter-reaction. Thus, in December 2005, Latvia introduced no less than a constitutional ban on same-sex marriage.[317] So, same-sex marriage is clearly one of the greatest family law controversies of our time, and it seems very likely that Europe will long remain divided upon this issue.

13.4.4. EQUALISATION OF THE RIGHTS OF SPOUSES

The equalisation of the legal rights of spouses represents one of the most impressive success stories of spontaneous convergence. As with most success stories, it does not require much elaboration. In the 1970s-1980s, Western European countries embraced formal legal equality between spouses, which had already been introduced in Russia and Scandinavia in the 1920s and in West Germany and Eastern European countries after the Second World War. By the end of the twentieth century, spousal equality, save for some remnants in the field of the law of names, had been achieved in every European country. The international human rights instruments did not initiate progressive developments in this area, but rather codified the common core already achieved through the progressive development of the substantive laws of the national states. It is illustrative that the initial reading of Articles 12 and 14 of the ECHR did not include the right of equality of the spouses within marriage. Only in 1984 was this right introduced into the European human rights law by the Seventh Additional Protocol.[318] Article 5 of this Protocol states that:

'Spouses shall enjoy equality of rights and responsibilities of a private law character between them, and in their relations with their children, as to marriage, during marriage and in the event of its dissolution.'

However, by the time the Protocol entered into force in 1988, this provision had very little to add to what had already been achieved in the various European countries by means of spontaneous parallel developments.

---

[316] Ibid.
[317] *NRC Handelsblad*, 22 December 2005.
[318] This Protocol is ratified by only 33 of the 44 Council of Europe Member States. For more details see: VAN GRUNDERBEECK, D., *Beginselen van personen- en familierecht. Een mensenrechtelijke benadering* (2003), p. 183, particularly note 774.

13.4.5. CONCLUDING REMARKS

Summing up the results of the preceding sections, is seems quite possible to speak of a convergence tendency in some particular fields of marriage law (for instance the equality of spouses). The international human rights instruments have generally played a rather modest role in this process. At the same time, new controversies emerge and marriage has remained a highly politicised and touchy issue. With the introduction of same-sex marriage, it was questioned in some quarters whether same- and opposite-sex marriage are one and the same institution. Some Belgian and Dutch scholars have suggested that this question should be answered in the negative, as same-sex marriage is a new sort of marriage, an 'incomplete' marriage severed of one of its indispensable pillars – the presumption of parentage,[319] a 'legal monster' resembling real marriage as much as alcohol-free whisky resembles a real one.[320] Consequently, same-sex marriage should be regarded as no more than a 'marriage-like institution'.[321] In progressive circles, including same-sex couples into the scope of marriage law is seen as a necessary step for purifying the institution of marriage of the last remnants of discrimination.[322] In their view, to present the exclusion of same-sex couples as necessary for the preservation of the institution of marriage, is similar to the presentation, in previous periods of history, of the exclusion of slaves, persons of different races or religions, and the subordination of women, as indispensable for the protection of the same institution of marriage.[323] The fact that the institution of marriage has survived the removal of these inequalities proves that marriage 'is an institution capable of change with time'.[324]

It is clear however, that the focal point of disagreement has shifted from the issues of spousal equality and secularisation to the issue of the heterosexual nature of marriage. The general conservative-progressive ideological divide continues to produce significant ideological differences from country to country. As everywhere in family law, within the margins of the overall modernisation tendency, the laws on marriage have continued to display particularities reflecting the dissimilar balance of political power between 'progressive' proponents and 'conservative' opponents of the

---

[319] SENAEVE, P., *Compendium van het Personen- en Familierecht*, part 3, (2003), No. 1489-2.

[320] NUYTINCK, A., 'De Wet openstelling huwelijk en de Wet adoptie door personen van hetzelfde geslacht' (2000), p. 214.

[321] SENAEVE, P., *Compendium van het Personen- en Familierecht*, part 3, (2003), No. 1489-2; RENCHON, J.-L., 'L'avènement du mariage homosexuel dans le Code civil Belge' (2004), p. 169.

[322] SWENNEN, F., 'Het "homohuwelijk" bestaat niet anno 2005' (2005), p. 67-68; YTTERBERG, H., 'All Human Beings are Equal, But Some Are More Equal than Others – Equality and Dignity without Equality in Rights?' (2002), p. 8.

[323] YTTERBERG, H., 'All Human Beings are Equal, But Some Are More Equal than Others – Equality and Dignity without Equality in Rights?' (2002), p. 9.

[324] Ibid.

modernisation of family law, resulting in different levels of secularisation and liberalisation of marriage law in each particular country. Thus, the differences within the marriage laws of the European countries remain rather significant. As we will see in the next chapter, the process of modernisation and liberalisation of marriage law resembles the process of the modernisation of divorce law. As the countries lagging behind take a step to reach the level of the vanguard countries and convergence is achieved in some aspect of marriage law (like for instance was the case with the equalisation of the position of the spouses), the latter take a further step (such as allowing same-sex marriage), a step which is at that moment completely unacceptable to the former. Thus, the developments go on and differences remain. As a result, the description Mary Ann Glendon made in the 1970s still retains its validity in the 2000s: 'on the ideological plane contemporary society is a museum of various conceptions of marriage'.[325]

---

[325] 'Christians who believe in the sacramental nature of marriage see it as an indissoluble tie. [...] Engels saw this Christian ideal of marriage as having been supplanted by bourgeois marriage in which economic considerations made every marriage a marriage of convenience and a form of prostitution; modern Marxists see the bourgeois marriage of Engels' time, organized around production, as being supplanted today by bourgeois marriage organized around consumption. The idea that marriage exists primarily for the personal fulfilment of the individual spouses and should last only so long as it performs this function is also in vogue'. GLENDON, M. A., 'Power and Authority in the Family: New Legal Patterns as Reflection of Changing Ideologies' (1975), p. 2.

CHAPTER 14
DIVORCE: HAS THE NO-FAULT REVOLUTION BROUGHT CONVERGENCE CLOSER?

14.1. INTRODUCTION

The law on divorce was deeply affected by the family revolution of the 1960s-1970s. The most important change was that divorce lost its social stigma and was no longer seen as 'a deviant act but rather part and parcel of a new concept of marriage and the family'.[1] This new image of divorce walked hand in hand with a 'mutation in the matrimonial model';[2] marriage was no longer perceived as life-long monogamy, but merely as serial monogamy.

Since the French Revolution, the law on divorce has been one of the most sensitive flash-points between the conservatives and the advocates of modernisation. The preceding chapters show that before the 1960s the conservative forces in Western Europe, save for few exceptions,[3] successfully managed to obstruct any far-reaching liberalisation (and in some countries even the very introduction) of divorce. Reforms were merely reluctantly allowed in under pressure of societal developments. From the 1960s on, the advocates of liberalisation (in Ireland, Portugal, Spain and Italy – of the (re)introduction) of divorce gained the upper hand. Although the political and ideological sensitivities of divorce issues still made compromise between the conservative and progressive camps an indispensable precondition of almost every divorce reform, the proponents of liberalisation were now in a far better position to determine the outcome of these compromises. The modernisation of divorce laws swiftly gained momentum. The transformation of divorce law also underwent a major qualitative change. Before this time, the liberalisation of divorce law amounted to, for the most part, a 'steady accumulation of specific grounds',[4] largely accomplished by

---

[1] COMMAILLE, J., 'Towards a New Definition of Divorce' (1980), p. 108.
[2] Ibid.
[3] Most notable exceptions were the radical reforms of divorce law in Portugal, Scandinavia, the Soviet Union and Republican Spain, discussed in Part III, Chapter 11.
[4] PHILLIPS, R., *Putting Asunder* (1988), p. 563.

adding 'new specific matrimonial offences and conditions' to already existing ones.[5] In the 1960s the main event of liberalisation became the introduction and the advance of no-fault divorce.

On the eve of the discussed period, fault-based divorce was still the only possible route to marriage dissolution in most Western European countries. In cases involving consenting spouses this led to the hypocrisy surrounding divorce by collusion. However, compared to the situation with contested divorce, divorce by collusion was not the major problem. The main problem was contested fault-based divorce. Firstly, the humiliating accusational procedure increased aversion and bitterness between the spouses and made their intimate life the subject of public scrutiny. Secondly, the 'guilty' spouse was, at least in theory, not entitled to obtain a divorce if an 'innocent' spouse opposed it. These inconveniences became less tolerable for the progressively minded populace in the revived spirit of individual freedom and the search for happiness and self-fulfilment typical of the new cultural climate of the 1960s. The right to dissolve an unhappy marriage was seen as a logical consequence of the right of every individual to seek happiness. From this individualistic perspective, the 'State had no right to prevent its citizens from pursuing such happiness [and] to make impossible or cumbersome the exercise of the natural right of divorce'.[6] The conservatives were concerned not so much with the hypocrisy of divorce by collusion, but with the ease of such divorce and the increase in the divorce rates. They still firmly believed that the State had 'an interest in the continuation of a marriage over and above the wishes of the parties involved',[7] and that divorce law should ensure these interests.

In the 1970s-1980s, the advocates of no-fault divorce were rather successful. Although fault did not disappear altogether from the divorce law of such important countries as England and Wales and France, fault ceased to be the only ground for divorce in all countries. However, the differences in the balance of political power from one European state to another have led to rather different compromises, on which the national divorce reforms were based. The following close up will show a selection of the various types of divorce reforms based on various kinds of compromises. Sweden again represents a rare case of non-constrained and non-compromised reform, which allowed for the introduction of immediate divorce on demand. Russia stands for the same result, reached in a more veiled and circumspect manner. The big three: England, Germany and France demonstrate how countries with quite similar starting points, choices at stake and principle political players, reached rather different outcomes in terms of the profundity of divorce reform. The compromise reached in Germany

---

5   Ibid.
6   RHEINSTEIN, M., *Marriage Stability, Divorce, and the Law* (1972), p. 196.
7   LEE, B., *Divorce Reform in England* (1974), p. 198.

brought about a rather liberal no-fault divorce law from the outset. The two French compromises, anno 1975 and 2004, resulted in fairly moderate laws that maintained fault as one of the divorce grounds but provided for a relatively easy divorce by consent. In England and Wales, the cautious reform of 1969 not only retained fault, but also made divorce by consent conditional to a rather lengthy period of separation. The inability to reach a workable compromise during the attempt to eradicate fault in 1996 resulted in a stillborn Family Law Act, which was based on the pursuit of rather irreconcilable objectives. Apart from these selections, I will further discuss in length two Catholic countries: Italy and Ireland. The (re-)introduction of divorce was delayed in these countries up to the second half of the twentieth century and involved a conflict of unprecedented vigour between conservative and progressive forces.

14.2. NON-COMPROMISED REFORMS: INTRODUCING DIVORCE ON DEMAND IN SWEDEN AND RUSSIA

14.2.1. SWEDEN: DIVORCE AS A PERSONAL RIGHT

Even before the Swedish legislature made a radical step in the liberalisation of divorce law in 1973, Swedish divorce law was one of the most permissive in Europe. Although fault grounds were retained in the reform of 1915, no-fault divorce for both contested and non-contested cases had been introduced into Swedish law in the beginning of the century.[8] Consensual divorce was possible after a relatively short period of separation: one year. At the same time, the pre-reform divorce law was still based upon a compromise between those, who accepted that divorce was an autonomous decision of the spouses, and those, who urged to retain State control over the dissolution of marriage. This compromise was no longer satisfactory when 'new radicalism'[9] came to dominate the Swedish political scene in the late 1960s. In the aforementioned Guidelines[10] for family law reform the objectives of the divorce reform were stated as follows: 'legislation should not under any circumstances force a person to continue to live under a marriage from which he wishes to free himself'.[11] Consequently, the concept of fault was to disappear entirely from Swedish divorce law.[12] Divorce on demand, available under classical Roman law and shortly reintroduced in Europe by

---

[8]   See Part III, Chapter 11, Section 11.2.1.
[9]   GYLLENSTEN, L., 'Swedish Radicalism in the 1960s: An Experiment in Political and Cultural Debate' (1972), p. 281.
[10] See Chapter 13, Section 13.3.1.
[11] Abstract of protocol in justice department matters, 15 Augustus 1969.
[12] 'The question of who is to blame for the break-up of the marriage ought to be irrelevant in the granting of divorce'. Abstract of protocol in justice department matters, 15 Augustus 1969.

Russian post-revolutionary law,[13] was the most important innovation of the new Swedish law. The choice for ideological neutrality and non-intervention of the State[14] signified the radical rejection of the traditional model of marriage dissolution regulation, based on the idea that divorce law could and should influence the social practise of divorce in order to buttress the stability of marriage. It was believed that the consequent application of the contractarian model of marriage required that marriage was to be entered into as a contract and to be dissolved like a contract.[15]

As result of these choices, the 1973 Law[16] reduced the State's intervention to a minimum, and the autonomous decision of the spouse(s) became the veritable ground for divorce. If both spouses agreed upon divorce and no minor children were involved, the divorce was required to be granted immediately upon their demand.[17] Not even a short period of reflection was required, even though not everyone agreed with the 'rationale that adult independent spouses do not need any time for reflection'.[18] However, the desire to respect the spouses' autonomy seems not to have been the only reason for the introduction of immediate divorce. Another, more pragmatic, reason was found in the increasing competition between the institution of marriage and the ever-growing non-marital cohabitation, which of course could be terminated without any delay or intervention of the State.[19] If a divorce was requested by only one of the spouses, or the spouses had minor children, the divorce was to be automatically granted if the demand for divorce was renewed after a six-month period of reflection. No inquiry into the reasons for divorce was to be held[20] and no defence against the divorce claim was possible. Hence, partly due to ideological and partly due to pragmatic reasons, Swedish law openly left the concept of the irretrievable breakdown of marriage behind and started, instead, to consider divorce in terms of entitlements

---

[13]   One of the opponents of the reform noticed: 'Perhaps it is a shocking idea that if one wants to understand the situation in the Sweden of tomorrow, one has to study Bolshevik Russia and the Rome of Antiquity'. SUNDBERG, J., 'Marriage or no Marriage' (1971), p. 233. According to him, introduction of divorce on demand to a certain extent revived the private and informal divorce of the times of classical Rome, which, together with the Soviet reforms of the 1920s, inspired the Swedish legislator.

[14]   AGELL, A., 'Should and Can Family Law Influence Social Behaviour?' (1998), p. 128.

[15]   SUNDBERG, J., 'Marriage or no Marriage. The Directives for the Revision of Swedish Family Law' (1971), p. 234.

[16]   Entered into force on 1 January 1974. In 1987 the rules on divorce were incorporated in the new Marriage Code. See: JÄNTERÄ-JAREBORG, M., Swedish Report concerning the CEFL Questionnaire on Grounds for Divorce and Maintenance Between Former Spouses (2003), http://www.law.uu.nl/priv/cefl > working field 1 > Sweden, p. 3.

[17]   Ibid, p. 4.

[18]   LÖGDBER, A., 'The Reform of Family Law in the Scandinavian Countries' (1978), p. 206.

[19]   Ibid.

[20]   JÄNTERÄ-JAREBORG, M., Swedish Report concerning the CEFL Questionnaire on Grounds for Divorce and Maintenance Between Former Spouses (2003) http://www.law.uu.nl/priv/cefl > working field 1 > Sweden, p. 4.

and rights.[21] All in all, the Swedish reform represents the most far-reaching, open and uncompromising divorce reform of the second part of the twentieth century.

14.2.2. RUSSIA: DE-FACTO DIVORCE ON DEMAND

The introduction of divorce on demand in Sweden was a matter of explicitly proclaimed policy. The Russian case represents the de-facto introduction of substantially the same institution in an indirect manner. Russian divorce law, prior to the new Family Code of 1995,[22] was considerably more liberal than Swedish pre-reform law. The divorce provisions of the 1969 Russian Family Code[23] were a mixture of the radical revolutionary law of the 1920s[24] and the conservative heritage of Stalin's time,[25] more or less released from the extremes of both. The main characteristics of the 1969 law were the availability of administrative divorce (abolished by Stalin and re-introduced in the late 1960s)[26] and the discrepancy between the formal ground for divorce (irretrievable breakdown) and actual practice. Spouses who agreed upon divorce and had neither minor children nor disputes regarding ancillary matters had resort to an administrative procedure. If one of those conditions was not met, the divorce case had to be heard in court. Although irretrievable breakdown of marriage formally remained the ground for both administrative and judicial divorce, no proof of breakdown was required in the administrative procedure. In a court procedure however, irretrievable breakdown of the marriage still had to be proven. If the court was not convinced that the marriage was irrevocably broken, it was entitled to dismiss the divorce petition, even against the wishes of both spouses.[27] Thus, as was the case in Sweden before the reform, the law was based on a compromise between respect for the autonomy of the spouses and State control of divorce. In practice this compromise led not to 'great' but rather to 'small' lies.[28] Spouses, who had agreed to divorce and had minor children, usually presented standard fictitious reasons for their divorce in order to avoid complications and to speed up the process. The most popular reasons were 'creation of a new family with another person' by one or both spouses and 'not living together as husband and wife for a significant period of time without an intention to resume cohabitation'.

---

21 BRADLEY, D., *Family Law and Political Culture* (1996), p. 71-72.
22 Russian Family Code of 8 December 1995, in force since 1 March 1996.
23 *Kodex Zakonov o Brake i Sem'ie RSFSR.*
24 See Part III, Chapter 11, Section 11.2.1.
25 See Part III, Chapter 11, Section 11.3.1.
26 By the 1968 *Osnovi zakonodatel'stva o brake i sem'e.*
27 For more details see: ANTOKOLSKAIA, M., *Semeinoe pravo* (1997), p. 79ff.
28 'The great lie' was the nickname of the Dutch practice of divorce by collusion on the ground of a false accusation of adultery that commenced with a decision of the Dutch Supreme Court passed in 1883. For the context see Part III, Chapter 10, Section 10.2.2.

The new divorce law was intended to put an end to this discrepancy between the law in the books and the law in action. The main concerns of the reform were diminishing State intervention and protecting the privacy of the spouses. Irretrievable breakdown of marriage still remained the formal divorce ground, but one of the assumptions behind the 1995 Code was that the spouses, and not the judge, are in the best position to decide whether their marriage has come to an end. The law explicitly prohibited the court to order the spouses to disclose the reasons for non-contested divorce. Non-contested divorce remained a matter of both administrative and court jurisdiction. The new Code extended the administrative procedure to the cases in which the spouses had disputes concerning ancillary matters. In such situation it became possible to first obtain an administrative divorce, and then go to court to litigate the ancillary matters. Consenting spouses with minor children were still required to go to court, but court jurisdiction was retained in these cases solely to ensure that the agreements concerning the children would not escape judicial scrutiny. The role of the court in non-contested cases was no longer different than that of the administrative body. Neither the court nor the civil registrar were entitled to investigate the reasons for divorce or to refuse to grant divorce. All they were allowed to do was rubberstamp the autonomous decisions of the spouses.

In regard to cases of contested divorce, there is an certain ambiguity in the new law that has led to a dispute concerning its interpretation. This ambiguity originates in a controversy as to the proper role of the State both within and outside the drafting team. The majority of the drafters were in favour of a slightly mitigated Swedish model.[29] They were of the opinion that divorce should be granted upon the demand of one of the spouses, without investigation of the grounds and irrespective the objections of the other spouse, but, differing from Sweden, only after a short period of reflection. However, some highly reputable scholars, including several judges of the Supreme Court, maintained that the State should retain its authority to verify whether or not a marriage has been irretrievably broken down. Although it clearly was the introduction of divorce on demand that was at stake, neither the words 'divorce on demand' nor references to Swedish law were used in the discussion. The debate simply centred on the way the irretrievable breakdown of marriage should be established. Finally, the advocates of divorce on demand more or less won; but the resulting law on contested divorce appeared to be not unambiguous. On the one hand, Article 22 of the Family Code states that 'marriage has to be dissolved if it is proven that further cohabitation of the spouses is no longer feasible'. Thus, as before, the irretrievable breakdown of marriage has to be proven. On the other hand, Article 22

---

[29] The author of this book was one of the six members of the drafting commission formed by the Committee on Women, Family and Youth Affairs of the *State Duma* of the Russian Federation (*Komitet po delam zhenshchin, sem'i i molodegi Gosydarstvennoy Dumy Rossiskoy Federatsii*).

(2) states that: 'marriage has to be dissolved if attempts to reconcile the spouses have failed and one of the spouses keeps insisting on divorce'. These attempts of reconciliation involve no more than the discretion of the court to postpone divorce up to three months. If after three months the petitioner renews his or her demand, the court is obliged to grant the divorce. In my view, the only way to reconcile the abovementioned provisions is to assume that according to the new law the renewal of the appeal for divorce constitutes an irrefutable presumption of the breakdown of the marriage. In this interpretation, it is clear that behind the façade of irretrievable breakdown, the new Russian law actually introduced divorce on demand, as easily obtainable as under Swedish law.[30]

The controversy as to the role of the State in cases of contested divorce was never completely settled. In became even sharper when the view that the judge should have authority to scrutinise the divorce grounds, received explicit support from the Supreme Court. The new Russian Code is silent as to the power of the court to inquire into the reasons of divorce in contested cases. The consequent application of its provisions seems to necessitate the conclusion that even in a hypothetical case when both spouses deliberately refuse to discuss their personal matters in court, divorce still has to be granted after a three-month delay.[31] This interpretation, however, was met with considerable opposition.[32] In 1998 the Supreme Court ruled in favour of the view that in order to establish the irretrievable breakdown of marriage, a judge is still entitled to require the spouses to disclose the reasons for divorce. As there was no support for this in the new Family Code, the Supreme Court had to resort to the provisions of the Code of Civil Procedure in order to create a procedural sanction for a refusal of the spouses. The Court included the duty of the spouses to divulge the reasons for divorce in contested cases into the list of formal procedural requirements prescribed for filing a divorce petition.[33] The effect of this decision is that if a petitioner in a contested divorce case refuses to specify the reason for divorce in his or her divorce petition, the court can order a stay in the divorce procedure until the petitioner satisfies this requirement. As such a stay has no time-limit, it is quite an effectual means to force spouses to disclose the reasons for divorce. The opponents of the authority of the judge to scrutinise the divorce grounds in contested divorce cases have pointed out that this interpretation is not only contrary to the design of contested divorce in the new Code, but also quite pointless. Whatever reasons the petitioner states in his or her divorce petition, they can be of no influence on the outcome of the case, as the new law leaves

---

[30]   The delay in case of contested divorce is even shorter under Russian law: three months in Russia and six month in Sweden.
[31]   ANTOKOLSKAIA, M., *Semeinoe pravo* (1999), p. 132-133.
[32]   NETCHAEVA, A., *Semeinoe pravo* (1998), p. 107; PCHELINTZEVA, L., *Semeinoe pravo* (1999), p. 154-156.
[33]   Directive No. 15 on 5 November 1998 entitled 'On the Application of the Legislation by Dissolving Divorce Cases,' item 7.

the court no room to attach any consequences to its appreciation of these reasons. If the petitioner renews his or her demand after a period of three months, the law gives the court no other choice than to grant the desired divorce order.[34]

To sum up, differing from Sweden, there was no room in Russia for a forthright, non-compromised introduction of divorce on demand. The new Code resorted to the accustomed concept of irretrievable breakdown and subsequent intervention of the Supreme Court has slightly curtailed its original intent to minimise State interference in unilateral divorce. The present situation is de-facto nonetheless clearly divorce on demand. Unilateral divorce must be granted if there is a renewal of the initial application three months after the initial filing, but formally the privacy of the spouses is no longer protected against the demand to disclose the reasons for the divorce.

14.3. IN THE BAN OF COMPROMISE: ENGLAND, FRANCE AND GERMANY

14.3.1. ENGLAND: AN UNWORKABLE COMPROMISE. A STORY OF A FAILED REFORM

Two reforms, two compromises

Two divorce reforms, undertaken in England and Wales in 1969 and 1996 respectively, provide one of the best illustrations of the compromise nature of most divorce reforms in Europe. The English case also clearly demonstrates that in the discussions surrounding the reforms, ideological inclinations often took precedence over regard for efficiency and pragmatic reasoning. In both reforms, the main discourse was between the conservatives, upholding the idea of State control upon marriage dissolution, and the proponents of the liberalisation of divorce law, advocating respect for the autonomous decision of the spouses to end their marriage.[35] In both cases, uneasy compromises were reached. The 1969 compromise resulted in a law that, as well as being rather conservative by European standards, was also fairly contradictory. While proclaiming the irretrievable breakdown of marriage as the sole ground for divorce, it retained the old fault grounds while introducing the possibility of no-fault divorce. Moreover, it proved to be rather inefficient in achieving one of the main

---

[34] ANTOKOLSKAIA, M., *CEFL* National Report for Russia: *Grounds for Divorce* (2003), p. 182-193.

[35] According to Cretney, the main concern of the proponents of the modernisation of divorce law was the 'recognition that the decision whether or not a marriage should be dissolved was one for the parties which the state was not in a position to question'. CRETNEY, S., *Family Law in the Twentieth Century* (2003), p. 391.

objectives of the reform, as it left too much room for divorce by collusion which it was supposed to put an end to. The compromise of 1996 appeared altogether unworkable and led to the stillborn 1996 Family Law Act.

The 1969 divorce reform

On the eve of the 1969 reform, the main problem of divorce law in England and Wales was that while the law in the books did not provide for divorce by mutual consent, consensual divorce by collusion was flourishing in practice. As late as 1956, nine members of the Royal Commission on Marriage and Divorce upheld the principle that divorce by consent was 'fundamentally incompatible with the concept of marriage', and that 'to give people the right to divorce themselves would be [...] disastrous for the nation'.[36] At the same time, in practice one could get a divorce 'as easily as a motor licence and rather more easily than a passport'.[37] The only condition was that the husband was prepared to behave 'like a gentlemen',[38] by playing guilty in a divorce procedure initiated by the wife. The problem of mass divorce by collusion was acknowledged by both the conservatives and their progressive opponents. However, the ways they proposed to solve it were rather in opposition to each other. The solution advocated by the proponents of liberalisation was simply to officially allow divorce by mutual consent without much enquiry and waiting time. The solution promoted by the conservatives was to make divorce law even more restrictive in order to make consensual divorce by collusion practically impossible. These two conflicting approaches made compromise rather difficult and largely determined the contradictory character of the 1969 divorce reform.

The reform was preceded by two important reports: one, *Putting Asunder*,[39] by a group of experts appointed by the Archbishop of Canterbury,[40] and another, *Reform of the Grounds of Divorce: the Field of Choice*,[41] by the Law Commission. Both the Law Commission and the Group of the Archbishop of Canterbury agreed that good divorce law should 'buttress rather than undermine the stability of marriage' and must 'enable the empty shell to be destroyed with the maximum fairness, and the minimum

---

[36] *Royal Commission on Marriage and Divorce* (Cmd. 6678, 156), Para. 69 (vii) and (viii). Cited in: CRETNEY, S., *Divorce Reform in England: Humbug and Hypocrisy or a Smooth Transition?* (1996), p. 41.

[37] HERBERT, A., 'Holy Deadlock' (1934), Cited in: CRETNEY, S., *Divorce Reform in England: Humbug and Hypocrisy or a Smooth Transition?* (1996), p. 41.

[38] Ibid.

[39] *Putting Asunder: a Divorce Law for Contemporary Society* (1966).

[40] This was a significant step on the part of the Church of England, which did not revoke its doctrine of indissolubility of marriage, but genuinely acknowledged that secular law may differ on this point from the law of the Church.

[41] LAW COMMISSION, *Reform of the Grounds of Divorce: the Field of Choice*, Law Commission (1966).

bitterness, distress and humiliation'.[42] They also shared the sentiment that matrimonial offence as a ground for divorce should be replaced by the irretrievable breakdown of marriage. The groups, however, held a different view on how the irretrievable breakdown should be established. The Archbishop's Group insisted that mutual consent of the spouses alone may not constitute sufficient proof of the breakdown. According to its report, *Putting Asunder*, admission of purely consensual divorce 'would virtually repudiate the community's interest in the stability of marriage, because a judge (the community representative) would take no effectual part in the proceedings'.[43] Therefore, *Putting Asunder* initially proposed a full inquest into the breakdown of marriage in every divorce case.[44] This perspective reflected a conservative idea to retain the State control of divorce and to rule out consensual divorce by collusion by making inquiry more stringent and divorce more difficult. Contrasted to the Archbishop's Group, the approach of the Law Commission was rather more pragmatic than ideological. The Commission considered a full inquest 'procedurally impracticable', and initially proposed to derive evidence of an irretrievable breakdown from a stated period of separation and absence of evidence to the contrary.[45] Thus, the spouses' autonomy would be admitted, albeit in a moderated form.

The compromise reached between the approaches of the two groups formed the basis of the Divorce Reform Act 1969.[46] According to this law, the irretrievable breakdown should be established without full inquest, but only upon proof of the existence of specific, listed circumstances.[47] Three of these 'circumstances' were 'the same old matrimonial faults':[48] adultery, desertion, and cruelty, which was now called 'unreasonable behaviour'.[49] In addition, two new no-fault 'circumstances' were added: two-years of de-facto separation followed by application for divorce by mutual consent, and five-year de-facto separation, followed by unilateral application, contested by the other spouse. As a result, 'the practical proposals to implement this new principle [irretrievable breakdown] were as conservative as the idea itself was radical'.[50] Still, the law of 1969 made an important step forward by allowing a 'guilty' spouse to obtain divorce against the will of an 'innocent' one. However, as the admission of such a 'Casanova's Charter' was a thorn in the flesh for the conservatives, a special hardship clause was introduced for the protection of an 'innocent' spouse. This hardship clause

---

[42]   Law Commission, *The Field of Choice* (1966), p. 10.
[43]   LEE, B., *Divorce Reform in England* (1974), p. 51.
[44]   Ibid, p. 46.
[45]   LAW COMMISSION, *The Field of Choice* (1966), p. 53.
[46]   Came into force on 1 January 1971. In 1973 consolidated into *the Matrimonial Causes Act*, which is still in force.
[47]   LEE, B., *Divorce Reform in England* (1974), p. 73.
[48]   STONE, L., *Road to Divorce* (1990), p. 307.
[49]   Ibid.
[50]   Ibid.

also ensured that the State would have the last word in a contested divorce procedure. In addition, it should be mentioned that under the 1969 Act the spouses could divorce and remarry without having all the practical consequences of divorce been settled.[51] The ancillary matters could be dealt with later, in a separate procedure(s). Considering the polarization of English society upon the issue of divorce, it is hardly surprising that even this rather conservative reform met substantial conservative opposition in and outside Parliament.[52]

Although the role of the State in marriage dissolution was a central issue of the debate surrounding the 1969 reform, a real breakthrough in this field came without much political debate by way of delegated legislation. The Government, unable to cope with the growing number of divorce petitions,[53] in 1973 introduced a so-called 'special procedure'[54] for a range of non-contested cases.[55] In 1977 this procedure was extended to all non-contested cases.[56] Since in reality almost all divorce petitions were non-contested, the special procedure became in practice the ordinary divorce procedure.[57] The special procedure allowed for the grant of a divorce without a court hearing or legal aid.[58] The State control of divorce thus became very much a fiction. The proponents of the strong role of the State mourned that under the special procedure, 'the court's inquisitorial role was reduced to ticking boxes followed by a short assessment of where, if true, the facts alleged would justify a decree'.[59] As a matter of fact, under the special procedure the time-span of a non-contested divorce case upon one of the fault grounds lasted, from petition to decree, less than four months.[60] This was a sharp contrast to the impossibility of obtaining a no-fault divorce by mutual consent any earlier than after two-years of de-facto separation. It is no wonder that most consenting couples opted for a shorter and cheaper fault-divorce by collusion, rather than for waiting for two years.[61] The emerging gap between the law in the books and the law in action once more accentuated the 'unsatisfactory nature of the

---

[51]   Although there was a statutory requirement to consider, but not settle, issues relating to children.
[52]   In Parliament most Labour and Liberals voted for the Act, and most Conservatives either refrained from voting or voted against it. LEE, B., *Divorce Reform in England* (1974), p. 73.
[53]   HALE, B., 'The Family Law Act 1996 – the death of marriage?' (1997), p. 6.
[54]   The description of the special procedure see: CRETNEY, S., 'Divorce Reform in England: Humbug and Hypocrisy or a Smooth Transition?' (1996), note 19, at p. 56.
[55]   Namely for certain cases where no minor children of the family were involved in. CRETNEY, S., *Family Law in the Twentieth Century* (2003), p. 382.
[56]   CRETNEY, S., *Family Law in the Twentieth Century* (2003), p. 382.
[57]   Ibid.
[58]   Ibid.
[59]   HALE, B., 'The Family Law Act 1996 – the death of marriage?' (1997), p. 6.
[60]   *Fourth Annual Report* of the Advisory Board in Family Law, 2000/2001, para. 3.5.
[61]   The Law Commission referred to 73% of divorce petitions being based on fault grounds. LAW COMMISSION, *The Ground for Divorce* (1990), para. 2.3.

compromise between offence-based facts and the breakdown principle'.[62] The net result of the 1969 reform, as supplemented by the special procedure, was that an easy consensual divorce without enquiry and waiting period was publicly kicked out of the front door, but shortly afterwards silently allowed to re-enter through the back entrance.

The stillborn 1996 Family Law Act

The dissatisfaction with this situation started to grow in the eighties.[63] Once again, it was very different aspects of the existing law that made both the proponents of liberalisation and the conservatives call for reform. While the advocates of liberalisation found existing divorce too difficult, the conservatives accused it of being too easy.[64] In 1988 the Law Commission published a Discussion Paper on the grounds for divorce, *Facing the Future*,[65] deprecating the current divorce law for being incoherent, hypocritical and too restrictive.[66] The Discussion Paper blatantly concluded that the objectives of the 1969 divorce reform, 'attaining maximum fairness and minimum bitterness', had failed due to the retention of the fault elements.[67] At the same time, the conservatives attacked the 1969 divorce law from the completely opposite position. Their main concerns were that the special procedure had introduced a 'divorce by post'[68] and had made divorce 'too easy'.[69] In 1993, the Conservative Government, then in office, contributed to the conservative criticism of the existing law in its consultation paper, *Looking to the Future. Mediation and the Grounds for Divorce*.[70] According to the Government, one of the problems with the current law was that it 'allow[ed] divorce to be obtained quickly and easily without the parties being required to have regard to the consequences' and 'does nothing to save

---

[62]   CRETNEY, S., 'Divorce Reform in England: Humbug and Hypocrisy or a Smooth Transition?' (1996), p. 42.

[63]   For an overview see: CRETNEY, S., *Family Law in the Twentieth Century* (2003), p. 385ff.

[64]   As the Law Commission summarised in its 1990 report, the disagreement was so great that there was not even consensus about what it meant to make divorce 'easier'. For the advocates of liberalisation, easy divorce meant a 'short or painless' one, whereas for the conservative it may mean something different. LAW COMMISSION, *The Ground for Divorce* (1990), para 3. 46.

[65]   LAW COMMISSION, *Facing the Future* (1988).

[66]   The Commission pointed out that it 'increased confusion for litigants', 'encouraged collusion', and that 'the ensuing hostility makes divorce more painful, not only for parties, but also for the children'. LAW COMMISSION, *Facing the Future* (1988), para. 3.48-3.50.

[67]   LAW COMMISSION, *Facing the Future* (1988), para. 3.48.

[68]   HALE, B., 'The Family Law Act 1996 – the death of marriage?' (1997), p. 6.

[69]   CRETNEY, S., MASSON, J., BAILEY-HARRIS, R., *Principles of Family Law* (2002), p. 297. Lady Brenda Hale complained that, "oddly enough, this summary [*Facing the Future*] did not emphasise one of the most serious criticisms of the present law: that it allows a couple to be divorced, and therefore to remarry, before all the practical consequences of their separation from one another have been decided'. HALE, B., 'The Family Law Act 1996 – the death of marriage?' (1997), p. 6.

[70]   LORD CHANCELLOR'S DEPARTMENT, *Looking to the Future* (1993).

marriages'.[71] The situation started more and more to resemble that of the time of the drafting of the 1969 divorce law. There was a consensus as to the need to reform the current law, but the conservative and progressive critics saw the objectives of such a reform in a completely different way.[72] The coming law was again doomed to become a compromise. There was a consensus, albeit not unanimous,[73] that fault should be dispensed with and that irretrievable breakdown should become the sole ground for divorce.[74] However, simply bringing the law in the books in line with the law in action, by allowing divorce by mutual consent without enquiry and without a long waiting period, appeared to be as impossible in the 1990s as it had been in the 1960s. The idea of immediate divorce by consent, combined with the possibility of a contested divorce after a stated period of separation, was rejected out of the fear that it 'would turn consent into a major bargaining chip'.[75] Still, by then even the conservatives had accepted that to require the court to establish a breakdown by a full enquiry would not work in practice.[76] The two remaining options were to introduce a lengthy mandatory period of separation, or a lengthy mandatory period of reflection, for both divorce by mutual consent and contested divorce.[77] The latter option was put forward in the 1996 Family Law Act.[78]

In 1990, the Law Commission produced a report with a draft Bill attached to it.[79] The Commission's proposal was relatively modern for European standards,[80] and suggested

---

[71] Ibid, Paras 5.6-10.

[72] Lady Brenda Hale pointed out that 'even if everyone agreed that the present system was indefensible, they did not agree about what could be done to improve it'. HALE, B., 'The Family Law Act 1996 – the death of marriage?' (1997), p. 6.

[73] The conservative proponents of retention of fault claimed that its removal 'would destroy the moral basis of the law of marriage and divorce'. See: HALE, B., 'The Family Law Act 1996 – the death of marriage?' (1997), p. 9. These arguments were eloquently verbalised by Baroness Young who said in the House of Lords that divorce law 'will influence behaviour. It will send a message and it will influence the cultural climate of our society. The message of no fault is clear. It is that breaking marriage vows, breaking a civil contract, does not matter. It undermines individual responsibility. It is an attack upon decent behaviour and fidelity. It violates common sense and creates injustice for anyone who believes in guilt and innocence'. Baroness Young, *Hansard (HL)*, vol. 569, col. 1638. Cited in: HALE, B., 'The Family Law Act 1996 – the death of marriage?' (1997), at p. 9.

[74] CRETNEY, S., 'Divorce Reform in England: Humbug and Hypocrisy or a Smooth Transition?' (1996), p. 42.

[75] HALE, B., 'The Family Law Act 1996 – the death of marriage?' (1997), p. 14.

[76] No one believed any longer in the possibility of a 'return to the full-blown divorce trials if the past'. HALE, B., 'The Family Law Act 1996 – the death of marriage?' (1997), p. 10.

[77] HASSON, E., 'Divorce reform in England, the case of the Family Law Act 1996' (2006), p. 277.

[78] Ibid, p. 278.

[79] LAW COMMISSION, *The Ground for Divorce* (1990).

[80] Although even this moderate proposal was criticised because it 'effectively constituted divorce by repudiation – after a one year waiting period – however unfair such repudiation might be'. CRETNEY, S., 'Divorce Reform in England: Humbug and Hypocrisy or a Smooth Transition?' (1996), p. 47.

that divorce should be granted after a one-year period of reflection.[81] There was no requirement to settle ancillary matters before obtaining a divorce order.[82] The role of the State was reinsured by retaining a hardship clause.[83] In addition, a number of procedural measures were designated to facilitate reconciliation and mediation.[84] The Commission's proposal received much support from professional groups working with families.[85]

In 1993 the Conservative Government published its Consultation Paper,[86] which was basically in line with the proposal of the Law Commission, save for the introduction of a compulsory 'information meeting'[87] and much heavier reliance upon mediation.[88] However, the 1995 definitive proposal by the Government[89] departed from both the earlier Governmental proposal and the proposals by the Commission in one fundamental point:[90] it was no longer possible to obtain a divorce unless all ancillary matters were first settled.[91]

In Parliament, the Bill became a matter of heated controversy.[92] The choices and the arguments 'were the same as they had always been'[93] in divorce matters. The conservatives, by then a minority in Parliament, did not succeed in their attempts to keep elements of fault within the grounds of divorce.[94] However, the concern to save

---

[81] The Law Commission rejected a requirement of a separation of one year, as it might cause hardship to the people, who currently rely upon adultery or behaviour, because they cannot afford to separate for two years. HALE, B., 'The Family Law Act 1996 – the death of marriage?' (1997), p. 13.

[82] CRETNEY, S., 'Divorce Reform in England: Humbug and Hypocrisy or a Smooth Transition?' (1996), p. 44.

[83] 'The court would only be able to refuse a divorce if divorce would result in grave financial or other hardship to one of the parties, and it would, in all circumstances, be wrong to dissolve the marriage' *Draft Bill* annexed to the report *The Ground for Divorce* (1990), para. 1.5.

[84] CRETNEY, S., 'Divorce Reform in England: Humbug and Hypocrisy or a Smooth Transition?' (1996), p. 44.

[85] For an overview see: HASSON, E., 'Divorce reform in England, the case of the Family Law Act 1996' (2006), p. 280.

[86] LORD CHANCELLOR'S DEPARTMENT, *Looking to the Future* (1993).

[87] LAW COMMISSION, *The Ground for Divorce* (1990), para. 8.1.

[88] Mediation was envisaged in a rather paternalistic and moralistic fashion. The Government said that it 'enables spouses to accept responsibility for the breakdown […] to address face to face the questions of fault and blame [and] offers an opportunity to address what went wrong with the marriage'. (LORD CHANCELLOR'S DEPARTMENT, *Looking to the Future* (1993), para. 7.5.) Stefan Cretney rightly affiliated such expectations with 'the re-education programmes associated with totalitarian regimes'. CRETNEY, S., 'Divorce Reform in England: Humbug and Hypocrisy or a Smooth Transition?' (1996), p. 50.

[89] LORD CHANCELLOR'S DEPARTMENT, *Looking to the Future* (1995).

[90] CRETNEY, S., 'Divorce Reform in England: Humbug and Hypocrisy or a Smooth Transition?' (1996), p. 46.

[91] LORD CHANCELLOR'S DEPARTMENT, *Looking to the Future* (1995), para. 2.34.

[92] HALE, B., 'The Family Law Act 1996 – the death of marriage?' (1997), p. 8.

[93] Ibid.

[94] Ibid, p. 12.

marriages was equally shared by both Conservative and Labour parties.[95] This concern led to some important modifications of the Bill. The initially proposed one-year period of reflection was kept only for non-contested divorces where no minor children were involved. In cases of contested divorce a defendant could ask for an additional six-month period of reflection. The general rule was that if a couple had children under the age of 16 years old, the period of reflection was automatically extended for six months[96] even if there was mutual consent to divorce.[97] But this was not all; in effect, getting divorced could take considerably longer because now all the ancillary matters had to be adjudicated within the same divorce procedure.[98] All in all, the conservatives had managed to turn the 'divorce clock back';[99] the newly proposed no-fault divorce made obtaining divorce more lengthy and difficult than existing fault-based divorce under the special procedure. Finally, the extremely complicated Bill became the infamous stillborn 1996 Family Law Act.[100]

The further history of the Family Law Act 1996 is known well enough. The Labour Government that came into office in 1997 initially intended to implement Part II, dealing with the substantive law on divorce and separation, in 2000.[101] However, due to the disappointment that arose from the piloting of the new procedure,[102] the Government withdrew its support for the Act, and in 2001 decided to ask Parliament to repeal it in due time.[103] Part III, governing legal aid for mediation in family matters, came into force in 1997, only to be repealed in 1999.[104] This Part made participation in mediation a compulsory step for getting legal aid.[105] A strong belief in the potential of mediation to solve the problems surrounding divorce in non-adversary manner

---

[95]   HASSON, E., 'Divorce reform in England, the case of the Family Law Act 1996' (2006), p. 281.

[96]   Sec. 7 of *Family Law Act* 1996.

[97]   This amendment was upheld by the House of Commons in spite of strong opposition from the part of child protection organisations. HALE, B., 'The Family Law Act 1996 – the death of marriage?' (1997), p. 15.

[98]   The requirement to settle ancillary matters and therefore 'to take responsibility for themselves' was rightly labelled by David Bradley as 'true conservatism'. BRADLEY, D., 'Comparative Law, Family Law and Common Law' (2003), p. 138.

[99]   HASSON, E., 'Divorce reform in England, the case of the Family Law Act 1996' (2006), p. 285.

[100]   Received Royal Assent at 4 July 1996.

[101]   HOME OFFICE, *Supporting Families. A Consultation Document* (1998), para. 4.42. See also: HASSON, E., 'Divorce reform in England, the case of the Family Law Act 1996' (2006), p. 289.

[102]   Lord Chancellor's Department, Nr. 159/99, cited in: HASSON, E., 'Divorce reform in England, the case of the Family Law Act 1996' (2006), at p. 290.

[103]   On 16 January 2001 the Government announced that it would repeal Part II of the Act. Lord Chancellor's Department, *Divorce Law Reform – Government Proposes to Repeal Part II of the Family Law Act 1996*, Press Notice 20/01.

[104]   Replace by *Access to Justice Act*.

[105]   Sec. 29 of the *Family Law Act* 1996. For more on mediation in this Act see: HASSON, E., 'Divorce reform in England, the case of the Family Law Act 1996' (2006), p. 291-292.

was one of the cornerstone policies upon which the 1996 Act was founded.[106] However, the brief implementation of the provisions on mediation proved that the hope that mediation would be a 'mass solution to the problem of divorce'[107] was much too optimistic.[108] Disappointment in the potential of mediation was probably one of the main reasons for the decision not to proceed with further implementation of the 1996 Act and to repeal its provisions on mediation.[109]

Many epitaphs have already been written for this Act, there is no need to add another one here. The story of the 1996 Act is probably one of the best recent examples of the impact of the conservative/progressive divide on family law policy.[110] On the progressive side of this divide, divorce was perceived as an individual right to dissolve a marriage that became unhappy;[111] 'a private matter into which the State should not intrude'.[112] Personalistic ethics demanded that the 'individual's needs and desires' should 'have priority over the general good or society's need for stable institutions'.[113] On the conservative side, it was firmly believed that marriage was 'for religious or other reasons [...] sacred or at least a superior form of family arrangement'.[114] Therefore, it was claimed that divorce is a 'matter of public concern and that the State has the right to restrict it'.[115] In line with the old transpersonalistic approach, the needs and desires of the individuals concerned were rendered not to be 'the ultimate arbiter'[116] in divorce cases. This unbridgeable conservative-progressive divide led to an unworkable compromise, one which only perpetuated what Stefan Cretney called a 'tradition of humbug and hypocrisy'.[117] According to Ezra Hasson, the nature of this compromise was to satisfy both the progressive-minded camp seeking to introduce

---

[106] CRETNEY, S., MASSON, J., BAILEY-HARRIS, R., *Principles of Family Law* (2002), p. 304-305.

[107] BAINHAM, A., 'Exciting Times in England – Children and Divorce' (2001), p. 75.

[108] The piloting of the 'information meetings', which were part of the new divorce procedure, revealed that only 7% of the couples involved in the pilots had decided to go for mediation. 39% had reported to be only strengthened in their intention to go to a solicitor. Lord Chancellor's Department, Nr. 159/99, cited in: HASSON, E., 'Divorce reform in England, the case of the Family Law Act 1996' (2006), note 95 at p. 290.

[109] CRETNEY, S., MASSON, J., BAILEY-HARRIS, R., *Principles of Family Law* (2002), p. 308; HASSON, E., 'Divorce reform in England, the case of the Family Law Act 1996' (2006), p. 289-290.

[110] It has been suggested that it was 'a deep ideological division which has made it so difficult to reformulate divorce law about which people could agree'. BAINHAM, A., 'Exciting Times in England – Children and Divorce' (2001), p. 76.

[111] Ibid, p. 75.

[112] Ibid.

[113] BROOKS, J., *Whose Fault Is It Anyway? Divorce and the Family Law Act 1996* (2000), p. 4.

[114] BAINHAM, A., 'Exciting Times in England – Children and Divorce' (2001), p. 76.

[115] Ibid.

[116] BROOKS, J., *Whose Fault Is It Anyway? Divorce and the Family Law Act 1996* (2000), p. 4.

[117] CRETNEY, S., 'Divorce Reform in England: Humbug and Hypocrisy or a Smooth Transition?' (1996), p. 52.

no-fault divorce, and the marriage-saving aspirations of the conservatives.[118] By trying to simultaneously pursue 'conflicting policy objectives',[119] the new law 'created a rich possibility of potentially unworkable contradictions'.[120] In the words of John Dewar, those conflicting policy objectives encompassed promoting autonomy and self-determination of the spouses through encouraging mediation and out-of-court agreements, and at the same time increasing State intervention through influencing spouses' behaviour via marriage saving policy.[121] Thereby, the Act endeavoured 'both to give parties greater autonomy while at the same time seeking to influence how they use[d] it'.[122] The result of this compromise was that 'the new law looked backwards'[123] and from the outset had little chance to work. David Bradley has suggested that, 'for all its appearance as liberal measure [...] the Family Law Act 1996, in fact complemented the political agenda of the recent Conservative administration'.[124] In the end everything turned full circle, and England and Wales had to fall back on the provisions of the 1969 Act.[125]

14.3.2. FRANCE: COMPROMISE OR CONSENSUS? DIVORCE À LA CARTE SURVIVES ALL REFORMS

The 1975 reform: introducing divorce à la carte

On the eve of the reforms of the 1970s, divorce in France had already had a long history of severe political controversy. As a renowned French scholar has put it: 'during more than two centuries of France's concern with the problem of divorce, the same ideologies confronted each other, the same arguments were put forward and the same sensibilities were affected'.[126] In the 1970s, French public opinion was as deeply split with regard to divorce as it had been ever since the Revolution; despite radical transformations in the 1960s, there still were '*les deux Frances*'.[127] The legal situation largely resembled the English one. While the law in the books allowed only fault-based divorce, in practise the proportion of consensual divorces by collusion was estimated

---

[118]   HASSON, E., 'Divorce reform in England, the case of the Family Law Act 1996' (2006), p. 285-286.
[119]   CRETNEY, S., *Family Law in the Twentieth Century* (2003), p. 389.
[120]   DEWAR, J., 'The Normal Chaos of Family Law' (1998), p. 477-478.
[121]   Ibid, p. 476.
[122]   Ibid.
[123]   HASSON, E., 'Divorce reform in England, the case of the Family Law Act 1996' (2006), p. 286.
[124]   BRADLEY, D., 'Comparative Law, Family Law and Common Law' (2003), p. 136.
[125]   The *Matrimonial Causes Act*, which incorporated the provisions of the *Divorce Reform Act 1969*, is still in force.
[126]   Speech of J. Foyer during the parliamentary debate of 28 May 1975. Cited in: FOYER, J., 'The Reform of Family Law in France' (1978), p.101.
[127]   RHEINSTEIN, M., *Marriage Stability, Divorce, and the Law* (1972), p. 195.

at one-fourth of the total number of cases.[128] Both the proponents of liberalisation and their conservative opponents called for reform,[129] but did not agree upon its direction. The proponents of liberalisation advocated for the complete abolition of fault-based divorce,[130] the conservatives opposed this idea, and the general public was hopelessly split.[131] Thus, as in England and Wales, the pending divorce reform was doomed to become a compromise. The Swedish model had been considered and rejected by the draftsmen.[132] Even a less far-reaching proposal to introduce divorce based solely on the ground of irretrievable breakdown of marriage was considered impossible.[133] At the same time, the French legislature was, more than the English one, prepared to admit divorce by mutual consent. In the end, the French divorce law of 1975,[134] drafted by the eminent scholar Jean Carbonnier, came to accommodate a mixed system of fault and no-fault grounds, the so-called *divorce à la carte*.[135] This system was believed to reflect the plurality of the conceptions of marriage held in the pluralistic French society.[136] Thus, the new law provided for a wide range of different routes to divorce, including a fault-based divorce-sanction; two forms of consensual divorce, and a unilateral divorce-remedy on the ground of irretrievable breakdown of marriage.[137] The fault grounds were preserved out of regard for the still popular view of divorce in the terms of culpability.[138] This was not without consequences, however. According to Commaille, after the reform, both doctrine and case law amply demonstrated that 'the notion of fault has permeated other types of divorce proceedings'.[139]

The most significant achievement of the 1975 law was its allowance of divorce by mutual consent without a long waiting period. The law provided for two forms of

---

[128]　FOYER, J., 'The Reform of Family Law in France' (1978), p.106.
[129]　According to an opinion poll that was conducted in the early 1970s, the majority of the respondents supported the divorce reform. DADOMO, C., 'The Current Reform of French Law of Divorce' (2004), p. 220.
[130]　This was suggested in a Bill by the socialist MP Gaston Deferre and a Bill by a group of communist MPs. MAHE, C., 'De Franse wetgever op weg naar afschaffing van "schuldscheiding' (2002), p. 17, note 5.
[131]　GLENDON, M. A., 'The French Divorce Reform Law of 1976' (1976), p. 201.
[132]　Ibid, p. 202.
[133]　In Carbonnier's words, such a divorce is merely 'a repudiation, a tragedy for a wife, the subject of horror for our Western societies', CARBONNIER, J., *Droit civil: La famille, l'enfant, le couple* (2002), p. 542.
[134]　Law of 11 July 1975 entered into force on 1 January 1976.
[135]　CARBONNIER, J., *Droit civil: La famille, l'enfant, le couple* (2002), p. 541.
[136]　CORNU, G., *Droit Civil, La famille* (2003), No. 312.
[137]　BÉNABENT, A., *Droit civil: La Famille* (2001), No. 228.
[138]　CARBONNIER, D., 'La question du divorce: mémoire à consulter' (1975), p. 118.
[139]　COMMAILLE, J., 'Towards a New Definition of Divorce' (1980), p. 106.

divorce by mutual consent:[140] divorce by joint application,[141] when spouses had to agree upon divorce and ancillary matters, and divorce by unilateral application accepted by the other spouse,[142] when an agreement on ancillary matters did not need to be reached.[143] Divorce by joint application gave the spouses the advantages of a non-contentious procedure (the spouses could have one attorney)[144] and of preservation of privacy (the reasons for divorce did not need to be disclosed).[145] However, the 'oppressive formality'[146] of consensual divorce rather diminished its attractiveness.[147] First, divorce by mutual consent was not possible during the first six months of marriage.[148] Secondly, the spouses had to appear before the judge twice, first for the initial application and then for the renewal of application after the three month period of reflection.[149] Moreover, the spouses had to produce a preliminary agreement on ancillary matters, followed by a definite agreement – both subject to judicial scrutiny.[150] These requirements put one spouse 'at mercy of the other'; should one spouse change his or her mind, the other had to restart the whole procedure using a different ground.[151] Another problem was that although the judge was not entitled to investigate the reasons for divorce, State control manifested itself in the obligation of the judge to investigate whether the consent of the each of the spouses was genuinely freely given and serious enough.[152]

Divorce by one spouse's acceptance of the other's application, also known as divorce by 'shared fault',[153] was a real innovation, peculiar to the French legal system.[154] Its main purpose was to 'de-dramatise' divorce and diminish the contentious elements of the divorce procedure.[155] This form of divorce consisted of two stages: a non-

---

[140] The categorisation of divorce by unilateral application accepted by the other spouse as divorce by mutual consent was not uncontroversial. For instance, Jean Carbonnier regarded it not a form of divorce by mutual consent but as a separate form of divorce. CARBONNIER, J., *Droit civil: La famille, l'enfant, le couple* (2002), p. 574.

[141] *Le divorce sur requête conjointe.* Art. 230-232 *Code Civil.*

[142] *Du divorce demandé par un époux et accepté par l'autre.* Art. 233-236 *Code Civil.*

[143] CHAUVEAU, V., CORNEC, A., 'France' (2002), p. 265.

[144] Art. 230 (2) *Code Civil.*

[145] BÉNABENT, A., *Droit civil: La Famille* (2001), No. 284.

[146] FERRÉ-ANDRÉ, S., 'A Pause in the Reform of French Family Law' (2004), p. 184.

[147] Only 41% of divorcing couples found recourse in this form of divorce. FERRÉ-ANDRÉ, S., 'A Pause in the Reform of French Family Law' (2004), p. 184.

[148] Art. 230 (3) *Code Civil.*

[149] BÉNABENT, A., *Droit civil: La Famille* (2001), No. 288-289.

[150] Ibid, No. 289-291.

[151] RUBELLIN-DEVICHI, J., 'How Matters Stand Now in Relation to French Law Reform' (2000), p. 155.

[152] Art. 232 *Code Civil.* BÉNABENT, A., *Droit civil : La Famille* (2001), No. 283.

[153] FERRAND, F., *CEFL National Report for France: Grounds for Divorce* (2003), p. 340.

[154] BÉNABENT, A., *Droit civil : La Famille* (2001), No. 293.

[155] Ibid, No. 296.

contentious one and a contentious one.[156] During the first stage, one of the spouses applied for divorce claiming that the continuation of marital life had become intolerable,[157] but without raising the question of fault. The other spouse acknowledged these facts and accepted the demand of divorce.[158] The judge examined the possibility of reconciliation and, if an attempt at reconciliation failed, confirmed the consent in principle of the spouses to divorce.[159] After that, the second, contentious, stage of the divorce procedure commenced. During this stage, the court[160] decided the ancillary matters.[161] As with divorce by joint application, this 'hybrid-procedure' also appeared to be 'too strictly formal', so that divorce by acceptance always remained no more than a marginal divorce form.[162]

Another new ground for divorce was the irretrievable breakdown of marriage. This ground enabled a 'guilty' spouse to abandon an 'innocent' one. The introduction of this 'divorce-repudiation' had been the matter of great political controversy,[163] which reached its zenith when the original Bill was replaced at the last minute by a more restrictive one. The Bill provided for three different modes of proof of irretrievable breakdown. The first mode of proof was subjective: the petitioning spouse had to convince the court that the marriage was permanently disrupted. The initial Bill did not require any stated period of such disruption. Thus, if the applicant managed to convince the court, divorce could be granted immediately. The second and the third modes of proving irretrievable breakdown were of an objective nature. The marriage was presumed to be irretrievably broken down if the spouses had lived apart for at least six years, or if the defendant-spouse had suffered a grave mental illness for at least six years.[164] However, at the last moment the Bill was modified by President Giscard d'Estaing, who took out the possibility of immediate unilateral divorce upon convincing the court that the marriage was permanently disrupted.[165] As a result, the 1975 law provided for unilateral divorce on the ground of irretrievable breakdown of marriage only after six years of living apart or six years of grave mental illness on the part of the defender. In the latter case, the petitioner also had to convince the court that the illness of his or her spouse had made the marriage community impossible and

---

[156] Ibid, No. 293.
[157] FERRAND, F., *CEFL National Report for France: Grounds for Divorce* (2003), p. 79-80.
[158] Ibid, p. 80.
[159] BÉNABENT, A., *Droit civil : La Famille* (2001), No. 296.
[160] Before 1994, separate judicial instances were involved during these stages: a family judge (*le juge aux affaires familiales*) during the first stage and the Tribunal de Grande Instance in the second stage. The law of 8 January 1993 made the family judge a universal forum for all divorce cases. FERRAND, F., *CEFL: Grounds for Divorce* for France (2003), p. 118.
[161] BÉNABENT, A., *Droit civil : La Famille* (2001), No. 293.
[162] FERRÉ-ANDRÉ, S., 'A Pause in the Reform of French Family Law' (2004), p. 184.
[163] BÉNABENT, A., *Droit civil : La Famille* (2001), No. 300.
[164] GLENDON, M. A., 'The French Divorce Reform Law of 1976' (1976), p. 207.
[165] Ibid.

that such community could not be expected to be restored in future.[166] In both cases, divorce could be refused if the defendant invoked a hardship clause.[167] Although the question of fault was not formally relevant for this procedure, the negative sentiment against this 'divorce-repudiation' was so strong that the petitioning spouse was treated as if she or he was guilty and the 'divorce ha[d] been awarded against him or her'.[168] As a result, the petitioner had to bear all the financial consequences of the divorce. The combination of the aforementioned disadvantages made divorce upon the irretrievable breakdown of marriage so unattractive that it was used by hardly 2% of all divorcing spouses.[169]

Fault was retained and, against the reformers hopes,[170] continued to remain one of the most popular grounds.[171] Almost all specific offences listed by the pre-reform law were now replaced by one general fault ground, defined as, 'grave or renewed violation of marital obligations which made maintaining marital life intolerable.[172] Alongside this general fault ground, only one specific offence was retained,[173] namely the condemnation for certain crimes.[174] The new law deprived adultery of its status as an absolute ground.[175] From this point on, adultery had to be treated as just a violation of marital obligations.[176] The 'purity' of the general fault ground was preserved by the *Cour de Cassation*, which tried to prevent its evolution into a kind of new 'objective ground'[177] by ensuring that both requirements, culpable behaviour and intolerability of marital life, were satisfied.[178] If both spouses were 'guilty', divorce could be brought on the ground of shared fault.

---

[166] FERRAND, F., *CEFL* National Report for France: *Grounds for Divorce* (2003), p. 402-403.

[167] Art. 240 *Code Civil*. BÉNABENT, A., *Droit civil: La Famille* (2001), No. 311 and 316.

[168] FERRAND, F., *CEFL* National Report for France: *Grounds for Divorce* (2003), p. 408-409.

[169] FERRÉ-ANDRÉ, S., 'A Pause in the Reform of French Family Law' (2004), p. 185.

[170] DEKEUWER-DÉFOSSEZ, F., *Rénover le droit de la famille: Propositions pour un droit adapté aux réalités et aux aspiration de notre temps* (1999), p. 75. Further referred to as: Report Dekeuwer-Défossez.

[171] On the eve of 2004 reforms fault grounds accounted for 42% of all divorce proceedings. FERRÉ-ANDRÉ, S., 'A Pause in the Reform of French Family Law' (2004), p. 185.

[172] Art. 242 *Code Civil*. The mere proof of a grave or continuous violation of marital obligations did not suffice for divorce; the spouses also had to convince the judge that such violation had made the continuation of marital life intolerable. See: DEKEUWER-DÉFOSSEZ, F., 'Impressions de recherches sur les fautes causes de divorces' (1985), p. 219-226.

[173] This fault ground was formulated as an absolute ground for divorce. Its retention has been considered to be a mere 'rarity'. BÉNABENT, A., *Droit civil: La Famille* (2001), No. 238.

[174] Art. 243 *Code Civil* referred to the crimes listed in art 131-1 of Criminal Code.

[175] Under the previous law, adultery was regarded as an absolute ground for divorce. That is to say that all that the petitioner had to prove was the adultery itself. No proof was required of the fact that marital life has been disrupted due to the adulterous behaviour of the respondent. This 'easy' proof had opened the gate to divorce by collusion.

[176] BÉNABENT, A., *Droit civil: La Famille* (2001), No. 238.

[177] FERRAND, F., *CEFL National Report for France: Grounds for Divorce* (2003), p. 339.

[178] Ibid, p. 340.

All in all, the compromise attained in France in 1975 was more capable of satisfying both the conservatives and the proponents of liberalisation than the either of the English compromises of 1969 and 1996. The greatest advantage of the French law above the English one was providing a rather quick divorce by mutual consent. However, the excessive formalism of divorce by mutual consent still encouraged spouses to resort to fault divorce by collusion.[179] In England, the inability to provide for divorce by mutual consent without a mandatory waiting period was the most serious deficiency of the 1969 reform. This very deficiency made the 1969 reforms unable to solve the problem of mass divorce by collusion. The French unilateral divorce on the ground of irretrievable breakdown was as restrictive as that provided by the English law.

Failure of no-fault bills. Retaining divorce à la carte

During almost thirty years of application of the 1975 law, several weaknesses became apparent.[180] One of the points of concern was that a spouse who wanted to end the marriage but possessed neither the consent of the other spouse nor the ability to instigate a fault procedure, 'remained a prisoner of the conjugal bond'[181] for at least another six years. Another disturbing factor was that the ever popular fault-based divorce appeared to 'aggravate conflict and destabilise family environment' and to be 'traumatic for everyone'.[182] Moreover, there was a general dissatisfaction with the length, complicity and the costs of divorce procedure.[183] It was clear that the compromise reached in the 1970s was no longer regarded satisfactory thirty years later, and the need for reform became widely realised.[184] In the late 1990s, preparations for reform were started by the left-wing Government that was formed after the elections of 1997. The Government commissioned several reports and studies, the most important of which became a report by the sociologist Irène Théry[185] and a report by the law professor Françoise Dekeuwer-Défossez.[186] The governmental concern for reforms had instigated a wide range of discussion. The major points of the reform

---

[179] This had been predicted by Glendon in 1976. GLENDON, M. A., 'The French Divorce Reform Law of 1976' (1976), p. 226. On an analysis of the practices of fault divorce by collusion, see: *Report Gélard* (2003), p. 12-19. Cited in: DADOMO, C., 'The Current Reform of French Law of Divorce' (2004), at p. 221.

[180] DADOMO, C., 'The Current Reform of French Law of Divorce' (2004), at p. 222.

[181] BÉNABENT, A., *Droit civil: La Famille* (2001), No. 230.

[182] FERRÉ-ANDRÉ, S., 'A Pause in the Reform of French Family Law' (2004), p. 186.

[183] DADOMO, C., 'The Current Reform of French Law of Divorce' (2004), p. 218.

[184] For more on the reasons for the reform see: DEKEUWER-DÉFOSSEZ, F., *Rénover le droit de la famille: Propositions pour un droit adapté aux réalités et aux aspiration de notre temps* (1999).

[185] THÉRY, I., *Couple, filiation et parenté aujourd'hui, Le droit face aux mutations de la famille et de la vie privée,* (1998). (Hereafter referred to as *Report Théry*).

[186] DEKEUWER-DÉFOSSEZ, F., *Rénover le droit de la famille: Propositions pour un droit adapté aux réalités et aux aspiration de notre temps* (1999). (Hereafter referred to as *Report Dekeuwer-Défossez*).

agenda were the abolition of fault-based divorce, the liberalisation of divorce on the ground of the irretrievable breakdown of marriage, and the de-formalisation of divorce by consent. However, it soon appeared that even the proponents of the modernisation of family law were divided into two groups.[187] The first group sought to introduce administrative divorce[188] but intended to preserve the plurality of divorce grounds, including the ground of fault.[189] The second group advocated eliminating fault-based divorce altogether.[190] The idea of administrative divorce met serious opposition,[191] and in spite of the benevolent interest of the Minister of Justice,[192] was dropped by the government.[193] Administrative divorce disappeared for awhile from the French political agenda.[194] The second group was initially more successful. Their strongest argument was that retention of fault necessitated inquiry into such vague and delicate matters as who was guilty in the breakdown of marriage; an inquiry that only fed enmity between the spouses.[195] It was even proposed to introduce a moderate form of unilateral divorce on demand in order get rid of the last remnant of the 'indissolubility logic', which had survived in the 1975 law in the form of the notion that marriage could only be dissolved upon proof of a cause.[196] Although both the *Report Théry* and the *Report Dekeuwer-Défossez* proposed to retain fault,[197] on the 26 June 2001 a Private Bill[198] aimed at the introduction of no-fault divorce was submitted to the French *Assemblée nationale*[199] by a socialist MP. The Bill intended to introduce a right to divorce and to reduce the number of divorce grounds to just two: divorce by consent and divorce based on the irretrievable breakdown of marriage.[200] Divorce upon

---

[187] BASTARD, B., 'Administrative Divorce in France: A Controversy Over a Reform that Never Reached the Statute Book' (2000), p. 79.

[188] One of the most influential proponents of administrative divorce was Irène Théry. Her first proposal dated from 1993. (THÉRY, I., *Le Démariage* (1993)). It was later worked out in the *Report Théry*.

[189] BASTARD, B., 'Administrative Divorce in France: A Controversy Over a Reform that Never Reached the Statute Book' (2000), p. 79.

[190] See, for instance, the articles in the *Gazette du Palais* by the family judge Danièle Ganancia ('Pour un divorce du XXI siècle' (1997), p. 16 and 33-39), and by the law professor Alain Bénabent ('Plaidoyer pour quelques réformes du divorce' (1997), p. 225-228.) Bénabent has even proposed introducing a modest form of unilateral divorce on demand. *Droit civil: La Famille* (2001), No. 100.

[191] The *Report Dekeuwer-Défossez* recommended caution regarding this matter. One of the most fervent opponents of administrative divorce, Jacqueline Rubellin-Devichi, argued that it would reduce marriage to mere cohabitation and jeopardise a weaker party. RUBELLIN-DEVICHI, J., 'How Matters Stand Now in Relation to French Law Reform' (2000), p. 155.

[192] BASTARD, B., 'Administrative Divorce in France: A Controversy Over a Reform that Never Reached the Statute Book' (2000), p. 76-77.

[193] Ibid, p. 72 ff.

[194] FERRAND, F., *CEFL National Report for France: Grounds for Divorce* (2003), p. 59.

[195] BÉNABENT, A., *Droit civil : La Famille* (2001), No. 100.

[196] Ibid.

[197] *Report Théry*, p. 113-115; *Report Dekeuwer-Défossez*, p. 85.

[198] Proposition de loi relative à la réforme du divorce, N° 3189, 26 June 2001.

[199] The Lower Chamber of the French Parliament.

[200] MAHE, C., 'De Franse wetgever op weg naar afschaffing van "schuldscheiding"' (2002), p. 20.

irretrievable breakdown could be obtained (1) after three-years de-facto separation; (2) when both spouses accepted that their marriage has broken down and request divorce; and (3) upon unilateral request after a period of reflection.[201] In line with the general European trend, more emphasis was placed on mediation.[202] This Bill was, however, curtailed by the *Sénat*,[203] which was not prepared to introduce no-fault divorce.[204] In October of the same year, another Private Bill aimed at the abolition of fault was introduced in the *Sénat* by Senator Nicolas About.[205] However, the political moment for the introduction of no-fault divorce in France was over when President Chirac was re-elected, and the Left lost their majority in the Parliament in June 2002. Following this change both Private Bills were made redundant and in October 2002 the Government announced a new reform.[206] The same year, a working group including 22 MP's, academics and practitioners was set up to elaborate a new Bill.[207] On 9 July 2003 the Government introduced to the *Sénat* a newly made Bill,[208] based on a modified version of the existing divorce *à la carte*. This Bill was, following the emergency procedure, promptly adopted by the *Sénat* on 4 January 2004 and by the *Assemblée nationale* on 12 may 2004 to become the Law of 26 May 2004.[209]

The new Law maintains the plurality of grounds of divorce: the new Article 229 *Code Civil* provides for divorce: (1) by mutual consent; (2) upon mutual acceptance of the breakdown of marriage; (3) upon the irretrievable breakdown of the conjugal bond; or (4) upon fault.[210] The main changes are in the modifications of these particular grounds. Divorce by joint application is importantly simplified and de-formalised.[211] Spouses who agree upon divorce may now acquire a divorce decree in one single hearing, provided the court approves their agreement on ancillary matters.[212] The second hearing is only necessary if the judge finds that the agreement regarding ancillary matters provides insufficient protection for the interests of the children or of one of the spouses.[213]

---

[201]   FERRAND, F., *CEFL National Report for France: Grounds for Divorce* (2003), p. 59.
[202]   Ibid, p. 59-60.
[203]   The Upper Chamber of the French Parliament.
[204]   DADOMO, C., 'The Current Reform of French Law of Divorce' (2004), p. 223.
[205]   Proposition de loi visant à remplacer la procédure de divorce pour faute par une procédure de divorce pour cause objective, N° 12, 10 octobre 2001.
[206]   DADOMO, C., 'The Current Reform of French Law of Divorce' (2004), p. 223.
[207]   Ibid, p. 223.
[208]   Le projet de loi relatif au divorce, C-389, 9 July 2003.
[209]   Law 2004-439 of 16 May 2004. Came into force on 1 January 2005.
[210]   'Le divorce peut être prononcé en cas: (-) soit de consentement mutuel; (-) soit d'acceptation du principe de la rupture du mariage; (-) soit d'altération définitive du lien conjugal, (-) soit de faute'.
[211]   BÉNABENT, A., *La réforme du divorce article par article* (2004), p. 38-39.
[212]   Art. 230 and 132 *Code Civil*.
[213]   The new Art. 232 (2) *Code Civil*.

Divorce by the acceptance by one spouse of the application of the other has been replaced by divorce by the mutual acceptance of the breakdown of marriage. The mutual acknowledgement of the fact that the marriage has broken down and the common intent to end the marriage have become sufficient for divorce.[214] In this way, divorce by acceptance is turned into a 'true and realistic divorce by mutual consent, in which parties' agreement relates only to recognition of the breakdown, not to the consequences'.[215] Divorce on this ground can be requested either by both spouses or by one of them.[216] The procedure is also simplified, and once acceptance is given, it can no longer be withdrawn.[217]

Divorce upon unilateral request on the basis of the irretrievable breakdown of marriage after six years of separation is changed into unilateral divorce on the basis of the irretrievable breakdown of marriage after a two-year de-facto separation. The reform of this ground is claimed to be the most essential departure from the previous law. It was accompanied by serious controversy, as in some quarters unilateral divorce was still equated with repudiation.[218] Not only has the period of separation been shortened from six to two years, more importantly the two-year separation now constitutes an irrefutable presumption of irretrievable breakdown of marriage.[219] This innovation has been interpreted as a general recognition of the right to divorce under French law.[220] The petitioning spouse is no longer bound to bear all the financial consequences of divorce; he or she is even entitled to compensatory payments. The hardship clause disappeared from the new law altogether.[221]

Divorce based upon fault has been retained because of the conviction that it still 'meets the needs of the majority of French people'.[222] The general definition of fault remained the same, while the last specific fault ground, the condemnation for certain crimes, has disappeared.[223] The invocation of fault as a ground for divorce no longer has any influence on the distribution of the financial burden of divorce.[224] It is hoped that due

---

[214]   FULCHIRON, H., 'The New French Divorce Law' (2005), p. 245.
[215]   FERRÉ-ANDRÉ, S., 'A Pause in the Reform of French Family Law' (2004), p. 185.
[216]   The new Art. 233 *Code Civil.*
[217]   The new Art. 233 (2) *Code Civil.*
[218]   MAHE, C., 'De Franse wetgever op weg naar afschaffing van "schuldscheiding"' (2002), p. 21-22
[219]   FULCHIRON, H., 'The New French Divorce Law' (2005), p. 246.
[220]   Ibid.
[221]   BÉNABENT, A., *La réforme du divorce article par article* (2004), p. 47.
[222]   FERRÉ-ANDRÉ, S., 'A Pause in the Reform of French Family Law' (2004), p. 184. Irène Théry affirmed that while the opponents of fault-based divorce claimed that it had been 'condemned by the history'; one cannot do away with the reality that the majority of French still opt for this form. *Le Figaro*, 29 December 19997, cited in: BASTARD, B., 'Administrative Divorce in France: A Controversy Over a Reform that Never Reached the Statute Book' (2000), p. 79.
[223]   BÉNABENT, A., *La réforme du divorce article par article* (2004), p. 49.
[224]   FULCHIRON, H., 'The New French Divorce Law' (2005), p. 247.

to the fact that it has become considerably more easy to obtain divorce upon the other grounds, fault-based divorce will be confined to 'situations of grave conflict or of violence which must be stopped'.[225] However, it is possible to predict that in the absence of immediate divorce on demand, the fault ground will remain attractive for a spouse who wants to end a marriage against the will of the other spouse, but does not wish to wait for two years.

Many commentators note that the 2004 divorce reform rested upon a broad consensus in both Chambers of the Parliament and within the academic community.[226] The new law was praised for its well-balanced and pacifying character.[227] The Minister of Justice described the reform as 'organised around three large axes: a law based on pluralism and respect of choice, a law of divorce more simple and more caring for the future, and a protective divorce law founded in responsibility'.[228] At the same time, it has been also observed that in contrast with the proposals launched in 2001, the general tone of the 2004 law was rather conservative.[229] On the whole, the 2004 divorce reform has been characterised as 'a matter of modernisation, not revolution'.[230] In general, the basis of the 2004 reform was again a compromise. The proponents of no-fault divorce had to accept that their attempt to abolish fault divorce had been lost.[231] Still, the French compromise of 2004 is of a rather different nature than the English one of 1996. In England and Wales the compromise of 1996 amounted to an attempt to reconcile irreconcilable ends, which led to an inconsistent and unworkable law. In France, the compromise between the progressive and conservative camps was achieved by creating different possibilities alongside each other in order to make both camps content. The English 1996 Family Law Act de-facto made divorce more lengthy and complicated than it was before. In contrast, the French 2004 law brought about a further liberalisation of divorce. Consensual divorce in France became more permissive than under German and English (both current and repealed) law, as the new French law provides for a quick and simple divorce by consent, regardless of whether there is agreement upon ancillary matters. The French divorce without consent is now

---

[225] FERRÉ-ANDRÉ, S., 'A Pause in the Reform of French Family Law' (2004), p. 186.
[226] DADOMO, C., 'The Current Reform of French Law of Divorce' (2004), p. 223.
[227] Ibid.
[228] (translation mine). 'La réforme qui vous est présentée s'ordonne autour de trois grands axes: un droit du divorce pluraliste et respectueux des choix, un droit du divorce plus simple et soucieux de l'avenir, un droit du divorce protecteur, fondé sur la responsabilité'. Presentation by the Minister of Justice Dominique Perben in the Sénat on 2 January 2004,
    http://www.senat.fr/seances/s200401/s20040107/s20040107001.html#int26
[229] BÉNABENT, A., La réforme du divorce article par article (2004), p. 8.
[230] FERRÉ-ANDRÉ, S., 'A Pause in the Reform of French Family Law' (2004), p. 184.
[231] Regrets to this point have been, among others, expressed by Christian Damodo ('The Current Reform of French Law of Divorce' (2004), p. 225) and by Alain Bénabent. BÉNABENT, A., La réforme du divorce article par article (2004), p. 37.

comparable with the German one, and significantly more liberal than that provided by the current English law.

14.3.3. GERMANY: A PRAGMATIC COMPROMISE

The German 1976 divorce reform had a better starting position than those in England and France, as the 1938 *Ehegesetz* already provided for divorce on the ground of the irretrievable breakdown of marriage. However, as divorce on this ground required three years of separation and was much more lengthy and difficult to obtain than on the ground of fault, Germany also wrestled with a severe problem of divorce by collusion. About 95% of divorce actions were brought on the ground of matrimonial offence, which enabled an immediate divorce by collusion, while only 5% of divorcing spouses chose to apply for divorce on the ground of the irretrievable breakdown of their marriage.[232] Such a wide gap between the law in the books and the law in action made a reform all but inevitable. There was a general consensus that the 'matrimonial offence principle ha[d] proved a failure [...] because it aggravated, rather than solved problems in many cases'.[233] The most important debates were around the same questions as in England: what is to constitute sufficient proof of the breakdown, and especially: should mutual consent be regarded as such proof? The position of the German legislature as to divorce by consent resembled that of the English one rather than that of the French one. As in England, divorce by consent became the focal point of controversy between the conservatives and the proponents of modernisation. All proposals to introduce an easily accessible divorce by consent in order to put an end to divorce by collusion were rejected. The conservatives claimed that legislative recognition of divorce by consent would 'reduce marriage to the level of [an] ordinary contractual obligation which can be disposed of freely'.[234] The habitual transpersonalistic argument, that divorce by consent 'ignores society's interest in stable marriage', was also employed.[235] As divorce by consent was rendered unacceptable, the two modes of proof of the breakdown of marriage that had also been discussed in England remained: the subjective mode, based on enquiry; and the objective mode, based on a stated period of separation. As in England, both secular and ecclesiastical circles agreed that the irretrievable breakdown of marriage should replace the fault grounds, but could not agree on how such breakdown should be proven. The Commission on Marriage Law established by the German Protestant churches came up with a proposal that was accepted by the Roman Catholic Study Group for Marriage

---

[232] GIESEN, D., 'The reform of Family Law in Germany' (1978), p. 120.
[233] Ibid, p. 353.
[234] Ibid, p. 359.
[235] Giesen's comment was that 'a marital union between two people doesn't exist for the sake of the institution'. Ibid.

Law. This proposal suggested a subjective mode of proof; divorce was to be granted if the court was convinced that the 'marital relationship has been destroyed so severely that no restoration [...] can be expected'.[236] Such mode of proof necessitated a full court inquiry. In 1970 the Congress of Representatives of the German Legal Profession (*Deutscher Juristentag*) rejected such inquiry and proposed an objective mode of proof: a fixed period of separation.[237]

As in England and France, the new German law was doomed to become a compromise.[238] Irretrievable breakdown became the sole ground for divorce. The general rule was that marriage could be dissolved if a court was convinced that the marriage had failed. That would of course have enabled the spouses to obtain consensual divorce without delay. However, due to a last minute concession to the Christian Democrats, who dominated the *Bundesrat*[239] and who considered unqualified divorce by mutual consent incompatible with the protection of marriage, the possibility of consensual divorce was restrained.[240] If the spouses have not been living apart for at least one year, marriage may only be dissolved under exceptional circumstances; the petitioner should attest that the continuation of marriage would lead to unreasonable hardship for him or her, resulting from causes that can be attributed to the other spouse.[241] If the spouses have been living apart for one year, mutual consent constitutes the irrefutable presumption of breakdown.[242] If the spouses have been living apart for three years, this constitutes the irrefutable presumption of breakdown, even in case of a unilateral application.[243] These two presumptions exemplify the legislature's choice for the objective mode of proof of breakdown; although, even if the breakdown of marriage is presumed, divorce is not granted automatically. The accessibility of divorce by consent is restricted by the requirement that the spouses should agree on all the consequences of their divorce.[244]

---

[236] *Eine Denkschrift der Familienrechtskommisson de Evangelischen Kirche in Deutschland* (1969), p. 17. Cited in: GIESEN, D., 'The reform of Family Law in Germany' (1978), p. 121.

[237] Ibid, p. 358.

[238] 'To the surprise of many people, the reform was finally achieved by a series of "ingenious" compromises in a vexed parliamentary situation. By these compromises, the legislature remarkably succeeded in avoiding clear and definite positions on many problems. It thus followed the time-honoured pattern of evading politically sensitive issues by adopting meaningless rules which serve to neutralize rival claims'. MÜLLER-FREIENFELS, W., 'The Marriage Law Reform of 1976 in the Federal Republic of Germany' (1979), p. 186.

[239] GLENDON, M.A., *The Transformation of Family Law* (1989), p, 179-180.

[240] Ibid.

[241] GOTTWALD, P., SCHWAB, D., BÜTTNER, E., *Family and Succession Law in Germany* (2001), p. 58.

[242] Para. 1566 I BGB. See: MARTINY, D., 'Family Law' (2005), p. 259.

[243] Para. 1566 III BGB. See: MARTINY, D., 'Family Law' (2005), p. 259.

[244] Para 630 Code of Civil Procedure. See: MARTINY, D., *German Report concerning the CEFL Questionnaire on Grounds for Divorce and Maintenance Between Former Spouses* (2003), http://www.law.uu.nl/priv/cefl > working field 1 > Germany, p. 16.

State control over divorce is further upheld by maintaining a hardship clause. This clause enables the court to deny a divorce even if breakdown is proven. If maintaining the marriage is in the interests of minor children, the court can apply the hardship clause ex officio and in principle can even deny a divorce by mutual consent.[245] In case of an unilateral application for divorce, the respondent spouse can try to bar divorce by proving that divorce would lead to exceptional hardship for him or her.[246] Initially, the Law of 1976 provided that no hardship clause could be invoked if the spouses have been living apart for five years.[247] This enabled Müller-Freienfels to suggest that this provision expressed 'the premise that the right to marriage and to divorce are fundamental and basic rights, indirectly constitutionally guaranteed by the Constitution'.[248] However, in 1980 the Federal Constitutional Court (*Bundesverfassungsgericht*) declared that the five-year cut-off contradicted the constitutional provision for special legal protection of marriage, and was therefore unconstitutional.[249] According to Mary Ann Glendon, this judicial intervention shifted the balance between State intervention and autonomy in such way that it became no longer possible to view divorce under German law as a right of an individual.[250]

14.4. FROM INDISSOLUBILITY TO DIVORCE: SPAIN, PORTUGAL, ITALY AND IRELAND

Alongside the introduction of no-fault divorce in the countries with a more or less long standing divorce tradition, no-fault divorce was adopted by some of the countries which previously had no divorce at all. In Portugal, Spain and Italy, divorce was introduced upon mixed fault and no-fault grounds. Ireland instantly embraced the principle of irretrievable breakdown. Malta remains the only European country that does not provide for divorce at all.

---

[245] GOTTWALD, P., SCHWAB, D., BÜTTNER, E., *Family and Succession Law in Germany* (2001), p. 59.
[246] Ibid, p. 59.
[247] GLENDON, M.A., *Abortion and Divorce in Western Law* (1987), p. 74.
[248] MÜLLER-FREIENFELS, W., 'The Marriage Law Reform of 1976 in the Federal Republic of Germany' (1979), p. 188.
[249] BVerfG 21 October 1980, *NJW* (1981), p. 108-109.
[250] GLENDON, M.A., *Abortion and Divorce in Western Law* (1987), p. 74.

14.4.1.   PORTUGAL AND SPAIN: REINTRODUCTION OF DIVORCE AFTER THE FALL OF DICTATORSHIP

Portugal

In Spain and Portugal, the re-introduction of divorce was clearly connected with the liberation from dictatorial regimes.[251] In Portugal, divorce was reintroduced for the Catholic part of the population in 1975,[252] the year the Carnation Revolution put an end to Salazar's rule. At first, the provisions of Salazar's 1966 Civil Code that allowed divorce for fault to non-Catholics were extended to the whole of the population.[253] In the following year no-fault divorce including divorce by mutual consent was introduced.[254] In 1995, Portugal became one of the few European countries allowing administrative divorce.[255]

Spain

In Spain, the changes following the end of Franco's regime after his death in 1975 were less sweeping than those brought about by the Carnation Revolution in Portugal. The reintroduction of divorce remained controversial in and outside[256] the Parliament.[257] The Socialists, the Communists, and a group of independent members of Parliament were the main proponents of divorce;[258] the governing UCD party was split upon the issue.[259] Other than in 1931, it was decided not to mention divorce in the Constitution.[260] Divorce was not reintroduced until 1981.[261] The divorce law of 1981 was considerably more restrictive than the law of 1932 had been.[262] It did not provide for an immediate divorce by mutual consent.[263] Direct divorce without a previous period of separation was possible only in one case: when the respondent spouse was

---

[251]   On the abolition on divorce during the dictatorial rule see Part III, Chapter 11, Section 11.3.1. In Spain, the process of democratisation symbolically started with the reform of family law. LANGNER, D., *Eheschließung und Ehescheidung nach spanischem Recht* (1984), p. 1.

[252]   SOTTOMAYOR, M., 'The Introduction and Impact of Joint Custody in Portugal' (1999), p. 249.

[253]   Ibid.

[254]   Decrees No. 261 of 27 May 1975 and No. 56 of 13 May 1976. SOTTOMAYOR, M., 'The Introduction and Impact of Joint Custody in Portugal' (1999), p. 249-250.

[255]   Decree No. 131 of 6 June 1995. DE OLIVEIRA, G., *CEFL National Report for Portugal: Grounds for Divorce* (2003), p. 48.

[256]   Some meetings of the pro-divorce lobbies were even bombed. PHILLIPS, R., *Putting Asunder* (1988), p. 578.

[257]   LANGNER, D., *Eheschließung und Ehescheidung nach spanischem Recht* (1984), p. 22-23.

[258]   Ibid, p. 23.

[259]   Ibid, p. 24.

[260]   Ibid, p. 22-23.

[261]   Act No. 30 of 7 July 1981.

[262]   See Part III, Chapter 11, Section 11.3.1.

[263]   LANGNER, D., *Eheschließung und Ehescheidung nach spanischem Recht* (1984), p. 102.

convicted for an attempt to kill the applicant spouse of his or her ascendants or descendants.[264] In all other cases, divorce could be granted only after one year of judicial separation[265] or two years of de-facto separation if both spouses agreed upon divorce; and only after five years of de-facto separation in the case of unilateral application.[266] As judicial separation was possible upon both fault[267] and no-fault[268] grounds, the Spanish divorce law of 1981 could be characterised as mixed-fault/no-fault based.

In 2005 the Socialist Government of Rodríguez Zapatero carried out a divorce reform[269] as uncompromising as the Swedish reform of 1973. Together with Sweden and Finland, Spain became one of the few European countries that openly admits divorce on demand. Thus, Spain repositioned itself from the back ranks to the vanguard of European divorce law.

14.4.2. ITALY: DIVORCE LAW AS A SYMBOL OF LIBERTY AND PROGRESS

In almost no other country has the political connotation of the divorce issue been as apparent as in Italy. Divorce there became 'a national issue of prime importance'.[270] The whole nation was split into *dovorzisti* and *anti-divorzisti*.[271] It has been noted that 'the political debate during parliamentary and extraparliamentary discussions of the legislative proposals for divorce [...] unconsciously assumed the character of an irrational but radical confrontation between progressives and conservatives'.[272] All the

---

[264] Art. 86 (5) Spanish *Civil Code*. MARTÍN-CASALS, M., *Spanish Report concerning the CEFL Questionnaire on Grounds for Divorce and Maintenance Between Former Spouses* (2003), http://www.law.uu.nl/priv/cefl > working field 1 > Spain, p. 7.

[265] The one-year term started from the moment of filing a petition for separation. Ibid, p. 8.

[266] Art. 86 Spanish *Civil Code*. Ibid, p. 7-9.

[267] The fault grounds for separation, among others, were:'desertion, marital infidelity, 'abusive or offensive conduct or 'any other serious or reiterated infringement of conjugal obligations'. Art. 82 Spanish Civil Code. MARTÍN-CASALS, M., *Spanish Report concerning the CEFL Questionnaire on Grounds for Divorce and Maintenance Between Former Spouses* (2003), http://www.law.uu.nl/priv/cefl > working field 1 > Spain, p. 2.

[268] Including the mutual consent of the spouses (Art. 81(1) Spanish *Civil Code*. MARTÍN-CASALS, M., *Spanish Report concerning the CEFL Questionnaire on Grounds for Divorce and Maintenance Between Former Spouses* (2003), http://www.law.uu.nl/priv/cefl > working field 1 > Spain, p. 2.

[269] By Law 15/2005 of 8 July 2005. On the new Spanish divorce law see: GARCÍA CANTERO, G., 'Family Law Reform in Differing Directions' (2006), p. 433-436.

[270] RHEINSTEIN, M., *Marriage Stability, Divorce, and the Law* (1972), p. 189.

[271] Ibid.

[272] POCAR, V., RONFANI, P., 'Family Law in Italy: Legislative Innovations and Social Change' (1978), p. 612.

---

parties to the left of the Christian Democrats supported divorce, so the Communists[273] found themselves in an unusual alliance with the Liberal party.[274] The Christian Democrats, together with the Extreme Right, opposed divorce.[275] It has been witnessed that at a certain point the divorce debate in Italy 'lost its original legal character and acquired a political or moral tone, with strong emotional and irrational implications'.[276] The arguments in this debate were 'liberty' and 'progress' put against the 'defence of sacred family values'.[277] Divorce reform was not feasible as long as the Christian Democrats, who unconditionally adhered to the principle of indissolubility, were ruling Italy, as they had ever since the Second World War.[278] However, the situation changed in 1962 when their traditional dominance was broken and a coalition Government that included the Socialists was formed.[279] Remarkably enough, on the eve of the divorce reform there was not only not enough popular support for divorce, but what support there was, was diminishing.[280] In 1968 the divorce Bill was brought to Parliament by two MPs, a socialist and a liberal.[281] In spite of the fact that a majority of Italians still opposed divorce, the Chamber of Deputies decided 'to lead rather than follow public opinion'[282] and approved the Divorce Bill in November 1969. The Bill successfully passed the Senate, was signed by the President and the new law came into force in December 1970.[283]

However, it turned out that the enactment of the divorce law was the beginning rather than the end of the political confrontation on this issue.[284] The constitutionality of divorce (its compatibility with the Concordat) was repeatedly, but unsuccessfully challenged before the Constitutional Court. The opponents of divorce launched a

---

[273] The communists supported divorce quite reluctantly as the commotion surrounding divorce threatened the durable co-operation with the Christian Democrats which they were eager to establish. See: ABSE, T., 'Italy: A New Agenda' (1994), p. 201-203.

[274] SGRITTA, G., TUFARI, P., 'Italy' (1977), p. 261.

[275] Ibid.

[276] POCAR, V., RONFANI, P., 'Family Law in Italy: Legislative Innovations and Social Change' (1978), p. 612.

[277] Ibid.

[278] The Christian Democrat party embraced the traditional concept of the family to the bitter end, taking positions even more inflexible than those maintained by the leaders of the ecclesiastical hierarchy, not to mention those of some minority Catholic movements. Ibid, p. 612.

[279] RHEINSTEIN, M., Marriage Stability, Divorce, and the Law (1972), p. 189.

[280] Roderick Phillips noticed that there was not a public opinion swing in favour of divorce that made divorce possible. On the contrary, when the divorce Bill was introduced, the surveys of public opinion showed that in 1955 56% of the population opposed divorce, but in 1959 this amount had increased to 61% and in 1962 to 69%. PHILLIPS, R., Putting Asunder (1988), p. 573.

[281] POCAR, V., RONFANI, P., 'Family Law in Italy: Legislative Innovations and Social Change' (1978), p. 618.

[282] PHILLIPS, R., Putting Asunder (1988), p. 573.

[283] Law No. 898, of 1 December 1970, came into force on 18 December 1970.

[284] LIBRANDO, V., 'The Reform of Family Law in Italy' (1978), p. 170.

campaign for a referendum on the abrogation of the law on divorce. Considering the initial lack of popular support for divorce, they counted on a certain victory. However, in the four years between the introduction of divorce and the referendum, which was finally held on 12 May 1974,[285] the opposition to divorce had considerably diminished.[286] The reasons for this were manifold. First of all, the immediate negative effects of divorce on the family and society predicted by the *anti-divorzisti* had failed to become manifest.[287] Secondly, the divorce debate had eventually shifted from moral to more pragmatic aspects of divorce.[288] Thirdly, as the divorce debate acquired more and more the status of a political confrontation between the left and the right, the unanimity of the Catholic front against divorce gradually waned.[289] As a result, public opinion shifted in favour of the divorce law at the very last moment and the *anti-divorzisti* quite unexpectedly lost the Referendum.[290] A survey of public opinion conducted in 1975 showed that the introduction of divorce in Italy had caused no trauma to the population in either urban or agricultural areas.[291]

The dual system of marriage celebration, introduced in Italy by the 1929 Concordat, resulted in some peculiarities for Italian divorce law. In the case of civil marriage, divorce dissolved the matrimonial bond; in case of religious marriage it only terminated the civil effects of marriage.[292] Although the new law provided for both fault and no-fault divorce, it was strongly dominated by fault.[293] Divorce without a previous judicial separation was possible only in rather exceptional cases; conviction of one of the spouses for a serious crime, non-consummation of marriage, or dissolution of marriage abroad by a foreign spouse. The normal way of obtaining divorce was a two-step procedure of first obtaining a judicial separation[294] and then converting it into divorce.[295] A judicial separation could be obtained at that time either

---

[285] POCAR, V., RONFANI, P., 'Family Law in Italy: Legislative Innovations and Social Change' (1978), p. 612.

[286] SGRITTA, G., TUFARI, P., 'Italy' (1977), p. 261-262.

[287] Ibid, p. 262.

[288] POCAR, V., RONFANI, P., 'Family Law in Italy: Legislative Innovations and Social Change' (1978), p. 612.

[289] Ibid.

[290] Only 41% voted for the abrogation of divorce law, in favour of maintaining divorce voted 59%. SGRITTA, G., TUFARI, P., 'Italy' (1977), p. 260-261.

[291] POCAR, V., RONFANI, P., 'Family Law in Italy: Legislative Innovations and Social Change' (1978), p. 621.

[292] LIBRANDO, V., 'The Reform of Family Law in Italy' (1978), p. 167.

[293] Roderick Phillips noticed that 'the principle of fault lay at the core of the 1970 legislation'. PHILLIPS, R., *Putting Asunder* (1988), p. 574.

[294] It was a judicial separation that the Italian law required. De-facto separation, started at least two years before the new law came into force, sufficed for divorce only during the transitional period. SGRITTA, G., TUFARI, P., 'Italy' (1977), p. 259.

[295] Ibid, p. 259.

upon one of the fault grounds provided by law,[296] or on the ground of mutual consent.[297] A liberal feature of the Italian divorce law was that a spouse solely responsible for the separation was allowed to petition for divorce.[298] Its restrictive nature was most apparent in the long period that was required before a separation could be converted into divorce. Even if both spouses agreed to convert the separation into divorce, this could take place only after five years of separation. If only the 'innocent' spouse asked for conversion, this term was extended up to six years. And if only the 'guilty' spouse wished to divorce, he or she had to wait for seven years.[299] The importance of fault significantly decreased in 1975, when all fault grounds for judicial separation were abolished[300] and the sole ground for separation became the facts leading to the conclusion that the 'continuation of cohabitation [is] intolerable or [will] prejudice severely the upbringing of the children'.[301] In 1987, divorce law was slightly liberalised by the introduction of divorce by joint application and the reduction of the period of separation required in a consensual divorce from five to three years.[302] However, even after that, Italian divorce law remained rather restrictive by European standards. Divorce still normally required a two-stage process and a long period of separation before the separation could be converted into divorce.[303] As in England, Germany and France, Italy's divorce law was doomed to be a compromise, designed to accommodate national legal and social traditions, political realities, and contemporary trends in European matrimonial law.[304] However, the step from indissolubility of marriage to a rather restrictive divorce was much more significant than the steps made at that time in any of the afore-described countries. The gap between the proponents and opponents of divorce that had to be bridged was wider than anywhere else. It can come as no surprise that the resulting compromise was more restrictive than elsewhere.

Many unsuccessful proposals to reform Italian divorce law have been made in recent years.[305] The most notable of them was made in 1997-1998, when a multi-party committee prepared a reform Bill that provided for the incorporation of divorce law into the Civil Code and introduced the possibility for divorce after three years of de-

---

[296] The grounds for separation for fault were provided by the 1942 Civil Code: adultery (simple by a wife, and constituting a grave injury, by a husband), wilful desertion, cruelty (Art. 151); convictions for certain crimes and some other matrimonial offences listed in the Art. 152-153.

[297] LIBRANDO, V., 'The Reform of Family Law in Italy' (1978), p. 171.

[298] Ibid, p. 172-173.

[299] SGRITTA, G., TUFARI, P., 'Italy' (1977), p. 259.

[300] Ibid.

[301] Art. 151 of Italian Civil Code. POCAR, V., RONFANI, P., 'Family Law in Italy: Legislative Innovations and Social Change' (1978), p. 634.

[302] PATTI, S., CEFL National Report for Italy: Grounds for Divorce (2003), p. 44.

[303] PHILLIPS, R., Putting Asunder (1988), p. 576.

[304] Ibid, p. 573-574.

[305] For an overview, see: PATTI, S., CEFL National Report for Italy: Grounds for Divorce (2003), p. 61.

facto separation instead of the currently required three years of judicial separation.[306] However, the passage of this Bill was obstructed by the Catholic-oriented parties that appeared on the Italian political stage after the break-up of the Christian Democratic Party.[307]

14.4.3. IRELAND: SHIFTING PARADIGMS OF NATIONAL IDENTITY

Introducing divorce was an even more challenging step for Ireland than for other Catholic countries such as Italy, Portugal and Spain. In the latter countries, the indissolubility of marriage was just one of the vested postulates of the Catholic religion. In Spain and Portugal, the introduction of divorce was associated with the short-lived republics of the first part of the twentieth century, and the abolition of divorce with the victory of the fascist regimes.[308] In Italy, the divorce discord became part of the general progressive-conservative political confrontation of the post-war period. In contrast, in Ireland the legal ban on divorce was of comparatively recent origin. It was introduced as late as 1937, some fifteen years after Ireland obtained independence from the British Empire.[309] As was explained above,[310] the peculiarities of Irish history made the indissolubility of marriage to be perceived as part of the national identity rather than some old, medieval, theological dogma.[311] It is no exaggeration to say that in Ireland the introduction of divorce involved not only a change of the constitution, but also a change of the national self-image. For that reason, the Irish reform provides a good illustration of both the flexibility and stiffness of culture and identity paradigms.[312]

In the period between the gaining of independence and the emergence of the divorce question in the 1980s, the life and self-consciousness of the Irish people underwent significant modification. Ireland experienced a late industrialisation and urbanisation

---

[306] LENTI, L., 'Recent Changes in the Judge-Made Law of Separation and Divorce and Perspectives on Law Reform' (2002), p. 218-219.

[307] Ibid, p. 218.

[308] See: Sections 11.2.1. and 11.3.1. of Part III..

[309] See Part III, Chapter 11, Section 11.3.1.

[310] See Part III, Chapter 11, Section 11.3.1.

[311] See DILLON, M., *Debating Divorce. Moral Conflict in Ireland* (1993), p. 14-15 and 21-24; JAMES, C., 'Cead Mile Failte. Ireland Welcomes Divorce: The 1995 Irish Divorce Referendum and the Family (Divorce) Act of 1996' (1997), Lexis.

[312] An analysis of this process is greatly facilitated by the insightful in-depth study of the socio-esthetical discourse that preceded the first Irish divorce referendum by Michele Dillon in his book *Debating Divorce. Moral Conflict in Ireland* (1993).

in the 1960s-70s,[313] and acceded to the EC in 1993.[314] The Irish became a more secular,[315] 'better educated and more well-travelled population'.[316] The practical incentives for the introduction of divorce spoke for themselves; 75,000 of the 3,5 million total population[317] were 'trapped in broken marriages',[318] and 22,9% of all Irish children were born out of wedlock.[319]

After careful preparation,[320] in April 1986 the Fine Gael/Labour coalition government announced their intent to hold a referendum on the withdrawal of the constitutional ban on divorce.[321] The pro-divorce camp consisted of the Labour party, most of the Fine Gael politicians, including the leader of the divorce campaign, Prime Minister FitzGerald, as well as an independent Divorce Action Group.[322] The anti-divorce camp was headed by the Anti-Divorce Campaign: an independent ad hoc group of lay Catholics.[323] The conservative party of De Valera, Fianna Fail,[324] then in opposition, officially adopted a neutral position. However, most of its individual members took a clear anti-divorce position.[325] The Irish Catholic hierarchy, in line with the post-Vatican II, new attitude of the Catholic Church towards worldly affairs, also officially chose for neutrality.[326] By doing so, the hierarchy recognised that 'civil legislation and Catholic teaching could be independent of each other',[327] and that Catholic 'morality and civil law do not necessarily coincide'.[328] Moreover, in a joint statement with regard to the first divorce referendum, the hierarchy acknowledged the right of Catholics 'to vote in good conscience in favour of divorce'.[329] Individual

---

[313]   Ibid, p. 25-26.
[314]   Ibid, p. 26.
[315]   For instance, in 1972 the constitutional provisions establishing the special position of the Catholic Church were removed. PRICE, C., 'Finding Fault with Irish Divorce Law' (1997), Lexis.
[316]   Ibid.
[317]   According to the data of the Central Statistics Office of Ireland for 1991.
[318]   FETTE, S., 'Learning From Our Mistakes: The Aftermath of the American Divorce Revolution as a Lesson to the Republic of Ireland' (1997) Lexis.
[319]   According to the data of the Central Statistics Office Ireland for 1985.
[320]   In 1983 the Joint Oireachtas Committee on Marriage Breakdown was established. The Committee received more than 700 submissions of different interest groups. Based thereon it presented a summary of the arguments for and against divorce. SHATTER, A., *Family Law in the Republic of Ireland* (1986), p. 244.
[321]   Ibid, p. 247.
[322]   DILLON, M., *Debating Divorce. Moral Conflict in Ireland* (1993), p. 31.
[323]   Ibid.
[324]   See Part III, Chapter 11, Section 11.3.1.
[325]   DILLON, M., *Debating Divorce. Moral Conflict in Ireland* (1993), p. 31-32.
[326]   Ibid.
[327]   Ibid, p. 92.
[328]   Ibid, p. 95.
[329]   Ibid, p. 97.

bishops, however, deviated from this official standpoint and raised their voice against divorce in the framework of their pastoral guidance.[330]

The arguments that were used for and against divorce had also notable peculiarities. Michele Dillon noticed that due to the absence of 'an established and well accepted discourse of individual rights' in Irish society,[331] advocating for divorce in terms of individual civil rights remained on the very margins of the divorce debate.[332] Thus, Prime-Minister FitzGerald, while introducing the Government's intent to hold a divorce referendum, laid the emphasis on communitarian rather than individualistic arguments for divorce, stressing that 'divorce would serve the balance of the social good'.[333] The promoters of divorce highlighted that not divorce, but marriage breakdown jeopardises the family and society and causes detriment to children.[334] They argued that the availability of divorce neither caused nor increased the incidence of marital breakdown, but rather allowed the victims of the breakdown the possibility to institutionalise their new relationships.[335] They stressed that the impossibility of remarriage victimised the children of subsequent relationships. As the parents could not legalise their new relationships, their children were bound to bear all the disadvantages of illegitimacy.[336] On the other side of the debate, the opponents of divorce, including the clergy, also relied on social rather than theological arguments against divorce.[337] Their argumentation[338] could be roughly summarised as follows: every Catholic should adhere to the theological doctrine of the indissolubility of marriage; however, the divorce debate is about civil law and not about religious law, therefore the position of the non-Catholic minority should also be considered, and thus the theological arguments alone do not suffice for the rejection of divorce. Nonetheless, the social costs of divorce are such that one does not need theological arguments to vote against it. These social costs lie in the fact that divorce undermines the institution of marriage and therefore the whole of the society,[339] causing suffering

---

[330]   Ibid.
[331]   Ibid, p.15.
[332]   Ibid, p. 62-64.
[333]   FitzGerald's press conference, "Today Tonight," April 32 1986. Cited in: DILLON, M., *Debating Divorce. Moral Conflict in Ireland* (1993), p. 33.
[334]   SHATTER, A., *Family Law in the Republic of Ireland* (1986), p. 245.
[335]   Ibid.
[336]   Ibid, p. 246.
[337]   PRICE, C., 'Finding Fault with Irish Divorce Law' (1997), Lexis.
[338]   Excellently analysed by Michele Dillon in his *Debating Divorce. Moral Conflict in Ireland* (1993), p. 31-69.
[339]   SHATTER, A., *Family Law in the Republic of Ireland* (1986), p. 244-245.

to women and children,[340] and laying additional burdens on the social welfare system and the taxpayer.[341]

During the first referendum held in 1986, the Anti-Divorce Campaign proved to be the most effective. Although right after the announcement of the referendum a national opinion poll had indicated that sixty-one percent of the voters supported the introduction of divorce, this support dropped as the referendum approached.[342] At the referendum, the constitutional amendment was rejected by a majority of nearly two to one.[343]

Six years later, in 1992, the Government started to prepare a second referendum on the removal of the constitutional ban on divorce. In its White Paper,[344] the Government proposed several drafts of the constitutional amendment, involving five different options. One of these was to give the *Oireachtas*[345] a power to legislate on divorce,[346] similar to the legislative power enjoyed by the parliaments of other European countries. The four other options involved embedding the regulation of divorce into the constitution itself,[347] thus making any subsequent legislation on divorce the matter of constitutional amendments.

The second referendum was held in 1995. The preceding campaign brought to mind many aspects of the divorce campaign of the 1980s. However, there were also some important differences. Firstly, all the main political parties, including Fianna Fail, now officially supported the removal of the constitutional ban.[348] Secondly, the influence of the Irish Catholic Church was at that time gravely undermined by a series of 'unseemly' sex scandals.[349] Another difference was that Europe's secularisation and openness had made notable progress in Ireland during the period between the two

---

[340] ibid, p. 245.
[341] MARSHALL, L., 'What God Has United Man Will Now Divide: Divorce Referendum Changes Law of 60 Years' (1997), Lexis.
[342] FETTE, S., 'Learning From Our Mistakes: The Aftermath of the American Divorce Revolution as a Lesson to the Republic of Ireland' (1997), Lexis.
[343] 935,843 votes were given against the amendment and 538,279 in favour of it. SHATTER, A., *Family Law in the Republic of Ireland* (1986), p. 250.
[344] *Marital Breakdown: A Review and Proposed Changes*, p.1 9104, Statutory Office, Dublin.
[345] The Irish Parliament.
[346] BURLEY, J., REGAN, F., 'Divorce in Ireland: The Fear, the Floodgates and the Reality' (2002), p. 206.
[347] Ibid.
[348] JAMES, C., 'Cead Mile Failte. Ireland Welcomes Divorce: The 1995 Irish Divorce Referendum and the Family (Divorce) Act of 1996' (1997), Lexis.
[349] Ibid.

referenda.[350] The voting population was younger and more urban.[351] The loss of the unique Catholic identity was still a prominent argument in the anti-divorce campaign;[352] however, by this time there was already a powerful competing self-image of a new, modern, Europe-conscious Irish identity. One of the prototypes of this new identity was the then-President, Mary Robinson, a woman who successfully combined her professional career as a lawyer, professor and politician with the role of a wife and mother – and on top of that she was Catholic, but married to a Protestant.[353]

On the 24 November 1995 the proponents of divorce won the second referendum by a close majority of 0.6%.[354] The road to divorce was opened. However, the divorce law introduced in 1996[355] is still the most restrictive in Europe. In contrast to other European countries the grounds for divorce are listed directly in the Constitution, which means that any subsequent modernisation of divorce will require another referendum.[356] Although the new law provides for no-fault divorce on the ground of the irretrievable breakdown of marriage, the conditions that have to be met in order to actually obtain a divorce make the dissolution of a marriage extremely difficult. The new Article 41.3.2 states that the court can grant a divorce only when the three following preconditions are simultaneously met: (1) the spouses have lived apart for a period of at least four years during the previous five years; (2) there is no prospect for their reconciliation; and (3) the court is satisfied with the provisions made for the spouse, children or any other dependent member of family.[357] Therefore, Irish law combines the usual objective criterion for marital breakdown (a long period of separation) with the subjective criterion that the court has to be convinced that there is no prospect for reconciliation. This makes obtaining a divorce in Ireland twice as difficult as in the countries with either a subjective or an objective criterion. On the one hand, the Irish law demands a long period of separation, no matter the circumstances of the case. On the other hand, even after this period has expired the court can still deny a divorce petition if the court is not convinced that reconciliation is

---

[350] It was suggested that the removal of the constitutional ban on divorce was a signal that Irish people now viewed themselves as a part of the European Community. MARSHALL, L., 'What God Has United Man Will Now Divide: Divorce Referendum Changes Law of 60 Years' (1997), lexis.

[351] JAMES, C., 'Cead Mile Failte. Ireland Welcomes Divorce: The 1995 Irish Divorce Referendum and the Family (Divorce) Act of 1996' (1997), Lexis.

[352] BURLEY, J., REGAN, F., 'Divorce in Ireland: the Fear, the Floodgates and the Reality' (2002), p. 208.

[353] JAMES, C., 'Cead Mile Failte. Ireland Welcomes Divorce: The 1995 Irish Divorce Referendum and the Family (Divorce) Act of 1996' (1997), Lexis.

[354] This time 50.3% voted in favour of removing the constitutional ban, and 49.7% against it. PRICE, C., 'Finding Fault with Irish Divorce Law' (1997), Lexis.

[355] The *Divorce Act* was passed on 27 November 1996 and came into force on 27 February 1997.

[356] BURLEY, J., REGAN, F., 'Divorce in Ireland: The Fear, the Floodgates and the Reality' (2002), p. 218.

[357] SHANNON, J., *CEFL National Report for Republic of Ireland: Grounds for Divorce* (2003), p. 84-86.

impossible.[358] In this way, the divorce petition can be dismissed even against the explicit wish of both spouses to end their marriage.[359]

The introduction of divorce legislation in Ireland was a matter of great significance, involving shifting paradigms of Irish national identity. It is suggested that the divorce discourse represented, in the first place, the culmination of a campaign to modernise Irish legislation and, in the second place, a watershed in the creation of a more pluralistic Irish society.[360] The introduction of divorce is seen as an important indication that Ireland has moved from a traditional, homogeneous, agrarian society to a heterogeneous, modern, urbanised society.[361] However, the tiny majority of votes in favour of divorce reveals that Irish society remained deeply divided upon the issue.[362] It is claimed to be more accurate to say that the majority of the Irish became tolerant enough to allow divorce to those who wish to have it, rather than that Ireland was really welcoming divorce.[363]

14.5. THE BREAKTHROUGH OF CONVERGENCE OR THE CONTINUANCE OF DIVERSITY?

14.5.1. WHAT'S IN A NAME? BEYOND THE FAULT – NO-FAULT DICHOTOMY

The advance of no-fault divorce throughout Western Europe has evoked the idea that Europe was moving towards a spontaneous harmonisation of family law. The momentum of the no-fault movement was so great that many reputable scholars saw it as a token of a spontaneous convergence of divorce law in Europe. It was even optimistically spoken of as 'entering into the period which is marked by a kind of *ius commune*'.[364] At a certain point it indeed looked this way: in 1960 fault-based divorce existed in thirteen Western European countries, divorce upon the irretrievable

---

[358]   EVERITT, N., 'Some Remarks on the Recent Developments of Divorce Law in the Republic of Ireland and England' (2001), p. 204.

[359]   WALLS, M., BERGIN, D., *The Law of Divorce in Ireland* (1997), p. 14.

[360]   MARTIN, F., 'From Prohibition to Approval: the Limitation of the 'No Clean Break' Divorce Regime in the Republic of Ireland' (2002), p. 224.

[361]   Ibid.

[362]   This time 50.3% voted in favour of removing the constitutional ban, and 49.7% against it. PRICE, C., 'Finding Fault with Irish Divorce Law' (1997), Lexis.

[363]   FETTE, S., 'Learning From Our Mistakes: The Aftermath of the American Divorce Revolution as a Lesson to the Republic of Ireland' (1997), Lexis.

[364]   NEUMAYER, K., 'General Introduction' (1978), p. 1. In a similar sense see also: PINTENS, W., VANWINCKELEN, C., *Casebook. European Family Law* (2001), p. 16 and PHILLIPS, R., *Putting asunder* (1988), p. 570.

breakdown of marriage in seven, and mutual consent divorce in six,[365] while four countries allowed no divorce at all. 'Twenty years later fault grounds had been retained in eight jurisdictions, and no-fault divorce had extended to twelve, as had mutual consent divorce'.[366] However, as the turn of millennium approached, the no-fault movement gradually lost some of its momentum. Attempts to get rid of the fault grounds failed in England and Wales in 1996, in France in 2005, and the current attempt in Belgium is probably about to fail as well.[367] Two Eastern-European countries, Latvia[368] and Lithuania,[369] have recently re-introduced fault grounds into their divorce law. This retroactive movement is consonant with the situation in regard to the so-called 'covenant marriages' in the US.[370]

The introduction of no-fault divorce on the ground of irretrievable breakdown of marriage was such a change compared to the fault-based divorce-sanction that it is understandable that many analysed the development of European divorce law mainly along the lines of the fault/no-fault dichotomy. However, with the passage of time it became clear that the situation is much more complicated. As long as many countries allowed divorce *exclusively* on the ground of fault, this analysis had its merits; in this situation the 'innocent' spouse had no other option than an infringing, accusational procedure while the 'guilty' spouse had no option at all except to purchase or coerce the cooperation of the 'innocent' party. Since nowadays not a single European country retains fault-based divorce as the sole ground,[371] the situation has utterly changed. The invocation of fault is now only one of the options among many, often providing the fastest route to a divorce. Thus, although the retention of fault grounds still has its

---

[365] PHILLIPS, R., *Putting Asunder* (1988), p. 570.

[366] Ibid.

[367] In Belgium the discussion surrounding divorce reform is still in process. The most recent Bill (Chamber 2005/2006, 2341/001), presented to the Parliament on 15 March 2006, suggests a system somewhat resembling that applied in England and Wales. The irretrievable breakdown of marriage is proclaimed to be the sole ground for divorce. This breakdown can be established upon the proof of specific 'circumstances'. Culpable behaviour is maintained among such circumstances (Art. 229 para. 3 CC).

[368] Introduced in 1993 by the restored Latvian Civil Code of 1937 (Art. 71-72 and 74).

[369] Introduced by Art. 3.60 of the 2000 Civil Code of Lithuania (in force since 1 July 2001). See also KASERAUSKAS, Š., 'Moving in the Same Direction'? Presentation of Family Law Reforms in Lithuania (2004), p. 330-331.

[370] Three American states, Louisiana (in 1991), Arizona (in 1999) and Arkansas (in 2001), have retreated from no-fault divorce by adopting legislation allowing a couple at the time of marriage to sign a 'covenant marriage' agreement, stating that they voluntary restrict the grounds for a possible future divorce to fault grounds. For the evaluation of this trend see: MAXWELL, N., 'Unification and Harmonisation of Family Law Principles: The United States Experience' (2003), p. 263-264. For an opposite opinion see: WARDLE, L., 'Divorce Reform at the Turn of the Millennium: Certainties and Possibilities' (1999), p. 783-800.

[371] MARTINY, D., 'Divorce and Maintenance Between Former Spouses – Initial Results of the Commission on European Family Law' (2003), p. 534.

(often symbolic) meaning, it no longer says a great deal about the permissiveness of the divorce law of a particular country, and the abolition of such grounds does not automatically mean that divorce becomes any easier. The unsuccessful attempt to remove fault grounds in England and Wales provides a good example. The current law offers spouses the possibility to obtain a fault-based divorce within four to six months,[372] whereas the repealed provisions of the Family Law Act of 1996 made it impossible to obtain a divorce decree earlier than after a one-year period of 'reflection', which was to be extended by six months, even for consenting spouses if they had children. In addition, although the Act removed the need to prove a reason for the breakdown of the marriage, the repealed system insisted that the couple should settle ancillary matters beforehand, 'which may be much harder than proving adultery, behaviour or separation'.[373]

The recent survey of current divorce law in Europe provided by the CEFL National Reports,[374] reveals a phenomenon that, paraphrasing Zweigert and Kötz,[375] could be called 'functional disequivalence'. It is easy to see that, confusingly enough, under one and the same designation of 'irretrievable breakdown'[376] virtually every type of divorce can be hidden, from fault-based (for instance England and Wales, Scotland, Greece and partly also Poland and Bulgaria) to divorce by consent (for example The Netherlands, Russia). If we look beyond these labels, we can roughly distinguish five more or less pure functional types of divorce grounds: (1) fault-based grounds, (2) irretrievable breakdown in the narrow sense of this term, (3) divorce on the ground of separation[377] for a stated period of time, (4) divorce by consent, and (5) divorce on demand.

In theory, **fault-based divorce** presupposes a court enquiry into a matrimonial offence, but the strictness of this inquiry has been watered down over time. For instance, in England and Wales the so-called 'special procedure' under which undefended divorces

---

[372] *Fourth Annual Report of Advisory Board in Family Law*, 2000/2001, para. 3.5. Cited in: CRETNEY, S., MASSON, J., BAILEY-HARRIS, R., *Principles of Family Law* (2002), p. 299, note 95.

[373] HALE, B., 'The Family Law Act 1996 – the death of marriage?' (1997), p. 9.

[374] The integral national reports are published on the CEFL website: http://www.law.uu.nl/priv/cefl > working field 1. An integrated vision is published in: BOELE-WOELKI, K., BRAAT, B., SUMNER, I. (eds.) *Grounds for Divorce* (2003).

[375] Zweigert and Kötz use the concept of 'functional equivalence'. ZWEIGERT, K., KÖTZ, H., *An Introduction to Comparative Law* (1998), p. 34 ff. See also: Section 1.3.1. of Part I.

[376] On the analysis of the grounds for the breakdown of marriage, as it is apparent from the *CEFL National Reports*, see: MARTINY, D., 'Divorce and Maintenance Between Former Spouses – Initial Results of the Commission on European Family Law' (2003), p. 537-540.

[377] The term 'separation' is used to denote the variable concepts of cessation of marital life as used in different jurisdictions.

are granted without any court hearing[378] more resembles an administrative divorce than the old-fashioned divorce trials. That, combined with the possibility of obtaining a divorce immediately, sometimes makes fault-based divorce attractive even for consenting spouses.

Divorce based upon **irretrievable breakdown** in the narrow sense is granted upon a subjective criterion alone: if the court is convinced that the marriage cannot be saved (for example Bulgaria, The Netherlands, Poland, Hungary), or upon a subjective as well as an objective criterion, such as a certain period of separation (for instance four years in Ireland, three years in Austria). In the jurisdictions that prescribe the subjective criterion alone, the court inquiry is nearly a dead letter in non-contested cases; however, in contested cases it may be quite intrusive, especially in countries like Bulgaria and Poland where allocation of the fault is required.[379] In the jurisdictions that combine subjective (convincing the court or other competent authority) and objective (period of separation) criteria, proving the breakdown is twice as difficult, as even after the stated period of separation has expired, the court can refuse a divorce if it is not convinced that the marriage has irretrievably broken down.

The jurisdictions where divorce is to be granted after the simple expiry of the stated **period of separation** often call this an irrefutable presumption of the irretrievable breakdown of a marriage, but sometimes consider it a separate ground (Norway). In both cases, however, a divorce is granted automatically and without further inquiry. The accessibility of divorce basically depends on the length of the separation period. These periods vary quite significantly (for instance six years in Austria, five years in England and Wales, four years in Switzerland and Greece, three years in Italy and Portugal, three years in Germany, two years in France and Belgium, and one year in Denmark, Norway and Iceland). As these periods are rather lengthy in most jurisdictions, this form of divorce is less attractive if a shorter route is available to the spouses.

In some jurisdictions **divorce by consent** is covered under the designation of irretrievable breakdown, and constitutes an irrefutable presumption thereof (for example Austria, the Czech Republic, Germany, The Netherlands, England and Wales, Russia, Scotland). In other countries consent is presented as a separate ground (for instance Belgium, Bulgaria, France, Greece, Portugal). In both cases, the court with competent authority grants divorce automatically and without inquiry into the reasons

---

[378]   CRETNEY, S., 'Divorce Reform in England: Humbug and Hypocrisy or a Smooth Transition?' (1996), note 19, at p. 56.

[379]   TODOROVA, V., 'National Report for Bulgaria' (2003), p. 406-408; MACZYNSKI, A., SOKOLOWSLI, T., 'National Report for Poland' (2003), p. 194.

for the divorce if the spouses have agreed thereon. However, most of the states still consider divorce by consent to be a dangerous diminishment of State control over divorce. The multiple restrictions of the right of divorce by consent often make it a less attractive and speedy form of divorce. Only Dutch and Russian law de-facto allow for divorce on the ground of simple consent without any further restrictions. In some countries, the marriage must be of a certain duration (for instance three years in Bulgaria, two years in Belgium, one year in the Czech Republic and Greece). Other countries allow consensual divorce only after a certain period of separation (for example two years in England and Wales and in Scotland, one year in Germany and Spain; six months in Austria, Denmark, the Czech Republic and Iceland). In most countries (Austria, Belgium, Bulgaria, Greece, Germany, Hungary, Denmark, Portugal) an agreement to divorce alone is not sufficient and the spouses are required to reach an agreement on ancillary matters as well. This list of restrictions reveals that most of these countries are still reluctant to recognise the autonomous decisions of the spouses alone as a sufficient ground for divorce. The State, in one way or another, has to protect the spouses from their own 'ill-considered' decisions.[380]

Divorce on demand, when each of the spouses is simply considered to be entitled to divorce irrespective of the objections of the other spouse, is explicitly recognised in Sweden, Finland and Spain, and indirectly in Russia. This is, beyond a doubt, the easiest form of divorce; fully respecting the autonomous decisions of the spouses, or even one of them, and accepting that the State is not capable of keeping a marriage intact against the will of even one of the spouses. The only State intervention in this kind of divorce is a short waiting period of six months for contested divorces or divorces with minor children in Sweden, for all divorces in Finland, and a possibility of a three-month reconciliation period for contested divorces under Russian law.

Many countries have not just one, but multiple grounds for divorce. In these countries, consenting spouses have the possibility of a kind of 'ground shopping'. Empirical data seems to suggest that spouses, assisted by their lawyers, are always able to choose the shortest way to divorce, just as water will always find its way to the lowest point.[381]

This rough survey illustrates that the differences between the current divorce laws in Europe can no longer be accurately described in terms of a simple division into fault and no-fault grounds. If we look at it not from the point of view of the fault/no-fault division, but rather from the point of view of the ease with which divorce can be

---

[380]   MARTINY, D., 'Divorce and Maintenance Between Former Spouses – Initial Results of the Commission on European Family Law' (2003), p. 536. Dieter Martiny also notes that 'consent seems to be a dangerous kind of marriage dissolution'. Ibid.

[381]   For instance, in England and Wales 68.6% are granted upon fault grounds. (LOWE, N., 'National Report for England and Wales' (2003), p. 103), as this proves to be the shortest route to a divorce.

obtained in terms of time, costs, extent of inquiry and obstacles, we can see that there is still much difference among divorce laws. One can compare, for instance, the Irish law, where the spouses must wait for four years for a divorce (and even then the judge is entitled to refuse it if he is not convinced that the breakdown of marriage is irretrievable or that the financial provisions for the spouse and any dependent members of the family are sufficient), and the Swedish immediate divorce on demand. It is quite observable that the distance between these two no-fault laws is still immense, and the difference is not just on the level of positive law, but also on the ideological level.[382] Thus, the common core of divorce law in Europe is, at present, rather scarce. Even if the fault grounds were to completely disappear from the European scenery in foreseeable future, which, considering that attempts to eliminate fault have recently failed in England, France and probably also in Belgium, might take some time, this event alone would not significantly increase the common core.

14.5.2. THE HARMONISING IMPACT OF INTERNATIONAL HUMAN RIGHTS INSTRUMENTS

The harmonising impact of international human law instruments on the law of divorce in Europe is much more limited than one would perhaps expect. Neither of these instruments protects the right to dissolve a broken marriage, as an individual human right.[383] The explanation lies in the political sensitivity of divorce matters. The only attempt to defend the right to divorce before the European Court of Human Rights, the twenty-years old case *Johnston and others v. Ireland*,[384] is very illustrative for this. In the *Johnston* case, Mr. Johnston, an Irishman, who many years previously had obtained a judicial separation from his first wife, and his second partner, challenged the Irish law that did not permit full divorce and remarriage. In this case the court refused to use a dynamic interpretation of Article 12, and instead referred to the *travaux préparatoires* of the Convention, in order to argue that the omission of the right to dissolve marriage was deliberate.[385] Further, the ECHR did not elaborate on the existence of a European 'common ground' regarding divorce. This is remarkable considering that at that moment only two Member States, the defendant Ireland and

---

[382] As Mary Ann Glendon has rightly mentioned, a legal system that requires a spouse to wait for several years for divorce [...] is obviously promoting a different marriage ideology than is fostered in a country where divorce is available on one party's demand in year or less'. GLENDON, M-A., *The Transformation of Family Law* (1989), p. 192.

[383] VAN GRUNDERBEECK, D., *Beginselen van personen- en familierecht. Een mensenrechtelijke benadering* (2003), p. 261 ff.

[384] *Johnston v. Ireland*. ECHR (1986).

[385] Ibid, para. 52–53.

Malta, had not introduced full divorce; thus, the 'great majority' of the States did share a consensus upon this matter. Instead, the Court stated without any reference that, 'having regard to the diversity of the practices followed and the situations obtaining in the Contracting States, the notion's requirements will vary considerably from case to case. Accordingly, this is an area in which the Contracting Parties enjoy a wide margin of appreciation in determining the steps to be taken to ensure compliance with the Convention'.[386] Finally, in spite of the persuasive plea by Judge De Meyer,[387] the Court refused to recognise the right to dissolve marriage as a right protected under the ECHR.

One could wonder how the same Court that has forbidden differing treatment of illegitimate children in the *Marckx* case[388] could come to such a decision in the Irish divorce case. The explanation seems to be that on 26 June 1986, some four days before the final deliberation in the *Johnston* case, the overwhelming majority of the Irish electorate had just rejected divorce in the first referendum. The absence of divorce in Ireland had therefore acquired the highest political legitimation.[389] There was little chance that the Irish government would simply acquiesce in an opposite decision on the part of the Court. Therefore it is quite plausible that 'the Court carefully backed down in the *Johnston* case in order to preserve its own authority'.[390] Considering the persistent conservative-progressive discourse in Europe in respect of family law, it seems convincing that the Court considered 'striking down laws that make some children "legitimate" and others "illegitimate" politically safer than intruding upon the divorce law in Ireland'.[391] The Court was probably quite right in not trying to deliver a decision that would clearly be politically unacceptable to the country concerned. However, the end result is that the Conventional level of protection on this particular subject was established at a very low common denominator indeed. As no such case was again brought before the Court, the *Johnston* case has never been overruled.

---

[386]   Ibid, para. 55.

[387]   Ibid, dissenting opinion of the Judge De Meyer, p. 35-40. For a detailed discussion of the *Marckx* case see: Section 16.2.

[388]   See: Section 16.2.

[389]   Paul Mahoney has stressed that 'the Court (and the Commission) should be careful not to allow that machinery to be used so as to enable disappointed opponents of some policy to obtain a victory in Strasbourg that they have been unable to obtain in the elective and democratic forum in their own country'. MAHONEY, P., 'Marvellous Richness of Diversity or Invidious Cultural Relativism?'(1998), p. 3.

[390]   JOHNSON, N., 'Recent Developments: the Breadth of Family Law Review Under the European Convention on Human Rights' (1995), p. 513.

[391]   Ibid.

What is less understandable than the unfortunate history of the *Johnston* case, is that the right to dissolve one's marriage is not incorporated in the EU Charter and the not-ratified EU Constitution. This is quite remarkable if one considers the overall European situation with regard to divorce at the beginning of the third millennium. One cannot know whether this was a deliberate omission or just an oversight. However, one practical implication of this omission has already become apparent. If divorce would have acquired the status of an individual human right in the EU Charter, Malta most probably would have been forced to introduce divorce as a precondition to its accedence to the EU.[392] Thus, for the time being the right to dissolve a marriage is protected neither under the ECHR nor under the EU law.

14.5.3. CONVERGENCE OF DIVORCE LAW?

It is perhaps confusing that the period of divorce law development which commenced after the 1960s has been dubbed by some reputable scholars as a period of undeniable of convergence,[393] while other eminent academics[394] do not see any convergence at all in this period. This can be partially explained by the fact that some scholars tend to give too much weight to the advance of no-fault divorce.[395] As was shown in this chapter, in spite of the optimistic expectations from the no-fault reforms, the difference between the divorce laws of the European countries in terms of costs, time and intervention into the private lives of the spouses is still very considerable. In reality, behind the labels 'fault' or 'no-fault' divorce, far-reaching dissimilarities are hidden.

Stephan Cretney was right in suggesting that:

'In any event the greatly diminished influence of religion and other ideological factors does not mean the divorce law has ceased to be acutely controversial. I believe the contrary to be true: what has happened is rather that the *emphasis* has changed. True, the *ground* for divorce no longer has the prominence it once had, but in its place there is concern with the *whole divorce process*: with how the legal system treats all the incidents and consequences of the breakdown.'[396]

---

[392] Since respect for Human Rights is a pre-condition to acceding to the EU, the recognition of the right to divorce as a human right protected under EU law would have put pressure on Malta to amend its legislation.
[393] See, for instance, NEUMAYER, K., 'General Introduction' (1978), p. 1; PINTENS, W., VANWINCKELEN, C., *Casebook. European Family Law* (2001), p. 16; PHILLIPS, R., *Putting asunder* (1988), p. 570.
[394] For example: BRADLEY, D., 'A Family Law For Europe? Sovereignty, Political Economy and Legitimating' (2003), p. 72-79.
[395] See, for instance, SCHWENZER, I., 'Methodological Aspects of Harmonisation of Family Law' (2003), p. 150.
[396] CRETNEY, S., 'Breaking the Shackles of Culture and Religion in the Field of Divorce' (2005), p. 8.

Another possible explanation for the difference in the appreciation of the period after the 1960s is that during this period there was an undeniable pan-European tendency towards the development of divorce law in the same direction, from more restrictive to more permissive divorce law. A closer look reveals that as in the periods before, the choices that were at stake, the ideological connotations, and the political colour of the principle players of the divorce debates were very similar everywhere. This overall development towards modernisation can be easily erroneously perceived as evidence of the convergence of divorce laws in Europe. At the same time, due to the difference in the balance of power between progressive and conservative forces, different countries responded to the pan-European challenges in dissimilar ways.[397] Thus, after the 1960's there was still significant divergence in both the pace and the profundity of the modernisation of family laws from one European country to another. This difference is seen by the opponents of convergence as evidence that divorce laws do not converge.

Thus, in order to answer the question of whether divorce laws in Europe converged after the 1960s, one needs to establish more similarity between present-day divorce laws as compared to the divorce laws on the eve of the period. Let's revisit the figures already referred to with regard to the advance of no-fault divorce. In 1960, four European countries did not admit any divorce at all: Ireland, Spain, Italy and Malta. Fault-based divorce existed in the vast majority of thirteen Western European countries.[398] Fault was the only ground for divorce in England and Wales, Scotland, France, The Netherlands etc. Divorce based upon the irretrievable breakdown of marriage existed in seven Western European countries that were, for the most part, the Scandinavian and the Eastern European countries. Divorce by mutual consent was allowed in six countries, including Belgium and West Germany.[399] Everywhere in Europe, except, perhaps the Scandinavian region, divorce was rare and quite difficult to obtain. Today the picture is rather different. Malta, the only European country that does not provide for a full divorce, could perhaps be seen as a mere relic. Fault grounds are still present in a considerable minority of the divorce laws, but no European country maintains fault as the sole ground for divorce. The liberalisation of divorce throughout the analysed period is therefore manifest. There is, however, no evidence that the differences between the divorce laws in the beginning of the period were greater than at the end thereof. The current map of divorce laws in Europe shows that these laws encompass all generations: fault-based divorce, divorce due to irretrievable breakdown, divorce by consent and divorce on demand. Fifty years ago, the most

---

[397]   BRADLEY, D., 'A Family Law For Europe? Sovereignty, Political Economy and Legitimation' (2003), p. 81.

[398]   PHILLIPS, R., *Putting Asunder* (1988), p. 570.

[399]   Ibid.

conservative countries did not allow divorce at all, while the most progressive countries provided for divorce by mutual consent or irretrievable breakdown, albeit surrounded by restrictions. Today, the most conservative country, Malta, has still failed to introduce divorce. Even if Malta is left to one side, there is a major difference between, for instance, the Irish law, on the one hand, and the Swedish immediate divorce on demand, on the other hand. This difference exists not just on the level of positive law, but also on a deep ideological level.[400]

Thus the common core of divorce law in Europe is at the current stage probably only slightly broader[401] than it was fifty years ago. The explanation is that although the tendency towards modernisation of divorce influences every European country, the pace of proceeding from stage to stage within the progressive development of divorce law is different.[402] This difference in pace seems to be a permanent factor. It is clear that the process of modernisation and liberalisation of divorce law resembles the process of the modernisation of marriage law. The historical sketch above shows that as the countries in the rearguard make a step towards modernisation (for instance introducing no-fault divorce), the vanguard countries make a further step forward (like introducing divorce on demand) so that the gap between them persists. Thus, as with marriage law, the developments go on and differences remain. When Phillips systematised divorce law in 1986, he felt that the newly introduced extremely permissive Swedish divorce law did not fit within his scheme. What he then perceived as breaking 'with the trend toward divorce law uniformity in Western Europe',[403] was in fact the beginning of a new generation of divorce laws: divorce on demand.

14.5.4. THE HARMONIZING POTENTIAL OF THE CEFL PRINCIPLES ON DIVORCE

An examination of the convergence of divorce law in Europe cannot be complete without at least a brief discussion of the harmonising potential of the contemporary

---

[400]   As Mary Ann Glendon has rightly mentioned, a legal system that requires a spouse to wait for several years for a divorce […] is obviously promoting a different ideology of marriage than that fostered in a country where divorce is available on one party's demand in a year or less'. GLENDON, M-A., *The Transformation of Family Law* (1989), p. 192.

[401]   Bradley has rightly predicted such an outcome. BRADLEY, D., 'A Family Law For Europe? Sovereignty, Political Economy and Legitimation' (2003), p. 97.

[402]   In the 1980s, Phillips had noticed: 'Needless to say, these pressures and reforms were far from uniform throughout Western society. They went further in Scandinavia, especially Denmark and Sweden, […] but countries such as Spain and the Republic of Ireland lagged behind the trends elsewhere'. PHILLIPS, R., *Putting Asunder* (1988), p. 561. This statement is no longer valid with regard to Spain.

[403]   PHILLIPS, R., *Putting Asunder* (1988), p. 571.

harmonisation activities undertaken by the *Commission on European Family* (CEFL).[404] The CEFL *Principles of European Family Law Regarding Divorce* were published in 2004.[405] These *Principles* were elaborated by an independent group of scholars, informally representing 22 jurisdictions of Western and Eastern Europe. The *Principles* are intended as non-binding models, which could facilitate and promote the voluntary bottom-up harmonisation of divorce law in Europe. This is to say, that the *Principles* could serve as a source of inspiration for national legislatures, contemplating a divorce law reform.[406]

The method of comparative-research based drafting, adopted by CEFL, is the same as that practiced by most other groups engaged in the harmonisation of European private law.[407] The first step is to draw up a comprehensive questionnaire. Such questionnaire, drafted from a comparative perspective, aims to cover all the variations within the European jurisdictions. Then the members of the CEFL deliver national reports in which the questions of the questionnaire are answered.[408] On the basis of these reports, the draft *Principles*, along with a comparative overview and the comments, are elaborated by the CEFL Organising Committee. Following a thorough discussion(s) of the draft *Principles* by the whole of the CEFL, the final draft is made by the Organising Committee.[409]

The CEFL *Principles* on divorce consist of no more than eighteen provisions. This illustrates that the *Principles* are not aimed at providing detailed regulation for every aspect of divorce law. The *Principles* are rather focused on only two important matters of divorce law: the grounds for divorce and the connection between divorce as such and the resolution of ancillary matters.

While drafting the *Principles* on the basis of the comparative materials delivered in the national reports, two methods are generally used: the so-called 'better law' and 'common core' methods.[410] While using the 'common core' method the drafters make use of a rule which is common for all or most of the relevant jurisdictions. One half

---

[404]   For more about the CEFL see: Sections 1.1. and 2.1.1. of Part I.
[405]   BOELE-WOELKI, K. et al, *Principles of European Family Law Regarding Divorce and Maintenance Between Former Spouses* (2004).
[406]   BOELE-WOELKI, K., 'Comparative Research-based Drafting of Principles of European Family Law' (2002), p. 182.
[407]   See Part I, Chapter 2, Section 2.2.1.
[408]   See note 374 in this Chapter.
[409]   See BOELE-WOELKI, K., 'The Working Method of the Commission on European Family Law' (2005), p. 15-41.
[410]   For more on these methods see: ANTOKOLSKAIA, M., 'The "Better Law" Approach and the Harmonisation of Family Law' (2003), 159-183.

of the *Principles* (nine out of eighteen) are drafted in this way.[411] The 'common core' is defined rather broadly: as a solution shared by 'a significant majority of legal systems'.[412] Therefore even the nine *Principles* drafted upon the 'common core' method are not fully representative of the level of spontaneous harmonisation of divorce law already achieved in Europe. If the common core would be described more narrowly, as a solution shared by *all* of the covered jurisdictions, only two *Principles* would qualify for it. These *Principles*, based on generally shared common core, are *Principle* 1:1 (1), laying down the admissibility as such of divorce,[413] and *Principle* 1:2 (1), stating that divorce requires a legal (administrative or judicial) process. With regard to the grounds for divorce and the connection between divorce as such and the adjudication of ancillary matters, no common core, equally shared by the entire 22 jurisdictions, could be found.

Even the application of the common core as broadly defined by the CEFL, has revealed its limits as a method of drafting of the *Principles*. These limits are two-fold. In a first kind of case, a common core does exist, but this common denominator lies below the drafters' requirement as to the quality and the modernity of the rules they wish to make. This is the case with respect to four *Principles*.[414] In a second kind of case, no common core can be extracted because the diversity of national laws is too great. This is the case with regard to another four *Principles*.[415] The solution for the drafters in both cases is to move towards the 'better law' method, and either to select the 'better' rule among the diverging rules existing in the national jurisdictions, or to formulate a new rule themselves.[416]

The 'Better law' method was used to draft the other half of the 18 *Principles*. The 'Better law' method is much more demanding than the 'common core' method. The choices represented in the various national solutions reflect different political compromises, reached on the national level[417] in the context of the pan-European conservative-progressive discord. By preferring one of those solutions above the other, the drafters unavoidably take sides in this political debate and implicitly express value judgements.

---

[411] See table 1 at p. 33-34 in BOELE-WOELKI, K., 'The Working Method of the Commission on European Family Law' (2005), p. 31.

[412] BOELE-WOELKI, K., 'The Working Method of the Commission on European Family Law' (2005), p. 31.

[413] Malta, the only European country not allowing divorce, is not covered by the CEFL Principles.

[414] See table 1 at p. 33-34, 'The Working Method of the Commission on European Family Law' (2005), p. 31.

[415] Ibid.

[416] See ANTOKOLSKAIA, M., 'The "Better Law" Approach and the Harmonisation of Family Law' (2003), p. 162.

[417] This has been put forward by David Bradley. BRADLEY, D., 'A Family Law For Europe? Sovereignty, Political Economy and Legitimation' (2003), p. 81.

As the harmonising influence of the *Principles* solely depends on its persuasive authority, such judgments obviously need extensive justification.

Several fundamental choices are made by the CEFL with regard to the grounds for divorce. In the first place, the *Principles* go beyond the irretrievable breakdown of marriage. Thereby they reflect the far-reaching watering down of the concept of irretrievable breakdown of marriage, described above. Two separate grounds are chosen by the CEFL on consensual and unilateral divorce. Mutual consent is explicitly made the ground for the divorce of spouses who both wish to dissolve their marriage.[418] This choice is based on the functional common core that can be found among the European jurisdictions. Although, consent is a formal ground for divorce in the minority of European countries,[419] the great majority of jurisdictions de-facto provide for divorce upon mutual consent under various headings. The CEFL, however, chooses for a very liberal 'minority' model of divorce by mutual consent. According to the *Principles* 1:4 – 1:7, no period of separation and no agreement on ancillary matters[420] is required for such divorce. Divorce can be granted immediately, without any period of reflection, if no minor children are involved and the spouses reach an agreement on the ancillary matters.[421] In allowing immediate divorce, the Commission drew on the Swedish solution, which is so far not followed by any other European country.

With non-consensual divorce, the CEFL has chosen for a one-year factual separation as the divorce ground.[422] The stated advantage of this solution is that it provides for a simple objective test, without any inquiry in matrimonial fault or breakdown of the marriage.[423] However, this 'better law' solution may be objected to, both by the countries with more restrictive legislation, requiring a longer period of separation, as well as by the countries with more permissive law, where the spouses do not have to wait for one year.

To complete the picture of permissive divorce rules incorporated in the CEFL *Principles*, it should be mentioned that the CEFL has chosen for a limited connection between divorce as such and the adjudication of ancillary matters. In both cases of

---

[418]   *Principle* 1:4.

[419]   See the comment to *Principle* 1:4. BOELE-WOELKI, K. et al, *Principles of European Family Law Regarding Divorce and Maintenance Between Former Spouses* (2004), p. 30.

[420]   Yet such agreement is strongly encouraged because immediate divorce, without a period of reflection, is made conditional upon its conclusion. Principle 1:5 (1) and (2).

[421]   *Principle* 1:5 (2).

[422]   *Principle* 1:8.

[423]   Comment to *Principle* 1:8. BOELE-WOELKI, K. et al, *Principles of European Family Law Regarding Divorce and Maintenance Between Former Spouses* (2004), p. 55.

consensual and non-consensual divorce, the authority competent to grant divorce is only obliged to decide upon the ancillary maters related to minor children.[424]

This brief analysis allows the conclusion that the CEFL *Principles* on divorce generally represent modern and permissive solutions. The content of the *Principles* clearly reveals the drafters' not always explicated choices within the conservative-progressive divide in Europe. It is still too early to predict what harmonising effect the *Principles* will have in Europe. The very instructive national reports and comparative surveys can undoubtedly save national legislatures contemplating divorce reforms a great deal of time and effort. Only the future can show whether the solutions elaborated by the CEFL will be able to inspire national lawmakers.[425]

---

[424] *Principles* 1:2 and 1:10.

[425] There is, however, already a first example of reference to the *Principles* in the discussion of the reform of national divorce law. The *Principles* were used by the Scottish legislature 'as a source for arguing for the amendment of the current law on divorce'. See BOELE-WOELKI, K., 'The principles of European family law: aims and prospects' (2005), p. 167.

CHAPTER 15
NON-MARITAL COHABITATION: FROM OUTLAW TO FUNCTIONAL ALTERNATIVE FOR MARRIAGE

15.1. THOSE WHO WILL NOT MARRY AND THOSE WHO CAN NOT MARRY: TWO DIFFERENT CATEGORIES UNDER THE SAME LABEL

15.1.1. SOCIAL AND IDEOLOGICAL CHANGE: SIMULTANEOUS EXISTENCE OF DIFFERENT HISTORICAL STAGES

From the 1960s on, Europe has witnessed a rapid and unprecedented rise of non-marital cohabitation. Cohabitation was always marginally present on the fringes of society as a marriage substitute for the poor,[1] those unable to obtain legal divorce, and, since the end of the nineteenth century, for avant-garde intellectuals with conscious objections to religious marriage. However, since it was outlawed from the High Middle Ages until the 1960s, cohabitation was, with a few qualifications, statistically and legally 'invisible'.[2] In contrast, as shown in Part II, concubinage was fairly well accepted in Europe before the High Middle Ages, both legally and socially.[3] Still, it is only with great caution that the concubinage of Roman and early medieval times can be compared with modern cohabitation outside marriage. Roman concubinage largely functioned as a surrogate marriage for unequals, who were often prohibited from marrying each other.[4] In early medieval society, concubinage was often just a form of having more than one wife at the same time.[5] Later, when the Church succeeded in banning simultaneous concubinage, it became a fairly acceptable premarital relationship between an upper class man and a woman of lower class. Roman and

---

[1] KIERNAN, K., 'The Rise of Cohabitation and Childbearing Outside Marriage in Western Europe (2001), p. 1.
[2] Ibid.
[3] For a brief synopsis of the history of concubinage in Europe see: BECKER, H-J., 'Die nichteheliche Lebensgemeinschaft (Konkubinat) in der Rechtsgeschichte' (1978), p. 13-38.
[4] See Part II, Chapter 3, Section 3.2.3.
[5] See Part II, Chapter 3, Section 3.3.3. and Chapter 4, Section 4.3.3.

medieval concubinage was no more than a second-rank union, with a modest legal effect for the concubine and little or no effect for her children. In contrast, the incidence, the social function, the societal acceptance, and the equal status of the offspring that characterise present-day cohabitation demonstrate that since its re-emergence in the 1960s, cohabitation has been transformed from the second-rate union of the distant past to a freely chosen and all but equal alternative to marriage. In addition, the popularity of extramarital cohabitation today is without precedent in European history. At the turn of the millennium, around 30% of all couples under 30 years old in Europe were cohabiting.[6] This expansion of non-marital cohabitation proceeded in stages. Drawing on the experience of Sweden, a renowned European forerunner in family reforms, Kathleen Kiernan has divided the recent developments of non-marital cohabitation into four stages.[7] During the first stage, cohabitation is no more than 'a deviant avant-garde phenomenon practiced by a small group' of progressive intellectuals.[8] In the second stage it becomes 'a prelude or a probationary period', after which the partners marry and have children.[9] In the third stage, cohabitation becomes socially 'acceptable as an alternative to marriage' and the birth of a child is no longer seen as a reason to marry.[10] During the fourth stage, cohabitation and marriage become 'indistinguishable' in respect to childrearing and social acceptance.[11] The growth of the popularity of cohabitation in Sweden is shown as follows: 1% in 1960, 7% in 1970, 13% in 1975, 21% of all couples in 1983,[12] and 70-73% of couples under 30 years old in 1997.[13] This illustrates the progression of cohabitation from one stage to another.

Although the expansion of cohabitation outside marriage is clearly a pan-European trend, its advance has been, and still is, quite uneven from one European region to another.[14] If one uses the classifications made by Kathleen Kiernan, it is easy to notice

---

[6]   The EU average for all age groups is 8%. Editorial Note, 'The European Picture of Cohabitation' (2001), p. 168. Cited in: TONER, H., *Partnership Rights, Free Movement, and EU Law* (2004) at p. 31.

[7]   KIERNAN, K., 'The Rise of Cohabitation and Childbearing Outside Marriage in Western Europe' (2001), p. 3.

[8]   Ibid. The rejection of marriage for ideological reasons and the choosing for an informal union (a so-called 'conscience marriage') appeared among Swedish progressive intellectuals since the late nineteenth century. MYRDAL, A., *Nation and Family. The Swedish Experiment in Democratic family and Population Policy* (1968), p. 40.

[9]   In Sweden in 1963 one third of all marriages were estimated to have involved a pregnant bride. POPENOE, D., *Disturbing the Nest. Family Change and Decline on Modern Societies* (1988), p. 170.

[10]   KIERNAN, K., 'The Rise of Cohabitation and Childbearing Outside Marriage in Western Europe' (2001), p. 3.

[11]   Ibid.

[12]   POPENOE, D., *Disturbing the Nest. Family Change and Decline on Modern Societies* (1988), p. 170.

[13]   Calculated on the basis of the date presented in KIERNAN, K., 'The State of European Unions: an Analysis of Partnership Formation and Dissolution' (2002), at p. 58.

[14]   For an overview of the popularity of cohabitation in various countries of Europe see: KREYENFELD, M., KONIETZKA, D., 'Rechtsstellung nichtehelicher Lebensgemeinschaften – Demographische Trends und gesellschaftliche Strukturen' (2005), p. 45-77, and especially the table on p. 69-73.

that European countries are spread among different stages.[15] The vanguard countries, like Sweden and Denmark, have already reached the fourth stage;[16] cohabitation is about to eclipse marriage there.[17] Countries like Finland and France are catching up with them. Germany, Great Britain, The Netherlands, Belgium, Austria and other countries with relatively high levels of cohabitation find themselves at the third stage. Southern European countries such as Greece, Italy, Spain and Portugal, as well as Ireland and Eastern Europe, where cohabitation is still a rather marginal phenomenon,[18] are spread amongst the first, second, and partly the third stage. As with divorce, where different generations of divorce law simultaneously exist in different European countries, 'the contemporanity of the non-contemporaneous' is also present in the area of cohabitation. Thus, the patterns of cohabitation characteristic to different stages co-exist simultaneously within the European countries.[19]

15.1.2. LEGAL RESPONSE TO SOCIAL CHANGE: A GREAT RANGE OF DIFFERENCE

In the beginning, legislation did not reflect the sweeping advance of cohabitation outside marriage; as it took time for the established policy of disregarding extramarital cohabitation to change. The traditional legal attitude towards cohabitation before the 1960s was, in fact, more prohibitive than disinterested. Depending on the time and place, the hostile legal policy[20] towards cohabitation varied from criminal sanctions[21]

---

[15]   KIERNAN, K., 'The Rise of Cohabitation and Childbearing Outside Marriage in Western Europe' (2001), p. 3.

[16]   Ibid.

[17]   KIERNAN, K., 'The State of European Unions: an Analysis of Partnership Formation and Dissolution' (2002), p. 75. The proportion of cohabiting couples in the age category under 30 years old is about 70-73% in Sweden and about 60% in Denmark, Finland and The Netherlands. Editorial Note, 'The European Picture of Cohabitation' (2001), p. 168. Cited in: TONER, H., *Partnership Rights, Free Movement, and EU Law* (2004) at p. 31.

[18]   KIERNAN, K., 'The State of European Unions: an Analysis of Partnership Formation and Dissolution' (2002), at p. 58. In the South European countries the proportion of cohabitating couples is estimated at about 1 to 2% of all couples. Editorial Note, 'The European Picture of Cohabitation' (2001), p. 168. Cited in: TONER, H., *Partnership Rights, Free Movement, and EU Law* (2004) at p. 31.

[19]   KIERNAN, K., 'The Rise of Cohabitation and Childbearing Outside Marriage in Western Europe' (2001), p. 3.

[20]   For a general overview, see: BECKER, H-J., 'Die nichteheliche Lebensgemeinschaft (Konkubinat) in der Rechtsgeschichte' (1978), p. 36-38.

[21]   Criminal sanctions against cohabitation, sometimes even accompanied with forced separation (e.g. the Bavarian Police Code), were formally in force in Italy until 1968, in Norway until 1972, and in some parts of Germany until 1970. BRADLEY, D., 'Regulation of Unmarried Cohabitation in West-European Jurisdictions – Determinants of Legal Policy' (2001), p. 22.

to a denial of the validity of gifts on behalf of cohabitees because they were considered to be contrary to the public morals.[22]

The legal acceptance of cohabitation proceeded in small steps. A first legal shift took place in the 1960s-70s; but although cohabitation was no longer penalised during this period, only few countries choose to support it with favourable legal policy. The clearest example was the Swedish Socialist Government, which in the late 1960s proclaimed a positive attitude[23] towards cohabitees. This became known as the 'neutrality' policy,[24] the principle that implies that the law should be 'neutral in relation to the different forms of living together and different moral views' and should 'not create unnecessary difficulties' for those who decide to create a family without marrying.[25]

However, even after the attitude towards cohabitation became more benevolent, the majority of European countries were reluctant to pass specific regulation with respect to non-marital cohabitation. Their reluctance was not a reflection of a conservative attitude alone, but was rather grounded in objections coming from different sides of the political spectrum. The blend of these arguments composed the doctrine of 'law-free space',[26] or non-regulation. One of the ideas behind this doctrine was the conservatives' fear that the legal regulation of cohabitation would weaken the institution of marriage.[27] Another reason for the reluctance to regulate cohabitation had to do with the liberals' concern for personal autonomy.[28] It was argued that if cohabitees voluntarily choose to avoid the legal regulation attributed to marriage,[29] the State should respect their choice and not try to impose another form of legal regulation on them.[30] Another ground for the non-regulation policy was the feminists'

---

[22] MEULDERS-KLEIN, M.-T., *La personne, la famille et le droit 1968-1998: trois décennies de mutations en occident* (1999), p. 23.

[23] AGELL, A., 'Family Forms and Legal Policies. A Comparative View form a Swedish Observer' (1999) p. 206.

[24] See SÖRGJERD, C., 'Neutrality: the Death or the Revival of the Traditional Family' (2005), p. 343-345.

[25] Committee Report (SOU 1972:41), p. 58. Cited in SÖRGJERD, C., 'Neutrality: the Death or the Revival of the Traditional Family' (2005), p. 342.

[26] '*Rechtfreie Raum*'.

[27] For a short account, see: FORDER, C., 'Civil Law Aspects of Emerging Forms of Registered Partnerships' (1999), p. 7. On the undesirability of creating 'two competing systems', see: AGELL, A., 'The Legal Status of Same-Sex Couples in Europe – A Critical Analysis' (2003), p. 131.

[28] For instance, Ruth Deech has argued that each of the basic ideas of individualism – the dignity of the individual, the autonomy, the privacy and the self-development – had its influence on the legislative non-intervention in the field of cohabitation. DEECH, R., 'The Case Against Legal Recognition of Cohabitation' (1980), p. 300.

[29] DEECH, R., 'The Case Against Legal Recognition of Cohabitation' (1980), p. 301.

[30] 'As the cohabitees have chosen *not* to marry, the conclusion in many countries appears to be that no *special* legislation should be introduced to regulate their mutual relationships'. AGELL, A., 'Family Forms and Legal Policies. A Comparative View form a Swedish Observer' (1999) p. 197-216. In the

fear that cohabitation regulation modelled on marriage would reinforce traditional gender-role divisions, resulting in women's dependency.[31] In addition, the multiplicity of different patterns of cohabitation[32] gave rise to the expectation that it would be impossible to design any general rules that are able to cover all those forms.[33]

However, at a certain stage the complete abstention of cohabitation regulation appeared to be unworkable. In several countries this first became apparent in the field of public law. The non-regulation of cohabitation had placed unmarried partners, one or both of whom were receiving social benefits or rent support, in a more privileged position than married couples. The latter were often supposed to support each other, while no such obligation existed for the former. This was not only hard to justify, but also directly encouraged cohabiting partners not to formalise their relationships. These inconsistencies had to be removed by equalising cohabitation with marriage in respect to social security and other fields of public law.[34] Once this step was made it appeared that the law was discriminating against cohabitees, as it treated them equal to spouses in cases when such equalisation accrued disadvantages for them,[35] yet not when it worked in their favour.[36] Therefore, further public law adjustments had to be enacted. With regard to private law, the controversy over the necessity for regulation remained much longer.[37] Yet, in particular the lack of legal protection for a weaker party, who was left empty-handed if cohabitation came to an end by death or separation, led to growing dissatisfaction.[38]

Eventually, the discussion surrounding the regulation of different-sex cohabitation came to be intertwined with same-sex couples' struggle for legal and social

---

same sense see: DEECH, R., 'The Case Against Legal Recognition of Cohabitation' (1980), p. 300-310. For an overview of the impact of the doctrine of the so-called law-free space (*Rechtfreie Raum*) in German legal writings, see: SCHRAMA, W., *De niet-huwelijkse samenleving in het Nederlandse en Duitse recht*, (2004), p. 394-395, and note 103. For an overview of the implication of this doctrine on Dutch case law, see: FORDER, C., *Het informele huwelijk: de verbondenheid tussen mens, goed en schuld* (2000), p. 30-36.

[31] O'DONOVAN, K., 'Legal Marriage –Who Needs It?' (1984), p. 118.

[32] MEULDERS-KLEIN, M.-T., 'Les concubinages: diversités et symboliques' (2002), p. 604-610.

[33] FORDER, C., 'Civil Law Aspects of Emerging Forms of Registered Partnerships' (1999), p. 7.

[34] GRAUE, E., 'Cohabitation Without Marriage as a Problem of Law and Legislative Policy in West Germany and other Codified Systems' (1980), p. 283.

[35] One of the earliest examples of such regulation is the amending of the Dutch social security law in 1965. As result of this amendment, cohabitation negatively affected basic social security payments received by the couple. WAALDIJK, K., 'Level of legal Consequences of Marriage, Cohabitation and Registered Partnership for Different-sex and Same-sex Partners: Comparative overview' (2005), p. 42.

[36] GRAUE, E., 'Cohabitation Without Marriage as a Problem of Law and Legislative Policy in West Germany and other Codified Systems' (1980), p. 284.

[37] FORDER, C., 'Civil Law Aspects of Emerging Forms of Registered Partnerships' (1999), p. 5.

[38] FORDER, C., 'European Models of Partnership Laws: The Field of Choice' (2000), p. 373.

recognition.[39] The problems of same-sex couples were from the outset rather different from those of different-sex cohabitees. The main problem of same-sex cohabitees was two-fold: they had no legal protection, and society did not recognise their relationships. Differing from opposite-sex cohabitees, the lack of legal protection for same-sex couples did not result from their own implicit or explicit choice not to marry, but from the legal impossibility to marry. In their struggle to resolve these problems, same-sex couples were confronted with a hostility that was incomparably stronger than that surrounding the recognition of heterosexual cohabitation. Their claim of recognition was considered 'unnatural' in some quarters of Western Europe as late as in 1995,[40] and this is often still true in Eastern Europe. Nonetheless, as a result of the time confluence, the discussion surrounding the regulation of 'non-marital cohabitation' came to embrace two rather different phenomena: the search for a legal solution for heterosexual cohabitees, who had more or less freely chosen not to marry, and the search for an optimal form of the institutionalisation of relationships between same-sex partners, who had no access to marriage.[41]

Albeit for different reasons, the legal regulation of both opposite- and same-sex cohabitation remained controversial for a long time. The accommodation of heterosexual cohabitation, partly by way of piecemeal adjustments of existing laws and partly by virtue of judicial activity, started in the 1970s. However, it has been rightly noticed that as late as the mid 1990s, 'the positive recognition of cohabitation within family law in Europe was, with exception of the Scandinavian countries, still minimal'.[42] Still, in the last decades of the twentieth century there was clearly a change of tide. The legal policy surrounding cohabitation generally evolved from ambivalent neutrality into the 'unequivocal acknowledgment, if not legitimating, of extra-marital relationships'.[43] This change entailed a dramatic shift 'from piecemeal legislation and judicial activity' to the enactment of specific legislation.[44] This specific legislation is, however, largely confined to the regulation of same-sex cohabitation alone. Opposite-sex couples only incidentally come into its orbit. Due to the influence of the 'non-regulation' doctrine, legislation in favour of non-institutionalised heterosexual cohabitation still represents a minority phenomenon in Europe.

---

[39]   SCHRAMA, W., *De niet-huwelijkse samenleving in het Nederlandse en Duitse recht,* (2004), p. 117.
[40]   Refered to in: BRADLEY, D., 'Regulation of Unmarried Cohabitation in West-European Jurisdictions – Determinants of Legal Policy' (2001), p. 40.
[41]   See also: FORDER, C., 'Civil Law Aspects of Emerging Forms of Registered Partnerships' (1999), p. 5-6.
[42]   WILLEKENS, H., 'Long Term Developments in Family Law in Western Europe: An Explanation'(1998), p. 59.
[43]   BRADLEY, D., 'Regulation of Unmarried Cohabitation in West-European Jurisdictions – Determinants of Legal Policy' (2001), p. 23.
[44]   PROBERT, R., BARLOW, A., 'Cohabitants and the law: recent European reforms' (2000), p. 76.

15.1.3. A WORKING SCHEME OF LEGAL MODELS FOR THE REGULATION OF NON-MARITAL COHABITATION

The large variety of legislative responses to extra-marital cohabitation has inspired several attempts to classify them.[45] Without prejudice to the academic value of other classifications, for the purposes of this study a classification scheme has been chosen based on a functional criterion – the 'level of legal consequences'[46] – recently introduced in a comparative study carried out by an international team headed by Kees Waaldijk.[47] On the basis of this criterion, the following legal models could be distinguished:

1. No regulation of cohabitation;
2. The piecemeal amendment of existing laws;
3. Specific legislation providing minimal protection to de-facto cohabitation;
4. Specific legislation providing limited protection to cohabitees that have concluded a cohabitation contract;
5. Specific legislation providing limited protection of cohabitation that falls somewhere between contract and status;
6. Registered partnership legislation providing a status almost equal to that of spouses (registered partnership 'Nordic style'); and
7. The opening up of marriage to same-sex couples.

It must be noticed that in many countries more than one of these models can be distinguished. The Netherlands is a strong example in this respect, as its legislation reflects at least four of these models: the piecemeal amendment of pre-existing legislation, giving very minimal protection to unregistered cohabitees; a significantly higher level of legal consequences for those who have signed a cohabitation contract; an all but equal to marriage status for registered partners; and fully equal marital status through the right to marry for both same- and opposite-sex couples. Other countries have chosen for fewer varieties. Swedish law, for example, reflects only two of these models; it provides a basic level of protection for non-institutionalised same- and opposite sex cohabitation, and a marriage-like protection by virtue of the institution of a registered partnership that is only open to same-sex couples.

---

[45] For an overview of a number of suggested classifications and his own version, see: Curry-Sumner, I., *All's Well that Ends Registered?* (2005), p. 307- 313.

[46] See: Waaldijk, K., 'Level of legal Consequences of Marriage, Cohabitation and Registered Partnership for Different-sex and Same-sex Partners: Comparative overview' (2005), p. 7.

[47] This comparative study of the legal consequences of marriage, institutionalised and non-institutionalised cohabitation in nine European countries resulted in the publication of a very interesting book: Waaldijk, K. (ed.) *More of Less Together: Level of legal Consequences of Marriage, Cohabitation and Registered Partnership for Different-sex and Same-sex Partners* (2005).

These legal models for the regulation of non-marital cohabitation[48] will be discussed below on the basis of a selection of representative examples.

15.2. MODEL 1: NO REGULATION OF COHABITATION

The legal policy toward cohabitation in some Eastern European countries is still at the stage Western European countries were at prior to 1960. One might be amazed to find Russia and most of the other countries of the former Soviet Union among this group, as these countries have an overall modern family law. The Russian reluctance to regulate cohabitation may appear even more surprising when one recalls that Russia, in the period between 1926 until 1944, pioneered the regulation of unmarried cohabitation by granting de-facto marriage a virtual equality to formal marriage.[49] However, at the basis of this absence of legal regulation lies a social reality that is rather different from that in most Western European countries. In this respect, the story of cohabitation in these countries is clearly another illustration of the potential of social engineering by legal means.

In 1944, when cohabitation lost its legal standing and unmarried couples were summoned to formalise their relationships,[50] informal spouses obediently marched to the registration offices to register as married couples. From then until perestroika, stable non-marital cohabitation all but disappeared in the Soviet Union. This was the result of practical reasons rather than a societal disapproval of cohabitation. A large proportion of the population still believed that love, not a marriage certificate, justified an affective union.[51] But those who considered cohabitation outside marriage would find themselves surrounded with grave practical problems. The law treated them as complete strangers to one another. In the totalitarian State, in which every step of its citizens was regulated, they were simply unable to obtain any accommodation together, or even share a room in a hotel or a student hostel. As marriage was the only route to privileges like these, even pre-marital cohabitation was basically ruled out. Disconnected from the West by the iron curtain, the Soviet Union did not experience the sexual revolution of the 1960s-70s. However, in the sixties after the death of Stalin, the Soviet regime became more lenient and pre-marital sexual relationships became

---

[48]   The opening up of marriage to same-sex couples was already discussed in Chapter 13, Section 13.3.2. (The Netherlands) and Section 13.4.3. (Belgium and Spain).

[49]   See Part III, Chapter 11, Section 11.2.1.

[50]   See Part III, Chapter 11, Section 11.3.1.

[51]   In the 1960s 91% of adults interviewed in Leningrad considered non-marital sex with someone they loved to be moral. KON, I., *Sexual'naia kul'tura v Rossii* (1997), 254. A public opinion survey of 1989 showed that only 22.5% considered unmarried cohabitation as always wrong, 33.5% found it admissible in certain cases and 33% considered it always admissible. Ibid, p. 266.

more common. For the reasons mentioned above, this did not lead to any notable increase of cohabitation. One should also take into consideration that, unlike their Western contemporaries, young people in the Soviet Union did not hold any resentment towards marriage. Russian youngsters did not see marriage as something traditional, old-fashioned or 'bourgeois', but rather associated it with romance and commitment. This may have had to do with the fact that marriage had already been secularised long ago, and the communist ideological clichés about 'socialist marriage' were no longer taken seriously. Also divorce was easy, cheap, and free of stigma. It is interesting to observe that the absence of a pre-marital 'trial' period of childless cohabitation, in combination with easy divorce, led to a diminishment of the stability of marriage. The dominant pattern of behaviour of Russian youngsters was to marry at an early age, as soon as they would have a serious affectionate relationship,[52] and to have a child almost immediately thereafter.[53] This resulted in one of the highest divorce rates in Europe.[54] With only slight exaggeration one could say that the Russian alternative for non-marital cohabitation was early and easy marriage combined with early and easy divorce.

As for same-sex cohabitation, it was virtually unthinkable before perestroika; a homosexual who would dare to come out at that time would either end up in prison[55] or a psychiatric clinic.[56] The example of the Soviet Union illustrates well enough that it is erroneous to attribute a negative attitude toward homosexuality exclusively to the influence of religion; Soviet homophobia was a purely secular phenomenon.

After perestroika and the disintegration of the Soviet Union, the situation gradually started to change. Heterosexual cohabitation dramatically increased,[57] and homosexual

---

[52] In 1996, the average age of first marriage in Russia was 24.4 for men and 22.2 for women. *Demoscope weekly*, N 13-14, 26 March- 8 April 2001 www.demoscope.ru/weekly .

[53] In 1999, mothers under the age of 20 were responsible for 12.6% of births. *Demoscope weekly*, N 13-14, 26 March- 8 April 2001 www.demoscope.ru/weekly.

[54] Divorce rates have been around 50 to 60% of all marriages ever since the end of the 1960s. Population of Russia. 2000. Divorce. Eighth annual demographic report of the Centre of Demography and Ecology of the Russian Academy of Science. www.demoscope.ru/weekly.

[55] Even consensual homosexual acts between adult males were subject to criminal punishment until 1993. At the time of its abolition, 73 men convicted for homosexual acts with consenting adults were in prison. ALEKSEEV, N., *Pravovoe regulirovanie polozgenia sexual'nikh men'shinstv* (2002), p. 199.

[56] It wasn't until 1999 that a homosexual orientation was removed from the official list of mental and behavioural pathologies. ALEKSEEV, N., *Gey-brak. Semeinii status odnopolikh par v mezgdynarodnom, natsional'nom I mestnom prave* (2002), p. 362.

[57] In Russia, there were 34 million married couples and 3 million cohabiting heterosexual couples in 2002 (almost 10% of all couples). (*The main results of the census of 2002*. www.gks.ru .) In 2001 almost 1/3 of all children (28.8) were born outside marriage. (*Demoscope weekly*, N 77-78, 26 Augustus-8 September 2002 www.demoscope.ru/weekly) Almost half (47.2%) of extramarital children are recognised by their fathers (*Demoscope weekly*, N 41-42, 5-18 November 2001 www.demoscope.ru/weekly), which suggests that those children were born to stable relationships.

couples made their first steps on the long road to legal and societal recognition.[58] However, despite this change, Russia and other countries of the former Soviet Union still remain part of a group that have a very low instance of non-marital cohabitation and an exceedingly low level of acceptance of same-sex relationships.[59] In Russia, Moldova and Belorussia, the advance of cohabitation did not result in any alteration to public or private law. The new Russian Family Code anno 1996 is as silent with respect to relations between cohabitees as the Napoleonic *Code Civil*. The marital status of the parents, however, is of no influence to parental responsibility once paternity is established.[60] Therefore, the parental rights of cohabitees are duly protected. Outside of this, the law gives cohabitees no protection at all. The new Russian Family Code made the legal position of cohabitating couples, who wish to adopt a child, even worse than it was before. The 1969 Code allowed two unmarried persons to adopt the same child (at that time, one thought of an adoption by two relatives of the child, rather than by two cohabitees). The new Code eliminated this possibility, with the intent being to rule out the very possibility of same-sex adoption. Property, as it relates to cohabitees, is subject to the general rules of the Civil Code, not the Family Code. No specific regulation was discussed when the Code was drafted, as at that time the lack of regulation regarding cohabitation was not considered to be problematic. Later, it was *de lege ferenda* proposed to analogously apply the rules of matrimonial property law regarding marriage settlements to the property agreements between cohabitees,[61] and the rules regarding maintenance agreements of spouses to the maintenance agreements of cohabitees.[62] However, a great number of technical legal problems partially bar this possibility. With respect to same-sex couples, it is also rather doubtful that a Russian court would be prepared to analogously apply the rules of family law to their property or maintenance arrangements. Cohabitees have no rights to intestate succession, and must pay the high taxes, designated for unrelated persons, when they inherit through a will.[63] They are also unable to benefit from tax-free donations between the spouses.[64]

---

[58] There is still not even approximate information on the instance of stable homosexual unions in Russia. ALEKSEEV, N., *Gey-brak. Semeinii status odnopolikh par v mezgdynarodnom, natsional'nom I mestnom prave* (2002), p. 363.

[59] In the first comprehensive work on the legal aspects of homosexuality published in Russia, it is noticed that 'the level of intolerance towards homosexuality increases with every step to the East'. ALEKSEEV, N., *Pravovoe regulirovanie polozgenia sexual'nikh men'shinstv* (2002), p. 170.

[60] Art. 61 Family Code. Joint custody irrespective of the nature of the relationship between the parents has always been a rule of Soviet family law. See: ANTOKOLSKAIA, M., *CEFL National Report for Russia: Parental Responsibility*, (2004), p. 98-101.

[61] ANTOKOLSKAIA, M., *Semeinoe pravo*, (1999), p. 157-158.

[62] Ibid, p. 235-237.

[63] ALEKSEEV, N., *Gey-brak. Semeinii status odnopolikh par v mezgdynarodnom, natsional'nom I mestnom prave* (2002), p. 376-377.

[64] ALEKSEEV, N., *Gey-brak. Semeinii status odnopolikh par v mezgdynarodnom, natsional'nom I mestnom prave* (2002), p. 378.

The situation regarding the regulation of cohabitation in Belorussia and Moldova, which used the Russian 1996 Family Code as a model, is generally the same as in Russia. The situation in Estonia, Latvia and Lithuania, which followed their own path, is under rapid change. The deficiency of the regulation of non-marital cohabitation in the former group of countries forms a sharp contrast with the modernity of the rest of their family laws. Although there are no bills at the moment with regard to cohabitation, academic interest in the matter is rapidly increasing.[65]

15.3. MODEL 2: THE PIECEMEAL AMENDMENT OF EXISTING LAWS

An uncoordinated and unsystematic adjustment of rules in various areas of private and public law by means of statutory amendments and judicial activity was, for decades, the only response the majority of European countries had to non-marital cohabitation.[66] For most of these countries, this period of patchwork adjustment was only a transitional stage, followed by the adoption of specific cohabitation legislation. However, the importance of the patchwork rules did not diminish in the 1990s, when many European countries made specific legislation for same-sex cohabitation. The old patchwork rules often remained the only source of regulation for extramarital opposite-sex cohabitation, which largely continued to remain 'in the shadow of the law'.[67] Even in countries that provide specific legislation for unmarried different-sex couples, the patchwork rules[68] are still relevant for those forms of cohabitation that fall outside the scope of specific laws.[69]

In public law, the amendment of general laws mainly provides for a more or less non-discriminatory treatment of cohabiting couples so that cohabitation does not accrue only disadvantages regarding social security benefits and taxes. In the field of private law however, it falls short of granting more than a minimal level of legal consequences.

---

[65]   Regulation of extramarital cohabitation was one of the hottest issues in the academic debate held in the framework of the conference dedicated to the 10th anniversary of the Family Code of 1995. Personal observations of the author during the conference 'Family and the Law', held in Moscow on the 5th- 6th December 2005 in the Russian Parliament and the Russian Law Academy.

[66]   PROBERT, R., BARLOW, A., 'Cohabitants and the law: recent European reforms' (2000), p. 76.

[67]   MARTIN, C., THÉRY, I., 'The PACS and Marriage and Cohabitation in France' (2001), p. 142.

[68]   See also, for Germany and the Netherlands: SCHRAMA, W., *De niet-huwelijkse samenleving in het Nederlandse en Duitse recht,* (2004); for Belgium: SENAEVE, P., *Compendium van het Personen- en Familierecht,* part 3 (2003), No. 2060-2108; for the development of the English case law: FREEMAN, M., LYON, C., *Cohabitation without marriage: an essay in law and social policy* (1983).

[69]   SCHRAMA, W., *De niet-huwelijkse samenleving in het Nederlandse en Duitse recht,* (2004), p. 118. In The Netherlands, Belgium, France, Germany etc., specific rules regulating cohabitation apply only after the required institutionalisation of the relationships.

The legal techniques in the general rules of private law that are used to accommodate unmarried cohabitation vary from resulting and constructive trusts, estoppels and contracts in the common law systems,[70] to justified enrichment, *société de fait* and contracts in the civil law systems.[71] Special attention has commonly been given to the protection of the tenancy right of the surviving partner.

15.4. MODEL 3: SPECIFIC REGULATION PROVIDING MINIMAL PROTECTION TO DE-FACTO COHABITATION: BETWEEN PATERNALISM AND AUTONOMY

15.4.1. INTRODUCTION

A third approach to the regulation of cohabitation implies that partners to stable relationships should be protected *ipso facto* of their cohabitation, irrespective of any formalisation of their relationships. Such policy is clearly ad odds with the 'law-free space' doctrine, which holds that the State should respect cohabitees' choice not to marry and, therefore, not have their relationships subjected to legal regulation. Several arguments against this doctrine have been put forward.[72] The most important of them is two-fold. Firstly, there is growing evidence that partners often do not take the required steps to formalise their relationships, not because they do not want legal protection,[73] but because they do not think about the legal implications of their relationships.[74] Recent surveys have shown that the non-institutionalisation of relationships is often grounded in a lack of knowledge regarding the applicable rules and the legal consequences of unmarried cohabitation, rather than in a well considered deliberate choice made by both cohabitees.[75] Secondly, one must bear in mind that sometimes the economically stronger partner deliberately frustrates the institutionalisation of cohabitation or the registration of marriage in order to deprive

---

[70] HOGGERTT, B., 'Ends and Means: The Utility of Marriage as a Legal Institution' (1980), p. 99.
[71] PROVERT, R., BARLOW, A., 'Cohabitants and the law: recent European reforms' (2000), p. 76.
[72] See: e.g. FORDER, C., *Het informele huwelijk: de verbondenheid tussen mens, doeg en schuld* (2000), p. 30-35; SCHERPE, J., 'The Legal Status of Cohabitants – Requirements for Legal Recognition' (2005), p. 287-291; SCHRAMA, W., *De niet-huwelijkse samenleving in het Nederlandse en Duitse recht*, (2004), p. 552 ff.
[73] SCHRAMA, W., *De niet-huwelijkse samenleving in het Nederlandse en Duitse recht*, (2004), p. 394-395
[74] See: FORDER, C., *Het informele huwelijk: de verbondenheid tussen mens, doeg en schuld* (2000), p. 31-33.
[75] Various surveys confirm this suggestion. See, for instance, for the Netherlands: SCHERF, Y., *Registered Partnership in the Netherlands. A quick scan* (1999); for Sweden in 1999. Committee Repost (SOU 1999:104), cited in: SÖRGJERD, C., 'Neutrality: the Death or the Revival of the Traditional Family' (2005), at p. 345; for England and Wales: SMART, C., STEVENS, P., *Cohabitation Breakdown* (2000). See also: FORDER, C., VERBEKE, A., 'Geen woorden maar daden', p. 498-501.

the weaker party of legal protection.[76] However, even in countries that have opted for the regulation of de-facto cohabitation, the 'law-free space' argument has always been present in the background. In fact, most legislatures have tried to find a certain balance between the paternalist protection of the weaker party and the respect of such party's autonomy, leaving him or her to the fate he or she has chosen. This explains why most Acts applicable to de-facto cohabitation tend to provide no more than a basic level of legal consequences.[77]

Another problem inherent to the de-facto approach has to do with the fact that opposite-sex cohabitation is far from homogenous. It encompasses a wide range of divergent social phenomena: short term relationships, trial pre-marital cohabitation, stable unions without children, quasi-marital unions with children, etc.[78] This diversity raises several questions: do all of these forms need legal regulation, or only some of them? Could different forms of cohabitation be regulated in the same way? The weight of these questions only increases if one adds to the variety of opposite-sex cohabitation the variety of social patterns in same-sex relationships.

The group of States providing for the regulation of de-facto cohabitation is comprised of countries as diverse as Sweden and Norway, former socialist Yugoslavia and Hungary, and South-European Portugal. An important difference among them is that Sweden, Norway and Slovenia combine two levels of regulation for unmarried cohabitation. The first level provides a limited regulation of de-facto cohabitation for those same- and opposite-sex cohabitees who do not want to institutionalise their relationships. The second level provides for the institution of registered partnership, which grants a quasi-marital status to same-sex couples who wish to institutionalise their relationships. In contrast, former Yugoslavia (with the exception of Slovenia and Serbia), Hungary and Portugal go no further than to provide a limited regulation of de-facto cohabitation for all possible forms of cohabitation.

---

[76]   FORDER, C., 'European Models of Domestic Partnership Laws: The Field of Choice' (2000), p. 381.
[77]   Slovenia and Serbia form an exception to this rule.
[78]   An insightful analysis of the various social forms of cohabitation and their implications for the legal regulation thereof was recently presented by Wendy SCHRAMA in her excellent dissertation, *De niet-huwelijkse samenleving in het Nederlandse en Duitse recht,* (2004), p. 95-98. This author classifies cohabitation into pre-marital, long-term and post-marital cohabitation. *Ibid.*

15.4.2. SWEDEN, NORWAY: REGULATION OF DE-FACTO COHABITATION WITH THE POSSIBILITY TO OPT OUT

Sweden

Sweden was the first European country to pass specific legislation on non-marital cohabitation after the 1960s. In the aftermath of the proclamation of the 'neutrality' policy,[79] the Unmarried Cohabitees Act was enacted in 1973. In 1987, it was replaced by a more comprehensive Cohabitees (Joint Homes) Act.[80] Before this Act entered into force, the Act on Homosexual Cohabitees made its provisions equally applicable to same-sex couples.[81] Thus, Sweden also became the first country where both same- and opposite-sex cohabitation acquired equal legal protection. The Act was applicable to unmarried partners *ipso facto* of their cohabitation, without a requirement of registration, contract or any other expression of intent to institutionalise their relationship. It has been noticed that the Act, 'force[d] certain rules on unmarried couples'.[82] The main purpose of the Act was to grant a weaker party some minimal protection if their relationship ceased.[83] Therefore, the protection provided by the Joint Homes Act was of rather limited scope and mainly covered only patrimonial relationships and some public law issues. Within the property relationships, the Act dealt only with the couple's joint dwelling, household chattels,[84] and transfer of tenancy, previously regulated in the 1973 Act.[85] The autonomy of the partners was protected by allowing them to 'opt out'. This level of protection was considered satisfactory for opposite-sex cohabitees, who deliberately chose not to marry, but not for same-sex couples, who had no resort to marriage. In order to meet their needs, registered partnership was introduced in 1994.[86]

In 1997, a Parliamentary Committee was appointed to evaluate the legislation on cohabitation.[87] The possibility of more extensive legislation on non-institutionalised cohabitation was considered and rejected, out of respect for the autonomy of those

---

[79] This policy was proclaimed in 1972 in the framework of the preparation of the *Unmarried Cohabitees Act*. Committee Report (SOU 1972:41). See: SÖRGJERD, C., 'Neutrality: the Death or the Revival of the Traditional Family' (2005), p. 343-345.

[80] SALDEEN, Å., 'Cohabitation Outside Marriage or Partnership' (2005), p. 504.

[81] Ibid, p. 504.

[82] SÖRGJERD, C., 'Neutrality: the Death or the Revival of the Traditional Family' (2005), p. 337.

[83] SALDEEN, Å., 'Cohabitation Outside Marriage or Partnership' (2005), p. 504.

[84] FORDER, C., 'National Report on Sweden' (1999), p. 4.

[85] BRADLEY, D., *Family Law and Political Culture* (1996), p. 98.

[86] See below.

[87] SALDEEN, Å., 'Cohabitation Outside Marriage or Partnership' (2005), p. 504.

cohabitees who did not wish to subject their relationships to legal regulation.[88] The stated aim of the new legislation went no further than to grant the weaker party 'a minimum level of economic protection'.[89] A proposal to make the applicability of the legislation conditional upon registration was also rejected as jeopardising the protective effect that the legislation actually aimed to provide.[90] Accordingly, the new Cohabitees Act,[91] which in 2003 replaced both the Joint Homes Act and the Act on Homosexual Cohabitees, was not significantly more extensive than its predecessors. The Cohabitees Act is applicable to two adult persons sharing the same household, living in a stable affective relationship, and not engaged in marriage or registered partnership with each other or someone else.[92] The Cohabitees Act grants no right to maintenance or intestate succession, but the surviving partner has a right to keep the value of the joint dwelling and joint household goods up to a stated amount.[93] The possibility of opting out remains intact.

Norway

In Norway, the 1991 Joint Household Act[94] was enacted almost three decades later. It goes significantly less far than the Swedish Joint Homes Act. Distinguishing itself from the Swedish Act, it is not restricted to marriage-like cohabitation but rather applies to every group of unmarried adult persons (including close relatives) who have shared a common household for two years or have a child in common. The Norwegian Act contains neither rules governing property relations in ongoing relationships, nor rules for the division of property if the relationships come to an end.[95] All the Act does

---

88   In the explanatory note to the government Bill it was stressed that, 'In contrast to marriage and registered partnership, a cohabitee relationship means that special legal rules become applicable to the cohabitation without any explicit desire or expression of will on the part of the cohabitees that they should apply. [… therefore] According to the Government the regulation of the cohabitation should also in the future be oriented towards providing legal solutions to primarily financial problems and to those matters where a practical need to protect the parties prevail'. Cited in SALDEEN, Å., 'Cohabitation Outside Marriage or Partnership' (2005), at p. 505.

89   Governmental Bill. Cited in SÖRGJERD, C., 'Neutrality: the Death or the Revival of the Traditional Family' (2005), at p. 336.

90   SALDEEN, Å., 'Cohabitation Outside Marriage or Partnership' (2005), p. 505.

91   Entered into force on 1 July 2003.

92   SÖRGJERD, C., 'Neutrality: the Death or the Revival of the Traditional Family' (2005), p. 337.

93   Ibid.

94   *Act relating to the Joint Residence and Household when a Household Community Ceases to Exist*, of 4 July 1991.

95   However there is extensive case law of the Norwegian Supreme Court governing these issues (*Norwegian Supreme Court Reports* 1978, p. 1352 and 1984, p. 497). According to this case law a cohabitee's indirect contributions in the household in the form of childcare and housekeeping chores will in many cases entitle him or her to co-ownership of a house or other property items acquired during the relationship for common use, irrespective of the title of legal ownership. (See Sverdrup, T., 'Maintenance as Separate Issue – The Relationships Between Maintenance and Matrimonial Property' (2005), p. 123, note 12). This case law has been codified with relations to spouses (section

is provide a member of a household the right to take over, against the market value of the items in question, the dwelling and household goods of the deceased or departed household member.[96] This right is not dependant on title of ownership or entitlement to tenancy. However, if the community is dissolved for any reason other than the death of one of its members, the effectuation of the right to take over is only possible when strong reasons justifying such transfer have been established.[97] For the sake of the parties' autonomy, even these already very limited rights can be further limited or excluded by agreement (opting out).[98] In 1999, a specially appointed governmental Commission published a report containing suggestions for a more profound regulation of non-marital heterosexual cohabitation,[99] which is still under discussion.

Other Nordic countries do not follow

In spite of comparable high levels of cohabitation and a long tradition to follow each other's example, the other Nordic counties have been rather reluctant to follow the path of Sweden and Norway. Thus, no special legislation on unmarried heterosexual and unregistered homosexual cohabitation exists in Denmark, Finland and Iceland. In Denmark, a comprehensive proposal to assimilate marriage and non-marital cohabitation was considered and rejected in 1968.[100] At the moment there is a proposal to grant cohabitees the mutual right of succession.[101] In Finland, a 1992 proposal to pass regulation concerning the division of common households was also rejected, partly out of respect for the decision of parties not to marry, and partly out of fear of creating a 'second class marriage'.[102] The reluctance to legislate on non-institutionalised cohabitation is by no means a token of a negative attitude towards cohabitation in the Nordic region. It is rather a manifestation of a different strategy of accommodating cohabitation through the development of case law and amendments to general rules.[103] The concern for respecting the choice of the cohabitees not to subject themselves to the regulation of marriage also plays a significant role.[104]

---

31 of the *Marriage Act*), but not yet with relation to cohabitees. ASLAND, J., 'Legislation on Informal Cohabitation in Norway' (2005), p. 298.

[96] FORDER, C., 'National Report on Norway' (1999), p. 4.

[97] RYRSTEDT, E., 'Legal Status of Cohabitants in Norway' (2005), p. 443.

[98] Ibid.

[99] For the content of these proposals see: ASLAND, J., 'Legislation on Informal Cohabitation in Norway' (2005), p. 295-312.

[100] BRADLEY, D., *Family Law and Political Culture* (1996), p. 156.

[101] See: *Betaenkning om revision af arvelovgivningen*, Betaenkning Nr. 1473, Ministry of Justice, Copenhagen 2006.

[102] FORDER, C., 'National Report on Finland' (1999), p. 4.

[103] According to Agell, 'the Supreme Courts of Denmark and Norway have developed principles that protect the weaker cohabitee, perhaps as efficiently as the Swedish Act'. AGELL, A., 'Family Forms and Legal Policies. A Comparative View form a Swedish Observer' (1999) p. 201.

[104] FORDER, C., 'European Models of Domestic Partnership Laws: The Field of Choice' (2000), p. 381.

15.4.3. FORGOTTEN VANGUARD: FORMER YUGOSLAVIA AND HUNGARY

It is often forgotten that Yugoslavia and Hungary were also among the countries that pioneered the regulation of non-marital cohabitation. Cohabiting couples in Yugoslavia enjoyed some protection by virtue of piece-meal reforms enacted after World War II.[105] However, the history of the regulation of unmarried cohabitation really started in 1974, when the newly adopted Federal Constitution of Yugoslavia placed the jurisdiction of family matters into the hands of the autonomies, which then enacted comprehensive family codes in the next decade.[106] As the level of non-marital cohabitation in Yugoslavia has always been relatively high,[107] the codes of Bosnia-Herzegovina,[108] Croatia,[109] and Serbia[110] extended some rules of matrimonial property and maintenance law to durable marriage-like relationships.[111] In 1992, the same was done in Macedonia.[112] In all Yugoslavian autonomies there were more or less the same pre-conditions for the application of those rules: cohabitation as husband and wife, a durable union, and the absence of impediments to marriage.[113] If those requirements were satisfied, matrimonial property law and the rules governing spousal maintenance obligations automatically applied to cohabitees, even without registration or contract. The personal relations of cohabitees and their inheritance rights remained unregulated.

Slovenia was a case apart among the Yugoslavian autonomies. Jens Scherpe has rightly pointed out that Slovenia represents Europe's most radical example of regulation of unmarried de-facto cohabitation (in 2005 followed by Serbia), without paying regard to the will of the parties.[114] As early as 1976, the Slovenian Marriage and Family Regulation Act completely assimilated durable cohabitation into marriage in almost all personal and property aspects.[115] The Act defined cohabitation as a durable non-

---

[105]   RIJAVEC, V., KRALJIC, S., 'Die Rechtsstellung nichtehelicher Lebensgemeinschaften in Slowenien' (2005), p. 376-377.

[106]   SARCEVIC, P., 'Cohabitation without Formal Marriage in Yugoslavian Law' (1980), p. 294.

[107]   Ibid, p. 293.

[108]   Introduced by the Family Law of 1980. See: BABIC, S., 'Family Law in Bosnia and Herzegovina' (1996), p. 67-68.

[109]   Introduced by the *Marriage and Family Relations* Act of 1978, and taken over by *Family Law* Act of 1998 and *Family Law* Act of 2003 currently in force.

[110]   Introduced by the *Marriage and Family Relations* Act of 1980.

[111]   MLADENOVIC, M. et al 'The Family in Post-Socialist Countries' (1998), p. 26.

[112]   By *Family Law* of 1992. See: KRALJIC, S., 'Consequences Deriving From Cohabitation-Relations Between Partners and Between Parents and Children' (2003), p. 357.

[113]   SARCEVIC, P., 'Cohabitation without Formal Marriage in Yugoslavian Law' (1980), p. 294-296.

[114]   SCHERPE, J., 'Einführung: Nichteheliche Lebensgemeinschaften als Problem für den Gesetzgeber'(2005), p. 9.

[115]   GEC-KOROŠEC, M., KRALJIC, S., 'The Influence of Validly Established Cohabitation on Legal Regulations Between Cohabitants on Slovene Law' (2001), p. 384.

---

formalised community of life between an unmarried man and a woman who were not legally prohibited from marrying each other.[116]

This example was followed by Serbia in 2005. Article 4 of the new Serbian Family Act[117] plainly extends all the rights and duties of spouses to opposite-sex cohabitees. Non-marital cohabitation is defined as 'the sustained cohabitation of a man and a woman between whom there are no marriage impediments'.[118]

In Hungary, the statutory regulation of non-marital cohabitation dates from 1977.[119] Different than in the Yugoslavian autonomies, the rules in Hungary on cohabitation are not situated among the family law provisions, but among the general provisions of the Civil Code.[120] These rules are applicable to a man and a woman living together without marriage in affective relationships and economic partnership and sharing the same household.[121] The legal regulation of cohabitation does not go any further than regulating the property relationships of cohabitees. For this purpose a special property regime of joint ownership is created in the Civil Code.[122]

Initially, both the former Yugoslavian autonomies and Hungary regulated only opposite-sex cohabitation. Considering the low level of acceptance of same-sex relationships in Eastern Europe, changes to this were not really to be expected in the short-term. The events, however, went rather differently. In 1995, the Hungarian Constitutional Court proclaimed the legal definition of cohabitation as an exclusively opposite-sex union to be discriminatory, and therefore unconstitutional.[123] The Court gave the legislature one year to adjust the law.[124] In 1996, the definition of non-marital cohabitation was amended and made gender-neutral. Thus, same-sex couples came

---

[116]   Article 12. GEC-KOROŠEC, M., KRALJIC, S., 'The Influence of Validly Established Cohabitation on Legal Regulations Between Cohabitants on Slovene Law' (2001), p. 384-385; GEC-KOROŠEC, M., RIJAVEC, V., 'Slovenia: Post-Independence Changes in Family Law Regulation' (1994-95), p. 489.

[117]   *Family Act of Republic of Serbia* of 17 February 2005 entered in force on the 1 of July 2005.

[118]   Art. 4 para. 1 of the *Family Act of Republic of Serbia*.

[119]   Introduced in *Civil Code* by the Act of 1977. SZEIBERT ERDÖS, O., 'Unmarried Partnerships in Hungary' (2005), p. 116.

[120]   In Hungary, as in other Eastern European States during the socialist period, family law was separated from civil law, considered as a separate branch of law, and the rules of the family were placed in special Family Codes or Acts, rather than in Civil Codes.

[121]   Para 685/A of the Hungarian Civil Code. See: SZEIBERT ERDÖS, O., 'Unmarried Partnerships in Hungary' (2005), p. 119.

[122]   Para 578/G(1) of the Hungarian Civil Code. See: SZEIBERT ERDÖS, O., 'Unmarried Partnerships in Hungary' (2005), p. 119 ff.

[123]   Decision No 14 of 8 March 1995. See: JESSEL-HOLST, C., 'Ansätze für eine rechtiche Regelung der gleichgeschlechtlichen Lebensgemeinschaften in Ungarn' (2000), p. 168-169.

[124]   JESSEL-HOLST, C., 'Ansätze für eine rechtiche Regelung der gleichgeschlechtlichen Lebensgemein-schaften in Ungarn' (2000), p. 169.

to enjoy the same protection as opposite-sex couples.[125] In 2003, Croatia also extended legal regulation regarding cohabitation to same-sex couples.[126] Same-sex unions acquired legal protection with respect to property and maintenance on the same terms as their opposite-sex counterparts.[127] In order to invoke legal protection, the same-sex cohabitees must live together in a community of life for at least three years.[128] They also may not be married or engaged in another same- or opposite sex marriage-like union. Other prerequisites include being the age of majority and not related to one another within degrees constituting impediments to marriage.[129] No registration or any other form of institutionalisation is required.

The above described developments in former Yugoslavia and Hungary are interesting for several reasons. Firstly, they preclude regarding a pro-active approach to regulation of non-marital cohabitation as an exclusively Western European phenomenon. However, the background of this approach is not exactly the same as in the West. What the Eastern European pioneers of regulation of unmarried cohabitation did have in common with their West European counterparts was the influence of similar modern ideas in the field of family and family law.[130] Yet, another important motive for the regulation of cohabitation in post-war Yugoslavia was similar to one of the main reasons for the equalisation of unmarried cohabitation with marriage in the Soviet Union in the 1920s; namely, concern for the vulnerable position of peasant women.[131] That does not mean that the regulation of cohabitation in Yugoslavia and Hungary could in any way be attributed to Soviet influence. The policy of protection of unmarried couples started to develop in these countries at a time when such policy had already been radically abandoned in the Soviet Union.[132]

The absence of the possibility to 'opt out' of regulation seems to indicate that the Yugoslavian and Hungarian legislatures had little regard for anything like the 'law free space' doctrine and did not find the imposition of legal regulation on unmarried cohabitees problematic. In the absence of a better explanation, this might perhaps be attributed to the great deal of paternalism typical for Socialist law.

---

[125] Ibid.
[126] Introduced by the *Same Sex Union* Act of 14 July 2003.
[127] HRABAR, D., 'The Protection of the Weaker Family Members: the Ombudsman for Children, Same-Sex Unions, Family Violence and Family Law' (2004), p. 116.
[128] Ibid, p. 115-116.
[129] Ibid.
[130] HRABAR, D., 'Legal Status of Cohabitants in Croatia' (2005), p. 399.
[131] Ibid.
[132] In the Soviet Union cohabitation was deprived of its status by the Act of 1944. See Part III, Chapter 11, Section 11.3.1.

Furthermore, the legal recognition of same-sex unions in Croatia is an interesting example of the prevalence of the 'political will over the majority public opinion'.[133] The Government and Parliament managed to promote a progressive law in a country with a rather negative attitude to homosexuality.[134] In Hungary, the same legal effect was reached as a result of judicial activism in a similarly hostile cultural environment.[135]

15.5. MODEL 4: SPECIFIC LEGISLATION PROVIDING LIMITED PROTECTION TO COHABITEES THAT HAVE CONCLUDED A COHABITATION CONTRACT

In several European counties the law provides for specific legal consequences when cohabiting couples conclude a cohabitation contract. Such a contract always requires that parties explicitly opt for it.[136] The scope of legal protection provided by such contracts differs significantly from country to country. In fact, because contract law generally allows concluding any contract that is not contrary to the mandatory rules of law, cohabitees are always free to draw up contracts regulating various aspects of the patrimonial relationships between them, whether there are any special statutory provisions or not.[137] This is of course quite different in regard of the rights of third parties, inheritance rights and all kinds of public law matters.[138] In these fields of law a cohabitation contract produces only the legal effects explicitly provided for by the national law in question.

An example of such law is that of The Netherlands. Dutch law attaches to a cohabitation contract (*samenlevingscontract*), made in the form of a notarial deed, far-reaching legal consequences in the field of inheritance, tenancy, pensions and tax law.[139] These

---

[133] HRABAR, D., 'The Protection of the Weaker Family Members: the Ombudsman for Children, Same-Sex Unions, Family Violence and Family Law' (2004), p. 115.

[134] Ibid, p. 115 and 117.

[135] According to sociological research carried out in 1995, the Hungarian population is so negative towards homosexuality that 95% of respondents would not allow their child to be friends with a homosexual, and only 2% would allow a homosexual to enter their house. *Equality: A Relevant Issue in the EU Accession Process*, Report of March 2001, ILGA-Europe, Brussels, p. 31.

[136] The idea that durable cohabitation can always be qualified as an implicit contract does not find much support in legal literature. SCHRAMA, W., *De niet-huwelijkse samenleving in het Nederlandse en Duitse recht* (2004), p. 382-384.

[137] SCHERPE, J., 'The Legal Status of Cohabitants – Requirements for Legal Recognition' (2005), p. 292.

[138] Ibid.

[139] SCHRAMA, W., *De niet-huwelijkse samenleving in het Nederlandse en Duitse recht* (2004), p. 373-376.

constitute financial and other advantages that have made such cohabitation contracts quite popular among cohabiting couples in the Netherlands.[140]

In contrast, many other European countries, like for instance Germany, do not provide for specific legislation on cohabitation contracts. In Germany unmarried partners can of course use such contract (*Partnerschaftsvertrag*) to regulate their internal patrimonial relationships, but the contract has almost no effect in regard to third parties, nor in the field of inheritance or public law.[141] In Germany the cohabitation contract is considerably less popular than in the Netherlands.[142]

15.6. MODEL 5: SPECIFIC LEGISLATION PROVIDING LIMITED PROTECTION OF COHABITATION THAT FALLS SOMEWHERE BETWEEN CONTRACT AND STATUS

15.6.1. THE WORST OF TWO WORLDS

Several countries, like France, Belgium and the Spanish Autonomous Communities (*Comunidades Autónomas*), as well as some Italian regions have chosen to provide only very limited protection, and only for those same- and opposite-sex couples who choose to undergo a prescribed form of registration.[143] Making no distinction between same-sex couples who are deprived of the possibility to marry and opposite-sex couples who have chosen not to marry, this approach actually combines the disadvantages of the protection of de-facto cohabitation and those of registered partnership. On the one hand, a couple receives as little protection as is offered in countries with regulation of de-facto cohabitation. On the other hand, this protection is granted only for those couples who are willing to undergo the prescribed registration. As a result, the problems of both groups remain largely unresolved. Same-sex couples are denied the benefits of the quasi-marital status attached to a registered partnership, and also the position of opposite-sex couples is hardly improved; most of them fall outside the scope of the regulation, because those who are unwilling to marry are in most instances

---

[140]   Statistics shows that about 50% of cohabiting couples in The Netherlands make a cohabitation contract. SCHRAMA, W., 'General Lessons for Europe Based on a Comparison of the Legal Status of Non-Marital Cohabitation in the Netherlands and Germany' (2005), p. 265.

[141]   Ibid, p. 377-380.

[142]   In 1985 no more than about 20% of cohabiting couples in Germany drew up a cohabitation contract. Ibid, p. 265.

[143]   With the exception of Catalonian law and the law of several other Spanish Autonomous Communities. See below.

not very much inclined to institutionalise their relationship in another way.[144] Being aware of these problems, the Catalonian legislature and the legislatures of some other Spanish Autonomous Communities tried to alleviate them by making somewhat different rules for same- and opposite-sex couples within one and the same law.[145]

It is rather common to treat the hybrid forms of regulation discussed in this paragraph, such as the French PACS, the Belgian statutory cohabitation and the unions regulated by the laws of Spanish Autonomous Communities, as a species of registered partnership.[146] Such classification is solely focused on the requirement for applicability of the cohabitation law, that these hybrids have in common with registered partnership, namely official registration. It disregards the level of legal consequences provided by such legislation.[147] Such a formal classification has its merits; to call all registered unions 'registered partnership' certainly has the beauty of simplicity. However, as pointed out above, for the purposes of this study a functional rather than formal approach has been chosen. Resembling registered partnerships in the formal requirement of registration, unions such as PACS are entirely different from partnerships when looked at from the point of view of the resemblance to marriage. Registered partnership 'Nordic style'[148] is based on a 'separate but equal' doctrine and grants the registered partners all or nearly all the benefits of marriage, except for its name. In contrast, the hybrids such as PACS stop half-way between status and contract, deliberately avoiding the approximation of institutionalised cohabitation and marriage.

15.6.2. THE FRENCH PACS: 'NEITHER A UNION NOR A CONTRACT'

By the time the *Pacte civil de solidarité* (PACS) was adopted in France in 1999, heterosexual cohabitation had already been fairly well accommodated by means of

---

[144]   See in the same sense STEINER, E., 'The spirit of the new French registered partnership law – promoting autonomy and pluralism or weakening marriage' (2000), p. 7.

[145]   See Section 15.6.4.

[146]   See, for instance: FULCHIRON, H., 'Pacs et partenariats enregistrés en DIP français' (2004), p. 92; COESTER, M., 'Same Sex Relationships: A Comparative Assessment of Legal Developments Across Europe (2002), p. 754.

[147]   Surprisingly, this approach is also taken by Kees Waaldijk, who made the level of legal consequences the focal point of his study. See WAALDIJK, K., 'Level of legal Consequences of Marriage, Cohabitation and Registered Partnership for Different-sex and Same-sex Partners: Comparative overview' (2005), p. 43. However, he does acknowledge the fundamental difference between the French PACS and Belgian statutory cohabitation, on the one hand, and the Nordic registered partnerships, on the other hand. In order to distinguish between these two forms Waaldijk dubs the former 'semi-marriages' and the latter 'quasi-marriages'. Ibid.

[148]   See Section 15.7.2.

case law and piecemeal legislation.[149] The position of same-sex couples was far less favourable, as the French *Cour de Cassation*[150] had explicitly excluded homosexual couples from the scope of legal protection that had developed by that time for heterosexual cohabitees.[151] It was public attention, drawn by the AIDS tragedy to the precarious legal position of same sex partners,[152] that eventually induced the legislature to act. In the 1990s, a number of different proposals were put forward by the left-wing parties.[153] However, it was only from 1997, when the left won the parliamentary elections and the socialist party included promulgation of legislation on cohabitation in its programme,[154] that these endeavours had a real chance.

The same year, the project of the *Contrat d'union civile et sociale* (CUCS) was presented.[155] The main features of the CUCS were the creation of a union upon registration in the Civil Registers and the placement of the 'partners' to this union (both same- and opposite-sex couples, but also a couple of friends or relatives) on equal footing with spouses in the field of property, social security and inheritance law.[156] This proposal was met with much criticism from both the right and the left sides of the political spectrum.[157] In the context of the perpetuating existence of '*les deux Frances*', the opposition from the right was perhaps no surprise. What is more interesting is that there was no unanimity among the left.[158] Many leftist MPs felt the necessity to provide at least some legal protection for same-sex couples; however, they also realised that 'a project obviously devoted to homosexual couples could be divisive'.[159] In a country, where homosexuality still lacked acceptance by the broad populace, 'most leftist MPs feared they would not be re-elected if they supported

---

[149]   See MARTIN, C., THÉRY, I., 'The PACS and Marriage and Cohabitation in France' (2001), p. 142-146. For an overview in English see: FORDER, C., 'National Report on France' (1999), p. 4-12.

[150]   In its decisions of 11 July 1989 (Cass. soc., Bull. civ. V, 514 and 515.) and again as late as 17 December 1997 (Cass. 3ᵉ civ., Bull. civ. III, nr. 225.) the *Cour de Cassation* ruled that the concept of marriage-like cohabitation is not applicable to same-sex couples.

[151]   BRAAT, B., 'Nieuw Frans relatierecht: de PaCS' (2000), p. 75.

[152]   STEINER, E., 'The spirit of the new French registered partnership law – promoting autonomy and pluralism or weakening marriage' (2000), p. 3.

[153]   For a more detailed account of these proposals, see: THÉRY, I., SCHULZ, M., 'La contrat d'union sociale en question' (1997), p. 159-211. For a helpful comparison of the proposals see the tables at the end of this article (p. 208-211). For an overview in English, see: FORDER, C., 'National Report on France' (1999), p. 14-15.

[154]   MARTIN, C., THÉRY, I., 'The PACS and Marriage and Cohabitation in France' (2001), p. 148.

[155]   *Contrat d'union civile et sociale. Proposition de loi nr.* 88 of 23 July 1997.

[156]   For more on this proposal see: THÉRY, I., SCHULZ, M., 'La contrat d'union sociale en question' (1997), p. 159-211.

[157]   For a synopsis in English, see: CURRY-SUMNER, I., *All's Well that Ends Registered?* (2005), p. 78.

[158]   MARTIN, C., THÉRY, I., 'The PACS and Marriage and Cohabitation in France' (2001), p. 148.

[159]   Ibid.

homosexuality'.[160] Thus, for camouflage purposes opposite-sex couples had to be included as well.[161]

In 1998, the Government commissioned two reports: one to a prominent sociologist, Irène Théry,[162] and another to law professor Jean Hauser.[163] Both reports came with new proposals for legislation that involved a step back from the CUCS.[164] At almost the same time, two socialist MPs were asked by the *Commission des Lois*[165] of the *Assemblée Nationale* to prepare a new project. This resulted in the first draft of the *Pacte Civil de Solidarité* (PACS), which was presented in May 1998.[166] The proposed law was designated for both same- and opposite-sex couples. According to the initial draft, the PACS would be registered by the same authority as marriage – the mayor. The union was intended to be as exclusive as marriage and the registration would create a new civil status, as marriage does. The matrimonial property regime and the rules governing the succession rights of spouses were initially intended to be equally applicable to the 'PACSed' couples.[167] Thus, according to the initial proposal the status of the partners was identical to that of spouses, except for the rules on divorce, the right to adopt children, and the presumption of parentage. Therefore the initial proposal closely resembled registered partnership legislation in creating a genuine 'quasi-marriage'.[168]

However, not even the Socialist majority in the *Assemblée Nationale* was prepared to go that far, out of the fear that giving non-marital cohabitation the status of 'quasi-

---

[160] Ibid.

[161] Ibid.

[162] THÉRY, I. *Couple, filiation et parenté aujourd'hui, Le droit face aux mutations de la famille et de la vie privée*, (1998).

[163] HAUSER, J., *Rapport: Mission de recherche Droit et Justice. Groupe de réflexion: conséquences financières de la séparation des couples. Thème: Pacte d'Intérêt Commun.*

[164] Jean Hauser's proposal was the *Pacte d'Intérêt Commun* (PIC), which was no more than a private contract regulating property relationships and available to everyone including spouses. In her report, Irène Théry proposed including a gender-neutral definition of cohabitation in the *Code Civil*. A cohabitation lasting more than two years would be, without any requirement of registration, equated to marriage in the field of tax and social security law. However, Théry describes that a half-year earlier she came with a more far-reaching proposal that she considered 'more complete and satisfying', namely: 'concubinage for all cohabiting couples *plus* registered partnership for same-sex couples, as in the northern European countries'. Yet, because this proposal was rejected by the homosexual movement as too 'communitarian', she did not put it into her official report. MARTIN, C., THÉRY, I., 'The PACS and Marriage and Cohabitation in France' (2001), p. 148 and note 7 at p. 157.

[165] The Commission for law.

[166] *Proposition de loi relative au pacte civil de solidarité*, presented on 28 May 1998 by Catherine Tasca, President of the *Commission des Lois* of the *Assemblée Nationale*. *http://www.adventice.com/ infogay/div008.htm* .

[167] Ibid.

[168] MARTIN, C., THÉRY, I., 'The PACS and Marriage and Cohabitation in France' (2001), p. 147.

marriage'[169] would undermine the institution of marriage.[170] Accordingly, the left failed to defend the Bill in Parliament, and lost the debate in the *Assemblée Nationale* in October 1998.[171] After this defeat the Bill had to be amended in order to remove almost all resemblance to marriage.[172] Registration by the mayor was replaced with registration by a court registry.[173] The property regime was changed from the limited community of acquests to co-ownership (*l'indivision*).[174] The equalisation to spouses with respect to succession and taxation was discarded.[175] The rules regarding the capacity to enter a PACS were made so vague that it was no longer clear whether it was open only for cohabiting couples or also for persons who simply shared the same household. These renovations enabled the Minister of Justice to declare the PACS to be something fundamentally different from marriage. She stated that in contrast to marriage, 'in PACS there [is] no celebration, no solemnities, no fidelity and no intention to found a family'.[176] The amended Bill was adopted by the *Assemblée Nationale* in December 1998.[177] However, even this curtailed Bill never managed to pass through the *Sénat*.[178] The impasse was broken only after the *Assemblée Nationale* adopted the Bill in a third reading on October 1999, thereby overruling the disapproval of the *Sénat*.[179] However, the constitutionality of the PACS was immediately challenged before the Constitutional Court (*Conseil Constitutionnel*). In November the *Conseil* confirmed the constitutionality of the PACS in general, but made its constitutionality conditional upon the requirement that the PACS should only be open to cohabiting couples, not to all household-sharers.[180] Finally, on 15 November 1999, the PACS was signed by the President and became law.[181] In 2006 the provisions of the PACS underwent substantial amending.[182]

---

[169]   '*Mariage bis*'.

[170]   MARTIN, C., THÉRY, I., 'The PACS and Marriage and Cohabitation in France' (2001), p. 149.

[171]   Many left-wing MPs were simply not present at the Parliament when the Bill was debated.

[172]   For a comparison between the PACS and marriage see: CABRILLAC, R., 'Libres propos sur le PACS (après l'adoption de texte en première lecture pas l'Assemblée Nationale)' (1999), p. 72.

[173]   *Greffe du tribunal d'instance*. Art. 515-3 *Code Civil*.

[174]   Art. 515-5 *Code Civil*, MÉCARY, C., LEROY-FORGEOT, F., *Le Pacs* (2000), p. 65-66.

[175]   MARTIN, C., THÉRY, I., 'The PACS and Marriage and Cohabitation in France' (2001), p. 149.

[176]   Speech by the Minister of Justice Elisabeth Guigou before the *Assemblée Nationale* on 3 November 1998. Cited in: STEINER, E., 'The spirit of the new French registered partnership law – promoting autonomy and pluralism or weakening marriage' (2000), p. 4.

[177]   *Proposition de loi relative au PACS*, nr. 108 of 9 Décembre 1998.

[178]   The *Sénat* has rejected the Bill three times.

[179]   Act. 45 of the Constitution empowers the *Assemblée Nationale* to overrule the decision of the *Sénat* if the *Sénat* three times refuses to adopt a Bill adopted by the *Assemblée Nationale*.

[180]   *Conseil Constitutionnel*. Decision 99-419 DC of 9 November 1999. See also: MOLFESSIS, N., 'PACS. Le Réécriture de la loi par le Conseil Constitutionnel' (2000), p. 270-272.

[181]   Loi 99/944 du 15 November 1999. For a synopsis of the passage of the Bill see: MÉCARY, C., LEROY-FORGEOT, F., *Le Pacs* (2000), p. 7-8.

[182]   By the Act no. 2006-728 of 23 June 2006, *Portant réforme des successions et des libéralités* . The amendments come into force on 1 January 2007.

The result of this troublesome history is an Act that provides cohabitees with an ambiguous legal standing, somewhere between contract and status.[183] On the one hand, the PACS seems to be purely contractual in nature.[184] As with a contract and differing from a marriage, a PACS is established by a simple written agreement[185] without any ceremonial requirements. Initially, subsequent registration of the PACS by a court office of the *tribunal d'instance* was not essential for the validity of the PACS inter partners; however, without such registration a PACS produced no effect with respect to third parties.[186] However, in 2006 the procedure of formation of the PACS has acquired a more public character. The new registration procedure includes the mentioning of the PACS and the name of the other partner in the margins of the birth certificates of the partners.[187] The legal effect of the PACS inter partners and with respect to third parties are made dependent upon registration.[188] The court office of the *tribunal d'instance* is charged to enquire into the capacity of the partners to conclude a PACS (age, impediments, and so on) while performing the registration,[189] which very much resembles the enquiry that precedes the celebration of a marriage.

The effect of a PACS on the civil and personal status of the partners is also ambiguous. On the one hand, entering into a PACS does not change the civil status of the parties.[190] On the other hand, the rules on PACS are situated in Book I of the *Code Civil* dealing with the law on persons and the family and not in Book III, which deals with patrimonial matters. This was interpreted as an indication that the PACS was not meant to be merely a property arrangement between cohabiters, but rather an institution of family law.[191] The personal status of the partners also seems to be unchanged as they are still free to marry someone else, without previous dissolution of the PACS. On the other hand, a PACS does touch upon the personal status of the parties, as PACSed partners are not allowed to conclude another PACS.[192]

---

[183] MARTIN, C., THÉRY, I., 'The PACS and Marriage and Cohabitation in France' (2001), p. 135; HAUSER, J., 'Pacte civil de solidarité (PACS). Statut civil des partenaires' (2000), p. 411.

[184] FULCHIRON, H., 'Pacs et partenariats enregistrés en DIP français' (2004), p. 92.

[185] LEMOULAND, J-J., 'Pacte civil de solidarité (PACS). Formation et la dissolution de Pacte Civil de Solidarité' (2000), p. 408.

[186] Ibid. The essentiality of the registration was initially a matter of controversy. See: CORNU, G., *Droit Civil, La famille* (2003), No 52 and LEMOULAND, J-J., 'Pacte civil de solidarité (PACS). Formation et la dissolution de Pacte Civil de Solidarité' (2000), note 9 at p. 408.

[187] Art. 515-3-1 (1) *Code Civil* as amended by the Act no. 2006-728 of 23 June 2006.

[188] Art. 515-3-1 (2) *Code Civil* as amended by the Act no. 2006-728 of 23 June 2006.

[189] LEMOULAND, J-J., 'Pacte civil de solidarité (PACS). Formation et la dissolution de Pacte Civil de Solidarité' (2000), note 9 at p. 407-408.

[190] MÉCARY, C., LEROY-FORGEOT, F., *Le Pacs* (2000), p. 62.

[191] CABRILLAC, R., 'Libres propos sur le PACS (après l'adoption de texte en première lecture par l'Assemblée Nationale), (1999), p. 71-72.

[192] FULCHIRON, H., 'Pacs et partenariats enregistrés en DIP français' (2004), p. 93.

The content of the PACS also evokes the image of a non-negotiable 'contract of adherence',[193] a 'contractual statute for a couple'[194] to determine their common life on a contractual basis,[195] rather than that of an ordinary contract. The provisions of the PACS contain a set of mandatory rules, providing for a limited scope of basic rights and duties imposed on partners, the so-called *régime primaire*. This mandatory regime covers a duty of mutual assistance,[196] joint and several liability for household debts,[197] and a right to succeed in tenancy.[198] The parties have no contractual freedom to change the rights and duties that fall within the *régime primaire*. Everything not covered by the *régime primaire* can be regulated by contract. As maintenance rights, the rights of intestate succession and property rights are not part of the *régime primaire*, the partners are free to regulate these by contract. Initially, if a contract did not provide otherwise, the property relations of the partners were governed by a regime called *l'indivision*.[199] Roughly described, this 'legal' regime boils down to co-ownership for almost all assets acquired for value during the existence of a PACS. In 2006, the statutory property regime applicable to the PACSed partners, has been changed into a regime of separation of property,[200] generally resembling the contractual regime of separation of property for which the spouses can opt for in their martial contract.[201]

The rules on the dissolution of a PACS stress its inferiority to marriage. A PACS does not form an obstacle to concluding a marriage with another person. A marriage of a PACSed partner does not require the prior dissolution of the PACS, but leads to the automatic termination of the PACS.[202] Other modes of dissolution of the PACS resemble neither the dissolution of a marriage, nor of a contract. Unlike marriage, a PACS can be dissolved by a joint declaration of the parties. Unlike contract, a PACS can be terminated unilaterally by each of the parties.[203]

All in all, a PACS provides same-sex couples with an ambiguous family status, with no real equality to opposite sex couples and with very limited statutory rights.[204] The

---

[193]   Ibid.
[194]   Ibid.
[195]   Ibid.
[196]   Art. 515-4 (1) *Code Civil.*
[197]   Art. 515-4 (2) *Code Civil.*
[198]   Art. 515-6 *Code Civil.*
[199]   Art. 515-5 *Code Civil.*
[200]   Art. 515-5 -515-5 -5 *Code Civil* as amended by the Act no. 2006-728 of 23 June 2006.
[201]   Provided by Art. 1536-1543 *Code Civil.*
[202]   Art. 515-7 (1 and 2) *Code Civil.* LEMOULAND, J-J., 'Pacte civil de solidarité (PACS). Formation et la dissolution du Pacte Civil de Solidarité' (2000), p. 409.
[203]   Art. 515-7 (3 and 4) *Code Civil.* LEMOULAND, J-J., 'Pacte civil de solidarité (PACS). Formation et la dissolution du Pacte Civil de Solidarité' (2000), p. 409.
[204]   The succession rights of the partners have been also improved by the Act no. 2006-728 of 23 June 2006.

problems of the vast majority of unmarried opposite-sex couples[205] also remain largely unresolved for the simple reason that those who have opted not to marry are not expected to be likely to register a PACS.[206] The improvements introduced in 2006 did not really change this situation.

15.6.3. THE BELGIAN STATUTORY COHABITATION: EQUALLY SUITABLE FOR A SAME-SEX COUPLE AS FOR 'A PRIEST AND HIS MAID'

The introduction of the institution of 'statutory cohabitation' in Belgium shows notable parallels with the events surrounding the elaboration of the PACS in France. As in France, by the time a specific law on cohabitation was drafted, case law had already developed certain civil law remedies for heterosexual cohabitees.[207] Following the example of the French 1992 proposal, two drafts were presented before the Belgian Parliament.[208] Both proposals equally covered homosexual and heterosexual unmarried couples. The first proposal for the regulation of non-marital cohabitation was commenced by the Flemish Socialists (SP) in 1993.[209] This proposal sought to introduce a multistage regulation for both same- and opposite-sex couples, a so-called 'bill of fare for love'.[210] One year later another proposal, which after its reintroduction in 1995 became known as the Moureaux-proposal, was launched by a broader spectrum of left-wing parties.[211] According to this proposal, the relations of unmarried cohabitees was to have been regulated by a registered cohabitation contract. The scope of protection offered by such a contract was broader than was suggested in the aforementioned 1993 proposal.[212] The contract provided that the property of the cohabitees would remain separate, but the assets to which a cohabitee could not prove

---

[205] The legislation of 1999 did provide for some relief for unregistered same-sex couples. Apart from creating the PACS, the same Act introduced a new gender-neutral legal definition of unmarried cohabitation. Therefore all the protection developed for unmarried and 'unPACSed' heterosexual couples, by case and statutory law, was extrapolated to 'unPACSed' same-sex couples.

[206] STEINER, E., 'The spirit of the new French registered partnership law – promoting autonomy and pluralism or weakening marriage' (2000), p. 7.

[207] For an overview see: SENAEVE, P., 'Familierechtelijke aspecten van ongehuwd samenwonen' (1997), p. 61-81.

[208] SENAEVE, P., 'De wettelijke samenwoning en het geregistreerde partnerschap in het Belgisch recht' (1998), p. 254.

[209] SENAEVE, P., 'Familierechtelijke aspecten van ongehuwd samenwonen' (1997), p. 105

[210] The proposal included: (1) de-facto cohabitation, without registration and contractual arrangements, governed by general civil law; (2) couples, who entered a cohabitation agreement; (3) a registered civil union, providing for rather limited protection. SENAEVE, P., COENE, E., 'Geregistreerd partnerschap. Pleidooi voor de institutionalisering van de homoseksuele tweerelatie (1998), p. 127.

[211] Proposal of 2 March 1994. Chamber, 1993/1994, 1340/1.

[212] For a short account of the Draft see: SENAEVE, P., COENE, E., 'Geregistreerd partnerschap. Pleidooi voor de institutionalisering van de homoseksuele tweerelatie (1998), p. 125-138.

his or her title were presumed to be common.[213] The cohabitees were entitled to maintenance after termination of the relationship,[214] and to a usufruct in case of intestate succession.[215] The proposals remained undiscussed as late as 1997 because 'the time was not ready for them yet'.[216] Finally in 1997, when on the regional level the Flemish Socialists and Christian Democrats reached a political agreement regarding the cohabitation legislation in Flanders, the federal Parliament also began to act.[217] During the Parliamentary discussion of the proposals, leading academics were invited to express their opinions.[218] After this discussion the political parties agreed on a 'compromise' proposal.[219] In contrast to the situation in France, the ideological background of the compromise in Belgium was less explicit. However, the upshot was an even more limited regulation than that provided by the French PACS. The fear of 'undermin[ing] the institution of marriage as a corner stone of society'[220] was so strong that the compromise-draft, which later became law,[221] turned out to be just a 'rest stump of a much more ambitious plot'.[222] During the discussion in the Senate, the Minister of Justice explicitly stated that the draft was merely 'a codification of the existing case law'.[223] The new law created no civil status[224] and provided for only a minimal, pragmatic regulation of the patrimonial relationships of the cohabiting

---

[213] Art. 228*octies* of the 1994 proposal, as amended in 1995. Chamber, 1995/1996, 170/1.

[214] Art. 228*decies* (2) of the 1994 proposal, as amended in 1995. Chamber, 1995/1996, 170/1.

[215] Art. 5 of the 1994 proposal, as amended in 1995. Chamber, 1995/1996, 170/1.

[216] SENAEVE, P., 'De wettelijke samenwoning en het geregistreerde partnerschap in het Belgisch recht' (1998), p. 255.

[217] Ibid.

[218] Among the recommendations made was a proposal to broaden the scope of the legislation in order to include every form of cohabitation, irrespective the sexual dimension of the relationship (proposed by E. Heyvaert. Report by D. VANDENBOSSCHE and F. LOZIE, p. 15. Chamber, 1997/1998, 170/8). Some experts stressed that the needs of heterosexual cohabitees, who do not want to marry, and homosexual cohabitees, who cannot marry, could never be met by one and the same regulation (put forward by P. Senaeve and A.-C. van Gysel. (Report by D. VANDENBOSSCHE and F. LOZIE, p. 23. Chamber, 1997/1998, 170/8). Several experts recommended granting homosexual cohabitees all the rights and obligations of marriage, without opening up marriage to them. To this end, an alternative institution of registered partnership was seen as the most appropriate solution (this was proposed by, for instance P. Sanaeve. (Report by D. VANDENBOSSCHE and F. LOZIE, p. 17-18. Chamber, 1997/1998, 170/8). Van Gysel brought forward a complete draft that provided for the regulation of cohabitation, applicable on the basis of two years of de-facto cohabitation, childbirth or registration Report by D. VANDENBOSSCHE and F. LOZIE, p. 26-28. Chamber, 1997/1998, 170/8.

[219] Report by D. VANDENBOSSCHE and F. LOZIE, p. 63. Chamber, 1997/1998, 170/8.

[220] The wording of MP Moureaux. Report by D. VANDENBOSSCHE and F. LOZIE, p. 50. Chamber, 1997/1998, 170/8).

[221] The Law on Introduction of the Statutory Cohabitation of 23 November 1998. The Law was adopted by the Chamber 19 March, by the *Senaat* (with amendments) on 16 July and finally by the Chamber on 29 October. SENAEVE, P., 'De wettelijke samenwoning en het geregistreerde partnerschap in het Belgisch recht' (1998), p. 255. Came into force on 1 January 2000.

[222] Senator Boutmans. Parliamentary Proceedings. *Senaat*, 15 July 1998, 1-209.

[223] Parliamentary Proceedings. *Senaat*, 15 July 1998, 1-209.

[224] SENAEVE, P., *Compendium van het Personen- en Familierecht*, part 3 (2003), No. 1510-2.

persons.[225] In order to stress the patrimonial rather than familial character of the new institution, the rules on statutory cohabitation were placed not in Book I of the Belgian Civil Code dealing with the persons and the family, but in Book III, containing the rules of patrimonial law.[226]

The Belgian legislature surpassed even the French in avoiding any resemblance to marriage.[227] Under the pressure of the Christian Democrats,[228] the rules of statutory cohabitation were applicable upon registration to any two unmarried persons living together, irrespective their gender, familial, sexual or affective bond. Thus, statutory cohabitation came to cover as wide a range of relationships as same- and opposite-sex couples, a mother and her adult daughter, two studying room mates, and even 'a priest and his maid'.[229] At the same time, a group of more than two persons, sharing the same household, fell outside the scope of statutory cohabitation. This solution was often criticised as arbitrary[230] and discriminatory.[231] It was suggested that if statutory cohabitation did not presuppose affective sexual relationships, there was no reason to include a parent living together with one adult child and to exclude a parent living together with two or more adult children.[232]

For the rest, the Belgian statutory cohabitation very much resembles the French PACS. The law on statutory cohabitation is criticised by Belgian politicians and scholars for failing to provide an adequate regulation for both target groups: same- and opposite-sex couples.[233] On the one hand, it leaves the bulk of opposite-sex cohabitees who are not willing to register their relationships outside its scope. On the other hand, it

---

[225] MOSSELMANS, S., 'De wet van 23 november 1998 tot invoering van de wettelijke samenwoning en het gelijkheidsbeginsel' (2000-2001), p. 1041.

[226] The Moureaux-proposal suggested placing the rules regulating cohabitation into Book I. In France the rules on PACS were also incorporated into Book I of the French *Code Civil.* SENAEVE, P., 'De Belgische 'wettelijke samenwoning' en het Franse 'Pacte civil de solidarité' (2000), p. 440-441.

[227] For a comparison of statutory cohabitation and marriage, see: SENAEVE, P., 'Proeve van synoptische vergelijking tussen het huwelijk en de wettelijke samenwoning' (1998), p. 164-165.

[228] In this way, the Christian-Democrats wished to provide minimal protection also to family members living in the same household. SENAEVE, P., 'De Belgische 'wettelijke samenwoning' en het Franse 'Pacte civil de solidarité'(2000), p. 442.

[229] Speach of Senator Raes in the *Senaat.* Palamentary Procedings. *Senaat* 15 July 1998, 1-109.

[230] MOSSELMANS, S., 'De wet van 23 november 1998 tot invoering van de wettelijke samenwoning en het gelijkheidsbeginsel' (2000-2001), p. 1044.

[231] See, for instance, the opinion of M.P. Laeremans. Report by D. VANDENBOSSCHE and F. LOZIE, p. 61. Chamber, 1997/1998, 170/8).

[232] MOSSELMANS, S., 'De wet van 23 november 1998 tot invoering van de wettelijke samenwoning en het gelijkheidsbeginsel' (2000-2001), p. 1044.

[233] See the Explanatory Note to the Proposal of 15 July 2003. Chamber, 2003, 0110/001, p. 4. Patric Senaeve has also repeatedly stressed that trying to realise such different objectives in one and the same law was doomed to fail. SENAEVE, P., 'Naar de invoering van het homohuwelijk in het Belgische recht?' (2002), p. 51.

continues the discrimination of same-sex couples[234] by giving only minimal protection to their patrimonial relationships, while providing no regulation at all for their 'intimate personal' relationships.[235]

15.6.4. THE LAWS OF THE SPANISH AUTONOMOUS COMMUNITIES: THE BENEFITS OF CREATIVE DIFFERENTIATION

In Spain, the absence of federal regulation on non-marital cohabitation[236] induced a flow of regional legislation.[237] The most interesting example is provided by the Catalonian Act on Couples in Stable Unions.[238] In 1998, Catalonia pioneered a law that became a model for the other Spanish Autonomous Communities. Although the Catalonian approach is generally the same as the one taken in France and Belgium, the Catalonian law is rather special compared to its French and Belgium counterparts. The most important difference of the Catalonian Stable Union Act is an ingenious attempt to solve the problems that arise from making one law for two different target-groups: same- and opposite-sex couples.[239] One of the challenges was to resolve the main problem of unmarried opposite-sex couples: the protection of the weaker party (usually a woman engaged in housekeeping and childrearing). Therefore, the Catalonian legislature made the Stable Union Act applicable to opposite-sex couples either upon their making a formal contract (in the form of a public deed), or on the ground of de-facto cohabitation during a period of two years, or after a birth of a common child.[240] Another challenge was to meet the needs of same-sex couples, who wished to institutionalise their relationships. As gender-related problems of protecting

---

[234]   SENAEVE, P., 'Naar de invoering van het homohuwelijk in het Belgische recht?' (2002), p. 51.

[235]   MOSSELMANS, S., 'De wet van 23 november 1998 tot invoering van de wettelijke samenwoning en het gelijkheidsbeginsel' (2000-2001), p. 1044.

[236]   In 2005, federal legislation opened up marriage for same-sex couples and thereby solved the problems of same-sex couples who wish to institutionalise their relationships. See Chapter, 13, Section 13.4.3.

[237]   At the this book was finalised, cohabitation legislation was passed in the following Autonomous Communities: Catalonia, (Law 10/1998, of 15 July 1998), Aragon (Law 6/1999 of the 26 March 1999), Navarre (Law 6/2000 of 3 July 2000), Balearic Islands (Law 18/2001 of 19 December 2001), Valencia (Law 1/2001 of 6 April 2001), Madrid (Law 11/2001 of 19 December 2001), Asturias (Law 4/2002 of 23 May 2002), Andalusia (Law 5/2002 of 16 December 2002), Canary Islands (Law 5/ 2003 of 6 March 2003), Basque Country (Law 2/2003 of 7 May 2003), Extremadura (Law 5/2003 of 20 March 2003) and Cantabria (Law 1/2005 of 16 May 2005). See for and overview: ASÍN CABRERA, 'La partenariat de droit espagnol: quel avenir pour une réglementation en droit international privé?' (2004), p. 76; GONZÁLEZ BEILFUSS, C., 'Private international law aspects of homosexual couples' (2006), p. 3.

[238]   Law No 10/1998 of 5 July 1998.

[239]   GONZÁLEZ BEILFUSS, C., 'Private international law aspects of homosexual couples' (2006), p. 3.

[240]   GARCÍA CANTERO, G., 'The Catalan Family Code of 1998 and Other Autonomous Region Law on de Facto Unions' (2001), p. 400.

the weaker party are much less an issue for same-sex couples, the Catalonian Act is made applicable to same-sex couples only if they explicitly and formally contract for it.[241] Some other Autonomous Communities (for instance Navarre, Aragon,[242] and Madrid[243]) also made their laws applicable to non-institutionalised de-facto unions, all on the basis of cohabitation during a stated period or having a common child, as well as to couples that make a formal contract. In contrast, in Valencia[244] and the Balearic Islands[245] formalisation of the union is the only route to its legal recognition.

Similar to the French PACS and the Belgian statutory cohabitation, the Catalonian Stable Union Act provides a minimum level of protection through mandatory rules (comparable to the French *régime primaire*), leaving the rest to the free disposition of the parties. A peculiarity of the Catalonian law is a positive discrimination in favour of same-sex couples. The mandatory rules grant them a limited right to succeed in intestacy, while the heterosexual couples do not enjoy such a right.[246] The reason for this is that same-sex partners are not allowed to marry, while the opposite-sex couples are.[247] This inventive differentiation, however, has not been followed by other Autonomous Communities, who all have chosen to treat same- and opposite-sex couples equally.[248]

The basic mandatory level of protection is more or less the same in the majority of the Autonomous Communities. The scope of protection is much broader than that found under the French PACS or the Belgian statutory cohabitation. Both partners have to contribute to the maintenance of the household.[249] If no agreement has been made, the property of the partners remains separate.[250] Heterosexual partners are allowed to adopt a child jointly, same-sex couples were initially allowed to adopt a

---

[241]   Art 19. See: ROCA, E., 'Same-Sex Partnerships in Spain: Family, Marriage or Contract?' (2001), p. 373.

[242]   Registration in an administrative register prescribed by Aragon Act serves only the purposes of good administration and is not a precondition for the application of the law. ROCA, E., 'Same-Sex Partnerships in Spain: Family, Marriage or Contract?' (2001), p. 373, note 31.

[243]   GARCÍA CANTERO, G., 'De Facto Unions Revisited' (2003), p. 407.

[244]   Ibid, p. 406.

[245]   MARTÍN-CASALS, M., 'Same-Sex Partnerships in the Legislation of Spanish Autonomous Communities' (2002), p. 60.

[246]   GARCÍA CANTERO, G., 'The Catalan Family Code of 1998 and Other Autonomous Region Law on *de Facto* Unions' (2001), p. 402.

[247]   MARTÍN-CASALS, M., 'Same-Sex Partnerships in the Legislation of Spanish Autonomous Communities' (2002), p. 63.

[248]   ASÍN CABRERA, 'La partenariat de droit espagnol: quel avenir pour une réglementation en droit international privé?'(2004), p. 76.

[249]   ROCA, E., 'Same-Sex Partnerships in Spain: Family, Marriage of Contract?' (2001), p. 375.

[250]   Ibid.

child jointly only in Navarre.[251] However, this prohibition has recently been lifted in most of the Autonomous Communities.[252] Upon the breakdown of the relationship, an economically weaker partner, who has been taking care of the household and the children or working in the business of the other partner without having been paid adequately, is entitled to compensation.[253] The economically weaker partner is also entitled to maintenance.[254] The basic provisions regarding intestate succession differ somewhat from one Autonomous Community to the other. As was already mentioned, Catalonian law allows only a same-sex partner to succeed in case of intestacy. The rest of the Autonomous Communities make no distinction between same- and opposite-sex couples. In Navarre and the Balearic Islands, partners' inheritance rights are equated with the inheritance rights of spouses.[255] Aragon law allows a surviving partner to retain household chattels.[256] In addition to the mandatory basic regime, couples are free to make contractual arrangements with respect to their relationships during and after cohabitation.[257]

The other provisions of the Spanish Acts are also rather similar. With respect to the capacity to establish a union, the laws of the other Autonomous Communities have followed the Catalonian example rather closely[258] and generally resemble French and Belgium law. As with French and Belgian law, the Spanish Autonomous Communities have created a legal regime for unmarried couples, that is in-between a status and a (explicit or implied)[259] contract.[260] The union has the same half-way effect on the partners' civil and personal status; they are neither married, nor free. They are not free, as an existing union precludes them from establishing another one. At the same time, their freedom is much less restricted than if they were married, namely the existence of a union does not preclude them from marrying someone else. Also, the absence of State control over the termination of a union is an argument against considering such unions a status.[261] Gabriel García Cantero even regards 'the legal force of [such

---

[251]   MARTÍN-CASALS, M., 'Same-Sex Partnerships in the Legislation of Spanish Autonomous Communities' (2002), p. 61.

[252]   See: GONZÁLEZ BEILFUSS, C., 'Private international law aspects of homosexual couples' (2006), p. 3.

[253]   ROCA, E., 'Same-Sex Partnerships in Spain: Family, Marriage or Contract?' (2001), p. 375.

[254]   Ibid.

[255]   GARCÍA CANTERO, G., 'De Facto Unions Revisited' (2003), p. 404 and 408.

[256]   ROCA, E., 'Same-Sex Partnerships in Spain: Family, Marriage or Contract?' (2001), p. 379.

[257]   Ibid, p. 106.

[258]   Ibid, p. 375.

[259]   When de-facto cohabitation is regarded sufficient for legal recognition of the partnership, the existence of a contract is implied. ROCA, E., 'Same-Sex Partnerships in Spain: Family, Marriage of Contract?' (2001), p. 373.

[260]   Encarna Roca has concluded that Catalonia made a preference for a contractual system while Navarre has chosen for a more marriage-like status. Ibid, p. 371.

[261]   As Encarna Roca has noticed, as the existence of the partnership 'depend[s] exclusively on the cohabitants' will, [...] the breakdown will only depend on their decision'. Ibid, p. 376.

a] union weaker than that of a contract'.[262] Indeed, in contrast to the termination of most contracts, a unilateral uncontrolled withdrawal from a union is always possible. Creating a union with such a weak legal standing is perhaps an appropriate solution for heterosexual couples, who need nothing more than basic protection, as they can always resort to marriage. However, such a weak union falls short of meeting the requirements of same-sex couples, who are not allowed to marry and therefore need more comprehensive regulation.

15.6.5. TRANSITORY LEGISLATION?

This hesitant approach in between protection of de-facto cohabitation and registered partnerships was in most cases the product of uneasy political compromises and self-imposed constraints. One of the motives behind these legislative initiatives was recognition of the need to give at least some legal protection to same-sex couples. In France and Belgium, enacting registered partnership legislation – the most straightfor-ward way to grant same-sex couples the benefits of marriage without opening marriage up to them – was considered and rejected out of fear for public opinion. To avoid speaking all too openly about same-sex couples it was preferred to 'mask the issue of the same-sex relationships behind the façade of cohabitation'.[263] In France, this resulted in legislation, equally applicable to affective partners in same- and opposite-sex relationships. In Belgium this led to the inclusion of any two adults who, regardless of the reason, share a household.

Catalonian law and the law of some other Spanish Autonomous Communities distinguish overtly between same- and different-sex couples and try to accommodate both under the same law by making it applicable to opposite-sex couples *ipso facto* of their cohabitation and to same-sex couples only upon a formal contract. Catalonian law also provides same-sex couples with more extensive statutory protection. This inventive approach meets the needs of both same- and opposite-sex couples much better than the approach of France and Belgium. Same-sex couples are allowed to institutionalise their relationships by concluding the required contract, and are thereby granted a rather significant level of statutory protection that can be upgraded by virtue of the same contract. In this way, the patrimonial needs of same-sex couples are more or less met. Immaterial needs however, such as the claim for a genuine status, equality and recognition, are much less accommodated, as the Catalonian Act only creates

---

[262] GARCÍA CANTERO, G., 'The Catalan Family Code of 1998 and Other Autonomous Region Law on *de Facto* Unions' (2001), p. 401.

[263] STEINER, E., 'The spirit of the new French registered partnership law – promoting autonomy and pluralism or weakening marriage' (2000), p. 13.

something half-way between status and contract. The 'Catalonian' approach is also more successful in the accommodation of the needs of unmarried opposite-sex couples. A basic protection of a weaker party in a non-marital opposite-sex relationship is insured by giving her or him the possibility to invoke protection *ipso facto* of cohabitation. As the mandatory level of such protection remains very basic, couples, who deliberately choose not to marry, are able to retain much of their 'law-free space'.

Both French and Belgian legislation and the legislation of the Spanish Autonomous Communities went no further than to create an inconsequential intermediary-construct; something which is 'neither a legal union nor a simple property contract'; 'neither public nor private', and providing 'neither recognition for same-sex couples nor its non-recognition'. These unsatisfactory results allow the suggestion that legislation based on the in-between approach will probably turn out to be merely 'transitory legislation'.[264] Indeed, Belgium and Spain have already moved to a second stage by opening marriage to same-sex couples.

In Belgium, the problem of homosexual cohabitees found its ultimate solution when in 2003 they were granted the possibility to marry.[265] The position of 'unregistered' heterosexual cohabitees remained problematic and became the subject of a series of legislative proposals.[266] The most radical solution was put forward in 2002.[267] It was suggested that the application of the Statutory Cohabitation Act should be limited to couples living in affective sexual relationships,[268] and at the same time, to extend the legal protection to unregistered couples that have lived together for two years or had a common child.[269] In Spain, the problem of same-sex couples was resolved in 2005, when federal law opened marriage to same-sex couples.[270] The relationships of non-married opposite-sex couples are still regulated on the level of the Autonomous Communities. In France, however, the reform of 2006 went no further than minor improvements.

---

[264]   This way the French *PACS* has been typified by Martin and Théry. MARTIN, C., THÉRY, I., 'The PACS and Marriage and Cohabitation in France' (2001), p. 151.
[265]   By Law *On Opening up Marriage for the Same Sex Persons* of 13 February 2003. Came into force on 1 July 2003.
[266]   The Proposal of 18 May 2000 aspired to extend the protection of statutory cohabitees, particularly in the field of succession. Chamber, 1999/2000, 0661/001.
[267]   By the Proposal of 12 November 2002. Chamber, 2002/2003, 2135/001. Reintroduced by the Proposal of 15 July 2003. Chamber, 2003, 0110/001.
[268]   Explanatory Note to the Proposal of 15 July 2003. Chamber, 2003, 0110/001, p. 8 and 12.
[269]   Explanatory Note to the Proposal of 15 July 2003. Chamber, 2003, 0110/001, p. 23.
[270]   Law 13/2005, of 1 July 2005.

15.6.6. RELEVANCE TO THE CONVERGENCE DEBATE

The history of the French PACS, the Belgian statutory cohabitation and the Spanish regional laws is rather illustrative for some of the arguments put forward in the convergence debate. There is a close geographical, religious and legislative proximity between these countries, and the patterns of elaboration of cohabitation legalisation were remarkably similar. In France and Belgium the initial drafts sponsored by the political left were rather far-reaching, and at this stage, both countries seemed to follow the example of the registered partnership legislation 'Nordic style'. However, in both cases the initial drafts were drastically curtailed as they were dragged through political compromises. As a result, very similar laws were adopted in both countries. Up to this point, this history seems to reinforce the argument that there is a strong correlation between law and culture. Further developments, however, do not. On the contrary, they seem to reinforce the argument of the relative autonomy of law, and provide a strong example of the political dimension of the development of family law. The legislative activism of the progressive Socialist-Liberal-Green Government in Belgium and of Socialist Federal Government in Spain finally led these countries to a dramatic breakthrough. In 2003, Belgium became the second European country to open marriage to same-sex couples. In 2005, Spain followed. All the cultural and religious constraints they have in common with neighbouring France remained in place; it was merely a difference in the balance of political power that enabled the Belgian and Spanish governments to promulgate its avant-garde legislation. In France, in contrast, introduction of same-sex marriage still seems out of question.[271]

15.7. MODEL 6: REGISTERED PARTNERSHIP LEGISLATION: PROVIDING A STATUS ALMOST EQUAL TO THAT OF SPOUSES. THE 'SEPARATE BUT EQUAL' APPROACH

15.7.1. INTRODUCTION

Before the time was ripe for same-sex marriage, the institution of registered partnership was the most forthright and uncompromised response to same-sex partners' demands for equality and recognition. In some countries, the introduction of registered partnership actually paved the way for the opening-up of marriage to same-sex couples. The idea of registered partnership 'Nordic style' as discussed in this

---

[271] For a recent state of affairs see: FULCHIRON, H., 'Mariage et partenariats homosexuels en droit international privé français' (2006) p. 411.

section, is based on the 'separate but equal' doctrine that involves giving same-sex couples nearly all the rights of married couples without granting their union the name of marriage.[272] Such a marriage-like institution is capable of giving same-sex partners adequate legal protection, while almost eliminating discrimination and greatly contributing to the social acceptance of same-sex couples.[273]

The model of registered partnership 'Nordic style' that later spread across Europe was first introduced in Denmark in 1989. In the following decade, the same model was adopted by the whole of the Nordic region:[274] in Norway in 1993, in Sweden in 1995, in Iceland in 1996 and in Finland in 2001.[275] In 1998, The Netherlands introduced the same model with one significant difference; registered partnership was opened to both same- and different-sex couples. In 2001, Germany and in 2006 Slovenia generally followed the Nordic example as well, but initially, due to political and constitutional constraints, went significantly less far in the equalisation of registered partnership with marriage. In 2004 a pattern of registered partnership similar to the Nordic model was introduced in the UK,[276] in 2005 in Switzerland,[277] and in 2006 in the Czech Republic.[278] Because of the origin and the influence of the Nordic model, the legislation of the countries of the Nordic region will first be discussed. Thereafter, some attention will be paid to two countries where this model has been significantly altered: The Netherlands and Germany.

---

[272] AGELL, A., 'Family Forms and Legal Policies. A Comparative View from a Swedish Observer' (1999) p. 208.

[273] Maarit Jänterä-Jareborg notices that 'It is generally believed that the legislation has contributed to a greater tolerance and acceptance of homosexual relationships in the Scandinavian societies'. JÄNTERÄ-JAREBORG, M., 'Parenthood for Same-Sex Couples: Challenges of Private International Law from a Scandinavian Perspective' (2006), *forthcoming*.

[274] Thus came into being what was thereafter dubbed the 'Scandinavian' or 'Nordic' model of registered partnership. See: JÄNTERÄ-JAREBORG, M., SÖRGJERD, C., 'The Experiences with Registered Partnership in Scandinavia' (2004), p. 577 ff.

[275] An English translation of the Nordic Acts on registered partnership could be found in: *Legal Recognition of Same-Sex Couples in Europe*, BOELE-WOELKI K., FUCHS, A. (eds.) (2003) *Legal Recognition of Same-Sex Couples in Europe*.

[276] By the *Civil Partnership* Act of 17 November 2004, entered into force on 5th December 2005. For more on this Act, see: CURRY-SUMNER, I., *All's Well that Ends Registered?* (2005), p. 203-255.

[277] By the Act *On Registered Partnership* of 18 June, entering into force on 1 January 2007. For information in English see: CURRY-SUMNER, I., *All's Well that Ends Registered?* (2005), p. 159-202.

[278] By the *Registered Partnership* Act of 15 March 2006. The act came into effect 3 months after its publication in the official Collection of Law. See: Press release of the Czech Gay & Lesbian League of 15 March 2006.

15.7.2. PARTNERSHIP NORDIC STYLE: RESEMBLING MARRIAGE IN ALL BUT NAME

All Nordic countries have chosen a very similar solution for homosexual couples who wish to institutionalise their relationships. In addition to the obvious choice to start at the beginning, the Nordic region is interesting for the purposes of this study for a number of other reasons. Their cultural, historical, religious[279] and geographical proximity, along with a standing tradition of legislative cooperation makes the Nordic experience especially interesting for an analysis of convergence processes. The Nordic countries also provide a 'parade example'[280] of the use of family law as a means to successful social engineering.[281] It is widely acknowledged that the registered partnership Acts have greatly contributed to the social recognition of same-sex relationships and paved the way to their equalisation with different-sex unions.[282] Sweden, Denmark and Iceland also provide a good illustration of a flexible and benevolent attitude to homosexual couples on the part of the churches.

Denmark pioneers

As early as in 1973, the Danish Marriage Committee had already considered opening marriage to same-sex couples.[283] The problems faced by same-sex partners were identified and considered. However, all Committee members except for one agreed that allowing same-sex couples to marry would constitute 'too fundamental a break with traditional marriage',[284] and would find no understanding abroad.[285] In 1984, upon the initiative of the Social Democrats and supported by the other left-wing parties and the Social Liberals, the Parliament set up a Commission for Elucidation of the Situation of Homosexuals in the Society.[286] The aim of the Commission was to recommend measures that would remove the existing discrimination against homosexuals.[287] However, before the Commission had finalised its report, the MPs for the Social Democratic Party, the Socialist People's Party and the Social Liberal Party

---

[279] All Nordic countries have an established Church, which is of the Lutheran (Protestant) denomination. In all countries, except for Sweden, these churches enjoy the status of State Church. The Swedish Church was separated from the State in 2000. JÄNTERÄ-JAREBORG, M., SÖRGJERD, C., 'The Experiences with Registered Partnership in Scandinavia' (2004), p. 585.

[280] Ibid, p. 596.

[281] Ibid.

[282] Ibid.

[283] First Report of the Marriage Committee (1973), p. 19. Cited in: BRADLEY, D., *Family Law and Political Culture* (1996), p. 152.

[284] Ibid.

[285] Ibid.

[286] NIELSEN, L., 'Family Rights and the "Registered Partnership" in Denmark' (1990), p. 297.

[287] BROBERG, M., 'The Registered Partnership for Same-Sex Couples in Denmark' (1996), p. 150.

proposed a Registered Partnership Bill, in January 1988.[288] This forced the Commission to hurry, and it produced a report the same year in which a close majority of the members (six) advised against the introduction of registered partnership, while the minority (five) supported the idea.[289] The rejection of registered partnership by the majority of the Commission was by no means a token of its disapproval of homosexuality.[290] The majority simply saw no need for the institutionalisation of same-sex relationships because it believed that a mere prohibition of discrimination on the ground of sexual orientation would be sufficient to effectively eliminate inequality.[291] It was also held that there was no need for specific legal protection of the weaker party in a same-sex relationship, because a gender-related role division is not typical for same-sex couples.[292] The Commission's minority, which advised in favour of registered partnership, stressed the symbolic value of the institution and argued that formal equality is an unavoidable first step in the process of achieving real equality.[293] In November 1988 the Bill was presented to the Parliament. The Bill provoked a fierce public debate, with some Christian groups leading the opposition.[294] After an extensive and passionate discussion, which was generally held along the lines delineated in the Commission's report,[295] the MPs were given free vote and the Bill was adopted on 26 May 1989.[296]

The approach of the new law is rather simple. It states that unless the Act explicitly provides otherwise, a registered partnership carries the same legal consequences as a marriage.[297] All provisions of Danish law referring to spouses and a marriage are declared to be applicable to registered partners.[298] Entering into a partnership is open only to persons of the same-sex who are not a party to a marriage or another registered partnership, and who are not related to each other within certain degrees.[299] In the

---

[288] LUND-ANDERSEN, I., 'The Danish Registered Partnership Act' (2003), p. 14.

[289] *Homoseksuelles vilkar*. Report of the Conditions of Homosexuals No 1127, 1988.

[290] BRADLEY, D., *Family Law and Political Culture* (1996), p. 153.

[291] BROBERG, M., 'The Registered Partnership for Same-Sex Couples in Denmark' (1996), p. 150.

[292] Ibid.

[293] Ibid.

[294] A small Christian Party employed homophobic arguments and threatened to initiate a referendum for abrogation of the law. However, it lost the elections and was not able to fulfil its threats. Also, the habitual argument that registered partnership would undermine the institution of marriage and radicalise the country in the eyes of the other countries, was put forward in Denmark against registered partnership. FORDER, C., 'National Report on Denmark' (1999), p. 8.

[295] BROBERG, M., 'The Registered Partnership for Same-Sex Couples in Denmark' (1996), p. 151.

[296] The Act *On Registration of Partnership* of 7 June 1989 came into force on 1 October 1989. LUND-ANDERSEN, I., 'The Danish Registered Partnership Act' (2003), p. 15.

[297] Section 3 of the Act. See: NIELSEN, L., 'Family Rights and the "Registered Partnership" in Denmark' (1990), p. 299.

[298] Section 3 (3) of the Act. See: BROBERG, M., 'The Registered Partnership for Same-Sex Couples in Denmark' (1996), p. 152.

[299] NIELSEN, L., 'Family Rights and the "Registered Partnership" in Denmark' (1990), p. 300.

same way as marriage, a registered partnership creates a genuine civil status. The mode of dissolution of registered partnership is the same as for that of a marriage.[300] The only exceptions to the treatment of registered partners as a married couple were initially related to the presumption of parentage, adoption, joint parental responsibility,[301] medically assisted procreation[302] and Church wedding. Unlike marriage, which can be solemnised through a civil or religious ceremony, a registered partnership could be concluded only through civil registration.[303]

The problem of a Church blessing for registered partners became the subject of a lengthy debate within the State (Lutheran) Church of Denmark. In 1997, a Committee appointed by the bishops reported that: 'the Church must take into account that [...] marriage is no longer the dominant framework for cohabitation and formation of a family; that registered partnership is not a threat to marriage'.[304] Further, the Committee took a personalistic stance, stating that 'church blessings are for people and not for institutions'.[305] Most importantly, the Committee concluded that 'registered partnership and homosexual relationships are not in conflict with Christian teaching and morality [...]. The biblical statements on homosexuality [are] of a culturally conditioned, historical nature, [and] the Bible should be read in the light of the culture and history of our own time'.[306] The conclusion of the Committee was that there were no in principle objections against introducing a ritual for the blessing of registered partnerships.[307] However, not the whole of the clergy was prepared to go that far. Finally a compromise solution was reached: a blessing was to be made possible, but individual priests were left free to decide whether they wished to perform such a ceremony.[308] In addition, the Committee outlined three possible forms of blessing, one of which is very close to the Church blessing, held after a civil registration of marriage.[309]

---

[300] Section 5 of the Act. See: BROBERG, M., 'The Registered Partnership for Same-Sex Couples in Denmark' (1996), p. 153.

[301] NIELSEN, L., 'Family Rights and the "Registered Partnership" in Denmark' (1990), p. 303.

[302] After heated debate, the Act *On Artificial Insemination* adopted in 1997 excluded single women and women living in same-sex relationships from the scope of its beneficiaries. (Section 3). All attempts to abolish this provision have so far failed. LUND-ANDERSEN, I., 'The Danish Registered Partnership Act' (2003), p. 19-21.

[303] NIELSEN, L., 'Family Rights and the "Registered Partnership" in Denmark' (1990), p. 300.

[304] Registered Partnership, Cohabitation and Blessing' report of 21 May 1997. Summarised by: LUND-ANDERSEN, I., 'The Danish Registered Partnership Act' (2003), p. 22.

[305] Ibid.

[306] Ibid.

[307] Ibid.

[308] LUND-ANDERSEN, I., 'Cohabitation and Registered Partnership in Scandinavia: The Legal Position of Homosexuals' (1998), p. 400.

[309] Ibid.

The problem of adoption was partially resolved in 1999,[310] when a registered partner was allowed to adopt and acquire joint parental responsibility over his or her step-children.[311] The full equalisation of registered partners with spouses in respect to adoption is now under discussion.[312]

Thus, under Danish law almost all differences between registered partnership and marriage either have been or are about to be abolished. Therefore it is argued that it is quite inexpedient to continue to maintain two different sets of rules on marriage and registered partnership with almost identical content.[313] It is suggested that at the moment the only the question is when the time will be ripe to abolish registered partnership, and to replace it with same-sex marriage.[314]

Norway follows

In Norway, a very similar law was adopted in 1993.[315] Unlike Denmark, Norway at that time already had legislation that provided cohabiting persons with a minimal scope of protection.[316] However, this legislation was not considered sufficient to meet the needs of same-sex couples, who are deprived of the capacity to marry. After a 1990 Private Members' proposal to introduce registered partnership found support with the Labour, Left Socialist and Progress Parties, the Government introduced its own Bill in 1992.[317] The objectives of the new legislation were delineated in the Proposition by the Ministry of Children and Family Affairs.[318] This Proposition stressed that the emotional and economical reasons same-sex couples have, when it comes to the desire for legal regulation of their relationship, are the same as the reasons held by spouses.[319] The Bill was broadly discussed and most of the comments regarding it were neutral or benevolent.[320] Unlike in Denmark, the Bill was rather badly received by Norway's religious circles. The majority of the bishops of the Norwegian State Church expressed their concern that the new law went too far and would therefore weaken the position of marriage in the society.[321] It was even suggested that the new law in fact introduced same-sex marriage, but 'for publicity reasons it is not being referred to by its correct

---

[310]   By Law of 2 June 1999.
[311]   SCHEPRE, J., 'Zehn Jahre registrierte Partnerschaft in Dänemark' (2000), p. 32-34.
[312]   LUND-ANDERSEN, I., 'The Danish Registered Partnership Act' (2003), p. 18-19.
[313]   Ibid, p. 23.
[314]   Ibid.
[315]   Act *On Registered Partnership for Homosexual Couples* of 30 April 1993 came into force on 1 August 1993.
[316]   By 1991 *Joint Household Act*, see above.
[317]   BRADLEY, D., *Family Law and Political Culture* (1996), p. 218-219.
[318]   Proposition for a Law *On Registered Partnerships, Ministry of Children and Family Affairs*, 1992-93.
[319]   LØDRUP, P., 'Registered Partnership in Norway' (1994), p. 388.
[320]   Ibid, p. 392.
[321]   LØDRUP, P., 'Registered Partnership in Norway' (1994), p. 392.

name'.[322] This view was not shared by the Faculty of Theology of the University of Oslo, which spoke up for the Bill.[323] The Bill was adopted by the Parliament with the only significant opposition being from the Christian People's Party.[324]

The content of the new law is almost identical to the Danish one. The law governing marriage is, with few exceptions, extended to registered partnership.[325] The exceptions regarding Church wedding, adoption,[326] joint parental responsibility,[327] and assisted reproduction[328] are the same as in Denmark. The only significant difference is that Norwegian law prescribes a ceremony for the registration of partnership that is rather different from the celebration of marriage.[329] So far, The Church of Norway continues to refuse registered partners a Church blessing.[330] Registered partners have been allowed to adopt a step-child since 2003.[331]

Sweden joins

In 1995, Sweden introduced registered partnership following the example of Denmark and Norway. However, it should not be forgotten that Sweden was the first European country to officially accept homosexual relationships, in 1973,[332] and granted homo- and heterosexual cohabitees equal rights as early as in 1987.[333] In 1978, the Government appointed the first Commission to investigate the situation of homosexuals. In its 1984 report,[334] the Commission rejected both the idea of same-sex

---

[322] Bishop of Bjørgvin. Proposition for a Law on Registered Partnerships, Ministry of Children and Family Affairs, 1992-93, p. 43. Cited in: BRADLEY, D., *Family Law and Political Culture* (1996), p. 219.

[323] LØDRUP, P., 'Registered Partnership in Norway' (1994), p. 392.

[324] Being a governing party, this not-socialist Christian party made repealing the Act *On Registered Partnership* one of the priorities of its policy. JÄNTERÄ-JAREBORG, M., SÖRGJERD, C., 'The Experiences with Registered Partnership in Scandinavia' (2004), p. 587.

[325] Section 3 of the Act.

[326] The right to adopt a child, advocated by homosexual organisations, was rejected on the ground that there was no sufficient research on the effects on children of growing up in same-sex households. FORDER, C., 'National Report on Norway' (1999), p. 15.

[327] BRADLEY, D., *Family Law and Political Culture* (1996), p. 221.

[328] FORDER, C., 'National Report on Norway' (1999), p. 16.

[329] Unlike the registration of marriage, partnership registrations had to be performed by the notary public. Ibid, p. 9.

[330] JÄNTERÄ-JAREBORG, M., SÖRGJERD, C., 'The Experiences with Registered Partnership in Scandinavia' (2004), p. 583.

[331] Ibid.

[332] In 1973 the Swedish Parliament endorsed homosexual relationships as 'perfectly acceptable'. BRADLEY, D., *Family Law and Political Culture* (1996), p. 101.

[333] Also stressed by David Bradley. Ibid.

[334] Commission Report *Homosexuals and Society*, SOU, 1984: 63.

marriage[335] and also that of registered partnership.[336] The arguments against registered partnership were, again, not an expression of a negative attitude towards homosexuality. It was merely out of concern for the well-being of same-sex couples that the Commission considered registered partnership to be an inappropriate solution. It was thought that public registration would unnecessarily expose homosexual couples and strengthen the existing prejudice against them instead of promoting social acceptance.[337] The Commission was nonetheless committed to grant same-sex cohabitees appropriate legal protection. This was partially realised through the 1987 Homosexual Cohabitation Act which extended the Cohabitees (Joint Homes) Act to same-sex partners. As discussed above,[338] this legislation applied to unmarried partners *ipso facto* of their cohabitation. However, placing same-sex couples, which were not allowed to marry, on the same footing as opposite-sex cohabitees, who chose not to marry, appeared to be unsatisfactory. In 1991, after partnership legislation was promulgated in Denmark, the Swedish Government set up a second Commission to investigate the possibility of adopting similar legislation in Sweden.[339] In 1993 the Commission proposed an Act on Registered Partnership, modelled after the Danish one.[340] The ideological foundation of the proposal was the acknowledgment of the equal value of homosexual love[341] and the commitment to the ideology of neutrality. The Commission's report explicitly stated that its members:

> 'do not feel it incumbent on society to have viewpoints concerning the way in which people choose to live together, society's task ought instead to be that of enabling people to live in accordance with their own preferences and personalities, not preventing them from doing so. So long this does not cause harm to others.'[342]

---

[335]   The Commission's Report avowed that opening up marriage for same-sex couples would turn the institution of marriage in something different that it currently was, because 'it is hardly possible to speak of marriage between two individuals of the same-sex, without defining marriage in a different way from that practised today'. Commission Report *Homosexuals and Society,* SOU, 1984: 63, p. 274.

[336]   Ibid, p. 30.

[337]   Ibid, p. 274-278.

[338]   See Section 15.4. 2.

[339]   SAVOLAINEN, M., 'The Finish and the Swedish Partnership Acts – Similarities and Divergences' (2003), p. 25.

[340]   Commission Report *Partnership,* SOU, 1993:98. A strong minority of the Commission opposed the proposal and suggested introducing a 'domestic partnership' for both same- and opposite-sex cohabitees as well as persons sharing households without having sexual or affective relationships. SAVOLAINEN, M., 'The Finish and the Swedish Partnership Acts – Similarities and Divergences' (2003), p. 25.

[341]   SALDEEN, Å., 'Sweden: Family Counselling, the Tortuous Liability of Parents and Homosexual Partnership' (1994-95), p. 519-520.

[342]   Commission Report *Partnership,* SOU, 1993:98, p, 30. Cited in: BRADLEY, D., *Family Law and Political Culture* (1996), p. 103.

The Commission also scrutinised theological and traditionalist arguments against homosexuality and conceded that it 'can find no justification for those allegations'.[343] The Commission concluded that adoption should not be allowed for homosexual couples 'as long as there was no consensus among researchers about the consequences for a child growing up in a homosexual family'.[344]

While the Commission produced its report, the political climate in Sweden had become more conservative. The centre-right coalition Government, formed in 1991, was deeply split upon the partnership proposal, and turned out to be unable to produce any governmental bill.[345] However, in Parliament the Liberals joined the Social Democrats and the Left Party in their support for the proposal.[346] Thus, the Parliamentary Legal Committee took the initiative from the hands of the Government, and drafted a Bill upon the Commission's proposal.[347] On 7 June 1994 the Parliament adopted the Registered Partnership (Family Law) Act.[348]

The Act as initially adopted was almost identical to the Danish one. The exceptions to the equalisation of partnership with marriage stipulated in the Act were also originally the same: presumption of parentage, joint parental responsibility, adoption and medically assisted procreation.[349] As in Denmark, a Church blessing of the registered partnership is possible in Sweden, provided a Church minister is prepared to perform it.[350]

In 1999, the Swedish Government appointed a Commission[351] charged with investigating children in homosexual families and to advise the Government on the possibility of allowing same-sex couples to adopt children and acquire joint parental responsibility.[352] In its report, submitted in 2001,[353] the Commission advised in favour

---

[343] Ibid.

[344] Commission Report *Partnership*, SOU, 1993:98, p, 30. Cited in: SALDEEN, Å., 'The Children's Ombudsman, Adoption by Homosexual Partners and Assisted Reproduction'(2004), p. 441.

[345] BRADLEY, D., *Family Law and Political Culture* (1996), p. 104.

[346] Ibid.

[347] SAVOLAINEN, M., 'The Finish and the Swedish Partnership Acts – Similarities and Divergences' (2003), p. 25.

[348] The Act came into force on 1 January 1995.

[349] SALDEEN, Å., 'Sweden: Family Counselling, the Tortious Liability of Parents and Homosexual Partnership' (1994-95), p. 520.

[350] JÄNTERÄ-JAREBORG, M., SÖRGJERD, C., 'The Experiences with Registered Partnership in Scandinavia' (2004), p. 586.

[351] Commission on Children in Homosexual Families, Directive 1999:5.

[352] SALDEEN, Å., 'The Children's Ombudsman, Adoption by Homosexual Partners and Assisted Reproduction'(2004), p. 441.

[353] Commission Report *Children in Homosexual Families*, SOU, 2001:10. Cited in: SALDEEN, Å., 'The Children's Ombudsman, Adoption by Homosexual Partners and Assisted Reproduction'(2004), p. 442 and 444

of allowing same-sex adoption, joint parental responsibility and medically assisted reproduction for women living in lesbian relationships.[354] The Commission's report was met with serious opposition from such authoritive Swedish organisations as the National Board of Health and Welfare, the Office of the Children's Ombudsman and the Faculty of Law of Uppsala University. They maintained that the Report subordinated the principle of the best interests of the child to the needs and perspectives of adults.[355] The Government, however, did not agree with this critique and based its Bill upon the Commission's report. The Bill stated that:

'As with other legislation, partnership and adoption are basically issues of values, primarily the view on the formation of the family and parenthood, which at the same time should be determined objectively and rationally.'[356]

It was further maintained that the legal recognition of the child-parent relationships would 'give an important signal to children who live with homosexual adults'.[357] After heavy discussion, the Bill was passed by Parliament in May 2002.[358] Accordingly, same-sex couples were equated with spouses in respect to adoption and joint parental responsibility.[359] Since 1 July 2005 lesbian couples have been granted the right to undergo assisted fertilization treatment at public hospitals. Upon the birth of the child, both women automatically acquire the right of legal parentage.[360]

Thus, the legal position of registered same-sex couples according to Swedish law became identical to that of spouses in all but the presumption of parentage and access to medically assisted procreation. The total equalisation is looked forward to in the very near future, as in 2005 the Swedish Government has appointed a Committee on Marriage and Partnership charged with investigating the possibility to open up marriage to same-sex couples.[361]

---

[354]   Ibid.
[355]   SALDEEN, Å., 'The Children's Ombudsman, Adoption by Homosexual Partners and Assisted Reproduction'(2004), p. 442.
[356]   Governmental Bill *Partnership and Adoption*, 2001/02:123 summarised in: ibid..
[357]   Ibid.
[358]   The new Law came into force on 1 February 2003.
[359]   Since 1 February 2003 registered partners can jointly adopt a foreign child. JÄNTERÄ-JAREBORG, M., SÖRGJERD, C., 'The Experiences with Registered Partnership in Scandinavia' (2004), p. 581.
[360]   JÄNTERÄ-JAREBORG, M., 'Parenthood for Same-Sex Couples: Challenges of Private International Law from a Scandinavian Perspective' (2006), p. 81.
[361]   Ibid.

Iceland adopts the same model

Iceland followed the example of its neighbours in 1996. The pre-history of the new legislation was also similar to that of the other countries. In 1992 the Icelandic Parliament appointed a Commission to examine the legal situation of homosexuals.[362] In its 1994 Report, the Commission proposed to introduce registered partnership legislation modelled on that of the other Nordic countries.[363] Accordingly, the Act on Confirmed Cohabitation[364] was enacted in February 1996.[365] The content of the Act is almost identical to the Danish and the Swedish ones. The exceptions regarding the presumption of parentage,[366] the Church wedding,[367] joint adoption[368] and medically assisted procreation[369] are also the same. A notable difference is the equalisation of confirmed partners with spouses and heterosexual cohabitants, in respect to the possibility of acquiring joint parental responsibility.[370]

Adoption of a step-child was made possible in 2000.[371] In 2003 the Government appointed a Commission to explore the issue of homosexual adoption and assisted reproduction.[372]

Finland: the same model with notable restrictions

Finland was the last Nordic country to introduce registered partnership. The content of the 2001 Finish Act[373] generally follows the patterns of the other Nordic countries; however, there are more exceptions to the equalisation of registered partners with spouses. As with Norway, rules governing marriage ceremony are not applicable to registered partnerships. But while the ceremony in Norway is different only in name and in fact is very similar to a civil registration of marriage, the differences in Finland are more significant. Although the authority competent to register a partnership is the same as for civil marriages, the registration procedure may not include a solemn

---

[362] FORDER, C., 'National Report on Iceland' (1999), p. 6.
[363] Ibid.
[364] Literal translation of Icelandic *staðfest samvist*. FRIDRIKSDÓTTIR, H., WAALDIJK, K., 'Iceland' (2005), p. 122.
[365] Act of 12 June 1996, came into force on 27 June 1996.
[366] FORDER, C., 'National Report on Iceland' (1999), p. 12.
[367] BJÖRGVINSSON, D., 'General Principles and Recent Developments in Icelandic Family Law' (1995), p. 226.
[368] Ibid.
[369] Ibid.
[370] FORDER, C., 'National Report on Iceland' (1999), p. 12.
[371] JÄNTERÄ-JAREBORG, M., SÖRGJERD, C., 'The Experiences with Registered Partnership in Scandinavia' (2004), p. 584.
[372] FRIDRIKSDÓTTIR, H., WAALDIJK, K., 'Iceland' (2005), p. 122.
[373] Act of 9 November 2001 entered into force on 1 March 2002.

ceremony comparable to wedding.[374] The legislation relating to spousal names is not applicable to registered partners.[375] On the other hand, from the outset the Finish law, like the Icelandic law, has allowed registered partners to obtain joint parental responsibility.[376] Joint adoption is not allowed, but each partner is allowed to adopt a child separately.[377] The draft law on medically assisted procreation seeks to give a single woman, irrespective of her sexual orientation, access to medically assisted procreation on terms equal to those applicable to a single heterosexual woman.[378]

15.7.3. THE NETHERLANDS: SAME- AND DIFFERENT-SEX COUPLES UNDER THE SAME ROOF

A particularity of The Netherlands was that the public and legislative debate regarding registered partnership[379] was for the most part parallel to the discussion surrounding same-sex marriage.[380] The discussion regarding the institutionalisation of same-sex relationships[381] actually started in 1990, when the Dutch Supreme Court acknowledged that there was not sufficient justification for certain legal effects to be attributed to marriage, but not to the durable cohabitation of two persons of the same sex.[382] Two weeks after this decision, a governmental Commission (which became known as the *Kortmann Commission I*)[383] was asked to deliver an advisory opinion regarding the legal recognition of various family forms. In 1991, the Commission proposed two forms of registration, a 'light' and a 'strong' one. The 'light' form of registration by the local administration was intended for those cohabiting couples who wished their

---

[374]   SAVOLAINEN, M., 'The Finish and the Swedish Partnership Acts – Similarities and Divergences' (2003), p. 30.

[375]   JÄNTERÄ-JAREBORG, M., SÖRGJERD, C., 'The Experiences with Registered Partnership in Scandinavia' (2004), p. 584.

[376]   SAVOLAINEN, M., 'The Finish and the Swedish Partnership Acts – Similarities and Divergences' (2003), p. 35.

[377]   Ibid, p. 36.

[378]   Ibid, p. 37.

[379]   For more on the introduction of registered partnership in the Netherlands see: WAALDIJK, C., 'Partnerschapsregistratie en huwelijk: toenemende rechtsgelijkheid voor geslachtsgelijke partners en hun kinderen' (2000), p. 126-182. For information in English, see: the contributions by Caroline FORDER to the International Survey of family law for 1994 (p. 361-362); 1995 (p. 360-361); 1997 (p. 259-264) and CURRY-SUMNER, I., *All's Well that Ends Registered?* (2005), p. 117-158. For information in German, see: BOELE-WOELKI, K., SCHRAMA, W., 'Die Rechtsstellung von Menschen mit homosexueller Veranlagung im niederländischen Recht' (2000), p. 51-113.

[380]   For a synopsis of the discussion in The Netherlands with regard to same-sex marriage, Section 13.3.2.

[381]   For more details see: WAALDIJK, C., 'Partnerschapsregistratie en huwelijk: toenemende rechts-gelijkheid voor geslachtsgelijke partners en hun kinderen' (2000), p. 128-130.

[382]   HR 19 October 1990, *NJ* (1992), p. 129.

[383]   Named after its chairman, professor C. Kortmann.

relationship to have no more than a limited public law effect.[384] The 'strong' form of registration by the Civil Registrar involved more marriage-like effects and was designated for all couples, who wanted far-reaching legal protections, including close relatives who maintained a common household.

As in the Nordic region, political circumstances played a crucial role in the adoption of partnership law. In August 1994, a Government without the participation of a Christian-Democrat party was formed. It was the first coalition Government of the Social-Democrats and the two Liberal parties which went into history under the name of 'Purple I'. In 1994 this Government produced a *Registration of Cohabitation Bill*,[385] which provided for the 'strong' form of registration alone. According to the Bill, only those couples, who were unable to marry (same-sex partners and close relatives), were allowed to benefit from such registration. Although the Bill tended to place registered partners on the same footing as spouses, there were 'numerous smaller and bigger differences between them'.[386] In 1995, a change of strategy was announced in a governmental Memorandum on *Life Forms in Family Law*.[387] Accordingly, the Bill was amended in such a way that persons related within certain degrees of kinship were excluded from its scope,[388] while opposite-sex couples were incorporated into it.[389] Most of the legal differences between marriage and partnership were removed.[390] It is important to note that the reasons for including opposite-sex couples into the scope of partnership legislation in The Netherlands were completely different from those that would later play an important role in France and Belgium.[391] In the Dutch context it had nothing to do with a desire to camouflage the legal recognition of same-sex cohabitation with a 'gender neutral' institution. On the contrary, inclusion of heterosexual couples was deemed to avoid the stigmatisation of same-sex couples in a separate 'second class marriage',[392] and to accentuate the equal value of same-sex

---

[384]   Both forms of registration were designated as optional: the 'light' form of registration should also only apply to those who had opted for it. Thus, the proposal did not solve the problem of de-facto cohabitants, not willing to undergo registration.

[385]   Second Chamber, 1993/1994, 23 761, No. 3, p.2.

[386]   WAALDIJK, C., 'Partnerschapsregistratie en huwelijk: toenemende rechtsgelijkheid voor geslachts- gelijke partners en hun kinderen' (2000), p. 128.

[387]   Second Chamber, 1994/1995, 22 700, No. 5.

[388]   It was concluded that there was little need for such registration. Second Chamber, 1994/1995, 22 700, No. 5. It was also feared that such registration could be abused, for instance in order to place one of the children in a more privileged position with regard to succession. BOER, J., de, *Personen- en familierecht* (2002), No. 556.

[389]   Second Chamber, 1994/1995, 23 761, No. 5.

[390]   WAALDIJK, C., 'Partnerschapsregistratie en huwelijk: toenemende rechtsgelijkheid voor geslachts- gelijke partners en hun kinderen' (2000), p. 129.

[391]   See Sections 15.6.1. and 15.6.2.

[392]   See FORDER, C., 'National Report on the Netherlands' (1999), p. 8; SCHRAMA, W., 'Registered Partnership in the Netherlands' (1999), p. 322.

relationships.[393] At the same time, the Government wished to provide heterosexual couples that were not willing to marry with an alternative form of institutionalisation of their relationships.[394] In spite of severe criticism, the availability of partnership registration for heterosexual couples has been upheld.[395]

The 1998 *Registered Partnership Act*[396] resembled the Nordic laws in everything except the inclusion of opposite-sex couples. The same technique[397] was used to achieve an equality between partnership and marriage in family law; most of the provisions of the law of marriage were simply declared to be applicable to registered partners.[398] In contrast, a different and more obscure technique was employed in public law.[399] All in all, registered partners were effectively placed on an equal footing with spouses. Registered partnership also created a new, genuine, civil status alongside marriage.[400]

The main differences between registered partnership and marriage were initially in the fields of legal parentage, parental responsibility and partnership dissolution. The difference with respect to paternity is the same as in the Nordic countries. However, this difference is much more questionable in The Netherlands, where the institution of registered partnership is also open to opposite-sex couples. The presumption of paternity on the part of a man, who is married to the mother of the child, is not extended to registered partners.[401] An opposite-sex partner of the mother of a child can acquire legal parentage via recognition of the child. A same-sex partner of the mother of a child is not allowed to recognise the child.[402] However, since the

---

[393] Second Chamber, 1994/1995, No 23 761 No. 7, p. 10. See also: BOER, J., de, *Personen- en familierecht* (2002), No. 556.

[394] Second Chamber, 1994/1995, No 23 761 No. 7, p. 10.

[395] For an overview of critique, see: SCHRAMA, W., 'Registered Partnership in the Netherlands' (1999), p. 322-323.

[396] Law of 5 July 1997, came into force on 1 January 1998.

[397] SCHRAMA, W., 'Registered Partnership in the Netherlands' (1999), note 18 at p. 313.

[398] For a detailed comparison of the position of the spouses and the registered partners in the field of private law, see: WAALDIJK, C., 'Partnerschapsregistratie en huwelijk: toenemende rechtsgelijkheid voor geslachtsgelijke partners en hun kinderen' (2000), p. 132-159.

[399] Instead of one general reference that all provisions related to spouses are applicable to the registered partners, as used by the Nordic legislatures, the Dutch legislature chose to list in the *Registered Partnership Adjustment Act* (17 December 1997) hundreds of specific laws, that had to be amended. Kees Waaldijk rightly assesses this operation as creating 'impenetrable chaos' in Dutch legislation. (WAALDIJK, C., 'Partnerschapsregistratie en huwelijk: toenemende rechtsgelijkheid voor geslachtsgelijke partners en hun kinderen' (2000), p. 159-162.) Some laws were simply forgotten and had to be adjusted later. Ibid.161.

[400] Second Chamber, 1996/1997, 23 761, No. 11, p. 11.

[401] Contrary to the advice of the *Kortmann Commission I*, which recommended extending the presumption of legal parentage to opposite-sex partnerships.

[402] Because a male partner of a child's mother can recognise this child, even when he is not the child's biological parent, there were suggestions that a lesbian partner or spouse of the mother of a child should acquire the same right. (For instance: LOENEN, T., 'Echte of onechte ouders' (1995), p. 95). However, the prevailing view still considers such an obvious partition from biological truth as a step

introduction of same-sex adoption in 2001,[403] a same-sex partner of the mother of a child is allowed to adopt her partner's child. The presumption of paternity was not extended to registered partnerships at the time of its introduction, because registered partnership is available for both same-sex and opposite-sex couples. Therefore it was considered objectionable to create a complicated dual regime in order to make the presumption of paternity solely applicable to opposite-sex couples.[404] Since marriage is now also available to same-sex couples, this argument is no longer valid. With marriage, a dual regime is created anyway, as the presumption of paternity is limited to opposite-sex spouses alone. This development seemed to allow the expectation that the presumption of paternity would soon at least be extended to opposite-sex registered partners. However, the legislature again appeared to be reluctant to amend parentage law in order to solve a problem regarding legal parentage. Instead, a different route, via the rules on adoption, was chosen to bring registered partnership closer to marriage in regard to the acquisition of legal parentage. The Secretary of State presented this choice in light of preserving differences between marriage and registered partnership.[405]

The rules regarding the parental responsibility of the partners were initially quite different from that of spouses.[406] However, in 2002[407] registered partnership was made all but equal to marriage with respect to parental responsibility.[408]

---

too far. It is claimed that making such a possibility available would turn the presumption of marital parentage into a complete fiction, because two women could never create a child. Therefore, the legislature has chosen to institutionalise the social parentage between a child, born within a homosexual relationship with the aid of artificial procreation techniques, and the same-sex partner of its parent, not by amending filiation law, but via adoption law. VLIET, F., 'Door de zij-ingang naar niemandsland?' (2000), 41-42.

[403] By Act of 21 December 2000 *On the Opening Up Adoption for the Persons of the Same Sex*, came into force on 1 April 2001.

[404] The partners were, however, allowed to apply for joint parental responsibility. Law of 30 October 1997, entered into force on 1 January 1998.

[405] First Chamber, 2001, 2, p. 42- 43.

[406] The spouses automatically acquire joint parental responsibility and, since 1998 as a rule retain it, even after divorce. (*The Joint Custody and Guardianship* Act 30 October 1997, came into force on 1 March 1998.). These rules were initially not extended to registered partners. See: LENTERS, H., 'Naam en gezag' (2000), p. 40-42.

[407] Act *On Automatic Joint Parental Responsibility of The Registered Partners* of 4 October 2001, came into force on 1 January 2002.

[408] Opposite-sex spouses and registered partners (the latter, provided they both are legal parents) acquire joint parental responsibility automatically (art. 1:253aa Dutch Civil Code). Same-sex spouses and registered partners can never jointly become legal parents of a child under the Dutch law, other than by way of adoption. A same-sex spouse or registered partner, who is not the parent of a child born 'within' a marriage or a partnership, automatically acquires joint parental responsibility together with the parent of the legal child charged with the sole parental responsibility, provided the child does not have any legal filiation links with another parent (art. 1:253sa). If a child has legal filiation links with another parent, the partner or spouse of the child's legal parent charged with sole parental responsibility, can acquired joint parental responsibility by means of a court order. (art. 1:253t).

The dissolution of a registered partnership is considerably easier than the dissolution of a marriage. This has much to do with the legislature's desire to provide for an alternative, more lenient institution for opposite-sex couples who have ideological objections to marriage. Unilateral dissolution of a partnership requires a judicial procedure that closely resembles the dissolution of marriage.[409] However, the dissolution of a partnership upon mutual consent is possible via an administrative procedure that is not available for the dissolution of a marriage. The possibility of a rapid administrative dissolution of registered partnership in combination with the possibility of converting a partnership into a marriage and vice versa[410] produced a rather dramatic side effect. Many married couples saw the chance to obtain a so-called 'lightning divorce'[411] through the conversion of their marriage into a partnership, and the subsequent dissolution of this partnership through an administrative procedure. A Private Bill aimed to both abolish the 'lighting divorce' and complete the uniformisation of the dissolution of marriages and registered partnerships has been rejected by the First Chamber on 20 June 2006.[412]

Since 2001, registered partnership exists in the Netherlands alongside same-sex marriage. While recommending that marriage should be opened to people of the same sex, the *Kortmann Commission II* suggested that once same-sex marriage was introduced, registered partnership should be abolished. However, this advice was not followed. Still, since the introduction of same-sex marriage, the future of registered partnership in the Netherlands has become uncertain.[413] Some scholars advocate the continuation of this institution, arguing that even after the introduction of same-sex marriage, registered partnership satisfies the need of those couples, mainly opposite-sex, who object to marriage.[414] Others maintain that with the introduction of same-sex

---

[409] VLAARDINGERBROEK, P., BLANKMAN, K. (et. al.), *Het hedendaagse personen- en familierecht* (2002), p. 114.

[410] This possibility was introduced by Act of 21 December 2000 *On the Opening Up Marriage for the Persons of the Same Sex.* This law came into force on 1 April 2001.

[411] 'Flitsscheiding'.

[412] Bill of the Act *On Dissolution of Marriage without Judicial Intervention and on Embodying in Legal Form the Continuation of Parentage after Divorce,* First Chamber, 2005-2006, 29 676, A-C. A governmental Bill seeking to rule out the 'lightning divorce' is currently under discussion in the Second Chamber. Bill of the Act *On Promoting Continuation of Parentage after Divorce and Responsible Divorce,* Second Chamber, 2005-2006, 30 145, No. 1-4.

[413] See BOELE-WOELKI, K., 'Registered Partnership and Same-Sex Marriage in the Netherlands' (2003), p. 51-52.

[414] See, for instance: DE BOER, J., *Personen- en familierecht* (2002), No. 556. The statistics of partnership registration became extremely confusing after 2001, when a 'lightning divorce' became possible, as the great majority of opposite-sex partnerships are likely to emerge as the result of the conversion of a marriage into a registered partnership by way of the first step in obtaining a 'lightning divorce'. (See: BOELE-WOELKI, K., 'Registered Partnership and Same-Sex Marriage in the Netherlands' (2003), p. 49-51.) However, even before the 'lightning divorce' almost ½ of all registered partnerships were between opposite-sex partners.

marriage, registered partnership has fulfilled its task and must be abolished for the sake of the coherence of the legal system.[415] In 2006, the Government commissioned specific research on the future of registered partnership.

15.7.4. GERMANY: PROTECTION OF SAME-SEX COUPLES VERSUS THE SPECIAL PROTECTION OF MARRIAGE

In 2001, registered partnership was introduced in Germany. Germany generally followed the Nordic example; however, the peculiarities of the German political and constitutional context lead to a number of important differences. Before registered partnership was introduced, both statutory and case law had already developed some remedies for the minimal[416] protection of so-called 'marriage-like relationships'.[417] However, the Federal Constitutional Court placed same-sex couples outside the notion of 'marriage-like relationships'.[418] The Court acknowledged the existing discrimination of same-sex couples, but ruled that such discrimination imposes no obligation on the legislature to pass specific regulation with regard to same-sex couples.[419] The position of same-sex couples was thus extremely unfavourable; on the one hand they were barred from marriage, on the other hand they were deprived of the protection given to marriage-like relationships. In order to improve this situation, a number of bills were proposed between 1995 and 1999.[420] However, the Government, dominated by

---

[415]   See, for example: SCHRAMA, W., *De niet-huwelijkse samenleving in het Nederlandse en Duitse recht*, (2004), p. 566.

[416]   Compared to other Western European countries, the protection provided in Germany was rather minimal. RUBELLIN-DEVICHI, J., 'La permanence des spécifiés nationales de droit de la famille' (1997), p. 73.

[417]   The legal definition of a marriage-like relationship, *Eheähnliche Gemeinschaft,* was given by the Federal Constitutional Court in 1992 (BVerfG 17 November 1992, *NJW* (1993), p. 643). For a recent analysis of the legal position of cohabitees, see: MARTINY, D., 'Rechtsprobleme der nichtehelichen Lebensgemeinschaft während ihres Bestehens nach deutschem Recht' (2005), p. 79-99. For the protection of patrimonial rights see: SCHRAMA, W., *De niet-huwelijkse samenleving in het Nederlandse en Duitse recht* (2004). For a synopsis on the protection in other areas, OSTNER, I., 'Cohabitation in Germany – Rules, Reality and Public Discourses' (2001), p. 96-99.

[418]   BVerfG 17 November 1992, *NJW* (1993), p. 643.

[419]   Ibid.

[420]   The Alliance 90/the Greens proposed a Bill in 1995, *On Introduction of the Right to Conclude a Marriage for Persons of the Same Sex;* and in 1997, a *Law Governing the Relationships of Non-Married Life-Cohabitation* (Bill of 14 March 1997). The latter Bill proposed a regulation for both same-and different-sex couples on the ground of de-facto cohabitation, or as an alternative, a registration by a notary public. In 1998, the Social Democratic Party proposed a Bill *On the Enforcement of the Duty of Equal Treatment Ordained by Art. 3 of the Constitution* (Bill of 9 March 1998). This Bill sought to resolve the problems of same-sex couples by extrapolating onto them almost all the rules of marriage law. In 1999, the Liberals – Free Democratic Party came with a proposal *On Regulation of the Legal Status of Registered Life Partnerships* (Bill of 23 June 1999). In 1999, the German Lesbian and Gay

the Christian-Democrats, was reluctant to promote them. In 1998, the *Bundesrat* summoned the Government to provide legislation for same-sex couples.[421] In 1999, a registered partnership for same-sex couples, dubbed a 'Hamburg marriage', was made possible in the Federal State of Hamburg.[422] It appeared that political changes were necessary before legislation on same-sex relationships could get a real chance. In the autumn of 1998, the so called 'red-green' coalition Government of the Social Democrats and the Green Party came into office. The introduction of a Registered Life Partnership for same-sex couples was part of their coalition agreement.[423] A year later the governmental Bill was elaborated.[424]

However, many obstacles still had to be overcome. The main particularity of Germany as compared with the above discussed countries was that any reform of marriage or cohabitation law had to be judged against Article 6 Paragraph 1 of the German Constitution, which grants special State protection to the institution of marriage.[425] The interpretation of the duty of the State to protect marriage as an institution (*Institutsgarantie*) prevailing at the time the partnership legislation was drafted, was that the legislature had 'a duty to privilege marriage in comparison to other legal institutions'.[426] From this so-called 'requirement of distance', the legal literature derived an implied prohibition to creating a quasi-marriage for same-sex couples (*Abbildungsverbot*) and a prohibition from placing unmarried persons in an equal or better position than that of spouses (*Konkurrenzschutzgebot*).[427] Therefore, the German legislature appeared to be caught between two irreconcilable tasks: to abolish the discrimination of same-sex couples, and at the same time to preserve the privileged position of marriage. Thus, the Nordic method of the general extrapolation of the bulk of marriage law to registered partnerships seemed out of the question.[428] In anticipation of an eventual constitutionality test by the Federal Constitutional Court, the

---

Federation presented a proposal *On Introduction of Life Partnership for Same Sex Couples* (Proposal of 1 July 1999). For a concise overview of these proposals, see: VERSCHRAEGEN, B., 'Gleichgeschlechtliche Beziehungen im Spiegel des Rechts' (2000), p. 68-71.

[421]   Referred to by SCHWAB, D., in: 'Eingetragene Lebenspartnerschaft – Ein Überblick' (2001), at p. 386.

[422]   By Law of 14 April 1999. Such registration, however, created for partners neither rights nor obligations. SCHLÜTER, W., HECKES, J., STOMMES, S., 'Die gesetzliche Regelung von außerehelichen Partnerschaften gleichen und verschiedenen Geschlechts im Ausland und die deutschen Reformvorhaben' (2000), p. 6.

[423]   STRICK, K., 'Gleichgeschlechtliche Partnerschaft – Vom Straftatbestand zum Status?'(2000), p. 82.

[424]   Bill of Law *On Termination of the Discrimination Against Same Sex-Communities; Life Partnerships.*

[425]   SCHLÜTER, W., HECKES, J., STOMMES, S., 'Die gesetzliche Regelung von außerehelichen Partnerschaften gleichen und verschiedenen Geschlechts im Ausland und die deutschen Reformvorhaben' (2000), p. 18.

[426]   THORN, K., 'The German Law on Same-Sex Partnerships' (2003), p. 85.

[427]   SCHLÜTER, W., HECKES, J., STOMMES, S., 'Die gesetzliche Regelung von außerehelichen Partnerschaften gleichen und verschiedenen Geschlechts im Ausland und die deutschen Reformvorhaben' (2000), p. 9-10.

[428]   Ibid, p. 10-12.

provisions on registered partnership were in many aspects drafted to be deliberately different from the provisions governing marriage.[429] In order to avoid any resemblance to marriage, even different terminology was invented.[430] The cautiously prepared Bill successfully passed the *Bundestag*, but was met with heavy resistance from the conservative majority of the *Bundesrat*. Due to the peculiarity of the German parliamentary system, not all federal laws need to be approved by the *Bundesrat*.[431] The Government did not wish to compromise the Bill, and in order to facilitate its passage decided to place those provisions that needed the approval of the *Bundesrat* (mainly provisions in the field of public law) in a Supplementary Act.[432] The result of this was quite unfortunate as the Supplementary Act failed to be passed by the *Bundesrat*.[433] Consequently, the new Life Partnership Act (LPartG)[434] was enacted with 'numerous loopholes which in some cases even counteract the legal effect aimed at by its provisions'.[435] The only reassuring event was that the new law successfully withstood the constitutionality test. On 17 January 2002, the Federal Constitutional Court interpreted the constitutional protection of marriage in such a way that, 'the constitution allows positive discrimination in favour of marriage but does not oblige the legislator to do so'.[436] The Court even called for the removal of the artificial difference between the new partnership and marriage.[437] This encouraged the Government to pursue the approximation between the new registered partnership and marriage. In June 2004, the MPs of the governing parties introduced a new Bill into the *Bundestag*. In December 2004, the Act on Amending the Life Partnerships removed most of the inconsequence of the initial Act.[438]

The initial Act strongly deviated from the liberal Nordic model. Some of the differences were removed in 2004 but a few others remain. The partnership legislation is still not

---

[429] SCHWAB, D., 'Eingetragene Lebenspartnerschaft- Ein Überblick' (2001), p. 386. Dieter Schwab noticed that no clear principle could be found behind this differentiation, so the selection was based on a certain degree of arbitrariness. Ibid.

[430] It is noticed that the newly created legal terms often had the sole purpose of distinguishing partnership from marriage, as there is no difference in regard to content. (THORN, K., 'The German Law on Same-Sex Partnerships' (2003), p. 87). For comparison of the partnership terminology with that of the marriage law, see: SCHWAB, D., *Familienrecht* (2003), No. 872.

[431] THORN, K., 'The German Law on Same-Sex Partnerships' (2003), p. 86.

[432] *Lebenspartnerschaftsgesetzergänzungsgesetz*, See: SIEGFRIED, D., WAALDIJK, K., 'Germany', 108.

[433] See THORN, K., 'The German Law on Same-Sex Partnerships' (2003), p. 86.

[434] Law *On Termination of the Discrimination Against Same Sex-Communities; Life Partnerships* of 16 February 2001. Came into force on 1 August 2001.

[435] THORN, K., 'The German Law on Same-Sex Partnerships' (2003), p. 86.

[436] BVerfG 17 July 2002, *NJW* (2002), p. 2543-2548. See: THORN, K., 'The German Law on Same-Sex Partnerships' (2003), p. 86-87.

[437] Ibid.

[438] Law of 15 December 2004, passed the *Bundesrat* on the 26 November 2004. Came into force on 1 January 2005.

incorporated in the BGB but was from the outset enacted as a separate law.[439]
Registered partnership is open to two persons of the same sex, not related within the
prohibited degrees and neither married nor engaged in another registered
partnership.[440] The monogamy principle is clearly visible in this provision. However,
the effect of entering into a registered partnership on the civil status of the partners
was not entirely clear in the initial act, as being engaged in a registered partnership
was not an impediment to concluding a marriage.[441] To a certain extent, the German
law resembled the French and the Belgian solution of not making a PACS or statutory
cohabitation an obstacle to entering into marriage. However, in France and Belgium
the entering of one of the partners into marriage leads to the automatic dissolution
of the PACS or statutory cohabitation, respectively. In Germany, this was not the case.
It was held to be highly improbable that the German legislature deliberately allowed
a person to be a party to both a partnership and a marriage at the same time.[442] The
explanation to this legal paradox was thought to be an 'astonishing oversight'[443] on
the part of the legislature. It was also suggested that it was possible to extend the
impediment of bigamy to registered partners by way of analogy.[444] Fortunately, the
problem was resolved by the amendment of 2004,[445] which made a standing registered
partnership an impediment to the registration of a marriage.

The original Bill provided that the partnership had to be registered by the authority
responsible for the registration of marriage, namely a Civil Registrar. However, when
the Bill was split, this provision was placed in the Supplementary Act that perished
in the *Bundesrat*. As a result, the competence to determine the authority charged with
partnership registration came into the hands of the *Länder*. Consequently, there is no
uniformity on the matter; in most of the *Länder* the competent authority is a civil
registrar or local administration, while in more conservative Bavaria, it is a notary
public.[446]

---

[439]   BOELE-WOELKI, K., 'Het Duitse *LPartG* verdient geen schoonheidsprijs' (2002), p. 1.
[440]   Para 1 LPartG. See also: SCHWAB, D., 'Eingetragene Lebenspartnerschaft – Ein Überblick' (2001),
        p. 389-390.
[441]   Initially registered partnership has not been added to the list of marriage impediments laid down
        in paragraph 1306 BGB.
[442]   DETHLOFF, N., 'The Registered Partnership Act of 2001' (2002), p. 173.
[443]   Ibid.
[444]   Ibid.
[445]   See now Paragraph 1306 BGB as amended by the Act *Amending the Life Partnerships Law* of 15
        November 2004.
[446]   THORN, K., 'The German Law on Same-Sex Partnerships' (2003), p. 88.

The personal legal effects of partnership registration are very close to those of marriage.[447] The partners are under an obligation of mutual care and support, and of 'the common arrangement of life' (*gemeinsame Lebensgestaltung*).[448] The succession rights of the partners also resemble the corresponding rights of spouses. The regulation of matrimonial property and maintenance,[449] on the contrary, was initially rather different. The reason for this was the expectation that there would be a less gender-related role division within same-sex couples, as they could not procreate together.[450] Unlike marriage, initially no legal property regime was created for registered partners. The partners could, however, create a property regime by a declaration made at the time of the registration of the partnership. They could basically choose between joint property, the separation of property, and the so-called 'community of equalisation' (*Ausgleichsgemeinschaft*). The latter was identical to the legal matrimonial property regime of deferred community of property (*Zugewinngemeinschaft*), but was, in accordance with the nature of the initial legislation, only different in name.[451] This situation was changed by the 2004 Act, when the legal regime of matrimonial property was overtly extended to registered partners. By the same amendment, registered partners were granted almost the same maintenance rights as spouses. The 2004 Act also allowed step-parent adoption by a partner of the parent of a child.[452] From the outset, the termination of a partnership has been rather similar to that of a marriage. The only exception was an unexplainable difference[453] in the length of the dissolution of a partnership, which was longer than the dissolution of a marriage. This difference was removed by the 2004 Amendment Act.[454] Therefore today, with the exception to adopt children commonly, the legal status of marriage and same-sex partnership is basically the same in the field of civil law. The 2004 Act only partially equalised partnership with marriage in respect to social security, pensions and taxes. Particularly in tax law same-sex partnerships are still not recognized by federal law.

---

[447] Nonetheless different terminology has been used. While spouses are under an obligation to maintain a conjugal community of life, partners are obliged to 'a common arrangement of life'. DETHLOFF, N., 'The Registered Partnership Act of 2001' (2002), p. 174.

[448] Art. 2 *LPartG*. See also: SCHWAB, D., 'Eingetragene Lebenspartnerschaft- Ein Überblick' (2001), p. 190-391.

[449] For dissimilarities in respect of maintenance see: ROLLER, S., 'Zweifelsfragen im Unterhaltsrecht der Lebenspartnerschaft'(2003), p. 1424-1427.

[450] ROLLER, S., 'Zweifelsfragen im Unterhaltsrecht der Lebenspartnerschaft'(2003), p. 1425.

[451] THORN, K., 'The German Law on Same-Sex Partnerships' (2003), p. 93.

[452] Para. 9 VIII LpartG.

[453] KAISER, D., '"Entpartnerung" – Aufhebung der eingetragenen Lebenspartnerschaft gleichgeschlecht-licher Partner' (2002), p. 873.

[454] Initially, in cases of marriage the required period of separation could start before the application for divorce, while in cases of partnership dissolution this term only started to run from the moment of application for dissolution. THORN, K., 'The German Law on Same-Sex Partnerships' (2003), p. 93. This difference is removed by the 2004 Act.

In the end one can conclude that after the constraints, imposed on the drafters of the initial partnership legislation by the restrictive interpretation of Article 6 Paragraph 1 of the Constitution, were removed, the German legislation came to very much resemble the Nordic model.

15.7.5. SPREAD OF THE PARTNERSHIP 'NORDIC' STYLE IN EUROPE: A RECENT SUCCESS STORY OF LEGAL TRANSPLANTATION

As the preceding sketch shows, the Danish partnership model has rapidly spread all over Europe. In the last two years, the countries with registered partnership 'Nordic style' have been joined by the UK, Switzerland, and the Czech Republic. The subsequent developments of these partnership laws have also gone along very much the same lines.[455] The initial discrimination against partners with regard to legal parentage, parental responsibility and adoption[456] is now tending to diminish everywhere. The countries, that initially went less far than the Danish model due to political constraints (for instance Finland and Germany), have almost completely upgraded their regulations in line with this model.

It has been suggested that the remarkable influence of the Danish model has to do with the fact that such transplantation of legislation was easier in the context of cohabitation than in other areas of family law, as to a certain extent the national legislatures were all starting 'with a blank canvas'.[457] However, the popularity of the Danish model may also be explained by virtue of its simplicity and straightforward untangling of the problems of same-sex couples. The simple extension of the rights and obligations of spouses to registered partners, except for when the law provides otherwise, proved to be the most convincing technique. The retention of the name and the standing of marriage for opposite-sex couples alone makes this model politically easier to attain than same-sex marriage. These features make the Danish model the obvious solution for countries that wish to accommodate the needs of same-sex couples in a non-discriminatory way, and, on the one hand, are not bound by too many political

---

[455]   This statement requires, however, a qualification even with regard to the Nordic countries. Maarit Jänterä-Jareborg observes that after adopting a similar model each Nordic country 'has acted on its own', which led to diverging solutions to remaining problems. Thus, acknowledging the basic similarity of the approach taken in the Nordic region, she questions 'whether it is accurate to refer to a "homogeneous" Scandinavian model on registered partnership'. JÄNTERÄ-JAREBORG, M., 'Parenthood for Same-Sex Couples: Challenges of Private International Law from a Scandinavian Perspective' (2006), p. 78.

[456]   Delineated by Caroline Forder, see: FORDER, C., 'Civil Law Aspects of Emerging Forms of Registered Partnerships' (1999), p. 9.

[457]   PROBERT, R., BARLOW, A., 'Cohabitants and the law: recent European reforms' (2000), p. 76.

constraints to create a marriage-like institution for same-sex couples,[458] but, on the other hand, are not (yet) prepared to open marriage as such to same-sex couples. It is interesting that all deviations from the Danish model have been made due to political constraints imposed on the national drafters, and all such deviations have led to legal constructs that missed the efficiency of the Danish original. The technique of equalising registered partnership with marriage except for when provided otherwise, is, perhaps, the most illustrative example. The Netherlands (with regard to public law), Germany, Switzerland and the UK all deviated from the Danish model at this crucial point and chose to specifically list all the situations in which partners were equalised with spouses.[459] Such deviation led to 'a complex array of legislative amendments often running into hundreds of pages',[460] incurring the considerable danger of oversights and mistakes.[461]

For these reasons, one may expect that the Danish model will remain popular in Europe. However, neither its popularity nor its technical perfection was able to persuade countries to follow it if the balance of political power did not favour such a step. The history of the French PACS and Belgian statutory cohabitation can illustrate this. It can be expected that this will remain the case in the future.

15.8. MODEL 7: THE ULTIMATE SOLUTION: SAME-SEX MARRIAGE

Opening marriage to same-sex couples is the ultimate form of recognition and equalisation for these couples. At the time the manuscript of this book went to the publisher, three countries, The Netherlands, Belgium and Spain, had pioneered the law on same-sex marriage. The wide-spread expectation among Nordic scholars is that it is only a matter of time before Nordic countries like Sweden and Denmark will follow.[462] At this point, the issue of the institutionalisation of homosexual cohabitation is commingled with the evolution of the concept of marriage. Therefore, the history of the introduction of same-sex marriage has already been discussed above, in the sections dealing with the law on marriage.[463]

---

[458] Like France and Belgium at the time of drafting legislation on PACS and statutory cohabitation.
[459] CURRY-SUMNER, I., *All's Well that Ends Registered?* (2005), p. 198.
[460] Ibid. The UK *Civil Partnership* Act counts 400 pages and the Dutch *Registered Partnership Amendment* Act contains amendments to more than 300 legal acts. Ibid, note 196.
[461] Ibid, p. 199.
[462] JÄNTERÄ-JAREBORG, M., SÖRGJERD, C., 'The Experiences with Registered Partnership in Scandinavia' (2004), p. 578; LUND-ANDERSEN, I., 'The Danish Registered Partnership Act' (2003), p. 23.
[463] See Chapter 13, Section 13.3.2. (The Netherlands) and Section 13.4.3. (Belgium and Spain).

15.9. HARMONISING EFFECT OF EUROPEAN HUMAN RIGHTS LAW

The picture with regard to the legal regulation of extramarital cohabitation in Europe is not complete without at least a brief account of the development of European Human Rights Law. It must be noted that European law as developed by the case law of the European Court of Human Rights in Strasbourg, EU legislation and case law of the European Court of Justice, has had a very modest influence on the legislation of the national states in the field of non-marital cohabitation. Instead of promoting the acknowledgment of new types of relationships on the national level, both courts have proved reluctant to go any further than the 'common standard' already achieved within the European states. Consequently, European law grants hardly any protection to intimate relationships that fall outside traditional marriage, defined as a heterosexual union based on 'the traditional "nuclear" family – that of a married heterosexual union'.[464] This cautious approach has to do with the ideologically controversial character of the issue of non-marital, and especially, same-sex relationships.

15.9.1. PROTECTION OF UNMARRIED COHABITATION UNDER THE EUROPEAN CONVENTION ON HUMAN RIGHTS

The European Court of Human Rights in Strasbourg (ECHR) has repeatedly stressed[465] that protection of family life, under Article 8 of the Convention, 'is not solely confined to marriage-based relationships and may encompass other de facto "family" ties where the parties are living together outside of marriage'.[466] However, while the Strasbourg Court acknowledges the existence of family life in a case involving a married couple simply by virtue of the existence of a formal marriage, in a case involving non-marital heterosexual cohabitation, the family life is only presumed to exist.[467] For such cases the ECHR has developed a so-called 'reality test'.[468] Accordingly, the Court has stated that 'when deciding whether a [non-marital] relationship can be said to amount to "family life", a number of factors may be relevant, including whether the couple live

---

[464] McGLYNN, C., 'Challenging the European Harmonisation of Family Law: Perspectives on "the Family" (2003), p. 219.

[465] The most important cases are *Marckx v. Belgium*, ECHR (1979), para 31; *Johnston v. Ireland*, ECHR (1986), para 56; *Keegan v. Ireland*, (1994), para 44; *Kroon v. the Netherlands* (1994), para 30; *X, Y. and Z. v. the United Kingdom*, ECHR, (1997), para 36.

[466] *Keegan v. Ireland*, ECHR (1994), para 44.

[467] SCHRAMA, W., *De niet-huwelijkse samenleving in het Nederlandse en Duitse recht* (2004), note 454 at p. 101.

[468] See: STALFORD, H., 'Concept of Family under EU law – Lessons from the ECHR' (2002), p. 413.

together, the length of their relationship and whether they have demonstrated their commitment to each other by having children together or by any other means'.[469]

The position of same-sex couples is considerably worse than that of their heterosexual counterparts. The ECHR has explicitly denied same-sex partners the protection of family life under Article 8 of the Convention.[470] All they can rely on is the protection of private life under the same Article 8, which can be invoked in situations involving the most notorious restraints on homosexual relationships.[471] Helen Toner reads in the most recent case law[472] an indication of a generally positive shift in the ECHR's attitude towards same-sex cohabitants.[473] However, it is equally possible to interpret the same decisions as a continuation of the deliberate avoidance of the recognition of the 'family life' of same-sex couples. This particularly applies to *Karner v. Austria*, in which the ECHR ruled that denying a surviving partner the right to succeed his deceased partner in tenancy because of the homosexual character of their relationship constitutes a violation of the right for respect for the home (Article 8, in conjunction with Article 14). This decision was again based on the protection of private, rather than family life. The Court considered deliberation on the existence of family life between the applicant and the deceased tenant, who lived as a couple for five years,[474] to be 'unnecessary'.[475] Thus, it seems that the Court deliberately missed the chance to part with the old limited approach,[476] based on denying same-sex couples the protection of family life and only granting them incidental protection of private life.

There is one more important difference in the way the ECHR treats same- and opposite-sex couples. In its deliberations on the protection of unmarried opposite-sex couples, the Strasbourg Court tends to compare the position of such couples with that of spouses – although this comparison does not favour the unmarried couples very

---

[469] *X, Y. and Z. v. the United Kingdom*, ECHR, (1997), para 38.

[470] *X. and Y. v. the United Kingdom*. ECHR, (1983), p. 220; *Kerkhoven and Hinke v. The Netherlands*. ECHR, (1992), para 1.

[471] For an overview, see: VAN GRUNDERBEECK, D., *Beginselen van personen- en familierecht. Een mensenrechtelijke benadering* (2003), p. 288 ff. For an overview in English, see: WINTEMUTE, R., 'Strasburg to the Rescue? Same-Sex Partners and Parents Under the European Convention' (2001), p. 713-729; and more recently, TONER, H., *Partnership Rights, Free Movement, and EU Law* (2004), p. 79-122; and forthcoming: MCGLYNN, C., *European Family Values: Families, Law and Policy in the European Union* (2006).

[472] *Salguiero da Silva Mouta v Portugal*. ECHR (2001); *Fretté v. France*. ECHR (2002) and *Karner v. Austria*, ECHR (2003). *L. and V. v. Austria*. ECHR (2003), not mentioned by Toner, should, in my view, be included in this list.

[473] Toner claims that 'in the light of these decisions the ECtHR's insistence that same-sex couple cannot enjoy "family life" together cannot be sustainable much longer'. TONER, H., *Partnership Rights, Free Movement, and EU Law* (2004), p. 84.

[474] *Karner v. Austria*. ECHR (2003), para 11-12.

[475] Ibid, para 33.

[476] Developed in 1981 in *Dudgeon,* and confirmed in 1983 in *X. and Y. v. the United Kingdom*.

much. The Court neither requires unmarried cohabitation to be placed on an equal footing with marriage,[477] nor considers the special protection of marriage to be a form of discrimination against unmarried couples.[478] The Strasbourg Court also acknowledges a broad margin of appreciation on the part of the Member States with regard to the passing or not passing of any specific legislation having to do with non-marital cohabitation.[479] Yet, when deciding cases relating to same-sex couples, the ECHR tends to compare them with unmarried heterosexual couples rather than spouses. In a number of judgments dealing with discrimination on the ground of sexual orientation,[480] the Court has come to the conclusion that providing a level of legal protection for homosexual couples that is different from the legal protection provided for unmarried heterosexual couples does not qualify as a form of prohibited discrimination under Article 14 ECHR, in conjunction with Article 8.[481] Lately, however, there have been some positive developments in this area. The ECHR has

---

[477] In *Johnston v. Ireland*, it was explicitly stated that '… the Court does not consider it is possible to derive from Article 8 an obligation on the part of Ireland to establish for unmarried couples a status analogous to that of married couples'. (*Johnston v. Ireland*. ECHR (1986), para 68). The same year the Commission stated in *Lindsay v. the United Kingdom* (EComHR (1986)) that marriage and non-marital cohabitation 'are not analogous situations. Though in some fields, the *de facto* relationship of cohabitees is now recognised, there still exist differences between married and unmarried couples, in particular, differences in legal status and legal effects. Marriage continues to be characterised by a corpus of rights and obligations which differentiate it markedly from the situation of a man and woman who cohabit'. (Ibid. para 181). 14 years later, in *Shackell v. the United Kingdom* (ECHR (2000)) the Court confirms this approach despite its acknowledgement that 'there may well now be an increased social acceptance of stable personal relationships outside the traditional notion of marriage'. This change of circumstance did not preclude the ECHR from concluding that 'marriage remains an institution which is widely accepted as conferring a particular status on those who enter it'.

[478] In *Marckx v. Belgium* the Court ruled that the law favouring the traditional family, based on marriage, 'aims at ensuring that family's full development and is thereby founded on objective and reasonable grounds relating to morals and public order'. (*Marckx v. Belgium*. ECHR (1979), para 40). This statement has been repeated in *Keegan v. Ireland*, and *McMichael v. the United Kingdom*. ECHR (1995).

[479] See *Saucero Gómez v. Spain*. ECHR (1999) and the analyses by SCHRAMA, W., *De niet-huwelijkse samenleving in het Nederlandse en Duitse recht* (2004), at p. 105-107.

[480] The first and most important decision was *Dudgeon v. United Kingdom*. ECHR (1981). Ytterberg reads in this judgment, and the judgments that came after it, a far reaching protection against discrimination on the ground of sexual orientation. (YTTERBERG, H., 'All Human Beings are Equal, But Some Are More Equal than Others – Equality and Dignity without Equality in Rights?' (2003), p. 1-2.) However, the prominent absence of sexual orientation amongst discrimination grounds listed in the Twelfth Additional Protocol to ECHR (2000, not yet in force) suggests a reluctance of the Council of Europe institutions to go further in this direction.

[481] In *Johnston v. Ireland*, the Court ruled that Articles 8 and 14 gave no reasons for establishing any special regime of protection for a particular category of unmarried couples, who were unable to marry (in this case a heterosexual couple, unable to marry due to the impossibility to dissolve a previous marriage). This statement applies mutatis mutandis to same-sex couples. (*Johnston v. Ireland*. ECHR (1986), para 68). The position of the Court has been confirmed in *S. v the United Kingdom*, ECHR, (1986) para 7; *C. and L.M. v. the United Kingdom*. ECHR (1989), para 2; and *B. v. the United Kingdom* ECHR (1990), para 2.

recently stated that 'differences based on sexual orientation require particularly serious reasons by way of justification',[482] and also that the States only enjoy a narrow margin of appreciation in such matters.[483]

The reasons for the reluctance of the European Court of Human Rights to take a more pro-active and innovative approach with regard to non-marital cohabitation are actually the same as those with regard to divorce law;[484] the Court does not feel enough political legitimacy to take a more active position, due to the absence of consensus in Europe with respect to the regulation of non-marital cohabitation.[485] The Court's own fairly recent reference to these reasons therefore deserves extensive citation:

> 'It is indisputable that there is no common ground on the question. Although most of the Contracting States do not expressly prohibit homosexuals from adopting where single persons may adopt, it is not possible to find in the legal and social orders of the Contracting States uniform principles on these social issues on which opinions within a democratic society may reasonably differ widely. The Court considers it quite natural that the national authorities, whose duty it is in a democratic society also to consider, within the limits of their jurisdiction, the interests of society as a whole, should enjoy a wide margin of appreciation when they are asked to make rulings on such matters. By reason of their direct and continuous contact with the vital forces of their countries, the national authorities are in principle better placed than an international court to evaluate local needs and conditions. Since the delicate issues raised in the case, therefore, touch on areas where there is little common ground amongst the member States of the Council of Europe and, generally speaking, the law appears to be in a transitional stage, a wide margin of appreciation must be left to the authorities of each State.'[486]

As a result, the level of protection of both opposite- and same-sex cohabitation provided by the ECHR case law barely goes further than the lowest common denominator of the national European legal systems.

---

[482]   *L. and V. v. Austria.* ECHR (2003), para 45.
[483]   *Karner v. Austria.* ECHR (2003), para 41.
[484]   See Chapter 14, Section 14.5.2.
[485]   MACDONALD, R. et al (eds.) *The European System for the Protection of Human Rights* (1993), p. 84 and 123; ARAI, Y., 'The Margin of Appreciation Doctrine in the Jurisprudence of Article 8 of the European Convention on Human Rights', (1998), p. 57; SCHRAMA, W., *De niet-huwelijkse samenleving in het Nederlandse en Duitse recht* (2004), p. 99-103
[486]   *Fretté v. France*, ECHR (2002), para 41.

15.9.2. PROTECTION OF UNMARRIED COHABITATION IN EU LAW

As to the European Union, there has always been a certain tension between progressive political statements made by some Community institutions with regard to unmarried couples and the restrictive approach taken in the EU binding instruments and the case law of the European Court of Justice. Two non-binding documents, the Recommendation of the Parliamentary Assembly of the European Council adopted in 1981, and especially the Resolution on the Equal Treatment of Homosexuals and Lesbians,[487] adopted by the European Parliament in 1994, provided a strong international impetus for the legal regulation of same-sex relationships.[488] As early as 1994, when only two European countries had introduced registered partnership in their domestic laws, the European Parliament called for the 'full rights and benefits of marriage [to] be made available to same-sex couples'. In 1997, the Parliament again went into action, this time with a Resolution against discrimination towards same-sex relationships. However, due to the weak position of the Parliament within the EU institutional framework, it was a long time before its activism witnessed a response from other Community institutions.

The European Court of Justice in Luxembourg (ECJ) has shown no reaction upon the Parliament's innovative political statements. In its case law,[489] the Court did not go one step further than the existing status quo within the Member States. In contrast with the ECHR, which has been more prepared to recognise heterosexual family relationships outside formal marriage, the ECJ developed a rather formalistic approach to family relationships. This approach was pithily summarised by Clare McGlynn as 'whereas marriage bequests the status of "family", divorce appears to take it away'.[490] Ever since the infamous *Reed* decision of 1968,[491] the notion of a 'spouse' has been interpreted in the context of the free movement of persons,[492] and includes only heterosexual relationships based on formal marriage.[493] As a result, the ECJ takes only

---

[487]   Resolution of 8 February 2004, *O.J.* C61/40.

[488]   See VERSCHRAEGEN, B., *Gleichgeschlechtliche "Ehen"* (1994), p. 32 ff.

[489]   For an overview of case law, see: VAN GRUNDERBEECK, D., *Beginselen van personen- en familierecht. Een mensenrechtelijke benadering* (2003), p. 296-313. For an overview in English, see: TONER, H., *Partnership Rights, Free Movement, and EU Law* (2004), p. 79-122; and forthcoming: MCGLYNN, C., *European Family Values: Families, Law and Policy in the European Union* (2006).

[490]   MCGLYNN, C., 'A Family Law for the European Union' (2000) at, p., 225.

[491]   *The Netherlands v. Reed.* ECJ (1986), 49.

[492]   Based on the Regulation 1612/68 of 15 October 1968, on the Freedom of Movement for Workers within the Community. *O.J.* (1968), p. 475. This Regulation was replaced in 2004 by the Directive 2004/38. See note 517 in this chapter.

[493]   In *Diatta v. Land Berlin* (ECR (1985)) the Court granted protection to a spouse after the actual separation of the parties because the marriage was not yet completely dissolved by divorce. This approach is confirmed in *Arauxo-Dumay v. Commission* (CFI (1993), para 28). Another confirmation

---

the existence of a formal marriage into consideration,[494] and not actual family life between the parties.[495] In 1998, in another standard case, *Grant v. South West Trains*, the ECJ ruled that denying pension rights to a same-sex partner, which according to the rules of the company were available to an opposite-sex partner with whom an employee 'had a "meaningful" relationship for at least two years',[496] did not violate the antidiscrimination provision of the Article 141 of the Equal Pay Directive. In explaining its reluctance, the Court referred to the fact that:

> 'in the present state of the law within the Community, stable relationships between two persons of the same sex are not regarded equivalent to marriage or stable relationships outside marriage between the persons of opposite sex'.[497]

However, one year after *Grant*, the Treaty of Amsterdam introduced a direct prohibition of discrimination on the ground of sexual orientation into primary Community Law.[498]

The tension between the innovative political statements of the European Parliament and the limited approach seen in the EC legal instruments and the ECJ case law persisted after the turn of millennium. In 2000, another Resolution of the European Parliament[499] called for the Member States to 'grant legal recognition of extramarital cohabitation, irrespective of gender', and to recognise 'registered partnerships of persons of the same sex and assign them the same rights and obligations as exist for registered partnerships between men and women'.[500] However, the Parliament again seemed to be ahead of its time. The most important EU human rights document – the European Charter of Fundamental Rights – goes significantly less far than the Parliament's call. Still, one of the most important improvements of the Charter is a clear and unambiguous prohibition of discrimination on the ground of sexual

---

of the same approach has been rightly derived from a more recent case, *Safet Eyüp v. Landesgeschaftsstelle des Arbeitsmarktsevice Vorarlberg.* ECJ (2000). See: TAMASI, L., RICCI, C., BARIATTI, S., 'Characterisation in Family Matters for Purposes of European Private International Law' (2006) forthcoming.

[494] With the exception of marriages of convenience.

[495] STALFORD, H., 'Concept of Family under EU law – Lessons from the ECHR' (2002), p. 413.

[496] *Grant v. South West Trains.* ECJ (1998), para 25.

[497] *Grant v. South West Trains.* ECJ (1998), para 35.

[498] Article 13 of the *Treaty of the European Communities*.

[499] European Parliament resolution *On Respect for Human Rights in the European* Union (1998-1999) (11350/1999 – C5-0265/1999 – 1999/2001(INI)).

[500] Ibid, p. 57. The next year this call was repeated in the European Parliament resolution *On the Situation as Regards Fundamental Rights in the European Union* (2000) (2000/2231(INI)), p, 84 and 85.

orientation.[501] Another important innovation is that Article 9 of the European Charter of Fundamental Rights and Article II-69 of the not-ratified European Constitution[502] disconnect the right to found a family from the right to marry. This was done to acknowledge the laws of those Member States that protect a family created outside marriage. Due to this mixture of innovativeness and caution, appreciation of the Charter on this point varied from careful optimism[503] to a fear that it would inspire 'sticking to the "rusty and trusty formulae of yesteryear" around which consensus already exists'.[504]

After the turn of the millennium, the approach taken by the Community Courts with regard to (same-sex) cohabitation generally remained as limited as their early case law. In 1999, in *D. v. the Council*,[505] the Court of First Instance (CFI) interpreted the notion of 'spouse' in the Staff Regulations to include only 'a relationship founded on civil marriage in the traditional sense of this term'.[506] A same-sex partnership, contracted under Swedish law, fell outside this notion. The justification for this restrictive approach was once again sought in 'the views prevailing within the Community as a whole',[507] which appeared to be characterised by 'the great diversity of laws [on recognition of same-sex relationships] and the absence of any general assimilation of marriage and other form of statutory union'[508] In 2001 the Court of Justice confirmed this decision.[509]

It is important to notice that the old restrictive approach, maintained by the CFI and ECJ, seems to be overruled by the latest Community legislation.[510] The Staff Regulations under discussion in *D. v. the Council* were amended in 2004; Community officials

---

[501]   Article 21 of the Charter. Its importance is highlighted by TONER, H., *Partnership Rights, Free Movement, and EU Law* (2004), p. 130-131.

[502]   *Treaty Establishing a Constitution for Europe.* O.J. C 310/01, 16 December 2004. On the history of the inclusion of the Charter in the Draft Constitution, see: DUTHEIL DE LA ROCHÈRE, J., 'The EU and the Individual: Fundamental Rights in the Draft Constitutional Treaty' (2004), p. 351-352.

[503]   TONER, H., *Partnership Rights, Free Movement, and EU Law* (2004), p. 144 ff.

[504]   WIELER, J., 'Editorial: Does the European Union Truly Need a Charter of Rights?' 6 *European Law Review* (2000), p. 95, cited in: MCGLYNN, C., 'Families and the European Union Charter of Fundamental Rights: progressive change or entrenching the status quo?'(2001) at p. 598. In the same sense, see also: MCGLYNN, C., 'Families and the European Union Charter of Fundamental Rights: progressive change or entrenching the status quo?'(2001), p. 582-598.

[505]   *D. v. the EU Council*, CFI (1999); for an analysis of this case, see: TONER, H., *Partnership Rights, Free Movement, and EU Law* (2004), p. 182-189.

[506]   *D. v. the Council*, CFI (1999); para 26. Cited in MCGLYNN, C., 'A Family Law for the European Union' (2000) at, p., 226.

[507]   *D. v. the Council.* ECJ (2001), para 49.

[508]   *D. v. the Council.* ECJ (2001), para 50.

[509]   *D. v. the Coincil.* ECJ (2001).

[510]   MEEUSEN J., PERTEGÁS, M., STRAETMANS, G., SWENNEN F., 'General report' (2006) forthcoming.

living in registered partnerships are now fully equated with spouses,[511] provided that the couple is in possession of an official legal document acknowledging their status, neither partner is in a marital relationship or in another non-marital relationship, the partners are not related to each other within the degrees that would exclude the possibility of marrying each other, and the partners have no legal access to marriage under their national law.[512] This amendment means, in the first place, that the legal effect of a partnership under this Regulation will be determined by the law of the State where the partnership was entered into. Thus, the decision in *D. v. the Council* would have been rather different under the amended Regulation, as the status of the partnership would have been determined according to Swedish law.[513] In the second place, by this amendment the Community legislature has introduced a kind of 'positive discrimination' in favour of those same-sex partners who did not have access to marriage under their national law.[514]

In 2000, the Community legislature passed a Directive prohibiting discrimination on the ground of sexual orientation, but only in the rather limited field of employment.[515] A significant step towards the recognition of unmarried couples under EU law is made in two recent directives, Directive 2003/86, on the Right to Family Reunification;[516] and Directive 2004/38, on the Rights of Citizens of the Union and their Family Members to Move and Reside Freely within the Territory of the Member States,[517] which were adopted by the Community legislature in 2003 and 2004, respectively. Directive 2003/86 explicitly leaves to the discretion of the Member States the decision of whether to extend the benefits of family reunification to unmarried cohabitants or registered partners.[518] The more far reaching proposal, made by Sweden during the discussion in the Council, to grant registered partners equal rights with spouses, was rejected by the majority of the delegations.[519] The free movement rights under the

---

[511]   The *Staff Regulations of Officials of the European Communities and the Conditions of Employment of Other Servants of the European Communities* (259/68), as amended by the Regulation of 22 March 2004 Nr. 723/2004. O.J. L 124, para 8.

[512]   Article 1(2)(c) of Annex VII to the *Staff Regulations*.

[513]   SWENNEN, F. 'Atypical Families in EU (Private International) Family Law' (2006), forthcoming..

[514]   The exact reasons for this have remained unrevealed. See critically: JESSURUN D'OLIVEIRA, H., 'Europese receptie van nieuwe familiepatronen: het opengestelde huwelijk' (2004), p. 170-171. Registered partners, who do have an access to marriage under national law, are granted a more limited protection under the amended Staff Regulations. See: TAMASI, L., RICCI, C., BARIATTI, S., 'Characterisation in Family Matters for Purposes of European Private International Law' (2006) forthcoming.

[515]   Directive 2000/78 EC, *O.J.*, 2000, L 303/16. For an extensive analysis of the impact of this directive see: WAALDIJK, K., BONINI-BARALDI, M., *Sexual orientation discrimination in the EU: national laws and the Employment Equality Directive* (2006).

[516]   Directive of 3 October 2003, 2003/86 EC, *O.J.* L 251/12.

[517]   Directive of 30 April 2004, 2004/38 EC, *O.J.* L 158/77.

[518]   Directive 2003/86, para 10.

[519]   Council Document 10857/02, p. 8. Cited by: TONER, H., *Partnership Rights, Free Movement, and EU Law* (2004) at p. 74.

Directive 2004/38 are granted to the spouse, and the 'partner, with whom the Union citizen has contracted a registered partnership, on the basis of the legislation of a Member State, if the legislation of the host Member State treats registered partnership as equivalent to marriage'.[520] This means that under this Directive the legal effects of the registered partnership are determined on the basis of the *law of the host Member State*. The proposal by the European Parliament that would have connected the effect of the partnership to the law of Member State where it was contracted, was rejected.[521] The reason for this rejection was that the Commission did not want to force a Member State that did not provide for registered partnership in its national law to recognise the effects of a registered partnership that has been contracted in another State.[522] The Directive also grants a weaker right to 'the partner with whom the Union citizen has a durable relationship'.[523] The adoption of uniform guidelines for the qualification of durable unregistered relationships, suggested by the European Parliament, was equally rejected by the Commission, in order to leave this issue to the competence of the host Member State.[524] Although such unregistered partners fall outside the scope of the free movement rights, the Directive obliges the Member State to facilitate their entry and residence 'according to its national law'.[525]

The discussions surrounding the drafts of both directives clearly revealed the difficulties involved in reaching a consensus with regard to the protection of unmarried cohabitees.[526] It can be concluded that, in spite of their obvious merits on the issue of non-marital relationships, the two instruments just discussed have no harmonising effect on the law of the Member States, as they deliberately refrain from imposing any autonomous EU standard.[527] It has been rightly noted that instead of developing such a standard, the EU legislature makes reference to national law in all controversial cases, 'such as the qualification of the register partner as "family member", equal treatment between registered partnership and marriage, or the assessment of stability of a de facto

---

[520]   Article 2 sub 2 (a) and (b) of the Directive 2004/38.

[521]   Amendment 15, Report, A5-0009/2003. Cited in: SWENNEN, F. 'Atypical Families in EU (Private International) Family Law'(2006), forthcoming.

[522]   Amended Proposal, COM (2003), 1999 final, p. 11. Cited in: SWENNEN, F. 'Atypical Families in EU (Private International) Family Law' (2006), forthcoming.

[523]   Article 3 sub 2 (b) of the Directive 2004/38.

[524]   *Travaux préparatoire* for the Directive 2004/38. Cited in: TAMASI, L., RICCI, C., BARIATTI, S., 'Characterisation in Family Matters for Purposes of European Private International Law'(2006), forthcoming.

[525]   Article 3 of the Directive 2004/38.

[526]   See TONER, H., *Partnership Rights, Free Movement, and EU Law* (2004), p. 60-78. The Commission has explained with regard to the Directive 2003/86 that: 'given the diversity in national legislation concerning those enjoying the right to family reunification, it does not seem possible at the moment to extend the obligation to allow entry and residence beyond the spouse and minor children'. Cited ibid at p. 72.

[527]   TAMASI, L., RICCI, C., BARIATTI, S., 'Characterisation in Family Matters for Purposes of European Private International Law'(2006), forthcoming.

relationship'.[528] The minimum level of protection thus guaranteed to registered and unregistered cohabiting couples by the EU law goes no further than the lowest common denominator, as the EU law does not impose any higher EU standard on Member States that have stayed behind with their legislation.[529] The only positive effect of the new instruments is that the EU no longer makes the protection of unmarried couples impossible under its law in cases like *D. v. the Council*, when the relevant national law does provide for such protection. On the whole, 'legislative and judicial caution seem to be fuelling each other'[530] when it comes to the recognition of non-marital cohabitation under Community law.

15.9.3. EUROPEAN HUMAN RIGHTS LAW HAS ALMOST NO HARMONISING EFFECT

The preceding sketch shows that European law has not and does not play an active part in either the promotion of the recognition of unmarried cohabitation, or in providing a harmonising effect on the national law of the European states. The decisions of both the ECHR and the ECJ seldom go any further than the lowest common denominator of protection of non-marital relationship already existing within Europe. It is therefore claimed that even when the European Human Rights law now hesitantly recognises family relationships between partners outside marriage, 'the "family" which [is] recognised is one which although does not demonstrate the formal bond of marriage, does exhibit the features of a traditional marriage'.[531] The level of protection provided by European law to different forms of stable extramarital relationships is rather uneven. As a rule, both the ECHR and the ECJ are much more inclined to grant protection to heterosexual marriage-like relationships than to same-sex cohabitation. The cautious approach adopted by all institutions developing European Human Rights law is hardly surprising, if one considers the problem of the democratic legitimisation of their decisions that European lawgivers have to face.[532] It seems quite clear that both the ECHR and the ECJ consider themselves to lack the political mandate to overrule compromises reached on the national levels with regard to such sensitive issues as the extension of marital protection to unmarried couples or the recognition of same-sex relationships.

---

[528]   Ibid..
[529]   See SWENNEN, F. 'Atypical Families in EU (Private International) Family Law' (2006), forthcoming. In a similar sense, see: TONER, H., *Partnership Rights, Free Movement, and EU Law* (2004), p. 73 ff.
[530]   TONER, H., *Partnership Rights, Free Movement, and EU Law* (2004), p. 265.
[531]   MCGLYNN, C., 'Challenging the European Harmonisation of Family Law: Perspectives on "the Family" (2003), p. 226.
[532]   See Chapter 12, Section 12.1.2.

15.10. CONVERGENCE OR DIVERGENCE OF COHABITATION LAWS?

The above presented overview shows that the legal policymakers in many European countries felt themselves compelled to respond in one way or another to the explosive growth of extramarital cohabitation in the past few decades. However, the diversity of their responses[533] is quite challenging to the convergence theory. This diversity is no superficial diversity of legal terms used by different national legislations for the same functional equivalent, but a real diversity in the level of protection of cohabitation, and the degree of its approximation to marriage.[534]

15.10.1. DIVERSITY OF NATIONAL REGULATIONS OF SAME- AND OPPOSITE-SEX COHABITATION

Although the legal regulation of same- and opposite-sex cohabitation are often considered and discussed together, the explanations for the diversity of legal solutions seem to differ between them. The common feature is that in both cases this diversity is predominantly politically determined.[535] However, the nature of the political choices made by the national legislatures with regard to the regulation of same- and opposite-sex cohabitation is rather different. This has partly to do with the fact that the need for legal protection on the part of opposite-sex couples, who choose not to marry, is at variance with the need of same-sex couples, who are not allowed to marry. Another significant difference is that a much heavier ideological lading is attached to the regulation of same-sex cohabitation.

With opposite-sex cohabitation alone, that is to say; when not combined with same-sex cohabitation, the difference in the national legislative responses seems to be grounded merely in the dissimilar national choices that have been made with regard to the balance between protecting the weaker party, on the one hand, and respecting the parties' autonomy, on the other hand. Societal recognition of non-marital opposite-sex cohabitation as such is, in most European countries, no longer a very controversial issue. Therefore, one can not say that the differences in the regulation of opposite-sex

---

[533]   For a concise comparative table for a number different legislative responses, see: AGELL, A., 'The Legal Status of Same-Sex Couples in Europe – A Critical Analysis' (2003), p. 125.

[534]   For a different conclusion with regard to non-marital registered relationships, see: CURRY-SUMNER, I., *All's Well that Ends Registered?* (2005), p. 266.

[535]   The importance of politics is also stressed in: FASSIN, E., 'Sociological Questions. An Epilogue to "More or Less Together"' (2005), p. 190.

cohabitation necessarily follow the lines of a conservative-progressive ideological divide.

In contrast, same-sex cohabitation is still a highly divisive matter. The issue of the acceptance of homosexuality as such continues to colour the background of legislative debates surrounding legislation on same-sex cohabitation in many European countries. For this reason, the national differences in regulation of same-sex cohabitation mainly reflect the measure of societal acceptance of homosexuality and the dissimilar political compromises reached with regard to the legal recognition of same-sex affective relationships. The differences in the regulation of same-sex cohabitation do tend to closely follow the lines of the conservative-progressive political divide.

15.10.2. REGULATION OF NON-INSTITUTIONALISED OPPOSITE-SEX COHABITATION: LESS POLITICAL, BUT HIGHLY DIVERSE

The spectre of the variety of forms of legal accommodation of non-institutionalised heterosexual cohabitation in Europe stretches from no regulation at all (Russia) to near equalisation with marriage (The Netherlands). This range of difference cannot be explained[536] merely by differences in the scale of popularity of cohabitation across Europe.[537] For example, Denmark and Finland have one of the highest levels of non-marital cohabitation, but no specific legislation on it; while The Netherlands, with a somewhat lower rate of different-sex cohabitation, almost equalises it with marriage. Unlike with marriage and divorce legislation, the difference in the regulation of heterosexual de-facto cohabitation reflects more than a pan-European, conservative-progressive, ideological divide.[538] The reason for this is the dilemma of the choice between a paternalistic policy, imposing regulation on unmarried partners without their explicit choice, on the one hand, and a liberal policy, respecting the partners' decision not to institutionalise their relationships, on the other hand. The doctrine of non-regulation, built upon 'progressive' liberal and feminist premises, is responsible for the legislative choice not to interfere with de-facto cohabitation. For this reason,

---

[536] For explanatory schemes see e.g.: BRADLEY, D., 'Regulation of Unmarried Cohabitation in West-European Jurisdictions – Determinants of Legal Policy' (2001), p. 22-50.

[537] FASSIN, E., 'Sociological Questions. An Epilogue to "More or Less Together"' (2005), p. 189; PROBERT, R., BARLOW, A., 'Cohabitants and the law: recent European reforms' (2000), p. 80. The influence of the demographic factors on the diversity of the legislative responses to cohabitation has been also addressed in: BRADLEY, D., 'Regulation of Unmarried Cohabitation in West-European Jurisdictions – Determinants of Legal Policy' (2001), p. 24-25.

[538] In a similar sense, see: ASÍN CABRERA, 'La partenariat de droit espagnol: quel avenir pour une réglementation en droit international privé?' (2004), p. 71.

even in countries with an overall progressive legislation on institutionalised cohabitation, like Denmark, The Netherlands, Iceland, and Germany, non-institutionalised cohabitation remains within a 'law free space'. Therefore even among the members of the 'progressive camp' who fully accept and support opposite-sex cohabitation outside marriage, there is still no consensus with regard to the most appropriate legislative policy towards it. However, there are some indications that a movement towards more consensus might be expected in the near future. It is possible to discern that during recent years the academic support for the pro-active regulation of marriage-like opposite-sex de-facto cohabitation has been steadily growing at the expense of the doctrine of non-regulation. It is becoming more and more accepted that the presence of common children provides sufficient justification for at least some protection of the weaker party to a non-institutionalised opposite-sex relationship.[539] Although this change of attitude has not yet been translated into practical legislative steps,[540] it seems possible to predict that once it reaches the legislative stage, it will trigger some convergence on this issue. However, one should not overestimate the possible extent of such convergence. Over time, more consensus might, indeed, be found for the automatic protection of de-facto cohabiting couples with children, and couples in long-term stable relationships. Nonetheless, the diversity of forms of opposite-sex de-facto cohabitation will remain a factor for the considerable variety of legal solutions adhered to in the European states.

15.10.3. INSTITUTIONALISED NON-MARITAL OPPOSITE-SEX COHABITATION: NO CONSENSUS

The attitude to institutionalised heterosexual cohabitation also varies quite significantly. In some countries (France, Belgium) its inclusion into the registration scheme was a by-product of the reluctance to legislate on same-sex couples alone. In contrast, in The Netherlands it was rather a manifestation of a neutrality policy, and will likely turn out to be only a transitory measure, as the future existence of the Dutch registered partnership is strongly under discussion. The great majority of European countries see no need for another institution for opposite-sex couples, as they are always considered to be able to avail themselves of marriage. At the same time, most of the countries providing for the institutionalisation of opposite-sex cohabitation give no

---

[539]   DEECH, R., 'The Case Against Legal Recognition of Cohabitation' (1980), p. 303; SCHRAMA, W., *De niet-huwelijkse samenleving in het Nederlandse en Duitse recht* (2004), p. 563 ff.; SCHERPE, J., 'The Legal Status of Cohabitants – Requirements for Legal Recognition,' p. 287-291.

[540]   Some proposals to this end have been made, for instance, in Norway. See: ASLAND, J., 'Legislation on Informal Cohabitation in Norway' (2005), p. 295-312.

hint of an intent to revise their choice.[541] Therefore, there is actually no indication to expect more convergence with regard to the institutionalisation of opposite-sex cohabitation.

15.10.4. SAME-SEX COHABITATION: IN THE MIDST OF THE CONSERVATIVE-PROGRESSIVE DISCORD

The situation as to the regulation of same-sex cohabitation in Europe strongly resembles the situation with divorce law. Both find themselves in the midst of political discord, dividing Europe as a whole and also each particular European country individually. The parallels to divorce law can be drawn even further. Since the 1970s there has been a clear pan-European tendency towards more acceptance and equalisation of same-sex cohabitation. The choices, the ideological connotations, and the political colour of the principle players in the debates surrounding the regulation of same-sex cohabitation are almost the same everywhere. The clear and direct influence of the model of partnership legislation, once it had been set up in Denmark, reinforces the image of a pan-European process.[542] However, due to the difference in the balance of power between the progressive and conservative sides of the political spectrum,[543] various European countries have given different responses to the problem of same-sex couples. On the basis of the above described classification scheme, focussing on the level of legal consequences, it is easy to discern very significant differences between the various forms of legislative responses. In the same way as with regard to divorce legislation, it is possible to trace a pan-European tendency towards more progressive and permissive legislation on same-sex cohabitation. In the period from the 1960s until the present, the legislative response in some countries gradually evolved from no regulation at all to opening up marriage. For instance, Belgium first introduced a limited form of protection that fell somewhere between the legal categories of status and contract by way of statutory cohabitation, and a few years later introduced same-sex marriage. The Netherlands started with registered partnership, then also opened marriage to same-sex couples. It is even suggested that registered partnership is in general no more than 'an intermediary form (and in social practice [...] a transitional stage) between informal cohabitation and marriage – and possibly a stepping stone towards opening of marriage to same-sex couples'.[544] This makes it tempting to build a kind of 'evolutionary theory' that explains the development of

---

[541]   Except for The Netherlands, which is considering the complete abolition of the institution of registered partnership.

[542]   See FORDER, C., 'Civil Law Aspects of Emerging Forms of Registered Partnerships' (1999), p. 9.

[543]   BRADLEY, D., 'A Family Law For Europe? Sovereignty, Political Economy and Legitimisation' (2003), p. 81.

[544]   FASSIN, E., 'Sociological Questions. An Epilogue to "More or Less Together"' (2005), p. 188.

cohabitation legislation as a pan-European evolution through different generations of same-sex cohabitation laws. As the following chart illustrates, it is possible to make an evolutionarily classification starting from the first generation, the piecemeal legislation, and ending with opening marriage to same-sex couples as the last generation providing for total equalisation with heterosexual marriage. In between, it is possible to distinguish generations corresponding to the above discussed legal models: specific legislation attaching limited consequences to de-facto cohabitation, cohabitation contract, half-way legislation rendering between status and contract (like the PACS), and registered partnership providing for an all but equivalent of marriage.[545]

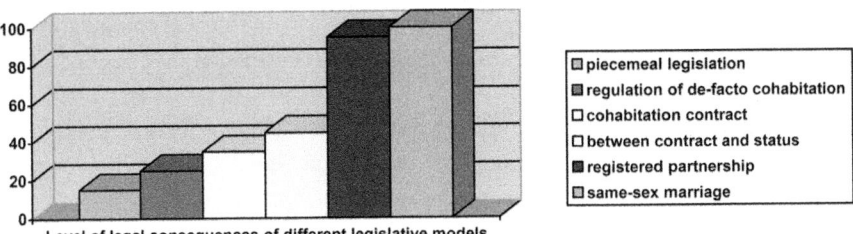

Level of legal consequences of different legislative models

- piecemeal legislation
- regulation of de-facto cohabitation
- cohabitation contract
- between contract and status
- registered partnership
- same-sex marriage

The idea of viewing different models of legislation for same-sex cohabitation as a kind of an evolutionary stepladder comes close to the suggested classifications of different generations of divorce law.[546] An obvious difference is of course that while the development of divorce law took almost four centuries, the different models of cohabitation legislation emerged within just four decades. Like the different generations of divorce law, the laws on same-sex cohabitation, belonging to different generations, simultaneously exist alongside each other in contemporary Europe, and sometimes even within one and the same jurisdiction.

However, just as with the 'evolutionary theory' of development of divorce legislation, an 'evolutionary theory' of development of legislation on same-sex cohabitation requires important qualifications. In the first place, as with divorce, it is necessarily to keep a clear distinction in mind between two questions: whether there is a tendency towards progressive development of legalisation on same-sex cohabitation, and

---

[545]   The percentage rates on the vertical axis of the chart are not based on any real figures and merely serve illustrative purposes.

[546]   The idea of 'generations' of same-sex cohabitation legislation requires qualification. It is true that every European country once had no cohabitation legislation at all, and that piecemeal adjustments of already existing legislation was the first step everywhere. However, when it comes to specific legislation, no 'evolution' is any longer traceable. For instance, registered partnership, one of the highest 'evolutional' forms of cohabitation legislation, was 'invented' much earlier than less far-reaching forms, such as PACS or statutory cohabitation.

whether there is a tendency towards convergence. A general tendency towards a higher level of acceptance, legal accommodation and approximation to marriage is clearly discernable. But, as with the example of divorce law, this does not necessarily imply a tendency towards convergence. To establish the occurrence of convergence one should be able to demonstrate that while cohabitation legislation is evolving in the same direction, the differences between the legislation of the various European countries are also steadily diminishing. This is clearly not the case. Before the 1960s there was an almost total uniformity of laws, corresponding to a pan-European consensus upon the non-acceptance of same-sex cohabitation. The growing acceptance is a common phenomenon, but so far this only called into being a whole range of differences and disagreements. Thus, in terms of convergence/divergence there is a clear tendency towards more diversity and less similarity in the field of regulation of cohabitation in general and same-sex cohabitation in particular.

In the second place, one should ask whether the evolutionary perspective of the development of the legislation on same-sex cohabitation reveals any tendency towards more convergence in the future. Again, as with divorce legislation, it is clearly observable that although all European countries tend to move in the same direction, the pace of their movement is rather unequal. Here too, can be distinguished between front-runners and those who stay behind, although the geographical orientation of this distinction does not always coincide with the same division as regards the permissiveness of divorce laws. In the field of divorce law the vanguard consists of the West- and East European countries, while the South European countries (with the exclusion of Spain and the inclusion of Ireland) are lagging behind. The axis of difference, therefore, generally lies North-South. With regard to the regulation of same-sex cohabitation the picture is different. Most Eastern-European countries (with the exception of The Czech Republic, Slovenia and Croatia), together with the South European countries (with the exception of Spain and to some extent Portugal) form the rearguard. The axis of difference here generally lies East-West rather than North-South. As in the field of modernisation of divorce law, while the countries in the rearguard are approaching one stage, the vanguard is already moving to the next. In this way the differences persist and the common core on the level of positive law remains rather limited.

These differences in pace generally reflect differences in the balance of political power between the progressive and conservative sides of the political spectrum, rather than anything that could be attributed to specific historical, cultural, or religious aspects of the countries concerned[547] – or even to a different level of acceptance of homosexuality in general. When the balance of political power shifts in favour of the progressive side, as happened in Belgium and Spain, even a country that traditionally belongs to the rearguard can become a true front-runner. As the above-discussed examples illustrate, legislation on same-sex relationships has so often been enacted merely because of the political will of the Government in office that it is impossible to dismiss this as accidental. For instance, the Croatian Government promoted legislation on same-sex relationships in disregard of the majority public opinion. The Socialist Government in Spain introduced same-sex marriage in a country that has long served as a paradigm of conservative Catholic culture. Socialist and liberal parties were responsible for the far-reaching partnership legislation in the Nordic countries. The political will of the particular Government in office was decisive for the introduction of registered partnership, and then same-sex marriage in the Netherlands, same-sex marriage in Belgium, and registered partnership in Germany and England and Wales. As the progressive-conservative divide in Europe gives no signs of waning, the development of same-sex partnership legislation cannot be expected to become 'a smooth linear progression to the same point',[548] and divergence of national laws will thus persist.

---

[547] The possible influence of legal traditions is analysed by David Bradley, who has found little dependency between the differences in the legal traditions and the divergence of the legislative models regarding cohabitation. BRADLEY, D., 'Regulation of Unmarried Cohabitation in West-European Jurisdictions – Determinants of Legal Policy' (2001), p. 25-26

[548] PROBERT, R., BARLOW, A., 'Cohabitants and the law: recent European reforms' (2000), p. 77.

CHAPTER 16
ILLEGITIMATE CHILDREN: FROM DISCRIMINATION TO EQUALITY AN EXAMPLE OF SUCCESSFUL HARMONISATION

16.1. FROM STIGMA TO FULL SOCIAL ACCEPTANCE

Since the 1960s, births of children outside of marriage have increased in Europe as rapidly as cohabitation. In 1970 the number of extramarital children did not exceed 5%; in 2003 this number had climbed to 30% of all new-borns.[1] In Sweden, the proportion of children born to unmarried parents now eclipses those born to parents who are married.[2] The growing number of extramarital births is generally caused by the rise of non-martial cohabitation rather than through an increase in single-parent mothers. Thus, although in England and Wales 40% of all children are currently born to unmarried parents, 75% of these parents live together.[3] The increase of births outside marriage has been accompanied by a rapidly growing social acceptance. Children born to parents who are unmarried but cohabiting are currently as accepted as those born to parents who are married. Single-mother parenthood has also lost its stigmatic character.

The public debate surrounding the status of illegitimate children provides one of the clearest examples of the conflict between the conservative transpersonalistic and the progressive personalistic approaches. Over the course of the twentieth century, the view that an extramarital child should not be punished 'for a wrong of which he was not guilty'[4] gained support. By the start of the twentieth century, the disgrace of those born out of wedlock and the legal deprivation traditionally attached to the status of

---

[1] Europe in figures. *Eurostat yearbook 2005*
[2] 56% of Swedish children are born to unmarried parents. Europe in figures. *Eurostat yearbook 2005*
[3] Figures for 2000. HAMILTON, C., 'England and Wales' (2002), p. 139.
[4] Report of the Committee on the Law of Succession in Relation to Illegitimate Persons (1966), para 19. Cited in: CRETNEY, S., *Family Law in the Twentieth Century. A History* (2003), p. 563.

'bastards' had already begun to be questioned in progressive corners of society.[5] However, for a long time in most of Europe[6] those who advocated for the improvement of the position of illegitimate children could achieve little more than the removal of some of the most notorious injustices. Due to the persistent perception that the equalisation of extramarital children would threaten marriage and the family, the old transpersonalistic stance continued to dominate the law until well into the 1960s. The statement by the Dutch Minister of Justice, cited in Chapter 11,[7] who in 1947 declared that illegitimate children, although perfectly 'innocent', should be nonetheless discriminated against in the name of 'the institution of marriage' and the 'interests of society as a whole', did not stand alone. As late as 1956 the English Royal Commission on Marriage and Divorce considered that extending legitimisation through the subsequent marriage of parents of adulterous children would constitute a 'threat to public morals' and lead to 'disastrous results for the status of marriage'.[8] The victory of the personalistic attitude towards illegitimate children after 1960s was part of the 'family revolution', typified by the general switch from the traditional monistic idea of marriage-based family as the only possible form of family, to the pluralistic idea of simultaneous co-existence of various family forms. By the turn of millennium, the whole discourse regarding the protection of public morals and the institution of marriage had become obsolete, as birth outside marriage was no longer considered to jeopardize morals or threaten the interests of society.

These far-reaching social, demographic and ideological changes progressively found their way into the law of every European State. Ultimately, the improvement of the position of illegitimate children was so comprehensive and radical that by the end of the period virtually every difference in the legal status between legitimate and illegitimate children had disappeared from the European legal scene.[9] Even the very term 'illegitimate' came to be seen as politically incorrect and has almost fallen into disuse.[10]

---

[5]   A good example of the change of public opinion is provided by the activities of English National Council for the Unmarried Mother and Her Child, which found considerable public support after its establishment in 1918. Ibid, p. 546.

[6]   With the only notable exception of the Nordic and Eastern European countries. See Part III, Chapter 11, Section 11.2.1.

[7]   See Section 11.3.3.

[8]   Cited in: CRETNEY, S., *Family Law in the Twentieth Century. A History* (2003), p. 546.

[9]   See in the same sense: SCHWENZER, I., 'Tensions between legal, biological and social conceptions of parentage' (2006), p. 2.

[10]   See VAN GRUNDERBEECK, D., *Beginselen van personen- en familierecht. Een mensenrechtelijke benadering* (2003), p. 325.

16.2. EUROPEAN HUMAN RIGHTS LAW AS A DRIVING FORCE OF MODERNISATION

In contrast to its rather limited contribution to the evolution of marriage, divorce and cohabitation law, European Human Rights law has played a crucial role with regard to the abolition of discrimination of extramarital children. To be sure, it was not so much the international conventions, but rather the case law of the European Court of Human Rights that became the vehicle for this abolition. Even so, some conventions have also had considerable influence on this process. The prohibition of discrimination on the ground of birth had already been incorporated in the 1948 Universal Declaration of Human Rights, and after that was habitually repeated in international human rights instruments.[11] In 1975,[12] a specific European Convention on the Legal Status of Children born out of Wedlock came into being under the auspices of the Council of Europe, and was ratified by 20 of 44 Member States of the Council of Europe.[13] The objectives of this Convention were twofold: promoting the equality of illegitimate children, and harmonising the filiation law of the participating States.[14] At present this Convention has become largely out-dated and is under the process of revision.[15]

However, it was not this specific convention, but rather Articles 8 and 14 of the European Convention on Human Rights, as interpreted in the ground-breaking *Marckx* judgment, that really changed the face of the law on children born out of wedlock in Europe. In *Marckx,* the European Court of Human Rights determined that Belgian law, which provided that an illegitimate child acquired legal filiation links with his or her mother not by virtue of birth (as was the case for a legitimate child), but via recognition by the mother, violated Articles 8 and 14 of the Convention.[16] The Court acknowledged that at the time the Convention was drafted, 'it was regarded as permissible and normal in many European countries to draw a distinction in this area between "illegitimate" and "legitimate" family'.[17] However, the ECHR chose to give Article 8 a dynamic-teleological interpretation by determining that the 'Convention must be interpreted in the light of present-day circumstances'.[18] The Court stated that presently the 'great majority' of member States 'ha[ve] evolved and [are] continuing to evolve, in company with the relevant international instruments, towards full

---

[11] For an overview see: ibid, note 1606 at p. 379.
[12] Came into force on 11 Augustus 1978.
[13] VAN GRUNDERBEECK, D., *Beginselen van personen- en familierecht. Een mensenrechtelijke benadering* (2003), p. 325.
[14] Ibid, p. 324.
[15] On the course of the preparations for revision see: Ibid.
[16] *Marckx v. Belgium.* ECHR (1979), para 41.
[17] Ibid. para 41.
[18] Ibid, para 41.

juridical recognition of the maxim *mater semper certa est*.[19] The ECHR also ruled that limiting the effects of recognition of an illegitimate child to the parents alone violated Article 8 in conjunction with Article 14.[20] The Court was so determined to prohibit the discrimination of 'illegitimate' children that it did not even refer to the margin of application of the States with regard to the matter of discrimination on the ground of birth.[21] It is also worth mentioning that the Court's conclusion in *Marckx*, that a consensus exists among the 'great majority' of countries, was mainly based on the forthcoming Convention on the Legal Status of Children born out of Wedlock, which at that time had been signed by ten, but only ratified by four, of the Contracting States.[22] Other discriminatory provisions of Belgian law, questioned in *Marckx*, stated that even after recognition, an illegitimate child was not entitled to inheritance through intestacy by the child's mother's family. Furthermore, an unmarred mother's capacity to make patrimonial dispositions on behalf of an illegitimate child was more limited than a married mother's capacity to make the same dispositions on behalf of a legitimate child. Striking down these discriminatory provisions, the ECHR dared to take an even bolder approach. The Court acknowledged that at the time of the decision such distinctions regarding the inheritance and patrimonial rights of illegitimate child were maintained in the majority of the European countries. Nonetheless, the ECHR chose to join the minority view of the six European countries that had abandoned this discriminatory attitude.[23] Ultimately, the Court held that differential treatment of illegitimate children, both with regard to inheriting from their parents' family and the capacity of the parents to make dispositions on behalf of such children, was a violation of Article 8 in conjunction with Article 14 ECHR.

Later ECHR case law regarding illegitimate children demonstrated that the *Marckx* decision was not off the cuff.[24] The Court proved to be determined to amplify and enforce the policy of abolishing discrimination against children born out of wedlock, commencing with *Marckx*. Some countries, including Belgium – the defendant in the *Marckx* case – were initially rather reluctant to accept the ECHR's activism. In 1985, the Belgian Cassation Court refused to acknowledge that the interpretation given to Article 8 ECRM in the *Marckx*-case had direct application in Belgium.[25] It took another

---

[19] Ibid, para 41. This maxim expresses the rule that the mother of a child is the woman who has given birth to the child.

[20] Ibid, para 45-49.

[21] SCHOKKENBROEK, J., 'The Prohibition of the Discrimination in article 14 of the Convention and the Margin of Appreciation' (1998), p. 22.

[22] *Marckx v. Belgium.* ECHR (1979).

[23] Ibid, para 52.

[24] *Abdulaziz at al v. the UK* v ECHR (1985); *Johnston and others v. Ireland.* EHRM, (1986) *Vermeire v. Belgium.* ECHR (1991); *Inze v. Austria.* ECHR (1987); *Mazurek v. France.* ECHR (2000); etc.

[25] Bv. Cass. 10 May 1985, *R.W.* 1985-86, 1848, cited in: SWENNEN, F., *Gezins- en familierecht in kort bestek* (2005), at p. 21.

decision against Belgium by the ECHR[26] before Belgium finally, in 1987, altered its filiation law.[27] In 1996, the Court made clear in *Johnston v. Ireland* that the requirement of non-discrimination is equally applicable to 'adulterous' children.[28] The determination of the ECHR to dispense with inheritance law's discrimination of extramarital children was confirmed in 2000, in *Mazurek v. France*.[29]

As a result of the European Court of Human Rights' continuous efforts to strike down all discriminatory national provisions against extramarital children, a 'highly uniform "European Family Law"'[30] has been created in this field. The European law governing the legal status of extramarital children has been complemented by a series of decisions regarding the relationship between unmarried parents and their children.[31] In general, child and parent-child law are the only areas of family law for which the ECHR has actually designed a 'whole Code of European Family Law'.[32] In these areas the European Court of Human Rights has managed to develop – and consequently impose on the European countries – an autonomous, higher standard of protection. Therefore, the level of protection granted by European law in the field of child-parent relationships is considerably higher than the common denominator of legal protection provided by the national laws on their own merits.

It is puzzling that European Human Rights law has reached significant achievements only in this, and a very few other[33] particular areas of family law. It is suggested that the Court's policy in this field has been determined by the political feasibility of this particular endeavour.[34] After the 1970s, the aspiration to put an end to discrimination against extramarital children and their unmarried parents rapidly lost its once controversial character and could count on an ever broadening European consensus. Apparently, 'striking down laws that make some children "legitimate" and others

---

[26]   *Vermeire v. Belgium.* ECHR (1991).
[27]   For more information see: 20-58. SWENNEN, F., *Gezins- en familierecht in kort bestek* (2005).
[28]   *Johnston v. Ireland.* ECHR (1986), para 74.
[29]   *Mazurek v. France.* ECHR (2000).
[30]   JOHNSON, N., 'Recent Developments: the Breadth of Family Law Review Under the European Convention on Human Rights' (1995), lexis.
[31]   The most notable among this decision are *Keegan v. Ireland.* ECHR (1994); *Kroon v. The Netherlands* ECHR (1995); *Mc.Michael v. the UK.* ECHR (1995); *X, Y and Z v. the UK.* ECHR (1997); *Hoffmann v. Germany.* ECHR (2001).
[32]   The famous mot portrayal from the dissenting opinion of Judge Sir Gerald Fitzmaurice in *Marckx v. Belgium.* ECHR (1979).
[33]   E.g. the equality of spouses.
[34]   JOHNSON, N., 'Recent Developments: the Breadth of Family Law Review Under the European Convention on Human Rights' (1995), lexis.

"illegitimate"[35] was estimated to be 'politically safer'[36] than getting involved in the highly controversial issues of divorce or same-sex relationships.

16.3. CHANGE OF NATIONAL LAWS: OVERALL EQUALISATION OF MARITAL AND EXTRAMARITAL CHILDREN

At the beginning of the 1960s, the Nordic and Eastern European countries were in a better starting position than the rest of Europe. Important improvements to the status of extramarital children had already taken place in the Nordic countries and the Soviet Union in the first part of the twentieth century.[37] Other Eastern European countries equalised marital and extramarital children soon after World War II.[38] The remaining inequalities were dispensed with in Denmark in 1960,[39] in Sweden in 1976,[40] in Norway – basically in 1956 and fully in 1981,[41] in Finland in 1975[42] and in 1983,[43] and in Iceland in 1992.[44] In the Soviet Union, both voluntary recognition and judicial establishment of paternity, previously abolished by the notorious Act of 8 July 1944,[45] were restored in 1968.[46]

In 1970,[47] West Germany became the first Western European country outside the Nordic region and Eastern Europe to genuinely equalise all children regardless of

---

35 Ibid.
36 Ibid.
37 See Part III, Chapter 11, Section 11.2.1.
38 E.g. in Bulgaria in 1945; in Czechoslovakia in 1950; in Hungary in 1946; in Poland in 1946 and 1950.
39 By the 1960 Law on the Legal Status of Children. SUNDBERG, J., 'Nordic Laws' (1971), p. 40.
40 See JÄNTERÄ-JAREBORG, M., CEFL National Report for Sweden: Parental Responsibilities (2005), p. 102.
41 BRADLEY, D., Family Law and Political Culture (1996), 210-211.
42 By the 1975 Law On Paternity. BRADLEY, D., 'Comparative Family Law and Political Process: Regulation of Sexual Morality in Finland' (1999), p. 183.
43 The Child Custody and the Rights to Access Act, 1983 granted extramarital children equal rights in the area of parental responsibility. See: KURKI-SUONIO, K., CEFL National Report for Finland: Parental Responsibilities (2005), p. 84.
44 By 1992 Law in Respect of Children. See: BJÖRGVINSSON, D., 'General Principles and Recent Developments in Icelandic Family Law' (1995), p. 227-228.
45 See: Section 11.3.1.
46 Restored in the Federal Fundamentals of Law on Marriage and the Family of 1968 and subsequently adopted in the Family Codes of the Republics.
47 In this year the Law of August 1969 (in force since 1 July 1970) was promulgated. See: GIESEN, D., 'The reform of Family Law in Germany' (1978), p. 131-134.

whether their parents were married when they were born.[48] The equalisation was finalised in reunified Germany in 1997.[49] In Austria the position of illegitimate children was generally improved in 1970.[50] In France the legal discrimination of extramarital children was generally abolished in 1972[51] and completely eradicated in 2005.[52] In 1975, after a long and tense political debate,[53] the position of illegitimate children was improved in Italy.[54] In Portugal discrimination of extramarital children was abolished in 1977.[55] In Switzerland separate legal treatment of illegitimate children was dispensed with in 1978.[56] In England and Wales, a number of substantial reforms were finalised in 1987.[57] In The Netherlands the equalisation was completed though the reforms of 1982[58] and 1997.[59]

It should be noted that although these reforms created a general status of equality for extramarital children, they did not eradicate each and every difference in legal treatment. There are still some differences remaining, mainly related to rules regarding the right to acquire the name and the nationality of the father, or to the attribution of parental responsibility.[60]

---

[48]   This had to do with the equality provision of Article 6(5) of the German Constitution, which allowed the Constitutional Court to put the legislature under pressure. See BOHNDORF, T., 'The New Legitimacy Law in Germany' (1970), p. 299-302.

[49]   By the *Gesetz zur Abschaffung der gesetzlichen Ambtspflegschaft und Neuordnung des Rechts der Beistandschaft*, 1997. See MARTINY, D., *CEFL National Report for Germany* (2005), p. 87.

[50]   By the 1970 Federal Act *On the New Regulation of the Legal Status of Children Born out of Wedlock*. See ROTH, M., *CEFL National Report for Austria: Parental Responsibilities* (2005), p. 77.

[51]   By the law of 3 January 1972. See FOYER, J., 'The Reform of Family Law in France' (1978), p. 93-101.

[52]   By *Ordonnance* of 4 July 2005. See FULCHIRON, H., 'Egalité, Vérité, Stabilité: The New French Filiation Law After the Ordonnance of 4 July 2005' (2006), p. 203-210.

[53]   The Christian Democrats were persistently opposed to equality between children born in and out of wedlock, especially in regard of 'adulterous' children. POCAR, V., RONFANI, P., 'Family Law in Italy: Legislative Innovations and Social Change' (1978), p. 624-625.

[54]   By the Law of 19 May 1975.

[55]   See DE OLIVEIRA, G., *CEFL National Report for Portugal: Parental Responsibilities* (2005), p. 98.

[56]   See HAUSHEER, H., *CEFL National Report for Switzerland: Parental Responsibilities* (2005), p. 104.

[57]   In this year the Family Reform Act removed the wording 'illegitimate' from the legal terminology. On the course of these reforms, see: CRETNEY, S., *Family Law in the Twentieth Century. A History* (2003), p. 525-565.

[58]   By the Law of 27 October 1982.

[59]   By the law of 24 December 1997. See DE BOER, J., *C. Assers' Handeling tot beoefening van het Nederlands burgerlijk recht. Personen- en familierecht* (2002), p. 494-496.

[60]   In Austria, Denmark, Germany, The Netherlands, Portugal, Sweden and Switzerland, the establishment of the paternity of an unmarried father does not automatically lead to the attribution of parental responsibility. Such attribution is only possible upon a joint application of the parents. BOELE-WOELKI, K., 'Parental Responsibilities – CEFL's Initial Results' (2005), p. 152-153.

16.4. FAR-REACHING HARMONISATION, BUT DIVERSITY REMAINS

As mentioned above, at the beginning of the discussed period the level of equalisation of marital and extramarital children throughout the European countries was quite uneven. Yet by the end of this period the laws on this particular issue had become rather similar, with all countries outlawing differential treatment between the two groups of children. Therefore, it can be concluded that the issue of equality of marital and extramarital children in Europe today has ceased to be a matter of diversity. The law governing the legal position of extramarital children provides a rare example of far-reaching harmonisation achieved by a convergence process induced by judicial activism of the European Court of Human Rights.

Now that the inequality of extramarital children has become a thing of the past, it seems possible to say that no political differences reflecting the progressive-conservative divide remain in this field within Europe. However, the uniformity on the fundamental issue of non-discrimination does not mean that all differences between national legislations have ceased to exist. Less important differences remain, especially in regard to the establishment of legal filiation links with the parents. Although these differences are also of a political nature, one cannot attribute them to a progressive-conservative divide.

Even after *Marckx*, some important differences still exist in the establishment of an unmarried mother's maternity. A great majority of European jurisdictions adhere to the rule that the mother of a child is the woman who has given birth to the child (*mater semper certa est*).[61] However, the Italian legal systems is still an exception to this rule.[62] The maternity of an unmarried mother can be established there by acknowledgement, in a judicial procedure, or by referring to the fact that the child has always been publicly known as the child of person in question. French law had long adhered to the same rule,[63] before the principle *mater semper certa est* was finally extended to unmarried mothers in 2005.[64] In addition, French, Luxembourgian, Spanish and Romanian law also allow a birth mother to remain legally anonymous. In France, such decision of the birth mother precludes the child from ever having the possibility of

---

[61] After *Marckx*, the principle *mater semper certa est* has been commonly considered to be the only way in which maternity can be established in compliance with Article 8 of the European Convention. For an overview of literature, see: VAN GRUNDERBEECK, D., *Beginselen van personen- en familierecht. Een mensenrechtelijke benadering* (2003), at p. 397.

[62] CESCHINI, R., 'Italy' (2002), p. 433.

[63] See CHAUVEAU, V., CORNEC, A., 'France' (2002), p. 286.

[64] FULCHIRON, H., 'Egalité, Vérité, Stabilité: The New French Filiation Law After the Ordonnance of 4 July 2005' (2006), p. 203.

establishing a maternal filial link through a judicial proceeding.[65] This French rule, long considered to be out of line with Article 8 of the Convention,[66] has recently been sustained by the ECHR.[67]

The great majority of European jurisdictions currently allow for both voluntary acknowledgement of a child by the child's unmarried father and for the establishment of paternity through a judicial procedure against the father's will.[68] There is, however, a clear distinction between the so-called 'free' and 'compulsory' establishment of paternity.[69] In countries with 'free' recognition, the establishment of paternity depends mainly on the will of the parents. Most jurisdictions make the voluntary recognition of a child by the father conditional upon the consent of the mother and/or the child, if the child has reached a certain age.[70] The mother's refusal to give consent to such a recognition can in most cases be substituted by the decision of a competent authority. Yet in some countries (for instance France, Austria and Switzerland) such consent is not required, though the mother and the child are allowed to contest the acknowledgement or to object to it.[71] In countries with a 'compulsory' establishment of paternity, like the Nordic countries and Germany before the reform of 1998,[72] the initiative of establishing parentage lies with the public authorities rather than the parents.[73] Also, the weight given to the biological truth varies significantly from one jurisdiction to another.

The differences just discussed do not really touch upon the equal status of extramarital children. The major political discord associated with this also belongs to the past. Unlike the choices surrounding the issue of equality, the remaining differences in filiation law are not connected to the conservative-progressive divide in Europe, but have to do with other, less fundamental discourses. It also seems rather unlikely that

---

[65] Since the Act of 18 January 1993. VAN GRUNDERBEECK, D., *Beginselen van personen- en familierecht. Een mensenrechtelijke benadering* (2003), at p. 398.

[66] See, for instance: MEULDERS-KLEIN, M.-T., 'The Status of the Father in European Legislations' (1996), at p. 493-494.

[67] *Odièvre v. France.* ECHR (2003).

[68] The laws of England and Wales and Ireland do not provide for voluntary recognition in the strict sense of this word.

[69] For this distinction see: FORDER, C., *Legal Establishment of the Parent Child Relationship: Constitutional Principles* (1995), p. 71-72 and MEULDERS-KLEIN, M.-T., 'The Status of the Father in European Legislations' (1996), at p. 499 ff.

[70] SCHWENZER, I., 'Tensions between legal, biological and social conceptions of parentage' (2006), p. 7.

[71] Ibid.

[72] VAN GRUNDERBEECK, D., *Beginselen van personen- en familierecht. Een mensenrechtelijke benadering* (2003), note 1708 at p. 402.

[73] MEULDERS-KLEIN, M.-T., 'The Status of the Father in European Legislations' (1996), at p. 499 -501.

those differences are determined by the particularities of national cultures.[74] Against this suggestion, it has been persuasively argued that the radical change to the long-standing tradition of establishing a legal filiation link with an unmarried mother, instigated by the *Marckx* judgment, has not created 'cultural shocks' in Belgium or any other European country.[75]

At the same time, neither can the diversity of present-day filiation laws be regarded as merely being diverse in the technical aspect of the chosen solutions. That is to say, this diversity is based on dissimilar political choices made with regard to the position of the parents, rather than merely a matter of dissimilar legal means to reach similar ends. For instance, the decision to leave the establishment of paternity to the free disposition of either one or both of the parents is clearly in accord with liberal ideas on family autonomy and the protection of the privacy of mother and child. The opposite choice – the compulsory establishment of paternity – is inspired by more of a paternalistic welfare-ist idea that the State has a duty to safeguard a child's interests in knowing his or her origins,[76] and having a legal father. It also has to do with the concern of strong welfare States like the Nordic countries and Germany[77] to restrain their own financial burdens.[78] The decision to grant a mother an unrestricted right to veto the recognition of a child by the child's father[79] generally reflects the feminist premise of the primacy of the mother's parental rights above those of the father.[80] In contrast, to allow the father to ask a competent authority to overrule the veto of the

---

[74] The cultural nature of these differences has been alleged by MEULDERS-KLEIN, M.-T., in 'Les problèmes de mise en œuvre de la Convention sur le statut des enfants nés hors mariage' (1995), p. 41-42, cited in: VAN GRUNDERBEECK, D., *Beginselen van personen- en familierecht. Een mensenrechtelijke benadering* (2003), at p. 335.

[75] PINTENS W., VANWINCKELEN, C., *Casebook European Family Law* (2001), p. 15.

[76] No absolute right to know ones origins can be derived from the case law of the ECHR. FORDER, C., 'Constitutional Principle and the Establishment of the Legal Relationship Between the Child and the Non-marital Father' (1993), p. 70; VAN GRUNDERBEECK, D., *Beginselen van personen- en familierecht. Een mensenrechtelijke benadering* (2003), at p. 339-350. However, in Germany the right to know one's origins has acquired the status of a fundamental constitutional 'personality' right. See: FORDER, C., 'Constitutional Principle and the Establishment of the Legal Relationship Between the Child and the Non-marital Father' (1993), p. 40-107. In 1994, the Dutch Supreme Court came to a rather similar conclusion. HR 15 April 1994, NJ, 608. For a brief account of the Dutch situation see: ANTOKOLSKAIA, M., 'Recent Developments in Dutch Filiation, Adoption and Joint Custody Law (2002), p. 769-799.

[77] The correlation between the high level of State support to families with children in the Nordic region and Germany and the compulsory establishment of paternity seems no coincidence.

[78] MEULDERS-KLEIN, M.-T., 'The Status of the Father in European Legislations' (1996), at p. 499

[79] See SCHRAMA, W., 'De betekenis van het EVRM voor de burgerlijke stand in de lidstaten van de CIEC' (1998), p. 223.

[80] Thus, in The Netherlands the introduction in 1998 of the possibility to overrule the veto of the mother was strongly opposed in Dutch feminist literature. See, for instance: HOLTRUST, N., DE HONDT, I., Note on HR 18 may 1990, in: HOLTRUST, N. (ed.), *Rechtspraak vrouwen en recht* (1992), p. 41-43).

mother is inspired by the opposite notion of equal rights for the (unmarried) father.[81] These dissents, although clearly of a less fundamental nature than the previous discrimination discords, still display no tendency of diminishing. Therefore, it seems rather unlikely that the legislative differences reflecting these discords will disappear in the near future.

In sum, the successful equalisation of the status of marital and extramarital children illustrates that the eradication of differences in some principle issues does not necessitate the total assimilation of laws in that particular area. Even total convergence with regard to the fundamental issue of non-discrimination against extramarital children does not automatically mean that the differences between the national laws on less fundamental points will also disappear.

---

[81] For an overview of other arguments see: VAN GRUNDERBEECK, D., *Beginselen van personen- en familierecht. Een mensenrechtelijke benadering* (2003), at p. 404-405.

CHAPTER 17
MATRIMONIAL PROPERTY LAW

17.1. 'THE NEW FAMILY AND THE NEW PROPERTY'[1]

The formation of national states in the nineteenth century significantly reduced the formerly indigestible patchwork of local legal regimes of marriage property.[2] Yet, on the eve of the 'family revolution' of the 1960s-1970s, matrimonial property law in Europe was still characterised by the diversity of legal regimes. These legal regimes can be roughly reduced to three basic models: the separation of property; the limited community of property; and the deferred community of property.

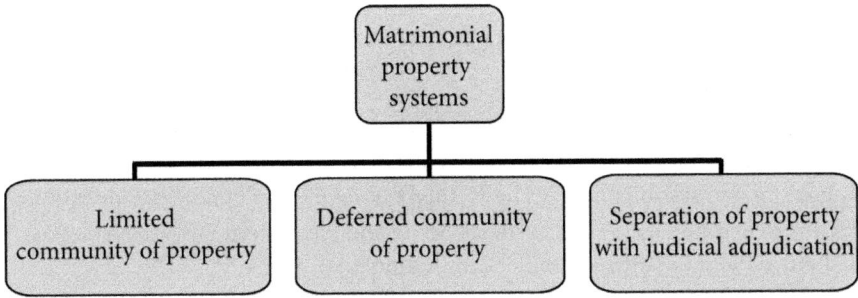

Around the 1960s all regimes equally faced the need to accommodate similar profound changes in family patterns. Historical analysis shows that irrespective of the particularities of a legal regime, marriage property law has always developed devices to safeguard the family assets that constitute the main source of wealth. In the Middle Ages this main form of wealth was land; in modern times, capital. In her well-known book,

---

1   This paragraph is named after the book by Mary Ann GLENDON *The New Family and the New Property* (1981).

2   I remind the reader that the legal regime of matrimonial property is the regime which in the continental legal systems governs the spousal property relationship by default if the spouses have not concluded a marital contract. In all continental jurisdictions the spouses are more or less free to opt for a contractual regime of marriage property by way of concluding a marital contract. In contrast, the common law system has no general notion of legal regime and marital contract (see below). Due to the limited scope of this study, the analysis in this and the previous chapters covers the legal regimes of marriage property only.

after which this section is named, Mary Ann Glendon, demonstrates that at present the bulk of the families do not rely for their subsistence upon land or family capital, but rather on professions and work-related benefits.[3] The other major changes that influenced marriage property law all over Europe were the emancipation of women, the increase of female employment, the change of the economic function of marriage,[4] and the dramatic rise of divorce rates. These changes confronted all matrimonial property legal systems with the need to accommodate such new principles as equality, autonomy and solidarity of the spouses. The principle of equality requires granting women an equal right to the administration of their separate property and the common fund (if any such fund exists under the regime in question).[5] The principle of autonomy necessitates allowing each spouse to freely dispose of his or her property during the marriage. The principle of solidarity is enrooted in the modern model of the partnership-marriage. In such a marriage each spouse is availed an equal share of family assets regardless of the way he or she contributes to their acquisition: child rearing and household work or paid job and business activities.[6] This principle also calls for legal devices to safeguard the main family assets (both common and personal) from any irresponsible actions of either of the spouses.

17.2. LIMITED COMMUNITY OF PROPERTY SYSTEMS

By the second part of the twentieth century universal community of property remained in just one European country: The Netherlands. All other countries (for instance France, Belgium, Italy, Spain, Portugal, Malta and the Eastern European countries) had moved to some form of limited community of property.

17.2.1. FRANCE: COMMUNITY OF ACQUESTS

On the eve of the discussed period, France had a system of community of movables and acquests, introduced by the Napoleonic Code in 1804. To remind the reader,

---

[3] Glendon refers here to a seminal article by Charles Reich 'The New Property', *73 Yale L.J.* (1963-640, p. 1245-1257. Cited in: GLENDON, M.A., *The New Family and the New Property* (1981), at p. 3.
[4] As Harry Willekens puts it: 'Marriage is not any longer in the first place an institution for the management and transmission of the means of production, but it has become a *social security* institution concerned with the management and distribution of income and of durable consumption goods'. WILLEKENS, H., 'Explaining Two Hundred Years of Family Law in Western Europe' (1997), p. 673-74.
[5] VERBEKE, A. et al, 'European marital property law' (1995), p. 464.
[6] VERBEKE, A., *Goederenverdeling bij echtscheiding* (1991), p. 403-404.

under this system the immovable property owned by each spouse before marriage, together with the property acquired during the marriage by gift or inheritance as well the assets of purely personal use, constituted the separate funds of the respective spouses. The rest fell into the common fund.[7] In 1907 the wife was granted the right to administer her own earnings, but the rest of common fund remained under the all but exclusive administration of the husband.[8]

During the 1965 reform[9] the community of movables and acquests was transferred into the community of acquests only. Since then all premarital property remains outside the common fund.[10] The common property presently consists of the assets acquired by the spouses during the marriage (with exception of the assets acquired by gift or inheritance,[11] and assets of purely personal nature),[12] as well the income from personal property.[13] Each of the spouses enjoins the exclusive power to administer his or her separate property.[14] The Act of 1965[15] did not do away with the exclusive right of the husband to administer the common fund, yet this right was subjected to important restrictions.[16] As time passed, the unequal position of women with regard to the administration of the common fund came to be considered increasingly problematical in light of the requirements of International Human Rights Law.[17] Yet, this inequality was only abolished in 1985.[18] Since then the common fund has been under the concurrent administration of both spouses.[19] In addition, a special regime of administration was created in order to safeguard the most important family assets belonging to the common fund. Therefore, the consent of both spouses is required, for instance, for donating common property; conveying the matrimonial home and household goods to third parties, as well as disposing of immovable property and property belonging to an enterprise.[20]

---

[7]   See Part III, Chapter 9, Section 9.2.6.
[8]   GLENDON, M.A., *The Transformation of Family Law* (1989), p. 117.
[9]   Act of 13 June 1965 *Réforme des régimes matrimoniaux*.
[10]   Art. 1403 CC.
[11]   Art. 1405 CC.
[12]   Art. 1404 CC.
[13]   Art. 1401 CC.
[14]   Art. 1428 CC.
[15]   In 1980 and 1983, wives of farmers and small entrepreneurs acquired the right to co-administration of the respective properties. GLENDON, M.A., *The Transformation of Family Law* (1989), p. 120.
[16]   Ibid, p. 117.
[17]   Ibid.
[18]   By Act of 23 December 1985, *Égalité des époux dans les régimes matrimoniaux en de parents dans la gestion des biens des enfants mineurs*.
[19]   Art. 1421 CC.
[20]   *Fonds de commerce*. See: BRAAT, B., ODERKERK, M., STEENHOFF, G., *Huwelijksvermogensrecht in rechtvergelijkend perspectief* (2000), p. 123.

Although the spouses are entitled to opt for another regime of matrimonial property by way of concluding a marital contract,[21] their contractual freedom is not unlimited. Thus the spouses are not allowed to choose for the total separation of property or for the dotal system, as those systems are considered to be incompatible with the principle of equality of the spouses. They are also not allowed to set aside the mandatory provisions of the articles 1388-1399 CC, governing the basic rights and duties of the spouses – the so-called primary regime.[22]

In case of termination of marriage by death or divorce, the common fund is, as a rule, equally divided between the spouses (and/or their heirs). However, exceptions to the principle of equal division are possible. Thus, the judge can assign the matrimonial home to one of the spouses with or without compensation.[23] Another possibility of deviation from equal division is to grant one of the spouses a so-called *prestation compensatoire*, in the form of periodical payments[24] or reallocation of property.[25]

17.2.2. ITALY: FROM SEPARATION OF PROPERTY TO LIMITED COMMUNITY OF PROPERTY

In Italy the reform of 1975[26] replaced the traditional legal regime of separation of property (the dotal system) with a limited community system, which under previous law functioned as one of the optional systems.[27] It is interesting to notice that the choice of the legislature for a community system was determined not by its popularity, but rather by the intent to promote genuine equality of the spouses and to improve the position of the housewife.[28] The Italian legal regime of marital property generally resembles the French one. The most notable difference is that, while in France the incomes from the separate property fall into the common fund, in Italy they constitute a separate, residual fund.[29] During the marriage the residual fund remains the separate property of the respective spouses, but in case of termination of marriage, it becomes

---

[21] *Contat de mariage*. For more on the marital contract, see: Ibid, ff.
[22] *Statut fondamental de la famille*. See: Ibid, p. 112-113.
[23] Ibid, p. 141-142.
[24] Ibid, p. 151.
[25] Ibid, p. 141.
[26] Introduced by the Act of 19 May 1975, On Family Law Reform.
[27] For more on Italian law see: COMANDE, G., National report 'Italy' (2003).
[28] GABRIELLI G., GUBEDDU, M., *Il regime patrimoniale dei coniugi*, Giuffré, Milan, 1997, p. 12-13. Cited in: BRAAT, B., ODERKERK, M., STEENHOFF, G., *Huwelijksvermogensrecht in rechtvergelijkend perspectief* (2000), note 5 at p. 154.
[29] *Comunione de residuo*. See: COMANDE, G., National report 'Italy' (2003), p. 8.

part of the common assets, subject to division.[30] In this respect, the Italian system displays a certain resemblance to the deferred community of property.

17.2.3. OTHER WESTERN-EUROPEAN COUNTRIES WITH COMMUNITY OF PROPERTY REGIMES

In Belgium the legal regime of matrimonial property was initially established by the French Code Napoleon in 1804. This Code is still in force; and, although the subsequent developments took place independently of France, the current Belgian system of community of acquests is still very close to the French one.[31] The same generally applies to Luxemburg. The legal regime of marriage property established by the Spanish Civil Code, the regime of community of acquests,[32] is also very similar to the French one. The main reforms of this regime law took place in 1975[33] and 1981.[34] This regime, however, does not apply to the whole of the country. The Spanish Autonomous Communities, with the power to legislate in civil matters, have enacted their own laws providing for different legal regimes of marriage property.[35] The legal regime[36] in Portugal is also the community of acquests, resembling the French one.[37] This regime is regulated by the 1966 Portuguese Civil Code. In 1977 the rules of matrimonial property law were brought in line with the 1976 Constitution, proclaiming the equality of men and women.[38] In The Netherlands there is presently a Bill in Parliament that seeks to replace the currently existing universal community

---

[30]   COMANDE, G., National report 'Italy' (2003), p. 8.

[31]   For more on the Belgian system see: PINTENS, W., VAN DER MEERSCH, B., VANWINCKELEN, C., *Inleiding tot het Familiaal Vermogensrecht* (2002), p. 21 ff.

[32]   *Sociedad de gananciales*. For more on the Spanish system see: CHECA MARTINEZ, M., National Report 'Spain' (2003), p. 6.

[33]   Law of 5 May 1975.

[34]   Matrimonial Property Act of 19 May 1981.

[35]   CHECA MARTINEZ, M., National Report 'Spain' (2003), p. 4. The legal regime in Catalonia and in the Balearic Islands is the total separation of property; in Aragon – the community of movables and acquests; in Navarra – the community of acquests; and in some provinces of the Basque Country and in Extremadura – the universal community of property. Ibid, p. 10.

[36]   Calling this system 'the legal regime' requires a qualification, as in two cases the mandatory system of separation of property automatically applies. Separation applies if one of the spouses has reached the age of sixty years old or if the marriage was celebrated without official investigation in the marriage impediments. DE SAUSA MACHADO, A., 'Portugal' (2002), p. 530.

[37]   Art.1717 of the Portuguese Civil Code. For more on the Portuguese system see: FRADA DE SOUSA, A., National Report 'Portugal' (2003).

[38]   By the Act of 25 November 1977 *d'adapter le Code à la Constitution de 1976 (dans le domaine des régimes matrimoniaux, il s'agissait surtout d'établir entre les époux des rapports patrimoniaux marqués du sceau de l'égalité.* FRADA DE SOUSA, A., National Report 'Portugal' (2003).

with a limited community system, closely resembling the French community of acquests.[39]

17.2.4. LIMITED COMMUNITY SYSTEMS IN EASTERN EUROPE

The limited community of property was introduced in the Eastern European states after World War Two, under the influence of the example of the Soviet Union.[40] Yet, the limited community regimes survived the disintegration of Soviet Union[41] and the end of the Eastern Block.[42] In contrast to Western Europe, problems such as granting spouses equal rights or improving the position of a housewife were resolved from the outset. The current matrimonial property regimes largely resemble the French community of acquests.[43] However, there are also some significant differences. The most notable difference is that the increase of value of the separate property of each of the spouses remains separate property and is not subjected to division upon the termination of the marriage. This can only be different if the non-owner spouse manages to prove his or her monetary or labour contribution to the increase of the other spouse's property.[44] Before the Perestroika, the legal regime of marital property in Eastern Europe was strictly mandatory. Deviation from this regime by way of marital contract was not allowed for a long time. This possibility was not introduced

---

[39] Draft Law No. 28 867 'On Modification of the Statutory Community of Assets'. See also: REINHARTZ, B., 'De nieuwe voorstellen ter aanpassing van de wettelijke gemeenschap van goederen' (2006), p. 3-14.

[40] The limited community of property was introduced in the Soviet Union in 1926. See: Part III, Chapter 11, Section 11.2.1.

[41] Limited community regimes still exist in all European former Soviet-Union states. See: art. 60 of the Family Code of Ukraine (2004); art. 14-15 of the Family Act of Estonia (1994); art. 3.87-3.88 of the Civil Code of Lithuania; art. 89 and 91 of the Civil Act of Latvia (1994); art. 19 of the Family Law Act of Moldova (2000) and art. 23 of the Family Code of Belorussia.

[42] The limited community regimes remain the legal regimes in all post-socialist Eastern European countries. See, e.g. art. 13 of the *Family Code* of Bulgaria (1968), limited community is also intended to be maintained in the Bulgarian Draft Family Code, which is currently in progress; art. 143 of the *Civil Code* of the Czech Republic (1964, as amended in 1998); and art. 195 of the *Family Act* of Serbia (2005).

[43] For Hungarian law see: WEISS, E., 'Remarks on Certain Aspects of the Codification of Family Law' (2002), p. 183-197; for Russian, Ukrainian and Belorussian law see: ZHYLINKOVA, I., 'Property Relations of Spouses in Slavonic Post-Soviet Countries (Ukraine, Russia, Belarus)', (2004), p. 483-490; for Estonian law see: KULLERKUPP, K., 'Family Law in Estonia' (2001), p. 98-201; for Lithuanian law see: KESERAUSKAS, S., 'Moving in the Same Direction'? Presentation of Family Law Reforms in Lithuania', p. 323-327; for Serbian law see: DRAŠKIĆ, M., KOVAČEK STANIĆ, G., 'The New Family Act of Serbia' (2006), p. 372-373.

[44] See, e.g. art. 37 of the Russian *Family Code* (*a contrario*); art.168-170 Family Act of Serbia; art. 91 (4) of the Civil Act of Latvia; art. 19-21 of the Family Code of Bulgaria.

460

until the 1990s.[45] Another distinction is that the administration of the common fund is not exercised by the spouses concurrently, but commonly.[46] Thus, in theory the consent of both spouses is required for every transaction. However, with regard to ordinary transactions conducted by one of the spouses, there is a rebuttable presumption that the other consented.[47] The conveyance of immovable property, transactions requiring the form of a notarial deed and some other important transactions require an explicit formal consent on the part of both spouses.[48] Yet another difference is in the division of property upon divorce. The general rule is equal division. However, in many Eastern European systems the judge has the discretional power to reduce the share of a spouse who wasted common property or did not contribute to it without a serious reason (like unemployment or illness).[49]

17.3. DEFERRED COMMUNITY OF PROPERTY SYSTEMS

The system of deferred community of property was developed in the Nordic region in the beginning of the twentieth century and was later introduced in Germany, Austria, Greece and Switzerland.[50] The word 'deferred' denotes that the forming of the community is postponed until the moment of the termination of marriage.[51] Thus, as long as the marriage exists, the property of the spouses remains separate, but if the marriage is terminated, the spouses are entitled to share each other's wealth.

The forms of such sharing differ from the pooling and subsequent division of the property in kind (in natura) in Sweden, Norway and Denmark, to the monetary compensation of the half of the surplus in Germany and Switzerland; and a mixture

---

[45] E.g. in 1986 in Hungary, in 1994 in Latvia; in 1995 in Russia, in 1998 in the Czech Republic and Estonia, in 1999 in Belorussia; in 2000 in Moldova; in 2001 in Lithuania; in 2004 in Ukraine, and in Serbia in 2005.

[46] E.g. art. 65 (1) of the *Family Code of Ukraine; art. 17 (2) of the Family Act of Estonia; art. 3.92 para. 1 of the Civil Code* of Lithuania; art. 21 (1) of the *Family Law Act* of Moldova, art. 145 (1) of the *Civil Code* of the Czech Republic.

[47] E.g. art. 65 (2) of the *Family Code* of Ukraine; art. 17 (3) of the *Family Act* of Estonia; art. 3.92 para. 2 of the *Civil Code* of Lithuania; art. 21 (2) of the *Family Law Act* of Moldova.

[48] E.g. art. 65 (3) of the *Family Code* of Ukraine (2004); art. 17 (4) of the *Family Act* of Estonia; art. 3.92 para. 3 of the *Civil Code* of Lithuania; art. 21 (2) and (5) of the *Family Law Act* of Moldova; art. 145 (1) of the *Civil Code* of the Czech Republic.

[49] E.g. Art. 39 of the Russian *Family Code*; Art. 70 of the Ukrainian *Family Code*; Art. 24 of the Belorussian *Marriage and Family Code*; Para 18 of the *Family Act* of Estonia,

[50] The precursors of the deferred community systems were nineteenth-century matrimonial property regimes of Hungary and Austria.

[51] On the merits of this term, see: AGELL, A., 'Division of Property upon Divorce from a European Perspective' (1998), p. 6-7.

of these two systems in Finland, Greece and Austria. As a genuine 'community' of assets is formed upon termination of marriage only in the systems that provide for a division of property in kind (in natura), some authors reserve the term 'deferred community' only for the systems prescribing such division.[52] The systems entitling a spouse only to a monetary compensation of the value of the surplus are then called 'participation systems'[53] or even 'separation of property systems'.[54] However, it was rightly concluded that the differences between those two ways of sharing are 'of a technical nature'.[55] These distinctions do not make much difference with regard to the economic outcome of the division. It was also accurately submitted that one system sometimes flows into the other, so that often no 'clear cut distinction' between them can be made.[56] Thus, in the countries with 'real' deferred community systems, each of the spouses has the right to retain the assets previously belonging to his or her separate fund. If the value of these assets exceeds the spouse's share, he or she has to pay monetary compensation to the other spouse.[57] In Finland, Austria and Greece the way of division, monetary compensation or division of property in kind (in natura), depends upon the decision of the debtor-spouse or a judge. For these reasons, all systems without community during marriage and with subsequent division upon termination of marriage will be discussed in this chapter under the same header of 'deferred community of property'.

17.3.1. NORDIC DEFERRED COMMUNITY SYSTEMS

Deferred community of property was introduced in the whole of the Nordic region in the beginning of the twentieth century.[58] The introduction of this regime instantly solved both the problem of inequality and the problem of the autonomy of the spouses: each spouse has the right to administer his or her property during the marriage. At the same time, the needs of a housewife are also fully protected,[59] as at the end of marriage the separate funds are pooled together and then equally divided between the spouses. In Denmark, Sweden and Norway the division of property upon termination of marriage occurred in natura. In Finland the spouse-debtor has the right to choose

---

[52] See, for instance: VERBEKE, A., *Goederenverdeling bij echtscheiding* (1991), p. 29; Dieter Henrich distinguishes four different types of regimes within deferred community system. HENRICH, D., 'Zur Zukunft des Güterrechts in Europa' (2002), p. 1522.
[53] E.g. STEENHOFF, G., 'A Matrimonial Property System for the European Union?' (2004), p. 2-3.
[54] BRAAT, B., ODERKERK, M., STEENHOFF, G., *Huwelijksvermogensrecht in rechtvergelijkend perspectief* (2000), p. 294.
[55] VERBEKE, A. et al, 'European marital property law' (1995), p. 463.
[56] Ibid, p. 464.
[57] Ibid, p. 463.
[58] See Part III, Chapter 11, Section 11.2.1.
[59] AGELL, A., 'Division of Property upon Divorce from a European Perspective' (1998), p. 9.

between division in natura and paying monetary compensation.[60] Under the deferred community of property regime, no common fund automatically exists during the marriage,[61] so family assets are independently administered by each of the spouses. However, this requires the most important family assets to be safeguarded. Therefore the right of the spouses to independently administer their property is restricted with regard to the most important family assets, such as the matrimonial home, household goods and certain other property. Transactions with those assets normally require the consent of the other spouse, even if that spouse is not a co-owner.[62]

The systems that were initially adopted in the Nordic countries resembled the system of universal community of property rather than the limited community of acquests. When a marriage came to an end, all marital and pre-marital property of the spouses was to be pooled together in order to be divided between the spouses. However, as with the growing of the divorce rates marriage evolved from a union for life into a kind of a 'serial monogamy', spouses sharing in each other's premarital assets became less and less self-evident. For these reasons all Nordic systems have been modified in the direction of a limited community of property. Norway introduced this modification in the most straightforward way. The 1991 Norwegian Marriage Act has plainly withdrawn pre-marital property and property acquired by way of gift or inheritance from the division.[63] In Sweden,[64] Denmark[65] and Finland[66] all marital and premarital property is as a rule still subjected to division. The main statutory exceptions are assets acquired by gift or inheritance under the explicit condition, made by the donator or testator, that these assets will be excluded from the division.[67] However, these countries have also developed devices to avoid a possibly unreasonable outcome of the equal division of the entire patrimony of the spouses. Accordingly, Swedish,[68] Danish[69] and

---

[60] VERBEKE, A. et al, 'European marital property law' (1995), p. 463.

[61] In all Nordic countries, common funds can exist if spouses have agreed that certain assets will be owned by them jointly. In Norway there is also a statutory possibility for the creation of joint property during the marriage. The 1991 Norwegian *Marriage Act* (Sec. 31 Para 3) codified a rule, developed earlier in the case law of the Supreme Court, that allows a housewife who is running a household and taking care of children to become co-owner of the house acquired during the marriage by her husband on his name and with his income. SVERDRUP, T., 'Maintenance as a Separate Issue – the Relationship Between Maintenance and Matrimonial Property' (2005), p. 123.

[62] E.g. Ch. 7, Sec 5 of the Swedish *Marriage Code*; Sec 28-39 of the Finnish *Marriage Act*; Sec. 18-19 of the Danish Act *Regarding Legal Effects of Marriage*, Sec. 32-33 of the Norwegian *Marriage Act*.

[63] SVERDRUP, T., 'Maintenance as a Separate Issue – the Relationship Between Maintenance and Matrimonial Property' (2005), p. 127.

[64] For more on the Swedish system, see: SCHIRATZKI, J., National Report 'Sweden' (2003).

[65] For more on the Danish system, see: NIELSEN, L., National Report 'Denmark' (2003).

[66] For more on the Finish system, see: GOTTBERG, E., National Report 'Finland' (2003).

[67] Chapter 7, Sec 2 of the Swedish *Marriage Code*, Sec 28a of the Danish Act *Regarding Legal Effects of Marriage*; Sec. 25 of the Finnish *Marriage Act*.

[68] Chapter 12, Sec. 1 of the Swedish *Marriage Code*.

[69] Sec. 56 of the Danish Act *Regarding Formation and Dissolution of Marriage*.

Finish[70] law grants judges a discretionary power to deviate from the equal division, taking special circumstances into consideration (most commonly the length of marriage[71] and the activities of the spouses in the common household). Another possibility to deviate from the equal division is created in order to protect the interests of one of the spouses from the other spouse's misuse of his or her right to administer his or her property.[72] The introduction of statutory limitations similar to the Norwegian ones is currently being discussed in these countries.[73]

In case of divorce, a spouse who owns certain property has the right, as a rule, to claim specific items of that property to be included in his or her share.[74] In Denmark,[75] Sweden[76] and Norway,[77] the matrimonial home and household goods form the most notable exception to this rule, as the court has discretion to attribute them to the spouse who needs them most. In Finland the matrimonial home is not subject to a special regime of division.[78] In Denmark, Sweden and Norway, the right to occupy the matrimonial home is normally attributed to the spouse who is considered to need it more. In most cases that is the spouse with whom the children come to reside after divorce. The attribution of the matrimonial home and household chattels, however, normally does not influence the spousal share by division, and thus has to be compensated by other property.[79] All deferred community systems protect one spouse in case of bankruptcy of the other.[80]

---

[70]   Sec. 103b of the Finnish *Marriage Act*.

[71]   Anders Agell points to the recommendation made in Sweden in the *travaux préparatoires* with regard to the adjustment of the division of property in accordance with the length of marriage. This recommendation proposes to deviate from equal division if a marriage has lasted for less then 5 years. In such cases, for each year of marriage, 20% of the property of each of the spouses is recommended to be subjected to division. Thus, if a marriage has lasted two years, 40% of the property would be divided; if marriage lasted for three years this would increase to 60%, and so forth. AGELL, A., 'Division of Property upon Divorce from a European Perspective' (1998), p. 11.

[72]   For Denmark see: NIELSEN, L., National Report 'Denmark' (2003), p. 12; for Sweden see: SCHIRATZKI, J., National Report 'Sweden' (2003), p. 17-18; for Finland see: GOTTBERG, E., National Report 'Finland' (2003), p. 17; for Norway see: Sec. 63 of the Norwegian *Marriage Act*.

[73]   SVERDRUP, T., 'Maintenance as a Separate Issue – the Relationship Between Maintenance and Matrimonial Property' (2005), p. 127.

[74]   E.g. Sec. 91 of the Finnish *Marriage Act*; Ch. 18 Sec 1 of the Swedish *Marriage Code*; Sec. 66 of the Norwegian *Marriage Act*.

[75]   NIELSEN, L., National Report 'Denmark' (2003), p. 12; for Sweden SCHIRATZKI, J., National Report 'Sweden' (2003), p. 16.

[76]   SCHIRATZKI, J., National Report 'Sweden' (2003), p. 16.

[77]   Sec. 67 of the Norwegian *Marriage Act*.

[78]   GOTTBERG, E., National Report 'Finland' (2003), p. 16.

[79]   See: for Denmark NIELSEN, L., National Report 'Denmark' (2003), 12; for Sweden SCHIRATZKI, J., National Report 'Sweden' (2003), p. 16; for Norway Sec. 67d and Sec 70 of the Norwegian *Marriage Act*.

[80]   In Demark, Sweden and Norway, when the debts of one spouse exceed his or her assets, debts are not divided between the spouses (NIELSEN, L., National Report 'Denmark' (2003), 11; Sweden SCHIRATZKI, J., National Report 'Sweden' (2003), p. 15; Sec. 58b of the Norwegian *Marriage Act*).

17.3.2. THE GERMAN 'COMMUNITY OF SURPLUS'

In Germany the pre-reform system of matrimonial property was the system of separation of property with community of administration entrusted to the husband.[81] The reform of this system became inevitable when, in 1949, Article 3 of the Constitution proclaimed the equality of men and women.[82] However, no statutory measures were taken within the four-year term the Constitution gave the legislature to adjust the existing law, and in 1953 the equality provision of the Article 3 became self-executing.[83] There was a consensus that the only regime that could be imposed by the courts in order to satisfy the constitutional requirement was the regime of separation of property.[84] This regime existed until 1957, when the long-awaited statutory reform finally came. The Equality Law 1957[85] introduced the current legal regime of deferred community of property (*Zugewinngemeinshaft*),[86] which is referred to in English as 'the community of surplus', 'the community of gains' or 'the community of increase'. As in the Nordic region, the property of the spouses under this regime remains separate during the marriage. Each of the spouses is, as a rule, free to administer his or her own assets.[87] The restrictions of the right of independent administration are also similar to those in the Nordic countries. In addition, each spouse needs the other's consent in order to dispose of his or her property 'in its entirety'.[88] Similar to Nordic law, the spouses share in the increase of each other's wealth upon termination of marriage. However, at this point similarity ends. In most of the Nordic countries property is pooled into community and then divided in kind (in natura). In contrast, in Germany no pooling and subsequent division takes place. Instead the surplus of each of the spouses is calculated, and then the spouse with a larger surplus has to pay half of the difference to the other one.[89] The way the surplus is calculated resembles the Norwegian system's division of marital property. The premarital property of the spouses is not counted in the calculation of the surplus, only the increase of its value during the marriage. Assets acquired during the marriage by gift or inheritance are regarded as 'premarital property'.[90]

Also in Finland no division of spouses' property takes place in case of bankruptcy GOTTBBERG, E., National Report 'Finland' (2003), p. 16.

[81]   The *Verwaltungsgemeinschaft* was introduced by the BGB. See Part III, Chapter 10, Section 10.2.4.

[82]   MÜLLER-FREIENFELS, W., 'Family Law and the Law of Succession in Germany' (1967), p. 424.

[83]   GLENDON, M. A., 'Power and Authority in the Family: New Legal Patterns as Reflection of Changing Ideologies' (1975), p. 7-8.

[84]   GLENDON, M.A., *The Transformation of Family Law* (1989), p. 117.

[85]   *Gleichberechtigungsgesetz.*

[86]   MÜLLER-FREIENFELS, W., 'Family Law and the Law of Succession in Germany' (1967), p. 426.

[87]   COESTER-WALTER, D., COERSTER, M., National Report 'Germany' (2003), p. 12.

[88]   Para 1365 BGB.

[89]   Para 1378 1 BGB. See GOTTWALD, P., SCHWAB, D., BÜTTNER, E., *Family and Succession Law in Germany* (2001), p. 113.

[90]   Para 1374 BGB. See COESTER-WALTER, D., COERSTER, M., National 'Germany' (2003), p. 15.

17.3.3. OTHER COUNTRIES WITH DEFERRED COMMUNITY OF PROPERTY

A regime of deferred community of property that resembles the Norway's was established in Austria in 1978.[91] The most notable difference between Austria and the other deferred community systems is that in Austria the division of property takes place according to the 'principle of fairness'[92] rather than equal division. The principle of fairness allows that a spouse who is the primary caretaker of children in addition to also having full-time employment may well receive 2/3 of the divisible property.[93] Another point of difference is that in Austria the divisible property is generally limited to those assets commonly used by the spouses during the marriage (like the matrimonial home and household goods, etc.) and the marital savings.[94] Both types of assets are divided separately. The division of property may take the form of re-allocation of property, awarding occupational rights with regard to the matrimonial home as well as monetary compensation.[95]

In Greece, the community of surplus replaced the traditional dotal system in 1983.[96] The Greek system mostly resembles the German one. There is, however, an important difference. Like the German law, the Greek law imposes on the spouses a mandatory compensation system.[97] However, under the Greek law one spouse is entitled to share in the other spouse's property only if the former spouse has contributed in the increase of the latter spouse's property.[98] As it is often difficult to calculate the spouses' contributions to one another's property, the law establishes a rebuttable presumption that such contribution amounts to one third of the debtor-spouse's property.[99] Thus, unlike in Germany, no principle of equal division exists under Greek law. Another difference is that a Greek judge has the discretionary power to determine the modus of division: via monetary compensation or via division in kind (in natura).[100]

---

[91] See: RECHBERGER, W., National Report 'Austria' (2003), p. 6.
[92] This results in equal division being the general rule, yet the court has wide discretion to divide the property differently. Para 83 (1) of the 1928 Austrian *Marriage Act* (*Ehegezetz*). See: RECHBERGER, W., National 'Austria' (2003), p. 19 -20.
[93] STEENHOFF, G., 'A Matrimonial Property System for the European Union?' (2004), p. 3.
[94] VERBEKE, A. et al, 'European marital property law' (1995), p. 462.
[95] Ibid, p. 468.
[96] MOUSTAIRA, E., National Report 'Greece' (2003), p. 5.
[97] VERBEKE, A. et al, 'European marital property law' (1995), p. 462.
[98] Such 'contribution' is interpreted rather broadly and includes among others: household work, 'psychological support' and 'creation of pleasant family ambiance', which enables the other spouse to execute his professional activities better. See: MOUSTAIRA, E., National Report 'Greece' (2003), p. 15-16.
[99] VERBEKE, A. et al, 'European marital property law' (1995), p. 466.
[100] Ibid, p. 467.

The participation in acquests[101] (*Errungenschaftsbeteiligung* or *participation aux acquêts*) became the legal regime of marriage property in Switzerland in 1988.[102] Four different funds are distinguished under the Swiss regime: the 'own' property (*Das Eigengut*) of the husband, the 'own' property of the wife, the acquests of the husband, and the acquests of the wife. Upon the termination of marriage the surplus of the acquests of each of the spouses is calculated, and the spouse with a larger surplus has to pay half of the difference to the other.[103] Other than in Germany, the increase in value of the pre-marital assets is not taken into consideration in the calculation of the surplus.[104]

17.4. THE SEPARATION OF PROPERTY SYSTEMS

The legal regime of separation of property exists in the common law countries: Great Britain and the Republic of Ireland, and in some civil law jurisdictions like the Spanish Autonomies of Catalonia and Balearic Islands.

17.4.1. ENGLAND AND WALES

The concept of 'matrimonial property regime', as understood in Continental Europe, is unknown in England and Wales.[105] The separation of property of husband and wife, introduced in 1882 by the Married Women's Property Act 1882,[106] entails that marriage does not bring any change to the property situation of the spouses. The proprietary relationship of the spouses after marriage in theory remains equal to that of complete strangers. However, in the second half of the twentieth century the separation of property of husband and wife was eroded by numerous piecemeal statutory and case law amendments.[107] It is held to be a 'moot point' whether these various provisions 'can in truth be said to amount to a "matrimonial property regime."'[108] Another important difference between the English and continental systems

---

[101] For more on the Swiss system see: GRAHAM-SIEGENTHALER, B., 'Switzerland' (2002), p. 670, 673-674 and 681-682.
[102] Ibid, p. 673.
[103] HENRICH, D., 'Zur Zukunft des Güterrechts in Europa' (2002), p. 1522.
[104] PINTENS, W., 'Europeanisation of Family Law' (2003), p. 10.
[105] CLARKSON, C., HILL, J., THOMPSON, M., National Report 'United Kingdom. England' (2003), p. 5.
[106] See Part III, Chapter 10, Section 10.2.4.
[107] CRETNEY, S., MASSON, J., BAILEY-HARRIS, R., *Principles of Family Law* (2003), p. 104.
[108] CLARKSON, C., HILL, J., THOMPSON, M., National Report 'United Kingdom. England' (2003), p. 5.

is that in England and Wales it is generally at present not possible to deviate from the 'legal' regime by concluding a marital contract.[109]

The disadvantages of separation of property for married women had already become apparent during World War II.[110] The separation system had introduced formal equality, but it did not allow women engaged in childrearing and household activities any possibility to share in the income of their husbands. Brenda Hoggett and David Pearl indicate three main problems with separation of property: unfairness, uncertainty and dependence on the discretion of the courts for adjustments.[111] The generally felt dissatisfaction with the separation system called for reforms. These were to solve two problems. One objective was to give housewives a better possibility to share in the family assets (especially in the matrimonial home and the household goods). The other point was to create a system availing the spouses more predictability and certainty. Starting with the Morton Commission of 1956[112] a whole range of reform proposals suggested introducing a fixed system of property rights in the form of a community of property for all assets, or at least for the matrimonial home.[113] There has, however, always been a considerable body of opinion objecting any form of fixed property rights and making a case for continuation of the traditional discretional system.[114] The 'struggle' for a statutory community regime was, in the words of Stephan Cretney, eventually 'quietly abandoned'.[115]

In the absence of a statutory reform, the Court of Appeal developed, in the 1950s-1960s under the leadership of Lord Denning, case law interpreting the Married Women's Property Act as empowering the judge to reallocate to property of the spouses as 'he

---

[109]   Such contracts are traditionally regarded as legally unenforceable and irrelevant to the exercise of the courts discretionary power to re-allocate the spouses' property. However, recently some shift in the direction of giving more weight to marital contracts has been monitored. Ibid, p. 11.

[110]   By that time it became clear 'that separation of property would not achieve justice for married women in the conditions prevalent in the second half of the twentieth century'. CRETNEY, S., *Family Law in the Twentieth Century* (2003), p. 114-115.

[111]   HOGGERTT, B., PEARL, D., *The Family, Law and Society* (1991), p. 141.

[112]   Royal Commission on Marriage and Divorce. The majority of the Commission rejected a far reaching proposal for a statutory community of property regime, but proposed joint ownership of savings from household money and statutory protection of the right to occupy the matrimonial home. CRETNEY, S., *Family Law in the Twentieth Century* (2003), p. 124-125.

[113]   The most notable are the Law Commission's *Working Paper on Family Property Law* (1971); First Report on *Family Property: A New Approach* (Law Com. No 53, 1973); *Third Report on Matrimonial Property* (Law Com. No. 86, 1978); *Family Law: Matrimonial Property* (Law Com. No 175, 1988) and Discussion *Paper Sharing Homes* (2002). See for an overview: CRETNEY, S., *Family Law in the Twentieth Century* (2003), p. 136-141.

[114]   First Report on *Family Property: A New Approach*, Law Com. No 53, 1973, para 10, cited in: HOGGERTT, B., PEARL, D., *The Family, Law and Society* (1991), at p. 155.

[115]   CRETNEY, S., *Family Law in the Twentieth Century* (2003), p. 136.

thinks fit'.[116] The result of decisions on the property matters upon divorce became less unfair, though 'even more uncertain'.[117] This line of case law was, however, brought to an end in 1969 by the decision of House of Lords in *Pettitt v. Pettitt*.[118] In this case, it was ruled that the court has no power to vary spouses' property rights and that the beneficial entitlement between spouses has to be determined according to the general rules of law without regard to their relations by marriage.[119]

Parallel to the case law developments, a series of statutory amendments were made in order to improve to position of married women. The Married Women's Property Act 1964 entitled a wife to half of the savings from housekeeping. However, the real solution to the problem came only with the Matrimonial Causes Act 1973, which gave the court the discretionary power to make a fair re-distribution of the spouses' assets by way of granting ancillary relief upon divorce.[120] The overriding objective of such distribution was the achievement of a fair outcome.[121] Article 25 of the Act states that in exercising its discretional power the court should take into consideration a number of circumstances. The new provisions more or less resolved the problem of fairness, but did so at expense of the predictability and certainty. The remaining problem was that until their case was decided by the court the spouses could neither influence[122] nor predict their property situation after divorce. In 1988 the Law Commission evaluated the rules determining ownership of property by the spouses according to the Matrimonial Causes Act as 'arbitrary, uncertain and unfair'.[123] The high costs of adjudication could be added to this list.

In addition to these general developments, a special regime for the matrimonial home has been created at law and in equity over the course of the last decades. If one of the spouses is a legal owner, equity can give the other spouse a beneficiary interest in the house. To this effect the equitable instruments of implied, resulting[124] and

---

[116] CRETNEY, S., MASSON, J., BAILEY-HARRIS, R., *Principles of Family Law* (2003), p. 104-106.
[117] HOGGETT, B., PEARL, D., *The Family, Law and Society* (1991), p. 142.
[118] *Pettitt v. Pettitt* [1970] *AC* 777; [1969] 2 *All ER* 385.
[119] LOWE, N., 'The English approach to the division of assets upon family breakdown' (1999), p. 48-49.
[120] CRETNEY, S., MASSON, J., BAILEY-HARRIS, R., *Principles of Family Law* (2003), p. 105.
[121] Ibid.
[122] The spouses cannot effectively regulate their property relationships by a marital contract, as such does not restrict the discretional power of the judge to re-allocate the property as it thinks fair.
[123] *Family Law: Matrimonial Property*, Law Com. No 175, 1988, para. 1.4.
[124] Resulting trust is presumed when one of the spouses contributes to the acquisition of a house put into the name of the other spouse. CLARKSON, C., HILL, J., THOMPSON, M., National Report 'United Kingdom. England' (2003), p. 7.

constructive[125] trusts, as well as the doctrine of proprietary estoppel,[126] are employed.[127] In addition to the equitable mechanisms, the Matrimonial Proceedings and Property Act 1970 allows a spouse who contributed in money or value to the improvement of property of the other spouse to claim a property right in this property.[128] It is important to mention that in cases of divorce all above-described rules are subject to the overriding discretionary power of the court to reallocate property in order to achieve a fair outcome.[129] The occupational rights of a spouse who cannot claim a beneficial interest were first protected under the Matrimonial Home Act 1967, and are presently guaranteed by the provisions of Part IV of the Family Law Act 1996. This Act gives a spouse occupying a matrimonial home that is legally owned by the other spouse, a right to stay in it.[130] A spouse not occupying the matrimonial home has a right to enter and occupy it.[131] A spouse without a proprietary interest in matrimonial home can also prevent the spouse who owns the home from disposing of it.[132]

After the turn of the millennium, the principle of equal division was introduced into English law. This happened in a fairly undramatic way; not by the reform of statutory law, but through judicial activism. In 2000, in the leading case *White v. White*, Lord Nicholls stated that equal division should be considered as 'a starting point',[133] and that 'a judge would always be well advised to check his tentative views against the yardstick of equal division. As a general guide, equality should be departed from only if, and to the extent that, there is good reason for doing so.'[134] However, the cases reported after *White v. White* initially showed that equal division remained more an exception than the rule, as the judges continued to give the wives less than 50% of the

---

[125] Constructive trust can be found if the spouses intended the house, put on the name of one of then, to become their shared ownership, provided that the other spouse has suffered detriment in reliance on that shared intention. Ibid.

[126] The doctrine of estoppel prevents one spouse from asserting strict legal rights when it would be unconscionable or unjust to do so. CRETNEY, S., MASSON, J., BAILEY-HARRIS, R., *Principles of Family Law* (2003), p. 136. Estoppel is mostly applied if one spouse moves into a house of the other, the other spouse makes him or her to believe that he or she will be given interests in this house, and in reliance on this belief the latter spouse acts to his or her detriment. CLARKSON, C., HILL, J., THOMPSON, M., National Report 'United Kingdom. England' (2003), p. 8.

[127] For detailed information see: CRETNEY, S., MASSON, J., BAILEY-HARRIS, R., *Principles of Family Law* (2003), p. 109-160

[128] Ibid, p. 104.

[129] CLARKSON, C., HILL, J., THOMPSON, M., National Report 'United Kingdom. England' (2003), p. 8.

[130] S. 3o (2) of the Family Law Act 1993.

[131] S. 33 of the Family Law Act 1993. See: CLARKSON, C., HILL, J., THOMPSON, M., National Report 'United Kingdom. England' (2003), p. 9.

[132] CLARKSON, C., HILL, J., THOMPSON, M., National Report 'United Kingdom. England' (2003), p. 10.

[133] *White v. White* [2000] *2 FLR,* per Lord Cooke of Thorndon, p. 999.

[134] *White v. White* [2000] *2 FLR,* per Lord Nicholls of Birkenhead, p. 989. For an analysis of this case, see: FREEMAN, M. (ed.), 'Exploring the Boundaries of Family Law in England in 2000' (2002), p.134-137.

marital property.[135] This situation came to an end in 2002, when the Court of Appeal stated in *Lambert v. Lambert* that deviation from equal division could be only justified by exceptional circumstances.[136] The exceptional circumstances are not listed in the judgment, but the courts are summoned to interpret this concept narrowly. Thorpe LJ specifically clarified that 'it is unacceptable to place greater value on the contribution of a breadwinner than that of the homemaker'.[137] The line of *White* was continued in *Miller v. Miller* and *MacFarlane v. MacFarlane*, [138] decided by the House of Lords on the 24th of May 2006. It was stated in the leading opinion of Lord Nicholls that even in case of a short marriage the yardstick of equality is to be applied to all property acquired during the marriage otherwise than by inheritance or gift, without distinction between 'business and investment' assets and 'family assets'.[139]

To end with, it can be concluded that although the English legislature introduced neither a fixed system of property rights nor a community of property system, more or less the same result was reached in the most recent case law. The traditional discretional system formally has remained unchanged. However, the equal division rule established in *White v. White* and strengthened in *Lambert v. Lambert, Miller v. Miller and MacFarlane v. MacFarlane*, actually resolved both the problem of the protection of property rights of the housewife and the problem of predictability and certainty. These developments allowed several comparatists to suggest that the English case law came close to de-facto establishment of a kind of deferred community of property.[140]

17.5. CONVERGENCE OF MATRIMONIAL PROPERTY LAW?

17.5.1. DIFFERENT OPINIONS REGARDING THE EXISTENCE OF CONVERGENCE

Both the existence of convergence in matrimonial property law and the possibility of its harmonisation in present-day Europe are rather controversial subjects. Already in 1989 Mary Ann Glendon suggested that various systems of matrimonial property have 'partially converged insofar as separate property systems had adopted devises to

---

[135] CLARKSON, C., HILL, J., THOMPSON, M., National Report 'United Kingdom. England' (2003), p. 13.
[136] *Lambert v. Lambert, EWCA Civ* 1685 [2002] 3 *FCR* 673, [2003] 1 *FLR*, p. 139.
[137] *Lambert v. Lambert, EWCA Civ* 1685 [2002], Thorpe LJ, para. 27.
[138] *Miller v. Miller* and *MacFarlane v. MacFarlane* [2006] *UKHL* 24; [2006]1 *AC* 1.
[139] Ibid. Per Lord Nicholls of Birkenhead, paras. 17-24.
[140] PINTENS, W., 'Europeanisation of Family Law' (2003), p. 12.

increase sharing of property between the spouses, and community property systems had adopted devices to provide for more independence in management'.[141] Recently Dieter Martiny emphasized, building on the conclusions of a study commissioned by the European Commission in 2003,[142] that apart from the differences between the regimes, 'there is also much common ground' in the field of matrimonial property law.[143] Matrimonial property law was the first field of family law to have been suggested to be suitable for deliberate harmonisation. In 1995 Anders Agell pointed to the possibility of elaborating an optional matrimonial property regime, which would be open to parties of international marriages.[144] Agell's proposal was instantly embraced by various scholars.[145] The idea of an optional marriage property regime appeared to be so appealing because, in contrast to other fields of family law, matrimonial property law leaves room for contractual freedom of the parties. At present all continental European countries more or less allow the spouses to deviate from a legal regime of matrimonial property in favour of a contractual regime. Therefore an optional regime could be created without significant modification of existing laws.[146]

However, other authors submit that convergence in the field of matrimonial property law remains rather limited.[147] This conclusion is derived from the fact that matrimonial property systems in Europe are currently divided into two 'fundamentally different types': the limited community of property, adhered to in the Roman legal systems and in Eastern Europe, and the deferred community of property, enacted in the Nordic region and in the Germanic legal systems.[148] It is also suggested that the differences between the deferred and the limited community systems cannot easily be

---

[141] GLENDON, M.A., *The Transformation of Family Law* (1989), p. 117.
[142] *Analyse comparative des rapports nationaux et propositions d'harmonisation consortium* (2003).
[143] MARTINY D., 'A New Matrimonial Property Regime for Europe' (2004), p. 3.
[144] AGELL, A., 'Towards Uniforming Spouses' Property Rights Especially in International Marriages?' (1995), p. 63-80.
[145] E.g. STEENHOFF, G., 'Op weg naar een Europees familierecht' (1999), p. 27; VERBEKE, A., 'Perspectives for an International Marital Contract' (2001); HENRICH, D., 'Zur Zukunft des Güterrechts in Europa' (2002), p. 1526; ANTOKOLSKAIA, M., 'Enkele gedachten over de harmonisatie van het familierecht in Europa' (2002); STEENHOFF, G., 'A Matrimonial Property System for the European Union?' (2004); MARTINY D., 'A New Matrimonial Property Regime for Europe' (2004) ; BRAAT, B., *Indépendance et interdépendance patrimoniales des époux dans le régime matrimonial légal des droits français, néerlandais et suisse* (2004), p. 417.
[146] VERBEKE, A., 'Perspectives for an International Marital Contract' (2001), p.192.
[147] E.g. PINTENS, W., VANWINCKELEN, C., *Casebook. European Family Law* (2001), p. 20-21; PINTENS, W., VAN DER MEERSCH, B., VANWINCKELEN, C., *Inleiding tot het Familiaal Vermogensrecht* (2002), p. 13-14; STEENHOFF, G., 'A Matrimonial Property System for the European Union?' (2004), p. 4; BOELE-WOELKI, K., 'Divorce in Europe: Unification of Private International Law and Harmonisation of Substantive Law' (2002), p. 23.
[148] PINTENS, W., 'Europeanisation of Family Law' (2003), p. 9. BOELE-WOELKI, K., 'Divorce in Europe: Unification of Private International Law and Harmonisation of Substantive Law' (2002), p. 23.

reconciled.[149] This divide is aggravated by the existence of one more completely different marital property system – the separation of property system of the common law countries.[150] For these reasons, the CEFL has for the moment considered matrimonial property unsuitable for drafting any *Principles of European Matrimonial Property Law.*[151]

The differing appreciations of the level of convergence in the field of matrimonial property law could be explained by the fact that the various researches are looking for similarities and differences on two different levels: the functional level of functional solutions, on the one hand; and the formal level of legal techniques, concepts and rules, on the other.

17.5.2. COMPARISON ON THE FUNCTIONAL LEVEL: COMPARING FUNCTIONAL SOLUTIONS

Matrimonial property law is less political. More consensus on the objectives of reforms

Taking the beginning of the twentieth century as a starting point, one can see that the modification of the matrimonial property regimes has been no less profound than the transformations in the field of divorce law. However, there is one notable difference in the process of the reforms. It is rightly noted by Mary Ann Glendon that although the law governing the financial consequences of divorce has 'more obvious and immediate impact on people's lives',[152] its reform was much less controversial than the reform of the divorce law itself. This is no wonder. As was discussed in chapter 14, the modification of divorce law in Europe stands in the centre of the conservative/progressive discord. In the framework of the divorce law reforms the 'conservatives' and 'progressives' generally pursue quite opposite policy objectives: making divorce more difficult or easier, respectively. In contrast, in the field of matrimonial property law there is much more consensus with regard to the main objectives of the reforms.[153] These objectives, ensuring the equality of the spouses and finding a proper

---

[149] HENRICH, D., SCHWAB, D. (eds.), *Eheliche Gemeinschaft, Partnerschaft und Vermögen im europäischen Vergleich* (1999); PINTENS, W., 'Europeanisation of Family Law' (2003), p. 10.

[150] PINTENS, W., 'Europeanisation of Family Law' (2003), p. 11.

[151] See BOELE-WOELKI, K., 'Divorce in Europe: Unification of Private International Law and Harmonisation of Substantive Law' (2002), p. 23.

[152] GLENDON, M.A., *Abortion and Divorce in Western Law* (1987), p. 108.

[153] Thus, Dieter Martiny discerns a 'considerable mass of fundamental agreement'. MARTINY D., 'A New Matrimonial Property Regime for Europe' (2004), p. 3. See in the similar sense also: BRAAT, B., ODERKERK, M., STEENHOFF, G., *Huwelijksvermogensrecht in rechtsvergelijkend perspectief* (2000), p. 271; ANTOKOLSKAIA, M., 'Enkele gedachten over de harmonisatie van het familierecht in Europa' (2002), p. 8.

balance between the principles of autonomy and solidarity, do not find much objection in either the 'conservative' or 'progressive' circles. Thus, the discussions surrounding the reforms of matrimonial property law are more technical rather than political.[154] These discussions mainly concern either the legal-technical methods of achieving the stated objectives (for example the English discourse with regard to the introduction of a community of property system or continuing with the system based on judicial discretion), or the details of the particular balance between the principles of solidarity and equality.

The basic commonality of the objectives made various marital property regimes grow closer to each other.[155] Mary Ann Glendon accurately mentioned in the early 1980s that as result of the assimilation of legal regimes, traditional comparison based on the division between the community and the separate property systems becomes less revealing.[156] Instead, she suggested a functional comparison along the lines of regulation of property relationships of the spouses existing in the context of ongoing marriage and termination of marriage by death or divorce.[157]

Recent examples of functional comparison

Several attempts of such functional comparison have been undertaken in the recent years. In 1998, Anders Agell showed considerable diversity in the outcome of the application of the rules from different European jurisdictions to one and the same case of division of property upon divorce between hypothetical spouses: Adam and Eva.[158] Most notable is his conclusion that those differences do not follow the lines dividing various matrimonial property systems, but rather go across these lines.[159] Another, more extensive study, was made by Bente Braat, Marieke Oderkerk and Gert Steenhoff in 2000.[160] In this study several jurisdictions,[161] representing different matrimonial property regimes, were evaluated on the basis of such functional criteria as: fairness, equality, flexibility and protection of the spouses, and so on. The authors discern a certain commonality on the level of functional equivalence,[162] but found no common

---

[154] See PINTENS, W., VANWINCKELEN, C., *Casebook. European Family Law* (2001), p. 21; ANTOKOLSKAIA, M., 'Enkele gedachten over de harmonisatie van het familierecht in Europa' (2002), p. 8; PINTENS, W., 'Europeanisation of Family Law' (2003), p. 12, note 45.

[155] GLENDON, M.A., *The New Family and the New Property* (1981), p. 57.

[156] Ibid, p. 58.

[157] Ibid.

[158] AGELL, A., 'Division of Property upon Divorce from a European Perspective' (1998), p. 1-20.

[159] Ibid, p. 9-16.

[160] BRAAT, B., ODERKERK, M., STEENHOFF, G., *Huwelijksvermogensrecht in rechtvergelijkend perspectief* (2000).

[161] Denmark, Germany, Italy, England, France, Italy and Sweden.

[162] BRAAT, B., ODERKERK, M., STEENHOFF, G., *Huwelijksvermogensrecht in rechtvergelijkend perspectief* (2000), p. 271ff.

core at all with regard to the legal techniques and the legal rules.[163] An in-depth study, based on the functional comparison of the impact of the principles of autonomy and solidarity on Swiss, French and Dutch law, was made in the dissertation of Bente Braat, which appeared in 2004.[164] The conclusion of this scrutiny is that inter-spousal solidarity is better ensured in the systems with community during the marriage, while the autonomy of spouses is more prominent in the deferred community (in terminology of Braat, the participation) systems.[165]

The ambit of the present study makes going into details fairly impossible. In the following two sections I will limit myself to a very general functional comparison. Such rough comparison certainly misses the precision and comprehensiveness of the last-mentioned studies. However, abstracting from the details sometimes reveals the general lines more clearly.

Formal and de-facto equality of the spouses

The objective of the formal legal equality of the spouses is successfully attained in all European legal systems.[166] In all countries with a community of property, the spouses have an equal right to administer their separate funds, and an equal right to administer the common fund (concurrent administration in the Western European countries and common administration in Eastern European countries). In the systems without community during the marriage,[167] each spouse has a right to administer her or his own assets. The restrictions with regard to disposing of specially protected assets (like the matrimonial home and household goods) apply equally to husbands and wives. Also, the rules governing the division (or the re-allocation) of property upon divorce are entirely gender neutral.

The picture with regard to the de-facto equality of the spouses is less bright. With regard to the administration of property, only the limited community systems place a housewife on equal footing with her husband who 'earns' the property. However, one community system, namely the Dutch universal community, does not give a housewife such an equal right. Under Dutch law each spouse administers the assets

---

[163] Ibid; STEENHOFF, G., 'A Matrimonial Property System for the European Union?' (2004), p. 4.

[164] BRAAT, B., *Indépendance et interdépendance patrimoniales des époux dans le régime matrimonial légal des droits français, néerlandais et suisse* (2004).

[165] Ibid, p. 416.

[166] BRAAT, B., ODERKERK, M., STEENHOFF, G., *Huwelijksvermogensrecht in rechtvergelijkend perspectief* (2000), p. 245.

[167] All kinds of deferred community systems and the system of separation of property operate functionally rather similarly due to one fundamental common feature – an absence of community of property during the marriage. For this reason, in the framework of this functional analysis they will be discussed together unless separate examination is necessary.

that he or she has brought into the community.[168] Remarkably enough, this modus of administration is maintained in the Bill, proposing the introduction of a limited community system.[169]

In all systems without community a housewife has no right to participate in the administration of the family assets, as all of them fall into the separate fund of the husband.[170] This deficiency is, however, somewhat compensated by granting a non-owning spouse the right of co-administration with respect to the matrimonial home and most other important family assets, owned by the other spouse. A special protection of the matrimonial home is a common feature of all systems without community during the marriage. The list of the other specially protected assets, and thus the level of the de-facto equality of a non-working housewife, varies significantly from one jurisdiction to another.

Thus, in general the community systems favour the de-facto equality of the spouses in the most straightforward and effective manner. The systems without community partially reach the same results via an indirect way of special protection of the most important family assets. However, as the Dutch universal community system gives a housewife as little protection as the systems without community, it can be concluded that even the differences in the level of de-facto equality do not strictly follow the lines between the various systems of matrimonial property.

Solidarity versus autonomy

The explanation of the many differences between the functional solutions reached in the various European jurisdictions to matrimonial property law problems lays in the fact that the principle of autonomy and the principle of solidarity point in opposing directions, and that each jurisdiction has found a specific balance between these two conflicting ends.[171]

---

[168] Article 97 of Book 1 of the Dutch Civil Code.

[169] See: Draft Law 'On Modification of the Statutory Community of Assets', Second Chamber, 2005/2006, 28 867, No. 9 and 10. See also: REINHARTZ, B., 'De nieuwe voorstellen ter aanpassing van de wettelijke gemeenschap van goederen' (2006), p. 8.

[170] In order to prevent such a situation, the Norwegian law has established a legal presumption of spousal co-ownership with regard to the matrimonial home and other property acquired for common use, provided that they both contributed to the acquisition of such property. (Sec. 32, Para 5 of the Norwegian *Marriage Act*). Housekeeping and childrearing is regarded as sufficient contribution from the part of the wife. See: SVERDRUP, T., 'Maintenance as a Separate Issue – the Relationship Between Maintenance and Matrimonial Property' (2005), p. 123.

[171] See VERBEKE, A., *Goederenverdeling bij echtscheiding* (1991), p. 402-404 ; and more recently: BRAAT, B., *Indépendance et interdépendance patrimoniales des époux dans le régime matrimonial légal des droits français, néerlandais et suisse* (2004), p. 43.

The objective of the autonomy of the spouses is, in general, better achieved in the systems without community.[172] In these systems each spouse remains during the marriage the legal owner of his or her property, and the principle of solidarity comes into stage only when the marriage comes to an end. However, in these jurisdictions the principle of solidarity necessitates protection of the most important family assets from ill-considered administration by a spouse-owner.[173] Therefore, all countries with the separation of property during marriage one way or another limit the power of the spouse-owner to independently dispose of the matrimonial home. As has been mentioned above, the scope of the other specially protected assets differs significantly from one country to another. For instance, in England special protection does not actually go any further than the matrimonial home. In the Nordic countries, disposition of the household goods and some other property acquired for common use also requires the consent of the spouse non-owner. In Germany the list of transactions requiring consent of the other spouse is complemented by the acts of disposition of the property 'in its entirety'.

In the countries with limited community of property, the principle of autonomy is more subordinate to the principle of solidarity.[174] In these jurisdictions both spouses jointly administer the common fund; in Western Europe by way of concurrent, and in Eastern Europe by way of common administration. However, a closer look at the limited community systems reveals much more autonomy of the spouses than the principle of joint administration may suggest. In countries with concurrent adminis-tration, each of the spouses is, as a rule, allowed to independently perform ordinary transactions with regard to the common assets. The countries with common administration reach the same result by way of a statutory presumption of the consent of the other spouse to ordinary transactions performed by either of them. With transactions involving the most important family assets, both spouses have to act jointly in all limited community systems. The list of specially protected assets in the limited community jurisdictions is generally more extensive than in the jurisdictions without community during marriage. Special protection of the matrimonial home, however, constitutes the common core of both systems with and without community.[175]

---

[172] Alain Verbeke et al call the principle of autonomy 'the cornerstone of a system of separation of property'. VERBEKE, A. et al, 'European marital property law' (1995), p. 455. See also the conclusion of Bente Braat. BRAAT, B., *Indépendance et interdépendance patrimoniales des époux dans le régime matrimonial légal des droits français, néerlandais et suisse* (2004), p. 416.

[173] See BRAAT, B., ODERKERK, M., STEENHOFF, G., *Huwelijksvermogensrecht in rechtvergelijkend perspectief* (2000), p. 267-268.

[174] BRAAT, B., *Indépendance et interdépendance patrimoniales des époux dans le régime matrimonial légal des droits français, néerlandais et suisse* (2004), p. 416.

[175] See also: MARTINY D., 'A New Matrimonial Property Regime for Europe' (2004), p. 3; PINTENS, W., VAN DER MEERSCH, B., VANWINCKELEN, C., *Inleiding tot het Familiaal Vermogensrecht* (2002), p. 13; BRAAT, B., ODERKERK, M., STEENHOFF, G., *Huwelijksvermogensrecht in rechtvergelijkend perspectief* (2000), p. 272.

This brief sketch shows that as to the administration of property a rather similar functional result with regard to reconciling the spouses' autonomy and solidarity is reached in the systems with and without community, despite the different starting points.

The principle of solidarity requires much more than just special protection from ill-considered administration of the most important family assets. The essence of the principle of solidarity is best epitomised by the modern model of the partnership-marriage. In such a marriage, each spouse is availed an equal share of family assets regardless of the way he or she contributes to their acquisition: child rearing and household work or paid job and business activities.[176] At present in the vast majority of the countries with both community and separation of property during the marriage,[177] the principle of equal sharing is the general rule.[178] Moreover, recent developments show that equal division has become the general rule not only in the limited and deferred community systems, but even in the English system of separation of property.

However, the differences in the extent of the spousal solidarity still remain rather significant. The initial starting point of most systems is the sharing in all pre-marital and post-marital assets. This rule is based on the 'extreme' notion of solidarity.[179] According to this broad, old notion, solidarity involves a total community of life and property, and the extent of the patrimonial community does not depend on the contributions of the spouses.[180] This form of sharing still exists in The Netherlands, the last country with a universal community system. This rule still operates as a starting point in several countries with deferred community: Sweden, Denmark and Finland. One might be amazed by the fact that this same 'extreme' solidarity is also operative in the English separation of property system, as the court has the discretional power to reallocate all assets of the spouses, no matter when or how they were acquired.[181]

However, such a broad notion of solidarity is more consonant to the earlier concept of the life-long-marriage than to the modern reality of 'serial monogamy'. Tone Sverdrup has accurately pointed to a general tendency towards increasingly linking the division of matrimonial property to the contributions (financial and non-market)

---

[176] VERBEKE, A., *Goederenverdeling bij echtscheiding* (1991), p. 403-404.
[177] The most notable exceptions are Greece and Austria.
[178] See for an overview: VERBEKE, A., *Goederenverdeling bij echtscheiding* (1991), p. 405-411.
[179] PINTENS, W., 'Europeanisation of Family Law' (2003), p. 10.
[180] SVERDRUP, T., 'Maintenance as a Separate Issue – the Relationship Between Maintenance and Matrimonial Property' (2005), p. 122.
[181] See: BRAAT, B., ODERKERK, M., STEENHOFF, G., *Huwelijksvermogensrecht in rechtvergelijkend perspectief* (2000), p. 254 in particular note 4.

of the spouses.[182] This tendency finds its expression in the exclusion from the division of premarital assets and assets acquired during the marriage by way of gift or inheritance.[183] In the vast majority of European countries, the solidarity-based sharing is linked to the contributions made by the spouses during the marriage.[184] The contribution of the spouse engaged in housekeeping and childrearing is generally equated to the financial contribution of the other spouse. This modern concept of solidarity is equally embraced by countries with deferred community of property (like Norway, Germany, Greece, Switzerland and Austria) and in countries with limited community. In all of these jurisdictions, a spouse does not share in property that he or she did not contribute to; namely the pre-marital property of the other spouse and property acquired by the other spouse during the marriage by way of gift or inheritance. Some authors suggest this modus of sharing to be the fairest compromise between the solidarity and the autonomy of the spouses.[185]

Within this last group of countries, the degree of solidarity is lowered even further in Italy and the Eastern European countries, which have a limited community system, and in Switzerland, which has a deferred community system. In Italy, the income from premarital assets are also excluded from the community during the marriage, and can only be divided upon divorce, provided that this fund still exists at that time. In the Eastern European countries, both the income from separate property and the increase of this property's value are excluded not only from the community, but also from the division upon termination of marriage, unless the non-owner spouse proves his or her contribution to the increase in value. In Switzerland the increase of the value of pre-marital assets is not taken into consideration in the calculation of the surplus that has to be divided among the spouses upon divorce. Walter Pintens suggests that such further limitations represent a positive development towards an even more limited version of solidarity.[186]

---

[182] SVERDRUP, T., 'Maintenance as a Separate Issue – the Relationship Between Maintenance and Matrimonial Property' (2005), p. 122.

[183] In all the above-mentioned jurisdictions, a donator or a testator can exclude the gift or inheritance from the community. In Sweden, Denmark and Finland a judge has the discretional power to limit the sharing in pre-marital property, and statutory limitations are currently being discussed (Ibid, p. 127). The Netherlands is about to introduce a limited community regime. In England the issue of division of pre-marital assets and assets acquired by inheritance and gift was recently discussed in *Miller v. Miller* and *MacFarlane v. MacFarlane* ([2006] *UKHL* 24; [2006] 1 *AC* 1). It was suggested that the yardstick of equality may not apply with full force to pre-marital and inherited assets if marriage was of short duration. See Lord Nicholls of Birkenhead, paras 21-25; Lord Mance, para. 168, and Baroness Hale of Richmond, para. 152.

[184] SVERDRUP, T., 'Maintenance as a Separate Issue – the Relationship Between Maintenance and Matrimonial Property' (2005), p. 122.

[185] See, for instance: VERBEKE, A., *Goederenverdeling bij echtscheiding* (1991), p. 419. Also Walter Pinters depict this degree of solidarity as 'equal and justified'. PINTENS, W., 'Europeanisation of Family Law' (2003), p. 10.

[186] See: PINTENS, W., 'Europeanisation of Family Law' (2003), at p. 12.

This overview shows that on the level of functional equivalence the differences in the degree of sharing in various jurisdictions are still rather significant. A convergence tendency is discernible with regard to two points: the limitation of the divisible property to assets that the spouses have contributed to during the marriage, and the equal division of those assets. At the same time it is rather clear that there is no correlation between the degree of sharing and a particular type of matrimonial property regime. The differences in the level of sharing visibly go across the lines dividing the various matrimonial property systems.

Concluding remarks

At the end of this brief functional comparison, it is possible to conclude that there seems to be a substantial common core of functional solutions to the same problems reached in the various matrimonial property systems. The remaining differences have mainly to do with the differing balances struck in the various jurisdictions between autonomy and solidarity. The differences with regard to ensuring the de-facto equality and the autonomy of the spouses are rather substantial. These differences generally coincide with the division between the different matrimonial property systems. Systems with a community during the marriage are (with the exception of The Netherlands) better at attaining de-facto equality of the spouses. Systems without community during the marriage are more successful in ensuring the autonomy of the spouses.[187] The differences concerning the level of solidarity are more considerable. These differences are linked with the scope of the divisible property, which seems to have no connection with a particular property system.

17.5.3. COMPARISON ON THE FORMAL LEVEL: COMPARING LEGAL TECHNIQUES, CONCEPTS AND RULES

In contrast with a comparison on the functional level, a comparison of matrimonial property laws in Europe on the formal level reveals little commonality. The great quantity of formal differences can be explained by a number of factors.

No common past, no shared conceptual language

In the first place, the absence of a common legal past in the field of matrimonial property law predetermines the absence of a shared conceptual language.[188] In the

---

[187] BRAAT, B., *Indépendance et interdépendance patrimoniales des époux dans le régime matrimonial légal des droits français, néerlandais et suisse* (2004), p. 416.

[188] As has been discussed in Chapter 5, matrimonial property law was not part of the uniform medieval uniform canon law that formed the *ius commune* of the bulk of the other fields of family law.

other fields of family law (like marriage, divorce, extramarital cohabitation, illegitimacy) both civil and common law countries have inherited from the medieval *ius commune* such shared core concepts, as 'marriage impediments', 'annulment', 'separation of bed and board', 'full divorce', 'illegitimacy', 'legitimisation', and so on. As matrimonial property law was no part of the medieval *ius commune* of family law, such basic concepts of the continental law as 'matrimonial property',[189] 'matrimonial property regime' or 'marital contract'[190] are unknown in the common law countries. The concept of 'family assets', used in the common law countries instead of the continental notion of 'matrimonial property', has no uniform interpretation in England, and is said to have 'no legal meaning'.[191] Moreover, a close linkage of matrimonial property law with the general law of property makes the conceptual and legal technical differences between the common and the civil law countries even stronger.[192] Taking an even broader view, one will see that civil and common law countries resolve matrimonial property law problems with the help of the rather dissimilar general legal concepts and techniques of their domestic legal systems. For instance the common law systems use such specific common law instruments as trusts, legal and beneficial ownership, and estoppel; and the civil law countries employ typical civil law concepts like marriage contracts, good faith, *imprévision*, and so on.

Similar functional results via different legal techniques

In the second place, within the civil law systems the countries with different types of matrimonial property regimes achieve functionally similar results with the help of fairly dissimilar technical means.[193] Even a brief analysis of the legal techniques employed in the various systems of matrimonial law necessitates discussing a whole range of varieties.

Thus, de-facto equality of the spouses is aimed for rather differently in the various civil law systems. In the limited community systems de-facto equality is realised via granting the spouses the right of joint administration of the common funds. In the jurisdictions without community during the marriage, more or less the same result is aimed for via the technique of special protection of the most important family assets, primarily the matrimonial home and the household goods. In continental countries this

---

[189]   While the countries of Continental Europe use the term matrimonial property, the common law countries use the term 'matrimonial property rights' VERBEKE, A., 'Perspectives for an International Marital Contract' (2001), p. 193-200; MARTINY, D., 'A New Matrimonial Property Regime for Europe' (2004), p. 1.

[190]   VERBEKE, A. et al, 'European marital property law' (1995), p. 447.

[191]   CRETNEY, S., MASSON, J., BAILEY-HARRIS, R., *Principles of Family Law* (2003), p. 102.

[192]   PINTENS, W., 'Europeanisation of Family Law' (2003), p. 12.

[193]   See in the same sense: BRAAT, B., ODERKERK, M., STEENHOFF, G., *Huwelijksvermogensrecht in rechtvergelijkend perspectief* (2000), p. 271.

technique involves that the specially protected assets cannot be alienated by the spouse-owner without the consent of the other spouse.

Different techniques are also used for establishing a balance between the principle of autonomy and the principle of solidarity. The jurisdictions without community ensure the autonomy of the spouses via the route of separate legal ownership during the marriage. The 'solidarity correction' is achieved in these regimes by means of the technique of special protection of the most important family assets. The countries with limited community systems safeguard the autonomy of the spouses by using two different legal techniques: that of the concurrent administration in Western Europe, and that of the common administration with the presumption of consent of the non-acting spouse in Eastern Europe. The 'solidarity correction' is attained in these jurisdictions by requiring the explicit joint consent of the spouses for disposing of the most important family assets. There is much diversity in the legal techniques employed for the protection of the non-acting spouse and third parties against the unauthorised acts of administration performed by one of the spouses.[194]

The techniques of attaining the principle of solidarity with regard to spousal sharing of the family assets are also rather dissimilar. In the countries with community of property during the marriage fair sharing is achieved by means of equal division of the common fund upon termination of marriage. In the countries with deferred community of property two different techniques are used. The first technique involves pooling together and then equally dividing the property in kind (in nature) upon termination of marriage. The other technique involves the monetary calculation of the surplus with subsequent equal monetary division of its value. In the separation of property system of the common law countries, the sharing is achieved via a completely different technique of granting the court a discretionary power to re-allocate the property of the spouses upon divorce.

17.5.4. CONCLUSION: MUCH FUNCTIONAL COMMON CORE, LITTLE CONVERGENCE OF LEGAL TECHNIQUES, CONCEPTS AND RULES

This brief analysis of matrimonial property law in Europe shows that, on the one hand, there is much common core on the level of functional solutions; and on the other hand, very limited common core on the level of legal techniques, rules and concepts. On the technical level there is also hardly any convergence discernable between the

---

[194] See BRAAT, B., ODERKERK, M., STEENHOFF, G., *Huwelijksvermogensrecht in rechtvergelijkend perspectief* (2000), p. 268-269.

different matrimonial property systems. Only the English separation of property system exhibits, since *White* and *Lambert,* some tendency to evolve in the direction of a deferred community system.

The limited and deferred community systems are equally capable of reaching the objectives of present-day matrimonial property law. Yet, in the technical sense these systems are really very dissimilar, as they come to more or less the same functional results from two almost opposing starting points. Each of these systems has its advantages and disadvantages,[195] so it is not really possible to claim that one of them is better than the other.[196]

For the perspectives for harmonisation the consequences of these findings are two-fold. Firstly, the commonality of the principle objectives and the existence of a broad functional common core indicate that harmonisation of matrimonial property law would be politically much more feasible, as compared to the fields of family law with more controversial objectives and less functional common core (like marriage, divorce, extramarital cohabitation). Another argument for the suitability of matrimonial property law for deliberate harmonisation is the contractual freedom that allows spouses to deviate from a legal regime. This opens the possibility of elaborating an optional regime for international marriages, existing alongside the national legal regimes, rather than a mandatory regime setting aside the national legal regimes.[197] At the same time, there are also factors that diminish the suitability of matrimonial property law for harmonisation. The persistent cross-system difference in the legal techniques of achieving similar functional results denotes that any deliberate attempt of harmonisation would be very difficult to attain.[198]

An option reconciling these contradictive indications has been repeatedly suggested by various scholars. This is not to try replacing the deferred and the limited community of property by one single 'European' optional regime,[199] but rather to suggest two

---

[195] See briefly: PINTENS, W., 'Europeanisation of Family Law' (2003), p. 10.

[196] See in the same sense: STEENHOFF, G., 'A Matrimonial Property System for the European Union?' (2004), p. 4 and BRAAT, B., *Indépendance et interdépendance patrimoniales des époux dans le régime matrimonial légal des droits français, néerlandais et suisse* (2004), p. 416.

[197] AGELL, A., 'Division of Property upon Divorce from a European Perspective' (1998), p. 18. VERBEKE, A., 'Perspectives for an International Marital Contract' (2001), p.192.

[198] See in the same sense: PINTENS, W., VAN DER MEERSCH, B., VANWINCKELEN, C., *Inleiding tot het Familiaal Vermogensrecht* (2002), p. 14.

[199] Some scholars expressed their preference for elaborating one single European model. Thus, Dieter Martiny; and Alan Verbeke propose drafting such a model on the basis of a deferred community system (VERBEKE, A., 'Perspectives for an International Marital Contract' (2001), p.193 ff; MARTINY D., 'A New Matrimonial Property Regime for Europe' (2004), p. 8-10). Gert Steenhoff suggests a slightly modified German system as a single model (STEENHOFF, G., 'A Matrimonial Property System

optional 'European' regimes for international marriages: one based on the deferred and one based on the limited community of property.[200]

---

[200]   for the European Union?' (2004), p. 7). Dieter Henrich has expressed a preference for the Swiss participation in acquests. HENRICH, D., 'Zur Zukunft des Güterrechts in Europa' (2002), p. 1526; This method has been repeatedly suggested by Dieter Martiny (MARTINY, D., 'Is Unification of Family Law Feasible or Even Desirable?' (1998), p. 165; and (2004), p. 321.) and by Walter Pintens (PINTENS, W., VANWINCKELEN, C., *Casebook. European Family Law* (2001), p. 21; PINTENS, W., 'Europeanisation of Family Law' (2003), p. 11) and in PINTENS, W., 'Harmonisatie in het huwelijksgoederenrecht' (2005), p. 247. See also: ANTOKOLSKAIA, M., 'Enkele gedachten over de harmonisatie van het familierecht in Europa' (2002), p. 8-10; BRAAT, B., *Indépendance et interdépendance patrimoniales des époux dans le régime matrimonial légal des droits français, néerlandais et suisse*, (2004), p. 417.

PART V
CONCLUSION

CHAPTER 18
CONCLUSION

18.1. INTRODUCTION

At the end of this long journey through the history of family law in Europe it is time to suggest solutions to the questions that were presented at the beginning of this book. As was explained in the first chapter, the main objective of this book is to examine the merits of the cultural constraints argument for the debate surrounding the harmonisation of family law. As a reminder to the reader, the cultural constraints argument suggests that family law is unsuitable for harmonisation because the family laws of the individual European countries are deeply imbedded in their unique national cultures and history. Proponents of the cultural constraints argument submit that family laws in Europe are not converging and some of them even deny that family laws have ever really converged in the past. The current diversity of family law is an emanation of the irredeemable dissimilarity of national cultures. Thus, any attempt to harmonise family law is doomed to failure.

As was suggested in the first Part of this book, the cultural constraints argument gives rise to two main questions. The first is whether family law has converged in the past and currently converges in the present. This question has been examined in the preceding chapters through a historical-comparative survey of the developments in several core fields of family law in Europe during the last two millennia. The conclusions that can be derived from this research will be discussed in the first section of this chapter. The second question is whether convergence and deliberate harmonisation of family law are possible at all. To the extent that the answer to this second question does not already follow from the answer to the first, it will be examined in the second section of this chapter. There I will discuss more specifically the contention that family law is imbedded in unique national culture. In the third and last section of this chapter, I will address the implications of the conclusions of the two previous sections for the deliberate harmonisation of family law.

18.2. CONVERGENCE PAST AND PRESENT

18.2.1. MOVEMENT TOWARDS MODERNISATION AND MOVEMENT TOWARDS CONVERGENCE: THE IMPORTANCE OF A CLEAR DISTINCTION

After discussing two thousand years of developments in several core fields of family law it should be possible to suggest an answer to the question of whether family laws in Europe have converged in the past and are converging at present. Looking through the history of family law during the whole of the last two millennia rather than at selected short-term periods allows this issue to be seen from a broader perspective. It then becomes visible that the history of family law in Europe more closely resembles a spiral rather than a linear process. During the first spin of this spiral, the permissive Classical Roman family law was replaced by the restrictive canon family law of the Middle Ages. Through the second spin, the medieval canon family gave way to the permissive law of our times. The informal, secular, private character of Classical Roman family law almost disappeared at the end of the High Middle Ages only to return again in our times, albeit as part of a much more sophisticated legal system. The last part of this spiral development shows an evolution, which, for the reasons explained in Chapter 2, can be called 'progressive'.[1] Thus, the last centuries of the development of family law in Europe can be depicted as progressive evolution, the pace of which varied from time to time and from one country to another, but its direction has clearly been the same everywhere: from patriarchal, restrictive, transpersonalistic, to modern, permissive, personalistic laws.[2] The studies of several renowned scholars support this vision. The image of progressive evolution clearly follows from the seminal work of Mary-Ann Glendon.[3] Extensive historical study of divorce law in Europe brought Roderick Phillips to the same conclusion.[4] According to Harry Willekens: 'Changes in different legal systems do not take place simulta-

---

[1] See Part I, Chapter 2, Section 2.2.2.

[2] I have already argued elsewhere that 'looking at the history of family law in Europe, it is possible to see that ever since the Middle Ages, when canon family law was uniform, all European countries were developing in the same direction. The substance, the tendencies and the driving forces of the reform of family law were essentially the same everywhere. The only true differences are in the timing.' See: my 'Development of Family Law in Western and Eastern Europe: Common Origins, Common Driving Forces, Common Tendencies' (2003), p. 65. Earlier, Harry Willekens had come to a similar conclusion. See WILLEKENS, H., 'Explaining Two Hundred Years of Family Law in Western Europe' (1997), p. 60.

[3] GLENDON, M-A., *The Transformation of Family Law* (1989).

[4] Phillips notices that 'for the most part, the history of divorce since the sixteenth century has been one of movement away from the Roman Catholic doctrines of marriage. This movement has varied in place and significance over time and place and has not always followed a lineal progression.' PHILLIPS, R., *Putting asunder* (1988), p. 1.

neously nor at the same pace, but when change occurs the direction is always the same'.[5] David Bradley also acknowledges that 'general trends – liberty, equality and secularity – are clearly apparent in the family laws of developed countries'.[6]

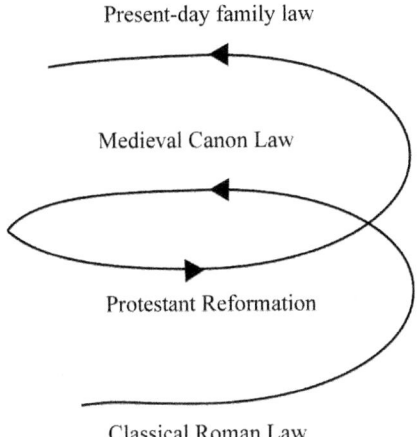

Present-day family law

Medieval Canon Law

Protestant Reformation

Classical Roman Law

As was indicated above, the spiral development of family law in Europe during the last two millennia can be divided into two major periods: from the Roman times till the Protestant Reformation, and from the Reformation till the present. The main event of the first period is the development from the diversity, composed of Roman law and various barbarian customary laws, to the uniformity of the medieval canon family law. This period could be considered as an era of overwhelming 'convergence'; that is, in the meaning of 'approximation of laws', not in the meaning of a spontaneous process. The mediaeval family law unification by no means occurred spontaneously, but was the result of considerable and deliberate efforts on the part of the Catholic Church. In the sixteenth century the Reformation divided Europe into Protestant and Catholic countries. Thereby the period of uniformity of canon family law and the legislative monopoly of the Catholic Church in family matters came to an end. The Enlightenment, the French Revolution and the subsequent Restoration brought about further division. Ever since the Enlightenment, Europe has been split by the ideological discord between the 'progressive' camp, seeking modernisation of family law under the influence of the ideas of the Enlightenment, on the one hand, and the 'conservative' camp, opposing this modernisation in the name of 'traditional' family values, on the

---

[5]   WILLEKENS, H., 'Explaining Two Hundred Years of Family Law in Western Europe' (1997), p. 60. See in the same sense also ANTOKOLSKAIA, M.V., 'Development of Family Law in Western and Eastern Europe: Common Origins, Common Driving Forces, Common Tendencies' (2003), p. 52-69.

[6]   BRADLEY, D., *Family Law and Political Culture* (1996), p. 238.

other.[7] In general, it is possible to conclude that the Reformation theology and later the Enlightenment progressive thought instigated the second period of development of family law in Europe: from the medieval uniformity to the present-day diversity. When compared to the first period, the main characteristic of this second period is undoubtedly increasing divergence rather than convergence.

The existence and importance of the convergence tendency during the second period is the main issue of the present-day convergence/divergence debate. The proponents of the cultural constraints argument allege the persistence and even increase of the differences, while the opposite side suggests that the tendency towards convergence came to dominate family at least in the last part of the twentieth century. The persistence of this debate finds its explanation in the fact that after the Reformation the development of family law in all European countries generally followed the same pattern, but the profundity and pace of these developments differed significantly.[8] The proponents of the idea of convergence lay the emphasis on the overall similarity of these developments, while its opponents stress the difference in profundity and pace.

From the sixteenth century onwards, the driving forces of this progressive evolution – the Reformation, the Enlightenment, the industrialisation, the urbanization, liberalism, socialist and feminist ideas, and so on – were pan-European events. Also the general economic, social and political developments in the whole of Europe were rather similar. Therefore the evolution of family law also displayed similarities on the general level in the sense that under the impact of pan-European cultural, economic and ideological trends the family laws of different countries were moving in the same direction – from a traditional restrictive family law, built upon communitarian, transpersonal premises, to a more permissive family law, based upon modern personalistic ideology.

The existence of a century long pan-European modernisation trend, however, does not necessarily mean that there is also a tendency towards convergence.[9] David Bradley

---

[7]   It is worth noting here that in domestic debates the cultural constraints argument is by far more popular in the 'conservative' camp. Rodolfo Sacco has mentioned that 'The ideology of cultural self-sufficiency is merely the name given to the ideology of cultural delay'. SACCO, R., 'Diversity and Uniformity in the Law' (2001), p. 177.

[8]   Mary Ann Glendon suggested that 'the degree and timing of changes in patterns of family relationships differed according to regions and population groups'. GLENDON, M.A., The New Family and the New Property (1981), p. 12.

[9]   In a number of my earlier works I erroneously derived evidence of convergence from the fact that family laws in Europe were evolving in the same direction. See 'Geschiedenis van het familierecht: gelijke ontwikkeling' (1999); p. 33-65; 'Gezamenlijke tendensen en beginselen' (1999); p. 65-81; 'The Process of Modernisation of Family Law in Eastern and Western Europe: Difference in Timing, Resemblance in Substance' (2000); 'Development of Family Law in Western and Eastern Europe: Common Origins, Common Driving Forces, Common Tendencies' (2003), p. 52-69.

rightly warns against such a short-cut in reasoning.[10] Convergence is brought on by this similar evolutionary development only when, within the framework of this development, the differences between national family laws are steadily diminishing. It is therefore important to distinguish between two questions: whether there is a general tendency towards modernisation of family law in Europe, on the one hand; and whether there is a general tendency towards convergence of the family laws of the European countries, on the other.

The answer to the first question is obviously in the affirmative. For the purposes of this book, this conclusion is of great significance. The overall similarity of the development of family law towards modernisation calls for a fundamental qualification of the thesis of the embedment of family law in unique national cultures, and therefore of the cultural constraints argument. Yet it is clear that there has always been a significant divergence in pace and profundity of modernisation of family laws from one European country to another. The examinations in the preceding chapters suggest that from all societal factors that one could consider, it is above all the differences in the balance of political power between 'progressive' and 'conservative' forces, that make the various countries respond to the pan-European challenges in dissimilar ways.[11] For those who oppose the idea of convergence, the ensuing differences constitute the evidence that family laws did not converge in the past and do not converge in the present.

The answer to the second question seems less unambiguous. On the basis of the image of the spiral development of family law, I have just submitted that the main characteristic of the period from the Reformation onwards is increasing divergence rather than convergence. Nonetheless, this period witnessed several episodes that were clearly characterised by increased similarity on the pan-European or regional level. The most notable example of pan-European developments is the spread of the Napoleonic *Code Civil* over a large part of Europe in the early nineteenth century. The best example of successful regional approximation of family laws is the twentieth-century Nordic co-operation. It is worth mentioning, that in both cases the approximation of laws was a result of deliberate harmonisation activities, rather than a spontaneous convergence process.

---

[10]   BRADLEY, D., 'A Note on Comparative Family Law: Problems, Perspectives, Issues and Politics,' p. 10.

[11]   See also, BRADLEY, D., 'A Family Law For Europe? Sovereignty, Political Economy and Legitimation' (2003), p. 81.

18.2.2. HAVE FAMILY LAWS BEEN CONVERGING?

It seems impossible to suggest a sensible answer to this question without further delineation of the period one is talking about. Except for the examples mentioned above, the historical overview of the preceding chapters reveals no evidence of durable diminishment of diversity before the second half of the twentieth century. In the 1960s-1970s the acceleration of modernisation of family law throughout Western Europe led the scholars of that time to believe that Europe had started to move towards spontaneous harmonisation. Thus, Jacques Fayer wrote in 1978: 'a classical aphorism of comparative law, that while the law of property and obligations tends towards homogeneity, family law remains the seat of national idiosyncrasies [...] which has been beyond dispute for some ten year ago', is losing its validity as 'the laws of the majority of the countries of Western Europe tended to converge towards a uniform model, and this evolution has been very rapid.'[12] In 1989 Mary-Ann Glendon submitted that 'despite contrasts in the legal and political context of law reforms, the national difference among Western family law systems have diminished steadily over the past two decades.'[13] Some scholars still support this interpretation,[14] while others deny its merits.[15]

It seems that any unqualified contention of the existence of convergence can only be based on the analysis of a period with a relatively short time-span. Several choices of such a period would predetermine an outcome confirming the existence of convergence. For instance, if one takes as a starting point the transitional period of the beginning of the twentieth century, when dissimilarities between the countries had become sharper due to the radical breakthroughs in Scandinavia, Russia and Portugal, and compares this with the present time, one will no doubt be led to conclude that similarity has increased. A similar picture arises if one chooses to compare the initial period of the radical reforms commencing in the 1960s-1970s, when some European countries were already affected by these reforms while others kept their old laws, with the present situation, when the rearguard have significantly caught up with the vanguard.

However, since the perception that family laws are converging is clearly associated with the ongoing process of modernisation, it seems logical to compare the present-day

---

[12] FOYER, J., 'The Reform of Family Law in France' (1978), p. 75.

[13] GLENDON, M.A., *The Transformation of Family Law* (1989), p. 1.

[14] Thus, Roderick Phillips asserts that 'in Europe the movement towards uniformity is more evident [than in the USA].' PHILLIPS, R., *Putting Asunder* (1988), p. 570. In the same sense see also: PINTENS, W., VANWINCKELEN, C., *Casebook. European Family Law* (2001), p. 16.

[15] See for instance, BRADLEY, D., 'Convergence in Family Law: Mirrors, Transplants and Political Economy' (1999), p.128.

situation not with some moment when this process accelerated (for instance the first radical reforms in the early twentieth century, or the mass radical reforms commenced in the 1960s), but rather with the situation that existed on the eve of the period of modernisation. This would be the state of affairs before the implementation of the Enlightenment ideas into family law, so roughly at the middle of the eighteenth century. The period thus defined – just about the last 250 years – seems to be the one to produce the outcome most relevant to the convergence/divergence debate of our time. An investigation of this period allows one to examine the fruits of the family law modernisation up to the present as a whole, not just a limited episode of it.

The analysis of this period gives no indication that the level of similarity of family laws as a whole has become higher now, than it was 250 years ago. This remains the case if one compares family laws on the level of functional equivalence, and disregards the outer forms and technical details. The following summary shows that the level of diversity/similarity not only varies in time but also differs significantly from one field of family law to the other. Let's reiterate the developments that were discussed in the preceding chapters.

Marriage

Before the 1960s the laws of European countries uniformly recognised only one form of intimate relationships: legal marriage.[16] In contrast, in the Europe of today a whole range of varieties of such relationships are legally recognised:[17] heterosexual and homosexual marriage, registered partnerships, intermediary forms between a status and a contract *a la* PACS, and non-institutionalised cohabitation. Two hundred and fifty years ago, the unanimity with which Europe regarded the concept of marriage as a heterosexual union was total and self-evident. Today, a new controversy regarding opening up marriage for homosexuals and transsexuals has turned this uniformity into a heated controversy. Thus, in the area of marriage law, one single uniform legal concept of marriage and one single legal form of intimate relationships has been replaced by a variety of diverging legal concepts and forms.

In the field of spousal equality the picture is rather different. The high level of similarity of 250 years ago (women everywhere were legally subordinate to their husbands as the head of the family) has evolved through a period of considerable diversity (due

---

[16]   Mary Ann Glendon concluded that 'by the turn of the twentieth century, Western family law systems had come to share, generally speaking, a common set of assumptions. Domestic relations were organized around a unitary conception of the family as marriage centred and patriarchal. Marriage was treated as an important support institution and a decisive determinant of the social status of spouses and children.' GLENDON, M.A., *The Transformation of Family Law* (1989), p. 291.

[17]   MEULDERS-KLEIN, M.-T., 'Les concubinages: diversités et symboliques' (2002), p. 606.

to differences in pace of the equalising of the rights of the spouses) towards an almost total similarity in our time (the spouses are all but completely legally equal everywhere in Europe). There and back again, so to say. Moreover, the whole issue of the equality of men and women in family relationships has become a matter of mandatory European Human Rights law. This is an interesting example of a particular issue where modernisation could be considered 'completed'. As was explained in Chapter 2, the expectation that legal evolution leads to more similarity is strongly related to the notion that such evolution involves the progress to some higher stages of a more or less universal nature.[18] It appears that in respect of the particular issue of spousal equality, this expectation has become true. This certainly constitutes a powerful argument against the cultural constraints argument, and is therefore highly relevant for the purposes of this book. I will return to this issue later. But as to our present inquiry it should be noted that on the balance of things, even at this particular issue modernisation as a whole did not bring forth any convergence, as it was modernisation that in the first place disturbed the universality of spousal inequality that existed 250 year ago.

Divorce

In the Catholic part of Europe divorce as such did not exist at all in the mid-eighteenth century. The only possibility to terminate marriage there was annulment. The Protestant and Orthodox countries provided for divorce upon a limited number of fault grounds. The difference between those countries that did not permit divorce and those that allowed for divorce was, of course, a very significant one. However, a more homogeneous picture arises if one analyses these laws from a functional perspective: the availability of divorce or annulment in terms of accessibility and costs in time, money and infringement in the private life of the spouses. Two hundred and fifty years ago divorce was almost as rare, costly, time-consuming and difficult to obtain, as annulment.

An analysis of present-day divorce laws reveals that it should be concluded that diversity has more likely increased than the opposite – even if one leaves aside Malta, the only remaining European country not allowing divorce, as if it were merely the exception that proves the rule. No European country any longer maintains fault as the only divorce ground. However, fault is still preserved alongside other grounds in a significant number of European jurisdictions. On the other side of the spectrum, an easy divorce on demand has been introduced in Sweden, Finland, Spain and indirectly in Russia. A functional analysis of the current divorce legislation leads to the conclusion that the fault/no-fault dichotomy is no longer indicative of the

---

[18]   See Part I, Chapter 2, Section 2.2.2.

availability and accessibility of divorce. Looking at the accessibility of divorce in terms of costs in time, money and infringement in private life reveals considerable differences between countries with an easy, rapid and cheap divorce without inquiry and separation or a waiting period (for example the immediate divorce in Sweden) and countries with time and money consuming divorces with extensive judicial inquiry and a long period of separation (for example the four year separation in Ireland).

Extramarital cohabitation

Europe was unanimous, 250 years ago, in giving non-marital cohabitation no legal standing. Now there is a hesitant unanimity in recognising that the rights of cohabitees should be protected one way or another. However, there is a whole range of legal forms employed for providing such protection. The level of institutionalisation of both same- and opposite-sex cohabitation varies, from granting cohabitees only some limited rights in the field of public and private law, to a complete functional equivalent to marriage (registered partnership 'Nordic style'). There is also a persistent diversity in Europe regarding how far the State should go in imposing regulation on opposite-sex couples who have chosen not to institutionalise their relationship.

Position of extramarital children

Two hundred and fifty years ago, illegitimate children were strongly disadvantaged everywhere in Europe. At present, the legal status of children born to unmarried parents exhibits only some rudimentary differences as compared to the status of children whose parents are married. As the equality of marital and extramarital children is now mandatorily prescribed by European Human Rights law, the remaining differences can be expected to disappear in the near future. Along with the equality of the spouses, the law governing the status of extramarital children provides a second example of a case where modernisation could be considered more or less 'completed'. Important as that may be, it should be noted here that this law was no less similar at the beginning of modernisation than it is at its 'end'.

Matrimonial property

Contrary to the laws on marriage, divorce, cohabitation and illegitimacy, the matrimonial property laws of the European countries do not share a common legal past. However, this seems to make little difference with regard to the issue of convergence and divergence. The matrimonial property law of mid-eighteenth century Europe was typified by a great diversity of regimes, each applying different legal techniques in order to achieve similar objectives: enabling the husband to use his wife's property to the benefit of the family, on the one hand, and simultaneously safeguarding the heritable property of the wife for her children and kin, on the other. This similarity of objectives predetermined a considerable level of similarity on the functional level. Irrespective of the matrimonial property regime, the law was generally characterised by reserving for the husband the right to administer his wife's property, and by the legal incapacity of married women.

From the end of the nineteenth century until the 1980s matrimonial property law experienced a period of transition from the old, male dominated model to the modern model, based on the equality of the spouses. This transitional period was characterised by large differences between the vanguard and the rearguard countries. During this period the spousal equality in patrimonial matters and the legal capacity of married women were highly controversial politically issues.

At present this transitional period has all but ended. Diversity of legal regimes of matrimonial property law from country to country is as typical for contemporary matrimonial property law as it was 250 years ago. Yet these technically different legal regimes display a far-reaching commonality on the functional level because the objectives of the modern matrimonial property law are the same everywhere in Europe. The common functional objectives of present-day matrimonial property law are ensuring the equality of the spouses and achieving a proper balance between the principles of solidarity and autonomy. With respect to the formal equality of the spouses the similarity of the laws of various European countries is almost total. Irrespective of the matrimonial property regime, a woman is everywhere in Europe fully legally capable, and all European legal systems provide both spouses with equal rights of administration of their own property and (where such funds exists) of the common funds. The issues of equality of the spouses in patrimonial matters and the legal capacity of married women have completely lost their controversial character. On the functional level, however, a considerable similarity can be delineated in regard to the de-facto equality of the spouses, as well the balance between the principles of autonomy and solidarity, but the level of similarity here is noticeably lower.

A two-fold conclusion can be derived from this analysis. On the one hand, matrimonial property law in Europe has reached a rather high level of similarity both on the level of the objectives of the regulation and on the level of the actual accomplishment of these objectives. On the other hand, these functionally similar results are achieved in the various systems of matrimonial property law by means of dissimilar legal techniques. The main differences between these techniques go along the lines of the two main systems of matrimonial property in present-day Europe: the system of limited community of property and that of deferred community of property. In regard to these systems and techniques there is very little similarity, and this will most likely remain to be the case.

Thus, the level of similarity of matrimonial property law in Europe seems to have come full circle in the last 250 years. The technical diversity of legal regimes combined with a similarity of objectives and a considerable functional equivalence is typical both for the end and the beginning of this period.

Conclusion

The answer to whether family laws in Europe have converged in the past is dependent on the period one has in mind. Convergence has definitely existed in certain periods, fields and places. However, the main characteristic of the whole period from the Reformation onwards is an increasing divergence rather than convergence. In the light of the fact that the modernisation of family law is considered to be the main driving force behind convergence, it is interesting to note that during the period of modernisation as a whole, convergence cannot be considered to have been the prevailing tendency either. On the contrary, apart from the limited differentiation that already came into being during the Reformation, it was the differences in the profundity and pace of modernisation that led to the diversity of family law in the first place. It is above all the acceleration of the modernisation of family law in the second half of the twentieth century, and especially from the 1960s onwards, that has in turn led to a diminishment of this diversity and created a perception that convergence, rather than divergence, is the main effect of modernisation. Among the fields of family law analysed in this book, there are two examples where this development has come full circle, and the present situation shows the same high level of similarity as did the situation of 250 years ago: the equality of the spouses, and the equality of children born in and outside wedlock. On these particular issues, a point has been reached (namely: full legal equality) from which it seems reasonable to expect that it will not be the subjected to major changes in the foreseeable future. Here, modernisation could be considered 'completed'. The remaining question seems to be whether similar developments are taking place in the other fields of family law. Can what is presently going in family law in Europe be considered as the 'final part' of modernisation, in the sense that what first has diverged because of differences in profundity and pace, is now converging again?

18.2.3. ARE FAMILY LAWS CONVERGING AT PRESENT?

The paradox of Zeno – yet the other way around

The analysis of the more recent history of family law in the preceding chapters reveals many examples of the phenomenon that, at the same time that the countries which lag behind in the modernisation of family law make a step forward (for example by giving limited protection to same-sex couples or introducing no-fault divorce), the countries in the vanguard of modernisation make another step forward (like allowing same-sex marriage or introducing divorce on demand), so that the gap between them remains. This phenomenon seems to be so persistent that it leads one to expect that the rearguard will never catch up with the vanguard and lasting convergence will never take place. Paraphrasing the paradox of Zeno, it is possible to ask whether or not Achilles could overtake a tortoise, but it is quite clear that a tortoise could hardly ever overtake Achilles, unless it suddenly sprouts wings. It is interesting to see that in family law, there are some historical examples of tortoises sprouting wings and overtaking Achilles. Such were the breakthroughs in the modernisation of family law following the Portuguese Revolutions of 1910 and the Russian Revolution of 1917, or the introduction of divorce on demand and same-sex marriage in 2005 in 'Catholic' Spain. But these are more exceptions than rules. Normally the tortoises (generally the South European countries plus Ireland) remain slow and the Achilleses (for example the Nordic countries) keep moving fast. As the countries lagging behind in, for instance, the liberalisation of divorce approach one stage, the vanguard has already moved to the next, and in this way the distance persists, and the common core on the level of positive law remains limited.

The end of history of family law?

The question to be answered here is whether this process will come to an end when some 'final' stage of evolution is reached, as seems to be the case with spousal equality and the equality of children born in and outside wedlock. It seems possible to say that if family law is everywhere evolving from less permissive to more permissive, there must be a point in the future where the highest level of permissiveness will be reached by all so that no further development will be possible. One could oppose the picture of ongoing competition between Achilleses and tortoises with the suggestion that all Achilleses and tortoises will unavoidably meet each other at the finish line. It could for instance be suggested that divorce on demand is the final point of the development of divorce law. Perhaps the same could be suggested of same-sex marriage. Comprehensive convergence could be expected if the countries that presently have divorce on demand and same-sex marriage have thereby reached the summit of the modernisation of divorce, marriage and same-sex cohabitation law, where they will sooner or later be joined by the other countries that are developing in the same direction but at a lesser speed. This would be the 'final point' of family law evolution – a kind of 'end of history'. At this point the family laws of all European countries would have reached uniformity by way of a spontaneous modernisation/convergence process.

At this point in our analysis, the reader is reminded of the close relationship between the harmonisation/cultural constraints debate and the Modernity/post-modernist discord that was delineated in Chapter 2.[19] As was noted there, the ultimate objective of the harmonisation of law is not just approximation for the sake of uniformity, but rather the improvement of law via approximation. In this respect there is a clear relation between deliberate harmonisation efforts and the 'unfinished Modernity project'. It is the 'Modernity' modus of thinking that leads one to believe in the possibility of emancipating man and improving human conditions according to the law of reason and universally valid values. However, there are no contemporary supporters of the modernisation of family law that claim that this modernisation will ever actually be 'finished'. The 'end of history' may have been suggested by several religious[20] and political theories;[21] there has been no such undertaking in the field of family law. And for good reasons, I would say, as such interpretation of the modernisation process of family law seems far too speculative[22] Although for some particular issues, like the equalisation of the position of spouses and illegitimate children, 'final points' of modernisation appear to be very well conceivable, this does not say much

---

[19]   See Part I, Chapter 2, Section 2.3.

[20]   E.g. the Christian eschatological expectations of the Second Coming.

[21]   E.g. Marxism. Karl Marx perceived as the 'end of history' the time when class distinctions no longer exist. The most recent announcement of the 'end of history' in the field of ideological evolution was made by Francis Fukuyama, who described it as the universalisation of Western liberal democracy as the final form of human government. FUKUYAMA, F., *The End of History and the Last Man* (1992).

[22]   Also Willekens pointed out that a general trend towards similar developments does not allow implying 'that all legal systems [...] are fated to develop towards the same horizont.' WILLEKENS, H., 'Explaining Two Hundred Years of Family Law in Western Europe' (1997), p. 60.

about the overall development of family law. No one could claim to know how family law will develop further. How could one know whether divorce on demand will be the final point of development of divorce law? It is certainly not less plausible that divorce law will develop further. Divorce on demand granted by a state official could evolve into a private informal declaration, a kind of *repudium,* given by one spouse to the other without any involvement of the State, as it was in classical Roman law. Or maybe at some stage of history, marriage and divorce will not be regulated by law at all? Maybe some day the legal regulation of civil marriage will become superfluous, as legal protection will be given on the basis of de-facto relationships? Maybe same-sex couples, once genuine equality has been acquired, will no longer be interested in the status civil marriage can grant them? Without a crystal ball, we can only guess about the future. If we stop guessing and return to the solid ground of facts, there is no sound indication that the ongoing evolution of family law will come to an end in the near future.

The arrival of an 'end point' of developments in family law is also rather unlikely because technical developments, like medically-assisted procreation, surrogate motherhood and – who knows – perhaps even cloning, keep generating new challenges for family law. New possibilities like these continue to provide food for new controversies, which will keep diversity of family laws existing. There are also family law problems that can not be described in simple terms of modernisation or protection of human rights. These are dilemmas involving merely conflicts of interest between two individuals. Who should be considered the legal mother of a child born from a surrogate mother: the genetic mother, or the woman who has carried the child? Whose interests should be protected when a child wishes to have the name of its begetter revealed, appealing to one's right to know ones origins, and the mother opposes this, referring to the protection of her private life? Such dilemmas know no obvious solution and will probably remain a source of unending disagreement among the European legislatures.

18.2.4. CONVERGENCE AND THE CULTURAL CONSTRAINTS ARGUMENT

From the preceding analysis it can be concluded that modernisation of family law takes place everywhere in Europe, but differences are not disappearing. Although there have been clear instances of convergence at certain times and in regard to certain issues, and although these have certainly become more significant from the 1960s onwards, there is no indication that what is going on at present is a general tendency towards convergence. To this extent, the proponents of the cultural constraints argument seem to be right, although those among them who deny any historical evidence of convergence altogether, are clearly wrong.

However, it seems that this is less relevant to the validity of the cultural constraints argument than is generally presupposed. More important is that the preceding chapters provide no evidence whatsoever that this persistence of diversity has anything to do with the embedment of family law in unique national cultures and history. On the contrary, the overall similarity of the modernisation of family law, and the pan-European character of both the driving and the opposing forces that shape this evolution, suggest that what goes on in family law is very much determined by pan-European, rather than national factors. It appears to be merely the differences in the pace of this evolution, and not its course and content, that find their explanation in the peculiarities of the national level. The preceding chapters have provided many indications that the main determinant for the differences in profundity and pace of the modernisation of family laws in Europe are national differences in the balance of political power between 'progressive' proponents and 'conservative' adversaries of the modernisation of family law. It is politics, rather than culture, that makes the various countries respond to similar pan-European challenges in dissimilar ways.

18.3. IS FAMILY LAW IMBEDDED IN UNIQUE NATIONAL CULTURE?

18.3.1. INTRODUCTION

Against the suggestion that politics, and not culture, determines national family laws, it could be argued that the political affairs of a given country are simply an integral part of its culture, or are determined by it, and that the cultural constraints argument cannot be defeated by pointing at the predominant significance of national politics for the evolution of family law. It seems therefore relevant to take a closer look at what, exactly, is meant by 'culture' in the context of the cultural constraints argument. In this section the notion of 'national culture' in the context of the cultural constraints argument will be analysed in the light of the historical material presented in the preceding chapters.

The assumptions constituting the cultural constraints argument could be summarised as follows. First, it is suggested that laws are ingrained in the culture of the countries in which they operate. Secondly, it is assumed that each country has its own particular national culture which influences the respective law. Thirdly, it is presupposed that each of these national cultures is unique to the country concerned and that these national cultures are not moving any closer to each other. The final reckoning is that due to their embedment in the unique national cultures, laws are not converging spontaneously and cannot be harmonised deliberately.

Culture can be defined in many different ways. A general definition of culture could be that it is the 'heritage of art, science and ideas'.[23] The issue is to what extent such heritage should be considered 'national' when it comes to the elements that are relevant to family law. Pierre Legrand clearly perceives the 'cultureness' of law from a national perspective,[24] and so do many others. For instance also Laurence Friedman, who has extensively explored the concept of 'legal culture', tends to believe that each country has its unique particular culture.[25]

18.3.2. ARE NATIONAL FAMILY CULTURES INTERNALLY HOMOGENEOUS?

The first relevant issue is to what extent the national cultures within Europe are internally homogenous. It is rightly noticed that the culture of a given country 'may be understood as a vast diversity of overlapping cultures; some relatively local, some, more universal'.[26] Laurence Friedman speaks in this respect of 'a dazzling array of cultures' within a single culture.[27] One of the important points of distinction between these sub-cultures is their ideological affiliation. Thus, Friedman delineates the conservative culture and the liberal culture and 'all sorts of variants and subgroups' between them.[28]

This internal cultural diversity is especially manifest in family ideology and the discourse on family legislation. As was discussed in the preceding chapters, ever since the Enlightenment the political life of Europe has been split by an ideological conservative/progressive discord.[29] All ideological trends since the Enlightenment, like the Restoration, nineteenth century liberalism, socialism, feminism, and so on, are of a pan-European nature. All these trends generated their own sets of values with regard to family and family law. The corresponding progressive-conservative divide does not coincide with State boundaries, but rather has split every particular European

---

[23]   HICKS, S., 'A Model of Society for the Comparative Study of Law' (1997), p. 215.
[24]   Legrand speaks in this sense of the 'Frenchness' of French law. LEGRAND, P., *Fragments on Law-as-Culture* (1999), p. 5.
[25]   FRIEDMANN, L., *The Legal System: A Social Science Perspective* (1975), p. 199.
[26]   COTTERRELL, R., 'The Concept of Legal Culture' (1997), p. 20.
[27]   FRIEDMANN, L., *The Republic of Choice: Law, Authority and Culture* (1990), p. 213.
[28]   FRIEDMANN, L., *Total Justice* (1985), p. 98.
[29]   See in particular Part III, Chapter 9, Section 9.3.1.

502

country. This does not refer to the growing multiculturalism resulting from immigration from non-European countries.[30] What is meant is that the innate population in each particular European country is split into various different 'cultures' that are affiliated to the corresponding ideologies. A clear example is France. Max Rheinstein noticed that since the Revolution of 1789, France has been split up into '*les deux Frances*', a progressive and a conservative one, and has shown how much the subsequent history of French family law was affected by the struggle between those two camps.[31] Describing the 1975 reform of French divorce law, Mary Ann Glendon concludes that at the end of the twentieth century the French society was still divided into the same '*les deux Frances*'.[32] Italy is also a good example. As Valerio Pocar and Paola Ronfani put it: 'It is important to remember that Italy today still presents major contrasts in culture and daily usage between industrialized zones and those with a predominantly agricultural economy, between town and country, between North and South. As result there are many different family structures, which cannot be integrated into a single abstract model. The same consideration applies to the whole discourse on family legislation.'[33] Everywhere in Europe, the modernity of family patterns and family culture differs greatly from one social environment to another. The ideas an urban family of highly educated young professionals have about family and family law, differ significantly from the corresponding ideas of a rural family of middle-aged traditional farmers in any European country, be it Italy, Sweden, Malta or the Netherlands. Franz Rothenbacher concisely labelled this phenomenon 'the contemporaneity of the noncontemporaneous'.[34] Each country has of course a predominant ideology regarding family law matters, which is generally the ideas of the majority of the population or the *élites dirigeante*.[35] Thus the pertinent family law is either a reflection of the predominant values, or a compromise between the values of the various groups.

Sometimes the ongoing struggle between the conservative and progressive 'cultures' in the field of family law comes to the forefront of ideological confrontation. The Irish and Italian divorce referendums are good illustrations of this phenomenon.[36] The history of family law reform shows that most confrontations finally result in legislation based on compromises. Only every now and then is one side able to clearly overpower

---

[30]   On this and other aspects of multiculturalism see: ÖRÜCÜ, E., *The Enigma of Comparative Law* (2004), p. 123-132.

[31]   RHEINSTEIN, M., *Marriage Stability, Divorce, and the Law* (1972), p. 195.

[32]   GLENDON, M. A., 'The French Divorce Reform Law of 1976' (1976), p. 201.

[33]   POCAR, V., RONFANI, P., 'Family Law in Italy: Legislative Innovations and Social Change' (1978), p. 629.

[34]   ROTHENBACHER, F. 'Social Change in Europe and its Impact on Family Structures'(1998), p. 21.

[35]   I am indebted to Esin Örücü for this term. See her *Critical Comparative Law: Considering Paradoxes for Legal Systems in Transition* (1999), p. 86.

[36]   See for instance: DILLON, M., *Debating Divorce. Moral Conflict in Ireland* (1993).

the other. For example, the conservative side managed to turn the clock back with the abolition of divorce in France after the Restoration in 1816 and in Spain under Franco in 1939. More often it is the progressive side that manages to achieve a certain breakthrough, like the introduction of divorce on demand in Sweden and Spain and of same-sex marriage in The Netherlands, Belgium and Spain.

It is worth noting that there is an objective difference between 'conservative' and 'progressive' family law that is relevant here. Family law built upon a conservative 'culture' is often rather restrictive. Population groups representing minority 'cultures' are also subjected to the restrictions of that law, although they do not share its underlying convictions. A good example is the first Irish divorce referendum of 1986, when 63.5% of the electorate voted against the introduction of divorce and 36.5% voted in favour.[37] As the legal possibility to obtain a divorce does not compel anyone to divorce, the result of the referendum meant that the majority of the Irish population denied not only themselves but also the dissenting minority the right to dissolve their marriage. Therefore these minorities often have the feeling that their rights are being infringed in an undemocratic manner;[38] as in the infamous *Johnston* case, where the plaintiffs maintained that the impossibility of obtaining a divorce in Ireland infringed on their right to family life and the right to marry – protected under articles 8 and 12 of the European Convention on Human Rights.[39] Family law built upon a progressive 'culture', however, is generally more permissive. This means that cultural groups representing a more conservative ideology are left enough room to arrange their family life in their own way. They have, of course, to accept the existence of permissive law, which is sometimes met with difficulty. For instance, not everyone in The Netherlands was happy with fact that marriage was opened up for same-sex couples, as some felt that this way also 'their marriage' was being deteriorated.[40] Still, providing more options for everyone is a relevant advantage of permissive law above restrictive law in this 'multicultural' context.

---

[37] JAMES, C., 'Ireland Welcomes Divorce: The 1995 Irish Divorce Referendum and The Family (Divorce) Act of 1996, 8 *Duke Journal of Comparative & International Law* 1997, Lexis).

[38] As Will Kymlicka has noted, 'the state unavoidably promotes certain cultural identities, and thereby disadvantages others'. KYMLICKA, W., *Multicultural Citizenship: A Liberal Theory of Minority Rights* (1995), p. 108.

[39] See: *Johnston v. Ireland.* ECHR (1986), and the dissenting opinion of Judge De Mayer.

[40] VAN MOURIK, M., 'Wettelijke en contractuele vormgeving van affectieve relaties' (1999), p. 67-68.

18.3.3. THE PAN-EUROPEAN CHARACTER OF NATIONAL CONSERVATIVE AND PROGRESSIVE 'SUBCULTURES'

If one accepts that the culture of each particular country is not internally homogeneous, the question arises to what extent the subcultures, in which national cultures are divided, are unique to the countries concerned. As was discussed above and in the preceding chapters, the 'subcultures' relevant to family ideology and law generally correspond with the ideological conservative/progressive divide that has characterised the political life of Europe since the Enlightenment. Both the 'conservative' and 'progressive' family ideologies are clearly of a pan-European nature, as both have their own rank and file in each European country. Sometimes this is a majority, sometimes a tiny stratum. The countries with modern family laws also have population groups with a conservative family 'culture' and the countries with conservative family laws always have population groups that represent the most modern views on family life. Laurence Friedman notices that adherents of specific attitudes 'tend to cohere, to hang together, to form clusters of related attitudes'.[41] The members of the affiliated cultural groups understand each other across the borders, often looking abroad to support their ideas, and they repeatedly call on the European courts to adjudicate their confrontations with their compatriot opponents.

Thus the elements of national culture that are relevant to family law are in general anything but unique. On the other hand, as the influence of different (sub)cultures varies from country to country,[42] national differences in prevailing family ideology and law can certainly not be disregarded. Yet it seems clear that in the field of family ideology and law there exist not so much unique national cultures, but rather a pan-European conservative and a pan-European progressive culture, and a whole range of varieties in between. There are of course all kinds of national peculiarities that contribute to the rich cultural, ideological and political palette that is Europe, but their significance as a determinant of family policy and law pales before the dominance of pan-European ideological conservative and progressive trends.

---

[41]   FRIEDMANN, L., *Total Justice* (1985), p. 98.
[42]   Roger Cotterrell has rightly noticed that legal ideology is more strongly linked with social power than other elements of legal culture. COTTERRELL, R., 'The Concept of Legal Culture' (1997), p. 23.

18.3.4. LEGAL CULTURE

Introduction

If the other elements of national culture that are relevant to family law are not, or at least not predominantly, of a unique national character, the question arises whether perhaps *legal* culture is. The proponents of the cultural constraints argument seldom refer to the embedment of family law directly in culture in general. It more often suggested that family laws are embedded in one particular element of culture, namely legal culture. Thus, Pierre Legrand speaks of the embedment of law in a subjective component of legal culture: legal *mentalité*. Marie-Thérèse Meulders-Klein suggests that family law constitutes the hard core of any legal culture.[43] This reference to legal, rather than general culture, allows the suggestion that, while general family 'cultures' are not unique to the particular European states, the legal cultures are. This possibility calls for some inquiry into the notion of legal culture.

What is legal culture? Deep and surface levels of legal cultures

Legal culture is a particular element of general culture: a kind of translation of general culture into the language of legal concepts, techniques and ideas. The issue of legal culture receives much attention at present and has no shortage of literature,[44] so I will have to confine myself to only a few references. As was mentioned above, the concept of legal culture is extensively explored in various works of Laurence Friedman. Friedman defines legal culture as 'ideas, attitudes, values and opinions about law, the legal system, and legal institutions of some given population'.[45] Within a legal culture Friedman primarily distinguishes between the professional and the common legal culture.[46] Mark van Hoecke and Mark Warrington introduce the concept of 'paradigm' in order to describe the hard core of legal cultures more specifically.[47] To such 'paradigmatical' aspects of legal culture they attribute: (1) a concept of law; (2) a theory of valid legal sources; (3) a methodology of law; (4) a theory of argumentation; (5) a theory of legitimation of law; (6) a common basic ideology.[48] Within those paradigms of legal culture Van Hoecke and Warrington distinguish between different levels. The 'common ideology, common moral convictions form the *deep* level, which eventually

---

[43] MEULDERS-KLEIN, M-T., 'Towards a European Civil Code of Family Law' (2003), p. 109.
[44] For an overview see: NELKEN, D., 'Comparing Legal Cultures' (1997), p. 1-9.
[45] FRIEDMANN, L., 'Some Thoughts on Comparative Legal Culture' (1990), p. 53.
[46] FRIEDMANN, L., *The Legal System: A Social Science Perspective* (1975), p. 223.
[47] VAN HOECKE, M., WARRINGTON, M., 'Legal Cultures, Legal Paradigms and Legal Doctrine: Towards a New Model For Comparative Law' (1998), p. 513.
[48] Ibid, p. 514-515.

comes to dominate the other levels.'[49] On the basis of this differentiation they further distinguish between differences among legal cultures, which manifest themselves at the surface and the deep levels. The differences on the deep moral and ideological level are of paramount importance. The differences on the surface level (for example legal rules, legal concepts and legal techniques) are less important.[50] It is justly pointed out that 'once the moral choices have been made, legal techniques are used in such a way as to reach the desired result.'[51] In a similar way Hugh Collins remarks with regard to the contemporary harmonisation activities, that technical aspects of the differences in legal cultures are relatively easy to reconcile, while overcoming differences, based on dissimilar moral values 'encounter[s] a general tension between the project of harmonisation and respect for cultural diversity in Europe.'[52] This proposition strongly applies to family law, where almost every rule 'represent[s] a symbolic endorsement of particular moral ideas.'[53] The emphasis on the political and ideological aspects of legal culture laid by Van Hoecke, Warrington and Collins is narrowly related to the idea of the embedment of family law in the political aspects of society, put forward by Otto Kahn-Freund and David Bradley[54] and amply supported by the results of the examinations in the preceding chapters.

The legal cultures of common law and civil law

According to Pierre Legrand, the most important differences among the legal cultures in Europe lie across the axes of the common/civil law dichotomy.[55] Legrand postulates an irreconcilable discord between the civil law and the common law *mentalités*.[56] He suggests that 'there exist both common law and civil law *mentalité* – two different ways of thinking about the law, about what it is to have knowledge of law and about the role of law in society'.[57] Legrand presents the history of the relationship between common and civil law systems as a kind of perpetual 'epistemological war'.[58] Consequently, he resolutely denies any possibility of the evolution of common and

---

49   Ibid, p. 519.
50   Ibid.
51   Ibid.
52   COLLINS, H., 'European Private Law and the Cultural Identity of States' (1995), p. 363.
53   Ibid.
54   See: Part I, Chapter, 2, Section. 2.3.
55   MOCCIA, L., has traced the historical routes of this 'mental obsession with presumed division between Civil and Common law' in the 'oversimplified as well as nationalistically biased' attitude that emerged in the middle of the seventeenth century. 'Historical Overview of the Origins and Attitudes of Comparative Law' (1992), p. 611-619.
56   LEGRAND, P., 'European Legal Systems Are Not Converging' (1996), p. 62.
57   LEGRAND, P., 'Against a European Civil Code' (1997), p. 45.
58   For which he received a well-deserved acquisition of selective and tendentious 'rétrodiction' of legal history. CHAMBOREDON, A.., 'The Debate on a European Civil Code: For an "Open Texture"' (2000), p. 68.

civil law cultures toward each other and claims that even evident examples of growing proximity between legal solutions provided in civil and common law systems should be dismissed as illusions based on a fallacious reduction of law to legal rules.[59]

In contrast with Legrand's contentions, several authors[60] assert that convergence of civil and common law systems, albeit gradually and patchily,[61] has taken place on various levels. Basil Markesinis notes convergence on both the functional (similar solutions to similar problems) and the formal level (for example convergence in the sources law; and a growing rapprochement of judicial views).[62] In the preceding chapters it was shown that there is not much difference between the common law and civil law rules on marriage, divorce, cohabitation, the position of extramarital children, and even matrimonial property. John Merryman has accurately pointed out that similarity of rules alone 'is in most cases an unreliable indicator of convergence or divergence of legal systems'.[63] Yet he admits that similar rules often provide 'outward evidence of a deeper legal similarity'. A 'more convincing measure of convergence' has to be found, according to Merryman, 'in the extent to which legal systems in Civil and Common Law nations play out the fundamental values of Western culture.'[64] Application of this criterion reveals that the common and civil Law families 'are moving along parallel roads, towards the same destination.'[65] Mark van Hoeke and Mark Warrington conclude that 'there are still differences between common law and civil law, but they are very close to a point where there will no longer be *paradigmatical* differences. What will be left is some degree of differences, not of a fundamental nature.'[66]

These conclusions apply all the more to family law. The preceding chapters make it plain that there are no more differences on the level of legal ideology in respect of family laws between the common and civil law cultures than between the civil law countries internally. If one takes as a starting point that legal ideology is the most important element in determining the differences and similarities between legal

---

[59]   LEGRAND, P., *Fragments on Law-as-Culture* (1999), p. 83-84.

[60]   E.g. LEWIS, X., 'The Europeanisation of the Common Law' (1995), p. 47-61; ZIMMERMANN, R., 'Roman Law and European Legal Unity'(1998), p. 34-35; MERRYMAN, J., 'On the Convergence (and Divergence) of Civil Law and the Common Law' (1978), p. 195-233, MARKESINIS, B. (ed.), *The Gradual Convergence. Foreign Ideas Foreign Influences and English Law on the Eve of the 21ˢᵗ Century* (1994).

[61]   MARKESINIS, B., 'Learning from Europe and Learning in Europe' (1994), p. 30.

[62]   Ibid.

[63]   MERRYMAN, J., 'On the Convergence (and Divergence) of Civil Law and the Common Law' (1978), p. 230.

[64]   Ibid, p. 232-233.

[65]   Ibid, p. 233.

[66]   VAN HOECKE, M., WARRINGTON, M., 'Legal Cultures, Legal Paradigms and Legal Doctrine: Towards a New Model For Comparative Law' (1998), p. 501.

cultures, one must conclude that the alleged fundamental difference between common and civil law legal cultures, whatever its merits for other fields of law, does not apply to family law. The history of family law clearly shows that the choices that were made in the context of family law reforms, and the political debates surrounding these reforms, have always been and still very much are the same on the continent as on the British Isles. Moreover, not only the ideological, but also the formal elements of legal culture in family law are not different in common and civil law countries. The explanation for this is that the bulk of family law in the whole of Western Europe, with the only notable exception being matrimonial property law, is imbedded in a common legal past: the medieval uniform canon law. The two systems even share the same conceptual language. For a common law lawyer terms like 'separation of bed and board', 'annulment' or 'illegitimate child' sound as familiar as for his continental colleague. There is not even much difference in regard to the legal sources, as even in the common law countries family law is mainly an area of codified law.[67]

Conclusion

In the context of the cultural constraints argument, only differences in legal culture on the 'deep' level of legal ideology and moral convictions could be truly relevant, as differences on the 'surface' level of legal rules, concepts and techniques are relatively easy to overcome. The preceding chapters allow the conclusion that in regard to family law, the general similarity on the level of ideologies and morals between all countries in Europe is overwhelming. Because of the shared common past of the medieval uniform canon law, the differences on the 'surface' level are also less than in any other field of private law. It is clear that the conclusions presented above in regard to the alleged fundamental differences between the legal cultures of common law and civil law can only apply all the more to the civil law countries amongst each other. The conclusion of this brief excursus into legal culture is therefore that in regard to family law, legal cultures in Europe are not of a unique national character either; at least not in such a way that this should affect the conclusion previously drawn with regard to the other elements of national culture relevant to family law, namely that in the field of family ideology and law, there exist not so much unique national cultures but rather a pan-European conservative and a pan-European progressive culture, and a whole range of varieties in between.

---

[67]   KAHN-FREUND, O., 'Common Law and Civil Law – Imaginary and Real Obstacles to Assimilation' (1978), p. 150.

18.3.5. IS THERE A COMMON EUROPEAN FAMILY CULTURE?

The conclusion remains that the elements of national culture that are relevant to family law are in general anything but unique. Modernisation goes on everywhere in Europe, albeit sometimes at a very different pace, and both the driving and opposing forces that shape this evolution are of a pan-European character. Does this mean that we could speak of a common European family culture?

The proponents of the cultural constraints argument firmly postulate the uniqueness of national cultures, while their opponents tend to see the particularities of the national cultures within Europe within the broader context of a common European culture. Also Laurence Friedmann, who generally believes in the uniqueness of national cultures,[68] acknowledges the existence of such general phenomenon as modern culture or the culture of Modernity.[69] Although there is no definite agreement concerning the principal characteristics of the common European culture, some characteristics thereof are more or less unambiguous. Among such common features are named, for instance, individualism and rationalism,[70] personalism and intellectualism,[71] rights-consciousness and dissolution of traditional authority,[72] and respect for human rights.

However, these are only very general characteristics. They are not enough to constitute a general ideological consensus on particular issues of family law. As we have seen, on some of those issues such consensus does exist. The best examples are the above discussed common ideological standpoints on the equality of spouses and of children born in and outside wedlock. Yet, it is abundantly clear that on many other issues there is no such consensus. The consensus-forming potential of the European human rights instruments and courts is limited by the fact that they generally tend to go no further than the level of consensus which already exists among the Member States. Therefore there is not much hope that in the near future a shared notion of European human rights will form a basis of common ideology for the whole of family law.

The point is that the pan-European character of family law culture and ideology stands out the most if looked at from a historical perspective, abstracting from any particular point in time. However, if one considers the family law culture and ideology of the various countries of Europe as they stand at a certain point in time only, it is the

---

[68]   FRIEDMANN, L., *The Legal System: A Social Science Perspective* (1975), p. 199.
[69]   FRIEDMANN, L., *The Republic of Choice: Law, Authority and Culture* (1990), p. 198-199.
[70]   VAN HOECKE, M., WARRINGTON, M., 'Legal Cultures, Legal Paradigms and Legal Doctrine: Towards a New Model For Comparative Law' (1998), p. 503.
[71]   WIEACKER, F., 'Foundations of European Legal Culture' (1990), p. 1-29.
[72]   FRIEDMANN, L., 'Some Thoughts on Comparative Legal Culture' (1990), p. 57.

differences, rather than the similarities, that tend to strike the eye. It was concluded above that these are merely differences in the pace and profundity of the modernisation of family law that takes place everywhere in Europe. Yet it is clear that in the context of an evaluation of the cultural constraints argument, the national differences in prevailing family culture and ideology that exist at present, and in one form or another will most probably continue to do so, cannot be disregarded. It is therefore very possible to speak of a common European family culture, but not in the sense that the cultural constraints argument could be dismissed altogether because in reality there are no relevant differences among the national family cultures and ideologies in Europe. There definitely are such differences, and the analysis of convergence tendencies in the preceding sections suggests that for the foreseeable future, they will not disappear.

18.3.6. CONCLUSION

It is clear that the core assumption of the cultural constraints argument – the alleged embedment of family laws in unique and unchangeable national cultures – cannot be maintained. History plainly shows that in the field of family ideology and law there exist not so much unique national cultures, but rather a pan-European culture, which is not homogeneous but an amalgam of pan-European 'conservative' and pan-European 'progressive' culture. The relative influence of these two opposing family 'cultures' varies from country to country and from time to time. As was concluded above, it is national politics, rather than national culture, that determines the pertinent family laws.

The cultural constraints argument cannot be saved by the suggestion that national politics is just an element of national culture. This not because such classification is impossible in principle. Although a more precise description of the relationship between culture and politics would of course depend on the adopted definition of both concepts, it seems obvious that national culture can be considered an important determinant of the political affairs of a country, and perhaps the same can be said of the reverse relationship. The cultural constraints argument cannot be saved by such reasoning because it is not so much the element of 'culture' that is essential to it, but the elements of uniqueness and unchangeability. It are these elements that lie at the heart of the assumption that convergence and deliberate harmonisation of national family laws is impossible, not the contention that family law is determined by culture. As we have seen, the political factor that is the main determinant of the evolution of national family law is the balance of power between the local adherents of predominantly pan-European 'progressive' and 'conservative' family ideology. This balance of political power is obviously neither unique nor unchangeable. On the contrary, there are few things so variable as the political vicissitudes of a country and the outcome of democratic elections. Although one could of course say that a particular country has in general a more or less continuous 'conservative' or 'progressive' political character (for instance when comparing Malta to Sweden or Ireland to The Netherlands), the example of Spain introducing same-sex marriage soon after the electoral victory of the social-democrats under Rodríguez Zapatero makes it clear that the political determinants of the evolution of family law are very changeable indeed. One never knows how long such a statement would remain valid when it comes to family law.

All things considered, the conclusion can be none other than that the cultural constraints argument is beyond redemption. Its core assumptions cannot be upheld. Family law is not so much embedded in unique national culture and history, but rather in pan-European culture and history. Pertinent national family laws are determined by political, rather than cultural factors, and these are not unchangeable at all. And every now and then family laws do converge spontaneously. However, it remains to be seen what all this means for the deliberate harmonisation of family law.

18.4. IMPLICATIONS FOR THE DELIBERATE HARMONISATION OF FAMILY LAW

It hardly seems necessary to point out that the political course of the countries in Europe is determined on a national level. Since national family laws are based on national compromises between the adherents of 'progressive' and 'conservative' family ideology, any form of top-down harmonisation[73] of family law involves overruling such national compromises and substituting them with compromises reached on an European level. Considering the political sensitivity of the issue of national sovereignty, this is largely unfeasible. Any comprehensive top-down harmonisation would clearly go beyond the current mandate of the EU,[74] and certainly beyond the present political will of the Member States. This does not mean that top-down harmonisation of family law in Europe is altogether impossible, but rather that the room for such harmonisation is quite limited. As we have seen, in a limited number of particular fields of family law, top-down harmonisation has already been taking place for quite some time. Perhaps the best example is the binding harmonisation of the law governing the status of children born outside marriage by the case law of the European Court of Human Rights. However, the number of issues on which there exists sufficient pan-European political consensus to allow the European Courts to develop such case law is presently

---

[73] For a definition of top-down harmonisation see Part I, Chapter 2, Section 2.2.1.
[74] See the references in footnote 15 in Part I, Chapter 2, Section 2.2.1.

very limited. With regard to such core fields of family law as marriage, divorce and extramarital cohabitation, the political preconditions for any comprehensive top-down harmonisation are clearly not fulfilled. The historical overview presented in the preceding chapters gives no indication that this is going to change in the near future. This is why any comprehensive top-down harmonisation by way of binding instruments should be considered both infeasible and undesirable.

It is worth stressing that it is 'political' constraints, not so much 'cultural', that lead to this conclusion. European history has proven top-down harmonisation as such to be entirely possible. Even manifest cultural dissimilarities appear not to be a permanent obstacle. Several historical examples – like the medieval unification, the Russian post-revolutionary legislation, and the transplantation of Swiss family law into Turkey – show that the cultural embedment of family law does not preclude the acceptance of culturally rather alien family law rules, if the imposition of the new law is backed with enough pressure. As was pointed out at the end of Chapter 7, today any such undertaking is obviously ruled out by the imperatives of democracy and the protection of human rights.[75] Also in this respect, it is not so much cultural constraints that constitute the limits for the harmonisation of family law in Europe, but rather political ones. All in all, one could perhaps better speak of the 'political constraints argument'.

The negative estimation of the prospects for binding top-down harmonisation does not apply to attempts to promote voluntary bottom-up harmonisation.[76] The preceding analysis reveals no objections to academic initiatives, such as the CEFL, whose ambitions go no further than elaborating non-binding *Principles* of European family law. However, because of the strong political dimension of family law, the actual influence that these *Principles* will have on the national legislatures and judiciaries should not be overrated.

The last suggestion I would like to make is that it would seem to be a good thing if the awareness that, apart from the existing jurisdiction of the ECHR and ECJ, the political reality in Europe simply rules out any binding harmonisation of family law, would temper the discord between the proponents and the opponents of the idea of harmonisation of family law in Europe. The harmonisation enthusiasts could better recognize that the road to harmonisation is a long and thorny one, and that the current generation will probably not see any fruits of their efforts other than very instructive and inspiring scientific publications. The opponents of the idea of harmonisation should in turn realise that there is no real threat of any non-voluntary harmonisation. There is no reason for them to lose any sleep.

---

[75]   See Part III, Chapter 7, Section 7.3.
[76]   For a definition of bottom-up harmonisation see: Part I, Chapter 2, Section 2.2.1.

APPENDICES

BIBLIOGRAPHY

ABBOT, P., WALLACE, C., *The family and the New Rights*, Pluto Press, London, 1992.

ABSE, T., 'Italy: A New Agenda', in: ANDERSON, P., CAMILLER, P. (eds.), *Mapping the West European Left*, Verso, London, 1994, p. 189-217.

ADORNO, T., HORKHEIMER, M., *Dialektik der Aufklärung: philosophische Fragment*, Querido, Amsterdam, 1947.

AGELL, A., 'Towards Uniforming Spouses' Property Rights Especially in International Marriages?' in: the Proceedings of the 3rd European Conference on Family Law, Council of Europe, Cádiz, 1995, p. 63-80

AGELL, A., 'The Swedish Legislation on Marriage and Cohabitation: A Journey Without a Destination', *9 Scandinavian Studies in Law* (1980), p. 9-48.

AGELL, A., 'Should and Can Family Law Influence Social behaviour?' in: EEKELAAR, J., NHLAPO, T., *The Changing Family: International Perspectives on the Family and Family Law*, Hart Publishing, Oxford, 1998, p. 125-137.

AGELL, A., 'Division of Property upon Divorce from a European Perspective', in: POUSSON-PETIT, J. (ed.), *Droit Comparé des personnes et de la Famille. Liber Amicorum Marie-Thérèse Meulders-Klein*, Bruylant, Brussels, 1998, p. 1-20.

AGELL, A., 'Family Forms and Legal Policies. A Comparative View from a Swedish Observer', *38 Scandinavian Studies in Law* (1999) p. 197-216.

AGELL, A., 'Is There one System of Family Laws in the Nordic Countries', *3 European Journal of Law Reform* (2001), p. 313-329.

AGELL, A., 'The Legal Status of Same-Sex Couples in Europe – A Critical Analysis', in: BOELE-WOELKI, K., FURCHS, A. (eds.), *Legal Recognition of Same-Sex Couples in Europe*, Intersentia, Antwerp, 2003, p. 122-134.

AJANI, G., 'By Chance and Prestige: Legal Transplants in Russian and Eastern Europe', *43 The American Journal of Comparative law* (1995), p. 93-117.

ALBERIGO, G., KOMONCHAK, A. (eds.), *History of Vatican II*, Vol. IV, Peeters, Leuven, 2003, p. 310.

ALEKSEEV, N., *Pravovoe regulirovanie polozgenia sexual'nikh men'shinstv. Rossia v svete praktiki mezgdynarodnikx opganizaii I natsional'nogo zakonodatel'stva stran mipa (Legal Regulation of the Status of Sequel Minorities. Russia in the light of the perceives of the International organisation and national legislation of the foreign countries)*, Beck, Moscow, 2002.

ALEKSEEV, N., *Gey-brak. Semeinii status odnopolikh par v mezgdynarodnom, natsional'nom I mestnom prave (Gay-Marriage: A XXIst Century Puzzle. Family status of same sex coupes in International, National and Local Law*, Beck, Moscow, 2002.

ALPA, G., 'European Community Resolutions and the Codification of "Private Law", *2 European Review of Private Law* (2000), p. 321-333.

ALSTON, P. (ed.), *The EU and Human Rights*, Oxford University Press, Oxford, 1999.

AMRAM, D., *The Jewish law of Divorce According to Bible and Talmud*, Hermon Press, New York, 1968.

Analyse comparative des rapports nationaux et propositions d'harmonisation consortium, in: Asser-UCL, *Study on Matrimonial Property Regimes and the Property of Unmarried Couples in Private International Law and Internal Law*, European Commission, 2003 http://ec.europa.eu/justice_home/doc_centre/civil/studies/doc/regimes/report_regimes _030703_fr.pdf .

ANCEL, M., 'Matrimonial Property Law in France', in: FRIEDMANN, W. (ed.), *Matrimonial Property Law*, Stevens and Sons, London, 1955, p. 3-29.

ANDRUP, H., BUCHHOFER, B., ZIEGERT, K., 'Formal Marriage Under the Crossfire of Social Change', in: EEKELAAR, J., KATZ, S. (eds.), *Marriage and Cohabitation in Contemporary Society*, Butterworths, Toronto, 1980, p. 32-38.

ANSAY, T., WALLACE, D., *Introduction to Turkish Law*, 4th edn., Kluwer, The Hague, 1996.

ANTOKOLSKAIA, M., *Family Law (Semeinoe pravo)*, Jurist, Moscow, 1997.

ANTOKOLSKAIA, M., *Family Law (Semeinoe pravo)*, 2nd edn., Jurist, Moscow, 1999.

ANTOKOLSKAIA, M., 'Geschiedenis van het familierecht: gelijke ontwikkeling', 'Gezamenlijke tendensen en beginselen' en 'Drie voorbeelden van harmonisatie en unificatie van het Familierecht in de 20ste eeuw. Vergelijking van het onvergelijkbare?', in: ANTOKOLSKAIA, M., DE HONDT, W., STEENHOFF, G., *Naar een Europees Familierecht, Report for the Netherlands Comparative law Association*, Kluwer, Deventer, 1999, p. 33-106.

ANTOKOLSKAIA, M., The Process of Modernisation of Family Law in Eastern and Western Europe: Difference in Timing, Resemblance in Substance', *4.2 Electronic Journal of Comparative Law* (2000), http://law.kub.nl/ejcl/42/art42-1.html.

ANTOKOLSKAIA, M., 'De ontwikkeling van het Russische familierecht vanaf de Bolsjewistische revolutie: een poging tot verklaring', *70 Tijdschrift voor Rechtsgeschiedenis*, 2002, p. 137-171.

ANTOKOLSKAIA, M., 'Recent Developments in Dutch Filiation, Adoption and Joint Custody Law, *3 Familia* (2002), p. 781-804.

ANTOKOLSKAIA, M., BOELE-WOELKI, K., ' Dutch Family Law in the 21st Century: Trend-Setting and Struggling Behind at the Same Time', in: HONDIUS, E., JOUSTRA, C. (eds.), *Netherlands Reports to the Sixteenth International Congress of Comparative Law, Brisbane 2002*, Intersentia, Antwerp, 2002, p. 53-74.

ANTOKOLSKAIA, M., 'Enkele gedachten over de harmonisatie van het familierecht in Europa', *1 Tijdschrift voor Familie- en Jeugdrecht* (2002), p. 4-10

ANTOKOLSKAIA, M., 'The Harmonisation of Family Law: Old and New Dilemmas' *1 European Review of Private Law* (2003), p. 28-49.

ANTOKOLSKAIA, M., 'Development of Family Law in Western and Eastern Europe: Common Origins, Common Driving Forces, Common Tendencies', *28 Journal of Family History* (2003), p. 52-69.

ANTOKOLSKAIA, M., 'Russian Report concerning the CEFL Questionnaire on Grounds for Divorce and Maintenance Between Former Spouses', http://www.law.uu.nl/priv/cefl > Working Field 1 > Russia

ANTOKOLSKAIA, M., *CEFL* National Report for Russia: Grounds for Divorce, in: BOELE-WOELKI, K., BRAAT, B., SUMNER I. (eds.), *European Family Law in Action*, Vol. I: Grounds for Divorce, European Family Law Series No. 2, Intersentia, Antwerp, 2003.

ANTOKOLSKAIA, M., 'The "Better Law" Approach and the Harmonisation of Family Law', in: BOELE-WOELKI, K. (ed.), *Perspectives for the Unification and Harmonisation of Family Law in Europe*, European Family Law Series No. 4, Intersentia, Antwerp, 2003, p. 159-183.

ANTOKOLSKAIA, M., 'Objectives and Values of Substantive Family Law', in: MEEUSEN J., PERTEGÁS, M., STRAETMANS, G., SWENNEN F. (eds.), *European Family Law for the European Union*, Intersentia, Antwerpen, 2006, forthcoming.

APELDOORN, L., *Geschiedenis van het Nederlandsche huwelijksrecht voor de invoering van de Fransche wetgeving*, Holland, Amsterdam, 1925.

ARAI, Y., 'The Margin of Appreciation Doctrine in the Jurisprudence of Article 8 of the European Convention on Human Rights' (1998) *16 Netherlands Quarterly of Human Rights 1*, p. 41- 61.

ARGYRIADIS, A., 'Reform of Family Law in Greece', CHLOROS, A. (ed.), *The Reform of Family Law in Europe*, Kluwer, Boston, 1978, p.139-149.

ASÍN CABRERA, 'La partenariat de droit espagnol: quel avenir pour une réglementation en droit international privé?', in: *Aspects de droit international privé des partenariats enregistrés en Europe*: actes de la XVIe Journée de Droit international privé du 5 mars 2004 à Lausanne, organisée conjointement par l'Institut suisse de Droit comparé et le Centre de Droit comparé, de Droit européen et de Législations étrangères, Université de Lausanne, Schulthess, Lausanne, 2004, p. 71-85.

ASLAND, J., 'Legislation on Informal Cohabitation in Norway', in: BOELE-WOELKI, K. (ed.), *Common Core and Better Law in European Family Law*, Intersentia, Antwerp, 2005, p. 295-304.

BABIC, S., 'Family Law in Bosnia and Herzegovina', in: BAINHAM, A. (ed.), *The International Survey of Family Law*, Martinus Nijhoff, The Hague, 1996, p. 51-68.

BAETEMAN, G., 'The Original System of the Code Napoleon in Belgium and Holland', in: KIRALFY, A. (ed.), *Comparative Law of Matrimonial Property*, Sijthoff, Leiden, 1972, p. 1-18.

BAETEMAN, G., 'The Modern Belgian Law', in: KIRALFY, A. (ed.), *Comparative Law of Matrimonial Property*, Sijthoff, Leiden, 1972, p. 18-62.

BAINHAM, A., 'Exiting Times in England – Children and Divorce', *International Family Law* (2001), p. 71-77.

BAINHAM, A., 'Men and Women Behaving Badly: Is Fault Dead in English Family Law?', *21 Oxford Journal of Legal Studies*, 2001, p. 219-238.

BAKER, J., 'Why the History of English Law Has Not Been Finished', *59(1) Cambridge Law Journal*, (2000), p. 62-85.

BAKER, J., *An Introduction to English Legal History*, 4th edn., Butterworths, London, 2002.

BART, J., *Histoire du droit privé de la chute de l'Empire romain au XIXe siècle*, Montchrestein, Paris, 1998.

BASEDOW, J., 'Codification of Private Law in the European Union: the making of a Hybrid', *1 European Review of Private Law* (2001), p. 35-49.

BASTARD, B., 'Administrative Divorce in France: A Controversy Over a Reform, that Never Reached the Statute Book', in: MACLEAN, M. (ed.), *Making Law for Families*, Hart Publishing, Oxford, 2000, p. 72-91.

BECKER, H-J., 'Die nichteheliche Lebensgemeinschaft (Konkubinat) in der Rechtsgeschichte', in: LANDWEHR, G., *Die nichteheliche Lebensgemeinschaft,* Vandenhoeck und Ruprecht, Göttingen, 1978, p. 13-38.

BELIAKOVA, A., Introductory article, in: VOROGEIKIN, E.M. (ed.), *Semeinoe pravo evropeiskikh zarubezhnukh sotsialiaticheskikh stran,* Progress, Moskou, 1979, p. 5-23.

BELLOMO, M., *The Common Legal Past of Europe 1000-1800,* transl. by Cocharane, L., The Catholic University of America Press, Washington D.C., 1995.

BÉNABENT, A., 'Le Liberté individuelle et le mariage', *Revue trimestrielle de droit civil* (1973), p. 440-495

BÉNABENT, 'Plaidoyer pour quelques réformes du divorce,' *Recuiel Daloz de doctrine de jurisprudence et de légis hebdomadaire,* (1997), p. 225-228.

BÉNABENT, A., *Droit civil: La Famille,* 10ᵉ éd, Litec, Paris, 2001.

BÉNABENT, A., *La réforme du divorce article par article,* Defrénois, Paris, 2004.

BENTHAM, J., *The Theory of Legislation,* Routledge and Paul, London, 1950.

BERMAN, H., *Law and Revolution. The Formation of the Western Legal Tradition,* Harvard University Press, Cambridge, Massachusetts, 1983.

BJÖRGVINSSON, D., 'General Principles and Recent Developments in Icelandic Family Law', in: BAINHAM, A. (ed.), *The International Survey of Family Law,* Martinus Nijhoff, The Hague, 1995, p. 215-237.

BOELE-WOELKI, K., 'Principles and Private International Law. The UNIDROIT Principles of International Commercial Contract and the Principles of European Contract law', 4 *Uniform Law Review* 1996, p. 652-678.

BOELE-WOELKI, K., 'De prijs van het homohuwelijk,' *6 Tijdschrift voor Familie- en Jeugdrecht,* (1999), p. 113.

BOELE-WOELKI, K., 'Registered Partnerships: Legislation in the Netherlands', in: *Current Problems in the in the Law of Persons,* CIEC, Strasburg, 1999, p. 43-53.

BOELE-WOELKI, K., SCHRAMA, W., 'Die Rechtsstellung von Menschen mit homosexueller Veranlagung im niederländischen Recht', in: BASEDOW, J. et al (eds.), *Die Rechtsstellung gleichgeschechtlicher Lebensgemeinschaften,* Mohr, Tübingen, 2000, p. 51-113.

BOELE-WOELKI, K., 'Het Duitse *LPartG* verdient geen schoonheidsprijs,' *1 Tijdschrift voor Familie- en Jeugdrecht,* (2002), p. 1.

BOELE-WOELKI, K., BRAAT, B., SUMNER, I. (eds.) Grounds for Divorce, Intersentia, Antwerp, 2003.

BOELE-WOELKI, K., 'Comparative Research-based Drafting of Principles of European Family Law', in: M. Faure et al. (eds.), *Towards a European Ius Commune in Legal Education and Research,* Intersentia, Antwerpen, 2002, p. 170-185.'

BOELE-WOELKI, K., 'Divorce in Europe: Unification of Private International Law and Harmonisation of Substantive Law', in: LEMAIRE, H., VLAS, P. (eds.), *Met recht verkregen. Bunder Opstellen aangeboden aan Mr. Ingrid S. Joppe,* Kluwer, Deventer, 2002, p. 17-28.

BOELE-WOELKI, K., 'B(l)oeiend vergelijkend familierecht: de Commission on European Family Law', in: BOELE-WOELKI, K., BRANTS, C., STEENHOFF, G. (eds.), *Het plezier van de rechtsvergelijking. Opstellen over unificatie en harmonisatie van het recht in Europa aangeboden aan prof. mr. E. H. Hondius,* Kluwer, Deventer, 2003, p. 141-159.

BOELE-WOELKI, K., 'Registered Partnership and Same-Sex Marriage in the Netherlands', in: BOELE-WOELKI, K., FURCHS, A. (eds.), *Legal Recognition of Same-Sex Couples in Europe,* Intersentia, Antwerp, 2003, p. 41-53.

BOELE-WOELKI, K. (ed.), *Perspectives for the Unification and Harmonisation of Family Law in Europe,* European Family Law Series No. 4, Intersentia, Antwerp, 2003.

BOELE-WOELKI, K., 'Het WODC rapport: De gekozen achternaam', *3 Familie- en Jeugdrecht* (2003), p. 36-43.

BOELE-WOELKI, K. et al, *Principles of European Family Law Regarding Divorce and Maintenance Between Former Spouses,* European Family Law Series No. 7, Intersentia, Antwerp, 2004.

BOELE-WOELKI, K. (ed.), *Common Core and Better Law in European Family Law,* European Family Law Series No. 10, Intersentia, Antwerp, 2005.

BOELE-WOELKI, K. 'Parental Responsibilities – CEFL's Initial Results', in: BOELE-WOELKI, K. (ed.), *Common Core and Better Law in European Family Law,* European Family Law Series No. 10, Intersentia, Antwerp, 2005, p. 141-168.

BOELE-WOELKI, K., 'The Working Method of the Commission on European Family Law', in: BOELE-WOELKI, K. (ed.), *Common Core and Better Law in European Family Law,* European Family Law Series No. 10, Intersentia, Antwerp, 2005, p. 15-41.

BOELE-WOELKI, K., 'The principles of European family law: aims and prospects', 2 Utrecht Law Review (2005), p. 160-168. hrrp://www/utrechtlawreview.org >Volume 1> issue 2 (December) 2005.

BOEVE, L., '*Gaudium et Spet* and the Crisis of Modernity: The End of the Dialogue with the World?' in: LAMBERIGTS, M., KENIS, L., *Vatican II and Its Legacy*, Peeters, Leuven, 2002, p. 83-95.

BOHNDORF, T., 'The New Legitimacy Law in Germany', *19 International and Comparative Law Quarterly* (1970), p. 299-308.

BÓNÉ, 'Comparaison entre le droit au divorce dans la République Batave (1798-1806) et dans l'Allgemeines Landrecht für die der Preussischen Staaten,' in: DAUCHY, S., DEMARS-SION, V. (eds.), *Juges et Criminels, Etudes en hommage à Renée Matinage*, Lille l'Espace Juridique, Lille, 2001, p. 173-186.

BONELL, M., 'Unification of Law by Non-Legislative Means', *The American Journal of Comparative Law* (1992), p. 617-633.

BOOR, E., 'Blijft vaders wil wet?', *3 Familie- en Jeugdrecht* (2003), p. 54-60.

BRAAT, B., ODERKERK, M., STEENHOFF, G., *Huwelijksvermogensrecht in rechtsvergelijkend perspectief*, Kluwer, Deventer, 2000.

BRAAT, B., 'Nieuw Frans relatierecht: de PaCS', *4 Familie- en jeugdrecht* (2000), p. 75-81.

BRAAT, B., *Indépendance et interdépendance patrimoniales des époux dans le régime matrimonial légal des droits français, néerlandais et suisse*, Staempfli, Berne, 2004.

BRAAT, B., ODERKERK, M., STEENHOFF, G., in: BOELE-WOELKI, K. (ed.), *Huwelijksvermogensrecht in rechtvergelijkend perspectief,* Kluwer, Deventer, 2000.

BRADLEY, D., *Family Law and Political Culture.* Scandinavian Laws in Comparative Perspective. Sweet & Maxwell, London, 1996.

BRADLEY, D., 'Antecedents of Finnish Family Laws: Legal Traditions, Political Culture and Social Institutions', *2 Legal History,* (1998).

BRADLEY, D., 'Equality and Patriarchy: Family Law and Sate Feminism in Finland', *26 International Journal of Sociology and Law* (1998), p. 197-212.

BRADLEY, D., 'Convergence in Family Law: Mirrors, Transplants and Political Economy', 6 *Maastricht Journal of European and Comparative Law* (1999), p. 128-150.

BRADLEY, D., 'Comparative Family Law and Political Process: Regulation of Sexual Morality in Finland', *2 Journal of Law and Society* (1999), p. 175-191.

BRADLEY, D., 'Regulation of Unmarried Cohabitation in West-European Jurisdictions – Determinants of Legal Policy', *15 International Journal of Law, Policy and the Family* (2001), p. 22-50.

BRADLEY, D., 'Comparative Law, Family Law and Common Law', *1 Oxford Journal of Legal History* (2003), p. 127-146.

BRADLEY, D., 'A Family Law For Europe? Sovereignty, Political Economy and Legitimation', in: BOELE-WOELKI, K. (ed.), *Perspectives for the Unification and Harmonisation of Family Law in Europe*, European Family Law Series No. 4, Intersentia, Antwerp, 2003, p. 65-104.

BRADLEY, D., 'A Note on Comparative Family Law: Problems, Perspectives, Issues and Politics,' *Oxford University Comparative Law Forum* (2005), www.ouclf.iuscomp.org.

BRANDENBURGSKII, J., Presentation at the dispute on the family in the House of Soviets, *48-49 ECU* (1925), p. 1504

BRAS, G., Le 'Canon law', in: CRUMP, C., JACOB, E. (eds.), *The Legacy of the Middle Ages*, The Clarendon Press, Oxford, 1951, p. 321-363.

BRAUNEDER, W., 'Europäisches Privatrecht; aber was ist es?' *Zeitschrift für Neuere Rechtsgeschichte ZfNRG*, (1993), p. 225-235.

BRESC, H., 'Europe: Town and Country (Thirteenth-Fifteenth Century)'in: BURGUIERE, A., KLAPISCH-ZUBER, C., SEGALEN, M., ZONABEND O. (ed.)., A History of the Family. Vol. I. Distant Worlds, Ancient Worlds, Polity Press, Oxford, 1996.

BRISSAUD, J., *A History of French Private Law*, transl. By Howell, R., Murray, London, 1912.

BRISTOW, J., *What Paul Really Said About Women. An Apostle's Liberating View on Equality in Marriage, Leadership, and Love,* Harper, San Francisco, 1991.

BROBERG, M., 'The Registered Partnership for Same-Sex Couples in Denmark', *2 Child and Family Law Quarterly* (1996), p. 149-155.

BROMLEY, P., *Family Law*, 4th edn., Butterworth, London, 1971.

BROOKE, N., *The Medieval Idea of Marriage*, Oxford University Press, Oxford, 1989.

BROOKS, J., *Whose Fault Is IT Anyway? Divorce and the Family Law Act 1996,* Grove Books, Cambridge, 2000.

BRUNDAGE, J., 'Concubinage and Marriage in Medieval Canon Law', *1 Journal of Medieval History* (1975), p. 1-17.

BRUNDAGE, J., 'Marriage and Sexuality in the Decretals of Pope Alexander III', in: *Miscellanea Rolando Bandinell Papa Alessandro III*, Nelle Sede Dell' Accademia, Siena, 1986, p. 59- 83.

BRUNDAGE, J., *Law, sex, and Christian society in medieval Europe*, Chicago Univ. Press, Chicago, 1987.

BRUNDAGE, J., *Medieval Canon Law*, Longman, London, 1995.

BUENO MEDINA, L., 'The Spanish Partnership Legislation', in: BOELE-WOELKI, K. (ed.), *Common Core and Better Law in European Family Law,* Intersentia, Antwerp, 2005, p. 305-313.

BÜRGE, A., *Römisches Privatrecht. Rechtsdenken und gesellschaftlische Varankerung. Eine Einführung*, Wissenschaflische Buchgesellschaft, Darmstadt, 1999.

BURGE, W., *Commentaries on Colonial and Foreign Laws Generally and in Their Conflict with Each other and With the Law of England*, V. II and III, Sweet and Maxwell, London, 1908-1910.

BURGUIÈRE, A., LEBRUN, F., 'Prince, Priest and Family' in: BURGUIÈRE, A. KLAPISCH-ZUBER, C., SEGALEN, M., ZONABEND O. (eds.), A History of the Family. Vol. II. The impact of Modernity, Polity Press, Cambridge, 1996.

BURLEY, J., REGAN, F., ' Divorce in Ireland: the Fear, the Floodgates and the Reality', *16 International Journal of Law, Policy and the Family* (2002), p. 202-222.

BUSSANI, M., MATTEI, U., 'The Common Core Approach to European Private Law' *Columbia Journal of European Private Law* (1997-98), p. 339-356.

BUSSCHERE, C., de, 'Wet van 23 november 1998', *1 Praktijk notarius*, (1999), p. 19-25.

CABRILLAC, R., 'Libres propos sur le PACS (après l'adoption de texte en premiere lecture pas l'Assemblée nationale), *Recueil Dalloz* (1999), p. 71-74.

CAENEGEM, R., *European Law in the Past and the Future: Unity and Diversity of Two Millennia*, Cambridge University Press, Cambridge, 2002.

CALVIN, J., *A harmony of the Gospels, Mathew, Mark and Luke*, St. Andrew Press, Edinburgh, 1972, Vol. I and II.

CALVIN, J., *Calvin's Commentary to Lev.* in: *Calvin's Commentaries*, Oliver and Boyd, Edinburgh, 1843-1859.

CAMERON, R., *Frederick William Maitland and the History of English Law*, Greenwood Press, Publishers, Westport, Connecticut, 1977.

CAPPELLETTI, M., SECCOMBE, M., WEILER, J., 'General Introduction', in: CAPPELLETTI, M., KOHNSTAMM, M., *New Perspectives for a Common Law of Europe*, Sijthoff, Leiden, 1978, p. 3-71.

CARBONNIER, J., 'Terre et ciel dans le droit français du mariage', in: RIPERTS, G., VABRES, H., at al, *Le droit privé français au milieu du XXe siècle: études offertes à Georges Ripert*; Vol.1: E ´tudes générales. Droit de la famille, Pichon et Durand-Auzias, Paris, 1950.

CARBONNIER, J., *Flexible droit: textes pour une sociologie du droit sans rigueur*, 3ᵉ ed, Pichon et Durand-Auzias, Paris, 1971.

CARBONNIER, D., 'La question du divorce: mémoire à consulter', D. 1975. Chron., p. 115-122.

CARBONNIER, J., *Droit civil*; T. 2, *La famille, l'enfant, le couple*, 21ᵉ éd, Press Universitaires de France, Paris, 2002.

CARBONNIER, J., 'Le Code Civil' reprinted in : *Le Code Civil 1804-2004. Livre du Bicentenaire*, Dallos, Paris, 2004, p. 17-37. Originally published in 1986.

CAROZZA, G., 'Propter Honoris Respectum: Uses and Misuses of Comparative Law in International Human Rights: Some Reflections of the Jurisprudence of the European Court of Human Rights', (1998) 5 *Notre Dame Law Review* p. 1217-1237.

CARUSO, D., 'The Missing View of the Cathedral: The Private Law Paradigm of European Legal Integration', 3 *European Law Journal* (1997), p. 3-32.

CASEY, J., *The History of the Family*, Basil Blackwell, Oxford, 1989.

CASSIDY, J., 'An Undergraduate Course in Comparative legal Studies', in: *Monismus oder Pluralismus der Rechtskulturen?* Proceedings of the 13ᵗʰ World Congress, *Rechtstheorie,* (1997), p. 201-207.

CASTILLO, M., 'The Dilemmas of Postmodern Individualism', in: LIEDMAN, S-E. (ed.), *The Postmodernist Critique of the Project of Enlightenment,* Rodopi, Amsterdam, 1997, p. 135-148.

CESCHINI, R., 'Italy', in: HAMILTON, C., PERRY, A., *Family Law in Europe,* Butterworths, London, 2002, p. 401-437.

CHAMBOREDON, A., 'Form v Substance? An Ideological Venture Beyond the Dichotomy in European Law of Contracts', *1 ERPL* (2000), p. 237-247.

CHAMBOREDON, A., 'The Debate on a European Civil Code: For an "Open Texture"', in: VAN HOECKE, M., OST, F. (eds.), *The Harmonisation of European Private Law,* Hart, Oxford, 2000, p. 63-99.

CHAUVEAU, V., CORNEC, A., 'France', in: HAMILTON, C., PERRY, A., *Family Law in Europe,* Butterworths, London, 2002, p. 251-291.

CHECA MARTINEZ, M., National Report 'Spain', in: Consortium Asser-UCL, *Study on Matrimonial Property Regimes and the Property of Unmarried Couples in Private International Law and Internal Law,* European Commission, 2003, http://ec.europa.eu/justice_home/doc_centre/civil/studies/doc/regimes/spanish_report_en.pdf .

CHLOROS, A., *Yugoslav Civil Law: History, Family, Property,* Clarendon Press, Oxford, 1970.

CHLOROS, A., *The Reform of Family Law in Europe,* Kluwer, Deventer, 1978.

CHIN-A-FAT, B., *Scheden: (ter)echter zonder rechter? Een onderzoek naar de meerwaarde van scheidingsbemiddeling,* Sdu Uitgevers, The Hague, 2004.

CLANCHY, M., 'Law and Love in the Middle Ages', in: BOSSY, J. (ed.), *Disputes and Settlements: Law and Human Relations in the West,* Cambridge University Press, Cambridge, 1983.

CLARK, D., 'The Idea of the Civil Law Tradition', in: CLARK, D. (ed.), *Comparative and Private International Law. Essays in Honour of J. H. Merryman on his Seventieth Birthday,* Duncker and Humblot, Berlin, 1990, p. 23-12.

CLARKSON, C., HILL, J., THOMPSON, M., National Report 'United Kingdom. England', in: Consortium Asser-UCL, *Study on Matrimonial Property Regimes and the Property of Unmarried Couples in Private International Law and Internal Law,* European Commission, 2003, http://ec.europa.eu/justice_home/doc_centre/civil/studies/doc/regimes/english_report_en.pdf.

CLIVE, E., 'Marriage: An Unnecessary Legal Concept', in: EEKELAAR, J., KATZ, S. (eds.) *Marriage and Cohabitation in Contemporary Society,* Butterworths, Toronto, 1980, p. 71-72.

COENE, E., 'Wetsontwerp Aangaande de Wettelijke Samenwoning', *4 Echtscheidingsjournaal* (1998), p. 67-68.

COESTER, M., 'Same Sex Relationships: A Comparative Assessment of Legal Developments Across Europe,' *4 FamPra* (2002), p. 748-764.

COESTER-WALTER, D., COERSTER, M., National Report 'Germany', in: Consortium Asser-UCL, *Study on Matrimonial Property Regimes and the Property of Unmarried Couples in Private International Law and Internal Law,* European Commission, 2003,

http://ec.europa.eu/justice_home/doc_centre/civil/studies/doc/regimes/german_report
_en.pdf .

COHEN, E., *The Crossroads of Justice. Law and Culture in Late Medieval France*, Brill, Leiden, 1993.

COING, H., 'Die europäische Privatrechtsgeschichte der neueren Zeit als einheitliches Forschungsgebiet', *1 Ius Commune* (1967), p. 1-33.

COING, H., *Die ursprüngliche einheit der Europäischen rechtswissenschaft*, Franz Steiner Verlag GMBH, Wiesbaden, 1968.

COING, H., 'European Common Law: Historical Foundations,' in: CAPPELLETTI, M., KOHNSTAMM, M., *New Perspectives for a Common Law of Europe*, Sjithoff, Leyden, 1978, p. 31-44.

COING, H., *Europäisches Privatrecht*, Vol. 1, Beck, Munich, 1985.

COLIN, A., CAPITANT, H., *Traité de droit civil* Vol. 1 *Introduction générale. Institutions civiles et judiciaires, personnes et famille*, Dalloz, Paris, 1957.

COLLINS, H., 'European Private Law and the Cultural Identity of States', *European Review of Private Law* (1995), p. 353-365.

COLOMER, A., 'The Modern French Law', in: KIRALFY, A. (ed.), *Comparative Law of Matrimonial Property*, Sijthoff, Leiden, 1972, p. 80-114.

COMANDE, G., National report 'Italy', in: Consortium Asser-UCL, *Study on Matrimonial Property Regimes and the Property of Unmarried Couples in Private International Law and Internal Law*, European Commission, 2003, http://ec.europa.eu/justice_home/ doc_centre/civil/studies/doc/regimes/italy_report_en.pdf.

COMMAILLE, J., 'Towards a New Definition of Divorce', in: TROST, J. (ed.), *Family in Change*, International Library, Västerås, 1980, p. 105-112.

COMMAILLE, J. et al, *Le divorce en Europe Occidentale: le loi en le nombre*, Groupe International de Rechercher sur le Divorce, 1983.

COMMAILLE, J., 'Lez métamorphoses de la gestion politique de l'univers privé des individus', in: RUBELLIN-DEVICHI, J., Des concubinages: droit interne, droit international, droit compare, Litec, Paris, 2002, p. 19-29.

COMTE, O., Letter to John Stuart Mill from 5 October 1843 published in: *The correspondence of John Stuart Mill and Auguste Comte*, Transaction Publishers, New Brunswick, 1995, p. 186-193.

CORBETT, P., *The Roman Law of Marriage*, 2nd edn., The Clarendon Press, Oxford, 1969 (first edn. 1930).

CORBIER, M., 'Divorce and Adoption as Roman Familial Strategies' in: RAWSON, B. (ed.), *Marriage, Divorce, and Children in Ancient Rome*, The Clarendon Press, Oxford, 1991, p. 47-98.

CORNU, G., *Droit Civil, La famille*, 8e éd, Montchrestien, Paris, 2003.

COTTERRELL, R., 'The Concept of Legal Culture', in: NELKEN, D. (ed.), *Comparing Legal Cultures*, Dartmouth, Aldershot, 1997, p. 13-31.

COTTERRELL, R., 'Is there a logic of legal transplants?' in: NELKEN, D., FEEST, J. (eds.), *Adapting legal cultures*, Hart, Oxford (2001), p. 70-92.

CRETNEY, S., 'Divorce Reform in England: Humbug and Hypocrisy or a Smooth Transition?', in: FREEMAN, M. (ed.), Dartmouth, Aldershot, 1996, p. 39-61.

CRETNEY, S., MASSON, J., BAILEY-HARRIS, R., *Principles of Family Law*,(7th edn.), Sweet and Maxwell, London, 2003.

CRETNEY, S., 'Breaking the Shackles of Culture and Religion in the Field of Divorce', in: BOELE-WOELKI, K. (ed.), *Common Core and Better Law in European Family Law,* Intersentia, Antwerp-Oxford, 2005, p. 3-15.

CRETNEY, S., *Family Law in the Twentieth Century. A History*, Oxford Univ. Press, Oxford, 2003.

CROOK, J., *Law and Life in Rome*, Cornell University Press, Ithaca New York, 1984.

CSILLAG, P., *The Augustan Laws on Family Relations,* Akadémiai Kiadó, Budapest, 1976.

COULON, J-M., TEILLER, M-N., SERRAND FRANCE, E., *Réflexions et propositions sur la procédure civile: rapport au ministre de la justice*, La Documentation française, Paris, 1997.

CURRY-SUMNER, I., *All's well that ends registered? The Substantive and Private International Law Aspects of Non-Marital Registered Relationships in Europe*, Intersentia, Antwerp-Oxford, 2005.

CYPIN, V., *Cerkovnoe pravo, (Ecclesiastical Law)* MFTI, Moscow, 1996.

CYPIN, V., 'O kanonakh s tolkovaniami episkopa Nicodima (Milosha)', in: *Pravila Provoslavnoi Cerkvi s kommentariami Nokodima episkopa Dalmatinsko-Istriiskogo (Rules of the Orthodox Church with the Comments of Nicodim Bishop of Dalmatian-Istria)* Vol. I and II, (first edited in 1912), Sviato-Troitskaia Segieva Lavra, Sergiev Pasad, 1996, p. V-XIII.

DADOMO, C., 'The Current Reform of French Law of Divorce', *International Family Law* (2004), p. 218-225.

DAUDET, P., *Études sur l'histoire de la juridiction matrimoniale: les origines carolingiennes de la compétence exclusive de l'Église (France et Germanie),* Sirey, Paris, 1933.

DAVID, R., 'The International Unification of Private Law', in: *International Encyclopaedia of Comparative Law*, Vol. 2, 65, Chapter 5, J.C.B. Mohr, Tubingen, Paris, 1971.

DAWSON, C., The Making of Europe: an Introduction to the History of European Unity, Meridian Books, Cleveland, 1956.

DE BLÉCOURT, A, (edited by Fischer, H.,) *Kort begrip van het oud-vaderlands burgerlijk recht,* Wolters, Groningen, 1950.

DE BOER, J., 'A whole code of family law: book 1 BW getoetst aan het EVRM', in: BLANKMAN, K., ROBERTS, W. (eds.), *Het EVRM en het Nederlandse en Belgische personen- en familie-en jeugdrecht,* W.E.J. Tjeenk Willink, Zwolle, 1987, p. 3-32.

DE BOER, J., *C. Assers' Handeling tot beoefening van het Nederlands burgerlijk recht. Personen-en familierecht*, Kluwer, Deventer, 2002.

Declaration on Religious Liberty (Vatican II *Dignitatis Humanae*, 7 December 1966), Eerdmans Publishing, Grand Rapids, 1984.

DE CRUS, P., 'Legal Transplants: Principles and Pragmatism in Comparative Family Law', in: HARDING, A., ÖRÜCÜ, E., *Comparative Law in the 21st Century*, Institute of Advanced Studies, 2002, p. 101-119.

DEECH, R., 'The Case Against Legal Recognition of Cohabitation', in: EEKELAAR, J., KATZ, S. (eds.), *Marriage and Cohabitation in Contemporary Society,* Butterworths, Toronto, 1980, p. 300-312.

DE FUNIAK, W., VAUGHN, M., 'Why Community Property is so Misunderstood – Knowing its Origins is the Key', *Community Property Journal* (1974), p. 97-116.

DE GROOT, G.-R., 'Op weg naar een Europees personen- en familierecht?', *1 Ars Aequi* (1995), p. 29-32.

DEKEUWER-DÉFOSSEZ, F., 'Impressions de recherches sur les fautes causes de divorces,' Recueil Le Dalloz, Chroniques (1985), p. 219-226.

DEKEUWER-DÉFOSSEZ, F., *Rénover, le droit de la famille: Propositions pour un droit adapté aux réalités et aux aspiration de notre temps: Rapport au Garde des Sceaux, Ministre de la justice,* La Documentation française, Paris, 1999.

DEKEUWER-DÉFOSSEZ, F., 'Codifier de droit de la famille?', in: *Le Code civil 1804-2004. Libre du Bicentenaire,* Dallos, Paris, 2004, p. 218-230.

DE OLIVEIRA, G., 'A European Family Law? Play it again, and again ... Europe!', *12 Tijdschrift voor familie- en jeugdrecht* (2000), p. 272–277.

DE OLIVEIRA, G., *CEFL* National Report for Portugal: *Parental Responsibilities,* in: BOELE-WOELKI, K., BRAAT, B., SUMNER I. (eds.), *European Family Law in Action,* Vol. II: *Parental Responsibilities,* European Family Law Series No. 2, Intersentia, Antwerp, 2005.

DE OLIVEIRA, G., 'Portuguese Report concerning the CEFL Questionnaire on Grounds for Divorce and Maintenance Between Former Spouses', http://www.law.uu.nl/priv/cefl > Working Field 1 > Portugal.

DE OLIVEIRA, G., *CEFL* National Report for Portugal: Grounds for Divorce, in: BOELE-WOELKI, K., BRAAT, B., SUMNER I. (eds.), *European Family Law in Action,* Vol. I: Grounds for Divorce, European Family Law Series No. 2, Intersentia, Antwerp, 2003.

DERRIDA, J., *The Other Heading. Reflections on Today's Europe,* Indiana University Press, Bloomington, 1992.

DE SAINT EXUPÉRY, A., *Le petit prince,* Gallimard, Paris, 1946.

DE SAUSA MACHADO, A., 'Portugal', in: HAMILTON, C., PERRY, A., *Family Law in Europe,* Butterworths, London, 2002, p. 522-543.

DE SAUSA SANTOS, B., 'Law: A Map of Misreading. Towards a Postmodern Conception of Law', *14 Journal of Law and Society* (1987), p. 279-299.

DETHLOFF, N., 'The Registered Partnership Act of 2001', in: BAINHAM, A. (ed.), *The International Survey of Family Law,* Jordan Publishing, Bristol, 2002, p. 171-181.

DETHLOFF, N., 'Arguments for the Unification and Harmonisation of Family Law in Europe', in: BOELE-WOELKI, K. (ed.), *Perspectives for the Unification and Harmonisation of Family Law in Europe,* European Family Law Series No. 4, Intersentia, Antwerp, 2003, p. 37-65.

DETHLOFF, N., KROLL, K., 'The Constitutional Court as Driver of Reforms in German Family Law', in: BAINHAM, A. (ed.), *The International Survey of Family Law,* Jordan Publishing, Bristol, 2006, p. 217-233.

DEWAR, J., 'The Normal Chaos of Family Law', *4 Modern Law Review,* (1998), p. 467-485.

DE WITTE, B., The Convergence Debate', *3 Maastricht Journal of European and Family Law* (1996), p. 105-107.

DICEY, A., *Lectures on the Relations Between Law and Public Opinion in England During the Nineteenth Century,* 2nd edn., Macmillan, London, 1963.

DILLON, M., *Debating Divorce. Moral Conflict in Ireland.* The Univ. Press of Kentucky, Lexington, 1993.

DIXON, S., *The Roman Family,* The Johns Hopkins University Press, Baltimore and London, 1992.

DIXON, S., 'The Sentimental Ideal of the Roman Family' in: RAWSON, B. (ed.), *Marriage, Divorce, and Children in Ancient Rome*, The Clarendon Press, Oxford, 1991, p. 99-113.

D'OLIVERCRONA, K., 'Précis historique de l'origine et du développement de la communauté de biens entre époux', *11 Revue historique de droit française et étranger* (1865).

DÖLLE, H., *Familienrecht*, V. 2, Müller, Karlsruhe, 1964.

DONAHUE, C., 'Roman Canon Law in the Medieval English Church: Stubbs Vs. Maitland Re-examined After 75 Years in the Light of Some Records From The Church Courts', *72 Michigan Law Reviews* (1974), p. 647-708

DONAHUE, C., 'The Policy of Alexander III's Consent Theory of Marriage', in: KUTTNER, S. (ed.), *Proceedings of the Fourth International Congress of Medieval Canon Law*, Biblioteca Apostolica Vaticana, Vatican City, 1975, p. 251-281.

DONAHUE, C., 'The Canon Law on the Formation of Marriage and Social Practice in the Later Middle Ages', *Journal of Family History* (1983), p. 144-158.

DONAHUE, C., 'English and French Marriage Cases in the Later Middle Ages: Might the Difference be Explained by Differences in the Property Systems?' in: BONFIELD, L. (ed.), *Marriage, Property, and Succession*, Dunker and Humbolt, Berlin, 1992, p. 339-367.

DRAŠKIC, M., KOVACEK STANIC, G., 'The New Family Act of Serbia', in: BAINHAM, A. (ed.), *The International Survey of Family Law*, Jordan Publishing, Bristol, 2006, p. 357-374.

DREW, K., *Law and Society in Early Medieval Europe*, Variorum Reprints, London, 1988.

DROBNIG, U., *Private Law in the European Union*, Kluwer, The Hague, 1996.

DROBNIG, U., 'Scope and General Rules of a European Civil Code', *5 European Review of Private Law* (1997), p. 489-495.

DUBY, G., *Medieval Marriage Two Models from Twelfth-Century France*, The John Hopkins University Press, Baltimore, 1978.

DUBY, G., *Ridder, vrouw en priester* (transl.), 2nd edn., H.J.W. Becht, Amsterdam, 1985.

DUFFY, S., 'Catholicism's Search for a New Self-Understanding', in: FAGIN, D. (ed.), *Vatican II. Open Questions and New Horizons*, Michael Glazier, Wilmington, 1984, p. 9-38.

DUMON, W., KOOY, G., *Echtscheiding in België en Nederland*, Van Loghum Slaterus, Deventer, 1983.

DURSTON, C., *The Family in English Revolution*, Basil Blackwell, Oxford, 1989.

DUTNEIL DE LA ROCHÉRE, J., 'The EU and the Individual: Fundamental Rights in the Draft Constitutional Treaty', *41 Common Market Law Review* (2004), p. 345-354.

ELSHTAIN, J., *Public Man, Private Woman: Women in Social and Political Thought*, Martin Robertson, Oxford, 1981.

ELWOOD, R., *Inessa Armand: Revolutionary and Feminist*, Cambridge University Press, Cambridge, 1992.

ENGELS, F., Letter to K. Schmidt in Marx, K., Engels, R., *Complete Works*, Book, 37, Politizdat, Moscow.

ENGELS, F., *The Origin of the Family, Private Property and the State*, Penguin Books, Harmondsworth, Middlesex, 1985.

ESMEIN, A., *Le mariage en Droit Canonique*, 2nd edn., Recueil Sirey, Paris, 1929-1935.

Europe in Figures, Eurostat Yearbook 2005, European Commission, Brussels, 2005.

EVERITT, N., 'Some Remarks on the Recent Developments of Divorce Law in the Republic of Ireland and England', *I Familia* (2001). p. 199-220.

EWALD, W., *Social Structure and Law. Theoretical and Empirical Perspectives*, Sage Publications, Newbury Park, 1990.

EWALD, W., 'Comparative Jurisprudence (II): The Logic of Legal Transplants', *43 The American Journal of Comparative Law* (1995), p. 489-510.

EWALD, W., 'The Jurisprudential Approach to Comparative Law: A Field Guide to 'Rats', *46 The American Journal of Comparative Law* (1998), p. 701-707.

FASSIN, E., 'Sociological Questions. An Epilogue to "More or Less Together"', in: WAALDIJK, K. (ed.), *More of Less Together: Level of legal Consequences of Marriage, Cohabitation and Registered Partnership for Different-Sex and Same-Sex Partners*, Institut National d'Etudes Démographiques, Paris, 2005, p. 187-182.

FAURHOLT, J., FEDERSPOEL, P., *Recent Danish Legislation on the Relations of Husband and Wife*, Nielsen and Lydische, Copenhagen, 1927.

FEENSTRA, R., 'Family, Property and Succession in the Province of Holland during the Sixteenth, Seventeenth and Eighteenth Century', in: BONFIELD, L. (ed.), *Marriage, Property, and Succession*, Dunker and Humbolt, Berlin, 1992, p. 37-53.

FELDBLUM, C., 'The Limitations of Liberal Neutrality Arguments in Favour of Same-Sex Marriage', WINTEMUTE, R., ANDENÆS, M., M., *Legal Recognition of Same-Sex Partnership. A Study of National, European and International Law*, Hart Publishing, Oxford, 2001, p. 55-74.

FELL, C, CLARK, C., WILLIAMS, E., *Women in Anglo-Saxon England and the impact of 1066*, British Museum, London, 1984.

FERRAND, F., *CEFL* National Report for France: Grounds for Divorce, in: BOELE-WOELKI, K., B. BRAAT, B., SUMNER I. (eds.), *European Family Law in Action*, Vol. I: Grounds for Divorce, European Family Law Series No. 2, Intersentia, Antwerp, 2003.

FERRÉ-ANDRÉ, S., GOUTTENOIRE-CORBUT, A., FULCHIRON, H., 'Work in Hand for the Reform of French Family Law', in: BAINHAM, A. (ed.), *The International Survey of Family Law*, Jordan Publishing, Bristol, 2003, p. 163 -186.

FESTY, P., 'On the New Context of Marriage in Western Europe. Data and Perspectives', *6 Population and Development Review* (1980), p. 311-315.

FETTE, S., 'Learning From Our Mistakes: The Aftermath of the American Divorce Revolution as a lesson to the Republic of Ireland', *7 Indiana International and Comparative Law Review* (1997) lexis.

FLETCHER, J., 'The New Look in Christian Ethics', *Harvard Divinity Bulletin* (1959), p. 7- 18.

FOCKEMA ANDREAE, S., *Bijdragen tot de Nederlandsche Rechtsgeschiedenis*, Part 1, De Erven F. Bohn, Haarlem, 1888.

FORDER, C., 'Constitutional Principle and the Establishment of the Legal Relationship Between the Child and the Non-marital Father: A Study of Germany, the Netherlands and England', *7 International Journal of Law and the Family* (1993), p. 40-107.

FORDER, C., 'An Identity Crisis – The Outer Limits of Euthanasia, The abolition of Chivalry and The Adventurous Provisions', in: BAINHAM, A. (ed.) *The International Survey of Family Law*, Martinus Nijhoff, The Hague, 1994, p. 357-361.

FORDER, C., *Legal Establishment of the Parent Child Relationship: Constitutional Principles*, Maastricht Univ. Press, Maastricht, 1995.

FORDER, C., 'Un Undutchuble Family Law: Partnership, Parenthood, Social Parenthood, Names and Some Article 8 ECHR Case Law', in: BAINHAM, A. (ed.), *The International Survey of Family Law,* Martinus Nijhoff Publishers, The Hague, 1997, p. 259-309.

FORDER, C., 'Civil Law Aspects of Emerging Forms of Registered Partnerships', paper to Fifth European Conference on Family Law *Civil Law Aspects of Emerging Forms of Registered Partnerships. Legally Regulate Forms of Non-Marital Cohabitation and Registered Partnerships,* The Hague, 1999.

FORDER, C., 'National Report on Sweden', paper to Fifth European Conference on Family Law *Civil Law Aspects of Emerging Forms of Registered Partnerships. Legally Regulate Forms of Non-Marital Cohabitation and Registered Partnerships,* The Hague, 1999.

FORDER, C., 'National Report on Finland', paper to Fifth European Conference on Family Law *Civil Law Aspects of Emerging Forms of Registered Partnerships. Legally Regulate Forms of Non-Marital Cohabitation and Registered Partnerships,* The Hague, 1999.

FORDER, C., 'National Report on Norway', paper to Fifth European Conference on Family Law *Civil Law Aspects of Emerging Forms of Registered Partnerships. Legally Regulate Forms of Non-Marital Cohabitation and Registered Partnerships,* The Hague, 1999.

FORDER, C., 'National Report on Denmark', paper to Fifth European Conference on Family Law *Civil Law Aspects of Emerging Forms of Registered Partnerships. Legally Regulate Forms of Non-Marital Cohabitation and Registered Partnerships,* The Hague, 1999.

FORDER, C., 'National Report on Iceland', paper to Fifth European Conference on Family Law *Civil Law Aspects of Emerging Forms of Registered Partnerships. Legally Regulate Forms of Non-Marital Cohabitation and Registered Partnerships,* The Hague, 1999.

FORDER, C., 'National Report on the Netherlands', paper to Fifth European Conference on Family Law *Civil Law Aspects of Emerging Forms of Registered Partnerships. Legally Regulate Forms of Non-Marital Cohabitation and Registered Partnerships,* The Hague, 1999.

FORDER, C., 'National Report on France', paper to Fifth European Conference on Family Law *Civil Law Aspects of Emerging Forms of Registered Partnerships. Legally Regulate Forms of Non-Marital Cohabitation and Registered Partnerships,* The Hague, 1999.

FORDER, C., 'European Models of Domestic Partnership Laws: The Field of Choice', *17 Canadian Journal of Family Law* (2000), p. 371-454.

FORDER, C., *Het informele huwelijk: de verbondenheid tussen mens, goed en schuld,* Kluwer, Deventer, 2000.

FORDER, C., 'Opening Up Marriage to Same Sex Partners and Providing Adoption by Same Sex Couples, Managing Information on Sperm Donor, and Lots of Private International Law', in: BAINHAM, A. (ed.), *The International Survey of Family Law,* Jordan Publishing, Bristol, 2000, p. 239-277.

FORDER, C., 'Marry or Not to Marry: than is the Question', in: BAINHAM, A. (ed.), *The International Survey of Family Law,* Jordan Publishing, Bristol, 2004, p. 301-320.

FORDER, C., VERBEKE, A., 'Geen worden maar daden. Algemene rechtsvergelijkende conclusies en aanbevelingen,' in: FORDER, C., VERBEKE, A. (eds.), *Gehuwd of niet: maakt het iets uit?,* Intersentia, Antwerp, 2005, p. 489-640.

FOUCAULT, M., *The Archaeology of Knowledge,* transl. by Sheridan Smith, A., Tavistock Publishers, London, 1972.

FOUCAULT, M., *Ervaring en waarheid. Duccio Trombadori in gesprek met Michel Foucault*, Te Elfder Ure, Nijmegen, 1985.

FOYER, J., 'The Reform of Family Law in France', in: CHLOROS, A. (ed.), *The Reform of Family Law in Europe*, Kluwer, Deventer, 1978, p. 75-111.

FRADA DE SOUSA, A., National Report 'Portugal', in: *Study on Matrimonial Property Regimes and the Property of Unmarried Couples in Private International Law and Internal Law*, European Commission, 2001, http://ec.europa.eu/justice_home/doc_centre/civil/studies/doc/regimes/portugal_report_fr.pdf.

FRANK, R., 'Marriage in the Middle Ages: Marriage in Twelfth- and Thirteenth-Century Scandinavia,' *4 Viator* (1973), p. 474.

FREEMAN, M., LYON, C., *Cohabitation without marriage: an essay in law and social policy*, Gower, Aldershot, 1983.

FREEMAN, M., 'Some Reflections on Gay Marriages at the Beginning of the Twenty-First Century', in: RUBELLIN-DEVICHI, J., Des concubinages: droit interne, droit international, droit compare, Litec, Paris, 2002, p. 357-373.

FREEMAN, M. (ed.), 'Exploring the Boundaries of Family Law in England in 2000', in: BAINHAM, A. (ed.), *The International Survey of Family Law*, Jordan Publishing, Bristol, 2002, p. 133-152.

FRIDRIKSDÓTTIR, H., WAALDIJK, K., 'Iceland', in: WAALDIJK, K. (ed.) More of Less Together: Level of legal Consequences of Marriage, Cohabitation and Registered Partnership for Different-sex and Same-sex Partners, Institut National d'Etudes Démographiques, Paris, 2005, p. 121-136.

FRIEDMAN, L., *The Legal System: A Social Science Perspective*, Russell Sage Foundation, New York, 1975.

FRIEDMAN, L., *Total Justice*, Russel Sage Foundation, New York, 1985.

FRIEDMAN, L., *The Republic of Choice: Law, Authority and Culture*, Harvard Univ. Press, Cambridge Massachusetts, 1990.

FRIEDMAN, L., 'Some Thoughts on Comparative Legal Culture', in: CLARK, D. (ed.), *Comparative and Private International Law. Essays in Honour of J. H. Merryman on his Seventieth Birthday*, Duncker and Humblot, Berlin, 1990, p. 49-57.

FRIEDMANN, W., *Law in Changing Society*, Stevens, S.I., 1959.

FROWEIN, J., SCHULHOFER, S., SHAPIRO, M., 'The Protection of Fundamental Human Rights as a Vehicle of Integration', in: CAPPELLETTI, M. (ed.), *New Perspectives for a Common Law of Europe*, Sijthoff, Leyden, 1978, p. 231-248.

FUKUYAMA, F., *The End of History and the Last Man*, Free Press, New York, 1992

FULCHIRON, H., FERRÉ-ANDRÉ, S., GOUTTENOIRE, A., 'A Pause in the Reform of French Family Law', in: BAINHAM, A. (ed.), *The International Survey of Family Law*, Jordan Publishing, Bristol, 2004, p. 183-188.

FULCHIRON, H., 'Pacs et partenariats enregistrés en DIP français', in: *Aspects de droit international privé des partenariats enregistrés en Europe*: actes de la XVIe Journée de Droit international privé du 5 mars 2004 à Lausanne, organisée conjointement par l'Institut suisse de Droit comparé et le Centre de Droit comparé, de Droit européen et de Législations étrangères, Université de Lausanne, Schulthess, Geneva, 2004, p. 85-104.

FULCHIRON, H., 'The New French Divorce Law', in: BAINHAM, A. (ed.), *The International Survey of Family Law,* Jordan Publishing, Bristol, 2005, p. 241-251

FULCHIRON, H., 'Mariage et partenariats homosexuels en droit international privé français', *2 Revue internationale de droit compare* (2006), p. 409-438.

FULCHIRON, H., 'Egalité, Vérité, Stabilité: The New French Filiation Law After the Ordonnance of 4 July 2005', in: BAINHAM, A. (ed.), *The International Survey of Family Law,* Jordan Publishing, Bristol, 2006, p. 203-210.

FUSZARA, M., LACIAK, B., '"Pro-Family Policy" in Poland in the Nineties', in: MACLEAN, M. (ed.), *Making Law for Families,* Hart Publishing, Oxford, 2000, p. 117-136.

GAIRO, T., 'Römisches Recht, Romanistik und Rechtsraum in Europa', *22 Ius Commune* (1995), p. 1-16.

GANANCIA, D., 'Pour un divorce du XXI siécle,' *108-109 Gazette du Palais,* 18-19 April 1997, p. 16 and 33-39.

GARCÍA CANTERO, G., 'The Catalan Family Code of 1998 and Other Autonomous Region Law on *de Facto* Unions', in: BAINHAM, A. (ed.), *The International Survey of Family Law,* Jordan Publishing, Bristol, 2001, p. 397-404.

GARCÍA CANTERO, G., 'De Facto Unions Revisited', in: BAINHAM, A. (ed.), *The International Survey of Family Law,* Jordan Publishing, Bristol, 2003, p. 413-410.

GARCÍA CANTERO, G., 'Family Law Reform in Differing Directions', in: BAINHAM, A. (ed.), *The International Survey of Family Law,* Jordan Publishing, Bristol, 2006, p. 431-438.

GARDNER, J., *Women in Roman Law and Society,* Croom Helm, London and Sydney, 1986.

GARDNER, J., *Family and Familia in Roman Law and Life,* The Clarendon Press, Oxford, 1998.

GAUNT, D., NYSTRÖM, L., 'The Scandinavian Model', in: BURGUIERE, A., KLAPISCH-ZUBER, C., SEGALEN, M., ZONABEND O. (eds.), *A History of the Family.* Vol. II. *The impact of Modernity,* Polity Press, Cambridge, 1996, p. 476-501.

GEC-KOROŠEC, M., RIJAVEC, V., 'Slovenia: Post-Independence Changes in Family Law Regulation', *33 Journal of Family Law* (1994-95), p. 485-493.

GEC-KOROŠEC, M., KRALJIC, S., 'The Influence of Validly Established Cohabitation on Legal Regulations Between Cohabitants on Slovene Law', in: BAINHAM, A. (ed.), *The International Survey of Family Law,* Jordan Publishing, Bristol, 2001, p. 383-395.

GÉLARD, P. *Rapport n° 120 au nom de la commission des Lois constitutionnelles, de législation, du suffrage universel, du Règlement et d'administration générale (1) sur le projet de loi relatif au divorce,* 2003-2004.

GELLNER, E., *Postmodernism, Reason and Religion,* Routledge, London, 1992.

GENKIN, D., NOVITZKII, I, RABINOVICH, N, *Istoriia sovetskogo semeinogo prava 1917-1947,* Juridicheskaia Literatura, Moscow, 1949.

GIES, F., GIES, J., *Marriage and the Family in the Middle Ages,* Harper & Row, New York, 1989.

GIESEN, D., 'Divorce Reform in Germany', *4 Family Law Quarterly,* 1973, p. 351-379.

GIESEN, D., 'The reform of Family Law in Germany', in: CHLOROS, A. (ed.), *The Reform of Family Law in Europe,* Kluwer, Deventer, 1978.

GILCHRIST, J., *Canon Law in The Age of Reform, 11th-12th Centuries,* Aldershot, Variorum, 1993.

GLENDON, M.A., 'Power and Authority in the Family: New Legal Patterns as Reflection of Changing Ideologies', *23 The American Journal of Comparative Law* (1975), p. 1-33.

GLENDON, M.A., 'The French Divorce Reform Law of 1976', *24 The American Journal of Comparative Law* (1976), p. 199-228.

GLENDON, M.A., 'Marriage and the State: the Withering Away of Marriage', *4 Virginia Law Review* (1976), p. 663-720.

GLENDON, M.A., *The New Family and the New Property,* Butterworth, Toronto, 1981.

GLENDON, M.A., *Abortion and Divorce in Western Law,* Harvard Univ. Press., Cambridge Mass., 1987.

GLENDON, M.A., *The Transformation of Family Law,* The University of Chicago Press, Chicago and London, 1989.

GLENDON, M.A., *Rights Talks: The Impoverishment of Political Discourse,* New York Press, New York, 1991.

GLENN, P. 'Reception and Reconciliation of Laws', in: *Monismus oder Pluralismus der Rechtskulturen?* Proceedings of the 13th World Congress, *Rechtstheorie* (1997), p. 209-214.

GLICK, T., 'Sexual Reforms, Psychoanalysis, and the Politics of Divorce in Spain in the 1920 and 1930s', *1 Journal of the History of Sexuality* (2003), p. 68-97.

GOFFART, W., *Barbarians and Romans A.D. 418-584 The Technique of Accommodation,* Princeton University Press, Princeton, 1980.

GONZÁLEZ BEILFUSS, C., 'Spanien und Portual', in: SCHERPE, J., YASSARI, N. (eds.), *Die Rechtsstellung nichtehelicher Lebensgemeinschaften,* Mohr Siebeck, Tübingen, 2005, p. 249-277.

GONZÁLEZ BEILFUSS, C., 'Private international law aspects of homosexual couples', Spanish National Report for the *XVIIth Congress of the International Academy of Comparative Law* (2006), http://www2.law.uu.nl/priv/AIDC/index1.asp .

GOODY, J., *The Development of the Family and Marriage in Europe,* Cambridge University Press, Cambridge, 1983.

GOODY, J., 'Introduction' in: *The impact of Modernity,* Vol. II of BURGUIERE, A. KLAPISCH-ZUBER, C., SEGALEN, M., ZONABEND, O. (ed.), *A History of the Family,* Polity Press, Cambridge, 1996.

GOODY, J., *The European Family. An Historical-Anthropological Essay.* Blackwell, Oxford, 2000.

GORDLEY, J., 'Comparative Legal Research: Its Function in the Development of Harmonised Law', *43 The American Journal of Comparative Law* (1995), p. 555-567.

GORECKI, J., 'Moral Premises of Contemporary Divorce Laws: Western and Eastern Europe and the United States,' in: EEKELAAR, J., KATZ, S. (eds.) *Marriage and Cohabitation in Contemporary Society,* Butterworths, Toronto, 1980, p. 124-130.

GOTTBERG, E., National Report 'Finland', in: Consortium Asser-UCL, *Study on Matrimonial Property Regimes and the Property of Unmarried Couples in Private International Law and Internal Law,* European Commission, 2003, http://ec.europa.eu/justice_home/doc_centre/civil/studies/doc/regimes/finish_report_en.pdf.

GOTTWALD, P., SCHWAB, D., BÜTTNER, E., *Family and Succession Law in Germany,* Beck, München, 2001.

GRAHAM-SIEGENTHALER, B., 'Switzerland', in: HAMILTON, C., PERRY, A., *Family Law in Europe,* Butterworths, London, 2002, p. 661-701.

GRAUE, E., 'German Law', in: KIRALFY, A. (ed.), *Comparative Law of Matrimonial Property,* Sijthoff, Leiden, 1972, p. 114-179.

GRAUE, E., 'Cohabitation Without Marriage as a Problem of Law and Legislative Policy in West Germany and other Codified Systems', in: EEKELAAR, J., KATZ, S. (eds.), *Marriage and Cohabitation in Contemporary Society,* Butterworths, Toronto, 1980, p. 282-292.

GRAVESON, R., 'The Backgrounds of the Century', in: GRAVESON, R., CRANE, F. (eds.) *A Century of Family Law 1857-1957,* Sweet and Maxwell, London, 1957, p. 1-20.

GROUP OF ARCHBISHOP OF CANTERBURY, *Putting Asunder: a Divorce Law for Contemporary Society,* S.P.C.K., London, 1966.

GRUBBS, J., *Law and Family in Late Antiquity The Emperor Constantine's Marriage Legislation,* The Clarendon Press, Oxford, 1995.

GUICHARD, P., CUVILLIER, J-P., 'Barbarian Europe', in: BURGUIERE, A., KLAPISCH-ZUBER, C., SEGALEN, M., ZONABEND O. (eds.), *A History of the Family.* Vol. I. *Distant Worlds, Ancient Worlds,* Polity Press, Oxford, 1996.

GYLLENSTEN, L., 'Swedish Radicalism in the 1960s: An Experiment in Political and Cultural Debate', in: HANCOCK, D, SJOBERG, G. (eds.), *Politics in the Post-Welfare State: Responses to the New Individualism,* Columbia Univ. Press, New York, 1972, p. 279-302.

HAAZEN, O., 'Comparative Law and Economics en het Europees privaatrecht als ongemengd rechtsstelsel', *73 Nederlands juristenblad* (1998), p. 1227-1233.

HADERKA, J., 'A Half-Hearted Family Law Reform of 1998', in: BAINHAM, A. (ed.), *The International Survey of Family Law,* Jordan Publishing, Bristol, 2000, p. 119-130.

HALE, D., 'The Family Law Act 1996 – the death of marriage?', in: Bridge, C., *Family Law Towards the Millennium: Essays for P M Bromley,* Butterworths, London, 1997, p. 1-31.

HALLER, M., 'Austria', in: CHESTER, P., *Divorce in Europe,* Nijhoff, Leiden, 1977.

HAMILTON, C., PERRY, A., *Family Law in Europe,* Butterworths, London, 2002.

HAMILTON, C., 'England and Wales', in: HAMILTON, C., PERRY, A. (eds.), *Family Law in Europe,* Butterworths, London, 2002, p. 95-163.

HANS-BALZ, P., *Ehe und Familie für homosexuelle Paare?: Rechtliche und ethische Aspekte,* ISE Bern, 1994.

HARRINGTON, J., *Reordering Marriage and Society in Reformed Germany,* Cambridge Univ. Press, Cambridge, 1995.

HASSON, E., 'Divorce reform in England, the case of the Family Law Act 1996', in: ANTOKOLSKAIA, M. (ed.), *Herziening van het echtscheidingsrecht. Administratieve echtscheiding, mediation, voortgezet ouderschap,* SWP, Amsterdam, 2006, p. 274-301.

HAUSER, J., Mission de recherche Droit et Justice. Groupe de réflexion: conséquences financières de la séparation des couples. Thème: Pacte d'Intérêt Commun Rapport à Madame Elisabeth Guigou, Ministre de La Justice, Garde des Sceaux, http://www.adventice.com/infogay.

HAUSER, J., 'Pacte civil de solidarité (PACS). Statut civil des partenaires.' *9 JCP- La Semaine Juridique, Edition Notariale et Immobilière* (2000), p. 411-415.

HAUSHEER, H., *CEFL* National Report for Switzerland: *Parental Responsibilities,* in: BOELE-WOELKI, K., BRAAT, B., SUMNER I. (eds.), *European Family Law in Action,* Vol. II: *Parental Responsibilities,* European Family Law Series No. 2, Intersentia, Antwerp, 2005.

HEER, F., *The Medieval World. Europe 1100-1350,* Weidenfield and Nicolson, London, 1962.

HEIJDEN, M., *Huwelijk in Holland,* Bert Bakker, Amsterdam, 1998.

HELMHOLZ, R., *Marriage Litigation in Medieval England,* Cambridge University Press, Cambridge, London, 1978.

HELMHOLZ, R., *Canon Law and the Law of England,* The Hambledon Press, London, 1987.

HELMHOLZ, R., 'Conflicts Between Religious and Secular Law: Common Themes in the English Experience', *12 Cardozo Law Review* (1991), p. 707-728.

HELMHOLZ, R., *The Spirit of Classical Canon Law,* Univ. of Georgia Press, Athens and London, 1996.

HENRICH, D., 'Zur Zukunft des Güterrechts in Europa', *49 Zeitschrift für das gesamte Familienrecht* (2002), p. 1521-1526.

HENRICH, D., SCHWAB, D. (eds.), *Eheliche Gemeinschaft, Partnerschaft und Vermögen im europäischen Vergleich,* Gieseking, Bielefeld, 1999.

HESSELINK, M., *De redelijkheid en billijkheid in het Europese privaatrecht,* Kluwer, Deventer, 1999.

HESSELINK, M., *The New European Legal Culture,* Kluwer, Deventer, 2001.

HICKS, S., 'A Model of Society for the Comparative Study of Law', in: *Monismus oder Pluralismus der Rechtskulturen?* Proceedings of the 13th World Congress, *Rechtstheorie,* (1997), p. 215-222.

HODSON, D., GREEN, M., SOUZA, N., DE, 'Lambert – Shutting Pandora's Box', *1 Family Law* (2003), p. 37-45(9).

HOGGERTT, B., 'Ends and Means: The Utility of Marriage as a Legal Institution', in: EEKELAAR, J., KATZ, S. (eds.), *Marriage and Cohabitation in Contemporary Society,* Butterworths, Toronto, 1980, p. 94-103.

HOGGERTT, B., PEARL, D., *The Family, Law and Society. Cases and Materials,* 3rd edn., Butterworths, London, 1991.

HOHNERLEIN, M., 'Konturen eines einheitlichen europäischen Familien- und Kindschaftsrecht – die Rolle der Europäischen Menschenrechtskonvention', *4 European Legal Forum* (2000-01), p. 252-260.

HOLDSWORTH, W., *A History of English Law,* 2nd edn., Methuen, London, V. 3 and 5, 1945.

HOLLISTER, W., *Anglo-Norman Political Culture and the Twelfth-Century Renaissance,* The Boydell Press, Woodbridge, 1997.

HOLTRUST, N., DE HONDT, W., Note on HR 18 May 1990, in: HOLTRUST, N. (ed.), *Rechtspraak vrouwen en recht,* Ars Aequi Libri, Nijmegen, 1992, p. 38-43.

HOME OFFICE, *Supporting Families. A Consultation Document* (1998), HMSO, London.

HONDIUS, E., *Naar een Europees burgerlijk recht,* preadvies Vereniging Burgerlijk recht, Vermande, Lelystad 1993.

HONDIUS, E., 'European Private Law –Survey 2002-2004', *6 European Review of Private Law* (2004), p. 855-899.

HÖRSTER, E., 'Does Portugal Need to Legislate on *De Facto* Unions?' *13 International Journal of Law, Policy and the Family* (1999), p. 274-279.

HOUGH, A., 'The early Kentish 'divorce laws': a reconsideration of Æthelberht, chs. 79 and 80, *Anglo-Saxon England* 23 (1994), p. 19–34.

HRABAR, D., 'The Protection of the Weaker Family Members: the Ombudsman for Children, Same-Sex Unions, Family Violence and Family Law', in: BAINHAM, A. (ed.), *The International Survey of Family Law,* Jordan Publishing, Bristol, 2004, p. 111-122.

HRABAR, D., 'Legal Status of Cohabitants in Croatia', in: SCHERPE, J., YASSARI, N. (eds.), *Die Rechtsstellung nichtehelicher Lebensgemeinschaften,* Mohr Siebeck, Tübingen, 2005, p. 399-415.

HÜBNER, R., *History of Germanic Private Law,* transl. by Philbrick, F., Murray, London, 1918.

HÜBNER, H., 'Sinn und möglichkeiten retrospektiver Rechtsvergleichung', in: MUSIELAK, H-J., SCHURIG, K. (eds.), *Festschrift für Gerhard Kegel,* Kohlhammer, Stuttgart, 1987, p. 235-252.

HUSSEY, J. (ed.), *The Cambridge Midlevel History,* V. IV The Byzantine Empire, Part II Government, Church and Civilisation, Cambridge University Press, Cambridge, 1967.

HUUSSEN, A., *De codificatie van het Nederlandse huwelijksrecht 1795-1838,* Holland Universiteits Pers, Amsterdam, 1975.

IHERING, R., *Geist des römischen Recht auf den verrscheidenen Stufen siener Entwicklung,* Drud and Berlag, 1891.

JACOBSEN, G., 'Sexual Irregularities in Medieval Scandinavia', in: BULLOUGH V., BRUNDAGE J., *Sexual Practices and the Medieval Church,* Prometheus Books, Buffalo, 1982.

JAMES, C., 'Cead Mile Failte. Ireland Welcomes Divorce: The 1995 Irish Divorce Referendum and the Family (Divorce) Act of 1996', *8 Duke Journal of Comparative and International Law,* (1997), lexis.

JAMES, M., 'The Illegitimate and Deprived Child', in: GRAVESON, R., CRANE, F. (eds.), *A Century of Family Law 1857-1957,* Sweet and Maxwell, London, 1957, p. 39-56.

JAMES, M., 'The English Law of Marriage', in: GRAVESON, R., CRANE, F. (eds.), *A Century of Family Law 1857-1957,* Sweet and Maxwell, London, 1957, p. 20-39.

JÄNTERÄ-JAREBORG, M., *Swedish Report concerning the CEFL Questionnaire on Grounds for Divorce and Maintenance Between Former Spouses* (2003) http://www.law.uu.nl/priv/cefl > working field 1 > Sweden

JÄNTERÄ-JAREBORG, M., 'Unification of International Family Law in Europe – A Critical Perspective', in: BOELE-WOELKI, K. (ed.), *Perspectives for the Unification and Harmonisation of Family Law in Europe,* European Family Law Series No. 4, Intersentia, Antwerp, 2003, p. 194-216.

JÄNTERÄ-JAREBORG, M., SÖRGJERD, C., 'The Experiences with Registered Partnership in Scandinavia', *3 FamPra* (2004), p. 577-597.

JÄNTERÄ-JAREBORG, M., *CEFL* National Report for Sweden: *Parental Responsibilities,* in: BOELE-WOELKI, K., B. BRAAT, B., SUMNER I. (eds.), *European Family Law in Action,* Vol. II: *Parental Responsibilities,* European Family Law Series No. 2, Intersentia, Antwerp, 2005.

JÄNTERÄ-JAREBORG, M., 'Parenthood for Same-Sex Couples: Challenges of Private International Law from a Scandinavian Perspective', in: TOMLJENOVIC, V., ERAUW, J., VOLKEN, P. (eds.), *Universalism, Tradition and the Individual. Liber Memorialis Petar Sarcevic,* Sellier, München, 2006, p. 75–91.

JARASS, H., PIEROTH, B., *Grundgesetz für die Bundesrepublik Deutschland: Kommentar,* Beck, München, 2002.

JEPPESEN-DE BOER, C., 'Administratieve echtscheiding in Denmarken', *Tijdschrift voor Familie en Jeugdrecht* (2005), p. 231-235.

JESSEL-HOLST, C., 'Ansätze für eine rechtliche Regelung der gleichgeschlechtlichen Lebensgemeinschaften in Ungarn', in: BASEDOW, J. et al (eds.), *Die Rechtsstellung gleichgeschlechtlicher Lebensgemeinschaften,* Moch, Tübingen, 2000, p. 167-171.

JESSURUN D' OLIVEIRA, H., 'De Europese Commissie erkent het Nederlands huwelijk, Nederlands relatierecht in Europese Unie', *42 Nederlands juristenblad* (2001), p. 2035-2040.

JESSURUN D'OLIVEIRA, H., 'Europese receptie van nieuwe familiepatronen: het opengestelde huwelijk', in: CORSTENS, G., DAVIDS, W., VELDT-FOGLIA, M. (eds.), *Europeanisering van het Nederlands Recht,* Kluwer, Deventer, 2004, p. 159-177.

JOHNSON, N., 'Recent Developments: the Breadth of Family Law Review Under the European Convention on Human Rights' *36 Harvard International Law Journal, 513* (1995), lexis.

JOLOWICZ, H., Roman *Foundations of Modern Law,* 2nd edn., Clarendon Press, Oxford, 1961.

KAHN-FREUND, O., 'Matrimonial Property Law in England', in: FRIEDMANN, W. (ed.), *Matrimonial Property Law,* Stevens and Sons, London, 1955, p. 267-315.

KAHN-FREUND, O., 'On Uses and Misuses of Comparative Law', *1 Modern Law Review* (1974), p. 1-27.

KAHN-FREUND, O., 'Common Law and Civil Law – Imaginary and Real Obstacles to Assimilation', in: CAPPELLETTI, M. (ed.), *New Perspectives for a Common Law of Europe,* Sijthoff, Leyden, 1978, p. 137-168.

KAIRYS, D., *Politics of Law: a Progressive Critique,* Pantheon Books, New York, 1982.

KAISER, D., '"Entpartnerung" – Aufhebung der eingetragenen Lebenspartnerschaft gleichgeschlechtlicher Partner', *13 Zeitschrift für das gesamte Familienrecht* (2002), p. 866-873.

KANT, I., *The Philosophy of Law,* Clark, Edinburgh, 1887.

KANT, I., *Critique of Pure Reason,* St. Martin's Press, New York, 1965.

KANT, I., *Observations on the Fallings of the Beautiful and Sublime,* reprinted in: reprinted in OSBORNE, M., *Woman in Western Thought,* Random House, New York, 1979.

KARAMZIN, N., *The History of the State of Russia,* Eksmo, Moscow, 2003.

KASER, M., *Das römische Privatrecht,* Part I, 2. Aufl., Beck, München, 1971.

KASER, M., *Das römische Privatrecht,* Part II, 2. Aufl., Beck, München, 1975.

KASER, M., *Roman Private Law,* (transl.), University of South Africa, Pretoria, 1993.

KASER, M., KNÜTEL, R., *Römische Privatrecht,* 17th substantially adapted and completed edition, Beck, München, 2003.

KASERAUSKAS, Š., 'Moving in the Same Direction'? Presentation of Family Law Reforms in Lithuania', in: BAINHAM, A. (ed.), *The International Survey of Family Law,* Jordan Publishing, Bristol, 2004, p. 315-335.

KELLY, H., *The Matrimonial Trials of Henry VIII,* Stanford University Press, Stanford, California, 1976.

KENNEDY, E., 'Anticipations of Postmodernist Epistemology', in: LIEDMAN, S-E. (ed.), *The Postmodernist Critique of the Project of Enlightenment,* Rodopi, Amsterdam, 1997, p. 105-134.

KERAMEUS, K., 'Problems of Drafting a European Civil Code', *5 European Review of Private Law* (1997), p. 455-481.

KERR, C., *Industrialisation and Industrial Man,* Harvard Univ. Press, Cambridge Massachusetts, 1960.

KERR, C., *The Future of Industrial Societies: Convergence or Continuing Diversity?* Harvard Univ. Press, Cambridge Massachusetts, 1983.

KERTZER, D., SALLER, P., *The Family in Italy from Antiquity to the present,* Yale University Press, New Haven, 1991.

KESERAUSKAS, S., 'Moving in the Same Direction'? Presentation of Family Law Reforms in Lithuania', in: BAINHAM, A. (ed.), *The International Survey of Family Law*, Jordan Publishing, Bristol, 2004, p. 315-336

KHAZOVA O., 'Conclusion of Marriage', in: KUZNETZOVA, I. (ed.), *Commentary to the Russian Family Code*, Jurist, Moscow, 2000, p. 51-54.

KIERNAN, K., 'The Rise of Cohabitation and Childbearing Outside Marriage in Western Europe, *15 International Journal of Law, Policy and the Family* (2001), p. 1-21.

KIERNAN, K., 'The State of European Unions: an Analysis of Partnership Formation and Dissolution', in: MACURA, M., BEETS, G. (eds.), *Dynamics of fertility and partnership in Europe. Insights and lessons from comparative research*, V1, United Nations, New York, 2002, p. 57-76.

KIRALFY, A., 'The English Law', in: KIRALFY, A. (ed.), *Comparative Law of Matrimonial Property*, Sijthoff, Leiden, 1972, p. 180-197.

KOLLONTAY, A., *Sem'ia i kommunisticheskoe gosudarstvo*, N. Novgorod, Communist, 1918.

KON, I., *Sexual'naia kul'tura v Rossii* (*Sexual Culture in Russia*), O.G.I., Moscow, 1997.

KOOPMANS, T., 'Towards a New "*Ius Commune*", in: DE WITTE, B., FORDER, C. (eds.), *The common law of Europe and the future of legal education*, Kluwer, Deventer, 1992, p. 43-51.

KOSCHAKER, P., *Europa en het Romeinse recht*, Tjeenk Willink, Zwolle, 1995.

KÖTZ, H., 'A common Private Law For Europe: Perspective For the Reform of European Legal Education', in: DE WITTE, B., FORDER, C. (eds.), *The common law of Europe and the future of legal education*, Kluwer, Deventer, 1992, p. 31-41.

KÖTZ, H., 'Was erwartet die Rechtsvergleichung von der Rechtsgeschichte', *Juristen Zeitung* (1992), p. 19-22.

KOVACEK STANIC, G., 'Legal Reforms Concerning the Family', in: BAINHAM, A. (ed.), *The International Survey of Family Law*, Martinus Nijhoff Publishers, The Hague, 1995, p. 533-542.

KRALJIĆ, S., 'Consequences Deriving From Cohabitation-Relations Between Partners and Between Parents and Children', in: BOELE-WOELKI, K. (ed.), *Perspectives for the Unification and Harmonisation of Family Law in Europe*, European Family Law Series No. 4, Intersentia, Antwerp, 2003, p. 339-365.

KREYENFELD, M., KONIETZKA, D., 'Rechtsstellung nichtehelicher Lebensgemeinschaften – Demographische Trends und gesellschaftlishe Strukturen', in: SCHERPE, J., YASSARI, N. (eds.), *Die Rechtsstellung nichtehelicher Lebensgemeinschaften*, Mohr Siebeck, Tübingen, 2005, p. 45-77.

KRYGIER, M., 'Law as Tradition', *5 Law and Philosophy* (1986), p. 263-276.

KULLERKUPP, K., 'Family Law in Estonia', in: BAINHAM, A. (ed.), *The International Survey of Family Law*, Jordan Publishing, Bristol, 2001, p. 95-110.

KURKI-SUONIO, K., *CEFL National Report for Finland: Parental Responsibilities*, in: BOELE-WOELKI, K., BRAAT, B., SUMNER I. (eds.), *European Family Law in Action*, Vol. II: *Parental Responsibilities*, European Family Law Series No. 2, Intersentia, Antwerp, 2005.

KYMLICKA, W., *Multicultural Citizenship: A Liberal Theory of Minority Rights*, Clarendon Press, New York, 1995.

LACEY, T., (revised by Mortimer, R.) *Marriage in Church and State*, SPCK, London, 1947.

LAIOU, A., SIMON, D. (ed.), *Law and Society in Byzantium: Ninth-Twelfth Centuries*, Dumbarton Oaks Research Library and Collection, Washington D.C, 1994.

LANDO, O., 'Optional or Mandatory Europeanisation of Contract Law', *1 European Review of Private Law* (2000), p. 59-69.

LANDO, O., BEALE, H. (eds.), *Principles of European contract law Part. I and II* (combined and revised), Kluwer, The Hague, 2000.

LANDO, O., 'Can Europe Build Unity of Civil Law Whilst Respecting Diversity?', *1 Europa e diritto privato* (2006), p. 1-18.

LANGNER, D., *Eheschließung und Ehescheidung nach spanischem Recht,* Peter Lang, Frankfurt am Main, 1984.

LAROUCHE, P., 'Ius Commune Casebooks for the Common Law of Europe Presentation Progress Rationale,' *1 European review of private law* (2000), p. 101-110.

LASK, E., 'Rechtsphilosophie', in: Festschrift für Kuno Fischer *Die Philosophie im beginn des zwanzigsten Jahrhunderts,* Winter's Universitätsbuchhandlung, Heidelberg, 1907, p. 269-320.

LAW COMMISSION, *The Grounds for Divorce. The Field of Choice*, HMSO, London, 1966.

LAW COMMISSION, *Solemnisation of Marriage in England and Wales,* HMSO, London, 1973.

LAW COMMISSION, *Facing the Future. A Discussion Paper on the Grounds for Divorce*, HMSO, London, 1988.

LAW COMMISSION, *Family Law. The Grounds for Divorce.* HMSO, London, 1990.

LEE, B., *Divorce Reform in England,* Peter Owen, London, 1974.

LEFEBVRE, C., *Cours de doctorat sur l'histoire du droit matrimonial français .Le droit des gens mariés,* Sirey, Paris, 1908.

LEGRAND, P., 'Legal Traditions in Western Europe: The Limits of Commonality', in: JAGTENBERG, R., ÖRÜCÜ, E., and DE ROO, A. (eds.), *Transfrontier Mobility of Law,* Kluwer, The Hague, 1995, p. 63-84.

LEGRAND, P., 'European Legal Systems Are Not Converging', *45 International and Comparative law Quarterly,* 1996, p. 53-81.

LEGRAND, P., 'Against a European Civil Code', *Modern Law Review* (1997), p. 44-63.

LEGRAND, P., 'The Impossibility of Legal Transplants', *4 Maastricht Journal of European and Comparative Law* (1997), p. 111-124.

LEGRAND, P., *Fragments on Law-as-Culture,* Tjeenk Willink, Deventer, 1999.

LELEU, Y.H., 'De vermogensrechtelijke gevolgen van de wettelijke samenwoning. Commentaar bij de virtuele wet van 23 november 1998,' *6 Notarieel en fiscaal maandblad* (1999), p. 123-134.

LEMOULAND, J-J., 'Pacte civil de solidarité (PACS). Formation et la dissolution de Pacte Civil de Solidarité', *9 JCP La Semaine Juridique, Edition Notariale et Immobilière* (2000), p. 406-410.

LENIN, V., Letter to I.F. Armand of 24 January 1915, *Polnoe sobranie sochineniy,* V., 46, Institut marksizma-leninizma, Moskow, 1958-1965.

LENTERS, H., *De Rol van de rechter in de echtscheidingsprocedure,* Tjeenk Willink, Zwolle, 1986.

LENTERS, H., 'Naam en gezag', in: *Familie geregeld?* Preadvies voor koninklijke Notarieel Broederschap, Vermande, Lelystad, 2000, p. 15-69.

LENTI, L., 'Recent Changes in the Judge-Made Law of Separation and Divorce and Perspectives on Law Reform,' in: BAINHAM, A. (ed.), *The International Survey of Family Law,* Jordan Publishing, Bristol, Bristol, 2002, p. 207-219.

LEWIS, J., 'Debates and Issues Regarding Marriage and Cohabitation in the British and American Literature', *15 International Journal of Law, Policy and the Family* (2001), p. 159-184.

LEWIS, X., 'The Europeanisation of the Common Law', in: JAGTENBERG, R., ÖRÜCÜ, E., and DE ROO, A. (eds.), *Transfrontier Mobility of Law,* Kluwer, The Hague, 1995, p. 47-61.

LIBRANDO, V., 'The Reform of Family Law in Italy', in: CHLOROS, A. (ed.), *The Reform of Family Law in Europe,* Kluwer, Deventer, 1978, p. 151-182.

LIEFBROER, A., 'Het gezinsideaal: Van traditioneel naar modern' *3 Demos* (2002), http://www.nidi.knaw.nl/nl/demos/2002/.

LIPSTEIN, K., 'European Legal Education in the Future: Teaching the "Common Law of Europe"', in: DE WITTE, B., FORDER, C., *The Common Law of Europe and the Future of Legal Education,* Kluwer, Deventer, 1992, p. 255-265.

LOBINGIER, C., 'The Matrimonial Community: Its Origin and Diffusion. A Problem of Comparative Law', *4 American Bar Association Journal* (1928), p. 211-218.

LOCKE, J., Two Treatises of Government, (first published in 1690), Dent, London, 1978.

LOCKE, J., *Essay concerning Human Understanding,* Clarendon Press, Oxford, 1979.

LØDRUP, P., 'Registered Partnership in Norway', in: BAINHAM, A. (ed.), *The International Survey of Family Law,* Martinus Nijhoff, The Hague, 1994, p. 387-394.

LØDRUP, P., 'Comparative Studies of Nordic Law', *The ISFL Family Letter* (2004), p. 1.

LOENEN, T., 'Echte of onechte ouders: zorg als grondslag voor ouderschap', *4 Nemesis* (1995), p. 92-96.

LÖGDBERG, A., The Reform of Family Law in the Scandinavian Countries, in: CHLOROS, A. (ed.), *The Reform of Family Law in Europe,* Kluwer, Boston, 1978, p. 201-226.

LORD CHANCELLOR'S DEPARTMENT, *Looking to the Future. Mediation and the Grounds for Divorce.* HMSO, London, 1993.

LORD CHANCELLOR'S DEPARTMENT, *Looking to the Future. Mediation and the Grounds for Divorce.* HMSO, London, 1995.

LOWE, N., DOUGLAS, G., *Bromley's Family Law,* Butterworths, London, 1998.

LOWE, N., The English approach to the division of assets upon family breakdown, in: HENRICH, D., SCHWAB, D. (eds.), *Eheliche Gemeinschaft, Partnerschaft und Vermögen im europäischen Vergleich,* Gieseking, Bielefeld, 1999, p. 47-71.

LOWE, N., CEFL National Report for England and Wales: *Grounds for Divorce,* in: BOELE-WOELKI, K., B. BRAAT, B., SUMNER I. (eds.), *European Family Law in Action,* Vol. I: Grounds for Divorce, European Family Law Series No. 2, Intersentia, Antwerp, 2003.

LUIG, K., 'The History of Roman Private Law and the Unification of European Law, *5 Zeitschrift für Europäisches Privatrecht* (1997), p. 405-427.

LUND-ANDERSEN, I., 'Cohabitation and Registered Partnership in Scandinavia: The Legal Position of Homosexuals', in: EEKELAAR, J., NHLAPO, T., *The Changing Family: International Perspectives on the Family and Family Law,* Hart Publishing, Oxford, 1998, p. 398-404.

LUND-ANDERSEN, I., 'The Danish Registered Partnership Act', in: BOELE-WOELKI, K., FUCHS, A. (eds.), *Legal Recognition of Same-Sex Couples in Europe,* Intersentia, Antwerp, 2003, p. 13-23.

LUND ANDERSEN, I., KRABBE, L., 'Danish Report concerning the CEFL Questionnaire on Grounds for Divorce and Maintenance Between Former Spouses', http://www.law.uu.nl/priv/cefl > Working Field 1 > Denmark.

LUND-ANDERSEN, I., KRABBE, L., *CEFL* National Report for Denmark: *Grounds for Divorce,* in: BOELE-WOELKI, K., BRAAT, B., SUMNER I. (eds.), *European Family Law in Action,* Vol. I: Grounds for Divorce, European Family Law Series No. 2, Intersentia, Antwerp, 2003.

LUTHER, M., 'Vom ehelichen Leben', in: *Luther's Works,* Muhlenberg Press, Philadelphia, 1986.

LYOTARD, J-F., *Het postmoderne uitgelegd aan onze kinderen,* transl. Janssen, C., Kok Agora, Kampen, 1987.

MACDONALD, R. et al (eds.), *The European System for the Protection if Human Rights,* Martinus Nijhoff Publishing, Dordrecht, 1993.

MĄCZYŃSKI, A., SOKOLOWSLI, T., *CEFL* National Report for Poland: *Grounds for Divorce,* in: BOELE-WOELKI, K., BRAAT, B., SUMNER I. (eds.), *European Family Law in Action,* Vol. I: Grounds for Divorce, European Family Law Series No. 2, Intersentia, Antwerp, 2003.

MAHE, C., 'De Franse wetgever op weg naar afschaffing van "schuldscheiding', *1 Tijdschrift voor Familie- en Jeugdrecht* (2002), p. 16-24.

MAHONEY, P., 'Marvellous Richness of Diversity or Invidious Cultural Relativism?', *19 Human Rights Law Journal 1* (1998), p. 1-23.

MAITLAND, F., *Roman Canon Law in the Church of England,* (Six Essays), Burt Franklin, New York, 1968.

MAKARIY, *The History of the Russian Church,* book IV, part I and II, Spaso-Preobragenskiy Monastery, Moscow, 1996.

MALINTOPPI, A., 'Les relations entre l' unification et l'harmonisation du droit et la technique de l'unification ou de l'harmonisation par la voie d'accords internationaux" *UNIDROIT Annuaire,* Vol. II (1967-1968), p. 44-61.

MALMSTRÖM, Å., 'Die Zusammenarbeit der nordischen Staaten auf dem Gebiete der Gesetzgebung. Ergebnisse und Erfahrungen', in: ZWEIGERT, K., DAVID, R. (eds.). *Europäische Zusammenarbeit im Rechtswesen,* Mohr, Tübingen, 1955,

MALMSTRÖM, Å., 'Matrimonial Property Law in Sweden', in: FRIEDMANN, W. (ed.), *Matrimonial Property Law,* Stevens and Sons, London, 1955, p. 410-433.

MARKESINIS, B., 'Learning from Europe and Learning in Europe', in: MARKESINIS, B. (ed.) *The Gradual Convergence. Foreign Ideas Foreign Influences and English Law on the Eve of the 21ˢᵗ Century,* Clarendon Press, Oxford, 1994, p. 1-32.

MARKESINIS, B., 'Studying Judicial Decisions in the Common Law and the Civil Law: A Good Way of Discovering Similarities and Differences that Exist Between these Legal Families', in: VAN HOECKE, M., OST, F. (eds.), *The Harmonisation of European Private Law,* Hart, Oxford, 2000, p. 118-134.

MARKS, K., ENGELS, F., *Collected Works,* 10 Vol., International Publishers, New York, 1975.

MARSHALL, L., 'What God Has United Man Will Now Divide: Divorce Referendum Changes Law of 60 Years,' *26 Georgia Journal of International and Comparative Law* (1997) lexis.

MARTIN, C., THÉRY, I., 'The PACS and Marriage and Cohabitation in France', *15 International Journal of Law, Policy and the Family* (2001), p.135-158.

MARTIN, F., 'From Prohibition to Approval: the Limitation of the 'No Clean Break' Divorce Regime in the Republic of Ireland', *16 International Journal of Law, Policy and the Family* (2002), p. 223-259.

MARTÍN-CASALS, M., *Spanish Report concerning the CEFL Questionnaire on Grounds for Divorce and Maintenance Between Former Spouses* (2003), http://www.law.uu.nl/priv/cefl > working field 1 > Spain.

MARTÍN-CASALS, M., *CEFL* National Report for Spain: Grounds for Divorce, in: BOELE-WOELKI, K., BRAAT, B., SUMNER I. (eds.), *European Family Law in Action*, Vol. I: Grounds for Divorce, European Family Law Series No. 2, Intersentia, Antwerp, 2003.

MARTÍN-CASALS, M., 'Same-Sex Partnerships in the Legislation of Spanish Autonomous Communities', in: BOELE-WOELKI, K., FUCHS, A. (eds.), *Legal Recognition of Same-Sex Couples in Europe,* Intersentia, Antwerp, 2003, p. 54-67.

MARTÍNEZ-TORRÓN, J., *Anglo-American Law and Canon Law. Canonical Roots of the Common Law Tradition,* Duncker & Berlin, 1998.

MARTINY, D., 'Is Unification of Family Law Feasible or Even Desirable?', in: HARTKAMP et al (eds.), *Towards a European Civil Code,* Ars Aequi Libri, Nijmegen, 1998.

MARTINY, D., *German Report concerning the CEFL Questionnaire on Grounds for Divorce and Maintenance Between Former Spouses* (2003), http://www.law.uu.nl/priv/cefl > working field 1 > Germany

MARTINY, D., 'Is Unification of Family Law Feasible or Even Desirable?' in: *Towards a European Civil Code,* A. HARTKAMP et al (eds.), Ars Aequi Libri, Nijmegen, 2004, p. 307-333.

MARTINY, D., 'Divorce and Maintenance Between Former Spouses – Initial Results of the Commission on European Family Law', in: BOELE-WOELKI, K. (ed.), *Perspectives for the Unification and Harmonisation of Family Law in Europe*, European Family Law Series No. 4, Intersentia, Antwerp, 2003, p. 529-550

MARTINY, D., 'A New Matrimonial Property Regime for Europe' presentation at the *UK-German Judicial Family Law Conference*, Cardiff, 8-11 September, 2004.

MARTINY, D., *CEFL* National Report for Germany: *Parental Responsibilities,* in: BOELE-WOELKI, K., BRAAT, B., SUMNER I. (eds.), *European Family Law in Action*, Vol. II: *Parental Responsibilities*, European Family Law Series No. 2, Intersentia, Antwerp, 2005.

MARTINY, D., 'Rechtsprobleme der nichtehelichen Lebensgemeinschaft während ihres Bestehens nach deutschem Recht', in: SCHERPE, J., YASSARI, N. (eds.), *Die Rechtsstellung nichtehelicher Lebensgemeinschaften,* Mohr Siebeck, Tübingen, 2005, p. 79-99.

MARTINY, D., Family Law', in: ZEKOLL, J., REIMANN M. (eds.), *Introduction to German Law,* 2nd edn., Kluwer, Deventer, 2005, p. 251-270.

MARX, K., 'The German Ideology', in: JORDAN, Z. (ed.), *Karl Marx: Economy, Class and Social Revolution,* Nelson, London, 1972.

MASSFELLER, F., 'Matrimonial Property Law in Germany', in: FRIEDMANN, W. (ed.), *Matrimonial Property Law,* Stevens and Sons, London, 1955, p. 389-410.

MATTEI, U., *Comparative Law and Economics,* Univ. of Michigan Press, 1996.

MATWEEV, G., *Semeinoe pravo,* Juriducheskaia lliteratura, Moskow, 1985.

MAYALI, L., 'Note on the Legitimization by Subsequent Marriage from Alexander III to Innocent III' in: MAYALI, L., MOORE, R., HIST, F., *Family, Community and Cult of the Eve of the*

Gregorian Reform, in Transactions of the Royal Historical Society, Serie 50, Vol. 30, 1980, p. 49-69.

MCGLYNN, C., 'A Family Law for the European Union', in: J. SHAW (ed.), *Social Law and Policy in an Evolving European union*, Oxford Hart, 2000, p. 224-241.

MCGLYNN, C., 'Families and the European Union Charter of Fundamental Rights: progressive change or entrenching the status quo?', *26 European Law Review* (2001), p. 582-598.

MCGLYNN, C., 'The Europeanisation of family law', *1 Child and Family Law Quarterly* (2001), p. 35-49.

MCGLYNN, C., 'Challenging the European Harmonisation of Family Law: Perspectives on "the Family"', in: BOELE-WOELKI, K. (ed.), *Perspectives for the Unification and Harmonisation of Family Law in Europe*, European Family Law Series No. 4, Intersentia, Antwerp, 2003, p. 219-238.

MCGLYNN, C., *European Family Values: Families, Law and Policy in the European Union*, Cambridge Univ. Press, Cambridge, 2006.

MCNAMARA, J., WEMPLE, S., 'Marriage and Divorce in the Frankish Kingdom', (1976), in: STUARD, S., *Women in Medieval Society*, University of Pennsylvania Press, Philadelphia, 1976.

MCSWEENEY, B., *Roman Catholicism. The Search for Relevance*, Basil Blackwell, Oxford, 1980.

MÉCARY, C., LEROY-FORGEOT, F., *Le Pacs*, Press Universitaires de France, Paris, 2000.

MEEUSEN J., PERTEGÁS, M., STRAETMANS, G., SWENNEN, F., 'General report', in: MEEUSEN, J., PERTEGÁS, M., STRAETMANS, G., SWENNEN, F. (eds.), *International Family Law for the European Union*, Intersentia, Antwerpen, 2007, forthcoming.

MERRYMAN, J., *The Civil Law Tradition*, Stanford University Press, Stanford, Cal., 1969.

MERRYMAN, J., 'On the Convergence (and Divergence) of Civil Law and Common Law', in: Cappelletti, M. (ed.), *New Perspectives for a Common Law of Europe*, Sijthoff, Leyden, 1978, p. 195-233.

MEULDERS-KLEIN, M.-T., 'Les problèmes de mise en œuvre de la Convention sur le statut des enfants nés hors mariage', in: *Troisième Conférence européenne sur le droit de la famille*, Council of Europe, Strasburg, 1995, p. 41-64.

MEULDERS-KLEIN, M.-T., 'The Status of the Father in European Legislations', *44 The American Journal of Comparative Law* (1996), p. 487-520.

MEULDERS-KLEIN, M.-T., *La personne, la famille et le droit – 1968-1998: Trois décennies de mutations en Occident* Bruylant, Brussel, 1999.

MEULDERS-KLEIN, M.-T., 'Les concubinages: diversités et symboliques', in: RUBBELIN-DEVICHI, J., *Des concubinages: droit interne, droit international, droit compare*, Litec, Paris, 2002, p. 603-619.

MEULDERS-KLEIN, M.-T., 'Towards a European Civil Code of Family Law? Ends and Means', in: BOELE-WOELKI, K. (ed.), *Perspectives for the Unification and Harmonisation of Family Law in Europe*, European Family Law Series No. 4, Intersentia, Antwerp, 2003, p. 105-118.

MEYER, P., *Der römische Konkubinat nach den Rechtsquellen und den Inschriften*, Teubner, Leipzig, 1895.

MILL, J.S., *Auguste Comte and Positivism, Essays on Ethic, Religion, and Society*, in: ROBSON, A., ROBSON, J., *Sexual Equality: Writings by John Stuart Mill, Harriet Taylor, and Helen Taylor*, University of Toronto Press, Toronto, 1994. Butterworths, London, 1981.

MILL, J.S., *The Subjection of Women* (first published in 1869), 3rd edn., The M.I.T. Press, Cambridge & London, 1974.

MILL, J.S., 'Essays on Equality, Law, and Education', in: ROBSON, A., ROBSON, J., *Sexual Equality: Writings by John Stuart Mill, Harriet Taylor, and Helen Taylor,* University of Toronto Press, Toronto, 1994.

MILL, J.S., 'Article on Henry Saint-Simon', in: ROBSON, A., ROBSON, J., *Sexual Equality: Writings by John Stuart Mill, Harriet Taylor, and Helen Taylor,* University of Toronto Press, Toronto, 1994.

MILSOM, S., *Historical Foundations of the Common Law,* 2nd edn., Butterworth, London, 1981.

MILTON, J., 'The Doctrine and Discipline of Divorce, Restored to the Good of Both Sexes, from the Bondage of Canon Law', in: *Complete Prose Works of John Milton,* Yale University Press, New Haven, 1959, Vol. 2, p. 217-356.

MITTERAUER, M., SEIDER, R., *The European Family. Patriarchy and Partnership from the Milled Ages to the Present,* Basil Blackwell, Oxford, 1982.

MLADENOVIC, M., JANJIC-KOMAR, M., JESSEL-HOLST, C., 'The Family in Post-Socialist Countries', in: GLENDON M.A. (ed.), *International Encyclopaedia of Comparative Law,* Martinus Nijhoff Publishers, Dordrecht, 1998.

MOCCIA, L., 'Historical Overview of the Origins and Attitudes of Comparative Law', in: WITTE, B., DE, FORDER, C. (eds.), *The common law of Europe and the future of legal education,* Kluwer, Deventer, 1992, p. 609-620.

MOLFESSIS, N., 'Pacte Civil de Solidarité (PACS). Le Réécriture de la loi par le Conseil Constitutionnel', *6 Famille* (2000), p. 270-272.

MONTESQUIEU, C., *The Spirits of Laws,* Book 1, Chapter 3, University of California Press, Berkeley, 1977.

MOSSELMANS, S., 'De wet van 23 november 1998 tot invoering van de wettelijke samenwoning en het gelijkheidsbeginsel', *28 Rechtskundig weekblad* (2000-2001), p. 1041-1048.

MOSSIKER, F., *Napoleon and Josephine: The Biography of a Marriage,* Gollancz, London, 1965.

MOUSTAIRA, E., National Report 'Greece', in: Consortium Asser-UCL, *Study on Matrimonial Property Regimes and the Property of Unmarried Couples in Private International Law and Internal Law,* European Commission, 2003, http://ec.europa.eu/justice_home/ doc_centre/civil/studies/doc/regimes/greek_report_en.pdf.

MOUTOUH, H., 'Le question de la reconnaissance du couple homosexuel: entre dogmatisme et empirisme', Recueil Dalloz (1998), p. 369-372.

MÜLLER- FREIENFELS, W., 'Equality of Husband and Wife in Family Law', *8 International and Comparative Law Quarterly* (1959), p. 249-267.

MÜLLER-FREIENFELS, W., *Ehe und Recht,* Mohr, Tübingen, 1962.

MÜLLER-FREIENFELS, W., 'Family Law and the Law of Succession in Germany', *14 International and Comparative Law Quarterly,* (1967), p. 409-445.

MÜLLER-FREIENFELS, W., 'The Unification of Family Law', *16 The American Journal of Comparative Law* (1968-69), p. 175-218.

MÜLLER-FREIENFELS, W., 'The Marriage Law Reform of 1976 in the Federal Republic of Germany', *28 International and Comparative Law Quarterly* (1979), p. 184-210.

MÜLLER-GRAFF, P.-C., 'Privatrecht und Europäisches Gemeinschaftsrecht', in: MÜLLER-GRAFF, P.-C. (ed.), *Gemeinsames Privatrecht in der Europäischen Gemeinschaft*, (2nd edn.), Nomos, Baden-Baden, 1999, p. 267-298.

MYRDAL, A., *Nation and Family. The Swedish Experiment in Democratic family and Population Policy*, The M.I.T. Press. Cambridge, Massachusetts, 1968.

NATHAN, G., *The Family in Late Antiquity: the Rise of Christianity and the Endurance of Tradition*, Routledge, London, 2000.

NELKEN, D., 'Disclosing /Invoking Legal Culture: An Introduction', *4 Social and Legal Studies* (1995), p. 435-452.

NELKEN, D., 'Comparing Legal Cultures: An Introduction', in: NELKEN, D. (ed.), *Comparing Legal Cultures*, Dartmouth, Aldershot, 1997, p. 1-9.

NELKEN, D., 'Legal Transplants and Beyond: Of Disciplines and Metaphors', in: HARDING, A., ÖRÜCÜ, E., *Comparative Law in the 21st Century*, Institute of Advanced Studies, 2002, p. 19-34.

NETCHAEVA, A., *Family Law ('Semeinoe pravo')*, Jurist, Moscow, 1998.

NEUHAUS, P. et al, 'The Family in Religious and Customary Laws', in *International Encyclopaedia of Comparative Law*, Vol . IV *Persons and Family*, GLENDON, M-A (ed.), Mohr, Tübingen, Martinus Nijhoff Publishers, The Hague, Boston, London, 1983, p. 3-63.

NEUMAYER, K., 'The Role of Uniform Legal Science in the Harmonisation of the Continental Legal Systems', in: NEWMAN, R. (ed.), *Essays in Jurisprudence in Honour of Roscoe Pound*, Bobbs Merrill, Indianapolis, 1962.

NEUMAYER, K., 'General Introduction', in: CHLOROS, A. (ed.), *The Reform of Family Law in Europe*, Kluwer, Deventer, 1978.

NEUWAHL, N., ROSAS, A., *The European Union and Human Rights*, Nijhoff, The Hague, 1995.

NEVOLIN, K. *Istoria rossiiskikh grazhdanskikh zakonov*, St. Petersburg's University, St. Petersburg, 1851.

NEYENS, M., 'Entwicklungen in der luxemburger Familienrechtspolitik', in: JANS, B. HABISCH, A., STUTZER, E. (eds.), *Familienwissenschaftliche und familienpolitische Signale*, Vektor-Verlag, Grafschaft, 2000.

NIELSEN, L., 'Family Rights and the "Registered Partnership" in Denmark', *4 International Journal of Law and the Family* (1990), p. 297-305.

NIELSEN, L., National Report 'Denmark', in: Consortium Asser-UCL, *Study on Matrimonial Property Regimes and the Property of Unmarried Couples in Private International Law and Internal Law*, European Commission, 2003, http://ec.europa.eu/justice_home/ doc_centre/civil/studies/doc/regimes/denish_report_en.pdf.

NIETZSCHE, F., *Beyond Good and Evil*, reprinted in OSBORNE, M., *Woman in Western Thought*, Random House, New York, 1979.

NOTTAGE, L., *Convergence, Divergence, and the Middle Way in Unifying or Harmonising Private Law*, Badia Fiesolana, San Domingo, 2001.

NOWAK, L., 'On Postmodernist Philosophy: an Attempt to Identify Is Historical Sense', in: LIEDMAN, S-E. (ed.), *The Postmodernist Critique of the Project of Enlightenment*, Rodopi, Amsterdam, 1997.

NUYTINCK, A., 'De Wet openstelling huwelijk en de Wet adoptie door personen van hetzelfde geslacht', in: KORTMANN, S. et al (eds.), *Yin-Yang: bundel opstellen, op 12 mei 2000 aangeboden aan prof. mr. M.J.A. Van Mourik ter gelegenheid van z?n 25-jarig ambtsjubileum als hoogleraar*, Kluwer, Deventer, 2000, p. 213-222.

O'DONOVAN, K., 'Legal Marriage –Who Needs It?' *47 Modern Law review* (1984), p. 111-118.

OFFICE FOR NATIONAL STATISTICS, *Civil Registration: Vital Change. White Paper*, HMSO, London, 2002.

OFFICE FOR NATIONAL STATISTICS, *Civil Registration: Delivering Vital Change. Consultation Paper*, HMSO, London, 2003.

OGRIS, W., 'FRIEDELEHE', in: ERLER, A., KAUFMANN, E., WERKMÜLLER, D., *Handwörterbuch zur deutschen Rechtsgeschichte*, Schmidt, Berlin, 1971, No. 1293-1296.

O'HALLORAN, K., 'Ireland: The Family and the Law in a Divided Land', in: EEKELAAR, J., NHLAPO, T., *The Changing Family: International Perspectives on the Family and Family Law*, Hart Publishing, Oxford, 1998, p. 115-123.

OKIN, S., *Women in Western Political Thought*, Princeton Univ. Press, Princeton, 1979.

OKIN, S., 'Are Our Theories of Justice Gender-Neutral?' in: FULLINWIDER, F., MILLS, C., *The Moral Foundations of Civil Rights*, Rowman and Littlefield, Totowa, 1986, p. 125-143.

OLÁH, L., 'Policy Changes and Family Stability: the Swedish Case', *12 International Journal of Law, Policy and the Family* (2001), p. 118-134.

OLIVERCRONA, D.,'De la commuaute des biens entre époux d'aprés les anciennes lois des peuples scandinaves' *15 Revue critique de législation et de jurisprudence* (1859).

O'NEILL, W., *Divorce in The Progressive Era*, New Viewpoints, New York, 1973.

ÖRÜCÜ, E., 'Turkey: Reconciling Traditional Society and Secular Demands', *26 Journal of Family Law* (1987-1988), p. 221-225.

ÖRÜCÜ, E., 'Turkish Family Law: a New Phase', *30 Journal of Family Law* (1991-1992), p. 431-438.

ÖRÜCÜ, E., 'The Impact of European Law on the Ottoman Empire and Turkey', in: MOMMSEN, W., de MOOR, J. (eds.), *European Expansion and Law*, Oxford, Berg Publishers, 1992, p. 39-58.

ÖRÜCÜ, E., 'A Theoretical Framework for Transfrontier Mobility of Law', in: JAGTENBERG, R., ÖRÜCÜ, E., and ROO, A. DE. (eds.), *Transfrontier Mobility of Law*, Kluwer, The Hague, 1995.

ÖRÜCÜ, E., 'Turkish divorce law", *2 Migrantenrecht* (1996), p. 27-33.

ÖRÜCÜ, E., 'Turkey: Change Under Pressure' in: ÖRÜCÜ, E. et al (eds.), *Studies of Legal Systems: Mixed and Mixing*. Kluwer, The Hague, 1996, p. 89-111.

ÖRÜCÜ, E., 'Mixed and Mixing Systems: A Conceptual Search', in: *Studies in Legal Systems: Mixed and Mixing*, Kluwer, The Hague, 1996, p. 335-352.

ÖRÜCÜ, E., *Critical Comparative Law: Considering Paradoxes for Legal Systems in Transition. Report for the Netherlands Comparative law Association*, Kluwer, Deventer, 1999.

ÖRÜCÜ, E., 'Unde Venit, Quo Tendit Comparative Law?', in: HARDING, A., ÖRÜCÜ, E., *Comparative Law in the 21ˢᵗ Century*, Institute of Advanced Studies, 2002, p. 2-17.

ÖRÜCÜ, E., 'Family Law Enters the New Century', in: BAINHAM, A. (ed.), *The International Survey of Family Law*, Jordan Publishing, Bristol, 2004, p. 469-482.

ÖRÜCÜ, E., *The Enigma of Comparative Law. Variations on a Theme for the Twenty-first Century*, Martinus Nijhoff, Leiden, 2004.

ÖRÜCÜ, E., 'Looking at Convergence through the Eyes of a Comparative Lawyer', *2.9 Electronic Journal of Comparative Law* (2005), www.ejcl.org/92/art92-1.html.

OSTNER, I., 'Cohabitation in Germany – Rules, Reality and Public Discourses', *15 International Journal of Law, Policy and the Family* (2001), p. 88-101.

OZMENT, S., *When Fathers Ruled: Family Life in Reformation Europe*, Harvard University Press, Cambridge, Mass., 1983.

PAIS, S., 'De Facto Relationships and Same-Sex Relationships in Portugal', in: BAINHAM, A. (ed.), *The International Survey of Family Law*, Jordan Publishing, Bristol, 2002, p. 337-345.

PALMER, V., 'From Lerotholi to Lando: Some Examples of Comparative Law Methodology', *53 The American Journal of Comparative Law* (2005), p. 261-290.

Pastoral Constitution of the Church in the Modern World, Vatican II, *Gaudium en Spes*, 7 December, 1965, in: *Documents of Vatican II*, Eerdmans Publishing, Grand Rapids, 1984.

PATEMAN, C., *The Sexual Contract*, Polity Press, Cambridge, 1988.

PATTI, S., *CEFL* National Report for Italy: Grounds for Divorce, in: BOELE-WOELKI, K., BRAAT, B., SUMNER, I. (eds.), *European Family Law in Action*, Vol. I: Grounds for Divorce, European Family Law Series No. 2, Intersentia, Antwerp, 2003.

PAYER, P., *Sex and the Penitentials. The Development of a Sexual Code 550-1150*, University of Toronto Press, Toronto, London, 1984.

PCHELINTZEVA, L., *Family Law ('Semeinoe pravo')*, Norma-Infra, Moscow, 1999.

PELLIS, L., 'Het homohuwelijk: een bijzonder nationaal product', *6 Familie- en Jeugdrecht* (2002), p. 162-168.

PEREZ-BUSTAMANTE, R., 'La communauté de biens en histoire du droit espagnol', in: GANGHOFER, R. (ed.), *Le droit de la famille en Europe: son évolution depuis l'antiquité à nos jours: actes des jour*, Presses Universitaires de Strasbourg, Strasbourg, 1992, p. 542-554.

PERTEGÁS SENDER, M., 'Huwelijk tussen personen van hetzelfde geslacht in België: internrechtelijke en internationaalrechtelijke implicaties,' in: SENAEVE, P., SWENNEN, F., *De hervormingen in het personen- en familierecht 2002-3003*, Intersentia, Antwerp, 2003, p. 257-280.

PETERS, A., SCHWENKE, H., 'Comparative Law Beyond Post-Modernism', *49 International and Comparative Law Quarterly* (2000), p. 800-834.

PETTIT, P., 'Parental Control and Guardianship' in: GRAVESON, R., CRANE, F. (eds.), *A Century of Family Law 1857-1957*, Sweet and Maxwell, London, 1957, p. 56-88.

PHILLIPS, R., *Family Breakdown in Late Eighteenth Century France. Divorces in Rouen 1972-1803*, Clarendon Press, Oxford, 1980.

PHILLIPS, R., 'Remaking the Family: The Reception of Family Law and Policy during the French Revolution', in:

PHILLIPS, R., *Putting asunder: A history of divorce in Western Society*, Cambridge University Press, Cambridge, 1988.

PINTENS, W., 'Accentenverschuiving in de rechtsvergelijking', in: *Liber Amoricum Roger Blanpain*, die Keure, 1998, p. 785-794.

PINTENS, W., VANWINCKELEN, C., *Casebook. European Family Law*, Leuven Univ. Pers, Leuven, 2001.

PINTENS, W., 'Over cultuur, Europa en recht', in: DIRIX, E. et al. (eds.), *Liber Amiricorum Jacques Herbots*, Kluwer, Deurne, 2002, p. 311-323.

PINTENS, W., VAN DER MEERSCH, B., VANWINCKELEN, C., *Inleiding tot het Familiaal Vermogensrecht*, Univ. Pers Leuven, Leuven, 2002.

PINTENS, W., 'Europeanisation of Family Law', in: BOELE-WOELKI, K. (ed.), *Perspectives for the Unification and Harmonisation of Family Law in Europe*, European Family Law Series No. 4, Intersentia, Antwerp, 2003, p. 3-35.

PINTENS, W., 'Harmonisatie in het huwelijksgoederenrecht', *Tijdschrift voor Familie- en Jeugdrecht* (2005), p. 245-248.

PLANTZ, H., *Deutsche Rechtsgeschichte*, Bölau, Köln, 1981.

POCAR, V., RONFANI, P., 'Family Law in Italy: Legislative Innovations and Social Change', *4 Law and Society Review*, 1978, p. 607-644.

POKROVSKII, I., *Osnovnie problemi grazgdanskogo prava*, Pravo, Petrograd, 1917.

POLLOCK, F., MAITLAND, F., *The history of English Law before the time of Edward I*, Vol. I, 2nd edn, Cambridge, Cambridge, 1898.

POLLOCK, F., MAITLAND, F., *The history of English Law before the time of Edward I*, Vol. II, 2nd edn., Cambridge University Press, Cambridge, 1952.

POPENOE, D., Disturbing *the Nest. Family Change and Decline on Modern Societies*, Aldine de Gruyter, New York, 1988.

Pravila Provoslavnoi Cerkvi s kommentariami Nokodima episkopa Dalmatinsko-Istriiskogo (Rules of the Orthodox Church with the Comments of Nicodim Bishop of Dalmatian-Istria) *Vol. I and II, (first edited in 1912), Sviato-Troitskaia Segieva Lavra, Sergiev Pasad, 1996.*

PRICE, C., 'Finding Fault with Irish Divorce Law', *19 Loyola of Los Angeles International and Comparative Law Journal* (1997), lexis.

PROBERT, R., BARLOW, A., 'Cohabitants and the law: recent European reforms', *Deutsches und Europäisches FamilienRecht* (2000), p. 76-81.

PROBERT, R., 'Lord Hardwicke's Marriage Act – Vital Change 250 Years On?', *34 Family Law* (2004), p. 585-589.

PUHR, J., BREEST, A., 'Entwicklung des Begriffs der "eheähnliche Gemeinschaft" in der Rechtsprechung zum Sozialrecht', *36 Sozialrecht in Deutschland und Europa* (1997), p. 463-467.

RADBRUCH, G., *Grunzdzüge der Rechtsphilosophie*, Gelle and Meyer, Leipzig, 1914.

RAEVICH, S., 'Brarnoe i semeinoe pravo', in: MAGEROVSKII, D. (ed.), *Osnovy sovetskogo prava*, Gosudarstvennoe Izdatel'stevo, Moskou-Leningrad, 1927.

RAZ, J., *The morality of freedom*, Oxford, Clarendon Press, 1986.

RECHBERGER, W., National Report 'Austria', in: Consortium Asser-UCL, *Study on Matrimonial Property Regimes and the Property of Unmarried Couples in Private International Law and Internal Law*, European Commission, 2003, http://ec.europa.eu/justice_home/doc_centre/civil/studies/doc/regimes/austrian_report_en.pdf.

REGAN, M., *Family law and the Pursuit of Intimacy*, New York Univ. Press, New York, 1993.

REGAN, M., *Alone Together and the Meaning of Marriage,* Oxford Univ. Press, Oxford, 1999.

REINHARDT, G., et.al. (eds.), *Essays on The French Revolution: Paris and the Provinces*, Texas Univ. Press, Arlington, 1992.

REINHARTZ, B., 'De nieuwe voorstellen ter aanpassing van de wettelijke gemeenschap van goederen', *2 Tijdschrift voor Familie- en Jeugdrecht* (2006), p. 3-14.

RENCHON, J.-L., 'L'avènement du mariage homosexuel dans de Code civil Belge', *2 Revue de droit international et de droit comparé 81* (2004), p. 169-207.

REYNOLDS, P., *Marriage in the Western Church. The Christianization of Marriage During the Patristic and Early Medieval Periods*, Brill, Leiden, 1994.

RHEINSTEIN, M., *Marriage Stability, Divorce, and the Law*, Univ. of Chicago Press, Chicago, 1972.

RIGAUX F., 'Monism and Dualism within the Europeans Jurisdictions', in: HOECKE, M., VAN, OST, F. (eds.), *The Harmonisation of European Private Law*, Hart, Oxford, 2000, p. 133-166.

RIJAVEC, V., KRALJIC, S., 'Die Rechtsstellung nichtehelicher Lebensgemeinschaften in Slowenien', (eds.), *Die Rechtsstellung nichtehelicher Lebensgemeinschaften*, Mohr Siebeck, Tübingen, 2005, p. 175-399.

RITZER, K., *Formen, Riten und religiöses Brauchtum der Eheschliessung in den christlichen Kirchen des ersten Jahrtausends*, Aschendorff, Münster, 1962.

ROBINSON, J., *Honest to God*, SCM Press, London, 1967 (first published in 1963).

ROBINSON, O., FERGUS, T, GORDON, W., *An Introduction to European Legal History*, Professional Brooks Limited, Abingdon, 1985.

ROBSON, A., ROBSON, J., *Sexual Equality: Writings by John Stuart Mill, Harriet Taylor, and Helen Taylor*, University of Toronto Press, Toronto, 1994.

ROCA, E., 'Regulation of Same-Sex Relationships from a Spanish Perspective', in: MACLEAN, M. (ed.), *Making Law for Families*, Hart Publishing, Oxford, 2000, p. 95-115.

ROCA, E., 'Same-Sex Partnerships in Spain: Family, Marriage of Contract?', *3 European Journal of Law Reform* (2001), p. 365-382.

RODOTÀ, S., 'Le régime matrimonial en droit Italien', in: KIRALFY, A. (ed.), *Comparative Law of Matrimonial Property*, Sijthoff, Leiden, 1972, p. 223-248.

ROLLER, S., 'Zweifelsfragen im Unterhaltsrecht der Lebenspartnerschaft', *19 Zeitschrift für das gesamte Familienrecht* (2003), p. 1424-1427.

ROTH, M., *CEFL National Report for Austria: Parental Responsibilities*, in: BOELE-WOELKI, K., BRAAT, B., SUMNER I. (eds.), *European Family Law in Action*, Vol. II: *Parental Responsibilities*, European Family Law Series No. 2, Intersentia, Antwerp, 2005.

ROTHENBACHER, F. 'Social Change in Europe and its Impact on Family Structures', in: EEKELAAR, J., NHLAPO, T., *The Changing Family: International Perspectives on the Family and Family Law*, Hart Publishing, Oxford, 1998, p. 3-33.

ROUGHOL-VALDERON, D., 'La Divorce par Consentement Mutuel et le Code Napoléon', *Revue Trimestrielle de Droit Civil* (1975), p. 482-487.

ROUSSEAU, J-J. *Third Discourse on Political Economy* in: *Rousseau, J-J. Oeuvres completes*, V reprinted in OSBORNE, M., *Woman in Western Thought*, Random House, New York, 1979.

ROUSSEAU, J-J. 'Sophia' from *Emilius: or A New System of Education*, reprinted in OSBORNE, M., *Woman in Western Thought*, Random House, New York, 1979.

ROUSSELE, A., 'The Family under the Roman Empire: Signs and Gestures', in: BURGUIERE, A., KLAPISCH-ZUBER, C.,

RUBELLIN-DEVICHI, J., 'La permanence des spécifiés nationales de droit de la famille', in: CAMMAILLE, J., SINGLY, F. (eds.), *La Questions Familiale en Europe*, l'Harmattan, Paris, 1997, p. 61-80.

RUBELLIN-DEVICHI, J., 'How Matters Stand Now in Relation to French Law Reform', in: BAINHAM, A. (ed.), *The International Survey of Family Law*, Jordan Publishing, Bristol, 2000, p. 143-162.

RUBELLIN-DEVICHI, J., *Droit de la famille, 2001-2002*, Dalloz, Paris, 2001.

RYRSTEDT, E., 'Legal Status of Cohabitants in Norway', in: SCHERPE, J., YASSARI, N. (eds.), *Die Rechtsstellung nichtehelicher Lebensgemeinschaften,* Mohr Siebeck, Tübingen, 2005, p. 439-455.

SACCO, R., 'Legal Formants: A Dynamic Approach to Comparative Law' (Instalment II of II), *39 The American Journal of Comparative Law,* (1991), p. 343-401.

SACCO, R., 'Diversity and Uniformity in the Law', *49 The American Journal of Comparative Law* (2001), p. 171-189.

SAFLEY, T., *Let No Man Put Asunder: The Control of Marriage in the German Southwest. A Comparative study 1500-1600,* Sixteenth Century Journal Publishers, Kirksville, 1984.

SAFLEY, T., 'Canon Law and Swiss Reforms: Legal Theory and Practice in the Marital Courts of Zurich, Bern, Basel and St. Gall', in: HELMHOLZ, R. (ed.), *Canon Law in Protestant Lands,* Duncker and Humbolt, Berlin, 1992, p. 187-201.

SALDEEN, Å., 'Sweden: Family Counselling, the Tortuous Liability of Parents and Homosexual Partnership,' in: FREEMAN, M. (ed.), *17 Annual Survey of Family Law, 1993,* University of Louisville Journal of Family Law (1994-95), p. 513-521.

SALDEEN, Å., 'The Children's Ombudsman, Adoption by Homosexual Partners and Assisted Reproduction', in: BAINHAM, A. (ed.), *The International Survey of Family Law,* Jordan Publishing, Bristol, 2000, p. 439-449.

SALDEEN, Å., 'Cohabitation Outside Marriage or Partnership', in: BAINHAM, A. (ed.), *The International Survey of Family Law,* Jordan Publishing, Bristol, 2005, p. 503-509.

SARCEVIC, P., 'Cohabitation without Formal Marriage in Yugoslavian Law', in: EEKELAAR, J., KATZ, S. (eds.), *Marriage and Cohabitation in Contemporary Society,* Butterworths, Toronto, 1980, p. 293-299.

SAVOLAINEN, M., 'The Finnish and the Swedish Partnership Acts – Similarities and Divergences', in: BOELE-WOELKI, K., FUCHS, A. (eds.), *Legal Recognition of Same-Sex Couples in Europe,* Intersentia, Antwerp, 2003, p. 24-40.

SCAMMELL, J., 'Freedom and Marriage in Medieval England', *4 The Economic History Review,* Second Series, Vol. XXVII (1974), p. 523-537.

SCHÄFER, B., BANKOWSKI, Z., 'Mistaken Identities: The Integrative Force of Private Law', in: VAN HOECKE, M., OST, F. (eds.) *The Harmonisation of European Private Law,* Hart, Oxford, 2000.

SCHERF, Y., *Registered Partnership in the Netherlands. A quick scan,* WODC, 1999.

SCHERPE, J., 'Zehn Jahre registrierte Partnerschaft in Dänemark', *2 Deutsches und Europäisches FamilienRecht* (2000), p. 32-37.

SCHERPE, J., 'The Legal Status of Cohabitants – Requirements for Legal Recognition,' in: BOELE-WOELKI, K. (ed.), *Common Core and Better Law in European Family Law,* Intersentia, Antwerp-Oxford, 2005, p. 283-334.

SCHERPE, J., 'Einführung: Nichteheliche Lebensgemeinschaften als Problem für den Gesetzgeber', in: SCHERPE, J., YASSARI, N. (eds.), *Die Rechtsstellung nichtehelicher Lebensgemeinschaften,* Mohr Siebeck, Tübingen, 2005, p. 1-12.

SCHILLEBEECKX, E., *Het huwelijk: aardse werkelijkheid en heilsmysterie,* H. Nelissen, Bilthoven, 1963.

SCHIMMEL, R., *Eheschliessungen gleichgeschlechtlicher Paare?* Dunker and Humbolt, Berlin, 1996.

SCHIRATZKI, J., National Report 'Sweden', in: Consortium Asser-UCL, *Study on Matrimonial Property Regimes and the Property of Unmarried Couples in Private International Law and Internal Law*, European Commission, 2003, http://ec.europa.eu/justice_home/doc_centre/civil/studies/doc/regimes/swedish_report_en.pdf.

SCHLESINGER, R., 'The Past and Future of Comparative Law', *43 The American Journal of Comparative Law* (1995), p. 477-481.

SCHLESINGER, R. et al, *Comparative law: cases, text, materials*, (6th edn.), Foundation Press, New York, 1998.

SCHLÜTER, W., HECKES, J., STOMMES, S., 'Die gesetzliche Regelung von außerehelichen Partnerschaften gleichen und verschiedenen Geschlechts im Ausland und die deutschen Reformvorhaben', *2 Deutsches und Europäisches FamilienRecht* (2000), p. 1-18.

SCHMIDT, F., 'The Prospective Law of Marriage', *15 Scandinavian Studies in Law* (1971).

SCHMIDT, T., 'The Scandinavian Law of procedure in Matrimonial Causes', in: EEKELAAR J.M., KATZ N. (eds.), *The Resolution of Family Conflicts*, Butterwoths, Harvard, 1984, p. 78-98.

SCHOKKENBROEK, J., 'The Prohibition of the Discrimination in article 14 of the Convention and the Margin of Appreciation', *19 Human Rights Law Journal* (1998), p. 20-23.

SCHOPENHAUER, A., 'Studies in Pessimism', in: *Parerga and Paralipomena*, Allen and Unwin, 1890, reprinted in: OSBORNE, M., *Woman in Western Thought*, Random House, New York, 1979.

SCHRAMA, W., 'De betekenis van het EVRM voor de burgerlijke stand in de lidstaten van de CIEC', *Tijdschrift voor Familie- en Jeugdrecht* (1998), p. 222-234.

SCHRAMA, W., 'Registered Partnership in the Netherlands', *13 International Journal of Law, Policy and the Family* (1999), p. 315-327.

SCHRAMA, W., *De niet-huwelijkse samenleving in het Nederlandse en Duitse recht*, Kluwer, Amsterdam, 2004.

SCHRAMA, W., 'General Lessons for Europe Based on a Comparison of the Legal Status of Non-Marital Cohabitation in the Netherlands and Germany,' in: BOELE-WOELKI, K. (ed.), *Common Core and Better Law in European Family Law*, Intersentia, Antwerp-Oxford, 2005, p. 257-281.

SCHWAB, D., 'Eingetragene Lebenspartnerschaft- Ein Überblick', *7 Zeitschrift für das gesamte Familienrecht* (2001), p. 386-403.

SCHWAB, D., *Familienrecht*, 12. Aufl., Beck, Munich, 2003.

SCHWENZER, I., 'Registerscheidung', in: GOTTWALD, P., e.a. (ed.), *Festschrift für Dieter Henrich*, Gieseking, Bielefeld, 2000, p. 533-544.

SCHWENZER, I., 'Methodological Aspects of Harmonisation of Family Law', in: BOELE-WOELKI, K. (ed.), *Perspectives for the Unification and Harmonisation of Family Law in Europe*, European Family Law Series No. 4, Intersentia, Antwerp, 2003, p. 143-158.

SCHWENZER, I., 'Tensions between legal, biological and social conceptions of parentage' General Report for the *XVIIth Congress of the International Academy of Comparative Law* (2006), http://www2.law.uu.nl/priv/AIDC/index1.asp.

SEGALEN, M., ZONABEND O. (ed.), *A History of the Family*. Vol. I. *Distant Worlds, Ancient Worlds*, Polity Press, Oxford, 1996.

SELLIN, J., *Marriage and Divorce Legislation in Sweden*, University of Pennsylvania, 1922.

SEMIDVORKIN, N., Sozdanie pervogo brachno-semeinogo kodeksa, MGY, Moskow, 1989.

SENAEVE, P., 'Familierechtelijke aspecten van ongehuwd samenwonen, in: PINTENS, W., VAN DER MEERSCH, B. (eds.), *Ongehuwd samenwonen, Recyclagedagen 1996 van de Nederlands-talige Raad*, Kluwer, Antwerpen, 1997, p. 61-118.

SENAEVE, P., 'De wettelijke samenwoning en het geregistreerde partnerschap in het Belgisch recht', *11 Familie- en Jeugdrecht* (1998), p. 254-259.

SENAEVE, P., COENE, E., *'Geregistreerd partnerschap. Pleidooi voor de institutionalisering van de homoseksuele tweerelatie*, Maklu, Antwerp, 1998.

SENAEVE, P., 'Proeve van synoptische vergelijking tussen het huwelijk en de wettelijke samenwoning', *10 Echtscheidingsjournaal* (1998), p. 164-165.

SENAEVE, P., 'De Belgische 'wettelijke samenwoning' en het Franse 'Pacte civil de solidarité', in: Verbeke, A. et al (eds.), *Facetten van ondernemingsrecht. Liber Amicorum Professor Frans Bouckaert*, Leuven Univers. Press, Leuven, 2000, p. 437-453.

SENAEVE, P., 'Naar de invoering van het homohuwelijk in het Belgische recht?' *4 Echtscheidings-journaal* (2002), p. 50-52.

SENAEVE, P., *Compendium van het Personen- en Familierecht*, parts 1-3, Acco, Leuven, 2003.

SGRITTA, G., TUFARI, P., 'Italy', in: CHESTER, P., *Divorce in Europe*, Nijhoff, Leiden, 1977.

SHANLEY, M., *Feminism, Marriage and the Law in Victorian England, 1850-1895*, I.B. Tauris, London, 1989.

SHANNON, J., *CEFL* National Report for Republic of Ireland: *Grounds for Divorce*, in: BOELE-WOELKI, K., BRAAT, B., SUMNER I. (eds.), *European Family Law in Action*, Vol. I: Grounds for Divorce, European Family Law Series No. 2, Intersentia, Antwerp, 2003.

SHATTER, A., *Family Law in the Republic of Ireland*, 3rd edn., Wolfhound Press, Dublin, 1986.

SHEEHAN, M., *Marriage, Family, and Law in Medieval Europe: Collected Studies*, University of Toronto Press, Toronto, 1996.

SHERSHENEVICH, G., *Russkoe grazgdanskoe pravo (Russian Civil Law)*, Spark, Moscow, 1995.

SIEGFRIED, D., WAALDIJK, K., 'Germany', in: WAALDIJK, K. (ed.), *More of Less Together: Level of legal Consequences of Marriage, Cohabitation and Registered Partnership for Different-sex and Same-sex Partners*, Institut National d'Etudes Démographiques, Paris, 2005, p. 107-120.

SLOYAN, S., *Is Christ the End of the Law*, The Westminster Press, Philadelphia, 1978.

SMART, C., STEVENS, P., *Cohabitation Breakdown*, Family Policy Studies Centre, London, 2000.

SMITS, J., 'A European Private Law as a Mixed Legal System. Towards a Ius Commune through the Free Movement of Legal Rules', *5 Maastricht Journal of European and Comparative Law* (1998), p. 328-340.

SMITS, J., *The Good Samaritan in European Private law; On the Perils of Principles without a Programme and a Programme for a Future*, Kluwer, Deventer, 2000.

SMITS, J., *The Making of European Private Law. Towards a Ius Commune Europaeum as a Mixed legal System*, Intersentia, Antwerp, 2002.

SMITS, J., 'On Successful Legal Transplants in a Future *Ius Commune Europaeum*', in: HARDING, A., ÖRÜCÜ, E., *Comparative Law in the 21st Century*, Institute of Advanced Studies, 2002, p. 137-154.

SMYCZYNSKI, T., 'Das polnische Familienrecht im Reformprozeâ der staatlichen Ordnung', *Deutsches und Europäisches Familien Recht* (1999), p. 137-142.

SOLEM, E., *The Nordic Council and Scandinavian Integration*, Praeger, New York, 1977.

SOLOV'EV, C., *Rus' iznachal'naia (The Early Russia)*, in: *Istoria Rissii s drevneishih vremen (History of Russia from the Ancient Times)*, boek 1, Astrel, Moscow, 2001.

SOLOV'EV, C., *Istoria Rissii 1054-1462 (History of Russia 1054-1462)*, in: *Istoria Rissii s drevneishih vremen (History of Russia from the Ancient Times)*, books, II, Astrel, Moscow, 2001.

SOLOV'EV, C., *Istoria Rissii 1463-1584 (History of Russia 1463-1584)*, in: *Istoria Rissii s drevneishih vremen (History of Russia from the Ancient Times)*, books, III, Astral, Moscow, 2001.

SOLOV'EV, C., *Istoria Rissii 1584-1613 (History of Russia 1054-1462)*, in: *Istoria Rissii s drevneishih vremen (History of Russia from the Ancient Times)*, books, IV, Astrel, Moscow, 2001.

SÖRGJERD, C., 'Neutrality: the Death or the Revival of the Traditional Family', in: BOELE-WOELKI, K. (ed.), *Common Core and Better Law in European Family Law*, Intersentia, Antwerp-Oxford, 2005, p. 335-352.

SOTTOMAYOR, M., 'The Introduction and Impact of Joint Custody in Portugal', *13 International Journal of Law, Policy and the Family* (1999), p. 247-254.

SPIER, J., HAAZEN, O., 'The European Group on Tort Law ("Tilburg Group") and the European Principles of Tort Law', *Zeitschrift für Europäishes Privatrecht*, 1999, p. 469-493.

SPRUIT, J., *Enchiridium. Een geschiedenis van het Romeinse privaatrecht*, Kluwer, Deventer, 1994.

STALFORD, H., 'Concept of Family under EU law – Lessons from the ECHR', *16 International Journal of Law, Policy and the Family*, (2002), p. 410-434.

STEENHOFF, G., 'The Place of Legal History in the Teaching of Law and in Corporatists Formation', in: HONDIUS, E. (ed.), *Netherlands Reports to the Fifteenth International Congress of Comparative Law*, Intersentia, Antwerp, 1998, p. 1- 19.

STEENHOFF, G., 'Op weg naar een Europees familierecht', in: ANTOKOLSKAIA, M., DE HONDT, W., STEENHOFF, G., *Naar een Europees Familierecht, Report for the Netherlands Comparative law Association*, Kluwer, Deventer, 1999, p. 1-32.

STEENHOFF, G., 'A Matrimonial Property System for the European Union?' presentation at the *UK-German Judicial Family Law Conference*, Cardiff, 8-11 September, 2004.

STEINER, E., 'The spirit of the new French registered partnership law – promoting autonomy and pluralism or weakening marriage', *1 Child and Family Law Quarterly* (2000), p. 1-14.

STINTZING, H., 'Constitutional Values and Social Change – Case of German Marital and Family Law', *13 International Journal of Law, Policy and Family* (1999), p. 132-146.

STONE, M., *Marriage and Friendship in Medieval Spain. Social Relations According to the Fourth Partida of Alfonso X*, Peter Lang, New York, 1990.

STONE, L., *The Family, Sex and Marriage e in England 1500-1800*, Penguin Books, Harmondsworth, Middlesex, 1982.

STONE, L., *Road to Divorce. England 1530-1987*, Oxford Univ. Press, Oxford, 1990.

STRICK, K., 'Gleichgeschlechtliche Partnerschaft – Vom Straftatbestand zum Status?', *2 Deutsches und Europäisches Familienrecht* (2000), p. 82-94.

STUBBS, W., *Seventeen Lectures on the Study of Medieval and Modern History and Kindred Subjects Delivered at Oxford, Under Statutory Obligation in the Years 1867-1884*, S.n. Oxford, Oxford, 1990.

SUNDBERG, J., 'Nordic Laws', in: Rheinstein, M., e.a., *Das Erbrecht von Familienangehörigen*, Alfred Metzner Verlag, Frankfurt/M-Berlin, 1971.

SUNDBERG, J., 'Marriage or no Marriage. The Directives for the Revision of Swedish Family Law', *20 International and Comparative Law Quarterly* (1971), p. 223-238.

SVERDLOV, G., *Over het object en het systeem van het socialistisch familierecht (O predmete i sisteme sotsialisticheskogo semeinogo prava)*, Sovjetskoe gosudarstvo i pravo, 1 (1941).

SVERDRUP, T., '*CEFL National Report for Norway: Grounds for Divorce*', in: BOELE-WOELKI, K., BRAAT, B., SUMNER I. (eds.), *European Family Law in Action*, Vol. I: Grounds for Divorce, European Family Law Series No. 2, Intersentia, Antwerp, 2003.

SVERDRUP, T., 'Maintenance as a Separate Issue – the Relationship Between Maintenance and Matrimonial Property', in: BOELE-WOELKI, K. (ed.), *Common Core and Better Law in European Family Law,* Intersentia, Antwerp, 2005, p. 119-135.

Svod Zakonov Rossiyskoy Imperii. Zakoni Grazgdanskie, (Digest of the Laws of Russian Empire) V. 10, part 1, Petrograd, 1916.

SWENNEN, F., *Het huwelijk afschaffen?*, Intersentia, Antwerpen, 2003.

SWENNEN, F., 'Het "homohuwelijk" bestaat niet anno 2005', *5 Echtscheidingsjournaal* (2005), p. 66-68.

SWENNEN, F., *Gezins- en familierecht in kort bestek,* Intersentia, Antwerpen, 2005.

SWENNEN, F. 'Atypical Families in EU (Private International) Family Law,' in: MEEUSEN J., PERTEGÁS, M., STRAETMANS, G., SWENNEN, F. (eds.), *International Family Law for the European Union*, Intersentia, Antwerpen, 2007, forthcoming.

SZEIBERT ERDÖS, O., 'Unmarried Partnerships in Hungary', in: BOELE-WOELKI, K. (ed.), *Common Core and Better Law in European Family Law,* Intersentia, Antwerp-Oxford, 2005, p. 313-333.

SZRAMKIEWICZ, R., *Histoire du droit Français de la famille*, Dalloz, Paris, 1995.

TAMASI, L., RICCI, C., BARIATTI, S., 'Characterisation in Family Matters for Purposes of European Private International Law,' in: MEEUSEN J., PERTEGÁS, M., STRAETMANS, G., SWENNEN, F. (eds.), *International Family Law for the European Union*, Intersentia, Antwerpen, 2007, forthcoming.

TAYLOR, B., *Eve and the Jerusalem: Socialism and Feminism in the Nineteenth Century*, Virago Press, London, 1983.

TERRÉ, F., SIMLER, P., *Droit civil. Les régimes matrimoniaux*, 2ᵉ ed, Dalloz, Paris, 1994.

TEUBNER, G., *Autopoietic Law: A New Approach to Law and Society*, Walder de Gruyter, Berlin, 1988.

TEUBNER, G., 'Legal Irritants: Good Faith in British Law or How Unifying Law Ends Up in New Divergences', *61 Modern Law Review* (1998), p. 1-61.

THÉRY, I., *Le Démariage*, Odile Jacob, Paris, 1993.

THÉRY, I., SCHULZ, M., 'La contrat d'union sociale en question', *Revue Esprit* (1997), p. 159-211.

THÉRY, I., *Couple, filiation et parenté aujourd'hui: le droit face aux mutations de la famille et de la vie privée: rapport remis au Ministre de l'emploi et de la solidarité et au Garde des sceaux, Ministre de la justice*, Odile Jacob, Paris, 1998.

THIBEAUDOT, A-C., *Mémoires sur le Consulat, 1799 à 1804. Par un ancien conseiller d'état*, Ponthieu, Paris, 1827.

THIELEN, J., *Oude en nieuwe opvattingen over het ontstaat van de algehele gemeenschap van goederen*, Jongbloed en Zoon, 's-Gravenhage, 1965.

THIELEN, J., *Man ende wyb ne hebben nen twiet gut: man en vrouw hebben geen gedeeld goed* (Sachsenspiegel I.31.1): studie over de geschiedenis van het huwelijksgoederenrecht in Nederlandse en Belgische gewesten. Koninklijke Vermande, Lelystad, 2001.

THOMSON, J., 'The Reform of Family Law in England', in: CHLOROS, A. (ed.), *The Reform of Family Law in Europe*, Kluwer, Deventer, 1978, p. 43-74.

THOMSON, J., *Family Law in Scotland*, 3rd edn., Butterworths, Edinburgh, 1996.

THORN, K., 'The German Law on Same-Sex Partnerships', in: BOELE-WOELKI, K., FURCHS, A. (eds.), *Legal Recognition of Same-Sex Couples in Europe*, Intersentia, Antwerp, 2003, p. 84-98.

TIBBETTS, S., The *Two Laws. Studies in Medieval Legal History Dedicated to Stephan Kuttner*, The Catholic University of America Press, Washington D.C., 1990, p. 54-75.

TIERNEY, B., 'Villey, Ockham and the origin of individual rights', in: WITTE, J., ALEXANDER, F. (eds.), *The Weightier Matters of the Law: Essays on Law and Religion, a Tribute to Harold J. Berman*, 1988, p. 1-31.

TOBÍO, C., 'Marriage, Cohabitation and the Residential Independence of Young People in Spain', 15 *International journal of Law, Policy and the Family* (2001), p. 68-87.

TODD, E., *The Explanation of Ideology. Family Statures and Social Systems*, Basil Blackwell, Oxford, 1985.

TODOROVA, V., '*CEFL* National Report for Bulgaria: *Grounds for Divorce*', in: BOELE-WOELKI, K., B. BRAAT, B., SUMNER I. (eds.), *European Family Law in Action*, Vol. I: Grounds for Divorce, European Family Law Series No. 2, Intersentia, Antwerp, 2003.

TOMESEN, L., 'Ideeënstelsels die ten grondslag liggen aan het Europese cultuurdebat', in: TOMESEN, L., VOSSEN, G., *Denken over cultuur in Europa*, Bohn Stafleu, Houten, 1994, p. 3-21.

TOMLIJENOVIC, V., 'The Canonic Marriage – Revision of Croatian Family Law and Its Conflict of Laws Implication', in: BAINHAM, A., *The International Survey of Family Law*, Jordan Publishing, Bristol, 2003, p. 107-124.

TONER, H., *Partnership Rights, Free Movement, and EU Law*, Hart Publishing, Oxford, 2004.

TOTTIE, L., 'The Elimination of Fault in Swedish Divorce Law', in: EEKELAAR, J., KATZ, S. (eds.) *Marriage and Cohabitation in Contemporary Society*, Butterworths, Toronto, 1980, p. 131-137.

TOUBERT, P., 'The Carolingian Moment (Eight-Tenth Century)', in: BURGUIERE, A., KLAPISCH-ZUBER, C., SEGALEN, M., TRAER, J., *Marriage and the Family in the Eighteenth-Century France*, Cornell Univ. Press, Ithaca, 1980.

TREGGIARI, S., *Roman Marriage Iusti Coniuges for the Time of Cicero to the Time of Ulpian*, The Clarendon Press, Oxford, 1991.

TREGGIARI, S., 'Divorce Roman Style: How Easy and how frequent was it?' in: RAWSON, B. (ed.), *Marriage, Divorce, and Children in Ancient Rome*, The Clarendon Press, Oxford, 1991, p. 31-46.

TROITSKII, S., *Khristianskaia filisofia braka*, (Christian Philosophy of Marriage), Put, Moscow, 1995.

TROMPENAARS, B., *Pluriforme unificatie en uniforme interpretatie: in het bijzonder de bijdrage van UNCITRAL aan de internationale unificatie van het privaatrecht*, Kluwer, Deventer, 1989.

VAN DEN BERGH, G., '*Ius Commune*, A history With a Future', in: DE WITTE, B., FORDER, C. (eds.), *The common law of Europe and the future of legal education*, Kluwer, Deventer, 1992, p. 593-607.

VANDENBERGHE, H., *De juridische betekenis van het concubinaat*, Story-Scientia, Gent, 1970.

VAN DE WAL, N., *Manuale novellarum Justiniani: aperçu systématique du contenu des Novelles de Justinien*, 2nd edn., Groningue, Chimaira, 1998 (first ed. 1964).

VAN ERP, S., *Europees Privaatrecht: Postmoderne dilemma's en keuzen. Naar een methode van adequate rechtsvergelijking*, Kluwer, 1998.

VAN GERVEN, W. et al, *Torts. Scope of Protection*, Hart, Oxford, 1998,

VAN GERVEN, W., 'Harmonisation of private law: do we need it?', *41 Common Market Law Review* (2004), p. 505-532.

VAN GERVEN, W., 'Casebooks for the Common Law of Europe. Presentation of the Project', *Maastricht Journal* (1996), p. 67-70.

VAN GRUNDERBEECK, D., *Beginselen van personen- en familierecht. Een mensenrechtelijke benadering*, Intersentia, Antwerpen, 2003.

VAN HOECKE, M., WARRINGTON, M., 'Legal Cultures, Legal Paradigms and Legal Doctrine: Towards a New Model For Comparative Law,' *47 International and Comparative Law Quarterly*, (1998), p. 495-536.

VAN HOECKE, M., 'The Harmonisation of Private Law in Europe: Some Misunderstandings', in: VAN HOECKE, M., OST, F. (eds.), *The Harmonisation of European Private Law*, Hart, Oxford, 2000, p. 1-20.

VAN KLEFFENS, E, *Hispanic Law Until the End of the Middle Ages*, Edinburgh University Press, Edinburgh, 1968.

VAN MOURIK, M., 'Turbulentie in het familierecht', *Weekblad voor Privaatrecht Notariaat en Registratie* (1997), p. 397-400.

VAN MOURIK, M., 'Wettelijke en contractuele vormgeving van affectieve relaties,' in: *Het familierecht in het perspectief van de 21^e eeuw*, Kluwer, Deventer, 1999, p. 59-68.

VAN NIMWEGEN, V., BEETS, G., VAN DER ERF, R., 'De bevolking in Europa', *6 Demos* (2005), p. 44-48, http://www.nidi.knaw.nl/nl/demos/2005/.

VAN REIJEN, W., *De onvoltooide rede. Modern en postmodern*, Kok Agora, Kampen, 1987.

VAN WIEL, C., *History of Canon Law*, Peeters Press, Louvain, 1991.

VAN WYK, A., 'Theories on the Historical Origins of the Community of Property Between Spouses', in: DE VOS, W. et al (eds.), *Essays in Honour of Bem Beinart: Jura legesquie antiquiores necnon*, Juta, Cape Town, 1979, p. 279-293.

VARGA, C., 'European Integration and the Uniqueness' of National Legal Cultures', in: WITTE, B., DE, FORDER, C. (eds.), *The common law of Europe and the future of legal education*, Kluwer, Deventer, 1992, p. 721-733.

VEBERS, J., 'Family Law in Latvia: From Establishment of the Independent State of Latvia in 1918 to Restoration of Independence n 1993', in: BAINHAM, A., *The International Survey of Family Law*, Martinus Nijhoff Publishers, The Hague, 1997, p. 207-227.

VERBEKE, A., *Goederenverdeling bij echtscheiding*, MAKLU, Antwerpen, 1991.

VERBEKE, A., CRETNEY, S., GRAUERS, F., MALAURIE, P., OFNER, H., SAVOLAINEN, M., SKORINI-PAPARRIGOPOULOU, F., BURGHT, D., VAN DER, 'European marital property law, Survey 1988-1994', *3 European Review of Private Law* (1995), p. 445-482.

VERBEKE, A., 'Perspectives for an International Marital Contract', *2 Maastricht Journal of European and Comparative law* (2001), p. 189-200.

VERSCHELDEN, G., DEVOS, S., 'Kroniek van het Belgisch familierecht (1993-2001), *12 Tijdschrift voor familie- en jeugdrecht* (2002), p. 314-323.

VERSCHRAEGEN, B., *Gleichgeschlechtliche "Ehen"*, Medien und Recht, Vienna, 1994.

VERSCHRAEGEN, B., 'Gleichgeschlechtliche Beziehungen im Spiegel des Rechts', *2 Deutsches und Europäisches FamilienRecht* (2000), p. 64-75.

VIOLLET, P., *Précis de l'histoire du droit français: accompagné de notions de droit canonique et d'indications bibliographiques: sources, droit privé*, L. Larose et Forcel, Paris, 1886.

VLAARDINGERBROEK, P., BLANKMAN, K., (et. al.), *Het hedendaagse personen- en familierecht*, 3ᵉ druk, Tjeenk Willink, Deventer, 2002.

VLIET, F., 'Door de zij-ingang naar niemandsland? – Commentaar op het wetsvoorstel "adoptie van hetzelfde geslacht"', *2 Nemesis* (2000), p. 41-50.

VOLTERRA, E., *La conception du mariage d'apre`s les juristes romains*, La Garangola, Padova, 1940.

VON BAR, C., 'The Study Group on a European Civil Code', *Juridka Förenisngen i Finland*, (2000), p. 323-337.

VON BAR, C., 'Paving the Way Forward with Principles of European Private Law' in: GRUNDERMANN, S. (ed.), An *Academic Green Paper on European Contract Law*, Kluwer, The Hague, 2002, p. 137-148.

VON BOGDANDY, A., 'The European Union as a Human Rights Organisation? Human Rights and the Core of the European Union' (2000) *37 Common Market Law Reviews*, p. 1307-1338.

VON BÓNÉ, E., 'Der Einfluß des französischen Scheidunsrechts im Verenigten Königreich der Niederlande (1815-1830)', in: SCHULZE, R. (ed.), *Rheinishes Recht und Europäishe Rechtsgeschichte*, Duncker and Humblot, Berlin, 1998, p. 267-276.

VON HOYER, E., *Die Ehen minderen Rechts in der fränkischen Zeit*, Rohrer, Brünn, 1926.

VON SAVIGNY, F., *System des heutigen römischen Recht*, Veit, Berlin, 1840.

WAALDIJK, C., 'Het heteroseksuele exclusiviteit van het huwelijk na Hoge Raad 19 oktober 1990', *40 Ars Aequi* (1981), p. 47-56.

WAALDIJK, C., 'Beantwoording rechtsvraag. Homohuwelijk', *36 Ars Aequi* (1987), p. 644-650.

WAALDIJK, C., 'De voorgestelde Wet openstelling huwelijk', *10 Tijdschrift voor Familie- en Jeugdrecht* (1999), p. 198-208.

WAALDIJK, C., 'Partnerschapsregistratie en huwelijk: toenemende rechtsgelijkheid voor geslachtsgelijke partners en hun kinderen', in: *Familie geregeld?* Preadvies voor koninklijke Notarieel Broederschap, Vermande, Lelystad, 2000, p. 121-185.

WAALDIJK, K., 'Level of legal Consequences of Marriage, Cohabitation and Registered Partnership for Different-sex and Same-sex Partners: Comparative overview', in: WAALDIJK, K. (ed.), *More of Less Together: Level of legal Consequences of Marriage, Cohabitation and Registered Partnership for Different-sex and Same-sex Partners*, Institut National d'Etudes Démographiques, Paris, 2005, p. 7-48.

WAALDIJK, K., BONINI-BARALDI, M., *Sexual orientation discrimination in the EU: national laws and the Employment Equality Directive*, Asser Press, The Hague, 2006.

WAGNER, W., *Marriage, Property, and Law in Late Imperial Russia*, Clarendon Press, Oxford, 1994.

WALLS, M., BERGIN, D., *The Law of Divorce in Ireland*, Jordans, Bristol, 1997.

WARD, I., 'The Limits of Comparativism: Lessons from UK-EC Integration', *2 Maastricht Journal of European and Comparative law* (1995), p. 23-33.

WARDLE, L., 'Divorce Reform at the Turn of the Millennium: Certainties and Possibilities', *3 Family Law Quarterly 33* (1999), p. 783-800.

WATSON, A., *The Law of the Persons in the later Roman Republic*, The Clarendon Press, Oxford, 1967.

WATSON, A., *Rome of the XII Tables. Persons and Property*, University Press, Princeton, 1975.

WATSON, A., *The Evolution of Law*, Basil Blackwell, Oxford, 1985.

WATSON, A., *Roman Law and Comparative Law*, University of Georgia Press, Athens, 1991.

WATSON, A., *The State, Law And Religion Pagan Rome*, University of Georgia Press, Athens and London, 1992.

WATSON, A., *Legal Transplants. An Approach to Comparative Law*, 2nd edn., The University of Georgia Press, Athens and London, 1993.

WATSON, A., 'Aspects of Reception of Law', *44 The American Journal of Comparative Law*, (1996), p. 335-351.

WATSON, A., *Legal Transplants and European Private Law*, Metro, Maastricht, 2000.

WATSON, A., *Society and Legal Change*, Temple University Press, Philadelphia, 2001.

WEBER, M., *Ehefrau und Mutter in der Rechtsentwicklung*, Mohr, Tübingen, 1907.

WEISS, E., 'Remarks on Certain Aspects of the Codification of Family Law', *1-2 Acte Juridica Hungaria* (2002), p. 175-204.

WELSTEAD, M., 'Reshaping Marriage and the Family – The Gender Recognition Act 2004 and the Civil Partnership Act 2004,' in: BAINHAM, A. (ed.), *The International Survey of Family Law*, Jordan Publishing, Bristol, 2006, p.185-202.

WENDT, F., *The Nordic Council and Co-operation in Scandinavia*, Munksgaard, Copenhagen, 1959.

WESTBROOK, R., 'Property and the Family in Biblical Law', *Journal for the Study of the Old Testament*. Supplement Series 113.

WESTERHOF, L., 'Civiel effect voor het kerkelijk huwelijk?', *2 Nederlands juristenblad* (2002), p. 80-81.

WHEATON, R., HAREVEN, T. (eds.), *Family and Sexuality in French History*, University of Pennsylvania Press, Philadelphia, 1980.

WIARDA, J. (ed.), *C. Assers' Handeling tot beoefening van het Nederlands burgerlijk recht. Deel 1. Personenrecht 1ᵉ stuk Natuurlijke Personen en Familierecht*, 9[de] druk, Tjeenk Willink, Zwolle, 1957.

WIEACKER, F., 'Foundations of European Legal Culture', *38 The American Journal of Comparative Law* (1990), p. 1-29.

WIEACKER, F., 'Historical Models for the Unification of European Law", in: KRAWIETZ, W., et. al. (eds.), *Prescriptive Formality and Normative Rationality in Modern Legal Systems. Festschrift for Robert. S. Summers*, Dunker und Humbolt, Berlin, 1994, p. 297-306.

WIEACKER, F., *A history of private law in Europe: with particular reference to Germany*, (transl. by Tony Weir), Clarendon Press, Oxford, 1995.

WIJFFELS, A., 'A New Software-Package for an Outdated Operating System?', in: VAN HOECKE, M., OST, F. (eds.), *The Harmonisation of European Private Law*, Hart, Oxford, 2000.

WILLEKENS, H., 'Explaining Two Hundred Years of Family Law in Western Europe', in: WILLEKENS, H. (ed.), *Het gezinsrecht in de sociale wetenschappen*, Vuga, The Hague, 1997, p. 59-95.

WILLEKENS, H., 'Long Term Developments in Family Law in Western Europe: An Explanation', in: EEKELAAR, J., NHLAPO, T., *The Changing Family: International Perspectives on the Family and Family Law*, Hart Publishing, Oxford, 1998, p. 47-72.

WILLIAMS, D., *The Enlightenment*, Cambridge Univ. Press, Cambridge, 1999.

WINTEMUTE, R., 'Strasburg to the Rescue? Same-Sex Partners and Parents Under the European Convention,' in: WINTEMUTE, R., ANDENÆS, M., *Legal Recognition of Same-Sex Partnership. A Study of National, European and International Law*, Hart Publishing, Oxford, 2001, p. 713-729.

WITTE, J., *From Sacrament to Contract. Marriage, Religion, and Law in Western Tradition*, Westminster John Knox Press, Louisville, 1997.

WOKLER, R., 'The Enlightenment Project And Its Critics', in: LIEDMAN, S-E. (ed.), The Postmodernist Critique of the Project of Enlightenment, Rodopi, Amsterdam, 1997, p. 14-30.

WOLTER, U., Ius canonicum in jure civili: Studien zur Rechtsquellenlehre in der neueren Privatrechtsgeschichte, Böhlau, Cologne, 1975.

WOOD, I., 'Kings, Kingdoms and Consent', in: SAWYER, P., WOOD, I. (eds.), *Early Medieval Kingship*, School of History of Leeds, Leeds, 1979.

WORMALD, R., *The Making of English Law: King Alfred to the Twelfth Century*, Vol. 1, Blackwell, Oxford, 1999.

WORTMANN, S., 'Kroniek van het personen- en familierecht', *Nederlands Juristenblad* (2000), p. 1588 – 1593.

WORTMANN, S., 'Kroniek van het personen- en familierecht', *Nederlandse Juristenblad* (2001), p. 1541 – 1546.

WORTMANN, S., 'Zo zijn we niet getrouwd. De openstelling van het huwelijk voor personen van hetzelfde geslacht', *2 Ars Aequi* (2001), p. 82-87.

WORTMANN, S., 'Rechtsontwikkelingen in het personen- en familierecht: flitsscheidingen en verrekenbedingen', *Weekblad voor Privaatrecht Notariaat en Registratie* (2002), p. 165-172.

WOUTERS, J., 'The EU Charter of Fundamental Rights – Some Reflections on its External Dimension', *1 Maastricht Journal of European and Family Law* (2001), p. 3-10.

YTTERBERG, H., 'All Human Beings are Equal, But Some Are More Equal than Others – Equality and Dignity without Equality in Rights?' in: BOELE-WOELKI, K., FURCHS, A. (eds.), *Legal Recognition of Same-Sex Couples in Europe*, Intersentia, Antwerp, 2003, p. 1-11.

ZAGOROVSKII, I., *O razvode po russkomy pravy (On divorce under Russian Law)*, Tip. M. F. Zil'berberga, Kharknov, 1884.

ZAGOROVSKII, I., *Kurs semeinogo prava, (Course of Family Law)* Zertzalo, Moscow, 2003. (Reprint of the 1909 edition).

ZHISHMAN, J., *Das Eherecht der orientalischen Kirche*, Braumüller, Wenen, 1864.

ZHYLINKOVA, I., 'Property Relations of Spouses in Slavonic Post-Soviet Countries (Ukraine, Russia, Belarus),' in: BAINHAM, A. (ed.), *The International Survey of Family Law*, Jordan Publishing, Bristol, 2004, p. 483-490.

ZIMMERMANN, R., 'Roman-Dutch Jurisprudence and its Contribution to European Private Law' *66 Tulane Law Review*, 1992, p. 1685-1721.

ZIMMERMANN, R., 'Der europäische Character des englishen Rechts. Historische Verbindungen zwischen civil law und common law', *Zeitschrift für Europäishes Privatrecht* (1993), p. 4-51.

ZIMMERMANN, R., 'Rechtsvergelijking, Rechtsgeschiedenis en *ius commune*', *43 Ars Aequi* (1994), p. 12-19.

ZIMMERMANN, R., 'Civil Code and Civil Law. The "Europeanization" of Private Law Within the European Community and the Re-emergence of a European Legal Science', *Columbia Journal of European Law* (1994-1995), p. 63-105.

ZIMMERMANN, R., 'Savigny's Legacy Legal History, Comparative Law, and The Emergence of A European Legal Sience', *112 The Law Quarterly Review* (1996), p. 576-605.

ZIMMERMANN, R., *The Law of Obligations. Roman Foundations of the Civilian Tradition*, Clarendon Press, Oxford, 1996.

ZIMMERMANN, R., 'Roman Law and European Legal Unity', in: HARTKAMP A. et al (eds.), *Towards a European Civil Code*, Ars Aequi Libri, Nijmegen, 1998, p. 21-32.

ZIMMERMANN, R., 'Roman Law and European Legal Unity', in: *Towards a European Civil Code*, A. HARTKAMP et al (eds.), Ars Aequi Libri, Nijmegen, 1998, p. 21-41.

ZIMMERMANN, R., 'Roman Law and the Harmonisation of Private Law in Europe', in: *Towards a European Civil Code*, A. HARTKAMP et al (eds.), Ars Aequi Libri, Nijmegen, 2004, p. 21-43.

ZWAAN, T., *Familie, huwelijk en gezin in West-Europa Van Middeleeuwen tot moderne tijd*, Boom, Amsterdam, c. ZWEIGERT, K., KÖTZ, H., *An Introduction to Comparative Law*, Clarendon Press, Oxford, 1998.

TABLE OF CASES

EUROPEAN COURTS

European Court of Human Rights (ECHR)

I. v. the United Kingdom, ECHR, EHRM, Judgment of 11 July 2002, *Reports of Judgments and Decisions*, 2002.

Fretté v. France, ECHR, Judgement of 26 February 2002, Application 36515/97, 2002-I.

Hoffmann v. Germany, ECHR, Judgement of 11 October 2001, Application 34045/96.

Karner v. Austria, ECHR, Judgement of 24 July 2003, *Reports of Judgments and Decisions*, 2003-IX.

Odièvre v. France, ECHR, Judgement of 13 February 2003, Application no. 42326/98, 2003-III.

L. and V. v. Austria. ECHR, Judgement of 9 January 2003, Application 39392 and 39829/98, *European Human Rights Cases*, 12.2.2003.

B. and L. v. the United Kingdom, Judgement of 13 September 2005, Application 36536/02

European Commission of Human Right (EComHR)

Lindsay v. the United Kingdom. EComHR, Decision of 1 November 1986, D.R. 49.

European Court of Justice (ECJ)

Diatta v. Land Berlin. ECJ, case of 13 February 1985, *European Court Reports* (1985), 567.

The Netherlands v. Reed. ECJ, case of 17 April 1986, *European Court Reports* (1986), 1283.

Grant v. South West Trains Ltd. ECJ, case of 17 February 1998, C-249/96, European Court Reports (1998), I-621.

Safet Eyüp v. Landesgeschaftsstelle des Arbeitsmarktsevice Vorarlberg. ECJ, case of 22 June 2000, C-65/98, European Court Reports (2000), I-4747.

D. and the Kingdom of Sweden v. the Council. ECJ, appeal cases of 31 May 2001, C-122/99P and C-125/99P European Court Reports (2001), I-4319.

Court of First Instance (CFI)

D. v. the EU Council, CFI, case of 18 January 1999, T-264/97, *European Court Reports*, Stuff Cases (1999), I-A-I and II-1.

Arauxo-Dumay v. Commission. CFI, case of 17 June 1993, T-65/92, *European Court Reports* (1993), II-597.

NATIONAL COURTS

Belgium

Cour de Cassation/Hof van Cassatie (Supreme Court)

Cass. Belg. 10 May 1985, *Rechtskundig Weekblad* (1985-86), p. 1848

France

Conseil Constitutionnel (Constitutional Court)

Decision 99-419 DC of 9 November 1999

Cour de Cassation (Supreme Court)

Cass. Fr. (2 chambre civile) 2 February 1972, *Recueil Dalloz*, 1972, jur., 295
Cass. Fr. (chambre sociale) 11 July 1989, *Bulletin des arrêts de la Cour de Cassation* V, no. 514 and 515.
Cass. Fr. (3 chambre civile) 17 December 1997 *Bulletin des arrêts de la Cour de Cassation* III, no. 225.

Germany

Bundesverfassungsgericht (Constitutional Court)

BVerfG 29 July 1959, Neuen Juristischen Wochenschrift (1959), p. 1489-1490
BVerfG 11 October 1978, *Neuen Juristischen Wochenschrift* (1979), p. 595-596
BVerfG 28 February 1980, *Neuen Juristischen Wochenschrift* (1980), p. 689-690
BVerfG 21 October 1980, *Neuen Juristischen Wochenschrift* (1981), p. 108-109
BVerfG 21 Oktober 1980 55, 134, *Neuen Juristischen Wochenschrift* (1981), p. 180
BVerfG 30 November 1982, *Neuen Juristischen Wochenschrift* (1983), p. 511-512
BVerfG, 5 March 1991, *Neuen Juristischen Wochenschrift* (1991), p. 1602.
BVerfG, 4 October 1993, *Neuen Juristischen Wochenschrift* (1993), p. 3058
BVerfG, 17 July 2002, *Neuen Juristischen Wochenschrift* (2002), p. 2543-2548
BVerfG 17 November 1992, *Neuen Juristischen Wochenschrift* (1993), p. 643
BVerfG 17 July 2002, *Neuen Juristischen Wochenschrift* (2002), p. 2543-2548

England and Wales

House of Lords

Hyde v. Hyde and Woodmansee [1886]) *Law Reports (1st series)* P&D 130,
White v. White [2000] *2 Family Law Reports,* p. 981.
Bellinger v. Bellinger [2003] *2 Family Law Reports,* p. 1048.
Miller v. Miller and MacFarlane v. MacFarlane [2006] *UK House of Lords,* 24.

Court of Appeal

J v. S–T (*Formerly J*) Court of Appeal [1997] *1 Family Law Reports,* p. 402
Lambert v. Lambert Court of Appeal (Civil Division) 1685 [2002] 3 *FCR* 673, [2003] *1 Family
    Law Reports,* p. 139.

The Netherlands

Hoge Raad (Supreme Court)

HR 22 juni 1883, W 4924.
HR 19 October 1990, *Nederlandse Jurisprudentie* 1992, no 129.

Hungary

Magyar Köztársaság Alkotmánybírósága (Constitutional Court)

Decision 14/1995 of 8 March 1995 (III. 13.) AB, ABH 1995

EUROPEAN FAMILY LAW SERIES

1. *Legal Recognition of Same-Sex Couples in Europe*, K. Boele-Woelki and A. Fuchs (eds.)

2. *European Family Law in Action Volume I: Grounds for divorce*, K. Boele-Woelki, B. Braat and I. Sumner (eds.)

3. *European Family Law in Action Volume II: Maintenance Between Former Spouses*, K. Boele-Woelki, B. Braat and I. Sumner (eds.)

4. *Perspectives for the Unification and Harmonisation of Family Law in Europe*, K. Boele-Woelki (ed.)

5. *Family Law Legislation of the Netherlands*, I. Sumner and H. Warendorf

6. *Indépendance et interdépendance patrimoniales des époux dans le régime matrimonial légal des droits néerlandais, français et suisse*, B. Braat

7. *Principles of European Family Law Regarding Divorce and Maintenance Between Former Spouses*, K. Boele-Woelki, F. Ferrand, C. González Beilfuss, M. Jänterä-Jareborg, N. Lowe, D. Martiny and W. Pintens

8. *Inheritance Law Legislation of the Netherlands*, I. Sumner and H. Warendorf

9. *European Family Law in Action Volume III: Parental Responsibilities*, K. Boele-Woelki, B. Braat and I. Curry Sumner (eds.)

10. *Common Core and Better Law in European Family Law*, K. Boele-Woelki (ed.)

11. *All's well that ends registered?*, I. Curry-Sumner (ed.)

12. *Model Family Code – From a global perspective*, I. Schwenzer and M. Dimsey

13. *Harmonisation of Family Law in Europe. A Historical Perspective*, M. Antokolskaia